SCHAUM'S OUTLINE OF

MICROECONOMICS

Fourth Edition

MICROECONOMICS

Fourth Edition

DOMINICK SALVATORE, Ph.D.

Professor of Economics
Fordham University

SCHAUM'S OUTLINE SERIES

McGRAW-HILL

New York Chicago San Francisco Lisbon London
Madrid Mexico City Milan New Delhi San Juan
Seoul Singapore Sydney Toronto

The McGraw·Hill Companies

DOMINICK SALVATORE is Professor of Economics at Fordham University in New York. He is the author of the textbooks *Microeconomics: Theory and Applications*, 4th ed. (2003), *International Economics*, 8th ed. (2004), *Introduction to International Economics* (2005), and *Managerial Economics in a Global Economy*, 6th ed. (2006). He has also written the Schaum's Outline in *International Economics* (4th ed.) and co-authored Scham's Outlines in *Principles of Economics* (2nd ed.) and *Statistics and Econometrics* (2nd ed.). He also authored many other books. His research has been published in numerous leading scholarly journals and presented at national and international conferences.

Schaum's Outline of
MICROECONOMICS

1 2 3 4 5 6 7 8 9 10 CUS CUS 0 9 8 7 6

ISBN 0-07-146236-8

PREFACE

Microeconomic theory presents, in a systematic way, some of the basic analytical techniques or "tools of analysis" of economics. As such, it has traditionally been one of the most important courses in all economics and business curricula and is a requirement in practically all colleges and universities.

Being highly abstract in nature, microeconomic theory is also one of the most difficult courses and often becomes a stumbling block for many students. The purpose of this book is to help overcome this difficulty by approaching microeconomic theory from a learn-by-doing methodology. While the book is primarily intended as a supplement to all current standard textbooks in microeconomic theory, the statements of theory and principles are sufficiently complete to enable its use for independent study as well.

Each chapter begins with a clear statement of theory, principles, or background information, fully illustrated with examples. This is followed by a set of multiple-choice review questions with answers. Subsequently, numerous theoretical and numerical problems are presented with their detailed, step-by-step solutions. These solved problems serve to illustrate and amplify the theory, to bring into sharp focus those fine points without which the student continually feels on unsafe ground, and to provide the applications and the reinforcement so vital to effective learning.

The topics are arranged in the order in which they are usually covered in intermediate microeconomic theory courses and texts. As far as content, this book contains more material than is covered in one-semester courses in undergraduate microeconomic theory. Thus, while directed primarily at undergraduates, it can also provide a useful source of reference for M.A. students, M.B.A. students and businesspeople. There is no prerequisite for its study other than a prior course in or some knowledge of elementary economics.

The methodology of this book and much of its content have been tested in micro-economic theory classes at Fordham University. The students were enthusiastic and made many valuable suggestions for improvements. To all of them I am deeply grateful. I would like to express my gratitude to the entire Schaum staff of McGraw-Hill for their assistance and especially to Barbara Gibson and Adrinda Kelly.

This is the fourth edition of a book that has enjoyed a very gratifying market success and has been translated into nine languages (Spanish, French, Italian, Portuguese, Greek, Chinese, Japanese, Arabic, and Indonesian) and was reprinted in India and Taiwan. All the features that made the first and second editions successful were retained in the third edition.

The following revisions were included in this edition:

- A brand new chapter (Chapter 12) has been added on Game Theory and Oligopolistic Behavior. Game theory is one of the most important development in microeconomic theory and all texts now include it.
- A second new chapter (Chapter 15) has also been added on the Economics of Information. The economics of information is another important development in

microeconomic theory and reflects the fact that we now do live an information economy.

- Chapter 7 was expanded with the inclusion of Section 7.8 on The Cobb-Douglas Production Function, Section 7.9 on X-Inefficiency, and Section 7.10 on Technological Progress.
- New Section 11.6 on Transfer Pricing was added to new Chapter 11.
- Numerous additional examples, review questions, and problems and applications were included throughout the volume.

These additions should be very useful, particularly to the more eager undergraduate student, as well as to M.A. and M.B.A. students. Many other changes were also made throughout to reflect the numerous helpful comments that I received from the many professors and students who used the first two editions. Finally, the glossary of important economic terms and the sample midterm and final examinations were revised and expanded.

DOMINICK SALVATORE

CONTENTS

Theory and Problems of

MICROECONOMICS

Fourth Edition

CHAPTER 1

Introduction

1.1 THE PURPOSE OF THEORY

The purpose of *theory* is to predict and explain. A theory is a *hypothesis* that has been successfully tested. A hypothesis is tested not by the realism of its assumption(s) but by its ability to predict accurately and explain, and also by showing that the outcome follows logically and directly from the assumptions.

EXAMPLE 1. From talking to friends and neighbors, from observations in the butcher shop, and from our own behavior, we observe that when the price of a particular cut of meat rises, we buy less of it. From this casual real-world observation, we could construct the following general hypothesis: "*If* the price of a commodity rises, *then* the quantity demanded of the commodity declines." In order to test this hypothesis and arrive at a theory of demand, we must go back to the real world to see whether this hypothesis is indeed true for various commodities, for various people, and at different points in time. Since these outcomes would follow logically and directly from the assumptions (i.e., consumers would want to substitute cheaper for more expensive commodities) we would accept the hypothesis as a theory.

1.2 THE PROBLEM OF SCARCITY

The word *scarce* is closely associated with the word *limited* or *economic* as opposed to *unlimited* or *free*. Scarcity is the central fact of every society.

EXAMPLE 2. Economic resources are the various types of labor, capital, land, and entrepreneurship used in producing goods and services. Since the resources of every society are limited or scarce, the ability of every society to produce goods and services is also limited. Because of this scarcity, all societies face the problems of what to produce, how to produce, for whom to produce, how to ration the commodity over time, and how to provide for the maintenance and growth of the system. In a free-enterprise economy (i.e., one in which the government does not control economic activity), all these problems are solved by the price mechanism (see Problems 1.5 to 1.9).

1.3 THE FUNCTION OF MICROECONOMIC THEORY

Microeconomic theory, or *price theory*, studies the economic behavior of individual decision-making units such as consumers, resource owners, and business firms in a free-enterprise economy.

EXAMPLE 3. During the course of business activity, firms purchase or hire economic resources supplied by households in order to produce the goods and services demanded by households. Households then use the income received from the sale of resources (or their services) to business firms to purchase the goods and services supplied by business firms. The "circular flow" of economic activity is now complete (see Problem 1.11). Thus, microeconomic theory, or price theory, studies the flow of goods and services from business firms to households, the composition of such a flow, and how the prices of goods and services in the flow are determined. It also studies the flow of the services of economic resources from resource owners to business firms, the particular uses into which these resources flow, and how the prices of these resources are determined.

1.4 MARKETS, FUNCTIONS, AND EQUILIBRIUM

A *market* is the place or context in which buyers and sellers buy and sell goods, services, and resources. We have a market for each good, service, and resource bought and sold in the economy.

A *function* shows the relationship between two or more variables. It indicates how the value of one variable (the dependent variable) depends on and can be found by specifying the value of one or more other (independent) variables.

Equilibrium refers to the market condition which once achieved, tends to persist. Equilibrium results from the balancing of market forces.

EXAMPLE 4. The market demand function for a commodity gives the relationship between the quantity demanded of the commodity per time period and the price of the commodity (while keeping everything else constant). By substituting various hypothetical prices (the independent variable) into the demand function, we get the corresponding quantities demanded of the commodity per time period (the dependent variable) (see Problem 1.13). The market supply function for a commodity is an analogous concept—except that we now deal with the quantity supplied rather than the quantity demanded of the commodity (see Problem 1.14).

EXAMPLE 5. The market equilibrium for a commodity occurs when the forces of market demand and market supply for the commodity are in balance. The particular price and quantity at which this occurs tend to persist in time and are referred to as the equilibrium price and the equilibrium quantity of the commodity (see Problem 1.15).

1.5 COMPARATIVE STATICS AND DYNAMICS

Comparative statics studies and compares two or more equilibrium positions, without regard to the transitional period and process involved in the adjustment.

Dynamics, on the other hand, deals with the time path and the process of adjustment itself. In this book we deal almost exclusively with comparative statics.

EXAMPLE 6. Starting from a position of equilibrium, if the market demand for a commodity, its supply, or both vary, the original equilibrium will be disturbed and a new equilibrium usually will eventually be reached. Comparative statics studies and compares the values of the variables involved in the analysis *at* these two equilibrium positions (see Problem 1.17), while dynamic analysis studies how these variables *change over time* as one equilibrium position evolves into another.

1.6 PARTIAL EQUILIBRIUM AND GENERAL EQUILIBRIUM ANALYSIS

Partial equilibrium analysis is the study of the behavior of individual decision-making units and the working of individual markets, *viewed in isolation*.

General equilibrium analysis, on the other hand, studies the behavior of all individual decision-making units and all individual markets, *simultaneously*. This book deals primarily with partial equilibrium analysis.

EXAMPLE 7. The change in the equilibrium condition of the commodity in Example 5 was examined only in terms of what happens in the market of that particular commodity. That is, we abstracted from all other markets by implicitly keeping everything else constant (the "*ceteris paribus*" assumption). We were then dealing with partial equilibrium analysis. However, when the equilibrium condition for this commodity changes, it will affect to a greater or lesser degree and directly or indirectly the market for every other commodity, service, and factor. This is examined in general equilibrium analysis in Chapter 14.

1.7 POSITIVE ECONOMICS AND NORMATIVE ECONOMICS

Positive economics deals with or studies *what is*, or how the economic problems facing a society *are actually solved*.

Normative economics, on the other hand, deals with or studies what *ought to be*, or how the economic problems facing the society *should be solved*. This book deals primarily with positive economics.

EXAMPLE 8. Suppose that a firm pollutes the air in the process of producing its output. If we study how much additional cleaning cost is imposed on the community by this pollution, we are dealing with positive economics. Suppose that the firm threatens to move out rather than pay for installing antipollution equipment. The community must then decide whether it will allow the firm to continue to operate and pollute, pay for the antipollution equipment itself, or just force the firm out with a resulting loss of jobs. In reaching these decisions, the community is dealing with normative economics.

Glossary

Comparative statics It studies and compares two or more equilibrium positions, without regard to the transitional period and process involved in the adjustment.

Dynamics The study of the time path and process of adjustment to disequilibrium.

Equilibrium The market condition which once achieved tends to persist.

Function The relationship between two or more variables.

General equilibrium analysis The study of the behavior of individual decision-making units and all individual markets *simultaneously*.

Hypothesis An "if-then" statement usually obtained from a causal observation of the real world.

Market The place or context in which buyers and sellers buy and sell goods, services, and resources.

Microeconomic theory or price theory The study of the economic behavior of individual decision-making units such as consumers, resource owners, and business firms in a free-enterprise economy.

Normative economics The study of what *ought to be*, or how the economic problems facing the society *should be solved.*

Partial equilibrium analysis The study of the behavior of individual decision-making units and the working of individual markets, *viewed in isolation.*

Positive economics The study of *what is*, or how the economic problems facing a society *are actually solved.*

Scarce Limited, or economic (as opposed to unlimited, or free).

Theory A hypothesis that has been successfully tested.

Review Questions

1. A theory is (*a*) an assumption, (*b*) an "if-then" proposition, (*c*) a hypothesis, or (*d*) a validated hypothesis.

   Ans. (*d*) See Section 1.1 and Example 1.

2. A hypothesis is tested by (*a*) the realism of its assumption(s), (*b*) the lack of realism of its assumption(s), (*c*) its ability to predict accurately an outcome that follows logically from the assumption(s), or (*d*) none of the above.

   Ans. (*c*) See Section 1.1 and Example 1.

3. The meaning of the word "economic" is most closely associated with the word (*a*) free, (*b*) scarce, (*c*) unlimited, or (*d*) unrestricted.

Ans. (*b*) Economic factors and goods are those factors and goods which are scarce or limited in supply and thus command a price.

4. In a free-enterprise economy, the problems of what, how, and for whom are solved by (*a*) a planning committee, (*b*) the elected representatives of the people, (*c*) the price mechanism, or (*d*) none of the above.

Ans. (*c*) See Example 2.

5. Microeconomic theory studies how a free-enterprise economy determines (*a*) the price of goods, (*b*) the price of services, (*c*) the price of economic resources, or (*d*) all of the above.

Ans. (*d*) Because microeconomic theory is primarily concerned with the determination of all prices in a free-enterprise economy, it is often referred to as price theory.

6. A market (*a*) necessarily refers to a meeting place between buyers and sellers, (*b*) does not necessarily refer to a meeting place between buyers and sellers, (*c*) extends over the entire nation, or (*d*) extends over a city.

Ans. (*b*) Because of modern communications, buyers and sellers need not come face to face with one another to buy and sell. The market for some commodities extends over a city or a section therein; the market for other commodities may extend over the entire nation or even the world.

7. A function refers to (*a*) the demand for a commodity, (*b*) the supply of a commodity, (*c*) the demand and supply of a commodity, service, or resource, or (*d*) the relationship between one dependent variable and one or more independent variables.

Ans. (*d*) See Section 1.4. Demand functions and supply functions are *examples* of functions, but the term "function" is a completely general term and refers to the relationship between any dependent variable and its corresponding independent variable(s).

8. The market equilibrium for a commodity is determined by (*a*) the market demand for the commodity, (*b*) the market supply of the commodity, (*c*) the balancing of the forces of demand and supply for the commodity, or (*d*) any of the above.

Ans. (*c*) See Section 1.4 and Example 5.

9. Which of the following is *incorrect*?

(*a*) Microeconomics is concerned primarily with the problem of what, how, and for whom to produce.

(*b*) Microeconomics is concerned primarily with the economic behavior of individual decision-making units when at equilibrium.

(*c*) Microeconomics is concerned primarily with the time path and process by which one equilibrium position evolves into another.

(*d*) Microeconomics is concerned primarily with comparative statics rather than dynamics.

Ans. (*c*) Choice *c* is the definition of dynamics. Dynamic microeconomics is still in its infancy.

10. Which of the following statements is most closely associated with general equilibrium analysis?

(*a*) Everything depends on everything else.

(*b*) *Ceteris paribus.*

(*c*) The equilibrium price of a good or service depends on the balancing of the forces of demand and supply for that good or service.

(*d*) The equilibrium price of a factor depends on the balancing of the forces of demand and supply for that factor.

Ans. (*a*) General equilibrium analysis studies how the price of every good, service, and factors depends on the price of every other good, service, and factors. Thus, a change in any price will affect every other price in the system.

11. Which aspect of taxation involves normative economics? (*a*) the incidence of (i.e., who actually pays for) the tax, (*b*) the effect of the tax on incentives to work, (*c*) the "fairness" of the tax, or (*d*) all of the above.

Ans. (*c*) See Section 1.7.

12. Microeconomics deals primarily with

(*a*) comparative statics, general equilibrium, and positive economics,
(*b*) comparative statics, partial equilibrium, and normative economics,
(*c*) dynamics, partial equilibrium, and positive economics, or
(*d*) comparative statics, partial equilibrium, and positive economics.

Ans. (*d*) See Sections 1.5 to 1.7.

Solved Problems

THE PURPOSE OF THEORY

1.1 (*a*) What is the purpose of theory? (*b*) How do we arrive at a theory?

(*a*) The purpose of theory—not just economics theory but theory in general—is to predict and explain. That is, a theory abstracts from the details of an event; it simplifies, generalizes, and seeks to predict and explain the event.

(*b*) The first step in the process of arriving at an acceptable theory is the construction of a model or a hypothesis. A hypothesis is an "if-then" statement which is usually obtained from a casual observation of the real world. Inferences are then drawn from the hypothesis. If these inferences do not conform to reality, the hypothesis is discarded and a new one is formulated. If the inferences do conform to reality, the hypothesis is accepted as a theory (if it can also be shown that the outcome follows logically and directly from the assumptions).

1.2 (*a*) What is likely to happen to the quantity *supplied* of a particular cut of meat when its price rises? (*b*) Express your answer to part (*a*) as a general hypothesis of the relationship between the price and the quantity supplied of any commodity. (*c*) What must we do in order to arrive at a theory of production?

(*a*) When the price of a particular cut of meat rises, its quantity supplied is likely to increase (if a sufficiently long period of time is allowed for farmers to respond).

(*b*) The general hypothesis relating the quantity supplied of any commodity to its price can be stated as follows: "*If* the price of a commodity rise, *then* more of it will be supplied per time period, *ceteris paribus*." (*Ceteris paribus* means holding everything else constant.) In the rest of book we will use the word "commodity" to refer to goods (meat, milk, suit, shoes, automobiles, etc.) and services (such as housing, communication, transportation, medical, recreational and other services or intangibles).

(*c*) Suppose that through an investigation of the real-world behavior of many farmers (not just meat producers) and other producers, we find that, *ceteris paribus*, they do indeed increase the quantity of the commodity that they supply when the price of the commodity rises. Since we can also logically understand why a producer would want to increase the quantity supplied of the commodity when its price rises (because the producer's profits increase), we would then accept the hypothesis of part (*b*) as a theory. (As we will see in Chapter 6, however, a complete theory of production involves much more than this.)

1.3 Distinguish between (*a*) a hypothesis, (*b*) a theory, and (*c*) a law.

(*a*) A hypothesis is an "if-then" proposition usually constructed from a casual observation of a real-world event which represents a tentative and yet untested explanation of the event.

(*b*) A theory implies that some successful tests of the corresponding hypothesis have already been undertaken. Thus, a theory implies a greater likelihood of truth than a hypothesis. The greater the number of successful tests (and lack of unsuccessful ones), the greater the degree of confidence we have in the theory.

(*c*) A law is a theory which is always true under the same set of circumstances, as, for example, the law of gravity.

THE PROBLEM OF SCARCITY

1.4 Distinguish between (*a*) economic resources and (*b*) noneconomic resources.

(*a*) Economic resources, factors of production, or inputs refer to the services of the various types of labor, capital equipment, land (or natural resources), and (in a world of uncertainty) entrepreneurship. Since in every society these resources are not unlimited in supply but are limited or scarce, they command a price (i.e., they are *economic* resources).

(*b*) Economic resources can be contrasted with noneconomic resources such as air, which (in the absence of pollution) is unlimited in supply and free. In economics, our interest lies with economic resources, rather than with noneconomic resources.

1.5 (*a*) Why is "what to produce" a problem in every economy? (*b*) How does the price mechanism solve this problem in a free-enterprise economy? (*c*) In a mixed enterprise economy? (*d*) In a centralized economy?

(*a*) "What to produce" refers to thoese goods and services and the quantity of each that the economy should produce. Since resources are scarce or limited, no economy can produce as much of every good or service as desired by all members of society. More of one good or service usually means less of others. Therefore, every society must choose exactly which goods and services to produce and how much of each to produce.

(*b*) In a free-enterprise economy, the "what to produce" problem is solved by the price mechanism. Only those commodities for which consumers are willing to pay a price per unit sufficiently high to cover at least the full cost of producing them will be supplied by producers in the long run. By paying a higher price, consumers can normally induce producers to increase the quantity of a commodity that they supply per unit of time. On the other hand, a reduction in price will normally result in a reduction in the quantity supplied.

(*c*) In a mixed-enterprise economy such as ours, the government (through taxes, subsidies, etc.) modifies and, in some instances (through direct controls), replaces the operation of the price mechanism in its function of determining what to produce.

(*d*) In a completely centralized economy, the dictator, or more likely a planning committee appointed by the dictator or the party, determines what to produce. We in the West believe that this is inefficient. Even the Soviet Union (never a completely centralized economy) has been moving recently toward more decentralized control of the economy and toward greater reliance on the price mechanism to decide what to produce.

1.6 (*a*) Why is "how to produce" a problem in every economy? (*b*) How does the price mechanism solve this problem in a free-enterprise economy? (*c*) In a mixed-enterprise economy? (*d*) In a centralized economy?

(*a*) "How to produce" refers to the choice of the combination of factors and the particular technique to use in producing a good or service. Since a good or service can normally be produced with different factor combinations and different techniques, the problem arises as to which of these to use. Since resources are limited in every economy, when more of them are used to produce some goods and services, less are available to produce others. Therefore, society faces the problem of choosing the technique which results in the least possible cost (in terms of resources used) to produce each unit of the good or service it wants.

(*b*) In a free-enterprise economy, the "how to produce" problem is solved by the price mechanism. Because the price of a factor normally represents its relative scarcity, the best technique to use in producing a good or service is the one that results in the least dollar cost of production. If the price of a factor rises in relation to the price of others used in the production of the good or service, producers will switch to a technique which uses less of the more expensive factor in order to minimize their costs of production. The opposite occurs when the price of a factor falls in relation to the price of others.

(*c*) In a mixed-enterprise economy, the operation of the price mechanism in solving the "how to produce" problem is modified and sometimes replaced by a government action.

(*d*) In a centralized economy, this problem is solved by a planning committee.

1.7 (*a*) Why is "for whom to produce" a problem in every economy? (*b*) How does the price mechanism solve this problem? (*c*) Why does the government in a mixed-enterprise economy modify the operation of the price mechanism in its function of determining for whom to produce?

(*a*) "For whom to produce" refers to how the total output is to be divided among different consumers. Since resources and thus goods and services are scarce in every economy, no society can satisfy all the wants of all its people. Thus, a problem of choice arises.

(*b*) In the absence of government regulation or control of the economy, the problem of "for whom to produce" is also solved by the price mechanism. The economy will produce those commodities that satisfy the wants of those people who have the money to pay for them. The higher the income of an individual, the more the economy will be geared to produce the commodities the consumers want (if they are also willing to pay for them).

(*c*) In the name of equity and fairness, governments usually modify the workings of the price mechanism by taking from the rich (through taxation) and redistributing to the poor (through subsidies and welfare payments). They also raise taxes in order to provide for certain "public" goods, such as education, law and other, and defense.

1.8 (*a*) Identify the two types of rationing that the price mechanism performs over the time in which the supply of a commodity is fixed, (*b*) explain how the price mechanism performs the first of these two rationing functions, and (*c*) explain how the price mechanism performs its second rationing function.

(*a*) In a free-enterprise economy, the price mechanism performs two closely related types of rationing. First, it restricts the total level of consumption to the available output. Second, it restricts the current level of consumption so the commodity will last for the entire time period over which its supply is fixed.

(*b*) The price mechanism performs the first rationing as follows: If the prevailing price of a commodity would lead to a shortage of the commodity, that price would rise. At higher prices, consumers would buy less and producers would supply more of the commodity until the total level of consumption equaled the available output. The opposite would occur if the prevailing price of the commodity would lead to a surplus of the commodity. Thus, the price mechanism restricts the total level of consumption to the available production.

(*c*) The price of a commodity such as wheat is not so low immediately after harvest as to lead to the exhaustion of the entire amount of wheat available before the next harvest. Thus, the price mechanism rations a commodity over the entire time period during which its supply is fixed.

1.9 (*a*) In a free-enterprise economy, how does the price mechanism provide for the maintenance of the economic system? (*b*) How does it provide for economic growth? (*c*) Why and how does the government attempt to influence the nation's rate of economic growth?

(*a*) The maintenance of the economic system is accomplished by providing for the replacement of the machinery, buildings, etc., that are used up in the course of producing the current outputs. In a free-enterprise economy, output prices are usually sufficiently high to allow producers not only to cover their day-to-day production expenditures but also to replace depreciating capital goods.

(*b*) Economic growth refers to increases in real per capita income. An economy's rate of economic growth depends on the rate of growth of its resources and on the rate of improvement in its techniques of production or technology. In a free-enterprise economy, it is the price mechanism that to a large extent determines the rate of economic growth. For example, the prospect of higher wages motivates labor to acquire more skills. Capital accumulation and technological improvements also respond to expectations of profits.

(*c*) In the modern world, governments have made economic growth one of their top priorities. Economic growth is often wanted for its own sake. This is true for developed and underdeveloped nations, regardless of their form of organization. Serious concern for the environment has only been voiced recently. Governments have used tax incentives, subsidies, sponsored basic research, etc., to stimulate economic growth.

THE FUNCTION OF MICROECONOMIC THEORY

1.10 (*a*) Distinguish between microeconomics and macroeconomics. (*b*) What basic underlying assumption is made in studying microeconomics?

(*a*) Microeconomic theory or price theory deals with the economic behavior of *individual* decision-making units such as consumers, resource owners, and business firms as well as individual markets in a free-enterprise economy. This is to be contrasted with macroeconomic theory, which studies the *aggregate* levels of output, national income, employment, and prices for the economy viewed as a whole.

(*b*) In studying microeconomic theory, the implicit assumption is made that all economic resources are fully employed. This does not preclude the possibility of temporary disturbances, but monetary and fiscal policies are supposed to assure us a tendency toward full employment without inflation. During periods of great unemployment and inflation, microeconomics is overshadowed by the aggregate problems.

1.11 (*a*) Draw a diagram showing the direction of the flows of goods, services, resources, and money between business firms and households. (*b*) Explain why what is a cost to households represents income for business firms, and vice versa.

(*a*) A simple schematic *model* of the economy is shown in Fig. 1-1.

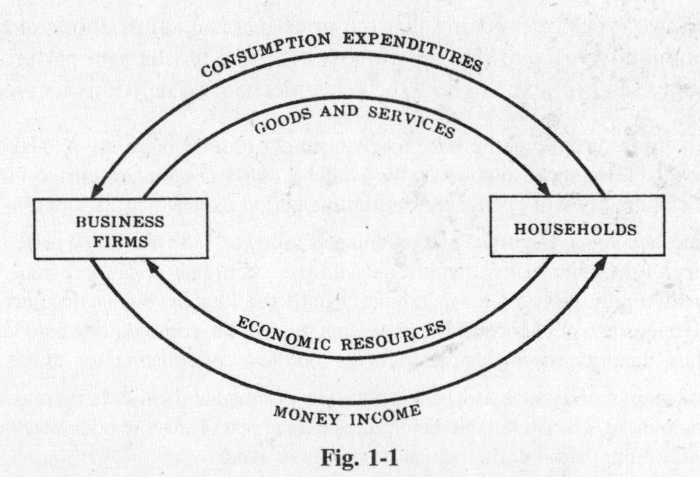

Fig. 1-1

(*b*) The top loop in Fig. 1-1 shows that households purchase goods and services from business firms. Thus, what is a cost or a consumption expenditure from the point of view of households represents the income or the money receipts of business firms. On the other hand, the bottom loop shows that business firms purchase the services of economic resources from households. Thus, what is a cost of production from the point of view of business firms represents the money income of households.

1.12 (*a*) With which of the five problems faced by every society is microeconomics primarily concerned? (*b*) With reference to the circular-flow diagram in Problem 1.11, explain how the prices of goods, services, and resources are determined in a free-enterprise economy.

(*a*) Of the five problems faced by every society, microeconomics is concerned primarily with the first three (i.e., what to produce, how to produce, and for whom to produce). The crucial step in solving these problems is the determination of the prices of the goods, services, and economic resources that enter the flows shown in the diagram of Problem 1.11 (hence the name "price theory").

(*b*) Households give rise to the demand for goods and services, while business firms respond by supplying goods and services. The demand and the supply of each good and service determine its price. In order to produce goods and services, business firms demand economic resources or their services. These are supplied by households. The demand and supply of each factor then determine its price. In microeconomics we study some of the best available models that explain and predict the behavior of individual decision-making units and prices. The empirical testing of these models is examined in other courses.

MARKETS, FUNCTIONS, AND EQUILIBRIUM

1.13 Suppose that (keeping everything else constant) the *demand function* of a commodity is given by $QD = 6000 - 1000P$, where QD stands for the market quantity demanded of the commodity per time period and P for the price of the commodity. (*a*) Derive the market *demand schedule* for this commodity. (*b*) Draw the market *demand curve* for this commodity.

(*a*) By substituting various prices for the commodity into its market demand function, we get the market demand schedule for the commodity as shown in Table 1.1.

Table 1.1

Price ($)	1	2	3	4	5	6
Quantity Demanded (per unit of time)	5000	4000	3000	2000	1000	0

(*b*) By plotting each pair of price-quantity values in the above market demand schedule as a point on a graph and joining the resulting points, we get the corresponding market demand curve for this commodity shown in Fig. 1-2.

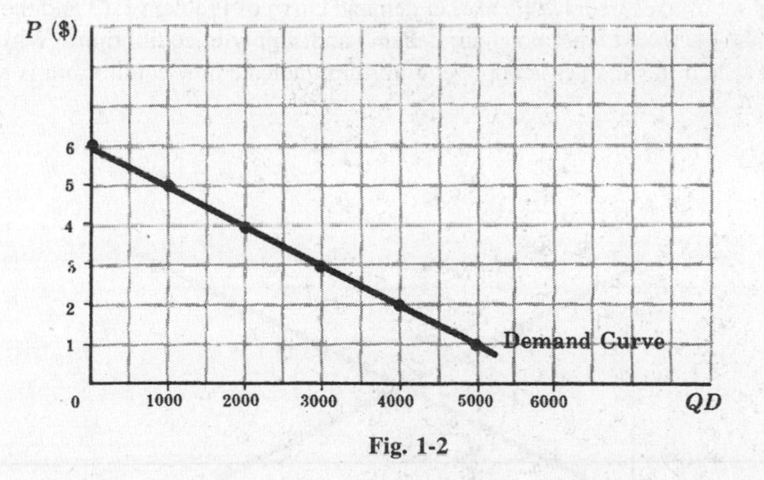

Fig. 1-2

(A more detailed discussion of demand functions, demand schedules, and demand curves is presented in Sections 2.1 to 2.4.)

1.14 Suppose that (keeping everything else constant) the *supply function* for the commodity in Problem 1.13 is given by $QS = 1000P$, where QS stands for the market quantity supplied of the commodity per time period and P for the price of the commodity. (*a*) Derive the market *supply schedule* for this commodity and (*b*) draw the market *supply curve* for this commodity.

(*a*) By substituting various prices for the commodity into its market supply function, we get the market supply schedule for this commodity as shown in Table 1.2.

Table 1.2

Price ($)	0	1	2	3	4	5	6
Quantity Supplied (per unit of time)	0	1000	2000	3000	4000	5000	6000

(*b*) By plotting each pair of price-quantity values in Table 1.2 as a point on a graph and joining the resulting points, we get the corresponding market supply curve for this commodity shown in Fig. 1-3.

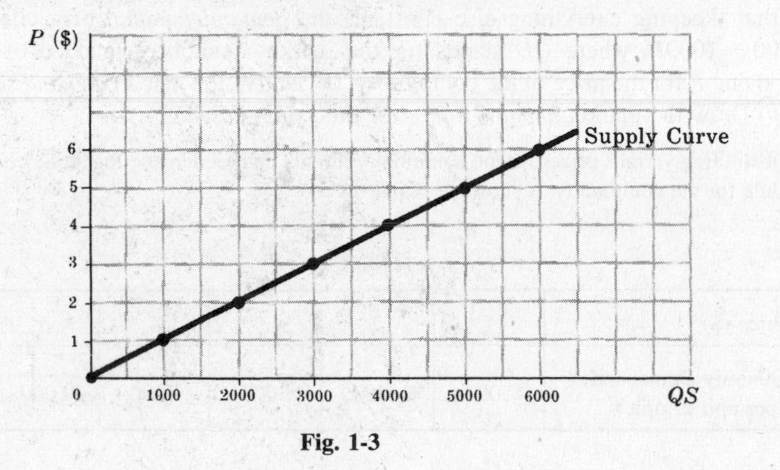

Fig. 1-3

(A more detailed discussion of supply functions, supply schedules, and supply curves is presented in Sections 2.2 to 2.8.)

1.15 (*a*) On one set of axes, redraw the market demand curve of Problem 1.13 and the market supply curve of Problem 1.14. (*b*) At what point are demand and supply in equilibrium? Why? (*c*) Starting from a position at which this market is not in equilibrium, indicate how equilibrium is reached.

(*a*)

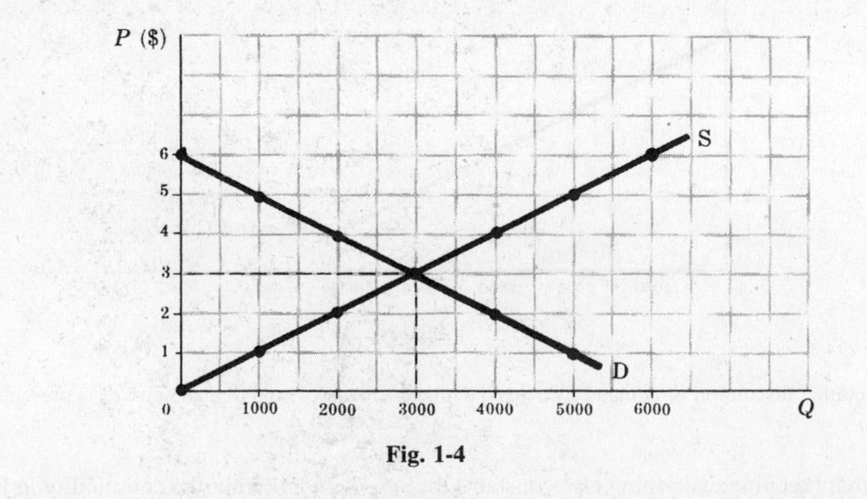

Fig. 1-4

(*b*) Demand and supply are in equilibrium when the market demand curve intersects the market supply curve for the commodity. Thus, at the price of $3, the quantity demanded of this commodity in the market is 3000 units per time period. This equals the quantity supplied at the price of $3. As a result, there is no tendency for the price and the quantity bought and sold of this commodity to change. The price of $3 and the quantity of 3000 units represent, respectively, the equilibrium price and the equilibrium quantity of this commodity.

(c) At $P > \$3$, $QS > QD$ and a surplus of the commodity develops. This will cause P to fall toward \$3. At $P < \$3$, $QD > QS$ and a shortage of the commodity develops. This will push P up toward \$3 (the symbol ">" means "larger than," while "<" means "smaller than").

(A more detailed discussion of equilibrium is presented in Sections 2.9 to 2.11.)

COMPARATIVE STATICS AND DYNAMICS

1.16 In what aspect of the variable involved in the analysis is (a) comparative statics interested? (b) dynamics interested?

(a) Comparative statics is interested only in the equilibrium values of the variables involved in the analysis. In microeconomics, these are the equilibrium price and the equilibrium quantity. Comparative statics thus implies an instantaneous adjustment to disturbances to equilibrium.

(b) Dynamics on the other hand, studies the movement over time of the variables involved in the analysis, as one equilibrium position evolves into another. More specifically, dynamic microeconomics studies how the price and quantity of a commodity change during the period of adjustment from one equilibrium point to another.

1.17 Suppose that the demand function for the commodity in Problem 1.13 changes to $QD' = 8000 - 1000P$. (a) Define the new market demand schedule for the commodity. (b) Draw the new market demand curve on a figure identical to that in Problem 1.15. (c) What are the new equilibrium price and quantity for this commodity?

(a)

Table 1.3

Price (\$)	1	2	3	4	5	6	7	8
QD'	7000	6000	5000	4000	3000	2000	1000	0

(b)

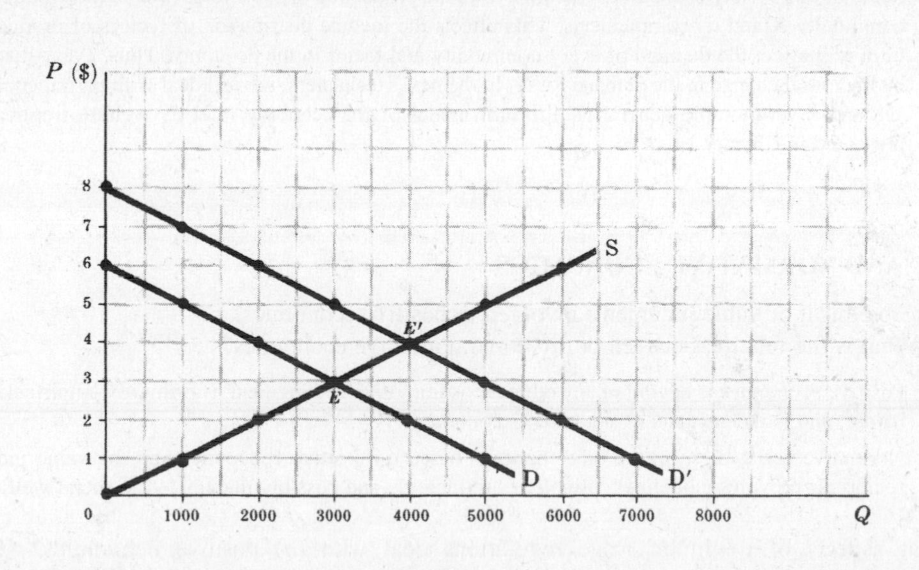

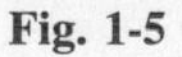
Fig. 1-5

(c) The new equilibrium price is \$4 and the new equilibrium quantity is 4000 units per time period. Comparative statics compares the value of P and Q at equilibrium points E and E'.

PARTIAL EQUILIBRIUM AND GENERAL EQUILIBRIUM ANALYSIS

1.18 (*a*) How does partial equilibrium analysis deal with the interconnections that exist between the various markets in the economy? (*b*) How does general equilibrium analysis deal with them? (*c*) Why do we deal primarily with partial analysis?

(*a*) In partial equilibrium analysis, we isolate for study specific decision-making units and markets, and abstract from the interconnections that exist between them and the rest of the economy. More specifically, we assume that the changes in the equilibrium conditions in our market do not affect any of the other markets in the economy and that changes in other markets do not affect the market under consideration.

(*b*) General equilibrium analysis examines the interconnections that exist among all decision-making units and markets, and shows how all parts of the economy are linked together into an integrated system. Thus, a change in the equilibrium conditions in one market will affect the equilibrium conditions in every other market, and these will themselves cause additional changes in or affect the market in which the process originally started. The economy will be in general equilibrium when all of these effects have worked themselves out and all markets are *simultaneously in equilibrium.*

(*c*) General equilibrium analysis is very complicated and time-consuming. We deal primarily with partial equilibrium analysis to keep the analysis manageable. Partial equilibrium analysis gives a first approximation to the results wanted. This approximation is better (and partial analysis more useful), the weaker the links between the market under study and the rest of the economy.

1.19 Suppose that the demand for commodity X rises in an economy in which there is no economic growth, and which is originally in general equilibrium. Discuss what happens (*a*) in the commodity markets and (*b*) in the factor markets.

(*a*) If, from an initial position of general equilibrium in the economy, the demand for commodity X rises, a new and higher equilibrium point for the commodity will be defined (see Problem 1.17). If we were interested in partial equilibrium analysis, we would stop at this point. However, the rise in the demand for commodity X will cause an increase in the demand for those commodities which are used together with X and a fall in the demand for the commodities which are substitutes for X. Thus, the equilibrium position of commodity X and its complements and substitutes will change.

(*b*) Some of this society's resources will shift from the production of substitutes of X to the production of more of commodity X and its complements. This affects the income distribution of factors of production which, in turn, will affect the demand of every commodity and factor in the economy. Thus, every market is affected by the initial change in the demand for X. In the next 10 chapters, we will deal with partial equilibrium analysis, and a very simple general equilibrium model of the economy (and its welfare implications) will be presented in Chapter 14.

POSITIVE AND NORMATIVE ECONOMICS

1.20 (*a*) Are ethical or value judgments involved in positive economics?
(*b*) What is the relation between positive and normative economics?

(*a*) Positive economics is devoid of any ethical position or value judgment, is primarily empirical or statistical in nature, and is independent of normative economics.

(*b*) Normative economics, on the other hand, is based on positive economics and the value judgments of the society. It provides guidelines for policies to increase and possibly maximize the social welfare.

1.21 What aspects of minimum wage regulations deal with (*a*) positive economics? (*b*) normative economics?

(*a*) The study of the actual or anticipated effect of minimum wage regulations on the economy is a study in positive economics. It involves the examination of which occupations (mostly unskilled) are or will be affected by the regulations, the extent of substitution of capital equipment for labor in production, which communities are or will be most affected, and what happens to the displaced workers.

(*b*) Having studied the actual or anticipated effect of minimum wages on the economy, society must decide if the trade-off between higher wages for some but less opportunity of employment for others is acceptable. At the same time, society must decide how much more taxes it wants to impose on the working population to raise the money to cover the resulting additional welfare payments for early retirement or for retraining the displaced workers. To answer these questions, society must make value judgments. (Welfare questions of this type will often be in the background of our discussion in subsequent chapter. A formal introduction to welfare economics will be presented in Chapter 14.)

CHAPTER 2

Demand, Supply, and Equilibrium: An Overview

2.1 THE INDIVIDUAL'S DEMAND FOR A COMMODITY

The quantity of a commodity that an individual is willing to purchase over a specific time period is a function of or depends on the price of the commodity, the person's money income, the prices of other commodities, and individual tastes. By varying the price of the commodity under consideration *while keeping constant the individual's money income and tastes and the prices of other commodities* (the assumption of *ceteris paribus*), we get the individual's *demand schedule* for the commodity. The graphic representation of the individual's demand schedule gives us that person's *demand curve*.

EXAMPLE 1. Suppose that an individual's demand function for commodity X is $Qd_x = 8 - P_x$ *ceteris paribus*. By substituting various prices of X into this demand function, we get the individual's demand schedule shown in Table 2.1. The individual's demand schedule for commodity X shows the *alternative* quantities of commodity X that the person is willing to purchase at various alternative prices for commodity X, while keeping everything else constant.

Table 2.1

P_x (\$)	8	7	6	5	4	3	2	1	0
Qd_x	0	1	2	3	4	5	6	7	8

EXAMPLE 2. Plotting each pair of values as a point on a graph and joining the resulting points, we get the individual's demand curve for commodity X (which will be referred to as d_x) shown in Fig. 2-1. The demand curve in Fig. 2-1 shows that *at a particular point in time, if* the price of X is \$7, the individual is willing to purchase one unit of X *over the period of time specified.* (The time period specified may be a week, a month, a year, or any other "relevant" length of time.) *If* the price of X is \$6, the individual is willing to purchase two units of X *over the specified time period*, and so on. Thus, the points on the demand curve represent *alternatives* as seen by the individual at a particular point in time.

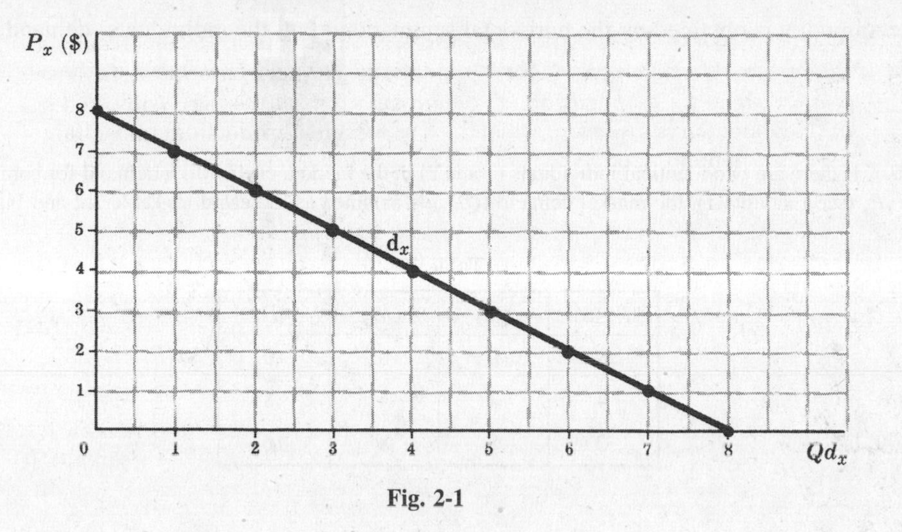

Fig. 2-1

2.2 THE LAW OF NEGATIVELY SLOPED DEMAND

In the demand schedule of Table 2.1, we see that the *lower* the price of X, the *greater* the quantity of X demanded by the individual. This *inverse* relationship between price and quantity is reflected in the *negative* slope of the demand curve of Fig. 2-1. With the exception of a very rare case (to be discussed in Chapter 4), the demand curve always slopes downward, indicating that at lower prices of a commodity, more of it is purchased. This is usually referred to as the *law of demand.*

2.3 SHIFTS IN THE INDIVIDUAL'S DEMAND CURVE

When any of the *ceteris paribus* conditions changes, the entire demand curve shifts. This is referred to as *a change in demand* as opposed to *a change in the quantity demanded*, which is movement along the same demand curve.

EXAMPLE 3. When an individual's money income rises (while everything else remains constant), the person's demand for a commodity usually increases (i.e., the individual's demand curve shifts up), indicating that at the same price that person will purchase more units of the commodity per unit of time. Thus, if the individual's money income rises, the individual's demand curve for steaks will shift up so that *at the unchanged steak price*, that person will purchase more steaks per month. Steak is called a *normal good*. There are, however, some commodities (such as bread and potatoes) whose demand curve usually shifts down when the individual's income rises. These are called *inferior goods*.

EXAMPLE 4. A change in the individual's tastes for a commodity also causes a shift in that person's demand curve for the commodity. For example, a greater desire on the part of an individual to consume ice cream causes an upward shift in the individual's demand curve for ice cream. A reduced desire is reflected in a downward shift. Similarly, the individual's demand curve for a commodity shifts up when the price of a substitute commodity rises, but shifts down when the price of a complement (a commodity used together with the one considered) rises. Thus, the demand for tea shifts up when the price of coffee (a substitute) rises but shifts down when the price of lemons (a complement of tea) rises (see Problems 2.7, 2.8, and 2.9).

2.4 THE MARKET DEMAND FOR A COMMODITY

The market or aggregate demand for a commodity gives the *alternative* amounts of the commodity demanded per time period, at various alternative prices, by *all* the individuals in the market. The market demand for a commodity thus depends on all the factors that determine the individual's demand and, in addition, on the number of buyers of the commodity in the market. Geometrically, the market demand curve for a commodity is obtained by the horizontal summation of all the individuals' demand curves for the commodity.

EXAMPLE 5. If there are two identical individuals (1 and 2) in the market, each with a demand for commodity X given by $Qd_x = 8 - P_x$ (see Example 1), the market demand (QD_x) is obtained as indicated in Table 2.2 and Fig. 2-2.

Table 2.2

P_x (\$)	Qd_1	Qd_2	QD_x
8	0	0	0
4	4	4	8
0	8	8	16

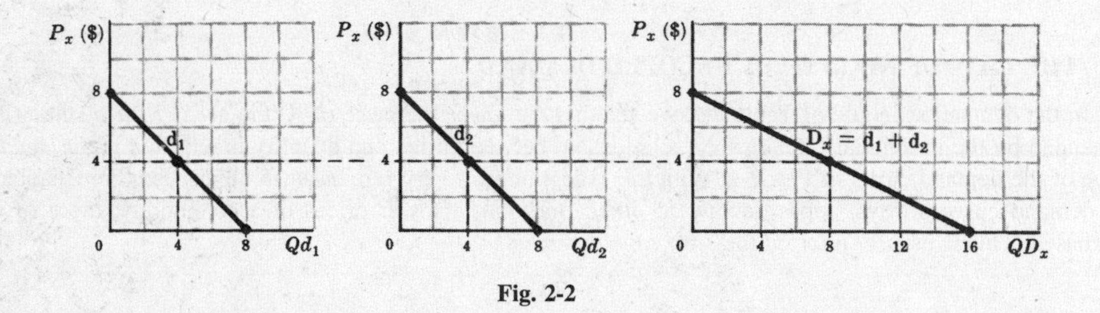

Fig. 2-2

EXAMPLE 6. If there are 1000 identical individuals in the market, each with the demand for commodity X given by $Qd_x = 8 - P_x$ *ceteris paribus* (*cet. par.*), the market demand schedule and the market demand curve for commodity X are obtained as follows (see also Table 2.3 and Fig. 2-3):

$$Qd_x = 8 - P_x \textit{ cet. par.} \quad \text{(individual's } d_x\text{)}$$
$$QD_x = 1000(Qd_x) \textit{ cet. par.} \quad \text{(market D}_x\text{)}$$
$$= 8000 - 1000P_x$$

Table 2.3

P_x (\$)	Qd_x
8	0
7	1000
6	2000
5	3000
4	4000
3	5000
2	6000
1	7000
0	8000

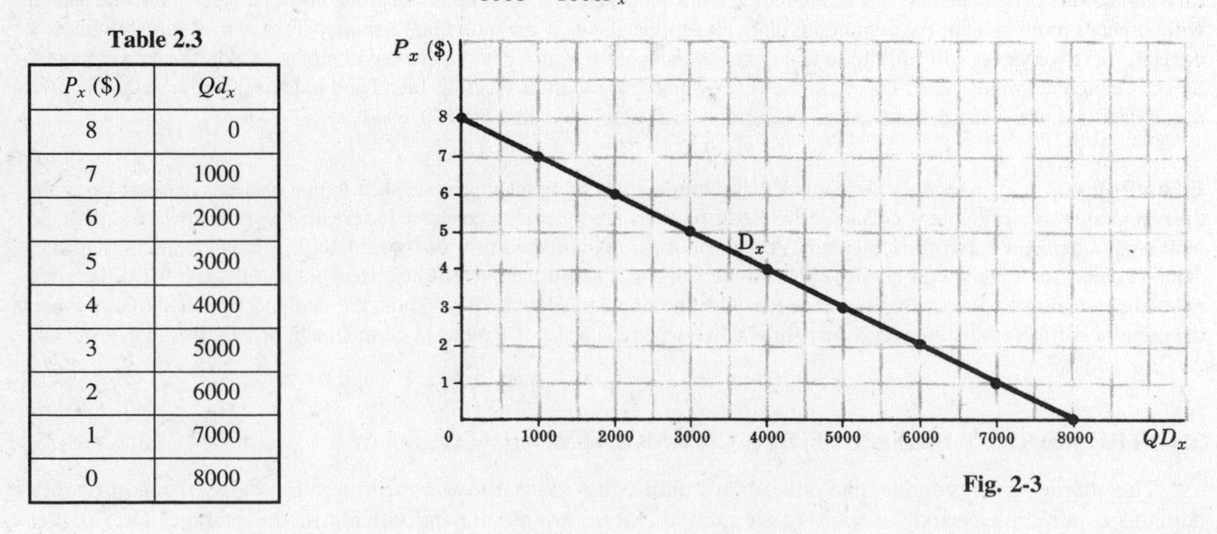

Fig. 2-3

The market demand curve for commodity X (D_x) will shift when the individual's demand curves shift (unless the shifts of the latter neutralize each other) and will change with time as the number of consumers in the market for X changes.

2.5 THE SINGLE PRODUCER'S SUPPLY OF A COMMODITY

The quantity of a commodity that a single producer is willing to sell over a specific time period is a function of or depends on the price of the commodity and the producer's costs of production. In order to get a producer's supply schedule and supply curve of a commodity, certain factors which influence costs of production must be held constant (*ceteris paribus*).

These are *technology, the prices of the inputs necessary to produce the commodity*, and for agricultural commodities, *climate and weather conditions*. By keeping all of the above factors constant while varying the price of the commodity, we get the individual producer's *supply schedule and supply curve*.

EXAMPLE 7. Suppose that a single producer's supply function for commodity X is $Qs_x = -40 + 20P_x$ *cet. par.* By substituting various "relevant" prices of X into this supply function, we get the producer's supply schedule shown in Table 2.4.

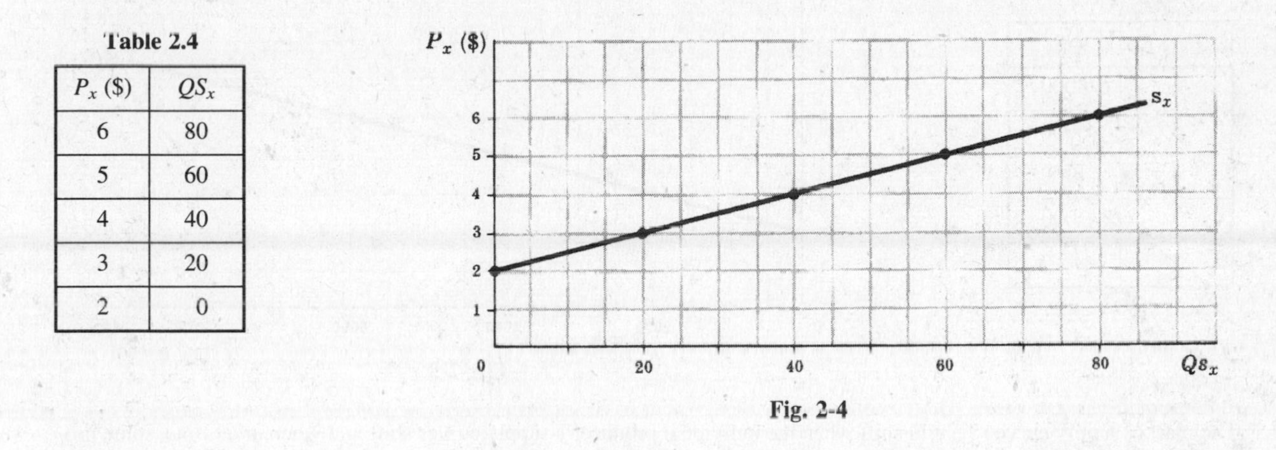

Table 2.4

P_x ($)	QS_x
6	80
5	60
4	40
3	20
2	0

Fig. 2-4

EXAMPLE 8. Plotting each pair of values from the supply schedule in Table 2.4 on a graph and joining the resulting points, we get the producer's supply curve (see Fig. 2-4). As in the case of demand, the points on the supply curve represent *alternatives* as seen by the producer *at a particular point in time*.

2.6 THE SHAPE OF THE SUPPLY CURVE

In the supply schedule of Table 2.4, we see that the *lower* the price of X, the *smaller* the quantity of X offered by the supplier. The reverse is, of course, also true. This *direct* relationship between price and quantity is reflected in the *positive* slope of the supply curve in Fig. 2-4. However, while in the case of the demand curve we can talk about "the law of negatively sloped demand," in the case of the supply curve we *cannot* talk of "the law of positively sloped supply." Even though the supply curve is *usually* positively sloped, it could also have a zero, infinite, or even negative slope, and no generalizations are possible.

2.7 SHIFTS IN THE SINGLE PRODUCER'S SUPPLY CURVE

When the factors that we kept constant in defining a supply schedule and a supply curve (the *ceteris paribus* condition) change, the entire supply curve shifts. This is referred to as a *change* or *shift in supply* and must be clearly distinguished from *a change in the quantity supplied* (which is a movement along the same supply curve).

EXAMPLE 9. If there is an improvement in technology (so that the producer's costs of production fall) the supply curve shifts *downward*. Thus downward shift is referred to as an *increase* in supply. It means that *at the same price* for the commodity, the producer offers more of it for sale per time period (see Problems 2.14 and 2.15).

2.8 THE MARKET SUPPLY OF A COMMODITY

The market or aggregate supply of a commodity gives the *alternative* amounts of the commodity supplied per time period at various alternative prices by *all* the producers of this commodity in the market. The market supply of a commodity depends on all the factors that determine the individual producer's supply and, in addition, on the number of producers of the commodity in the market.

EXAMPLE 10. If there are 100 identical producers in the market, each with a supply of commodity X given by $Qs_x = -40 + 20P_x$ *cet. par.* (see Example 7), the market supply (QS_x) is obtained as follows (see also Table 2.5 and Fig. 2-5):

$$Qs_x = -40 + 20P_x \ \textit{cet. par.} \quad \text{(single producer's } s_x\text{)}$$
$$QS_x = 100(Qs_x) \ \textit{cet. par.} \quad \text{(market } S_x\text{)}$$
$$= -400 + 2000P_x$$

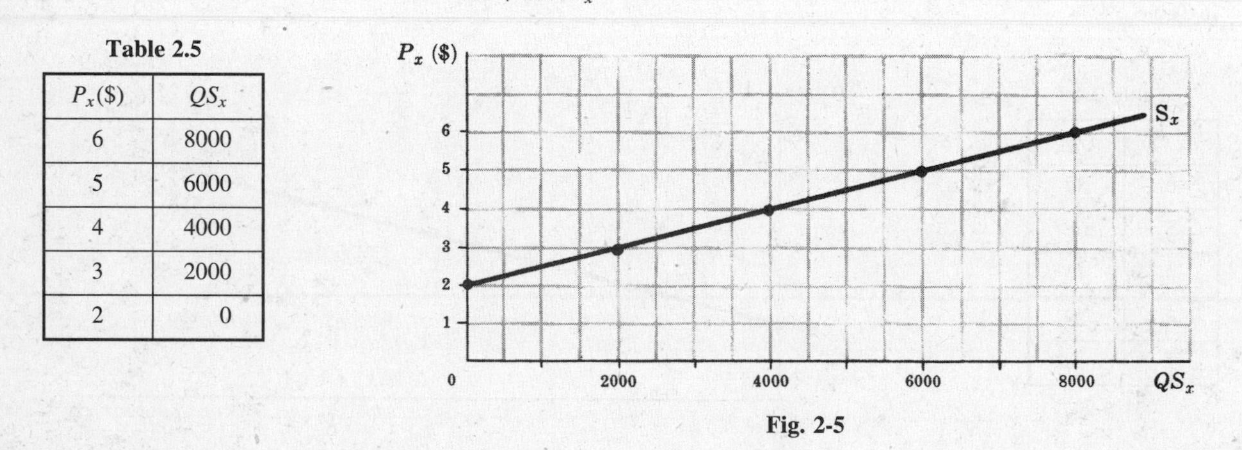

Table 2.5

P_x($)	QS_x
6	8000
5	6000
4	4000
3	2000
2	0

Fig. 2-5

The market supply curve (S_x) will shift when the individual producer's supply curves shift and when, over time, some producers enter or leave the market.

2.9 EQUILIBRIUM

Equilibrium refers to the market condition which, once achieved, tends to persist. In economics this occurs when the quantity of a commodity demanded in the market per unit of time equals the quantity of the commodity supplied to the market over the same time period. Geometrically, equilibrium occurs at the intersection of the commodity's market demand curve and market supply curve. The price and quantity at which equilibrium exists are known, respectively, as the *equilibrium price* and the *equilibrium quantity.*

EXAMPLE 11. From the market demand curve of Example 6 and the market supply curve of Example 10, we can determine the equilibrium price and the equilibrium quantity for commodity X as shown in Table 2.6 and Fig. 2-6. At the equilibrium point, there exists neither a surplus nor a shortage of the commodity and the market clears itself. *Ceteris paribus*, the equilibrium price and the equilibrium quantity tend to persist in time.

Table 2.6

P_x ($)	QD_x	QS_x	
6	2000	8000	
5	3000	6000	
4 ←	4000	4000 →	*Equilibrium*
3	5000	2000	
2	6000	0	

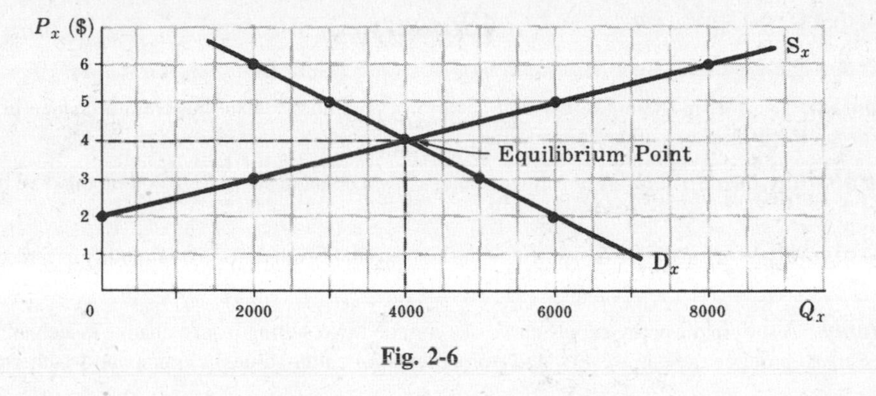

Fig. 2-6

EXAMPLE 12 Since we know that at equilibrium $QD_x = QS_x$, we can determine the equilibrium price and the equilibrium quantity mathematically:

$$QD_x = QS_x$$
$$8000 - 1000P_x = -4000 + 2000P_x$$
$$12{,}000 = 3000P_x$$
$$P_x = \$4 \quad \text{(equilibrium price)}$$

Substituting this equilibrium price either into the demand equation or into the supply equation, we get the equilibrium quantity.

$$QD_x = 8000 - 1000(4) \qquad \text{or} \qquad QS_x = -4000 + 2000(4)$$
$$= 8000 - 4000 \qquad\qquad = -4000 + 8000$$
$$= 4000 \quad \text{(units of } X\text{)} \qquad\qquad = 4000 \quad \text{(units of } X\text{)}$$

2.10 TYPES OF EQUILIBRIA

An equilibrium condition is said to be *stable* if any deviation from the equilibrium will bring into operation market forces which push us back toward equilibrium (see Example 13). If instead we move further away from equilibrium, we have a situation of *unstable equilibrium*. For unstable equilibrium to occur, the market supply curve must be *negatively sloped and less steeply inclined* than the (negatively sloped) market demand curve (see Problem 2.19).

EXAMPLE 13. The equilibrium condition for commodity X shown in Table 2.6 and Fig. 2-6 of Example 11 is stable. This is because, if for some reason the price of X rises above the equilibrium price of \$4, $QS_x > QD_x$ and a surplus of commodity X arises which will automatically push us back toward the equilibrium price of \$4. Similarly, if the price of X falls below the equilibrium price, the resulting shortage will automatically cause the price of X to rise toward its equilibrium level.

2.11 SHIFTS IN DEMAND AND SUPPLY, AND EQUILIBRIUM

If the market demand curve, the market supply curve, or both shift, the equilibrium point will change. *Ceteris paribus*, an increase in demand (an upward shift) causes an increase in both the equilibrium price and the equilibrium quantity. On the other hand, given the market demand for a commodity, an increase in the market supply (a downward shift in supply) causes a reduction in the equilibrium price but an increase in the equilibrium quantity. The opposite occurs for a decrease in demand or supply. If both the market demand and the market supply increase, the equilibrium quantity rises but the equilibrium price may rise, fall or remain unchanged (see Problem 2.23).

Glossary

Change in demand A shift in the entire demand curve of a commodity resulting from a change in the individual's money income or tastes, or prices of other commodities.

Change in the quantity demanded A movement along a given demand curve for a commodity as a result of a change in its price.

Change in the quantity supplied A movement along a given supply curve for a commodity as a result of a change in its price.

Change in supply A shift in the entire supply curve of a commodity resulting from a change in technology, the prices of the inputs necessary to produce the commodity, and (for agricultural commodities) climate and weather conditions.

Equilibrium The market condition which, once achieved, tends to persist. This occurs when the quantity of a commodity demanded equals the quantity supplied to the market.

Law of demand The inverse relationship between price and quantity reflected in the negative slope of a demand curve.

Stable equilibrium The type of equilibrium where any deviation from equilibrium brings into operation market forces which push us back toward equilibrium.

Unstable equilibrium The type of equilibrium where any deviation from the equilibrium position brings into operation forces which push us further away from equilibrium.

Review Questions

1. In drawing an individual's demand curve for a commodity, all but which one of the following are kept constant? (*a*) The individual's money income, (*b*) the price of other commodities, (*c*) the price of the commodity under consideration, or (*d*) the tastes of the individual.

Ans. (*c*) See Section 2.1.

2. The individual's demand curve for a commodity represents (*a*) a maximum boundary of the individual's intentions, (*b*) a minimum boundary of the individual's intentions, (*c*) both a maximum and a minimum boundary of the individual's intentions, or (*d*) neither a maximum nor a minimum boundary of the individual's intentions.

Ans. (*a*) For the various alternative prices of a commodity, the demand curve shows the *maximum* quantities of the commodity the individual intends to purchase per unit of time (one will take less if that is all one can get). We could similarly say that for various alternative quantities of a commodity per time period, the demand curve shows the *maximum* prices the individual is willing to pay.

3. A fall in the price of a commodity, holding everything else constant, results in and is referred to as (*a*) an increase in demand, (*b*) a decrease in demand, (*c*) an increase in the quantity demanded, or (*d*) a decrease in the quantity demanded.

Ans. (*c*) See Section 2.3.

4. When an individual's income rises (while everything else remains the same), that person's demand for a normal good (*a*) rises, (*b*) falls, (*c*) remains the same, or (*d*) any of the above.

Ans. (*a*) See Section 2.3.

5. When an individual's income falls (while everything else remains the same), that person's demand for an inferior good (*a*) increases, (*b*) decreases, (*c*) remains unchanged, or (*d*) we cannot say without additional information.

Ans. (*a*) See Section 2.3.

6. When the price of a substitute of commodity X falls, the demand for X (*a*) rises, (*b*) falls, (*c*) remains unchanged, or (*d*) any of the above.

Ans. (*b*) See Section 2.3.

7. When both the price of a substitute and the price of a complement of commodity X rise, the demand for X (*a*) rises, (*b*) falls, (*c*) remains unchanged, or (*d*) all of the above are possible.

Ans. (*d*) An increase in the price of a substitute, by itself, causes an increase in the demand for X. An increase in the price of a complement, by itself, causes a decrease in the demand for X. When both the price of a substitute and the, price of a complement of commodity X rise, the demand curve for X can rise, fall, or remain unchanged depending on the relative strength of the two opposing forces.

8. In drawing a farmer's supply curve for a commodity, all but which one of the following are kept constant? (*a*) Technology, (*b*) the prices of inputs, (*c*) features of nature such as climate and weather conditions, or (*d*) the price of the commodity under consideration.

Ans. (*d*) See Section 2.5.

9. A producer's positively sloped supply curve for a commodity represents (*a*) a maximum boundary of the producer's intentions, (*b*) a minimum boundary of the producer's intentions, (*c*) in one sense a maximum and in another sense a minimum boundary of the producer's intentions, or (*d*) none of the above.

Ans. (*c*) For various alternative prices of a commodity, the supply curve shows the maximum quantities of the commodity the producer intends to offer per unit of time. On the other hand, for various alternative quantities of the commodity per time period, the supply curve shows the minimum prices the producer must be given to offer the specified quantities.

10. If the supply curve of a commodity is positively sloped, a rise in the price of the commodity, *ceteris paribus*, results in and is referred to as (*a*) an increase in supply, (*b*) an increase in the quantity supplied, (*c*) a decrease in supply, or (*d*) a decrease in the quantity supplied.

Ans. (*b*) See Section 2.7.

11. When the market supply curve for a commodity is negatively sloped, we have a case of (*a*) stable equilibrium, (*b*) unstable equilibrium, or (*c*) any of the above is possible and we cannot say without additional information.

Ans. (*c*) See Section 2.10.

12. If, from a position of stable equilibrium, the market supply of a commodity decreases while the market demand remains unchanged, (*a*) the equilibrium price falls, (*b*) the equilibrium quantity rises, (*c*) both the equilibrium price and the equilibrium quantity decrease, or (*d*) the equilibrium price rises but the equilibrium quantity falls.

Ans. (*d*) A decrease in the market supply of a commodity refers to an upward shift in the market supply curve. With an unchanged market demand curve for the commodity, the new equilibrium point will be higher and to the left of the previous equilibrium point. This involves a higher equilibrium price but a lower equilibrium quantity than before.

Solved Problems

DEMAND

2.1 (*a*) Express in simple mathematical language what was discussed in Section 2.1.
(*b*) How do we arrive at the expression $Qd_x = f(P_x)$ *cet. par.*?

(*a*) What was said in Section 2.1 can be expressed in simple mathematical language as follows:

$$Qd_x = f(P_x, M, P_0, T)$$

where Qd_x = the quantity of commodity X demanded by the individual, over the specified time period
f = a function of, or depends on
P_x = the price of commodity X
M = the money income of the individual
P_0 = the prices of other commodities
T = the tastes of the individual

(*b*) By keeping constant the individual's money income, the prices of other commodities, and the individual's tastes, we can write

$$Qd_x = f(P_x, \bar{M}, \bar{P}_0, \bar{T})$$

where the bar on top of M, P_0, and T means that they are kept constant. The last mathematical expression is usually abbreviated as

$$Qd_x = f(P_x) cet.\ par.$$

This reads: The quantity of commodity X demanded by an individual over a specified time period is a function of or depends on the price of that commodity while holding constant everything else that affects the individual's demand for the commodity.

2.2 (*a*) What is the relationship between the expression $Qd_x = f(P_x)$ *cet. par.* and the expression $Qd_c = 8 - P_x$ *cet. par.* in Example 1?
(*b*) What is the relationship between "need" or "want" and "demand"?

(*a*) The expression $Qd_x = f(P_x)$ *cet. par.* is a *general* functional relationship indicating simply that Qd_x is a function of or depends on P_x when everything else that affects the individual's demand for the commodity is held constant. The expression $Qd_x = 8 - P_x$ *cet. par.* is a *specific* functional relationship indicating *precisely* how Qd_x depends on P_x. That is, by substituting various prices of commodity X into this *specific* demand function, we get the particular quantity of commodity X demanded by the individual per unit of time at these various prices. Thus, we get the individual's demand schedule and from it, the demand curve.

(*b*) The demand for a particular commodity arises because of its ability to satisfy a need or a want. However, the demand for a commodity, in an economic sense, arises when there is both a need for the commodity *and* consumers have the money to pay for it. Thus, demand really refers to *effective* demand rather than to simple need.

2.3 From the demand function $Qd_x = 12 - 2P_x$ (P_x is given in dollars), derive (*a*) the individual's demand schedule and (*b*) the individual's demand curve, (*c*) What is the maximum quantity this individual will ever demand of commodity X per time period?

(*a*)

Table 2.7

P_x ($)	6	5	4	3	2	1	0
Qd_x	0	2	4	6	8	10	12

(*b*) It should be noted that in economics, contrary to usual mathematical usage, price (the independent or explanatory variable) is plotted on the vertical axis while the quantity demanded per unit of time (the dependent or "explained" variable) is plotted on the horizontal axis (see Fig. 2-7). The reason for the negative slope of the individual's demand curve will be explained in Chapter 4.

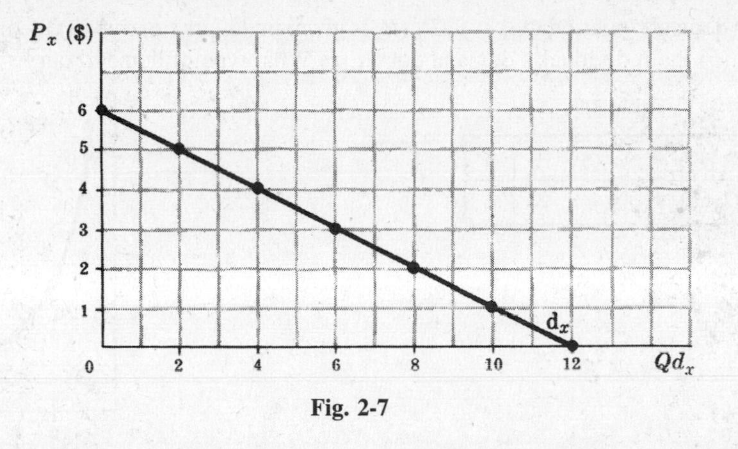

Fig. 2-7

(c) The maximum quantity of this commodity that the individual will ever demand per unit of time is 12 units. This occurs at a zero price. This is called *the saturation point* for the individual. Additional units of X result in a storage and disposal problem for the individual. Thus the "relevant" points on a demand curve are all in the first quadrant.

2.4 From the Individual's Demand Schedule (Table 2.8) for commodity X, (*a*) draw the individual's demand curve. (*b*) In what way is this demand curve different from the one in Problem 2.3?

Table 2.8
Individual's Demand Schedule

P_x ($)	6	5	4	3	2	1
Qd_x	18	20	24	30	40	60

(*a*)

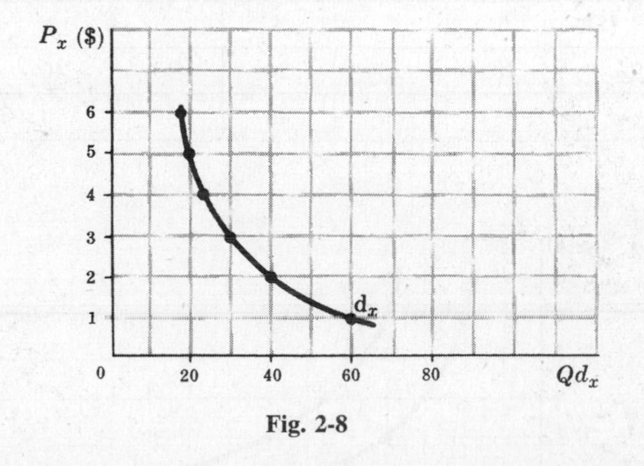

Fig. 2-8

(*b*) In this problem, the individual's demand is given by a curve, while in Problem 2.3 it was given by a straight line. In the real world, a demand curve can be a straight line, a smooth curve, or any other irregular (but usually negatively sloped) curve. For simplicity, in Problem 2.3 (and in the text) we dealt with a straight-line demand curve.

2.5 From the demand function $Qd_x = 8/P_x$ (P_x is given in dollars), derive (*a*) the individual's demand schedule and (*b*) the individual's demand curve, (*c*) What type of demand curve is this?

(*a*)

Table 2.9

P_x (\$)	1	2	4	8
Q_x	8	4	2	1

(*b*)

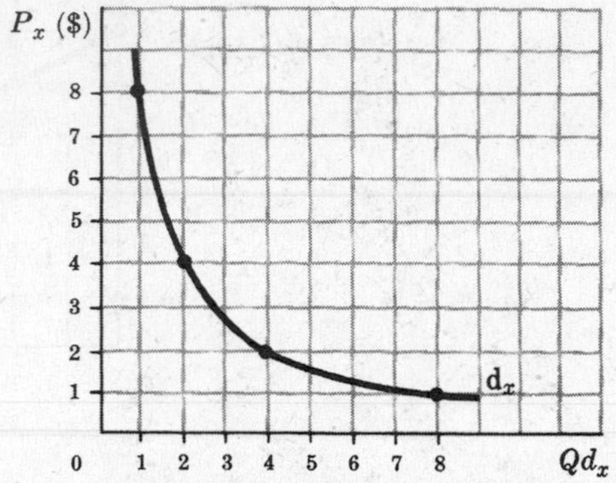

Fig. 2-9

(*c*) The demand curve in this problem is a rectangular hyperbola. As we move further away from the origin along either axis, the demand curve gets closer and closer to the axis but never quite touches it. This type of curve is said to be *asymptotic* to the axes. Economists sometimes use this type of demand curve because of its special characteristics. We will examine some of these special characteristics in the next chapter.

2.6 Table 2.10 gives two demand schedules of an individual for commodity X. The first of these (Qd_x) is the same as the demand schedule in Problem 2.4. The second (Qd'_x) resulted from an increase in the individual's money income (while keeping everything else constant), (*a*) Plot the points of the two demand schedules on the same set of axes and get the two demand curves, (*b*) What would happen if the price of X fell from \$5 to \$3 before the individual's income rose? (*c*) At the unchanged price of \$5 for commodity X, what happens when the individual's income rises? (*d*) What happens if at the same time that the individual's money income rises, the price of X falls from \$5 to \$3? (*e*) What type of good is commodity X? Why?

(*a*)

Table 2.10

P_x (\$)	6	5	4	3	2	1
Qd_x	18	20	24	30	40	60
Qd_x'	38	40	46	55	70	100

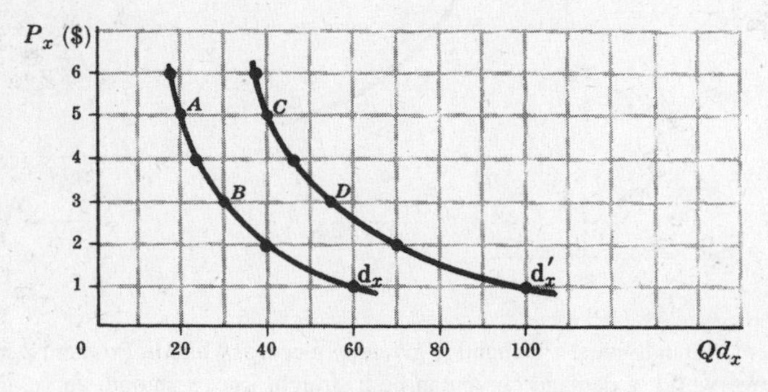

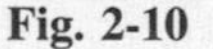
Fig. 2-10

(b) When the price of X falls from \$5 to \$3 before the individual's income rises, *the quantity of X demanded* by the individual increases from 20 to 30 units per time period. (This is movement along d_x in a downward direction, from point *A* to point *B* in the figure.)

(c) When the individual's income rises, that person's entire demand curve shifts up and to the right from d_x to d'_x. This is referred to as *an increase in demand*. At the unchanged price of \$5, the individual will now (i.e., after the shift) buy 40 units of X rather than 20 (i.e., the individual goes from point *A* to point *C*).

(d) When the individual's income rises while the price of X falls (from \$5 to \$3), the individual purchases 35 additional units of X (i.e., the individual goes from point *A* to point *D*).

(e) Since d_x, shifted up (to d'_x) when the individual's income rose, commodity X is a normal good for this individual. If d_x has shifted down as the individual's income rose, commodity X would have been an inferior good for this individual. In some cases, a commodity may be normal for one individual over some ranges of his or her income and inferior for another individual or for the same individual over different ranges of income (more will be said on this in Chapter 3).

2.7 The values in Table 2.11 refer to the change in an individual's consumption of coffee and tea at home when the price of coffee rises (everything else, including the price of tea, remains the same). (*a*) Draw a figure showing these changes, and (*b*) explain the figure drawn.

Table 2.11

	Before		After	
	Price (cents/cup)	Quantity (cups/month)	Price (cents/cup)	Quantity (cups/month)
Coffee	40	50	60	30
Tea	20	40	20	50

(*a*)

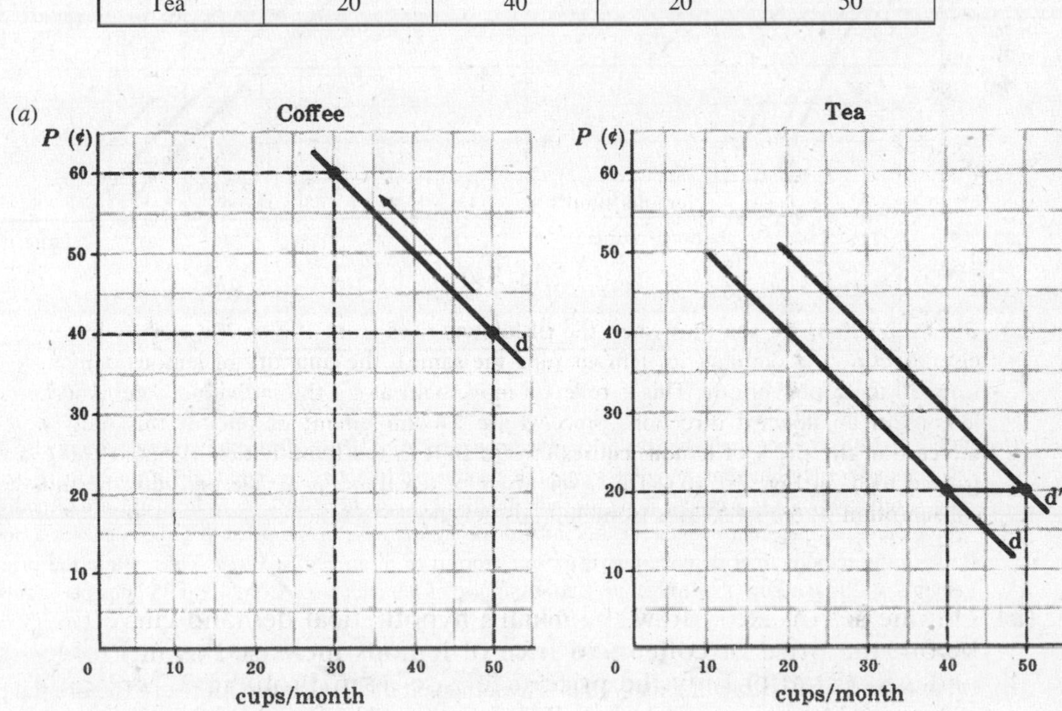

Fig. 2-11

(*b*) In Fig. 2-11 (*a*), we see that when the price of coffee rises; from 40¢ to 60¢ per cup (with everything else affecting the demand for coffee remaining the same), the quantity demanded of coffee falls from 50 to 30 cups per month. This is reflected by a movement along the individual's demand curve for coffee in an upward direction. Since tea is a substitute for coffee, the increase in the price of coffee causes an upward shift in the hypothetical demand curve for tea, from d to d′ in Fig. 2-11(*b*). Thus, with the price of tea remaining at 20¢ per cup, the individual's consumption of tea increases from 40 to 50 cups per month.

2.8 The values in Table 2.12 refer to the change in an individual's consumption of lemons and tea at home when the price of lemons rises (everything else, including the price of tea, remains the same). (*a*) Draw a figure showing these changes, and (*b*) explain the figure drawn.

Table 2.12

	Before		After	
	Price (cents/unit)	Quantity (units/month)	Price (cents/cup)	Quantity (units/month)
Lemons	10	20	20	15
Tea	20	40	20	35

(*a*)

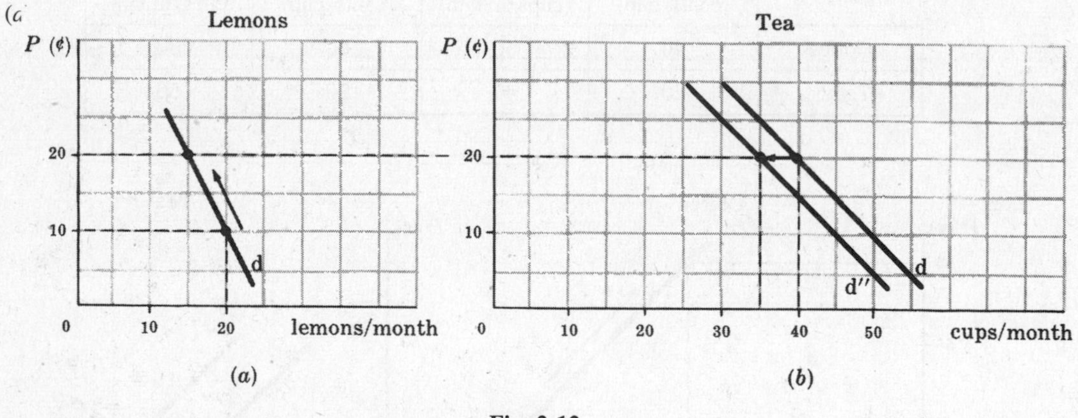

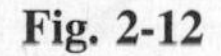
Fig. 2-12

(*b*) In Fig. 2-12(*a*), we see that when the price of lemons rises from 10¢ to 20¢ each (with everything else affecting the demand for lemons remaining the same), the quantity of lemons demanded falls from 20 to 15 per month. This is reflected by a movement along the individual's demand curve for lemons in an upward direction. Since lemons are a complement of tea for this individual, the increase in the price of lemons causes a downward shift in the hypothetical demand curve for tea, from d to d″ in Fig. 2-12(*b*). Thus, while the price of tea remains at 20¢ per cup, the individual's consumption of tea decreases from 40 to 35 cups per month.

2.9 (*a*) On one set of axes, draw the individual's hypothetical demand curve for tea (1) before the price of coffee and the price of lemons increased as in Problems 2.7 and 2.8, (2) after only the price of coffee rose as in Problem 2.7, (3) after only the price of lemons rose as in Problem 2.8 and (4) after *both* the price of coffee and the price of lemons rose as in Problems 2.7 and 2.8.

(*b*) Explain the completed graph.

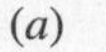
(*a*)

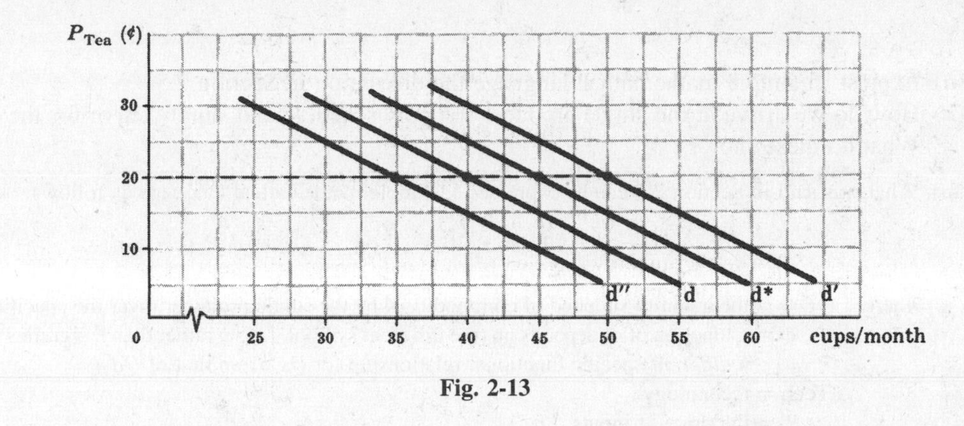

Fig. 2-13

(*b*) In Fig. 2-13, d represents the individual's hypothetical demand curve for tea *before* the price of coffee and the price of lemons rose; d″ is the individual's demand curve for tea *after* only the price of coffee (a substitute for tea) rose; d″ is the demand curve *after* only the price of lemons (a complement of tea) rose; and d* is the individual's hypothetical demand curve for tea *after both* the price of coffee and the price of lemons rose. Thus, at the unchanged tea price of 20¢ per cup, the individual increases consumption of tea to 45 cups per month when the price of coffee and the price of lemons increase as indicated in Problems 2.7 and 2.8.

2.10 Table 2.13 gives three individuals' demand schedules for commodity X. Draw these three demand curves on the same set of axes, and derive geometrically the market demand curve for commodity X (on the assumption that there are only these three individuals in the market for X).

Table 2.13

P_x ($)	Quantity Demanded (per unit of time)		
	Individual 1	Individual 2	Individual 3
6	9	18	30
5	10	20	32
4	12	24	36
3	16	30	45
2	22	40	60
1	30	60	110

From Table 2.13, we get

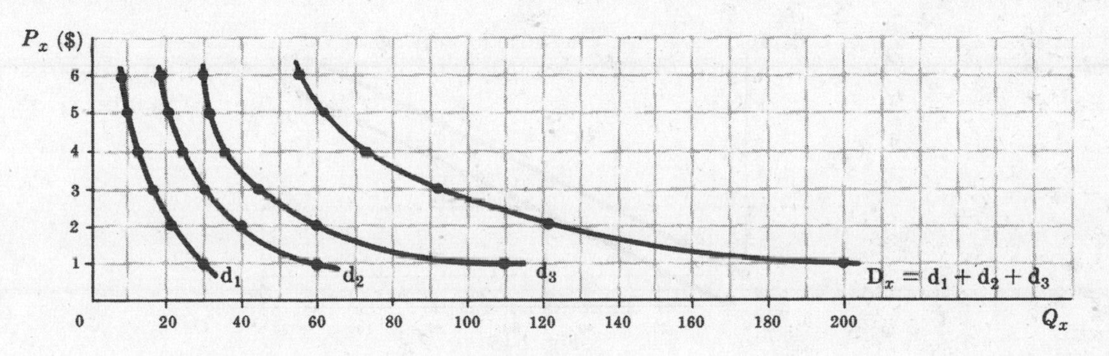

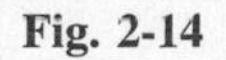
Fig. 2-14

SUPPLY

2.11 (*a*) Express in simple mathematical language the discussion in Section 2.5.
(*b*) How do we arrive at the single producer's supply schedule and supply curve for the commodity? What do these show?

(*a*) What was said in Section 2.5 can be expressed in simple mathematical language as follows:

$$Qs_x = \phi(P_x, \bar{\text{T}}\text{ech}, \bar{P}_i, \bar{F}_n) \qquad \text{or} \qquad Qs_x = \phi(P_x)\, cet.\ par.$$

where Qs_x = the quantity supplied of commodity X by the single producer, over the specified time period
ϕ = a function of or depends on (the different symbol, i.e., ϕ rather than f, signifies that we expect a *different* specific functional relationship for Qs_x from that of Qd_x)
Tech = technology
P_i = the price of inputs
F_n = features of nature such as climate and weather conditions. The bar on top of last three factors indicates that they are kept constant (the *cet. par.* condition).

The second general mathematical expression reads: The quantity of commodity X supplied by a producer over a specified time period is a function of or depends on the price of that commodity while certain other factors remain constant.

(b) $Qs_x = \phi(P_x)$ *cet. par.* is a *general* functional relationship. In order to derive the single producer's supply schedule and supply curve, we must get that person's *specific* supply function. The single producer's supply schedule and supply curve of a commodity show the *alternative* quantities of the commodity that the producer is willing to sell over a specified period of time at various alternative prices for commodity X, while keeping everything else constant. They show alternatives as seen by the producer at a particular point in time.

2.12 From the specific supply function $Qs_x = 20P_x$ (P_x is given in dollars), derive (*a*) the producer's supply schedule and (*b*) the producer's supply curve. (*c*) What things have been kept constant in the given supply function? (*d*) What is the minimum price that this producer must be offered in order to induce him or her to start supplying commodity X to the market?

(*a*)

Table 2.14

P_x ($)	6	5	4	3	2	1	0
QS_x	120	100	80	60	40	20	0

(*b*) The shape and location of a producer's supply curve (if it exists) depend on production and cost conditions (Chapters 6 and 8) and on the type of market organization in which the producer is operating (Chapters 9 to 12). From now on and unless otherwise specified, the supply curve will be taken to be positively sloped (its usual shape).

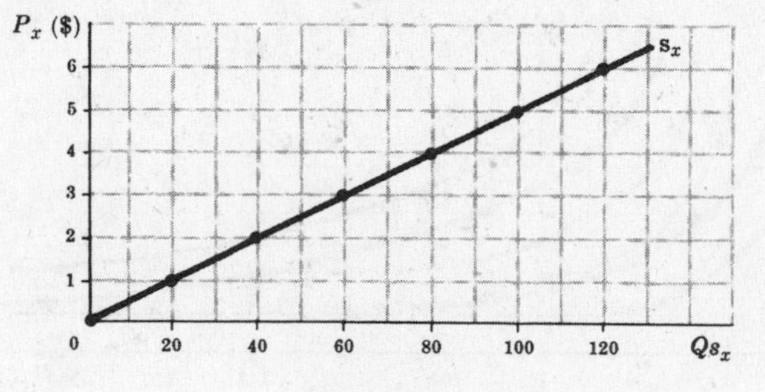

Fig. 2-15

(*c*) The things that are kept constant in defining a producer's supply schedule and in drawing the producer's supply curve are the technology in the production of the commodity, the prices of the inputs necessary to produce this commodity, and the features of nature (if X is an agricultural product).

(*d*) Any price above zero will induce the producer to place some quantity of commodity X on the market.

2.13 (*a*) From the producer's supply schedule for commodity X in Table 2.15, draw the supply curve. (*b*) In what way is this supply curve different from the one in Problem 2.12?

Table 2.15

P_x (\$)	6	5	4	3	2	1
Qs_x	42	40	36	30	20	0

(*a*)

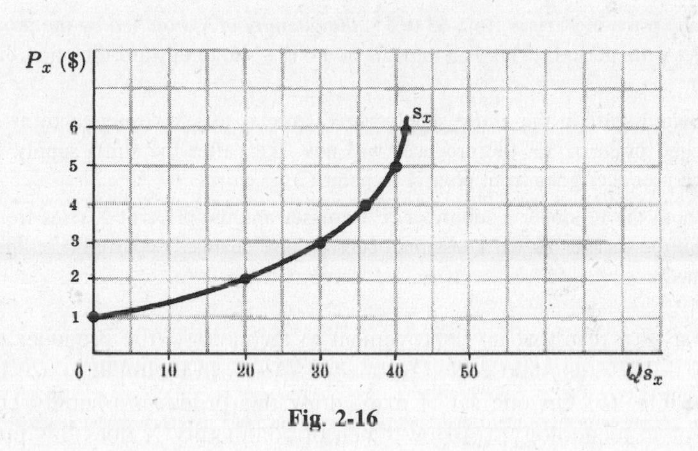

Fig. 2-16

(*b*) This producer's supply curve is given by a curve, while in Problem 2.12 it was given by a straight line. In the real world, a supply curve can be a straight line or a curve. For simplicity, in Problem 2.12 (and in the text) we dealt with a straight line (positively sloped) supply curve. Also to be noted is that according to the supply curve drawn above, the producer will begin to offer some quantity of X for sale only for prices above \$1.

2.14 Table 2.16 gives two supply schedules of a producer of commodity X. The first of these two supply schedules (Qs_x) is the same as the supply schedule in Problem 2.13. The second (Qs'_x) resulted from an increase in the prices of the inputs necessary to produce commodity X (everything else remained constant). (*a*) Plot the points of the two supply schedules on the same set of axes and get the two supply curves. (*b*) What would happen if the price of X rose from \$3 to \$5 before the shift in supply? (*c*) What quantity of commodity X will the producer place on the market at the price of \$3 before and after the supply curve shifted up? (*d*) What happens if at the same time the producer's supply of X decreases, the price of X rises from \$3 to \$5?

Table 2.16

P_x (\$)	6	5	4	3	2	1
Qs_x	42	40	36	30	20	0
Qs_x'	22	20	16	10	0	0

(*a*)

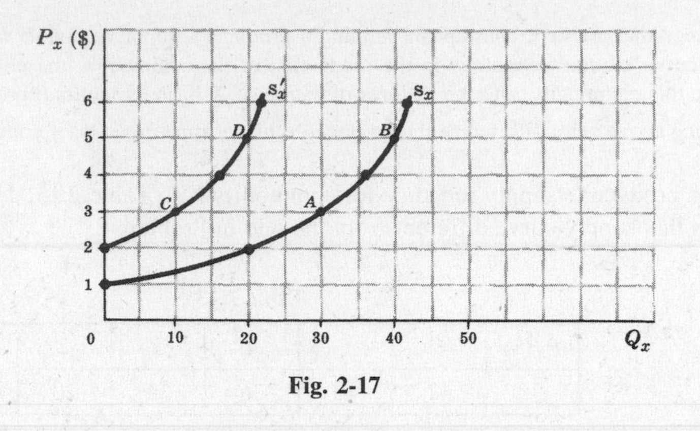

Fig. 2-17

(*b*) When the price of X rises from \$3 to \$5, *the quantity of X supplied* by the producer increases from 30 to 40 units per time period. (This is a movement along s_x in an upward direction, from point *A* to point *B* in the figure.)

(*c*) The upward shift in the entire supply curve from s_x to s_x' is referred to as *a decrease in supply*. At the unchanged price of \$3, the producer will now (i.e., after the shift) supply 10 units of X rather than 30 (i.e., the producer goes from point *A* to point *C*).

(*d*) When both the producer's supply of X decreases and the price of X rises from \$3 to \$5, the producer will place on the market 10 units less than before these changes occurred (i.e., the producer goes from point *A* to point *D*).

2.15 Suppose that as a result of an improvement in technology, the producer's supply function becomes $Qs_x' = -10 + 20P_x$ (as opposed to $Qs_x = -40 + 20P_x$ in Example 7). (*a*) Derive this producer's new supply schedule. (*b*) On one set of axes, draw this producer's supply curves before and after the improvement in technology, (*c*) How much of commodity X does this producer supply at the price of \$4 before and after the improvement in technology?

(*a*)

Table 2.17

P_x ($)	6	4	2	.5
Qs_x'	110	70	30	0

(*b*)

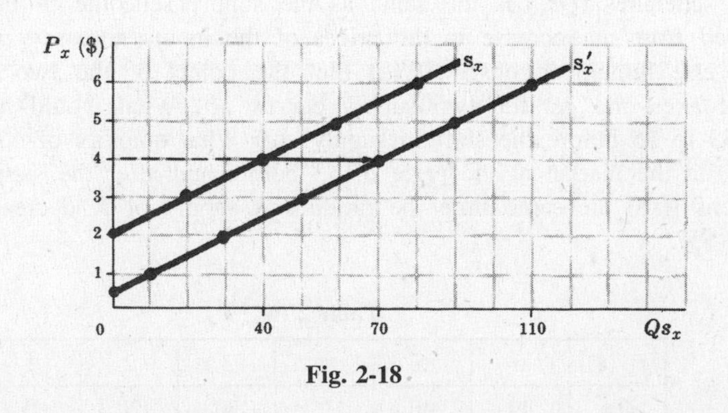

Fig. 2-18

(*c*) Before the supply curve increased (shifted down), the producer offered for sale 40 units of X at the price of \$4. After the improvement in technology, the producer is willing to offer 70 units of X at the same commodity price of \$4.

2.16 Table 2.18 gives the supply schedules of the three producers of commodity X in the market. Draw, on one set of axes, the three producers' supply curves and derive geometrically the market supply curve for commodity X.

Table 2.18

P_x (\$)	Quantity Supplied (per time period)		
	Producer 1	Producer 2	Producer 3
6	22	42	53
5	20	40	50
4	16	36	46
3	10	30	42
2	0	20	35
1	0	0	25
0	0	0	10

From Table 2.18, we get

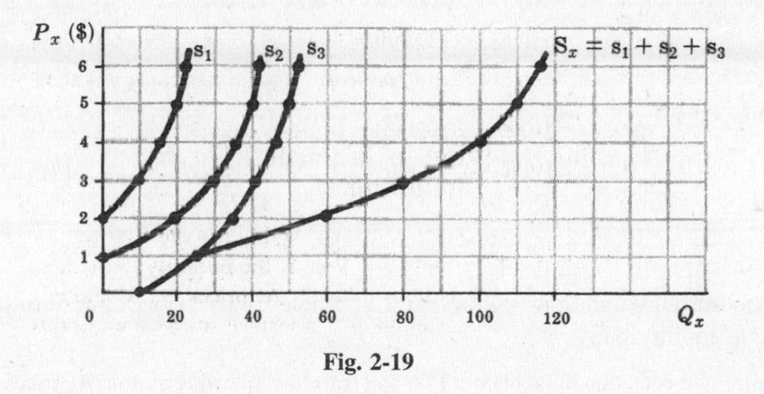

Fig. 2-19

This market supply curve was obtained by the horizontal summation of the three producers' supply curves for commodity X. (Some qualifications of this procedure will be discussed in Chapter 9.)

EQUILIBRIUM

2.17 There are 10,000 identical individuals in the market for commodity X, each with a demand function given by $Qd_x = 12 - 2P_x$ (see Problem 2.3), and 1000 identical producers of commodity X, each with a function given by $Qs_x = 20P_x$ (see Problem 2.12). (*a*) Find the market demand function and the market supply function for commodity X. (*b*) Find the market demand schedule and the market supply schedule of commodity X and from them find the equilibrium price and the equilibrium quantity. (*c*) Plot, on one set of axes, the market demand curve and the market supply curve for commodity X and show the equilibrium point. (*d*) Obtain the equilibrium price and the equilibrium quantity mathematically.

(*a*)

$$QD_x = 10{,}000(12 - 2P_x) \ \textit{cet. par.}$$
$$= 120{,}000 - 20{,}000P_x \ \textit{cet. par.}$$

$$QS_x = 1000(20P_x) \ \textit{cet. par.}$$
$$= 20{,}000P_x \ \textit{cet. par.}$$

(*b*) **Table 2.19**

P_x (\$)	QD_x	QS_x
6	0	120,000
5	20,000	100,000
4	40,000	80,000
3	60,000	60,000 ← Equilibrium
2	80,000	40,000
1	100,000	20,000
0	120,000	0

(*c*)

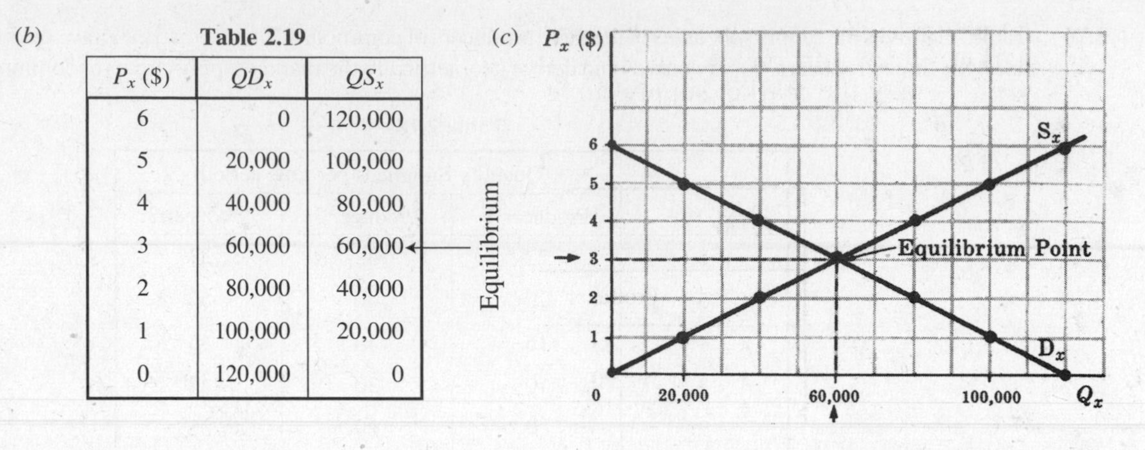

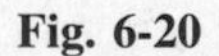

Fig. 6-20

(*d*)

$$QD_x = QS_x$$
$$120{,}000 - 20{,}000P_x = 20{,}000P_x$$
$$120{,}000 = 40{,}000P_x$$
$$P_x = \$3 \quad \text{(equilibrium price)}$$
$$QD_x = 120{,}000 - 20{,}000(3) \quad \text{or} \quad QS_x = 20{,}000(3)$$
$$= 60{,}000 \quad \text{(unit of X)} \qquad = 60{,}000 \quad \text{(units of X)}$$

2.18 (*a*) Is the equilibrium condition in Problem 2.17 stable? Why? (*b*) Define unstable equilibrium and *metastable* equilibrium.

(*a*) The equilibrium condition in Problem 2.17 is stable for the following reason. At prices above the equilibrium price, the quantity supplied exceeds the quantity demanded. A surplus results and the price is bid down toward the equilibrium level. At prices below the equilibrium level, the quantity demanded exceeds the quantity supplied. A shortage of the commodity arises and the price is bid up toward the equilibrium level. This is reflected in Table 2.20 and Fig. 2-21.

Table 2.20

P_x (\$)	QD_x	QS_x	Pressure on Price
6	0	120,000	downward
5	20,000	100,000	downward
4	40,000	80,000	downward
3	60,000	60,000	Equilibrium
2	80,000	40,000	upward
1	100,000	20,000	upward
0	120,000	0	upward

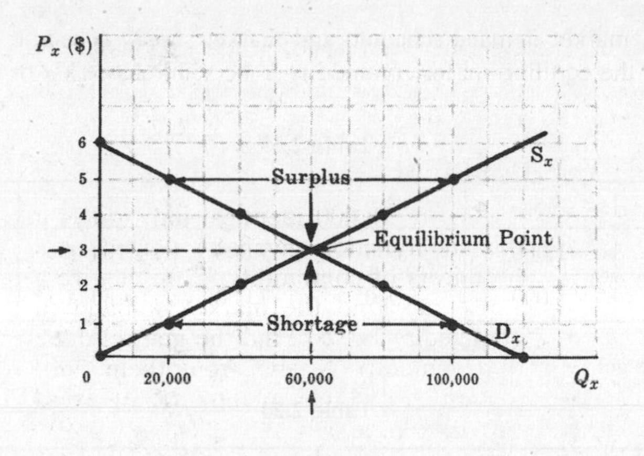

Fig. 2-21

(*b*) We have a situation of unstable equilibrium when a displacement from equilibrium brings into operation market forces that push us even further away from equilibrium. This occurs when the market supply curve has a smaller slope than the market demand curve for the commodity. In the unlikely case that the market demand curve and the market supply curve coincide, we have a situation of neutral or *metastable* equilibrium. Should this occur, a movement away from an equilibrium point does not activate any automatic force either to return to or to move further away from the original equilibrium point.

2.19 Table 2.21 gives the market demand schedule and the market supply schedule of commodity Y. Is the equilibrium for commodity Y stable or unstable? Why?

Table 2.21

P_y ($)	5	4	3	2	1
QD_y	5,000	6,000	7,000	8,000	9,000
QS_y	1,000	4,000	7,000	10,000	13,000

From Table 2.21, we get

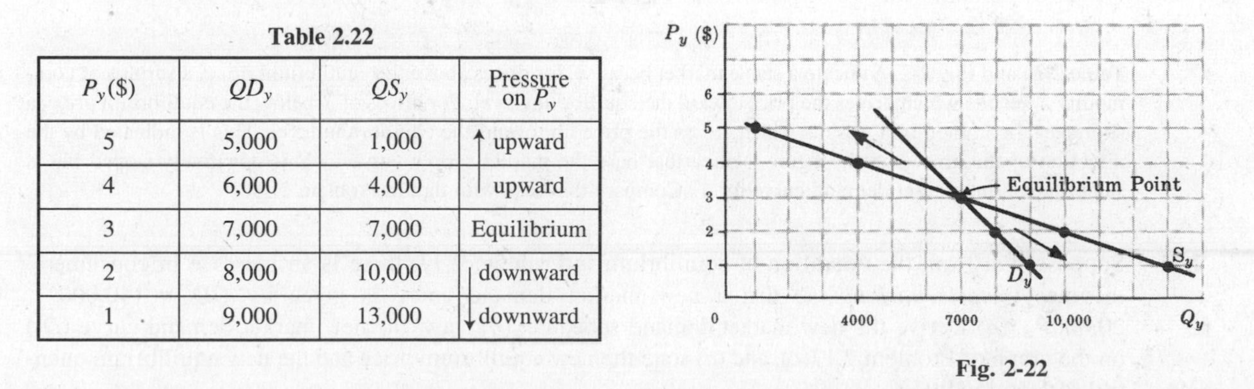

Table 2.22

P_y($)	QD_y	QS_y	Pressure on P_y
5	5,000	1,000	↑ upward
4	6,000	4,000	upward
3	7,000	7,000	Equilibrium
2	8,000	10,000	downward
1	9,000	13,000	↓ downward

Fig. 2-22

Table 2.22 and Fig. 2-22 show that the equilibrium price is $3 and the equilibrium quantity is 7000 units. If, for some reason, the price of Y rises to $4, the quantity demanded (6000 units) will exceed the quantity supplied (4000), creating a *shortage* (of 2000). This shortage will cause the price of Y to rise even more, and we move still further from equilibrium. The opposite occurs if a displacement causes the price of Y to fall below the equilibrium price. Thus, the equilibrium for commodity Y is unstable.

2.20 If commodity Y's market demand schedule and market supply schedule are instead those given in Table 2.23, would the equilibrium for commodity Y be stable, unstable or metastable? Why?

Table 2.23

P_y (\$)	5	4	3	2	1
QD_y	1,000	4,000	7,000	10,000	13,000
QS_y	5,000	6,000	7,000	8,000	9,000

From Table 2.23, we get

Table 2.24

P_y (\$)	QD_y	QS_y	Pressure on P_y
5	1,000	5,000	downward
4	4,000	6,000	downward
3	7,000	7,000	Equilibrium
2	10,000	8,000	upward
1	13,000	9,000	upward

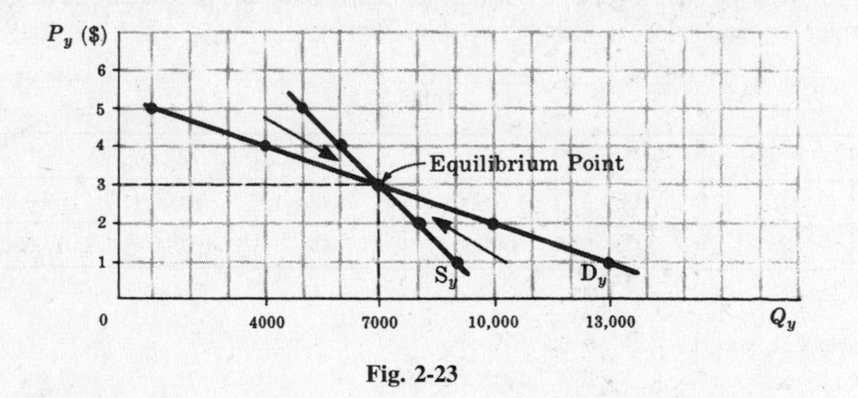

Fig. 2-23

Table 2.24 and Fig. 2-23 indicate a stable market because, for prices above the equilibrium price, a surplus of commodity Y results which drives the price toward the equilibrium level. For prices of Y below the equilibrium price, a shortage of commodity Y results which drives the price up toward the equilibrium level. This is indicated by the direction of the arrows in the figure. Notice that here the market supply curve of Y is negatively sloped but is steeper than the market demand curve for Y. Compare this case with that in Problem 2.19.

2.21 Suppose that from the condition of equilibrium in Problem 2.17, there is an increase in consumers' incomes (*ceteris paribus*) so that a new market demand curve is given by $QD'_x = 140{,}000 - 20{,}000P_x$. (*a*) Derive the new market demand schedule, (*b*) show the new market demand curve (D'_x) on the graph of Problem 2.17(*c*), and (*c*) state the new equilibrium price and the new equilibrium quantity for commodity X.

(*a*) **Table 2.25**

P_x (\$)	6	5	4	3	2	1	0
QD'_x	20,000	40,000	60,000	80,000	100,000	120,000	140,000

(*b*)

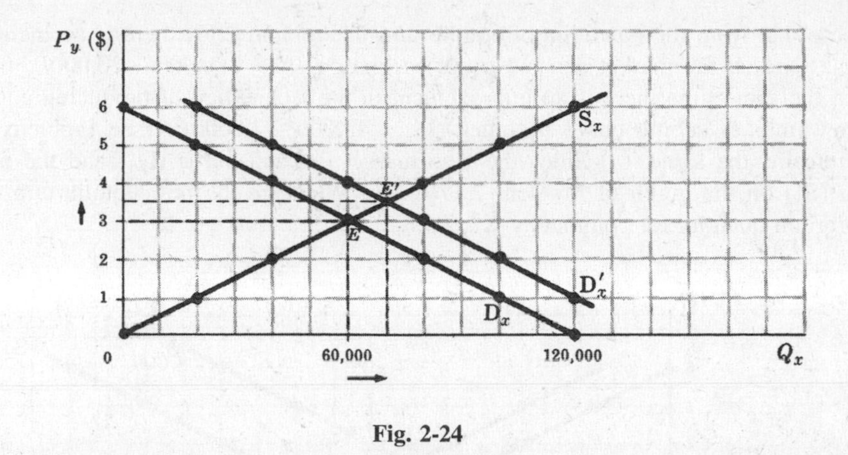

Fig. 2-24

(*c*) When D_x shifts up to D'_x (while everything else remains the same), the equilibrium price of X *rises* from $3 to $3.50. The equilibrium quantity of X rises from 60,000 to 70,000 units per time period.

2.22 Suppose that from the condition of equilibrium in Problem 2.17, there is an improvement in the technology of producing commodity X (*ceteris paribus*) so that a new market supply curve is given by $QS'_x = 40{,}000 + 20{,}000P_x$. (*a*) Derive the new market supply schedule, (*b*) show the new market supply curve (S'_x) on the graph of Problem 2.17(*c*), and (*c*) state the new equilibrium price and the new equilibrium quantity for commodity X.

(*a*)

Table 2.26

P_x ($)	6	5	4	3	2	1	0
QS'_x	160,000	140,000	120,000	100,000	80,000	60,000	40,000

(*b*)

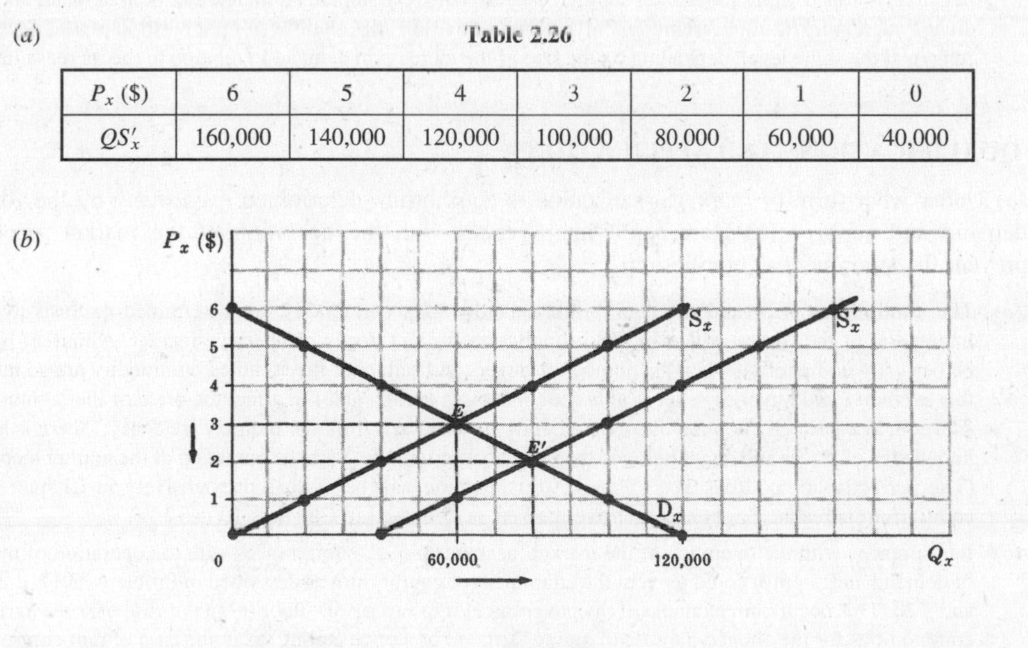

Fig. 2-25

(*c*) When S_x shifts down to S'_x (an increase in supply resulting from an improvement in technology, while everything else remains constant), the equilibrium price of X falls from $3 to $2. The equilibrium quantity of X rises from 60,000 to 80,000 units per time period.

2.23 Suppose that from the condition of equilibrium in Problem 2.17, there is an increase in consumers' incomes so that the market demand curve becomes $QD'_x = 140{,}000 - 20{,}000P_x$ (see Problem 2.21), and at the same time there is an improvement in the technology of producing commodity X so that the new market supply curve becomes $QS'_x = 40{,}000 + 20{,}000P_x$ (see Problem 2.22). Everything else remains the same. (*a*) Show the new market demand curve (D'_x) and the new market supply curve (S'_x) on the graph of Problem 2.17(*c*). (*b*) What are the new equilibrium price and the new equilibrium quantity for commodity X?

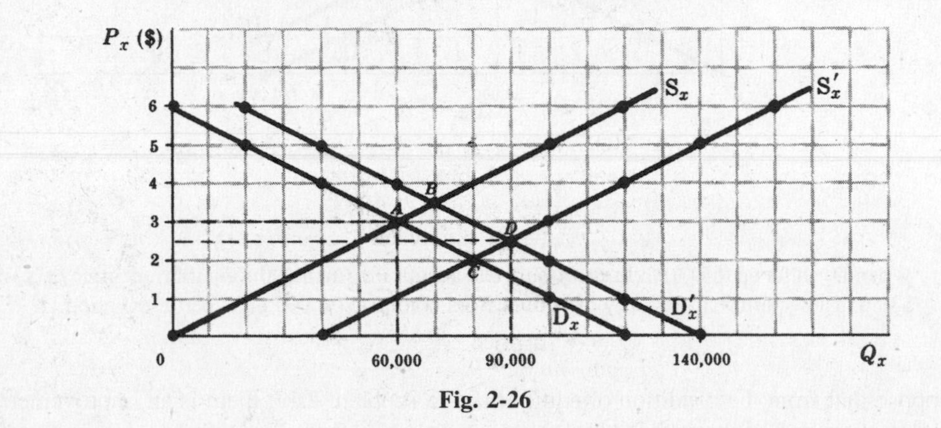

Fig. 2-26

(*b*) When D_x shifts to D'_x and S_x shifts to S'_x, the equilibrium price of X falls from $3 to $2.50. The equilibrium quantity rises from 60,000 to 90,000 units per time period. This corresponds to a movement from equilibrium point *A* to equilibrium point *D* in Fig. 2-26. (Point *B* represents the equilibrium point found in Problem 2.21. Point *C* corresponds to the equilibrium point found in Problem 2.22.) Thus, when the market demand curve is negatively sloped while the market supply curve is positively sloped, an increase in both demand and supply always increases the equilibrium quantity. At the same time, the equilibrium price can increase, decrease, or remain at the same level, depending on the size of the increase in demand in relation to the increase in supply.

SOME QUALIFICATIONS AND APPLICATIONS

2.24 (*a*) Under what form of market organization is equilibrium determined *exclusively* by the forces of demand and supply? (*b*) How could interferences with the operation of the market mechanism prevent the attainment of equilibrium?

(*a*) The equilibrium price and the equilibrium quantity of a commodity are determined exclusively by the interaction of the forces of demand and supply only in a *perfectly competitive* market. A market is said to be perfectly competitive when the number of buyers and sellers of the identical commodity are so numerous that no individual buyer or seller is able (or behaves as though able) to affect the price of the commodity. In addition, in a perfectly competitive market, entry into and exit from the industry are "easy," there is a perfect knowledge of prices and quantities, and there are no interferences with the operation of the market mechanism. (The perfectly competitive type of market organization will be discussed extensively in Chapter 9. How equilibrium is reached in noncompetitive markets is discussed in Chapters 10 to 12.)

(*b*) Interferences with the operation of the market mechanism (i.e., interferences with the operation of the forces of demand and supply) could prevent the attainment of equilibrium as described in Problems 2.17, 2.21, 2.22, and 2.23. This occurs, for example, if the government imposes a price floor (as in the case of some agricultural commodities for the alleged purpose of aiding farmers) or a price ceiling (as in the case of rent control for the alleged purpose of helping poor families). In such cases, the equilibrium price may not be attained and either a surplus or a shortage of the commodity results.

2.25 What happens if, starting from the position of equilibrium in Problem 2.17(*b*) and (*c*), the government (*a*) imposes a price floor of $4 on commodity X? (*b*) Imposes instead a price ceiling of $2 on commodity X?

(*a*) If P_x is not allowed to fall below $4, a surplus of 40,000 units of X will result per time period.

(*b*) If P_x is not allowed to rise above $2, a shortage of 40,000 units of X would result per time period. *Ceteris paribus*, this surplus or shortage would persist indefinitely and at the same level, time period after time period.

2.26 What happens if the government (*a*) grants a per-unit cash subsidy to all producers of a commodity or (*b*) collects instead a per-unit sales tax from all the producers of the commodity? (*c*) How is the imposition of a price floor or price ceiling different from the granting of a per-unit cash subsidy or the collecting of a per-unit sales tax from all the producers of a commodity?

(*a*) If the government grants a per-unit cash subsidy to all the producers of a commodity, the supply curve of each producer will shift downward by a vertical distance equal to the amount of the cash subsidy per unit. This is like a reduction in the costs of production; it has the same effect on the producers' supply curves and the market supply curve as an improvement in technology.

(*b*) The exact opposite to the result in part (*a*) occurs if instead the government collects a per-unit sales tax from each of the individual producers of commodity X.

(*c*) The imposition of a price floor or a price ceiling represents an interference with the operation of the market mechanism and as a result, the equilibrium point of the commodity may not be reached.

On the other hand, when the government grants a per-unit cash subsidy or collects a per-unit sales tax from all producers of the commodity, the equilibrium point will change *but it will still be determined by the intersection of the market demand curve and the market supply curve of the commodity*. The government is then said to be *working through the market* rather than interfering with its operation. In subsequent chapters, we will see that, in general, it is more efficient to work through the market mechanism than to interfere with its operation. (Additional qualifications to our concept of equilibrium were discussed in Chapter 1 under the headings of Comparative Statics and Partial Equilibrium.)

2.27 Suppose that from the condition of equilibrium in Problem 2.17, the government decides to grant a subsidy of $1 on each unit of commodity X produced to each of the 1000 identical producers of commodity X. (*a*) What effect does this have on the equilibrium price and quantity of commodity X? (*b*) Do consumers of commodity X reap any benefit from this?

(*a*) The subsidy causes each producer's supply curve and the market supply curve for X to shift down by a vertical distance equal to $1. The new market supply curve is indicated by S'_x and the new equilibrium point by E' in Fig. 2-27. The new equilibrium price for commodity X is $2.50 and the new equilibrium quantity is 70,000 units.

(*b*) Even though the subsidy was paid to producers of commodity X, consumers of this commodity also share in the benefit. Consumers now pay only $2.50 for each unit of X purchased rather than the $3 they paid before the subsidy was granted, and they now consume 70,000 rather than 60,000 units.

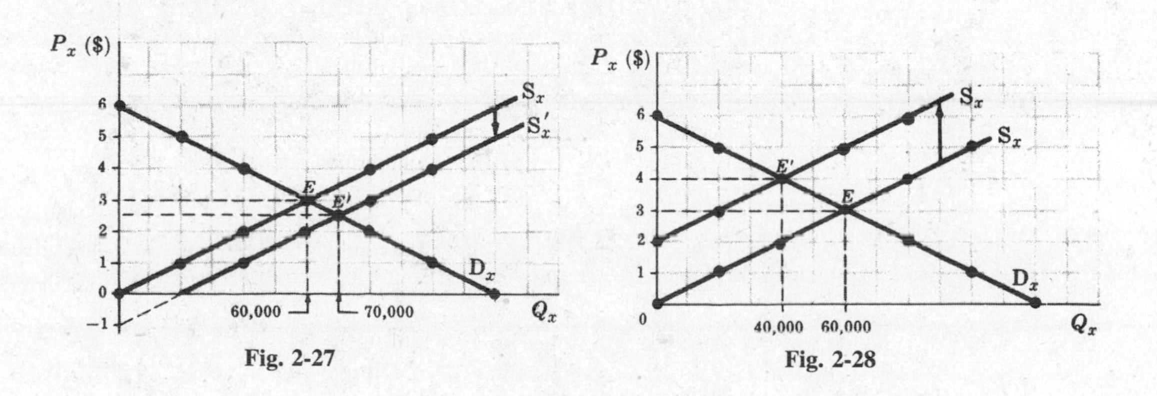

Fig. 2-27 Fig. 2-28

2.28 Suppose that from the equilibrium condition in Problem 2.17, the government decides to collect a sales tax of $2 per unit sold, from each of the 1000 identical sellers of commodity X. (*a*) What effect does this have on the equilibrium price and quantity of commodity X? (*b*) Who actually pays the tax? (*c*) What is the total amount or taxes collected by the government?

(*a*) The tax causes each seller's supply curve and the market supply curve for X to shift up by a vertical distance equal to $2. The new market supply curve is indicated by S'_x and the new equilibrium point by E' in Fig. 2-28. The new equilibrium price is $4 and the new equilibrium quantity is 40,000 units.

(*b*) Even though the government collects the tax from the seller, the consumer shares in the payment of the tax. After the imposition of the tax, consumers pay $4 for each unit of commodity X purchased (rather than $3 paid before the imposition of the tax) and consume only 40,000 units of X per time period (rather than 60,000). Sellers receive $4 per unit of X sold but retain only $2 per unit (the remaining $2 going to the government). Thus, of the tax of $2 per unit, $1 is paid by the consumer and $1 by the seller. In this case, the burden (or, as it is called, the *incidence*) of the tax falls equally on consumers and sellers. (We will return to the question of the incidence of a per-unit sales tax in the next chapter.)

(*c*) The total amount of taxes collected by the government is $80,000 per time period (i.e., the new equilibrium quantity of 40,000 units times the tax of $2 per unit).

CHAPTER 3

The Measurement of Elasticities

3.1 PRICE ELASTICITY OF DEMAND

The coefficient of *price elasticity of demand* (e) measures the percentage change in the quantity of a commodity demanded per unit of time resulting from a given percentage change in the price of the commodity. Since price and quantity are inversely related, the coefficient of price elasticity of demand is a negative number. In order to avoid dealing with negative values, a minus sign is often introduced into the formula for e. Letting ΔQ represent the change in the quantity demanded of a commodity resulting from a given change in its price (ΔP), we have

$$e = -\frac{\Delta Q/Q}{\Delta P/P} = -\frac{\Delta Q}{\Delta P} \cdot \frac{P}{Q}$$

Demand is said to be *elastic* if $e > 1$, *inelastic* if $e < 1$, and *unitary elastic* if $e = 1$.

EXAMPLE 1. Given the market demand schedule in Table 3.1 and market demand curve in Fig. 3-1, we can find e for a movement from point B to point D and from D to B, as follows:

Table 3.1

Point	P_x (\$)	Q_x
A	8	0
B	7	1000
C	6	2000
D	5	3000
F	4	4000
G	3	5000
H	2	6000
L	1	7000
M	0	8000

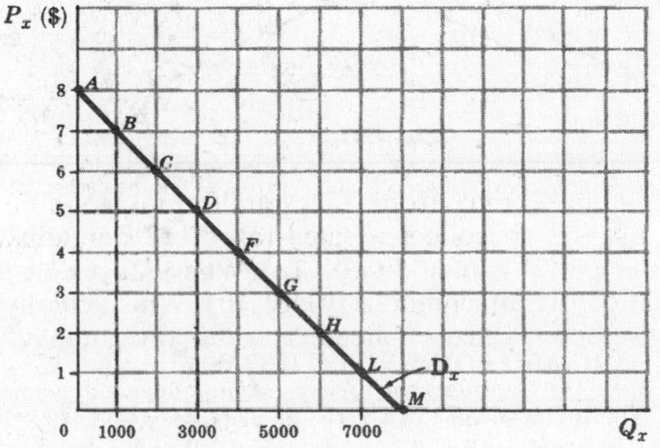

Fig. 3-1

From B to D, $$e = \frac{Q_D - Q_B}{P_D - P_B} \cdot \frac{P_B}{Q_B} = -\left(\frac{2000}{-2}\right)\left(\frac{7}{1000}\right) = 7$$

From D to B, $$e = \frac{Q_B - Q_D}{P_B - P_D} \cdot \frac{P_D}{Q_D} = -\left(\frac{-2000}{2}\right)\left(\frac{5}{3000}\right) \cong 1.67$$

(The symbol $\cong$ means *approximately equal to.*) Thus, we get a different value for e if we move from B to D than if we move from D to B. This difference results because we used a different base in computing the percentage changes in each case.

We can avoid getting different results by using the *average* of the two prices $[(P_B + P_D)/2]$ and the *average* of the two quantities $[(Q_B + Q_D)/2]$ instead of either P_B and Q_B or P_D and Q_D in the formula to find e. Thus,

$$e = -\frac{\Delta Q}{\Delta P} \cdot \frac{(P_B + P_D)/2}{(Q_B + Q_D)/2} = -\frac{\Delta Q}{\Delta P} \cdot \frac{P_B + P_D}{Q_B + Q_D}$$

Applying this modified formula to find e either for a movement from B to D or for a movement from D to B, we get

$$e = -\left(-\frac{2000}{2}\right)\left(\frac{12}{4000}\right) = 3$$

This is the equivalent of finding e at the point midway between B and D (i e., at point C).

EXAMPLE 2. Given the market demand schedule in Table 3.2 and the market demand curve in Fig. 3-2, we can find e for a movement from point C to point F, from F to C and midway between C and F, as follows:

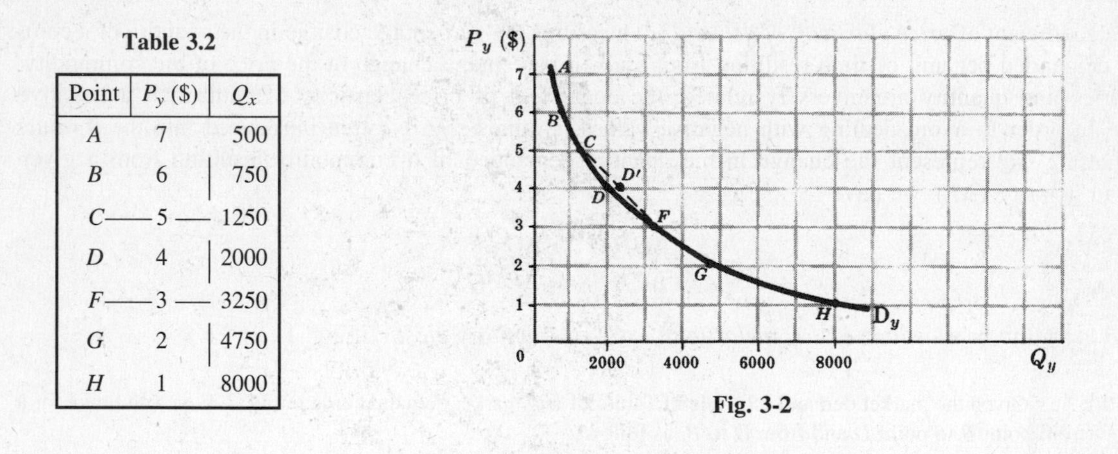

Table 3.2

Point	P_y (\$)	Q_x
A	7	500
B	6	750
C	5	1250
D	4	2000
F	3	3250
G	2	4750
H	1	8000

Fig. 3-2

From C to F, $$e = -\frac{\Delta Q}{\Delta P} \cdot \frac{P_C}{Q_C} = -\left(\frac{2000}{-2}\right)\left(\frac{5}{1250}\right) = 4$$

From F to C, $$e = -\frac{\Delta Q}{\Delta P} \cdot \frac{P_F}{Q_F} = -\left(\frac{-2000}{2}\right)\left(\frac{3}{3250}\right) \cong 0.92$$

At the point midway between C and F (point D' on the dashed chord),

$$e = -\frac{\Delta Q}{\Delta P} \cdot \frac{(P_C + P_F)}{(Q_C + Q_F)} = -\left(-\frac{2000}{2}\right)\left(\frac{8}{4500}\right) \cong 1.78$$

3.2 ARC AND POINT ELASTICITY

The coefficient of price elasticity of demand between two points on a demand curve is called *arc elasticity*. Thus, in Examples 1 and 2, we found arc elasticity. Later we will see that the coefficient of price elasticity of demand in general differs at every point along a demand curve. Arc elasticity is, therefore, only an estimate.

This estimate improves as the arc becomes smaller and approaches a point in the limit. *Point elasticity* of demand can be found geometrically as shown in Examples 3 and 4.

EXAMPLE 3. We can find the elasticity of the demand curve in Example 1 at point C geometrically as follows. (For easy reference, Fig. 3-1, with some modifications, is repeated here as Fig. 3-3.) Since we want to measure elasticity at point C, we have only a *single* price and a *single* quantity. Expressing each of the values in the formula for e in terms of distances, we get:

$$e = -\frac{\Delta Q}{\Delta P} \cdot \frac{P}{Q}$$

$$= \frac{NM}{NC} \cdot \frac{NC}{ON}$$

$$= \frac{NM}{ON} = \frac{6000}{2000} = 3$$

Note that this value of e is the same as that given by the modified formula in Example 1.

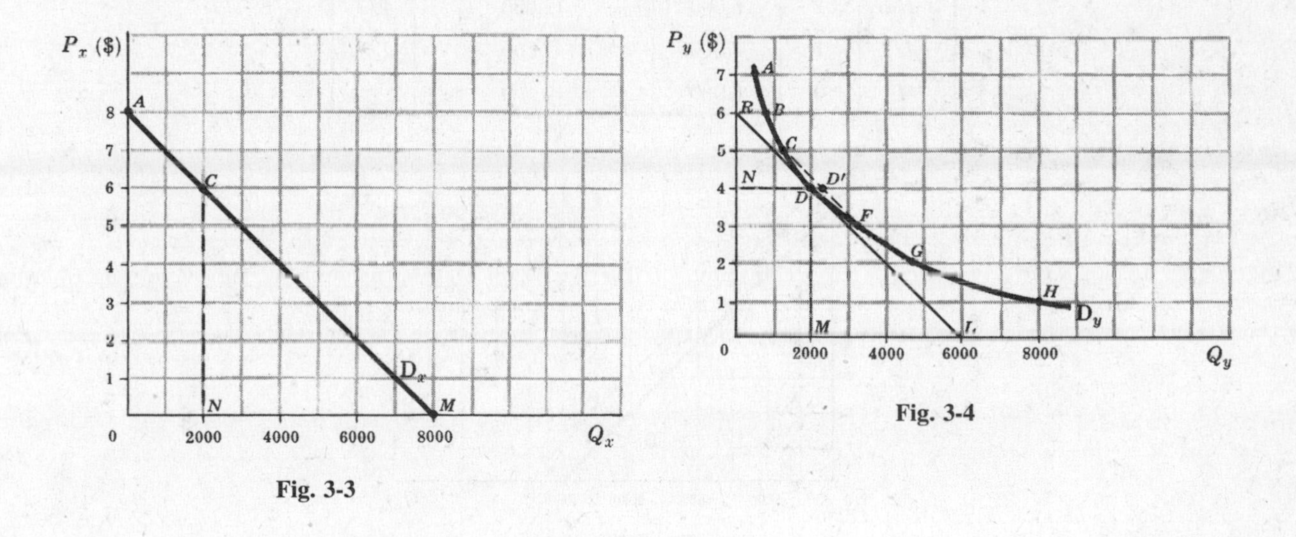

Fig. 3-3

Fig. 3-4

EXAMPLE 4. We can find e at point D for the demand curve of Example 2, as follows. (For easy reference, Fig. 3-2 with some modifications is repeated as Fig. 3-4.)

We draw a tangent to D_y at point D and then proceed as in Example 3. Thus,

$$e = \frac{ML}{OM} = \frac{4000}{2000} = 2$$

Notice that the price elasticity at D' (about 1.78 found in Example 2) differs slightly from the point elasticity of D_y at point D. The difference is due to the curvature of D_y and would diminish as C and F move closer to each other.

3.3 POINT ELASTICITY AND TOTAL EXPENDITURES

A straight-line demand curve (extended to both axes) is elastic above its midpoint, has unitary elasticity at the midpoint, and is inelastic below its midpoint (see Example 5). There are no such generalizations for curvilinear demand curves (see Problems 3.6 to 3.9). In the special case when a demand curve takes the shape of a rectangular hyperbola, $e = 1$ at every point on it (see Problem 3.8).

Regardless of the shape of the demand curve, as the price of a commodity falls, the total expenditures of consumers on the commodity (P times Q) rise when $e > 1$, remain unchanged when $e = 1$, and fall when $e < 1$ (see Example 5).

EXAMPLE 5. In Fig. 3-5 and Table 3.3, we find e at points B, C, D, F, G, H, and L for the demand curve of Example 1 and can observe what happens.to total expenditures on commodity X as P_x falls. At point B, $e = TM/OT = 7000/1000 = 7$ (see Fig. 3-5). The coefficient of price elasticity of D_x at other points is found in a similar way. As we approach point A, e approaches infinity. As we approach point M, e approaches zero. (For the factors affecting e, see Problem 3.10.)

Table 3.3

Point	P_x ($)	Q_x	Total Expenditures ($)	e
A	8	0	0	
B	7	1,000	7,000	7
C	6	2,000	12,000	3
D	5	3,000	15,000	5/3
F	4	4,000	16,000	1
G	3	5,000	15,000	3/5
H	2	6,000	12,000	1/3
L	1	7,000	7,000	1/7
M	0	8,000	0	

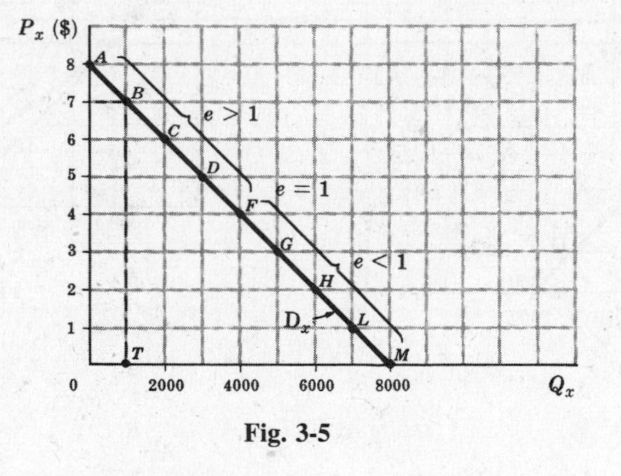

Fig. 3-5

3.4 INCOME ELASTICITY OF DEMAND

The coefficient of *income elasticity of demand* (e_M) measures the percentage change in the amount of a commodity purchased per unit time ($\Delta Q/Q$) resulting from a given percentage change in a consumer's income ($\Delta M/M$). Thus

$$e_M = \frac{\Delta Q/Q}{\Delta M/M} = \frac{\Delta Q}{\Delta M} \cdot \frac{M}{Q}$$

When e_M is negative, the good is inferior. If e_M is positive, the good is normal. A normal good is usually a *luxury* if its $e_M > 1$, otherwise it is a *necessity*. Depending on the level of the consumer's income, e_M for a good is likely to vary considerably. Thus a good may be a luxury at "low" levels of income, a necessity at "intermediate" levels of income and an inferior good at "high" levels of income.

EXAMPLE 6. Columns (1) and (2) of Table 3.4 show the quantity of commodity X that an individual would purchase per year at various income levels. Column (5) gives the coefficient of income elasticity of demand of this individual for commodity X *between* the various successive levels of available income. Column (6) indicates the range of income over which commodity X is a luxury, a necessity or an inferior good. Commodity X might refer to bottles of champagne. At income levels above $24,000 per year, champagne becomes an inferior good for this individual (who presumably substitutes rare and very expensive wines for champagne).

Table 3.4

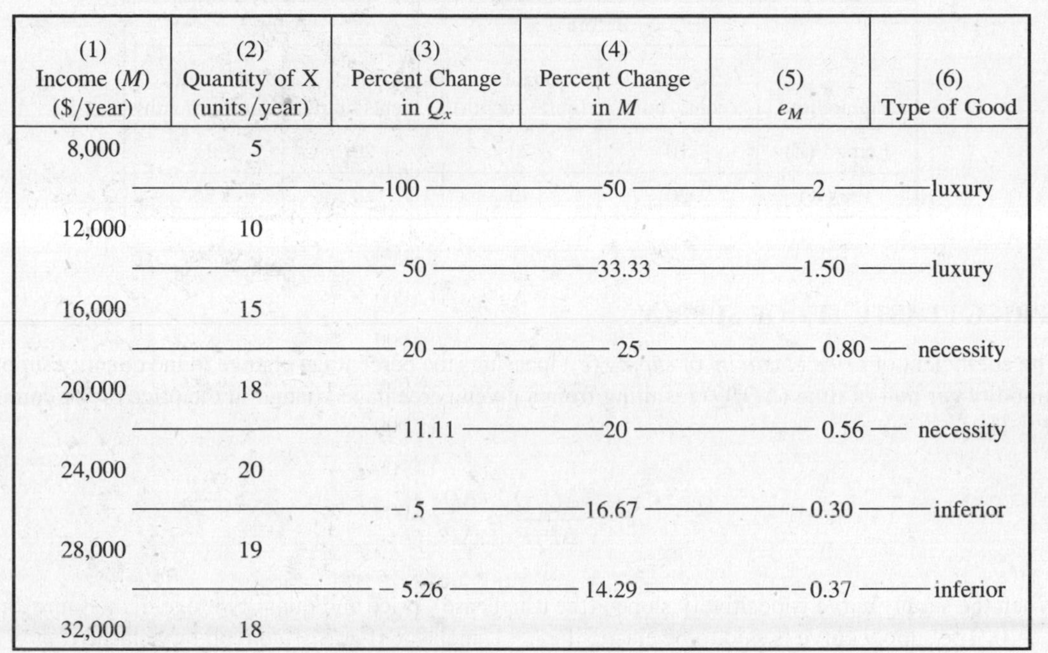

(1) Income (M) ($/year)	(2) Quantity of X (units/year)	(3) Percent Change in Q_x	(4) Percent Change in M	(5) e_M	(6) Type of Good
8,000	5				
		100	50	2	luxury
12,000	10				
		50	33.33	1.50	luxury
16,000	15				
		20	25	0.80	necessity
20,000	18				
		11.11	20	0.56	necessity
24,000	20				
		− 5	16.67	−0.30	inferior
28,000	19				
		− 5.26	14.29	−0.37	inferior
32,000	18				

3.5 CROSS ELASTICITY OF DEMAND

The coefficient of *cross elasticity of demand* of commodity X with respect to commodity Y(e_{xy}) measures the percentage change in the amount of X purchased per unit of time ($\Delta Q_x/Q_x$) resulting from a given percentage change in the price of Y($\Delta P_y/P_y$). Thus

$$e_{xy} = \frac{\Delta Q_x/Q_x}{\Delta P_y/P_y} = \frac{\Delta Q_x}{\Delta P_y} \cdot \frac{P_y}{Q_x}$$

If X and Y are substitutes, e_{xy} is positive. On the other hand, if X and Y are complements, e_{xy} is negative. When commodities are nonrelated (i.e., when they are independent of each other), $e_{xy} = 0$.

EXAMPLE 7. To find the cross elasticity of demand between tea (X) and coffee (Y) and between tea (X) and lemons (Z) for the data in the next table, we proceed as follows [Table 3.5(*a*) and (*b*) is the same as Tables 2.11 and 2.12 in Chapter 2]:

$$e_{xy} = \frac{\Delta Q_x}{\Delta P_y} \cdot \frac{P_y}{Q_x} = \left(\frac{+10}{+20}\right)\left(\frac{40}{40}\right) = +0.5$$

$$e_{xz} = \frac{\Delta Q_x}{\Delta P_z} \cdot \frac{P_z}{Q_x} = \left(\frac{-5}{+10}\right)\left(\frac{10}{40}\right) = -0.125$$

Since e_{xy} is positive, tea and coffee are substitutes. Since e_{xz} is negative, tea and lemons are complements. Problem 3.24 provides some empirical estimates of price, income, and cross elasticity of demand, while Problems 3.25 to 3.29 show some important applications of the concept of price elasticity of demand.

Table 3.5(*a*)

	Before		After	
Commodity	Price (cents/cup)	Quantity (units/month)	Price (cents/unit)	Quantity (units/month)
Lemon (Y)	40	50	60	30
Tea (X)	20	40	20	50

Table 3.5(*b*)

Commodity	Before		After	
	Price (cents/unit)	Quantity (units/month)	Price (cents/unit)	Quantity (units/month)
Lemon (Z)	10	20	20	15
Tea (X)	20	40	20	35

3.6 PRICE ELASTICITY OF SUPPLY

The coefficient of *price elasticity of supply* (e_s) measures the percentage change in the quantity supplied of a commodity per unit of time ($\Delta Q/Q$) resulting from a given percentage change in the price of the commodity ($\Delta P/P$). Thus

$$e_s = \frac{\Delta Q/Q}{\Delta P/P} = \frac{\Delta Q}{\Delta P} \cdot \frac{P}{Q}$$

When the supply curve is positively sloped (the usual case), price and quantity move in the same direction and $e_s > 0$. The supply curve is said to be elastic if $e_s > 1$, inelastic if $e_s < 1$, and unitary elastic if $e_s = 1$. Arc and point e_s can be found in the same way as arc and point e. When the supply curve is a positively sloped straight line, then, all along the line, $e_s > 1$, if the line crosses the price axis; $e_s < 1$, if it crosses the quantity axis; and $e_s = 1$, if it goes through the origin.

EXAMPLE 8. To find e_x for a movement from point *A* to point *C*, from *C* to *A* and midway between *A* and *C* (i.e., at point *B*) and midway between *C* and *F* (i.e., at point *D*) for the values of Table 3.6, we proceed as follows:

Table 3.6

Point	P_x (\$)	Q_x
A	6	8000
B	5	6000
C	6	4000
D	3	2000
F	2	0

From *A* to *C*,
$$e_s = \frac{\Delta P}{\Delta P} \cdot \frac{P_A}{Q_A} = \left(\frac{-4000}{-2}\right)\left(\frac{6}{8000}\right) = 1.5$$

From *C* to *A*,
$$e_s = \left(\frac{4000}{2}\right)\left(\frac{4}{4000}\right) = 2$$

At point *B*,
$$e_s = \frac{\Delta Q}{\Delta P} \cdot \frac{P_A + P_C}{Q_A + Q_C} = \left(\frac{4000}{2}\right)\left(\frac{10}{12{,}000}\right) \cong 1.67$$

At point *D*,
$$e_s = \frac{\Delta Q}{\Delta P} \cdot \frac{P_C + P_F}{Q_C + Q_F} = \left(\frac{4000}{2}\right)\left(\frac{6}{4000}\right) = 3$$

EXAMPLE 9. We can find e_s at points B and D geometrically from Fig. 3-6.

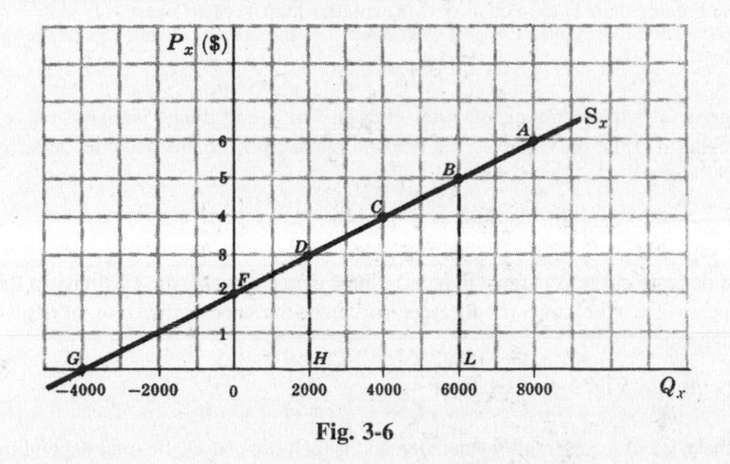

Fig. 3-6

At Point B, $$e_s = \frac{\Delta Q}{\Delta P} \cdot \frac{P_B}{Q_B} = \frac{GL}{LB} \cdot \frac{LB}{OL} = \frac{GL}{OL} = \frac{10{,}000}{6000} \cong 1.67$$

At point D, $$e_s = \frac{GH}{OH} = \frac{6000}{2000} = 3$$

To find point e_s, for a curvilinear supply curve, we draw a tangent to the supply curve at the point and then proceed as above (see Problems 3.21 and 3.22).

Glossary

Arc elasticity of demand The coefficient of price elasticity of demand between two points on a demand curve.

Cross elasticity of demand (e_{xy}) The ratio of the percentage change in the amount of commodity X purchased per unit of time to the percentage change in the price of commodity Y. If $e_{xy} > 0$, X and Y are substitutes; if $e_{xy} < 0$, X and Y are complements; and if $e_{xy} = 0$, X and Y are nonrelated (i.e., independent).

Income elasticity of demand (e_M) The ratio of the percentage change in the amount of a commodity purchased per unit of time to the percentage change in the consumer's income. If $e_M > 0$, the commodity is normal, and if $e_M < 0$, it is inferior; if $e_M > 1$, it is a luxury, and if $0 < e_M < 1$, it is a necessity.

Point elasticity of demand The coefficient of price elasticity of demand at a particular point on a demand curve.

Price elasticity of demand (e) The ratio of the percentage change in the quantity of a commodity demanded per unit of time to the percentage change in the price of the commodity. If $e > 1$, demand is elastic; if $e < 1$, demand is inelastic; and if $e = 1$, demand is unitary elastic.

Price elasticity of supply (e_s) The ratio of the percentage change in the quantity of a commodity supplied per unit of time to the percentage change in the price of the commodity.

Review Questions

1. If the percentage increase in the quantity of a commodity demanded is smaller than the percentage fall in its price, the coefficient of price elasticity of demand is (*a*) greater than 1, (*b*) equal to 1, (*c*) smaller than 1, or (*d*) zero.

   Ans. (*c*) See Section 3.1.

2. If the quantity of a commodity demanded remains unchanged as its price changes, the coefficient of price elasticity of demand is (*a*) greater than 1, (*b*) equal to 1, (*c*) smaller than 1, or (*d*) zero.

Ans. (*d*) See Section 3.1.

3. Arc elasticity gives a better estimate of point elasticity of a curvilinear demand curve as (*a*) the size of the arc becomes smaller, (*b*) the curvature of the demand curve over the arc becomes less, (*c*) both of the above, or (*d*) neither of the above.

Ans. (*c*) See Fig. 3-4 in Example 4.

4. If a straight-line demand curve is tangent to a curvilinear demand curve, the elasticity of the two demand curves at the point of tangency is (*a*) the same, (*b*) different, (*c*) can be the same or different, or (*d*) it depends on the location of the point of tangency.

Ans. (*a*) See point *D* in Fig. 3-4 of Example 4.

5. An increase in the price of a commodity when demand is inelastic causes the total expenditures of consumers of the commodity to (*a*) increase, (*b*) decrease, (*c*) remain unchanged, or (*d*) any of the above.

Ans. (*a*) See Section 3.3.

6. A fall in the price of a commodity whose demand curve is a rectangular hyperbola causes total expenditures on the commodity to (*a*) increase, (*b*) decrease, (*c*) remain unchanged, or (*d*) any of the above.

Ans. (*c*) See Section 3.3.

7. A negative income elasticity of demand for a commodity indicates that as income falls, the amount of the commodity purchased (*a*) rises, (*b*) falls, (*c*) remains unchanged, or (*d*) any of the above.

Ans. (*a*) See Section 3.4.

8. If the income elasticity of demand is greater than 1, the commodity is (*a*) a necessity, (*b*) a luxury, (*c*) an inferior good, or (*d*) a nonrelated good.

Ans. (*b*) See Section 3.4.

9. If the amounts of two commodities purchased both increase or decrease when the price of one changes, the cross elasticity of demand between them is (*a*) negative, (*b*) positive, (*c*) zero, or (*d*) 1.

Ans. (*a*) See Section 3.5.

10. If the amount of a commodity purchased remains unchanged when the price of another commodity changes, the cross elasticity of demand between them is (*a*) negative, (*b*) positive (*c*) zero, or (*d*) 1.

Ans. (*c*) See Section 3.5.

11. e_s for a positively sloped straight-line supply curve that intersects the price axis is (*a*) equal to zero, (*b*) equal to 1, (*c*) greater than 1, or (*d*) constant.

Ans. (*c*) See Example 9.

12. Which of the following elasticities measure a movement along a curve rather than a shift in the curve?

(*a*) The price elasticity of demand.
(*b*) The income elasticity of demand.
(*c*) The cross elasticity of demand.
(*d*) The price elasticity of supply.

Ans. (*a*) and (*d*). The price elasticity of demand and supply measures the relative responsiveness in quantity to the corresponding relative changes in the commodity price, keeping everything else constant. These are movements along a curve. The income elasticity and cross elasticity of demand measure shifts in demand.

Solved Problems

PRICE ELASTICITY OF DEMAND

3.1 (*a*) What does the *elasticity of demand* measure in general? (*b*) What do the *price elasticity of demand*, the *income elasticity of demand*, and the *cross elasticity of demand* measure in general?

(*a*) We saw in Chapter 2 that the amount of a commodity purchased per unit of time is a function of or depends on the price of the commodity, money incomes, the prices of other (related) commodities, tastes, and the number of buyers of the commodity in the market. A change in any of the above factors will cause a change in the amount of the commodity purchased per unit of time. The elasticity of demand measures the relative responsiveness in the amount purchased per unit of time to a change in any one of the above factors, while keeping the others constant.

(*b*) The *price elasticity of demand* measures the relative responsiveness in the quantity of a commodity demanded to changes in its price. The *income elasticity of demand* measures the relative responsiveness in the amount purchased to changes in money income. Similarly, the *cross elasticity of demand* measures the relative responsiveness in the amount purchased to changes in the price of a related commodity. The above elasticity concepts apply as much to the individual consumer's response as to the market response. However, we are primarily interested in the market responses.

3.2 Why don't we use the slope of the demand curve (i.e., $\Delta P/\Delta Q$) or its reciprocal (i.e., $\Delta Q/\Delta P$) to measure the responsiveness in the quantity of a commodity demanded to a change in its price?

The slope is not a useful measure since it is expressed in terms of the units of the problem. Thus by simply changing the units of the problem we can get a different slope. The use of the slope also would not allow us to compare in a meaningful way the degree of responsiveness of different commodities to changes in their prices. The coefficient of price elasticity of demand, relating as it does the *percentage* change in quantity to the corresponding *percentage* change in price, gives a measure which is *independent of the units of the problem* (i.e., e is a pure number).

3.3 For the market demand schedule in Table 3.7, (*a*) find the price elasticity of demand for a movement from point *B* to point *D*, from point' *D* to point *B*, and at the point midway between point *B* and point *D*. (*b*) Do the same for points *D* and *G*.

Table 3.7

Point	*A*	*B*	*C*	*D*	*F*	*G*	*H*
P_x($)	6	5	4	3	2	1	0
Q_x	0	20,000	40,000	60,000	80,000	100,000	120,000

(*a*) For a movement from *B* to *D*,

$$e = -\left(\frac{40{,}000}{-2}\right)\left(\frac{5}{20{,}000}\right) = 5$$

For a movement from *D* to *B*,

$$e = -\left(\frac{40{,}000}{2}\right)\left(\frac{3}{60{,}000}\right) = 1$$

At the point midway between *B* and *D* (i.e., at point *C*),

$$e = -\left(-\frac{40{,}000}{2}\right)\left(\frac{8}{80{,}000}\right) = 2$$

(*b*) For a movement from *D* to *G*,

$$e = -\left(\frac{40{,}000}{-2}\right)\left(\frac{3}{60{,}000}\right) = 1$$

For a movement from *G* to *D*,

$$e = -\left(\frac{-40{,}000}{2}\right)\left(\frac{1}{100{,}000}\right) = 0.2$$

At the point midway between *D* and *G* (i.e., at point *F*),

$$e = -\left(-\frac{40{,}000}{2}\right)\left(\frac{4}{160{,}000}\right) = 0.5$$

3.4 For the market demand schedule in Problem 3.3, (*a*) find *e* at point *C* *geometrically*, and (*b*) derive the formula for finding *e* geometrically at point C. (*c*) What happens to *e* as we approach point *A*? As we approach point *H*? Why?

(*a*) At point *C*,

$$e = \frac{LH}{OL} = \frac{80{,}000}{40{,}000} = 2$$

(see Fig. 3-7.)

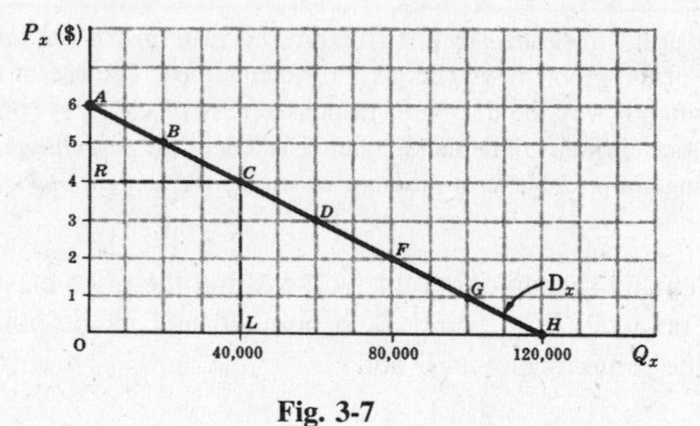

Fig. 3-7

(*b*)

$$e = -\frac{\Delta Q}{\Delta P}\cdot\frac{P}{Q} = \frac{LH}{\cancel{LC}}\cdot\frac{\cancel{LC}}{OL} = \frac{LH}{OL}$$

Notice that $\Delta Q/\Delta P$ is the reciprocal of the slope of D_x. Since the slope of a straight line remains constant

$$-\frac{\Delta Q}{\Delta P} = \frac{OH}{OA} = \frac{LH}{LC}$$

We have used LH/LC above in order to make the cancellations shown and express *e* as the ratio of two distances. The value of *e* at point *C* above coincides with the value found in Problem 3.3. By similar triangles

$$e = \frac{LH}{OL} = \frac{CH}{AC} = \frac{RO}{AR}$$

Thus, by dropping a perpendicular from any point on the demand curve to *either* the quantity or price axis, we can find the price elasticity of demand at that point as the ratio of the two distances defined.

(*c*) As we move toward point *A*, price elasticity increases and approaches infinity, since the numerator of the elasticity fraction increases while its denominator decreases. As we move toward point *H*, price elasticity decreases and approaches zero, since the numerator of the elasticity fraction decreases while its denominator increases.

3.5 (*a*) Find *e* geometrically at points *B*, *D*, *F*, and *G* for the market demand curve in Problem 3.4(*a*). What happens to total expenditures on commodity X as the price of X falls? (*b*) State and explain the general rule relating total expenditures on commodity X to *e* when P_x falls.

(a)

Table 3.8

Point	(1) P_x ($)	(2) Q_x	(3) Total Expenditures ($)	(4) e
A	6	0	0	
B	5	20,000	100,000	5
C	4	40,000	160,000	2
D	3	60,000	180,000	1
F	2	80,000	160,000	0.5
G	1	100,000	100,000	0.2
H	0	120,000	0	

(b) When the price of X falls, total expenditures rise as long as $e > 1$ (see Table 3.8). This is because as long as $e > 1$, the percentage increase in quantity (which by itself tends to increase total expenditures on commodity X) is greater than the percentage fall in price (which by itself tends to reduce total expenditures on X); therefore, total expenditures on X increase. Total expenditures reach a maximum when $e = 1$ and decline thereafter (see Table 3.8). The opposite occurs for price rises. Thus, total expenditures move in the opposite direction as prices when $e > 1$ and in the same direction as prices when $e < 1$.

3.6 For the market demand schedule in Table 3.9 (the same as in Example 2), *(a)* find the price elasticity of demand for a movement from point *A* to point *C*, from point *C* to point *A* and midway between *A* and *C*, and *(b)* do the same for points *F* and *H*.

Table 3.9

Point	*A*	*B*	*C*	*D*	*F*	*G*	*H*
P_y ($)	7	6	5	4	3	2	1
Q_y	500	750	1250	2000	3250	4750	8000

(a) For a movement from *A* to *C*,

$$e = -\left(\frac{750}{-2}\right)\left(\frac{7}{500}\right) = 5.25$$

For a movement from *C* to *A*,

$$e = -\left(\frac{-750}{2}\right)\left(\frac{5}{1250}\right) = 1.5$$

Midway between *A* and *C* (point *B′* in Fig. 3-8)

$$e = -\left(\frac{750}{2}\right)\left(\frac{12}{1750}\right) \cong 2.57$$

(b) For a movement from *F* to *H*,

$$e = -\left(\frac{4750}{-2}\right)\left(\frac{3}{3250}\right) \cong 2.19$$

For a movement from *H* to *F*,

$$e = -\left(\frac{-4750}{2}\right)\left(\frac{1}{8000}\right) \cong 0.3$$

Midway between F and H (point G' in Fig. 3-8)

$$e = -\left(-\frac{4750}{2}\right)\left(\frac{4}{11{,}250}\right) \cong 0.84$$

(For the elasticity from point C to point F, from F to C and midway between C and F, see Example 2.)

3.7 For the market demand schedule in Table 3.9, (*a*) find e at points B, G, and D and (*b*) state what happens to total expenditures on commodity Y when P_y falls.

(*a*) We can find e at points B and G geometrically from Fig. 3-8.

At point B, $$e = \frac{RN}{OR} = \frac{2500}{750} \cong 3.3$$

At point G, $$e = \frac{ML}{OR} = \frac{4000}{4750} \cong 0.84$$

At point D, $$e = 2$$

(see Example 2).

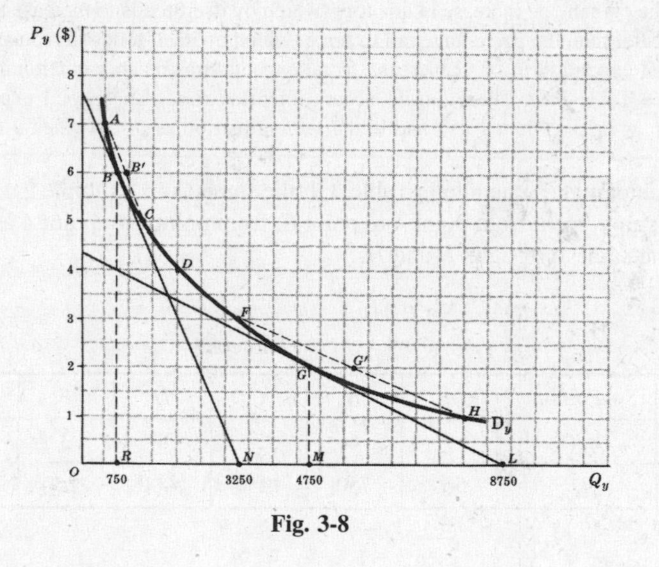

Fig. 3-8

(*b*) Column (3) of Table 3.10 shows that as P_y falls, total expenditures on commodity Y rise as long as $e > 1$ and fall when $e < 1$. Notice that as we move down along D_y, price elasticity falls. This is usually the case for curvilinear demand curves.

Table 3.10

Point	(1) P_y ($)	(2) Q_y	(3) Total Expenditures ($)	(4) e
A	7	500	3500	
B	6	750	4500	3.3
C	5	1250	6250	
D	4	2000	8000	2.0
F	3	3250	9750	
G	2	4750	9500	0.84
H	1	8000	8000	

3.8 (*a*) Show that when $QD_y = 600/P_y$ (a rectangular hyperbola), the total expenditures on commodity Y remain unchanged as P_y falls. (*b*) From (*a*), derive the value of e along the hyperbola. (*c*) Verify (*b*) by finding e geometrically at $P_y = \$4$ and at $P_y = \$2$.

(*a*)

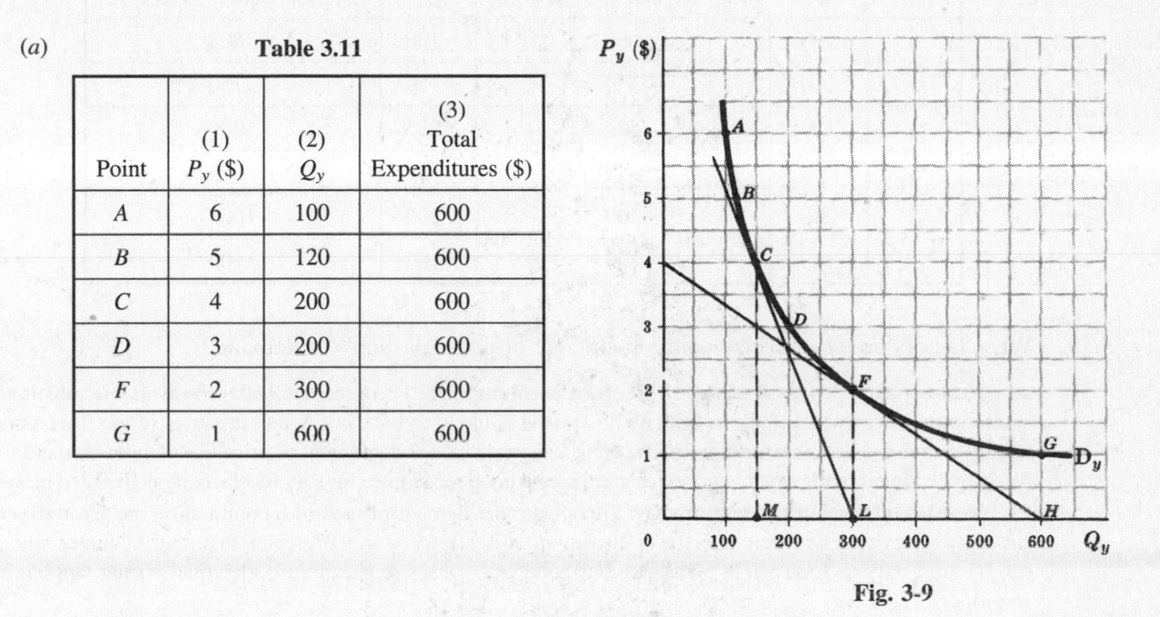

Table 3.11

Point	(1) P_y (\$)	(2) Q_y	(3) Total Expenditures (\$)
A	6	100	600
B	5	120	600
C	4	200	600
D	3	200	600
F	2	300	600
G	1	600	600

Fig. 3-9

(*b*) Since
$$QD_y = \frac{\$600}{P_y}$$

$(QD_y)(P_y) = \$600$ regardless of P_y. Thus, for any given percentage fall in P_y, QD_y will increase by the same percentage. Because the percentage changes in QD_y and P_y are always equal, $e = 1$ at every point on the rectangular hyperbola, D_y.

(*c*) See Fig. 3-9.

At point *C*,
$$e = \frac{ML}{OM} = \frac{150}{150} = 1$$

At point *F*,
$$e = \frac{LH}{OL} = \frac{300}{300} = 1$$

3.9 Table 3.12 gives two demand schedules. Using only the total expenditure criterion, determine if these demand curves are elastic or inelastic.

Table 3.12

P (\$)	6	5	4	3	2	1
Q_x	100	110	120	150	200	300
Q_z	100	150	225	325	500	1100

Since total expenditures on commodity X fail continuously as P_x falls [see column (3) of Table 3.13], $e < 1$ throughout the observed range of D_x. Total expenditures on commodity Z rise continuously as P_z falls [see column (5) of the table], so $e > 1$ throughout the observed range of D_z, D_x, D_z, and D_y (from Problem 3.8) are sketched in Fig. 3-10.

Table 3.13

(1) P($)	(2) Q_x	(3) Total Expenditures on X ($)	(4) Q_z	(5) Total Expenditures on Z ($)
6	100	600	100	600
5	110	550	150	750
4	120	480	225	900
3	150	450	325	975
2	200	400	500	1000
1	300	300	1100	1100

3.10 What factors govern the size of the coefficient of price elasticity of demand?

Number and closeness of substitutes for the commodity. The more and better the available substitutes for a commodity, the greater its price elasticity of demand is likely to be. Thus, when the price of tea rises, consumers readily switch to good substitutes such as coffee and cocoa, so the coefficient of price elasticity of demand for tea is likely to be high. On the other hand, since there are no good substitutes for salt, its elasticity is likely to be very low.

Number of uses of the commodity. The greater the number of uses of a commodity, the greater is its price elasticity. For example, the elasticity of aluminum is likely to be much greater than that of butter since butter can be used only as food while aluminum has hundreds of uses (e.g., aircraft, electrical wiring, appliances, and so on).

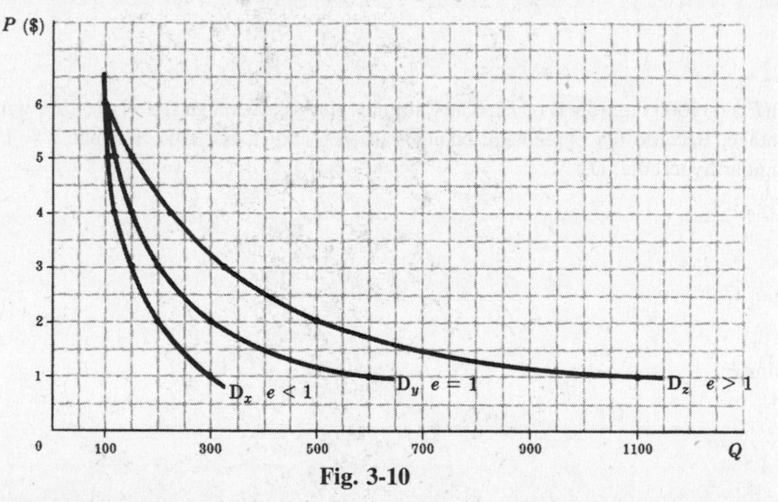

Fig. 3-10

Expenditures on the commodity. The greater the percentage of income spent on a commodity, the greater its elasticity is likely to be. Thus the demand for cars is likely to be much more price-elastic than that for shoes.

Adjustment time. The longer the period allowed for adjustment in the quantity of a commodity demanded, the more elastic its demand is likely to be. This is so because it takes time for consumers to learn of new prices and new products. In addition, even after a decision is made to switch to other products, some time may pass before the switch is actually made.

Level of price. If the ruling price is toward the upper end of the demand curve, demand is likely to be more elastic than if it were toward the lower end. This is always true for a negatively sloped straight-line demand curve and is usually true for curvilinear demand curves.

3.11 (*a*) Is the price elasticity of demand for Marlboro cigarettes greater than the price elasticity for cigarettes in general? Why? (*b*) What general rule can we infer from this?

(*a*) The price elasticity for Marlboro cigarettes is greater than the price elasticity for cigarettes in general because there are many more good substitutes for Marlboro (the many other brands of cigarettes) than substitutes for cigarettes in general (cigars and pipes).

(*b*) From the above we can infer the following general rule: The more narrowly a commodity is defined, the greater is its price elasticity of demand. Thus the price elasticity of demand for white bread is greater than that for bread in general; *e* for Chevrolets is greater than that for automobiles in general; and so on.

3.12 Suppose that two prices and their corresponding quantities (Table 3.14) are observed in the market for commodity X. (Frequently in the real world data can be obtained for only a few prices and quantities.) (*a*) Find the price elasticity of demand for commodity X between point *A* and point *B*. (*b*) What can be said about the shape of D_x between point *A* and *B*?

Table 3.14

Point	P_x ($)	Q_x
A	6.10	32,180
B	5.70	41,230

(*a*) Moving from *A* to *B*,

$$e = -\left(\frac{9050}{-0.40}\right)\left(\frac{6.10}{32{,}180}\right) \cong 4.29$$

Moving from *B* to *A*,

$$e = -\left(\frac{-9050}{0.40}\right)\left(\frac{5.70}{41{,}230}\right) \cong 3.13$$

Midway between *A* and *B*,

$$e = -\left(-\frac{9050}{0.40}\right)\left(\frac{11.80}{73{,}140}\right) \cong 3.64$$

In measuring price elasticity between points *A* and *B* above, the implicit assumption was made that money incomes, the prices of commodities related to commodity X, tastes, and the number of consumers in the market for X all remained unchanged. If this is indeed the case, then *A* and *B* represent two points on a single market demand for X. If one or more of the *ceteris paribus* conditions changed, then *A* and *B* represent points on different demand curves for X. Our measurement of price elasticity would then not have much meaning.

(*b*) The market demand curve for X can take any shape from point *A* to point *B*. If points *A* and *B* are very close to each other, knowledge of the exact shape of the demand curve between the two points is unnecessary and it does not make much difference how we measure price elasticity (from *A* to *B*, from *B* to *A*, or midway between *A* and *B*).

3.13 Sketch the demand curve given by $P_x = \$3$, and find its price elasticity.

In Fig. 3-11, d_x represents the demand curve for commodity X *faced by any single producer* in a competitive market. This demand curve indicates that the competitive producer can sell any amount at the going price of $3 per unit. If the producer raises the price, sales fall to zero. If she or he lowers the price, the total revenue falls unnecessarily.

Since the quantity can change without any corresponding change in price, we can determine from the elasticity formula that d_x has or approaches infinite price elasticity. Thus, when demand is horizontal (i.e., it has zero slope), its elasticity is infinite. When demand is vertical (i.e., it has infinite slope), its elasticity is zero. We will return to infinitely elastic demand curves in Chapter 9.

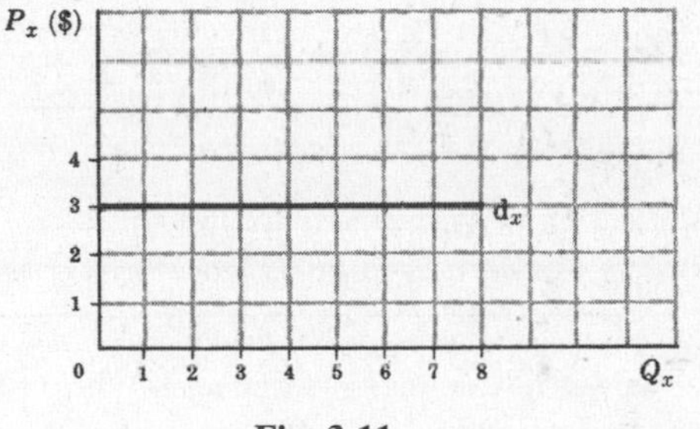

Fig. 3-11

INCOME ELASTICITY AND CROSS ELASTICITY OF DEMAND

3.14 Table 3.15 shows the quantity of "regular cuts of meat" that a family of four would purchase per year at various income levels. ("Regular cuts of meat" might refer to pork chops and pot roast; "superior cuts of meat" might refer to steaks and roast beef while "cheap cuts" to hamburger and chicken.) (*a*) Find the income elasticity of demand of this family for regular cuts of meat between the various successive levels of this family's income. (*b*) Over what range of income are regular cuts of meat a luxury, a necessity, or an inferior good for this family? (*c*) Plot on a graph the income-quantity relationship given above (measure income on the vertical axis and quantity on the horizontal axis). The resulting curve is called an *Engel curve*; such curves are discussed in greater detail in Chapter 4.

Table 3.15

Income ($/year)	4,000	6,000	8,000	10,000	12,000	14,000	16,000	18,000
Quantity (1b/year)	100	200	300	350	380	390	350	250

(*a*) See columns (5) and (6) of Table 3.16.

(*b*) At very low levels of income (here, $8000 per year or less), this family presumably consumes mostly cheap cuts of meat, regular cuts representing a luxury. At intermediate levels of income (here, between $8000 and $14,000 per year) regular cuts of meat become a necessity. At high levels of income (here, above $14,000), this family begins to reduce its consumption of regular cuts of meat and consumes more steaks and roast beef.

Table 3.16

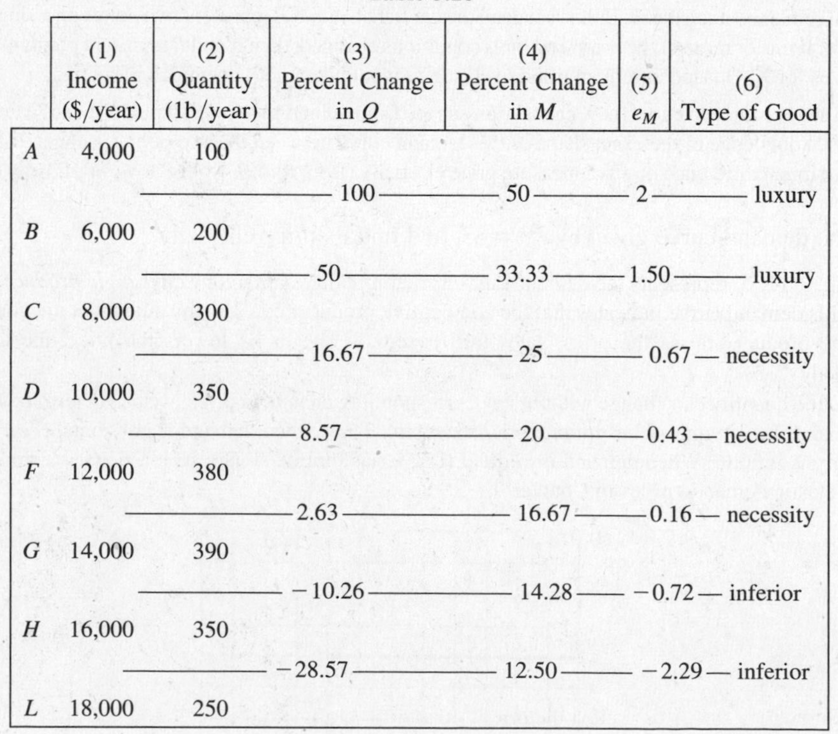

	(1) Income ($/year)	(2) Quantity (1b/year)	(3) Percent Change in Q	(4) Percent Change in M	(5) e_M	(6) Type of Good
A	4,000	100				
			100	50	2	luxury
B	6,000	200				
			50	33.33	1.50	luxury
C	8,000	300				
			16.67	25	0.67	necessity
D	10,000	350				
			8.57	20	0.43	necessity
F	12,000	380				
			2.63	16.67	0.16	necessity
G	14,000	390				
			−10.26	14.28	−0.72	inferior
H	16,000	350				
			−28.57	12.50	−2.29	inferior
L	18,000	250				

(c)

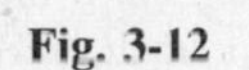

Fig. 3-12

3.15 (*a*) Does e_M measure movements along the same demand curve or shifts in demand? (*b*) How can we find the income elasticity of demand for the entire market? (*c*) Give some examples of luxuries, (*d*) Since food is a necessity, how can we get a rough index of the welfare of a family or nation?

(*a*) In measuring the income elasticity of demand, only income changes out of the factors affecting demand. Thus, while the price elasticity of demand (e) refers to a movement along a specific demand curve, the income elasticity of demand (e_M) measures a shift from one demand curve to another.

(*b*) In Problem 3.14(*a*) we found e_M for a single family. In getting the income elasticity of demand of a commodity for the entire market, Q would have to refer to the market quantity and M to the money income of all the consumers in the market (with the distribution of money incomes assumed to remain constant).

(*c*) Expenditures on education and travel are usually considered luxuries by most people.

(*d*) Roughly speaking, the smaller the proportion of income spent on food by a family or nation, the greater is its welfare.

3.16 (*a*) Find the cross elasticity of demand between hot dogs (X) and hamburgers (Y) and between hot dogs (X) and mustard (Z), for the data in Table 3.17. (*b*) State the *ceteris paribus* conditions in finding e_{xy} and e_{xz}.

Table 3.17

	Before		After	
Commodity	Price (dollars/unit)	Quantity (units/month)	Price (dollars/unit)	Quantity (units/month)
Hamburgers (Y)	3.00	30	2.00	40
Hot dogs (X)	1.00	15	1.00	10
Mustard (jar) (Z)	1.50	10	2.00	9
Hot dogs (X)	1.00	15	1.00	12

(*a*)

$$e_{xy} = \frac{\Delta Q_x}{\Delta P_y} \cdot \frac{P_y}{Q_x} = \left(\frac{-5}{-1}\right)\left(\frac{3}{15}\right) = +1$$

$$e_{xz} = \frac{\Delta Q_x}{\Delta P_z} \cdot \frac{P_z}{Q_x} = \left(\frac{-3}{0.50}\right)\left(\frac{1.50}{15}\right) = -0.6$$

Since e_{xy} is positive, hot dogs and hamburgers are substitutes. Since e_{xz} is negative, hot dogs and mustard are complements for this individual.

(*b*) In finding e_{xy}, we assumed that the prices of all other commodities (including the prices of X and Z), and the individual's money income and tastes remain unchanged. Similarly, e_{xz} measures the responsiveness in Q_x to a change in P_z only. Thus, like e_M, e_{xy} and e_{xz} measure shifts in the demand curve for X.

3.17 (*a*) Why is it that when two commodities are substitutes for each other, the cross elasticity of demand between them is positive while when they are complements it is negative? (*b*) How can we define an industry by using cross elasticities? What difficulties does this lead to?

(*a*) For two commodities which are substitutes, a change in the price of one, *ceteris paribus*, causes a change *in the same direction* in the quantity purchased of the other. For example, an increase in the price of coffee increases tea consumption and a decrease in the price of coffee decreases tea consumption. Thus the cross elasticity between them is *positive*. On the other hand, *ceteris paribus*, a change in the price of a commodity causes the quantity purchased of its complement to move *in the opposite direction*. Thus the cross elasticity between them will be *negative*. It should be noted that commodities may be substitutes over some range of prices and complements over others.

(*b*) High positive cross elasticities (indicating a high degree of substitutability) among a group of commodities can be (and frequently is) used to define the boundaries of an industry. This, however, may sometimes lead to difficulties. For example, how high should cross elasticities be among a group of commodities in order for us to include them in the same industry? In addition, if the cross elasticity of demand between cars and station wagons and between station wagons and small trucks is positive and very high but the cross elasticity between cars and small trucks is positive but low, are cars and small trucks in the same industry? In these and other cases, the definition of the industry adopted usually depends on the problem to be studied.

PRICE ELASTICITY OF SUPPLY

3.18 (*a*) What does the price elasticity of supply measure in general? (*b*) How does the length of the time of adjustment to a change in the price of a commodity affect the price elasticity of the supply of the commodity? Why? (*c*) Does the price elasticity between two points on the supply curve vary depending on whether we move up or down the supply curve? (*d*) What happens to total expenditures on a commodity when the commodity price rises along a positively sloped supply curve?

(*a*) The price elasticity of supply (e_s) measures the relative responsiveness or sensitivity in the quantity of a commodity supplied to changes in its price only. Thus e_s, as e, measures movements along the same supply curve.

(*b*) The longer the period of adjustment allowed for a change in the price of a commodity, the more elastic the supply curve of the commodity is likely to be. This is so because it takes time for producers to respond to price changes (we will return to this in Chapter 9).

(*c*) The arc elasticity of a straight-line or curvilinear supply curve varies depending on whether we move from one point on the supply curve to another or vice versa. As in the case of arc elasticity of demand, one way to avoid this is to find the price elasticity of supply at the midpoint of the chord through the two points.

(*d*) Along a positively sloped supply curve, an increase in price will always lead to an increase in the total revenue of the producer (which equals the total expenditures of consumers) regardless of the size of e_s. A reduction in price will always lead to a reduction in total revenue.

3.19 Prove that the supply curve given by $QS_x = 20{,}000P_x$, has unitary elasticity, and the supply curve given by $QS_y = 40{,}000 + 20{,}000P_y$, is inelastic. ($P_x$ and P_y are given in dollars.)

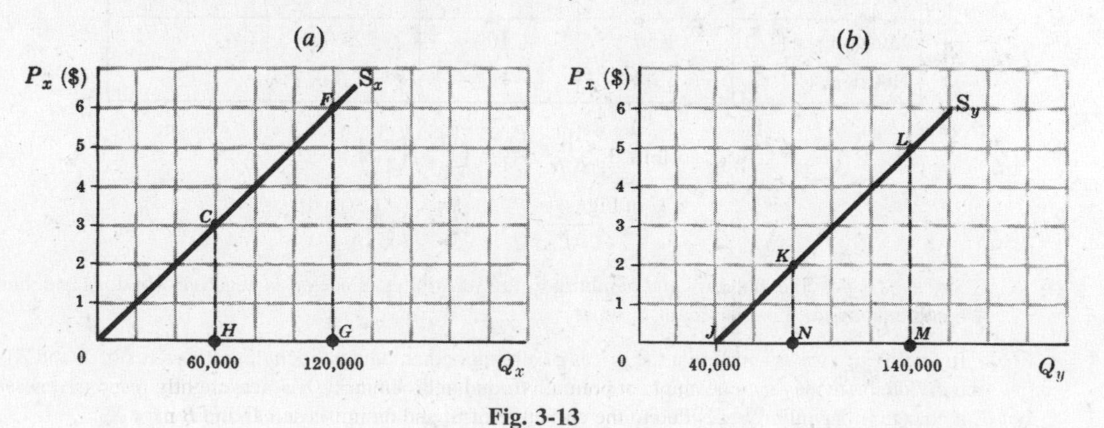

Fig. 3-13

As shown in Fig. 3-13(*a*),

$$\text{at point } C \text{ on S}, \qquad e_s = \frac{\Delta Q}{\Delta P} \cdot \frac{P_C}{Q_C} = \frac{OH}{HC} \cdot \frac{HC}{OH} = 1$$

$$\text{at point } F \text{ on S}_x, \qquad e_s = \frac{\Delta Q}{\Delta P} \cdot \frac{P_F}{Q_F} = \frac{OG}{GF} \cdot \frac{GF}{OG} = 1$$

As shown in Fig. 3-13(*b*),

$$\text{at point } K \text{ on S}_y, \qquad e_s = \frac{\Delta Q}{\Delta P} \cdot \frac{P_K}{Q_K} = \frac{JN}{NK} \cdot \frac{NK}{ON} = \frac{JN}{ON} < 1$$

$$\text{at point } L \text{ on S}_y, \qquad e_s = \frac{\Delta Q}{\Delta P} \cdot \frac{P_L}{Q_L} = \frac{JM}{ML} \cdot \frac{ML}{OM} = \frac{JM}{OM} < 1$$

What was found to be true for points *C* and *F* on S_x [Fig. 3-13(*a*)] is clearly true for all other points on S_x. Similarly, $e_s < 1$ all along S_y [Fig. 3-13(*b*)]. Thus, if a positively sloped straight-line supply curve goes through the origin, it has unitary elasticity; if it crosses the quantity axis, it is inelastic; and if it crosses the price axis (see Example 9), it is elastic.

3.20 From the supply schedule in Table 3.18, find arc e_s for a movement (*a*) from point *D* to point *B*, (*b*) from *B* to *D* and (*c*) midway between *D* and *B*.

Table 3.18

Point	P_y ($)	Q_y
A	6	6000
B	5	5500
C	4	4500
D	3	3000
F	2	0

(*a*) From *D* to *B*
$$e_s = \frac{\Delta Q}{\Delta P} \cdot \frac{P_D}{Q_D} = \left(\frac{2500}{2}\right)\left(\frac{3}{3000}\right) = 1.25$$

(*b*) From *B* to *D*
$$e_s = \left(\frac{-2500}{-2}\right)\left(\frac{5}{5500}\right) \cong 1.11$$

(*c*) Midway between *D* and *B*
$$e_s = \frac{\Delta Q}{\Delta P} \cdot \frac{P_D + P_B}{Q_D + Q_B} = \left(\frac{2500}{2}\right)\left(\frac{8}{8500}\right) \cong 1.18$$

3.21 Plot the supply schedule of Problem 3.20 and find e_s, *at* point *C*.

The elasticity of supply at point *C* in Fig. 3-14 is obtained by drawing a tangent to S_y at *C* and then proceeding as in Problem 3.19. Thus,

$$e_s = \frac{\Delta Q}{\Delta P} \cdot \frac{P_C}{Q_C} = \frac{OG}{GC} \cdot \frac{GC}{OG} = 1$$

Notice that the price elasticity of supply at point *C′* (found in Problem 3.20) differs slightly from the point elasticity of S_y *at* point *C*. The difference is due to the curvature of S_y and diminishes as *D* and *B* move closer to each other.

Also to be noted is that for any point on S_y to the left of C (e.g., point D), the tangent would cross the price axis and $e_s > 1$. For any point to the right of C (e.g., point B or point A), the tangent would cross the quantity axis and $e_s < 1$.

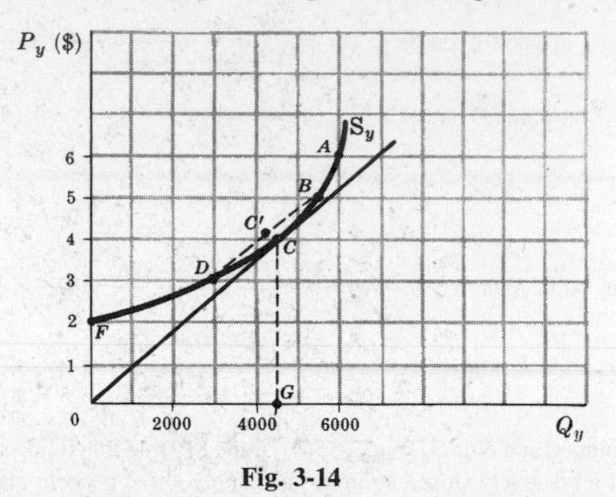

Fig. 3-14

3.21 From the supply schedule in Table 3.19, find arc elasticity for a movement (*a*) from point A to point C, (*b*) from C to A, and (*c*) midway between A and C. (*d*) Also find price elasticity of supply at point B.

Table 3.19

Point	A	B	C	D	F
P_x ($)	6	5	4	3	2
Q_x	6000	5500	4500	3000	0

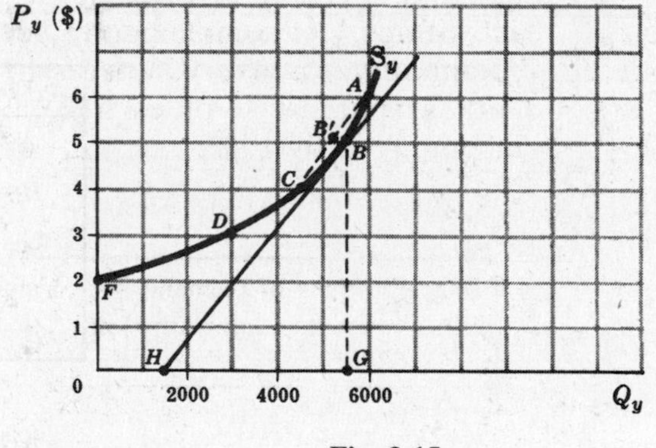

Fig. 3-15

(*a*) From A to C, $$e_s = \left(\frac{-1500}{-2}\right)\left(\frac{6}{6000}\right) = 0.75$$

(*b*) From C to A, $$e_s = \left(\frac{1500}{2}\right)\left(\frac{4}{4500}\right) \cong 0.67$$

(*c*) Midway between A and C (point B' in Fig. 3.15)

$$e_s = \left(\frac{1500}{2}\right)\left(\frac{10}{10{,}500}\right) \cong 0.714 \cong 0.71$$

(*d*) At point B, $$e_s = \frac{HG}{GB} \cdot \frac{GB}{OG} = \frac{HG}{OG} = \frac{4000}{5500} = 0.709 \cong 0.71$$

Notice, in Fig. 3-15, that the tangent to S_y at point B crosses the quantity axis and S_y is inelastic at point B.

3.23 On a single set of axes, draw a straight-line supply curve which is elastic, one that is inelastic, one that has unitary elasticity, one that has negative elasticity, one that has zero elasticity and one that has infinite elasticity.

If the supply curve takes the shape of a rectangular hyperbola, then [compare Problem 3.8(*b*)] $e_s = -1$.

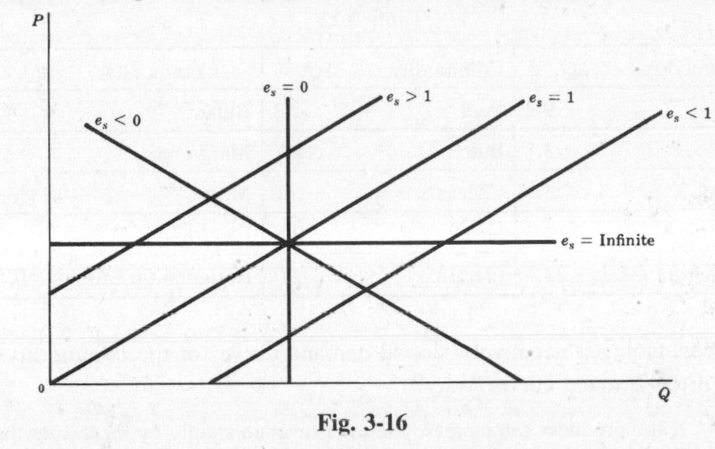

Fig. 3-16

SOME EMPIRICAL ESTIMATES AND APPLICATIONS OF ELASTICITY

3.24 Table 3.20 gives the estimated price, cross, and income elasticities for selected commodities in the U.S. or the U.K. (*a*) Indicate from the price elasticities (e) if the demand is elastic or inelastic; from the cross elasticities (e_{xy}) if the commodities are substitutes or complements; and from the income elasticity (e_M) whether the commodity is a luxury, a necessity, or an inferior good. (*b*) Indicate the change in the amount purchased of each commodity if the commodity price or the consumer's income rose by 10%.

Table 3.20

Price Elasticity of Demand		Cross Elasticity of Demand		Income Elasticity of Demand	
Commodity	e	Commodities	e_{xy}	Commodity	e_M
Beef	0.92	Beef, pork	0.28	Butter	0.42
Potatoes	0.31	Butter, margarine	0.67	Margarine	−0.20
Sugar	0.31	Cheese, butter	−0.61*	Meat	0.35
Electricity	1.20	Sugar, fruits	−0.28*	Electricity	0.20
Restaurant meals	2.27	Electricity, natural gas	0.2	Restaurant meals	1.48

*U.K.; all other, U.S.

Source: Schultz, *Theory and Measure of Demand*, University of Chicago Press, 1938; L. Taylor, "The Demand for Electricity: A Survey," *Bell Journal of Economics*, Spring 1975; H. Wold, *Demand Analysis*, New York, Wiley, 1953; L. Taylor and R. Halvorsen, "Energy Substitution in U.S. Manufacturing," *Review of Economics and Statistics*, November 1977; R. Stone, *The Measurement of Consumer's Expenditures and Behavior in the United Kingdom*, 1920–1938, vol. 1, Cambridge University Press, 1954.

(*a*) The answers are given in Table 3.21.

Table 3.21

Commodity	Type of Demand	Commodities	Type of Commodities	Commodities	Type of Commodity
Beef	Inelastic	Beef, pork	Substitutes	Butter	Necessity
Potatoes	Inelastic	Butter, margarine	Substitutes	Margarine	Inferior
Sugar	Inelastic	Cheese, butter	Complements	Meat	Necessity
Electricity	Elastic	Sugar, fruits	Complements	Electricity	Necessity
Restaurant meals	Elastic	Electricity, natural gas	Substitutes	Restaurant meals	Luxury

(*b*) The answers are given in Table 3.22.

Table 3.22

Commodity	ΔQ, %	Commodity	ΔQ, %	Commodity	ΔQ, %
Beef	9.2	Beef	2.8	Butter	4.2
Potatoes	3.1	Butter	6.7	Margarine	− 2.0
Sugar	3.1	Cheese	−6.1	Meat	3.5
Electricity	12.0	Sugar	−2.8	Electricity	2.0
Restaurant meals	22.7	Electricity	2.0	Restaurant meals	14.8

3.25 Should a producer, facing a negatively sloped demand curve for the commodity sold, operate in the inelastic range of the demand curve? Why?

No: as long as $e < 1$, the producer can increase the total revenue simply by increasing the commodity price. In addition, if the producer increases the price, less of this commodity will be consumed. The result would be a smaller output and smaller total costs of production. With total revenues rising and total costs falling, the producer's total profits (TR − TC) increase.

3.26 As a result of the high wage settlement in the New York City taxi strike of several years ago, taxi owners increased taxi fares. Was this the right decision?

The answer depends on the price elasticity of demand for taxi rides in New York City. If the demand for taxi rides is price-inelastic, the decision was correct (see Problem 3.25). If demand is elastic, then increasing taxi fares reduces the total revenue of taxi owners. In order to see what happened to the total profits of taxi owners, we must compare this decrease in total revenue with the change in total costs (higher wages for taxi drivers but fewer taxis and fewer taxi drivers).

Unfortunately, in the real world we often do not have (and it might be difficult) to get estimates of the elasticities necessary to reach correct decisions.

3.27 Prove the following results, assuming straight-line demand and supply curves, (*a*) For a given supply curve and a given equilibrium point, the more inelastic the demand curve, the greater the burden of a per-unit tax on the consumer. (*b*) For a given demand curve and a given equilibrium point, the more elastic the supply curve, the greater the burden of a per-unit tax on the consumer.

(*a*) In Fig. 3-17, S′ is the market supply curve after the imposition of a per-unit tax on producers. D_1, D_2, and D_3 are three alternative demand curves for the commodity. At the original equilibrium point (E), D_1 is more elastic than D_2 and D_2 is more elastic than D_3. Thus given the supply curve, the more inelastic the demand curve, the higher the new equilibrium price (after the imposition of the per-unit tax) and the greater the burden of the tax on consumers.

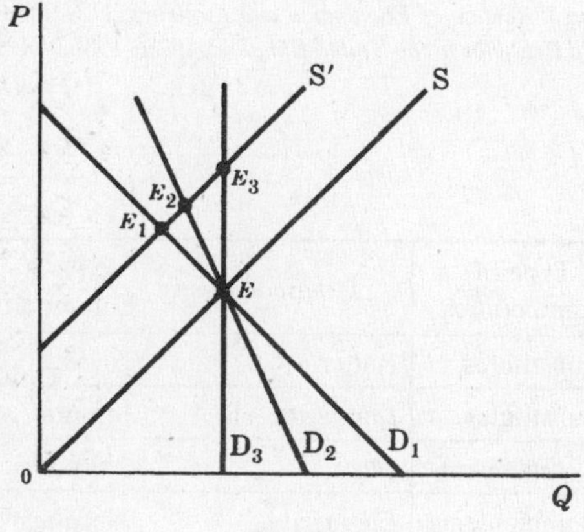

Fig. 3-17

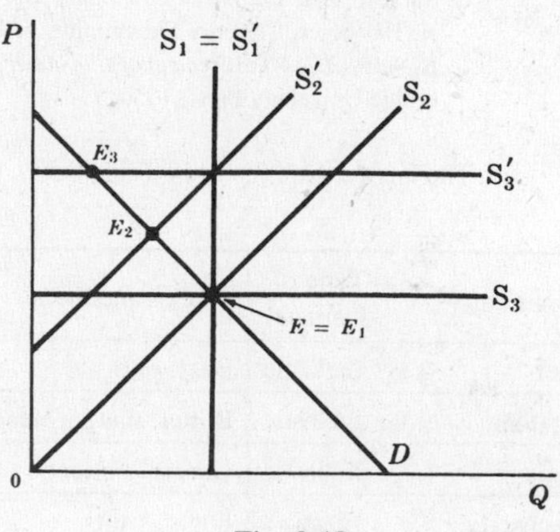

Fig. 3-18

(*b*) In Fig. 3-18, S_1, S_2, and S_3 are three alternative supply curves. S'_1, S'_2, and S'_3 are the new supply curves after the imposition of a per-unit tax on producers. S_1 has zero elasticity, S_2 has unitary elasticity, and S_3 has infinite elasticity. Thus, given the demand curve, the more elastic the supply curve, the higher the new equilibrium price (after the imposition of the per-unit tax), and the greater the burden of the tax on consumers.

3.28 If the market demand for agricultural commodities is price-inelastic, would a bad harvest lead to an increase or a decrease in the incomes of farmers as a group? Why?

A bad harvest is reflected in a decrease in supply (i.e., an upward shift in the market supply curve of agricultural commodities). Given the market demand for agricultural commodities, this decrease in supply causes the equilibrium price to rise. Since the demand is price-inelastic, the total receipts of farmers as a group increase. When the demand for an agricultural commodity is price-inelastic, the same result can be achieved by reducing the amount of land under cultivation for the commodity. This is done in some farm-aid programs.

3.29 With reference to Fig. 3-19, consider the following two farm-aid programs for wheat farmers. I. The government sets the price of wheat at P_2 and purchases the resulting surplus of wheat at P_2. II. The government allows wheat to be sold at the equilibrium price of P_1 and grants each farmer a cash subsidy of $P_2 - P_1$ on each unit sold. Which of the two programs is more expensive to the government?

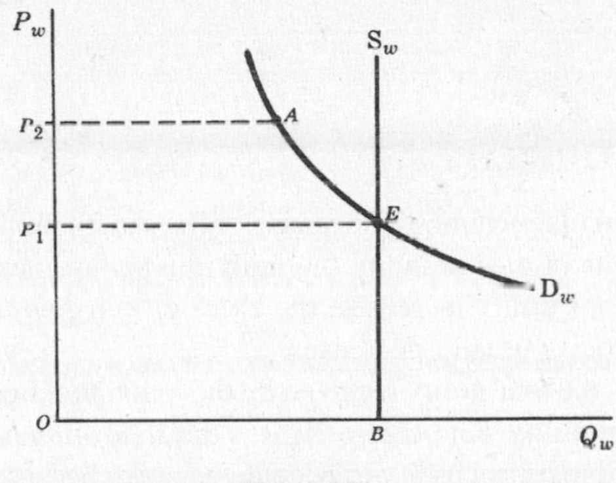

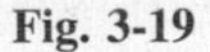

Fig. 3-19

Under both programs, the total receipts of wheat farmers as a group are the same (OP_2 times OB). The greater the fraction of this total paid by the consumers of wheat, the smaller the cost to the government. If D_w is elastic at every point of arc *AE*, consumers' expenditures on wheat would be greater under the second program, and so the second program would cost less to the government. If D_w is inelastic at every point of arc *AE*, consumers' expenditures on wheat would be greater under the first program, and so the first program would cost less to the government. If D_w has unitary elasticity at every point of arc *AE*, both programs would cost the same to the government. The way the above figure is drawn, the first program would cost less to the government. (We assumed no storage costs. We have also not considered what the government does with the surplus wheat and what is the effect of each of the two programs on the welfare of consumers.)

PRICE ELASTICITY WITH CALCULUS

***3.30** Find the price elasticity of demand (e) for the curvilinear demand function of the form $Q = aP^{-b}$

For this demand function, $dQ/dP = -abP^{-b-1}$ so that

$$e = -abP^{-b-1}\left(\frac{P}{Q}\right) = -b, \qquad \text{since } aP^{-b} = Q.$$

Thus, the demand function given is a rectangular hyperbola with the constant price elasticity of demand equal to $-b$.

CHAPTER 4

Consumer Demand Theory

4.1 TOTAL AND MARGINAL UTILITY

An individual demands a particular commodity because of the satisfaction or *utility* received from consuming it. Up to a point, the more units of a commodity the individual consumes per unit of time, the greater the *total utility* received. Although total utility increases, the extra or *marginal utility* received from consuming each additional unit of the commodity usually decreases.

At some level of consumption, the total utility received by the individual from consuming the commodity will reach a maximum and the marginal utility will be zero. This is the *saturation point*. Additional units of the commodity cause total utility to fall and marginal utility to become negative because of storage or disposal problems.

EXAMPLE 1. The first two columns of Table 4.1 give an individual's hypothetical total utility (TU) schedule from consuming various alternative quantities of commodity X per unit of time. (Utility is here assumed to be measurable in terms of a fictitious unit called the "util.") Note that up to a point, as the individual consumes more units of X per unit of time, TU_x increases. Columns (1) and (3) of the table show this individual's marginal utility (MU) schedule for commodity X. Each value of column (3) is obtained by subtracting two successive values of column (2). For example, if the individual's consumption of X goes from zero units to 1 unit, the TU_x goes from zero utils to 10 utils, giving a MU_x of 10 utils. Similarly, if the consumption of X rises from 1 unit to 2 units, the TU_x rises from 10 to 18, giving a MU_x of 8. Notice that as this individual consumes more and more units of X per unit of time, the MU_x falls.

Table 4.1

(1) Q_x	(2) TU_x	(3) MU_x
0	0	. . .
1	10	10
2	18	8
3	24	6
4	28	4
5	30	2
6	30	0
7	28	−2

EXAMPLE 2. If we plot the total and marginal utility schedules of Table 4.1, we get the total and marginal utility curves of Fig. 4-1. Since marginal utility has been defined as the *change* in total utility in changing consumption by one unit, each value of the MU_x has been recorded midway between the two levels of consumption, in part (*b*) of the figure. The saturation point ($MU_x = 0$) is reached when the individual increases consumption of X from 5 to 6 units. The falling MU_x curve illustrates the *principle of diminishing marginal utility.*

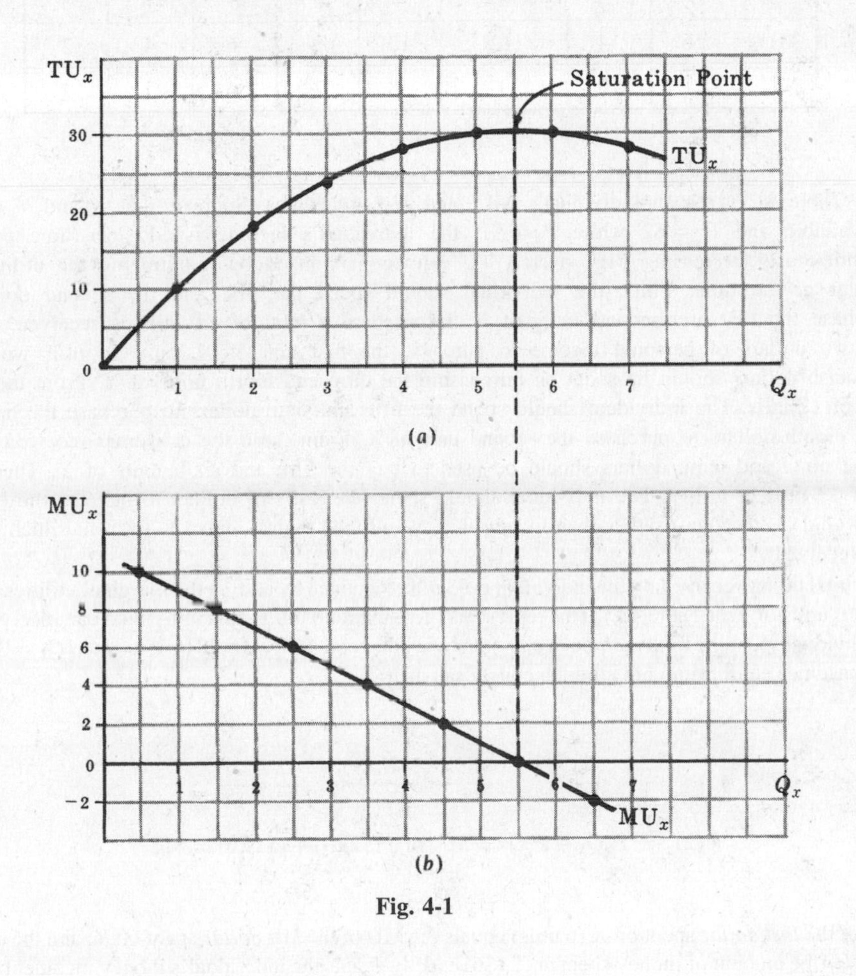

Fig. 4-1

4.2 CONSUMER EQUILIBRIUM

The objective of a rational consumer is to maximize the total utility or satisfaction derived from spending personal income. This objective is reached and the consumer is said to be *in equilibrium* when able to spend personal income in such a way that the utility or satisfaction of *the last dollar spent* on the various commodities is the same. This can be expressed mathematically by

$$\frac{MU_x}{P_x} = \frac{MU_y}{P_y} = \cdots$$

subject to the constraint that

$$P_xQ_x + P_yQ_y + \cdots = M \text{ (the individual's income)}$$

A derivation of the above equilibrium condition, in the case of two commodities, will be given in Section 4.7 (see also Problem 4.22).

Table 4.2

Q	1	2	3	4	5	6	7	8
MU_x	16	14	(12)	10	8	6	4	2
MU_y	11	10	9	8	7	(6)	5	4

EXAMPLE 3. Table 4.2 gives an individual's MU_x and MU_y schedules. Suppose that X and Y are the only two commodities available and $P_x = \$2$ while $P_y = \$1$; the individual's income is $12 per time period and is all spent. With continuously decreasing MU, overall TU can be maximized by maximizing the utility received from spending a dollar at the time. Thus, the individual should spend the first and the second dollars of personal income to purchase the first and second units of Y. From these a total of 21 utils is received. If the consumer spent the first two dollars of personal income to purchase the first unit of X, only 16 utils would be received. The third and fourth dollars should be spent on purchasing the third and fourth units of Y. From these the consumer receives a total of 17 utils. The individual should spend the fifth and sixth dollars to purchase the first unit of X and the seventh and eighth dollars to purchase the second unit of X. From these the consumer received 16 and 14 utils, respectively: The ninth and tenth dollars should be used to buy the fifth and sixth units of Y. These give the individual a total of 13 utils of utility. The individual should spend the last two dollars to buy the third unit of X (from which 12 utils would be received) rather than to buy the seventh and eighth units of Y (from which a total of only 9 utils would be received).

The overall total utility received by the individual is 93 utils (obtained by adding the marginal utilities of the first 3 units of X and the first 6 units of Y in Table 4.2). This represents the maximum utility this individual can receive from all expenditures. If the individual spent the total income in any other way, the total utility would be less when $Q_x = 3$, $Q_y = 6$, the two conditions for consumer equilibrium are simultaneously satisfied:

$$(1) \qquad \frac{MU_x}{P_x} = \frac{MU_y}{P_y} \quad \text{or} \quad \frac{12}{\$2} = \frac{6}{\$1}$$

$$(2) \qquad P_xQ_x + P_yQ_y = M \quad \text{or} \quad (\$2)(3) + (\$1)(6) = \$12$$

That is, the MU of the *last dollar* spent on X (6 utils) equals the MU of the *last dollar* spent on Y, and the *amount* of money spent on X ($6) *plus* the amount of money spent on Y ($6) exactly equals the individual's money income (of $12). The same two general conditions would have to hold for the individual to be in equilibrium if having purchased more than two commodities.

4.3 INDIFFERENCE CURVES: DEFINITION

A consumer's tastes and equilibrium can also be shown by indifference curves. An *indifference curve* shows the various combinations of commodity X and commodity Y which yield equal utility or satisfaction to the consumer. A higher indifference curve shows a greater amount of satisfaction and a lower one, less satisfaction. Thus, indifference curves show an ordinal rather than a cardinal measure of utility (see Problem 4.12*a*).

EXAMPLE 4. Table 4.3 gives points on three different indifference curves for a consumer. Plotting these points on the same set of axes and joining them by smooth curves, we get the three indifference curves shown in Fig. 4-2.

Table 4.3

Indifference Curve I		Indifference Curve II		Indifference Curve III	
Q_x	Q_y	Q_x	Q_y	Q_x	Q_y
1	10	3	10	5	12
2	5	4	7	6	9
3	3	5	5	7	7
4	2.3	6	4.2	8	6.2
5	1.7	7	3.5	9	5.5
6	1.2	8	3.2	10	5.2
7	0.8	9	3	11	5
8	0.5	10	2.9	12	4.9
9	0.3				
10	0.2				

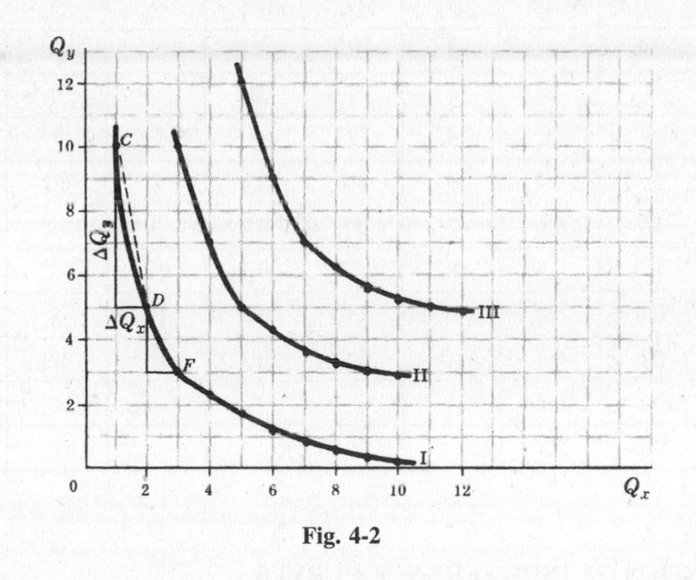

Fig. 4-2

EXAMPLE 5. All points on the same indifference curve yield the same satisfaction to the consumer. Thus the individual is indifferent between 10Y and 1X (point *C* on indifference curve I in Fig. 4-2) and 5Y and 2X (point *D*, also on indifference curve I). Points on indifference curve II indicate greater satisfaction than points on indifference curve I but less satisfaction than points on indifference curve III. Note, however, that the absolute amount of satisfaction is not specified. Thus, all we need is the *ordering* or *ranking* of a consumer's preferences to be able to draw these indifference curves.

4.4 THE MARGINAL RATE OF SUBSTITUTION

The *marginal rate of substitution* of X for Y (MRS_{xy}) refers to the amount of Y that a consumer is willing to give up in order to gain one additional unit of X (and still remain on the same indifference curve). As the individual moves down an indifference curve, the MRS_{xy} diminishes.

EXAMPLE 6. In moving from point *C* to point *D* on indifference curve I in Fig. 4-2, the individual gives up 5 units of Y in exchange for one additional unit of X. Thus, the $MRS_{xy} = 5$. Similarly, from point *D* to point *F* on indifference curve I, the $MRS_{xy} = 2$. On moving down the indifference curve, the individual is willing to give up less and less of Y in order to gain each additional unit of X (i.e., the MRS_{xy} diminishes). This is so because the less of Y and the more of X the individual has (i.e., the lower the point on the indifference curve), the more valuable is each remaining unit of Y and the less valuable is each additional unit of X to the individual. Therefore, the individual is willing to give up less and less of Y to get each additional unit of X, and the MRS_{xy} diminishes.

EXAMPLE 7. Table 4.4 shows the MRS_{xy} between the various points on indifference curves I, II, and III given in Table 4.3. It should be noted that the MRS_{xy} between two points on the same indifference curve is nothing else than the absolute (or positive value of the) slope of the chord between the two points. Thus, the MRS_{xy} between point *C* and point *D* on indifference curve I is equal to the absolute slope of chord *CD* (which is equal to 5, see Fig. 4-2). Also, as the distance between two points on an indifference curve decreases and approaches zero in the limit, the MRS_{xy} approaches the absolute slope of the indifference curve at a point. Thus, as point *C* approaches point *D* on indifference curve I, the MRS_{xy} approaches the absolute slope of the indifference curve at point *D*.

Table 4.4

Indifference Curve I			Indifference Curve II			Indifference Curve III		
Q_x	Q_y	MRS_{xy}	Q_x	Q_y	MRS_{xy}	Q_x	Q_y	MRS_{xy}
1	10	..	3	10	..	5	12	..
2	5	5	4	7	3	6	9	3
3	3	2	5	5	2	7	7	2
4	2.3	0.7	6	4.2	0.8	8	6.2	0.8
5	1.7	0.6	7	3.5	0.7	9	5.5	0.7
6	1.2	0.5	8	3.2	0.3	10	5.2	0.3
7	0.8	0.4	9	3	0.2	11	5	0.2
8	0.5	0.3	10	2.9	0.1	12	4.9	0.1
9	0.3	0.2						
10	0.2	0.1						

4.5 CHARACTERISTICS OF INDIFFERENCE CURVES

Indifference curves exhibit three basic characteritics: they are negatively sloped, they are convex to the origin, and they cannot intersect.

EXAMPLE 8. Since we are dealing with economic (i.e., scarce) goods, if consuming more of X, the individual must consume less of Y to remain at the same level of satisfaction (i.e., on the same indifference curve). Therefore, an indifference curve must be negatively sloped. It is also convex to the origin (see Fig. 4-2) because it exhibits diminishing MRS_{xy} (see Examples 6 and 7).

EXAMPLE 9. We can prove that indifference curves cannot intersect by looking at Fig. 4-3, which assumes the contrary. *G* and *H* are two points on indifference curve I, and as such they yield equal satisfaction to the consumer. In addition, *G* and *J* are two points on indifference curve II and they also yield equal satisfaction to the consumer. It follows that *H* and *J* are points of equal satisfaction, so that, by definition, they lie on the same indifference curve (and not on two different curves as assumed). Thus, it is impossible for indifference curves to intersect.

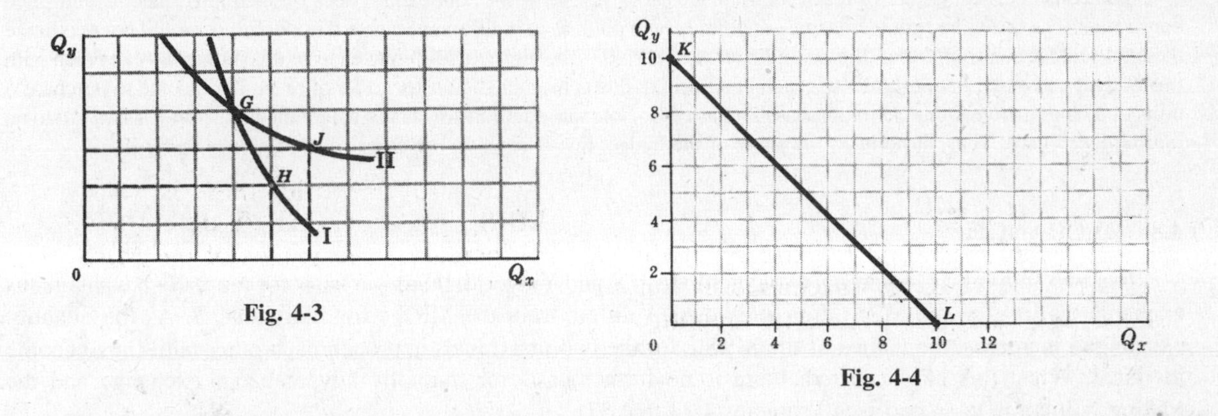

Fig. 4-3

Fig. 4-4

4.6 THE BUDGET CONSTRAINT LINE

The *budget constraint line* shows all the different combinations of the two commodities that a consumer can purchase, given his or her money income and the prices of the two commodities.

EXAMPLE 10. Suppose that $P_x = P_y = \$1$, that a consumer's money income is \$10 per time period and that it is all spent on X and Y. The budget line for this consumer is then given by line *KL* in Fig. 4-4. If the consumer spent all of her income on commodity Y, she could purchase 10 units of Y. This defines point *K*. If she spent all of her income on commodity X, she could purchase 10 units of X. This defines point *L*. By joining point *K* to point *L* by a straight line we define budget line *KL*. Budget line *KL* shows all the different combinations of X and Y that this individual can purchase given her money income and the prices of X and Y.

4.7 CONSUMER EQUILIBRIUM

A *consumer* is in *equilibrium* when, given personal income and price constraints, the consumer maximizes the total utility or satisfaction from his or her expenditures. In other words, a consumer is in equilibrium when, given his or her budget line, the person reaches the highest possible indifference curve.

EXAMPLE 11. By bringing together on the same set of axes the consumer's indifference curves (Fig. 4-2) and budget constraint line (Fig. 4-4), we can determine the point of consumer equilibrium. This is given by point *E* in Fig. 4-5.

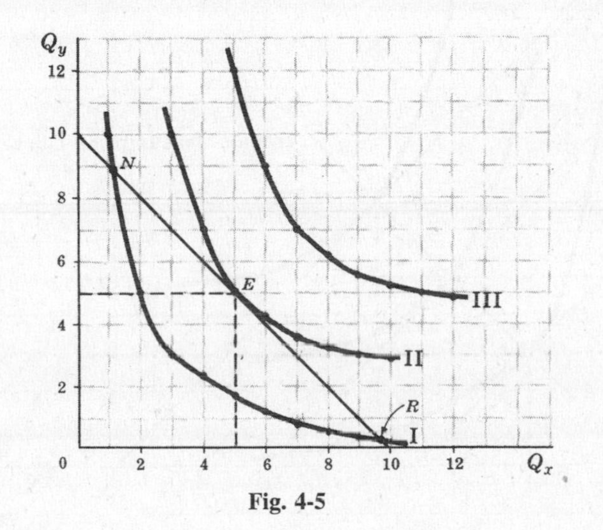

Fig. 4-5

The consumer would like to reach indifference curve III in Fig. 4-5, but cannot because of limited income and price constraints. The individual could consume at point N or at point R on indifference curve I, but doing so would not maximize the total satisfaction from expenditures. Indifference curve II is the highest indifference curve this individual can reach with this budget constraint line. In order to reach equilibrium, this consumer should spend \$5 of his or her income to purchase 5 units of Y and the remaining \$5 to purchase 5 units of X. Note that equilibrium occurs where the budget line is *tangent* to an indifference curve. Thus, at point E, the slope of the budget line is equal to the slope of indifference curve II.

4.8 EXCHANGE

In a two-individual (A and B), two commodity (X and Y) world, there is a basis for mutually advantageous exchange as long as the MRS_{xy} for individual A differs from the MRS_{xy} for individual B. As the quantity exchanged increases, the values of the MRS_{xy} for the two individuals approach each other until they become identical. When this has occurred, there is no further basis for mutually advantageous exchange and the trading will come to an end (see Problems 4.24 to 4.27).

4.9 THE INCOME-CONSUMPTION CURVE AND THE ENGEL CURVE

By changing the consumer's money income while keeping constant personal tastes and the prices of X and Y, we can derive the consumer's income-consumption curve and Engel curve. The *income-consumption curve* is the locus of points of consumer equilibrium resulting when only the consumer's income is varied. The *Engel curve* shows the amount of a commodity that the consumer would purchase per unit of time at various levels of total income.

EXAMPLE 12. If the consumer's tastes are given by the indifference curves of Fig. 4-2, if $P_x = P_y = \$1$, and if the consumer's money income (M) rises from \$6 to \$10 and then to \$14 per time period, then the consumer's budget lines are given, respectively, by lines 1, 2, and 3 in Fig. 4-6. Thus, when $M = \$6$, the consumer reaches equilibrium at point F on indifference curve I by purchasing 3X and 3Y. When $M = \$10$, the consumer reaches equilibrium at point E on indifference curve II by purchasing 5X and 5Y. When $M = \$14$, the consumer is in equilibrium at point S and purchases 7X and 7Y. By joining these points of consumer equilibrium, we get income-consumption curve FS in Fig. 4-6.

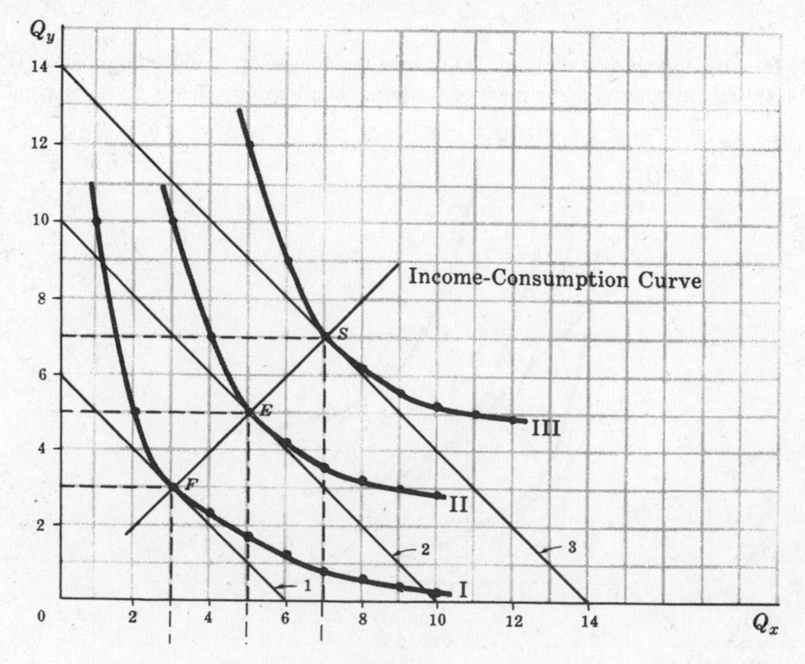

Fig. 4-6

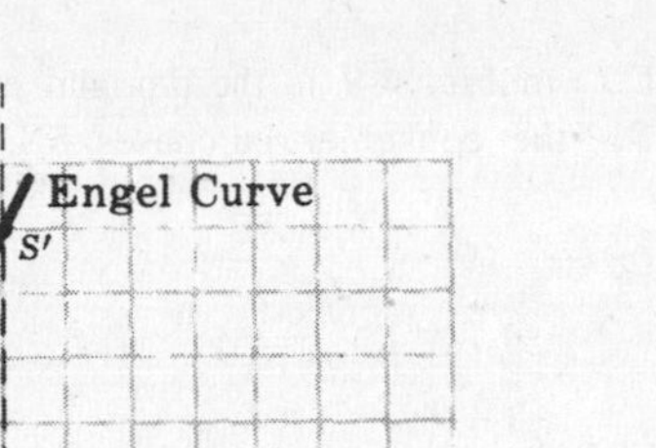
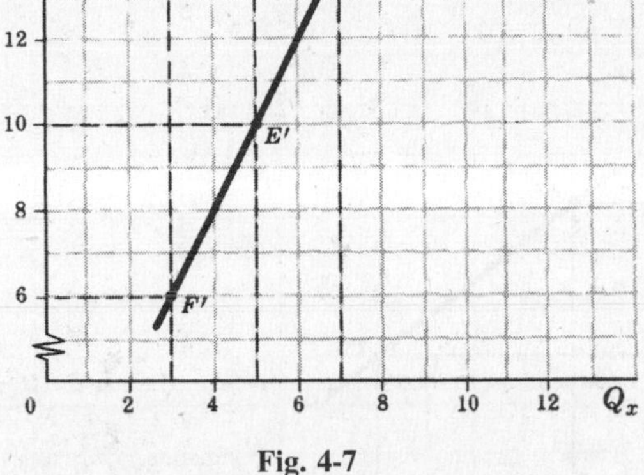

Fig. 4-7

EXAMPLE 13. Line $F'S'$ in Fig. 4-7 is the Engel curve for commodity X for the consumer of Example 12. It shows that when $M = \$6$, the consumer purchases 3X; when $M = \$10$, he or she purchases 5X, and when $M = \$14$, he or she purchases 7X. Since the Engel curve is positively sloped, $e_M > 0$ and commodity X is a normal good. When the Engel curve is negatively sloped, $e_M < 0$ and the good is inferior. We can further add that when the tangent to the Engel curve at a particular point is positively sloped and cuts the income axis, $e_M > 1$ and the commodity is a luxury at that point. If the tangent to the Engel curve is positively sloped and cuts the quantity axis, e_M is between zero and 1 and the commodity is a necessity (see Problem 4.29).

4.10 THE PRICE-CONSUMPTION CURVE AND THE CONSUMER'S DEMAND CURVE

By changing the price of X while keeping constant the price of Y and the consumer's tastes and money income, we can derive the consumer's price-consumption curve and demand curve for commodity X. The *price-consumption curve* for commodity X is the locus of points of consumer equilibrium resulting when only the price of X is varied. The consumer's *demand curve* for commodity X shows the amount of X that the consumer would purchase at various prices of X, *ceteris paribus*.

EXAMPLE 14. In Fig. 4-8 we see that when $P_x = P_y = \$1$ and $M = \$10$, the consumer is in equilibrium at point E on indifference curve II. This is the same as in Fig. 4-6. If P_x falls to \$0.50 while P_y and M remain unchanged, the budget line of the consumer rotates counterclockwise from KL to KJ. With this new budget line, the consumer is in equilibrium at point T where budget line KL is tangent to indifference curve III. By joining these points of consumer equilibrium, we get price-consumption curve ET in Fig. 4-8.

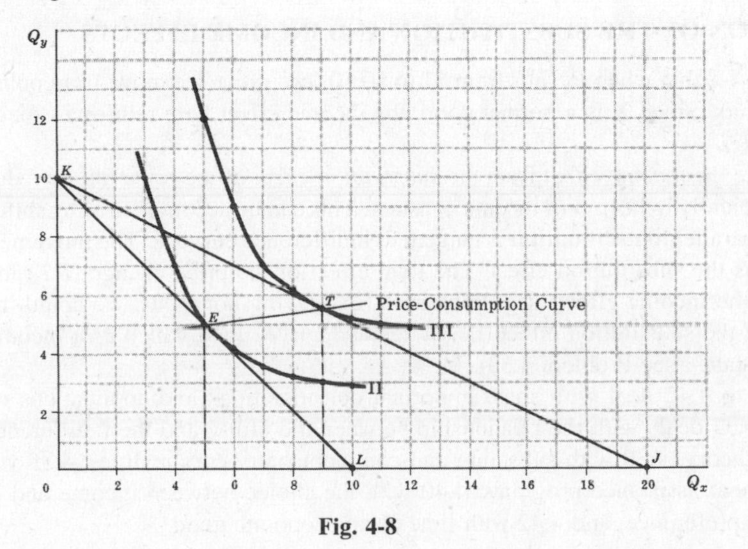

Fig. 4-8

EXAMPLE 15. Line $E'T'$ in Fig. 4-9 is the demand curve for commodity X for the consumer in Example 14. It shows that when $P_x = \$1$, the consumer purchases 5X, while when P_x falls to \$0.50, *ceteris paribus*, he or she purchases 9X.

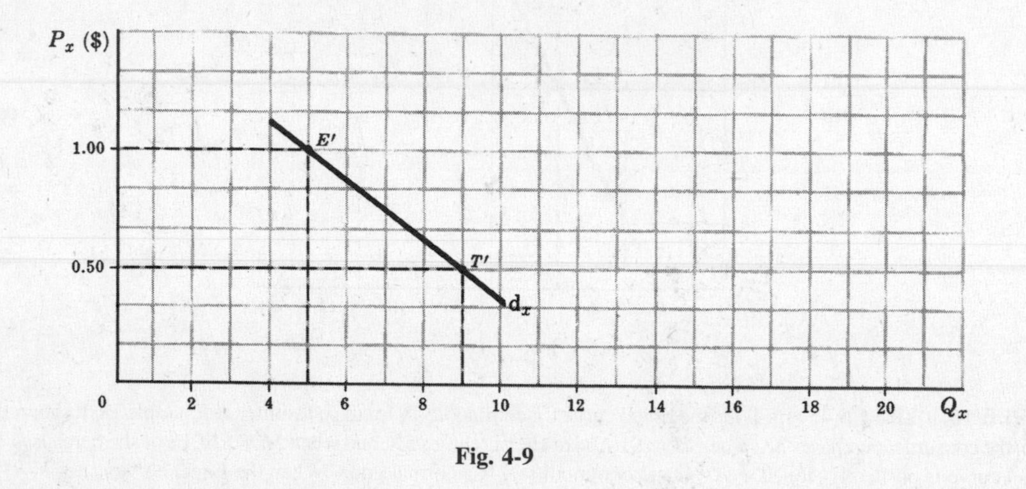

Fig. 4-9

When the slope of the price-consumption curve is positive as in Fig. 4-8, then d_x is inelastic. Thus, at $P_x = \$1$, this consumer buys 5X and spends \$5 on it. When P_x falls to \$0.50, the consumer buys 9X and spends \$4.50 on it. Since the amount spent on X falls when P_x falls, we know from Section 3.3 that d_x (in Fig. 4-9) is price-inelastic over arc $E'T'$

$$e = -\frac{\Delta Q}{\Delta P} \cdot \frac{P_{E'} + P_{T'}}{Q_{E'} + Q_{T'}} = -\frac{4}{-0.50} \cdot \frac{1.50}{14} \cong 0.86$$

When the slope of the price-consumption curve is zero, d_x is unitary price-elastic; when the slope of the price-consumption curve is negative, d_x is price-elastic (see Problem 4.30).

4.11 SEPARATION OF THE SUBSTITUTION AND INCOME EFFECTS

We saw in Fig. 4-8 that when P_x falls from \$1 to \$0.50 (*cet. par.*), we move from point E to point T and Q_x rises from 5 to 9 units. Since X is a normal good, the income effect here reinforces the substitution effect in causing the rise in Q_x.

We can separate the *income effect* from the *substitution effect* of the price fall by reducing the consumer's *money* income sufficiently to keep *real* income constant. This can be accomplished by shifting budget line KJ in Fig. 4-8 down and parallel to itself until it is tangent to indifference curve II. The movement along indifference curve II will give us the substitution effect. The total effect of the price change (ET) minus the substitution effect will give us the income effect (see Problem 4.32). Having done this, we could then derive a demand curve showing only the substitution effect (i.e., a demand curve along which *real* income rather than money income is kept constant—see Problem 4.32).

Problems 4.37 to 4.42 deal with some important considerations and applications of indifference curve analysis. Problem 4.37 deals with the relationship between the utility and the indifference curve approach to consumer demand theory, 4.38 with substitute and complementary commodities, 4.39 with the evaluation of alternative government assistance programs, 4.40 with the choice between income and leisure and overtime pay, 4.41 with time preference, and 4.42 with time as an economic good.

Glossary

Budget constraint line Shows all the different combinations of two commodities that a consumer can purchase, subject to a given money income and the prices of the two commodities.

Consumer equilibrium The point where a consumer maximizes the total utility or satisfaction, subject to a given income and price constraints.

Consumer's demand curve It shows the amount of a commodity the consumer would purchase at various prices, *ceteris paribus*.

Engel curve Shows the amount of a commodity that the consumer would purchase per unit of time at various levels of income.

Income-consumption curve The locus of points of consumer equilibrium resulting when only the consumer's income is varied.

Income effect The increase in the quantity purchased of a commodity with a given money income when the commodity price falls.

Indifference curve Shows the various combinations of two commodities which yield equal utility or satisfaction to the consumer.

Marginal rate of substitution (MRS_{xy}) The amount of commodity Y that a consumer is willing to give up in order to gain one additional unit of commodity X (and still remain on the same indifference curve).

Marginal utility (*MU*) The change in the total utility per unit change in the quantity of a commodity consumed per unit of time.

Price-consumption curve The locus of points of consumer equilibrium resulting when only the price of the commodity is varied.

Principle of diminishing marginal utility A concept stating that as an individual consumes more units of a commodity per unit of time, the total utility received increases, but the extra or marginal utility decreases.

Saturation point The point where the total utility received by an individual from consuming a commodity is maximum and the marginal utility is zero.

Substitution effect The increase in the quantity purchased of a commodity when its price falls (as a result of consumers switching from the purchase of other similar commodities).

Total utility (*TU*) The overall satisfaction that an individual receives from consuming a specified quantity of a commodity per unit of time.

Utility The property of a commodity that satisfies a want or need of a consumer.

Review Questions

1. When total utility increases, marginal utility is (*a*) negative and increasing, (*b*) negative and declining, (*c*) zero, or (*d*) positive and declining.

   Ans. (*d*) See Fig. 4-1.

2. If the MU of the last unit of X consumed is twice the MU of the last unit of Y consumed, the consumer is in equilibrium only if (*a*) the price of X is twice the price of Y, (*b*) the price of X is equal to the price of Y, (*c*) the price of X is one half of the price of Y, or (*d*) any of the above is possible.

   Ans. (*a*) See Example 3.

3. The statement $C = D = 10$ utils implies (*a*) an ordinal measure of utility only, (*b*) a cardinal measure of utility only, (*c*) an ordinal and a cardinal measure of utility, or (*d*) none of the above.

Ans. (*c*) Since an absolute amount of utility is specified, we have a cardinal measure of utility. When a cardinal statement is made, an ordinal statement is always implied (the reverse, however, is not true).

4. If an indifference curve were horizontal (assume X is measured along the horizontal axis and Y along the vertical axis), this would mean that the consumer is saturated with (*a*) commodity X only, (*b*) commodity Y only, (*c*) both commodity X and commodity Y, or (*d*) neither commodity X nor commodity Y.

Ans. (*a*) A horizontal indifference curve means that given the amount of Y, the consumer receives the same satisfaction regardless of the amount of X consumed. Therefore, the consumer is saturated with X. That is, the MRS_{xy} equals zero.

5. A consumer who is below the personal budget line (rather than on it) (*a*) is not spending all personal income, (*b*) is spending all personal income, (*c*) may or may not be spending all personal income, or (*d*) is in equilibrium.

Ans. (*a*) See Fig. 4-4.

6. At equilibrium, the slope of the indifference curve is (*a*) equal to the slope of the budget line, (*b*) greater than the slope of the budget line, (*c*) smaller than the slope of the budget line, or (*d*) either equal, larger, or smaller than the slope of the budget line.

Ans. (*a*) See Section 4.6.

7. If the MRS_{xy} for individual *A* exceeds the MRS_{xy} for individual *B*, it is possible for individual *A* to gain by giving up (*a*) X in exchange for more Y from *B*, (*b*) Y in exchange for more X from *B*, (*c*) either X or Y, or (*d*) we cannot say without additional information.

Ans. (*b*) Commodity X in relation to commodity Y is more valuable to individual *A* than to individual *B*; therefore, in order to gain, *A* should exchange Y with *B* for more X.

8. The Engel curve for a Giffen good is (*a*) negatively sloped, (*b*) positively sloped, (*c*) vertical, or (*d*) horizontal.

Ans. (*a*) See Section 4.9.

9. If the price-consumption curve for a commodity is horizontal at all relevant prices for it, the demand curve for this commodity is (*a*) horizontal, (*b*) positively sloped, (*c*) vertical, or (*d*) a rectangular hyperbola.

Ans. (*d*) When the price-consumption curve is horizontal for all the relevant prices of the commodity, the demand curve has unitary price elasticity throughout. Such a demand curve is a rectangular hyperbola.

10. The price-consumption curve for a straight-line demand curve extended to both axes (*a*) falls throughout, (*b*) rises throughout, (*c*) falls and then rises, or (*d*) rises and then falls.

Ans. (*c*) A straight-line demand curve extended to both axes is price-elastic above its midpoint (thus the price-consumption curve fails), and price-inelastic below its midpoint (and thus the price-consumption curve rises).

11. The substitution effect for a fall in the price of a commodity (*ceteris paribus*) is given by (*a*) a movement up a given indifference curve, (*b*) a movement from a higher to a lower indifference curve, (*c*) a movement down a given indifference curve, or (*d*) any of the above.

Ans. (*c*) See Section 4.11.

12. When *real* income rather than money income is kept constant in drawing a consumer's demand curve for a commodity, the demand curve is negatively sloped, (*a*) Always, (*b*) never, (*c*) sometimes, or (*d*) often.

Ans. (*a*) The only time we have a positively sloped demand curve for a commodity is when the income effect of the price change overwhelms the opposite substitution effect. When the consumer's real income is kept constant, we have no income effect (and the substitution effect always operates to increase the quantity of a commodity demanded when its price falls).

Solved Problems

TOTAL AND MARGINAL UTILITY

4.1 (*a*) With what is consumer demand theory concerned? (*b*) Why do we study consumer demand theory?

(*a*) Consumer demand theory is concerned with the individual's demand curve for a commodity—how it is derived and the reason for its location and shape. There are two different approaches to the study of consumer demand theory; the classical *utility approach* and the more recent *indifference curve approach.*

(*b*) We study consumer demand theory in order to learn more about the market demand curve for a commodity (which, as we have seen in Chapter 2, is obtained by the horizontal summation of all individuals' demand curves for the commodity).

4.2 From the TU_x schedule in Table 4.5, (*a*) derive the MU_x schedule, and (*b*) plot the TU_x and the MU_x schedules and indicate the saturation point.

Table 4.5

Q_x	0	1	2	3	4	5	6	7	8	9
TU_x	0	7	13	18	22	25	27	28	28	27

(*a*)

Table 4.6

Q_x	0	1	2	3	4	5	6	7	8	9
TU_x	0	7	13	18	22	25	27	28	28	27
MU_x	..	7	6	5	4	3	2	1	0	−1

(*b*)

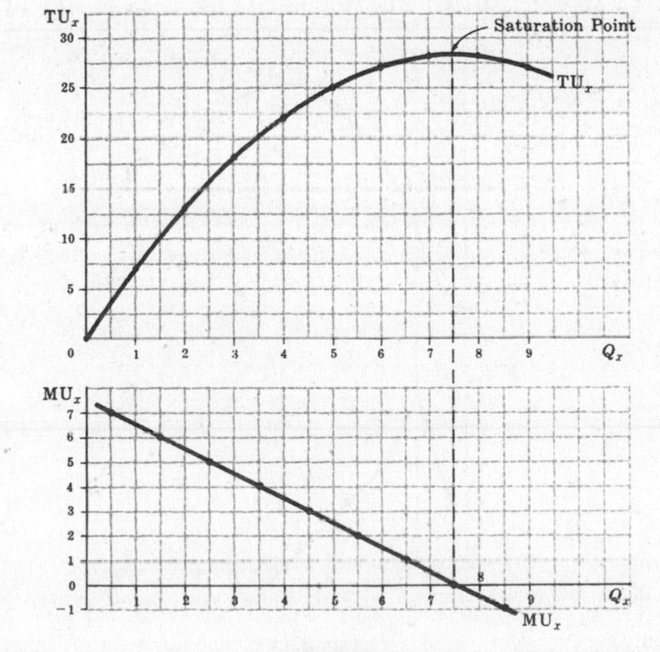

Fig. 4-10

Since $MU_x = \Delta TU_x / \Delta Q_x$, each value of MU_x has been recorded midway between successive levels of consumption. (For the same reason, the values of MU_x in Table 4.6 should have been recorded *between* successive values of the TU_x; however, this was not done so as not to complicate the table unduly.)

4.3 (*a*) Explain Table 4.6 if Q_x refers to the number of candy bars consumed per day by a teenager. (*b*) What does a utility function reflect?

(*a*) As the number of candy bars consumed per day increases, the total utility the teenager receives increases (up to a point). However, each additional unit consumed yields less and less extra or marginal utility. When the teenager increases consumption from 7 to 8 candy bars per day, the total utility is maximum and the marginal utility is zero. This is the saturation point. This teenager will not consume additional candy bars, even if they are free. Indeed, if given free more than 8 candy bars per day and the candy can not be resold, this teenager incurs the *disutility of disposing* (i.e., getting rid of) them.

(*b*) A utility function refers to a particular individual and reflects the tastes of this individual. Different individuals usually have different tastes and thus have different utility functions. Also, when the tastes of an individual change, the utility function also changes (shifts).

4.4 From the TU_y schedule in Table 4.7, (*a*) derive the MU_y schedule, and (*b*) plot the TU_y and the MU_y schedules and indicate the saturation point.

Table 4.7

Q_y	0	1	2	3	4	5	6	7
TU_y	0	4	14	20	24	26	26	24

(*a*)

Table 4.8

Q_y	0	1	2	3	4	5	6	7
TU_y	0	4	14	20	24	26	26	24
MU_y	..	4	10	6	4	2	0	−2

(*b*)

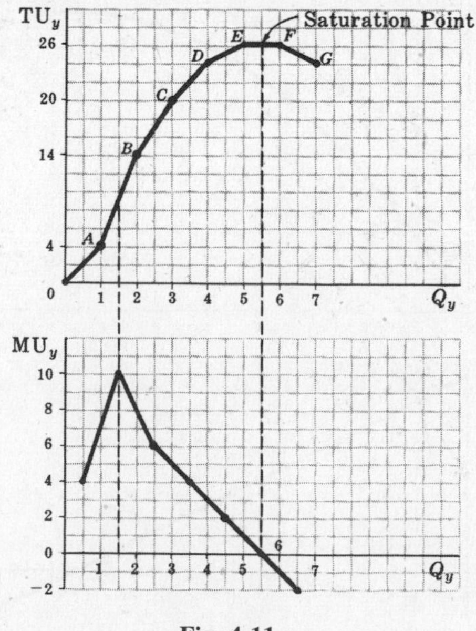

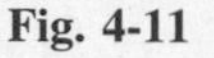
Fig. 4-11

It should be noted that in this case the MU_y, curves rises first and then falls.

4.5 (*a*) Using the values in Table 4.8, give a real-world case where the MU curve for a good might first rise and then fall. (*b*) Explain the shape of the MU_y curve in Fig. 4-11 in terms of the slope of the TU_y curve.

(*a*) Suppose a mother has two candy bars to give to her two little boys. If the two candy bars are different, an argument may arise between the children if both prefer the same candy bar. Suppose that the older boy (who cries the loudest) gets the preferred candy bar and refuses to share it with his little brother. The utility that the older boy receives from getting his preferred candy bar is only 4 utils (the argument and crying look away a great deal of his satisfaction in consuming the candy bar). Subsequently, the mother buys only the preferred type of candy bar so that now each child gets the same (preferred) candy bar. It is possible that the second unit of the preferred candy bar gives the older boy more utility (say, 10 utils) than the first since there is no arguing or crying now (see Table 4.8). Subsequently, additional units of the preferred candy bar give the older boy less and less additional utility.

Another example might be given by the first, the second, and subsequent martinis.

(*b*) The MU_y in Fig. 4-11 is equal to the average slope of the TU_y curve. For example, in going from 0 to 1 unit of Y consumed, the TU_y increases from 0 to 4 utils. Thus, the change in total utility resulting from increasing the consumption of Y by 1 unit is 4 utils. This is the MU_y and is equal to the slope of segment *OA* of the TU_y function in Fig. 4-11. Similarly, when the quantity of Y consumed per time period increases from 1 to 2 units, the total utility increases from 4 to 14 utils or by 10 utils. Thus the MU_y is 10 and is equal to the slope of the TU_y function between points *A* and *B*. Between points *E* and *F*, the TU is horizontal. Thus its slope, or the MU_y, is zero. To the right of point *F*, the TU_y is negatively sloped and so the MU_y is negative.

4.6 (*a*) Derive the MU curve geometrically from the TU curve of Fig. 4-12. (*b*) Explain the shape of the MU curve of part (*a*) in terms of the shape of the TU curve. (*c*) What is the relevant portion of the TU curve?

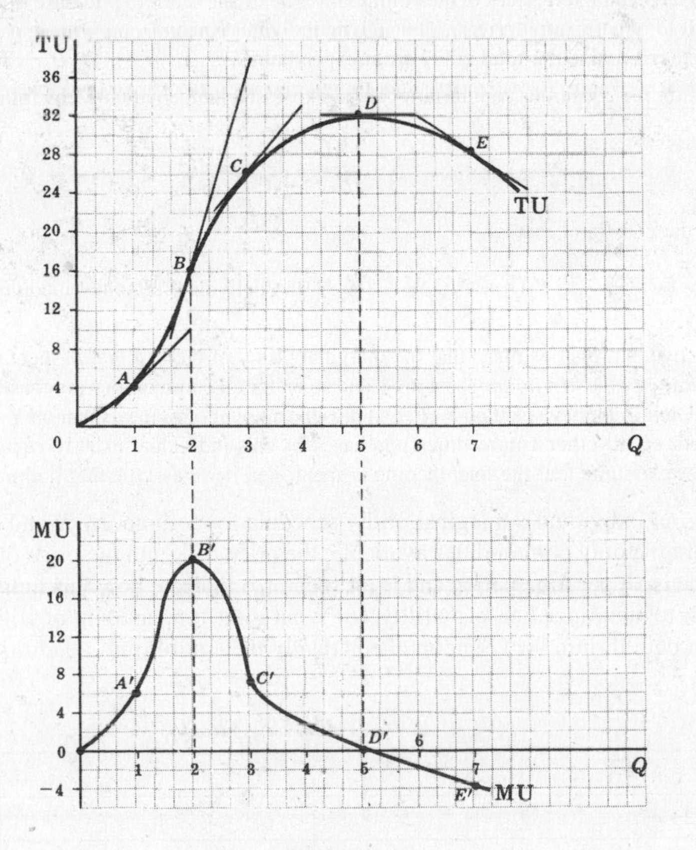

Fig. 4-12

(*a*) The MU curve is shown in Fig. 4-12. In this case, the TU function is a smooth or continuous curve. The MU corresponding to each point on the TU curve is given by the slope of the TU curve (or the slope of the tangent to the TU curve) at that point. Thus at point *A*, the slope of the TU curve is equal to 6. This corresponds to point *A*′ on the MU curve. At point *B*, the slope of the TU curve or the MU is equal to 20. This gives point *B*′. At *C*, *D*, and *E*, the slope of the TU curve is 7, 0, and −4, respectively. Thus we get points, *C*′, *D*′, and *E*′ on the MU curve. By joining points *O*, *A*′, *B*′, *C*′, *D*′, and *E*′ we get the MU curve corresponding to the given TU curve.

(*b*) As long as the TU curve faces up (from *O* to *B*), the TU is increasing at an increasing rate and the MU is rising. At point *B*, the TU curve changes direction (from facing up to facing down). At this point, the slope of the TU curve (the MU) is maximum. (In mathematics, *B* is called an *inflection point*.) Past point *B*, the TU curve faces down. That is, TU is increasing at a decreasing rate and MU is falling. At point *D*, the TU is maximum so the slope of the TU curve, or the MU, is zero. Past point *D*, the TU curve begins to fall so that the MU is negative.

(*c*) In textbooks, the TU function is usually given as a smooth curve and may or may not have a range over which it is increasing at an increasing rate. However, the economically relevant range of the TU curve is the portion over which the TU is rising at a declining rate (in the previous diagram, from point *B* to point *D*). This corresponds to the positive but declining range of the MU curve (i.e., from point *B*′ to *D*′). The reason for this will be discussed in Problem 4.9(*e*).

CONSUMER EQUILIBRIUM

4.7 (*a*) What constraints or limitations does the consumer face in seeking to maximize the total utility from personal expenditures? (*b*) Express mathematically the condition for consumer equilibrium. (*c*) Explain the meaning of your answers to part (*b*).

(*a*) In seeking to maximize the total utility from personal expenditures, the consumer faces an income and price constraint or limitation. That is, the consumer has a given and limited income over a specific period of time and faces given and fixed prices of the commodities he or she seeks to purchase (i.e., the individual consumer is too small to affect market prices). Thus, given individual income and price constraints, the rational consumer seeks to maximize the total utility from expenditures.

(*b*) The condition for consumer equilibrium can be expressed mathematically, as follows

$$\frac{\text{MU}_x}{P_x} = \frac{\text{MU}_y}{P_y} = \cdots$$

subject to the constraint that

$$P_xQ_x + P_yQ_y + \cdots = M \text{ (the individual's money income)}$$

(*c*) The above two expressions mean that the marginal utility of the *last dollar* spent on X must be equal to the marginal utility of the *last dollar* spent on Y and so on for all commodities purchased, subject to the constraint that the *amount* of money spent on X (P_xQ_x) plus the amount of money spent on Y (P_yQ_y) plus the amount of money spent on all other commodities purchased by this individual exactly equals the individual's money income (if we assume that the total income is spent; i.e., if we assume that nothing is saved).

4.8 Table 4.9 gives an individual's marginal utility schedule for commodity X and commodity Y. Suppose that X and Y are the only commodities available, the price of X and the price of Y are $1, and the individual's income is $8 per time period and is all spent. (*a*) Indicate how this individual should spend her income in order to maximize her total utility. (*b*) What is the total amount of utility received by the individual when in equilibrium? (*c*) State mathematically the equilibrium condition for the consumer.

Table 4.9

(1) Q	1	2	3	4	5	6	7	8	Total
(2) MU_x	11	10	9	8	7	6	5	4	60
(3) MU_y	19	17	15	13	12	10	8	6	100

(*a*) With continuously decreasing MU, overall TU can be maximized by maximizing the utility received from spending a dollar at the time. Thus, this individual should spend the first dollar of her income to purchase the first unit of Y. From this she receives 19 utils. If she spent this first dollar to purchase the first unit of X, she would receive only 11 utils. The individual should spend her second, third, fourth, and fifth dollars to purchase the second, third, fourth, and fifth units of Y. From these she received 17, 15, 13, and 12 utils, respectively. The individual should spend her sixth dollar to purchase the first unit of X (from which she receives 11 utils) rather than the sixth unit of Y (from which she would receive only 10 utils). Her seventh and eighth dollars should be spent on purchasing the sixth unit of Y and the second unit of X. Both give her 10 utils of utility. The individual cannot go on purchasing more units of X or Y because her income is exhausted.

(*b*) When this individual spends her income to purchase 2 units of X and 6 units of Y, her total utility is 107 utils (see Table 4.9). This represents the maximum utility this individual can receive from the expenditure. If this individual spent her income in any other way, the total utility would be less. For example, if she gave up the second unit of X to buy the seventh unit of Y, she would lose 10 utils and gain only 8 utils (see Table 4.9). Similarly, if she gave up the sixth unit of Y to purchase the third unit of X, she would lose 10 utils and gain only 9 utils. If she spent all of her income to purchase 8 units of X, she would receive only 60 units of utility [see row (2) of the table]. If she bought 8 units of Y, her total utility would be 100 utils [see row (3) of the table].

(*c*)
$$\frac{\mathrm{MU}_x}{P_x} = \frac{MU_y}{P_y} = \frac{10}{\$1} \quad \text{and} \quad P_xQ_x + P_yQ_y = (\$1)(2) + (\$1)(6) = \$8$$

4.9 Table 4.10 gives an individual's marginal utility schedule for commodity X and commodity Y. Suppose that the price of X and the price of Y are \$2, that the individual has \$20 of income per time period, and that he spends it all on X and Y. (*a*) State the equilibrium condition for this individual, (*b*) If "commodity" Y is savings, how would the equilibrium condition be affected? (*c*) Suppose that the MU of the fourth unit of Y was 7 utils rather than 8. What effect would this have on the equilibrium condition? (*d*) Suppose that the MU_x increased continuously as the individual consumed more of X [while the MU schedule for Y remained unchanged as indicated in row (3) of Table 4.10]. How should the consumer rearrange his expenditures to maximize his total utility? (*e*) Over what range of the MU function do consumers operate?

Table 4.10

(1) Q	1	2	3	4	5	6	7	8	9	10	11
(2) MU_x	16	14	11	10	9	8	7	6	5	3	1
(3) MU_y	15	13	12	8	6	5	4	3	2	1	0

(*a*)
$$\frac{MU_x}{P_x} = \frac{MU_y}{P_y} = \frac{8}{\$2}$$
$$P_xQ_x + P_yQ_y = (\$2)(6) + (\$2)(4) = \$20$$

(*b*) If Y referred to savings rather than to a consumption good and the MU_y schedule of row (3) represented the utility received by this individual from saving part of his income, the equilibrium condition for this consumer would remain completely unchanged. In order to maximize the total utility from his income, this consumer should spend \$12 of his income to purchase 6 units of commodity X and save the remaining \$8.

(*c*) If the MU of the fourth unit of Y was 7 rather than 8, in order to be in equilibrium this individual should buy a little more than 6 units of X and a little less than 4 units of Y. If the consumer could not purchase fractions of a unit of X and Y, then the individual could continue to buy 6 units of X (6X) and 4 units of Y (4Y), but now the equilibrium condition would hold only approximately and not precisely.

(*d*) If the MU_x [row (2) of the table] had been rising continuously rather than falling, this individual should spend all of his income to buy 10 units of X in order to maximize his total utility.

(*e*) Since in the real world we observe that consumers spend their income on many commodities rather than on a single one, consumers operate over the falling portion of the MU function. In addition, the MU function also becomes irrelevant past the saturation point, because the consumer would not be willing to get more of this commodity even if it were free. Thus, the relevant portion of the MU function is its positive but falling portion.

4.10 Why is water, which is essential to life, so cheap while diamonds, which are not essential to life, so expensive?

Since water is essential to life, the TU received from water exceeds the TU received from diamonds. However, the price we are willing to pay for each unit of a commodity depends not on the TU but on the MU. That is, since we consume so much water, the MU of the last unit of water consumed is very low. Therefore, we are willing to pay only a very low price for this last unit of water consumed. Since all the units of water consumed are identical, we pay the same low price on all the other units of water consumed.

On the other hand, since we purchase so few diamonds, the MU of the last diamond purchased is very high. Therefore, we are willing to pay a high price for this last diamond and for all the other diamonds purchased. Classical economists did not distinguish TU from MU and thus they were unable to resolve this so-called "water-diamond paradox."

INDIFFERENCE CURVES

4.11 Table 4.11 gives points on four different indifference curves for a consumer. (*a*) Sketch indifference curves I, II, III, and IV on the same set of axes. (*b*) What do indifference curves show?

Table 4.11

I		II		III		IV	
Q_x	Q_y	Q_x	Q_y	Q_x	Q_y	Q_x	Q_y
2	13	3	12	5	12	7	12
3	6	4	8	5.5	9	8	9
4	4.5	5	6.3	6	8.3	9	7
5	3.5	6	5	7	7	10	6.3
6	3	7	4.4	8	6	11	5.7
7	2.7	8	4	9	5.4	12	5.3

(*a*)

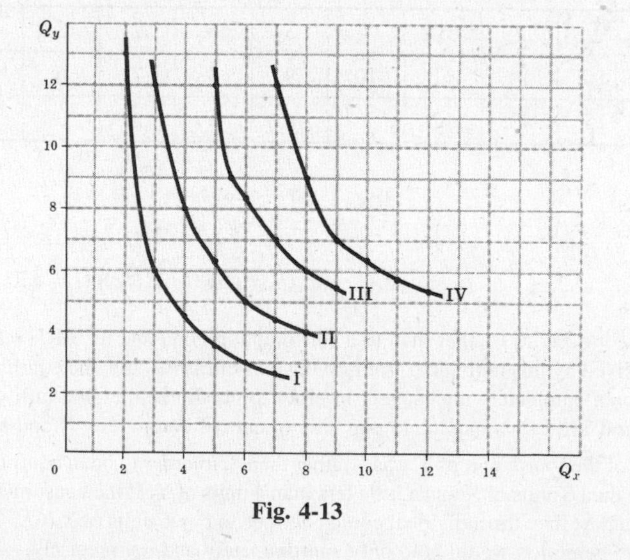

Fig. 4-13

(*b*) In difference curves are a graphic picture of a consumer's tastes and preferences (in utility analysis, the consumer's total utility curve introduced the tastes of the consumer). The consumer is *indifferent* among all the different combinations of X and Y on the same *indifference* curve but prefers points on a higher indifference curve to points on a lower one. Even though we have chosen to represent a consumer's tastes by sketching only 3 or 4 indifference curves here, the field of indifference curves is *dense* (i.e., there are an infinite number of them). All the indifference curves of a consumer give us the consumer's *indifference map.* Different consumers have different indifference maps. When the tastes of a consumer change, that person's indifference map changes.

4.12 (*a*) Is a cardinal measure of utility or satisfaction necessary in order to sketch a set of indifference curves? (*b*) What are the characteristics of indifference curves?

(*a*) In sketching a set of indifference curves, we need only an ordering or ranking of consumer preferences. A cardinal measure of utility or satisfaction is neither necessary nor specified. That is, we do not need to know either the absolute amount of utility that a consumer receives by being on a particular indifference curve or by how much utility increases when the consumer moves to a higher indifference curve. All we need to know to get the indifference curves of a consumer is whether the consumer is indifferent, prefers, or does not prefer each combination of X and Y to other combinations of X and Y.

(*b*) Indifference curves are negatively sloped, they are convex to the origin and do not cross. Indifference curves need not be and are usually not parallel to one another.

4.13 (*a*) Find the MRS_{xy} between all consecutive points on the four indifference curves of Problem 4.11. (*b*) What is the difference between MRS_{xy} and the MU_x?

(*a*) See Table 4.12.

(*b*) The MRS_{xy} measures the amount of Y a consumer is willing to give up to obtain one additional unit of X (and still remain on the same indifference curve). That is, the $MRS_{xy} = -(\Delta Q_y/\Delta Q_x)$. The MU_x measures the change in the total utility a consumer receives when changing the quantity of X consumed by one unit. That is, $MU_x = \Delta TU_x/\Delta Q_x$. In measuring the MRS_{xy}, both X and Y change. In measuring MU_x, the quantity of Y (among other things) is kept constant. Thus, the MRS_{xy} measures something different from the MU_x.

Table 4.12

I			II			III			IV		
X	Y	MRS_{xy}	X	Y	MRS_{xy}	X	Y	MRS_{xy}	X	Y	MRS_{xy}
2	13		3	12		5	12		7	12	
3	6	7	4	8	4	5.5	9	6	8	9	3
4	4.5	1.5	5	6.3	1.7	6	8.3	1.4	9	7	2
5	3.5	1	6	5	1.3	7	7	1.3	10	6.3	0.7
6	3	0.5	7	4.4	0.6	8	6	1	11	5.7	0.6
7	2.7	0.3	8	4	0.4	9	5.4	0.6	12	5.3	0.4

4.14 On the same set of axes, draw three indifference curves showing perfect substitutability between X and Y.

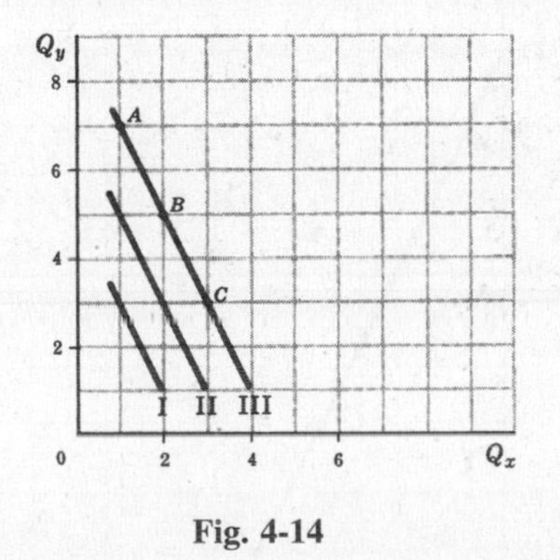

Fig. 4-14

For X and Y to be perfect substitutes, the MRS_{xy} must be constant. That is, no matter what indifference curve we are on and where we are on it, we must give up the same amount of Y to get one additional unit of X. For example, in going from point *A* to point *B* on indifference curve III, the MRS_{xy} equals 2. Similarly, in going from point *B* to point *C*, the MRS_{xy} is also equal to 2. If the indifference curves had throughout a slope of -1 (and thus a $MRS_{xy} = 1$), X and Y would not only be perfect substitutes but could be considered as being the

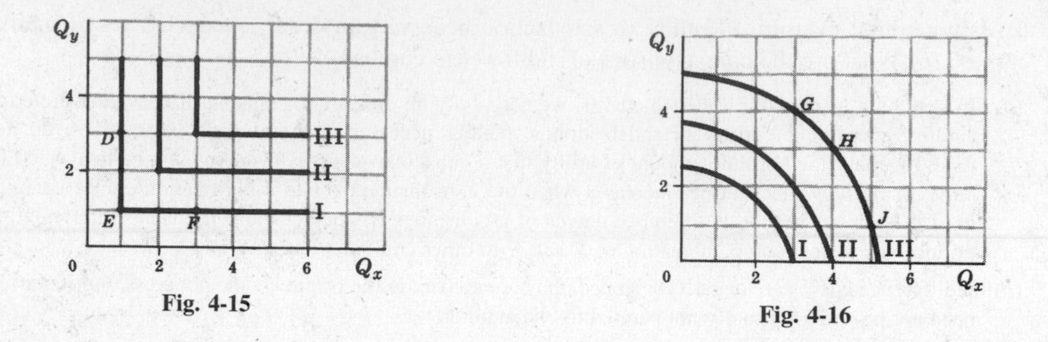

Fig. 4-15

Fig. 4-16

same commodity from the consumer's point of view. For example, X and Y could be two brands of beer and the consumer is indifferent as to which to drink.

4.15 On the same set of axes, draw three indifference curves showing perfect complementarity between X and Y.

Refer to Fig. 4-15. For X and Y to be perfect complements, the MRS_{xy} and the MRS_{yx} must both be equal to zero. For example, points *D*, *E*, and *F* are all on indifference curve I, yet point *F* involves the same amount of Y but more of X than point *E*. Thus, the consumer is saturated with X and so the $MRS_{xy} = 0$. Similarly, point *D* involves the same amount of X but more of Y than point *E*. Thus, the consumer is saturated with Y and so the $MRS_{yx} = 0$. Car and gasoline may be regarded as perfect complements. In general, indifference curves are neither straight lines nor right-angle bends, but show some curvature. The closer the shape of the indifference curve to a straight line, the greater the degree of substitutability between X and Y.

4.16 On the same set of axes, draw three indifference curves showing increasing MRS_{xy} as we move down the indifference curves.

The indifference curves in Fig. 4-16 are concave to the origin and thus show increasing MRS_{xy} as we move down the indifference curves. For example, in going from point *G* to point *H* on indifference curve **III**, the $MRS_{xy} = 1$. In going from *H* to *J*, the $MRS_{xy} = 2$. We will explore the implication which this type of indifference curve has for consumer equilibrium in Problem 4.23.

BUDGET CONSTRAINT LINE

4.17 Suppose that the price of commodity Y is \$1 per unit while the price of commodity X is \$2 per unit and suppose that an individual's money income is \$16 per time period and is all spent on X and Y. (*a*) Draw the budget constraint line for this consumer and (*b*) explain the reason for the shape and the properties of the budget constraint line in part (*a*).

(*a*)

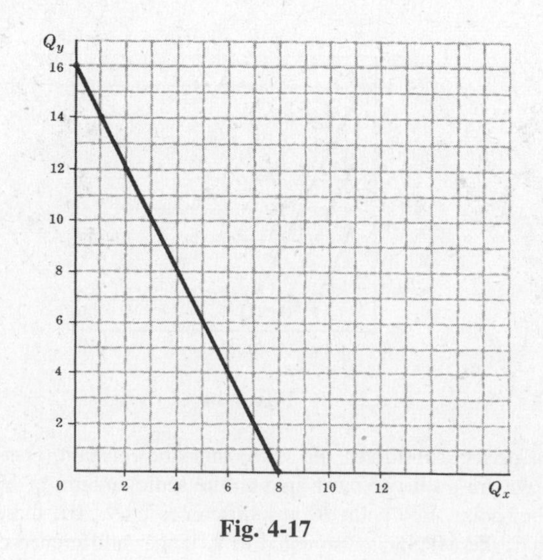

Fig. 4-17

(*b*) If this consumer spent all of his income on commodity Y, he could purchase 16 units of it. If he spent all of his income on commodity X, he could purchase 8 units of it. Joining these two points by a straight line, we get this consumer's budget constraint line. The budget constraint line gives us all the different combinations of X and Y that the consumer could buy. Thus he could buy 16Y and 0X, 14Y and 1X, 12Y and 2X, ..., 0Y and 8X. Note that for each two units of Y that the consumer gives up he can purchase one additional unit of X. The slope of this budget line has a value of -2 and remains constant. Also to be noted is that all points on the budget line indicate that the consumer is spending all of his income on X and Y. That is, $P_xQ_x + P_yQ_y = M = \$16$.

4.18 Given a consumer's money income (M), P_y and P_x, (*a*) indicate the quantity of Y the consumer could purchase if she spent all of her income on Y, (*b*) indicate the quantity of X the consumer could purchase if she spent all of her income on X, (*c*) find the slope of the budget constraint line in terms of P_x and P_y, and (*d*) find the *general* equation of the budget constraint line.

(*a*)
$$Q_{y0} = \frac{M}{P_y}, \quad \text{when} \quad Q_x = 0$$

(*b*)
$$Q_{x0} = \frac{M}{P_x}, \quad \text{when} \quad Q_y = 0$$

(*c*)
$$\text{slope} = \frac{\Delta Y}{\Delta X} = -\frac{Q_{y0}}{Q_{x0}} = -\frac{M/P_y}{M/P_x}$$
$$= -\frac{M}{P_y} \cdot \frac{P_x}{M} = -\frac{P_x}{P_y}$$

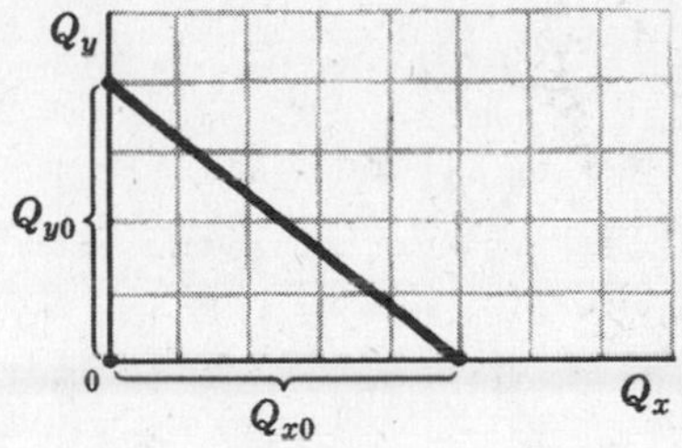

Fig. 4-18

(*d*) The general equation of a straight line can be written as $y = a + bx$, where a = y-intercept or the value of y when $x = 0$ and b = slope of the line. From the answer to part (*a*) we know that $a = M/P_y$ and from the answer to part (*c*) we know that $b = -P_x/P_y$.

Therefore, the general equation of the budget constraint line is

$$Q_y = \frac{M}{P_y} - \frac{P_x}{P_y} Q_x$$

By multiplying each term of the previous equation by P_y and then rearranging the terms, we get an equivalent way of expressing the equation of the budget constraint line. That is,

$$(P_y)\left(Q_y = \frac{M}{P_y} - \frac{P_x}{P_y} Q_x\right) \quad \text{gives} \quad P_yQ_y = M - P_xQ_x$$

By transposing the last term ($-P_xQ_x$) to the left of the equal sign, we get $P_xQ_x + P_yQ_y = M$.

4.19 (*a*) Find the *specific* equation of the budget constraint line in Problem 4.17. (*b*) Show an equivalent way of expressing the specific equation of the budget constraint line in part (*a*).

(*a*) In Problem 4.17, the y-intercept $(a) = M/P_y = \$16/\$1 = 16$. The slope of the budget line $(b) = -P_x/P_y = -2/1 = 2$. Therefore, the specific equation of the budget line in Problem 4.17 is given by $Q_y = 16 - 2Q_x$. By substituting various values for Q_x into this equation, we get the corresponding values for Q_y. Thus, when $Q_x = 0$, $Q_y = 16$; when $Q_x = 1$, $Q_y = 14$; when $Q_x = 2$, $Q_y = 12$; ...; when $Q_x = 8$, $Q_y = 0$.

(*b*) Another way to write the Problem 4.17 budget line equation is

$$(\$2)(Q_x) + (\$1)(Q_y) = \$16$$

By substituting various quantities of one commodity into this equation, we get the corresponding quantities of the other commodity that the consumer must purchase if he is to remain on his budget line. For example, if $Q_x = 2$, the consumer must purchase 12 units of Y if he is to remain on his budget line (i.e., if he is to spend all of his income of \$16 on X and Y).

CONSUMER EQUILIBRIUM

4.20 If the consumer's tastes are given by the indifference curves of Problem 4.10 and the total income and price constraints by the budget line of Problem 4.17, (*a*) find geometrically the point at which this consumer is in equilibrium and (*b*) explain why this is an equilibrium point; what is true of the slope of the indifference curve and the budget line at equilibrium?

(*a*)

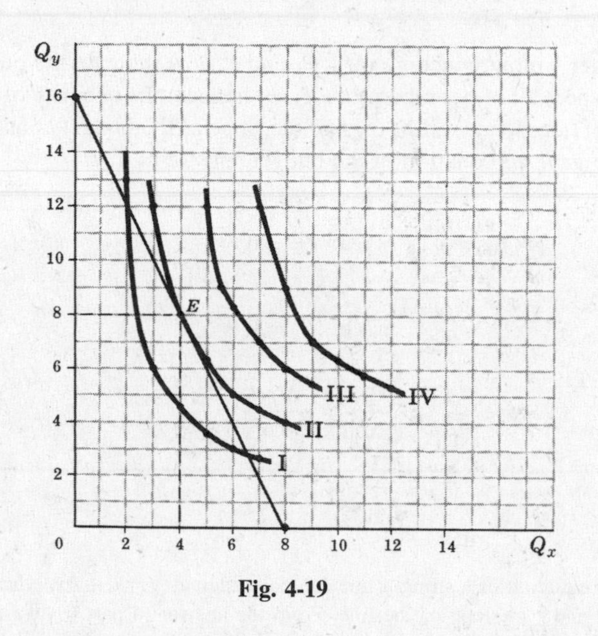

Fig. 4-19

(*b*) The consumer is in equilibrium at point *E*, where the budget line is tangent to the indifference curve II. Indifference curve II is the highest indifference curve that the consumer can reach given this particular budget line. Because they are tangent, the absolute slope of indifference curve II (MRS_{xy}) and the absolute slope of the budget line (P_x/P_y) are equal at point *E*. That is, at point *E*, $MRS_{xy} = P_x/P_y = 2$. Since the field of indifference carves, or the indifference map, is dense, one such point of tangency (and consumer equilibrium) is assured.

4.21 (*a*) Explain why points *G*, *D*, *C*, and *F* in Fig. 4-20 (which is the same as in Problem 4.20) are not points of consumer equilibrium. (*b*) Explain *in terms of the slopes of the indifference curves and the slope of the budget line* why a movement from point *C* to point *E* increases the consumer's satisfaction and (*c*) do the same for a movement from point *F* to point *E*.

(*a*) Given the price of X and the price of Y, the consumer's income is not sufficient to reach point *G* on indifference curve III (see Fig. 4-20). At point *D*, the consumer is on indifference curve I but is not spending all of her income. At points *C* and *F*, the consumer would be spending all personal income but is still on indifference curve I and thus is not maximizing her satisfaction.

(*b*) At point *C*, the absolute slope of indifference curve I (which indicates *what the consumer is willing to do*) exceeds the absolute slope of the budget line (which indicates *what this consumer is able to do in the market*). That is, starting at point *C*, this consumer is willing to give up more than 6 units of Y to obtain 1 more unit of X and still remain on indifference curve I (see Fig. 4-20). However, the consumer can get one additional unit of X in the market by giving up only 2 units of Y. Thus, by moving down the budget line from point *C* toward point *E*, the consumer increases her satisfaction.

(*c*) At point *F*, the absolute slope of the budget line is *greater* than the absolute slope of indifference curve I. This means that the consumer can obtain *more* of Y in the market than the individual is willing to accept in order to give up one unit of X. Thus, by moving up the budget line from point F toward point E, the consumer increases her satisfaction. At point E, the $\mathrm{MRS}_{xy} = P_x/P_y$.

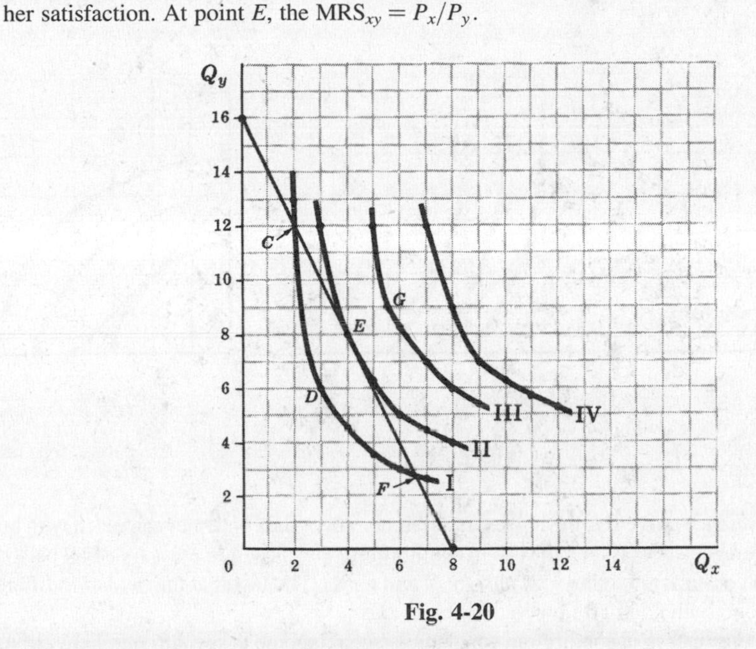

Fig. 4-20

4.22 (*a*) Express mathematically the condition for consumer equilibrium given by the indifference-curve approach. (*b*) Show that if a cardinal measure of utility exists, the condition in (*a*) reduces to

$$\frac{\mathrm{MU}_x}{P_x} = \frac{\mathrm{MU}_y}{P_y}$$

$$P_xQ_x + P_yQ_y = M$$

as given in Section 4.2.

(*a*) As shown in Problem 4.18, the consumer's budget line is given by the equation $P_xQ_x + P_yQ_y = M$. At the point where this budget line is tangent to an indifference curve, the absolute slope of the curve, MRS_{XY}, equals the absolute slope of the budget line, P_x/P_y (see Problem 4.20). Thus,

$$\mathrm{MRS}_{xy} = P_x/P_y$$

$$P_xQ_x + P_yQ_y = M$$

is the equilibrium condition under the indifference curve theory.

(*b*) Suppose that a consumer can measure utilities (and hence marginal utilities) numerically, and suppose that for some Q_x and Q_y, $\mathrm{MU}_x = 5$ utils, $\mathrm{MU}_y = 1$ util. Then the consumer would be willing to give up 5 units of Y for an additional unit of X, as the trade would not change that consumer's net utility. Thus, $\mathrm{MRS}_{xy} = 5$ for the given quantities and, in general, $\mathrm{MRS}_{xy} = \mathrm{MU}_x/\mathrm{MU}_y$. Substituting this expression into the first equation of part (*a*), we obtain

$$\frac{MU_x}{MU_y} = \frac{P_x}{P_y} \quad \text{or} \quad \frac{MU_x}{P_x} = \frac{MU_y}{P_y}$$

4.23 Draw a diagram showing that (*a*) if the indifference curves are convex to the origin but are everywhere flatter than the budget line, the consumer maximizes satisfaction by consuming only commodity Y, (*b*) if the indifference curves are convex to the origin but are everywhere steeper than the budget line, the consumer maximizes satisfaction by consuming only commodity X, and (*c*) if the indifference curves are concave to the origin, the consumer maximizes satisfaction by consuming either only commodity X or only commodity Y. (*d*) Would you expect indifference curves to be of any of these shapes in the real world? Why?

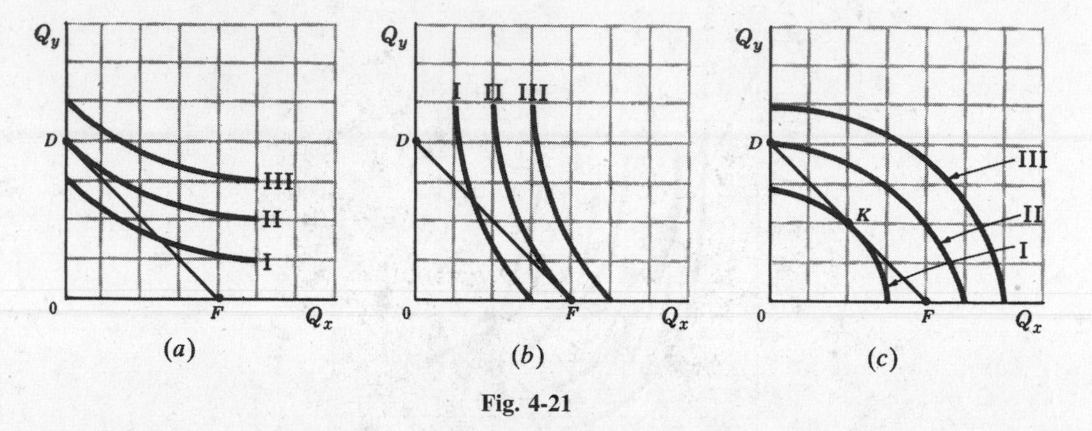

Fig. 4-21

In panel (*a*), indifference curve II is the highest indifference curve the consumer can reach with budget line *DF*. In order to reach indifference curve II (and thus be in equilibrium), the consumer must spend all personal income on commodity Y (i.e., the consumer must buy *OD* units of Y and no X). The fact that the field of indifference curves is dense always assures one such equilibrium point on the Y-axis.

In panel (*b*), the consumer is in equilibrium when all personal income is spent to purchase *OF* units of X (and no Y).

In panel (*c*), budget line *DF* is tangent to indifference curve I at point *K*. However, this is not the point at which the consumer is maximizing satisfaction since this person could reach indifference curve II by consuming only commodity Y (point *D*). Such equilibrium points as *D* in panel (*a*), *F* in panel (*b*), and *D* in panel (*c*) are called *corner solutions*.

(*d*) In the real world the consumer does not spend all income on a single commodity; therefore, indifference curves do not look like those shown in panels (*a*), (*b*), and (*c*).

EXCHANGE

4.24 Suppose that individual *A* and individual *B* possess together a combined total of 14 units of Y and 16 units of X. Suppose also that the tastes of individual *A* are represented by indifference curves I, II, and III in Fig. 4-22, while the tastes of individual *B* are given by indifference curves I′, II′, and III′, (with origin at O′). (What we have done here, essentially, is rotate *B*'s set of indifference curves by 180° and superimpose them on the figure of *A*'s indifference curves in such a way that the box formed has the specified dimensions of 14Y and 16X.) (*a*) What does every point inside (or on) the box represent? (*b*) Is there a basis for mutually advantageous exchange between individuals *A* and *B* at point *C*? Explain.

(*a*) Every point inside (or on) the box represents a particular distribution of the 14Y and 16X between individuals *A* and *B*. For example, point *C* indicates that *A* has 10Y and 1X, while *B* has 4Y and 15X.

(*b*) Since at point *C*, MRS_{xy} for individual *A* exceeds the MRS_{xy} for individual *B*, there is a basis for mutually advantageous exchange between individuals *A* and *B*. Starting from point *C*, individual *A* would be willing to give up 5Y to get one additional unit of X (and so move to point *D* on indifference curve I). Individual *B* would be willing to give up one unit of X in exchange for 0.4 of Y (and so move from point *C* to point *H* on indifference curve I′). Since *A* is willing to give up more of Y than necessary to induce *B* to give up one unit of X, there is a basis for exchange. In such an exchange, *A* will give up some Y in return for X from *B*.

4.25 Explain what happens if, starting from point *C* in Fig. 4-22, (*a*) individual *A* exchanges 3Y for 6X with individual *B*, (*b*) individual *B* exchanges 2X for 7Y with individual *A*, and (*c*) individual *A* exchanges 5Y for 4X with individual *B*.

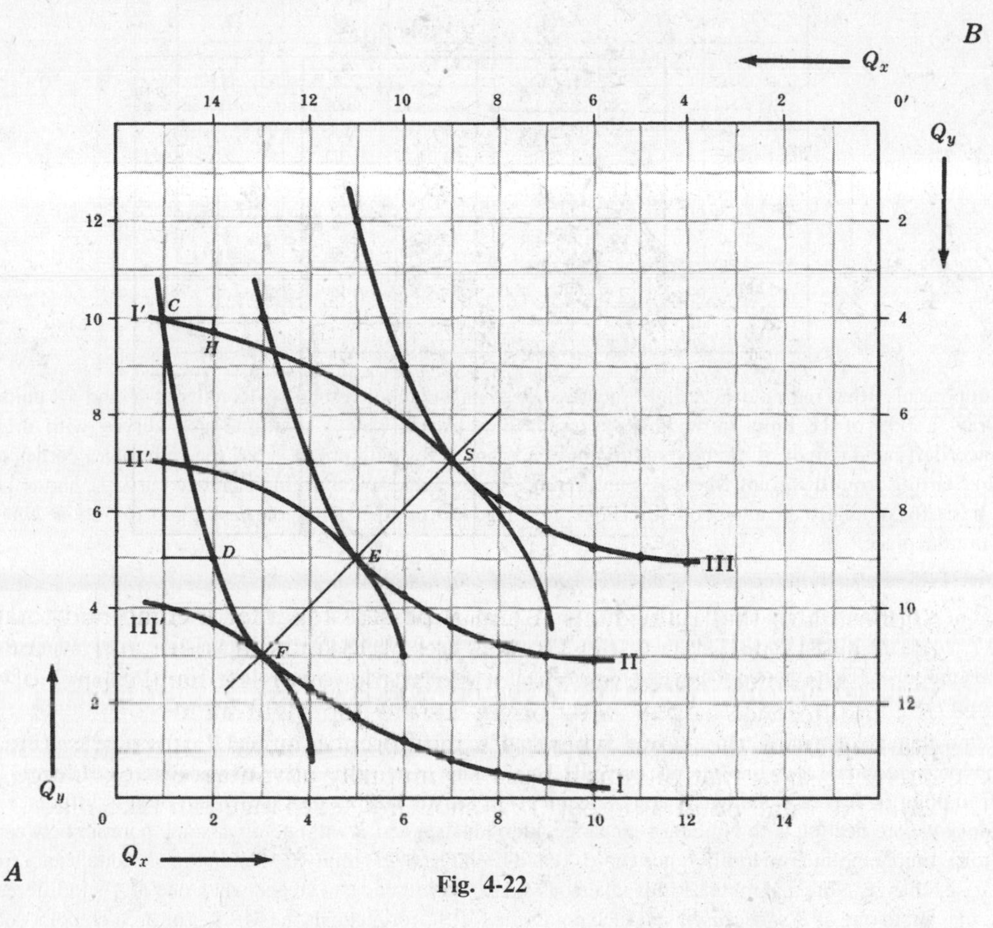

Fig. 4-22

(*a*) If *A* gives up 3Y in exchange for 6X from *B*, *A* would move from point *C* on indifference curve I to point *S* on indifference curve III, while *B* would move along indifference curve I′ from *C* to *S*. *A* would gain all of the benefit from the exchange while *B* would gain and lose nothing (since *B* would still be on indifference curve I′). At point *S*, indifference curves III and I′ are tangent and so their slopes are equal. This means that at point *S*, the MRS_{xy} for *A* equals the MRS_{xy} for *B* and so there is no basis for further exchange. (From point *S*, the amount of Y that *A* would be willing to give up to obtain one unit of X from *B* is not sufficient to induce *B* to part with one unit of X.)

(*b*) If *B* gave up 2X in exchange for 7Y from *A*, individual *B* would move from point *C* on indifference curve I′ to point F on indifference curve III′. In this case, all of the gains from this exchange would accrue to *B*. *A* would gain and lose nothing from this exchange since *A* would still be on indifference curve I. At point *F*, the MRS_{xy} for *A* equals the MRS_{xy} for *B* and so there is no further basis for exchange.

(*c*) Starting from point *C* on indifference curves I and I′, if individual *A* exchanges 5Y for 4X with individual *B* (and gets to point *E*), both *A* and *B* gain from the exchange since point *E* is on indifference curves II and II′. Joining points of tangency for the indifference curves of individual *A* and individual *B* we get *contract curve FS* (see Fig. 4-22). When *A* and *B* are not on the contract curve, either *A* or *B* or both can gain from exchange. When *A* and *B* are on the contract curve, no further gains from exchange are possible.

4.26 Suppose that the tastes of individual *A* are represented by indifference curves I, II, and III of Problem 4.10, while the tastes of individual *B* are given by the indifference curves of Table 4.13.

Table 4.13

I′		II′		III′	
Q_x	Q_y	Q_x	Q_y	Q_x	Q_y
11	10.5	13	11	14	13
12	8	14	8	15	10
12.5	7	15	6.8	16	8
13	6.2	16	6		
14	5				
15	3.9				
16	3				

Suppose also that individuals *A* and *B* possess together a combined total of 16 units of Y and 18 units of X. (*a*) Draw a box of 18 units in width and 16 units in height; plot *A*'s indifference curves with origin at the lower left-hand corner of the box and *B*'s indifference curves with origin at the top right-hand corner of the box. (*b*) Starting from the point where *A*'s indifference curve I intersects *B*'s indifference curve I′, show that there is a basis for mutually advantageous exchange. (*c*) Starting from the same point as in part (*b*), show *how* exchange can take place.

(*a*) Fig. 4-23 is usually referred to as an *Edgeworth box diagram.*

(*b*) Point *H* indicates that individual *A* has 13Y and 2X, while individual *B* has 3Y and 16X. At point *H*, the MRS_{xy} for *A* exceeds the MRS_{xy} for *B*. This means that *A* is willing to give up more of Y than necessary to induce *B* to give up one unit of X. Thus, there is a basis for mutually advantageous exchange in which *A* gives up some Y in return for X from *B*.

(*c*) A movement down indifference curve I′ from point *H* to point G leaves individual *B* at the same level of satisfaction but puts individual *A* on indifference curve III. On the other hand, a movement down indifference curve I from point *H* to point *D*, leaves individual *A* at the same level of satisfaction but puts individual *B* on indifference curve III′. Since we are dealing with voluntary exchange, individuals *A* and *B* will end up at some point in between *G* and *D* (for example, point *E* on indifference curves II and II′ in Fig. 4-23) implying that both individuals gain from voluntary exchange. Note that mutually advantageous exchange will come to an end when one of *A*'s indifference curves is tangent to one of *B*'s, because at all such points the MRS_{xy} for *A* equals the MRS_{xy} for *B*. Such points of tangency are assured by the fact that the fields of indifference curves are dense.

4.27 (*a*) How would we obtain the *entire* contract curve for Fig. 4-23? (*b*) What does a contract curve show? (*c*) Show that the condition necessary for mutually advantageous exchange using utility analysis is equivalent to that stated in Section 4.8.

(*a*) The line joining point *D* to points *E* and *G* in Fig. 4-23 gives a portion of the contract curve for *A* and *B*. By sketching many more indifference curves for *A* and *B* and joining all the points of tangency, we could obtain the entire contract curve. Such a curve would extend from point 0 to point 0′ and would be similar to the dashed line in Fig. 4-23.

(*b*) Any point not on the contract curve indicates that there is a basis for mutually advantageous exchange. Once the individuals are on the contract curve, they can obtain no further gain from exchange and the trading will come to an end. The greater *A*'s bargaining strength in relation to *B*'s in Problem 4.26(*c*), the closer individual *A* will end up to point *G* on the contract curve (see Fig. 4-23) and the greater the proportion of the gain from the exchange accruing to *A*. The greater *B*'s bargaining strength, the closer this individual will get to point *D* on the contract curve and the greater the proportion of the gain accruing to *B*.

(*c*) In utility analysis, the condition necessary for mutually advantageous exchange is MU_x/MU_y for $A \neq \text{MU}_x/\text{MU}_y$ for *B*. In this chapter we found that there is a basis for mutually advantageous exchange if the MRS_{xy} for $A \neq MRS_{xy}$ for B. However, we found in Problem 4.22 that $MU_x/MU_y = MRS_{xy}$. Therefore, we can state that exchange can take place if the MU_x/MU_y ($=MRS_{xy}$) for $A \neq MU_x/MU_y$ ($=MRS_{xy}$) for B.

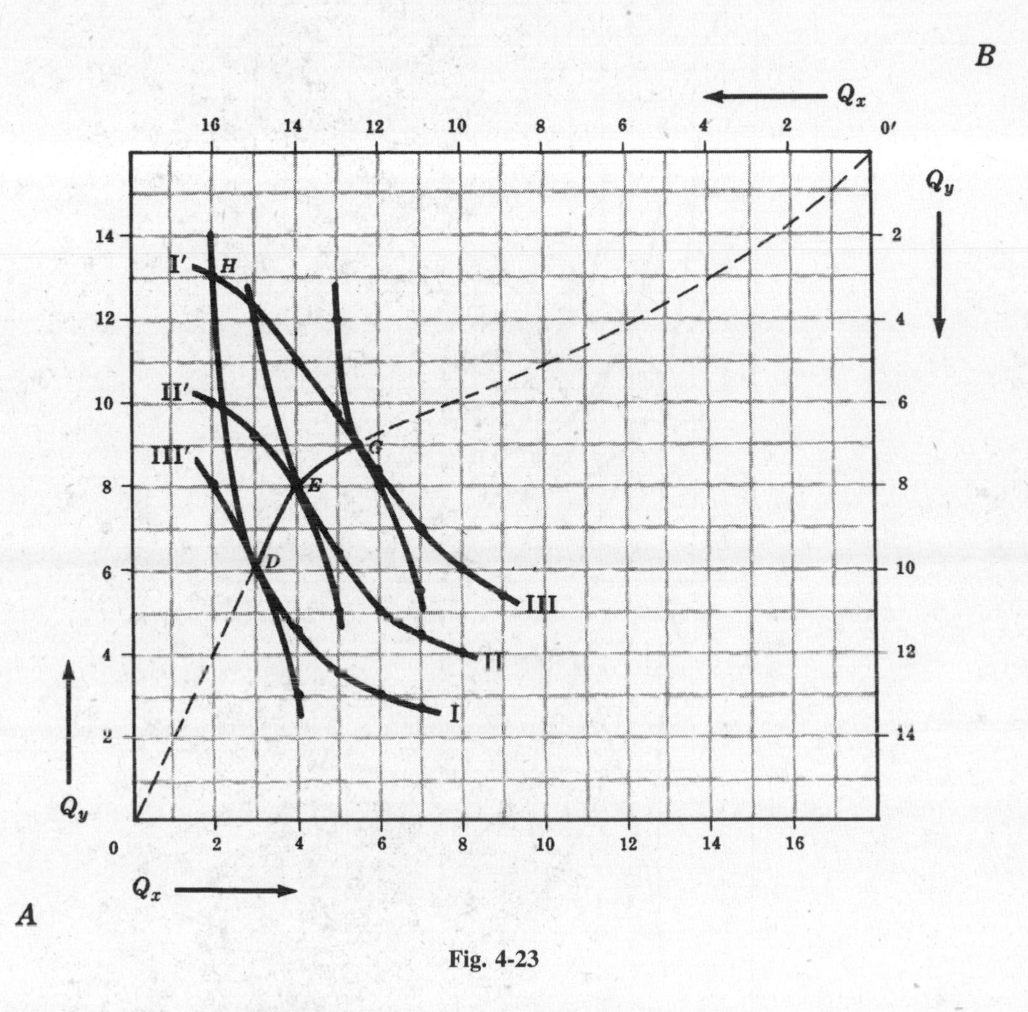

Fig. 4-23

THE INCOME-CONSUMPTION CURVE AND THE ENGEL CURVE

4.28 If the consumer's tastes are given by indifference curves I, II, and III of Problem 4.11 (and they remain unchanged during the period of the analysis), if the price of Y and the price of X remain unchanged at \$1 and \$2, respectively, and if the consumer's money income rises from \$12 to \$16 and then to \$20 per time period, derive the income-consumption curve and the Engel curve for this consumer.

In panel A of Fig. 4-24, budget lines 1, 2, and 3 are parallel to each other because P_x/P_y remains unchanged (at the value of 2). When the consumer's income is \$12 per time period, the consumer reaches equilibrium at point D on indifference curve I by purchasing 3X and 6Y. At an income of \$16, the consumer attains equilibrium at point E on indifference curve II by buying 4X and 8Y. At an income of \$20 per time period, the consumer reaches equilibrium at point G on indifference curve III by purchasing 5.5X and 9Y. Line DEG joins points of consumer equilibrium at different levels of income and is a portion of the income-consumption curve (ICC) for this consumer. (Even though line DEG was also a portion of the consumer's contract curve in Fig. 4-23 this was only a coincidence and need not be so.)

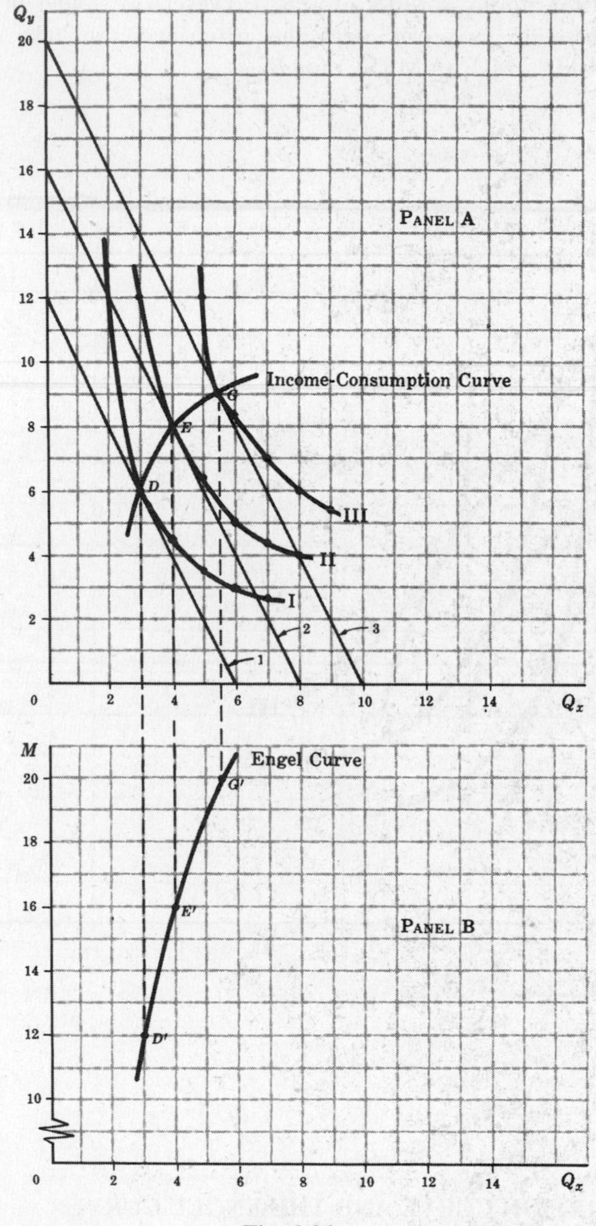

Fig. 4-24

Note that at points *D, E*, and G in panel A of Fig. 4-24, the

$$\mathrm{MRS}_{xy} = \frac{\mathrm{MU}_x}{\mathrm{MU}_y} = \frac{P_x}{P_y} = 2$$

Thus, as we move from one point of consumer equilibrium to another, both the MU_x and the MU_y can fall, rise or remain unchanged. All that is required for equilibrium is that the *ratio* of the MU_x to the MU_y remain constant and equal to the MRS_{xy} and P_x/P_y.

In panel B of Fig. 4-24, line $D'E'G'$ is a portion of this consumer's Engel curve for commodity X. It shows that at an income level of \$12 per time period, the consumer purchases 3 units of X; at an income level of \$16, he or she purchases 4X; and at an income level of \$20, this consumer purchases 5.5 units of X. Since the Engel curve for commodity X is positively sloped, e_M is positive and commodity X is a normal good.

4.29 For the income-quantity relationship in Table 4.14, (*a*) sketch the Engel curve and (*b*) determine if this commodity is a necessity, a luxury, or an inferior good at points *A, B, D, F, H,* and *L.*

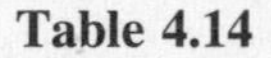

Table 4.14

Point	*A*	*B*	*C*	*D*	*F*	*G*	*H*	*L*
Income (\$/year)	4,000	6,000	8,000	10,000	12,000	14,000	16,000	18,000
Quantity (lb/year)	100	200	300	350	380	390	350	250

(*a*)

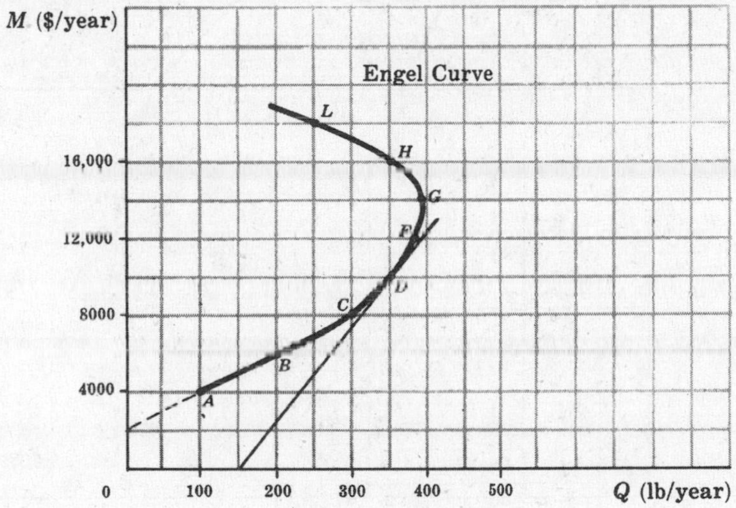

Fig. 4-25

(*b*) The tangent to the Engel curve at points *A* and *B* is positively sloped and cuts the income axis. Therefore, the income elasticity of demand is greater than one and the commodity is usually a luxury at those points (see Chapter 3, Problem 3.15). At points *D* and *F*, the slope of the tangent to the Engel curve is positive but cuts the quantity axis. Therefore, the income elasticity of demand is larger than zero but smaller than 1 and the commodity is a necessity at those points (see Chapter 3, Problem 3.14). At points *H* and *L*, the Engel curve is negatively sloped and the commodity is an inferior good.

THE PRICE-CONSUMPTION CURVE AND THE CONSUMER'S DEMAND CURVE

4.30 Suppose that from the point of consumer equilibrium in Problem 4.20, the price of X falls from \$2 per unit to \$1. (*a*) Find the new equilibrium point, sketch the price-consumption curve of this consumer for commodity X, and derive d_x. (*b*) Is d_x price-elastic, price-inelastic, or unitary price-elastic over this price range? (*c*) Does diminishing MRS_{xy} necessarily imply diminishing MU_x and MU_y? Is diminishing MU_x a prerequisite for d_x to be negatively sloped?

(a)

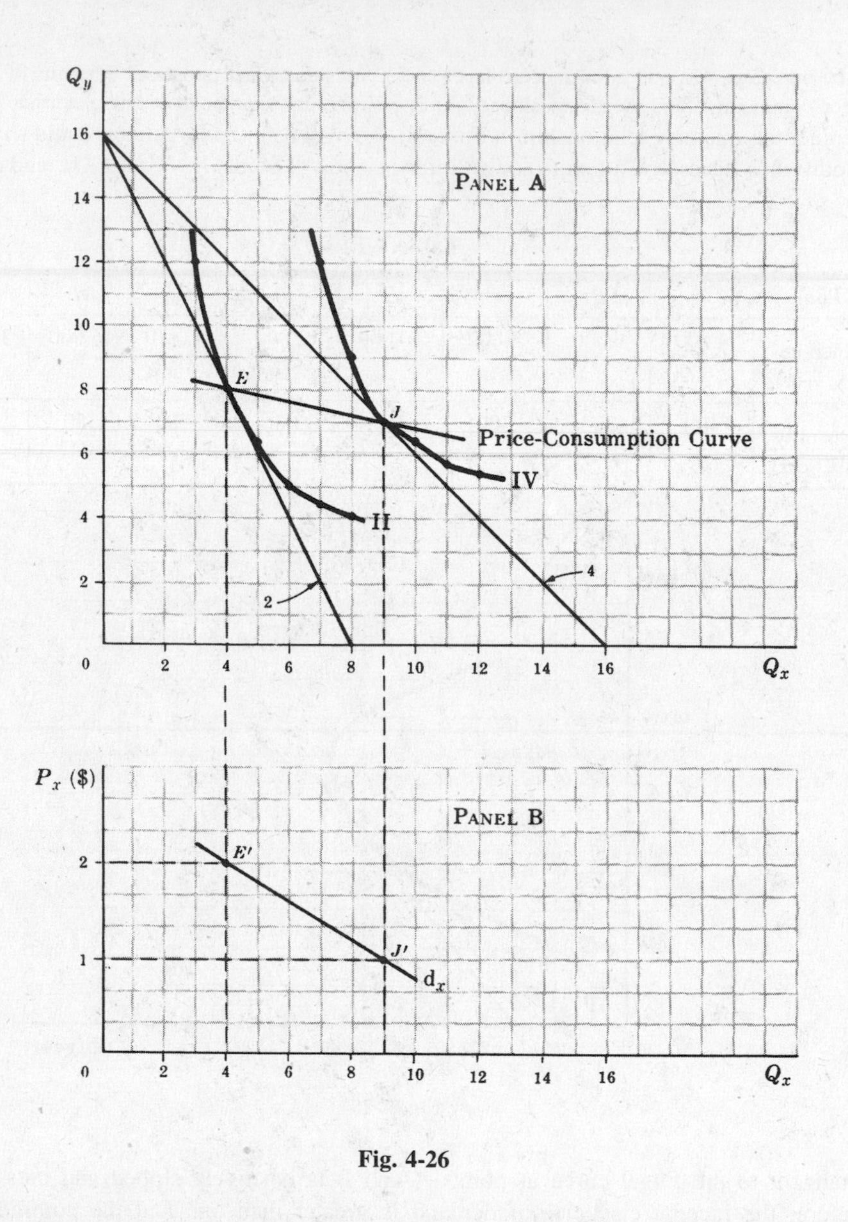

Fig. 4-26

In panel A of Fig. 4-26, point E is the original point of consumer equilibrium in Problem 4-20. When the price of X falls from \$2 to \$1 (*ceteris paribus*), we get budget line 4 and a new point of consumer equilibrium (point J on indifference curve IV). Joining point E to point J, we get a segment of the consumer's price-consumption curve (PCC) for commodity X. From the points of consumer equilibrium in panel A of Fig. 4-26, we can derive a segment of d_x (panel B).

(b) Since the PCC is negatively sloped, d_x is price-elastic over arc $E'J'$. [$e = -(5/-1) \cdot (3/13) = 15/33 \cong 1.15$; also, when the price of X falls from \$2 to \$1, the consumer increases expenditures on X from \$8 to \$9 per time period. Thus, d_x is price-elastic over arc $E'J'$.]

(c) At point E in panel A, the $MRS_{xy} = MU_x/MU_y = 2$. At point J, the $MRS_{xy} = MU_x/MU_y = 1$. Thus, in moving from point E to point J, the MRS_{xy} and the *ratio* of the MU_x to the MU_y falls. However, for the MU_x/MU_y to fall it is not necessary for the MU_x and the MU_y to fall. For example, the MU_x/MU_y can fall even if both the MU_x and the MU_y rise—as long as the rise in the MU_x is less than the rise in the MU_y. Therefore, diminishing MRS_{xy} does not *necessarily* imply diminishing MU_x and MU_y, and diminishing MU is not necessary to derive a negatively sloped demand curve.

4.31 In Fig. 4-27, the vertical axis measures a consumer's money income while the horizontal axis measures the quantity of X purchased by the individual per time period. Points *C*, *D*, and *E* refer to different equilibrium points resulting when only the price of X changes. (*a*) What would an indifference curve drawn on this set of axes show? (*b*) What does a clockwise rotation from budget line 1 to budget line 2 and then to budget line 3 imply for the price of X? (*c*) What type of demand curve can be derived from equilibrium points *C*, *D*, and *E*?

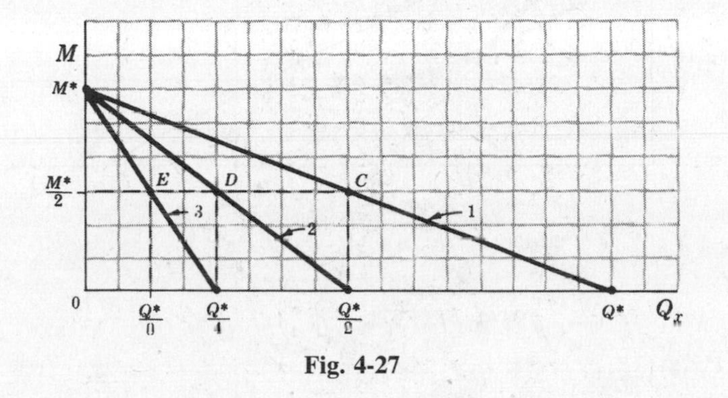

Fig. 4-27

(*a*) An indifference curve drawn on the set of axes in Fig. 4-27 would show the different combinations of money (not spent on X and thus available to buy other goods) and the quantity of commodity X purchased which yield equal satisfaction to this consumer.

(*b*) A clockwise rotation of budget line 1 to budget line 2 implies that the price of X *doubled* (since if the consumer spent all of his income on X, he would be able to purchase exactly half as much of X as before). Similarly, a clockwise rotation of budget line 2 to budget line 3 implies that the price of X has doubled again.

(*c*) Joining points *C*, *D*, and *E*, we get this consumer's PCC for commodity X. Since the PCC is horizontal, d_x would be unitary price-elastic over the arc defined. This is because as the price of X rises, the consumer buys fewer units of X but continues to spend the *same amount* (exactly one-half) of his income on X.

SEPARATION OF THE SUBSTITUTION AND INCOME EFFECTS

4.32 Panel A of Fig. 4-28 is identical to Fig. 4-8 in Example 14 except for budget line *K'J'*. Panel B is derived from panel A and is identical to Fig. 4-9 in Example 15 except for d'_x. (*a*) How was budget line *K'J'* obtained? What does it show? (*b*) What does a movement from point *E* to point *G* in panel A show? A movement from *G* to *T*? (*c*) How was d'_x in panel B obtained? What does it show?

(*a*) Budget line *K'J'* in panel A of Fig. 4-28 was obtained by shifting budget line *KJ* down and parallel to itself until it was tangent to indifference curve II. By shifting budget line *KJ* down, we reduced the consumer's money income. By shifting budget line *KJ* down until it was tangent to indifference curve II, we reduced the consumer's money income just enough to keep real income constant. (Note that according to this technique, the consumer's real income is kept constant if this consumer reaches the same indifference curve, before and after the price change. In the example we are discussing, the consumer's money income must be reduced by \$3 in order to keep real income constant.) Budget line *KJ* is shifted *parallel* to itself in order to keep the price of X in relation to the price of Y the same on budget line *K'J'* as it was on budget line *KJ*.

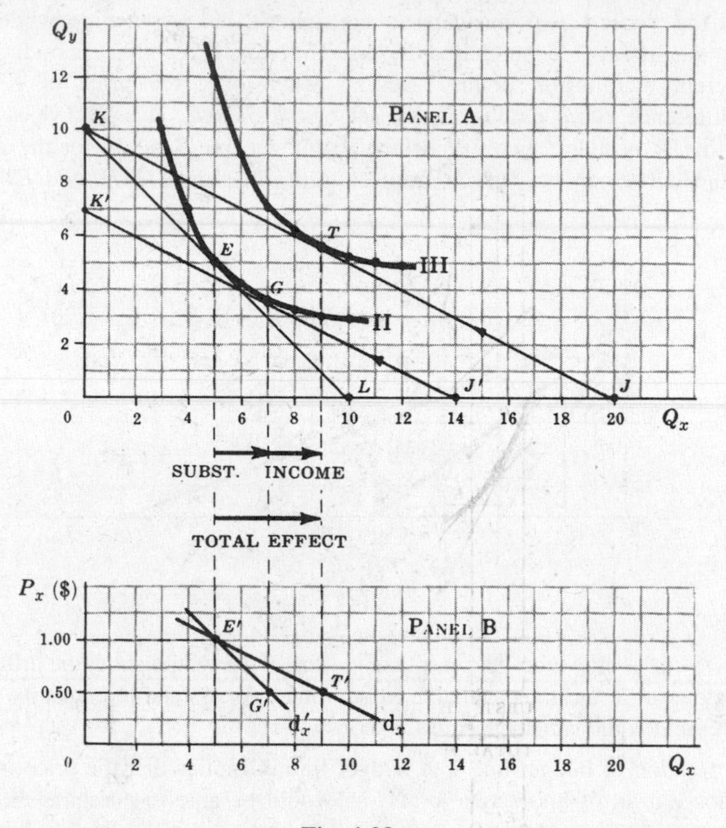

Fig. 4-28

(*b*) The movement from point *E* (on indifference curve II) to point *G* (also on indifference curve II) represents the substitution effect of the price change. The movement from point *G* (on indifference curve II) to point *T* (on indifference curve III) is the income effect of the price change. Thus, for the given price change

$$\text{Total Effect} = \text{Substitution Effect} + \text{Income Effect}$$
$$ET = EG + GT$$

(*c*) In panel B of Fig. 4-28, d'_x shows only the substitution effect of the price change. Thus, d'_x is the consumer demand curve for commodity X when the consumer's *real* rather than money income is kept constant. Some economists prefer this type of demand curve (i.e., d'_x) to the usual demand curve (that keeps money income constant). *Unless otherwise specified, by "demand curve" we will always refer to the traditional or usual demand curve.*

The technique for separating the income effect from the substitution effect shown in panel A of Fig. 4-28 is useful not only for deriving a demand curve along which real income is constant but also (and perhaps more importantly) because it is a very useful technique for analyzing many problems of great economic importance. Some of these are presented in the section on applications that follows.

4.33 Starting from Fig. 4-26, (*a*) separate the substitution effect resulting from the reduction in the price of X from \$2 to \$1 per unit (*ceteris paribus*), (*b*) derive the consumer's demand curve for commodity X when *real* income is kept constant, (*c*) with reference to the figure in parts (*a*) and (*b*), explain how you derived the demand curve for commodity X along which *money* income is kept constant, and (*d*) explain how you derived the demand curve for commodity X along which *real* income is kept constant.

(*a*) and (*b*)

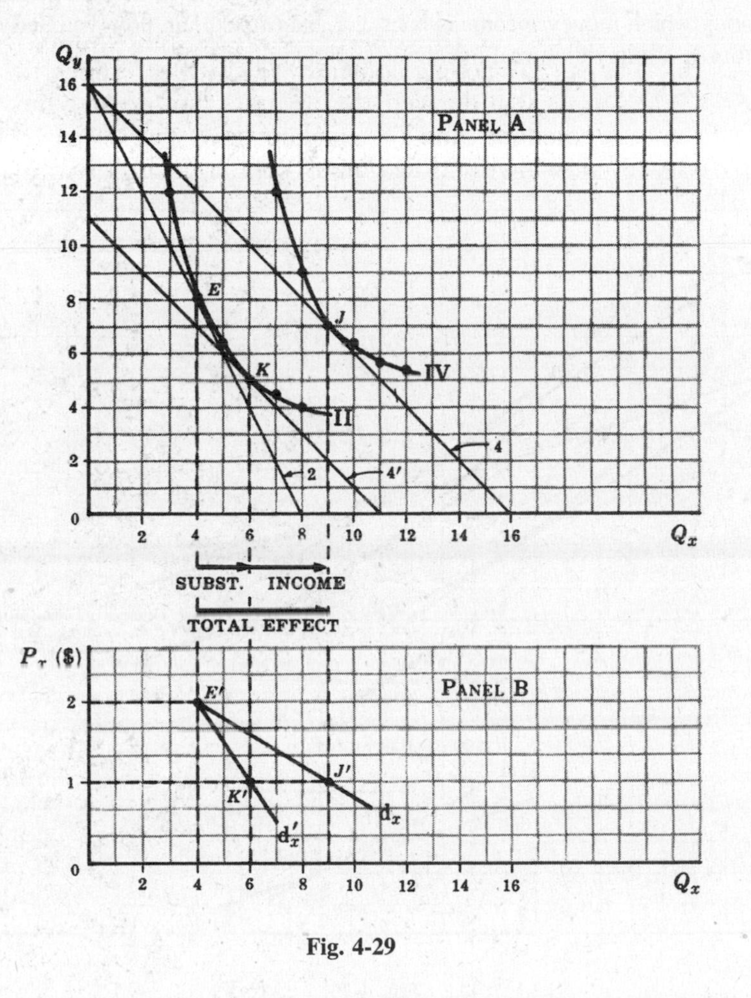

Fig. 4-29

(*c*) In panel A, the consumer moves from equilibrium point *E* (on budget line 2 and indifference curve II) to equilibrium point *J* (on budget line 4 and indifference curve IV) as a result of the reduction of P_x, *ceteris paribus*. Thus, when $P_x = \$2$, the consumer purchases 4X per time period (point E′ on d_x in panel B); when $P_x = \$1$, the consumer purchases 9X (point *J′* on d_x). Of the total increase in the quantity of X demanded, part is due to the substitution effect and the remainder is due to the income effect. (Since in Problem 4.28 we found that X is a normal good, both the substitution effect and the income effect work in the same direction.) Thus, as P_x falls (and we move along d_x in a downward direction), *the consumer's money income remains constant but real income increases*. To be noted is that in this example, the income effect is greater than the substitution effect. In the real world, the substitution effect is usually much stronger than the income effect.

(*d*) Many economists prefer to keep the consumer's *real* income constant in deriving a demand curve. One way to keep real income constant is to reduce the consumer's money income sufficiently to eliminate the income effect of the price change. In the previous figure, this is accomplished by shifting budget line 4 (parallel to itself) until it is tangent to indifference curve II. What we get is budget line 4′ which reflects the same *relative* prices as budget line 4, but \$5 less of money income. The movement from *E* to *K* along indifference curve II is then the substitution effect of the price change. The movement from *K* to *J* is the income effect of the price change; d'_x reflects only the substitution effect. Thus along d'_x, the consumer's *real* income is held constant. Note that d'_x is less price-elastic than d_x.

4.34 Starting from a position of consumer equilibrium (*a*) separate the substitution effect from the income effect of a *price rise* (*ceteris paribus*) for a normal good, (*b*) derive two demand curves for the commodity, one that keeps money income constant and the other that keeps real income constant, (*c*) with reference to the figure in parts (*a*) and (*b*), explain how you derived the demand curve for commodity X along which money income is constant, and (*d*) explain how you derived the demand curve for commodity X along which real income is kept constant.

(*a*) and (*b*) See Fig. 4-30.

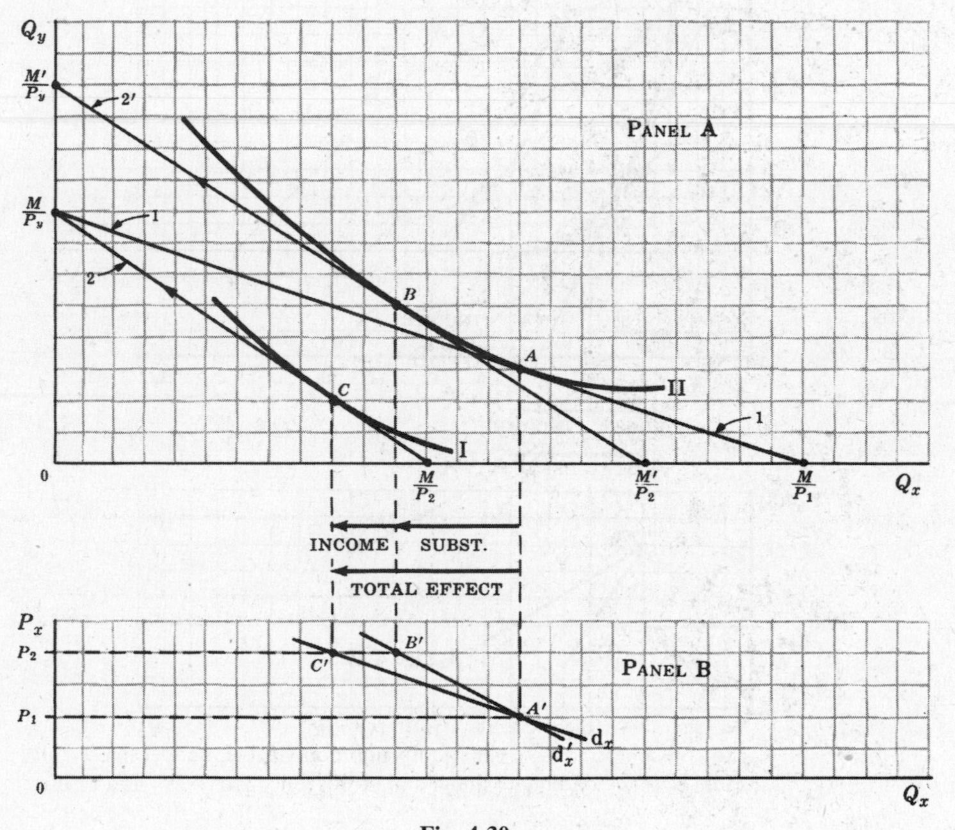

Fig. 4-30

(*c*) In panel A of Fig. 4-30, the consumer is originally in equilibrium at point *A* on budget line 1 and indifference curve II. This gives point *A*′ on d_x and d'_x in panel B. When the price of X rises from P_1 to P_2 (*ceteris paribus*), the consumer will be in equilibrium at point C on budget line 2 and indifference curve I. This gives point *C*′ on d_x; d_x is the usual demand curve along which *money* income is kept constant. The movement from *A* to *C* is the total effect of the price change. Since the commodity is a normal good, the substitution effect and the income effect reinforce each other in *reducing* the quantity of the commodity demanded per time period when its price *rises*.

(*d*) To derive d'_x we must isolate the income effect of the price change. We do that by shifting up budget line 2 parallel to itself until it is tangent to indifference curve II. This gives us budget line 2′. The upward shift from budget line 2 to budget line 2′ corresponds to an *increase* in the consumer's money income from *M* to *M*′ while keeping the same relative commodity prices given by the slope of budget line 2. Budget line 2′ is tangent to indifference curve II at point *B*. The movement along indifference curve I from *A* to *B* refers to the substitution effect of the price rise. The movement from *B* to *C* is the income effect; d'_x shows only the substitution effect of the price change. Thus along d'_x the consumer's *real* income is kept constant. Note that d'_x is less price-elastic than d_x.

4.35 Starting from position A of consumer equilibrium in Fig. 4-31, determine (*a*) the total effect of the reduction in P_x from P_2 to P_1, (*b*) the substitution effect, and (*c*) the income effect. (*d*) What type of good is commodity X?

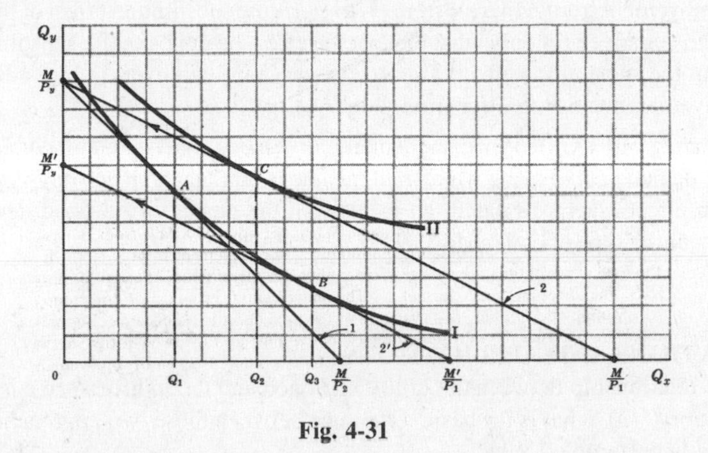

Fig. 4-31

(*a*) In Fig. 4-31, the consumer is originally in equilibrium at point A, budget line 1, and indifference curve I. When the price of X falls from P_2 to P_1 (*ceteris paribus*), the consumer will reach equilibrium at point C on budget line 2 and indifference curve II. The movement from A to C (or from Q_1 to Q_2) is the total effect of the price change.

(*b*) To find the substitution effect of the price reduction, we must eliminate the income effect from the total effect. This is accomplished by shifting down budget line 2 to budget line 2′. Budget line 2′ is tangent to indifference curve I at point B. The movement along indifference curve I from A to B (which equals Q_1 Q_3) is the substitution effect of the price change.

(*c*) Since the substitution effect (Q_1 Q_3) exceeds the total effect (Q_1 Q_2), the income effect must be opposite the substitution effect. The income effect is given by a movement from B to C and equals Q_3 Q_2.

(*d*) In this case, the income effect moves in the opposite direction from the substitution effect. Therefore, commodity X is an inferior good. However, commodity X is not a Giffen good because when the price of X falls, the quantity of X demanded per time period increases from Q_1 to Q_2 (the total effect). Note that in this case, the demand curve along which real income is constant would be more price-elastic than the demand curve along which money income is constant. However, both demand curves are negatively sloped.

4.36 Starting from a position of consumer equilibrium, (*a*) show the substitution effect and the income effect of a *price reduction* for a *Giffen good*. (*b*) Is the demand curve for a Giffen good along which *real* income is held constant positively sloped? Why?

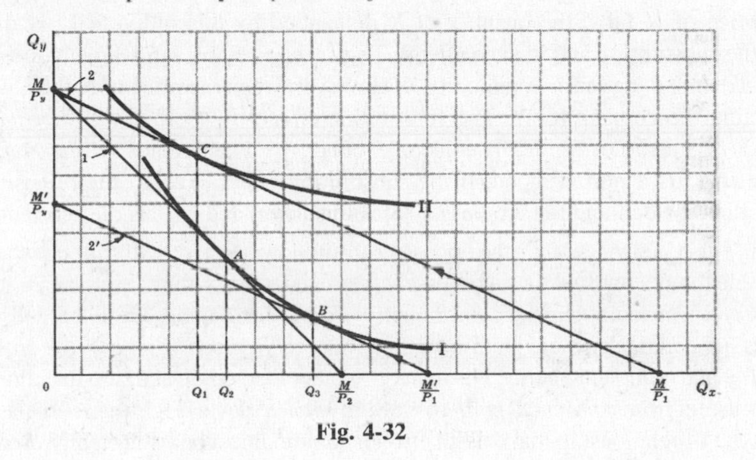

Fig. 4-32

(*a*) Point *A* is the original equilibrium point. When the price of X falls from P_2 to P_1 (*ceteris paribus*), the consumer will be in equilibrium at point *C*. The movement from *A* to *C* (or from Q_2 to Q_1) is the total effect of the price change. Commodity X is therefore a Giffen good, since as the price of X falls, the consumer buys less of it. The movement from *A* to *B* (or from Q_2 to Q_3) is the substitution effect of the price change. For the total effect to be negative, not only must the income effect be opposite the substitution effect, but it must also overwhelm the substitution effect. This occurs very rarely, if ever. In Fig. 4-32, the income effect is given by a movement from *B* to *C* (or from Q_3 to Q_1).

(*b*) Since we are dealing with a Giffen good, the demand curve along which *money* income is constant is *positively* sloped, but the demand curve along which *real* income is constant is *negatively* sloped. This is so because the substitution effect *always* results in an increase in the quantity of a good demanded when its price falls, regardless of the type of commodity we are dealing with.

SOME CONSIDERATIONS AND APPLICATIONS

4.37 (*a*) What is the relationship between the utility approach and the indifference curve approach to consumer demand theory? (*b*) What is the basic difference between these two approaches? (*c*) Which of these two approaches is preferable? Why?

(*a*) The indifference curve approach to the study of consumer demand theory can be used as an *alternative* to the older utility approach for the purpose of analyzing consumer behavior (such as equilibrium and exchange) and deriving a consumer demand curve for a commodity.

(*b*) The basic difference between the utility approach and the indifference curve approach is that the utility approach rests on the stronger and somewhat unrealistic assumption that utility is measurable in a cardinal sense, while the indifference curve approach requires only an *ordinal* measure of utility or satisfaction. That is, the indifference curve approach requires only that the consumer be able to decide whether one basket of goods yields more, equal, or less satisfaction than other baskets of goods, without the need to attach a specific number of utils of utility to each basket.

(*c*) Because the indifference curve approach requires only an ordinal (rather than a cardinal) measure of utility or satisfaction and also because it allows us to separate the income effect from the substitution effect of a price change more readily than the utility approach, many economists prefer the indifference curve approach over the utility approach. However, the student can learn much from both approaches.

4.38 Suppose that an individual spends all personal income on only three commodities: X, Y, Z. Assume that we know that X and Y are normal commodities and that X is a substitute for Y (in the sense that an individual who consumes more of X, must consume less of Y in order to remain at the same level of satisfaction, i.e., on the same indifference curve). (*a*) Explain how the substitution and income effects operate on commodities X and Y when the price of X falls, *ceteris paribus*. (*b*) Under what condition will the sign of e_{yx} be negative (even though we know that X and Y are substitutes)?

(*a*) When the price of X falls, the quantity of X demanded by this individual per unit of time increases because of the substitution and income effects. This is reflected by a movement down and along the negatively sloped demand curve for commodity X. However, when the price of X falls, we have two *opposing* forces affecting the demand for Y. The substitution effect, by itself, tends to *reduce* the demand for Y because X is a substitute for Y. The income effect, by itself, tends to *increase* the demand for Y because Y (as X) is a normal good. If the substitution effect exceeds the opposite income effect (the usual case), then the demand for Y falls (i.e., d_y shifts down) and e_{yx} has the "correct" (i.e., positive) sign.

(*b*) If the income effect is stronger than the opposite substitution effect, d_y will shift up when the price of X falls. This is possible though unusual. In such a case, e_{yx} will have the "wrong" sign (i.e., e_{yx} will be negative indicating that X and Y are complements even though we know that X and Y are in fact substitutes for each other).

There is a theoretically more precise method (than relying on the sign of the cross elasticity) to define substitutability and complementarity. However, this other method, in addition to being more complicated, is also not very useful from a *practical* point of view. In *empirical* work, it is the cross elasticity method of classifying the type of relationship that exists between commodities that is normally used, even though it may sometimes lead to the "wrong" conclusion.

4.39 Suppose that a "typical" poor family is in equilibrium at point *A* on budget line 1 and indifference curve I in Fig. 4-33. (At this point this family spends \$1000 of its income of \$5000 to purchase 100 units of food.) Suppose that now the government decides to lift this poor family's level of utility or satisfaction from indifference curve I to indifference curve II. (*a*) How can the government do this by subsidizing the family's consumption (i.e., paying part of the price) of food? (*b*) What would be the cost of this program to the government per "typical" poor family? (*c*) How else could the government achieve the same result? At what cost? (*d*) Why might the government still choose the more expensive program to achieve the desired results?

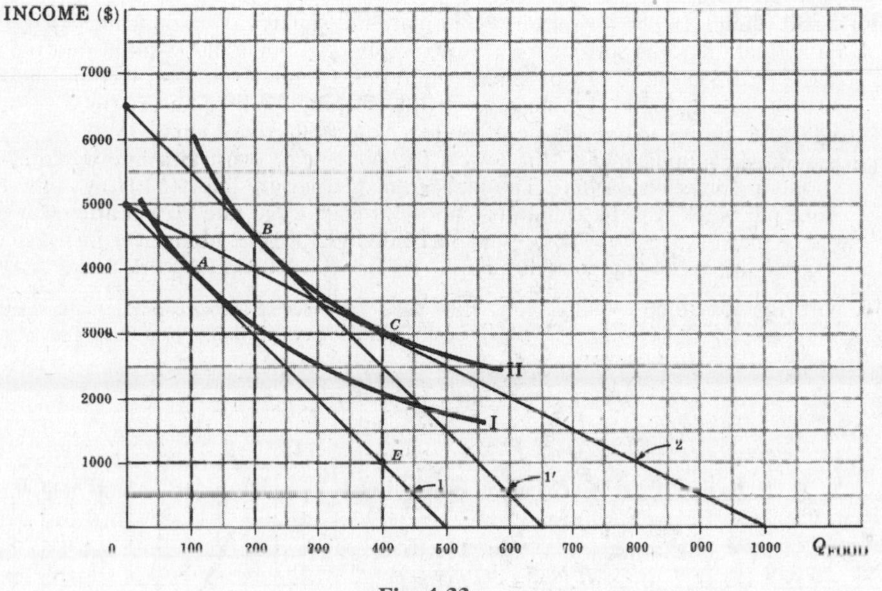

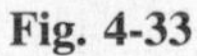
Fig. 4-33

(*a*) One way in which the government can lift this poor family's level of utility or satisfaction from point *A* on budget line 1 and indifference curve I to indifference curve II is by allowing this family to purchase food at *half* the market price, with the other half of the market price paid by the government. With this consumption subsidy on food purchases, this poor family would reach the new equilibrium point *C* on budget line 2 and indifference curve II.

(*b*) To reach point *C* with the above program, this poor family spends \$2000 of its income to purchase 400 units of food (see the figure). Without the subsidy, the family would have had to spend \$4000 of its income to purchase 400 units of food (point *E* in the figure). Thus, the cost of this program to the government would be \$2000 (*CE*) per "typical" poor family.

(*c*) The government could also achieve its objective of lifting this poor family's level of satisfaction from indifference curve I to indifference curve II by giving instead a cash subsidy of only \$1500. With this cash subsidy, the poor family would be in equilibrium at point *B* on budget line 1′ and indifference curve II. At point *B*, the family spends \$2000 of its income (of \$6500) to purchase 200 units of food (see Fig. 4-32).

(*d*) Even if it is more expensive, the government might still choose the first of these programs because it results in a greater increase in this family's consumption of food. This greater increase in the consumption of food may itself be an aim of the government aid program.

4.40 Panels A and B of Fig. 4-34 measure money income on the vertical axis and leisure time on the horizontal axis. Panel A shows that an individual has a maximum of 80 h per week available for either leisure or work. The individual's income is zero if 80 h is devoted to leisure and \$400 if 80 h is devoted to work. Point *A* shows the individual choosing 40 h of leisure and 40 h of work, with a total personal income of \$200 per week. Panel B shows various combinations of leisure and income that give the individual the same satisfaction. For example, the individual is indifferent between an income of \$450 and 10 h of leisure per week (point B) and an income of \$200 and 40 h of leisure (point A). However, with the same 40 h of leisure and an income of \$400, the individual would be at point G on indifference curve IV. (*a*) What is the wage rate, as indicated by the lowest income-leisure constraint line in panel A? The middle income-leisure line? The highest income-leisure line? (*b*) How many hours of work per week will the individual choose at each wage rate? (*c*) If after working 40 h per week at a wage of \$5 per hour the individual is offered an overtime wage rate of \$10 per hour, how many additional hours will the individual work?

(*a*) The wage rate (W) is always given by the slope of the income-leisure constraint line. The lower line in panel A indicates that if the individual works 80 hours per week for a weekly salary of \$400 or 40 h for \$200, then

$$W = \frac{\$400}{80\,\text{h}} = \frac{\$200}{40\,\text{h}} = \$5 \quad \text{per hour}$$

Similarly, with the middle line,

$$W = \frac{\$650}{80\,\text{h}} = \$8.125 \cong \$8.13 \quad \text{per hour}$$

Finally, with the top line,

$$W = \frac{\$800}{80\,\text{h}} = \$10 \quad \text{per hour}$$

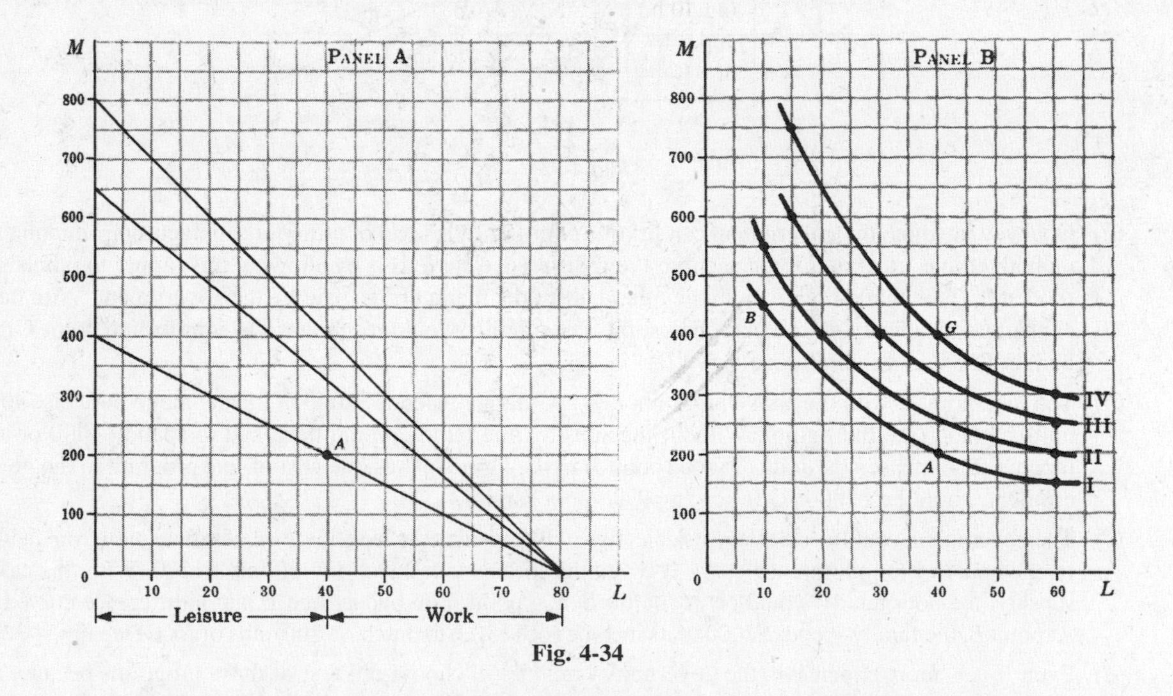

Fig. 4-34

(*b*) In Fig. 4-35, the indifference curves of panel B in Fig. 4-34 are superimposed on the income-leisure lines of panel A. At $W = \$5$, the individual is in equilibrium at point A by working 40 h per week for a weekly salary of \$200 and using the remaining 40 h per week for leisure. At $W \cong \$8.13$, the individual is in equilibrium at point F and works 50 h per week for a weekly salary of \$400. At $W = \$10$, the individual is in equilibrium at point G and goes back to working 40 h per week for the same weekly salary of \$400. Thus, at the very high $W = \$10$, the individual prefers more leisure to more work and the individual's supply curve for work slopes backward.

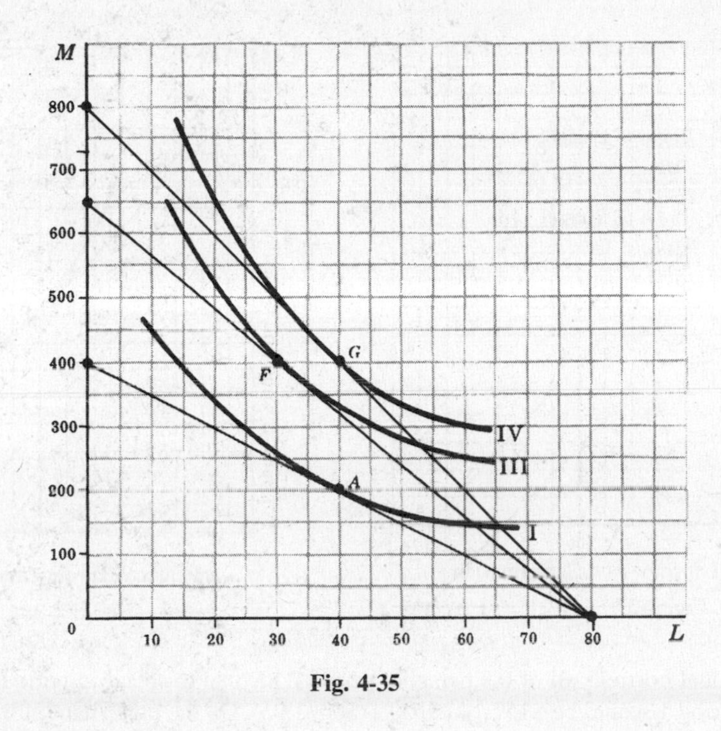

Fig. 4-35

(c) Fig. 4-36 shows that after working 40 h at $W = \$5$ (point A), the individual will work an additional 20 hours per week for a total of 60 h per week and a weekly salary of \$400 (point C) if the overtime wage rate is \$10 per hour (the slope of AC).

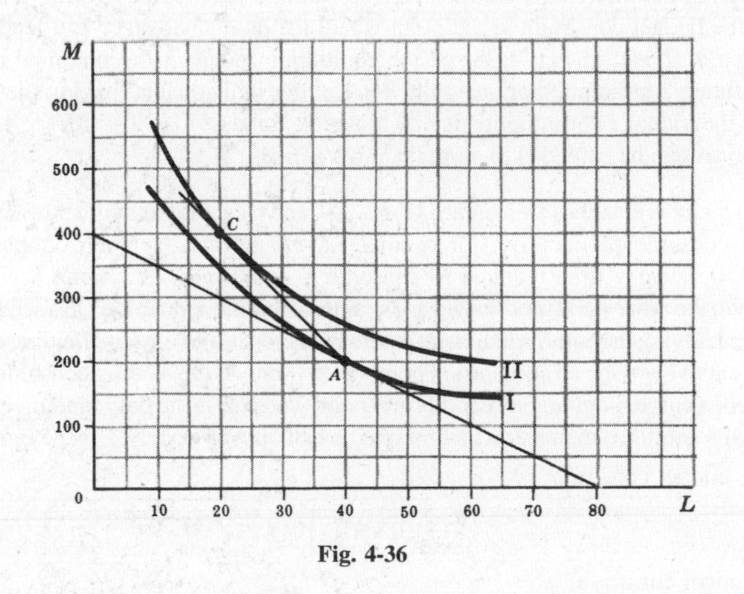

Fig. 4-36

4.41 Suppose that an individual's income is \$100 the year before retirement (period 1) and \$60 the year after retirement (period 2), and that net savings over the two periods are zero. If the individual can either borrow against future income or lend from present income at a 5% interest rate (r), (a) derive and plot the individual's budget constraint between period 1 and period 2. (b) If the individual is in equilibrium by transferring \$20 of income from period 1 to period 2, draw a figure showing how this equilibrium was reached. How much does this individual consume in period 1 and period 2 at equilibrium?

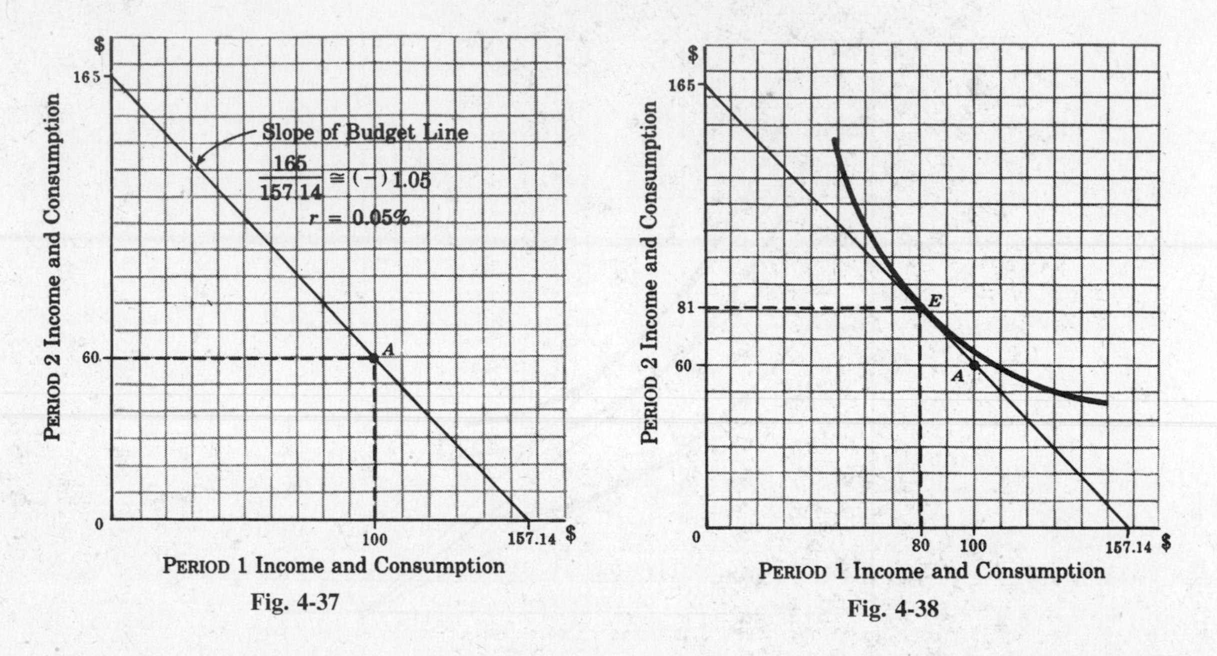

Fig. 4-37

Fig. 4-38

(*a*) If the individual borrows all of the personal period 2 income to spend in period 1, the level of expenditures in period 1 would be \$157.14 (\$100 + \$60/1.05). On the other hand, if the individual lends all of the personal period 1 income, the expenditures in period 2 would be \$165 [60 + (\$100 × 1.05)]. This gives the individuals the budget line shown in Fig. 4-37.

(*b*) For the individual to be in equilibrium by lending \$20 out of period 1 income, one of the indifference curves (showing this individual's utility derived from period 1 versus period 2 consumption) must be tangent to the budget constraint at the point where the individual saves and lends \$20 out of period 1 income. This is shown in Fig. 4-38. At the equilibrium point *E*, the marginal rate of substitution of present for future consumption or *time preference* of this individual is equal to the market rate of interest of 5%. The individual's consumption is \$80 in period 1 and \$81 [\$60 + (\$20 × 1.05)] in period 2. This type of analysis can be extended to more than two periods.

4.42 Suppose that an individual has an income, $M = \$100$, and a maximum number of hours, $T = 24$ per week, available to consume products X (for example, a movie) and Y (for example, a restaurant meal). $P_x = P_y = \$10$, and the time required to consume X and Y is $t_x = 2$ h and $t_y = 3$ h, respectively. (*a*) Derive and plot the money and time budget constraints of this individual. (*b*) On a separate graph, draw indifference curve I, giving the equilibrium point where both money and time are binding constraints; alternative indifference curve I′, giving an equilibrium point where *T* only is the binding constraint; and another alternative indifference curve, I′, giving an equilibrium point where *M* is the only binding constraint. (*c*) How can the individual's equilibrium position be improved when only *M* or only *T* is the binding constraint?

(*a*) The money budget constraint is

$$(\$10)\text{X} + (\$10)\text{Y} \leqslant 100$$

The time budget constraint is

$$(2\,\text{h})\text{X} + (3\text{h})\text{Y} \leqslant 24\,\text{h}$$

The inequalities indicate that the individual can be on or inside the particular budget lines shown in Fig. 4-39. To these, we might add X, Y $\geqslant 0$ to prevent negative values for X and Y.

(*b*) In Fig. 4-40, *OCEB* is the feasible region (or regions) which satisfies both constraints simultaneously. Point *E* is the equilibrium point at which both constraints are binding. Point *F* is an alternative equilibrium point where *T* only is the binding constraint, and point *G* is another alternative equilibrium point where *M* is the only binding constraint.

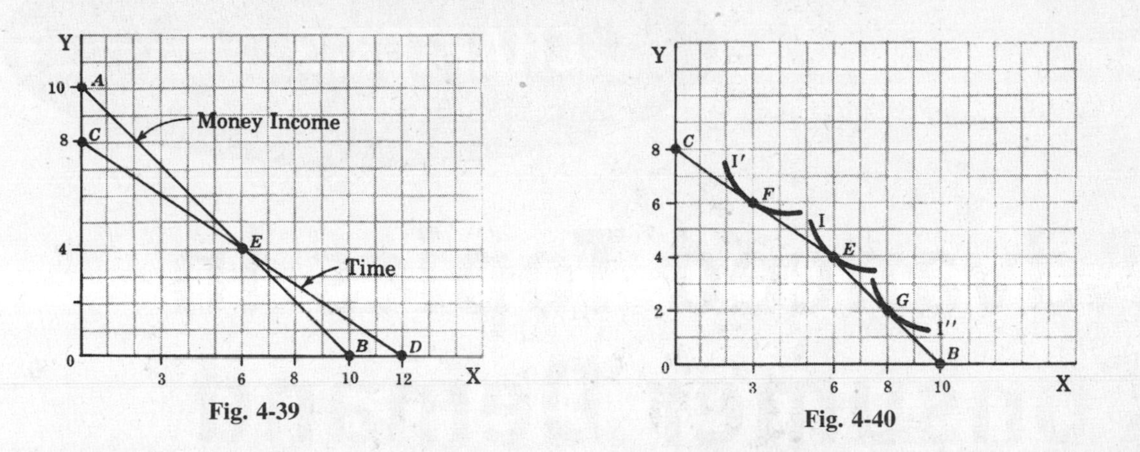

Fig. 4-39

Fig. 4-40

(*c*) When only M is the binding constraint, the individual can exchange for work part of the 24 h available for consumption. This will shift the individual's T constraint down and the M constraint up. The individual should keep on doing this until both the T and M constraints are binding, at a point analogous to E, where the individual will reach the highest possible indifference curve of type I″. When T only is the binding constraint, the individual should do the opposite, until both constraints become binding and it is possible to reach the highest possible indifference curve of type I′.

CONSUMER DEMAND THEORY WITH CALCULUS

***4.43** Starting with the utility function $U = U(X, Y)$, where X and Y refer, respectively, to the quantities of commodities X and Y, derive the expression for the slope of the indifference curve using calculus.

Taking the total differential and setting it equal to zero (since utility remains unchanged along a given indifference curve), we get

$$dU = \frac{\partial U}{\partial X} dX + \frac{\partial U}{\partial Y} dY = 0$$

(Note: ∂ = math symbol for partial derivative.)

Thus, the expression for the absolute slope of the indifference curve is

$$-\frac{dY}{dX} = \frac{\partial U/\partial X}{\partial U/\partial Y} = \frac{MU_X}{MU_Y} = MRS_{XY}$$

***4.44** Starting with utility function $U = U(X, Y)$ and budget constraint $P_X X + P_Y Y = M$, derive the equilibrium condition using calculus.

We start by forming function V, which incorporates the utility function to be maximized subject to the budget constraint set equal zero, and get

$$V = U(X, Y) + \lambda(M - P_X X - P_Y Y)$$

where λ is the Lagrangian multiplier. Taking the first partial derivative of V with respect to X and Y and setting them equal zero, we get

$$\frac{\partial V}{\partial X} = \frac{\partial U}{\partial X} - \lambda P_X = 0 \quad \text{and} \quad \frac{\partial V}{\partial Y} = \frac{\partial U}{\partial Y} - \lambda P_Y = 0$$

Dividing the first by the second equation, we get

$$\frac{\partial U/\partial X}{\partial U/\partial Y} = \frac{MU_X}{MU_Y} = MRS_{XY} = \frac{P_X}{P_Y}$$

CHAPTER 5

Advanced Topics in Consumer Demand Theory

5.1 THE SUBSTITUTION EFFECT ACCORDING TO HICKS AND SLUTSKY

The substitution effect of a price change defined in Section 4.11 and shown graphically in Problems 4.32 (Fig. 4-28) and 4.33 (Fig. 4-29) is known as the *Hicksian substitution effect*. This differs from the *Slutsky substitution effect*, which keeps real income constant by rotating the original budget line through the original equilibrium point until it is parallel to the new budget line after the price change. The movement from the original equilibrium point to the point where the rotated budget line is tangent to the higher (than the original) indifference curve represents the Slutsky substitution effect.

EXAMPLE 1. Figure 5-1 is the same as panel A of Fig. 4-28 except that budget line $K''J''$ has been added. Budget line $K''J''$ goes through point E (the original equilibrium point on budget line KL before the price change), is parallel to budget line KJ (after the price change), and is tangent to indifference curve II′ (which is higher than II). The movement from point E to point H (3X) is the Slutsky substitution effect, compared to the Hicksian substitution effect of 2X given by the movement from E to G. Note that Hicks keeps real income constant by keeping the consumer on the original indifference curve II. On the other hand, Slutsky keeps real income constant in the sense that the consumer could purchase the original basket of X and Y given by point E. The consumer, however, will move to point H on the higher indifference curve II′, so that the Slutsky substitution effect exceeds the Hicksian substitution effect. The Slutsky measure is generally preferred to the Hicksian measure because it relies on observable prices and quantities. The Slutsky demand curve (showing only the Slutsky substitution effect) is more elastic than the Hicksian demand curve, and both are less elastic than the usual demand curve showing both the substitution and income effects (see Problem 5.1).

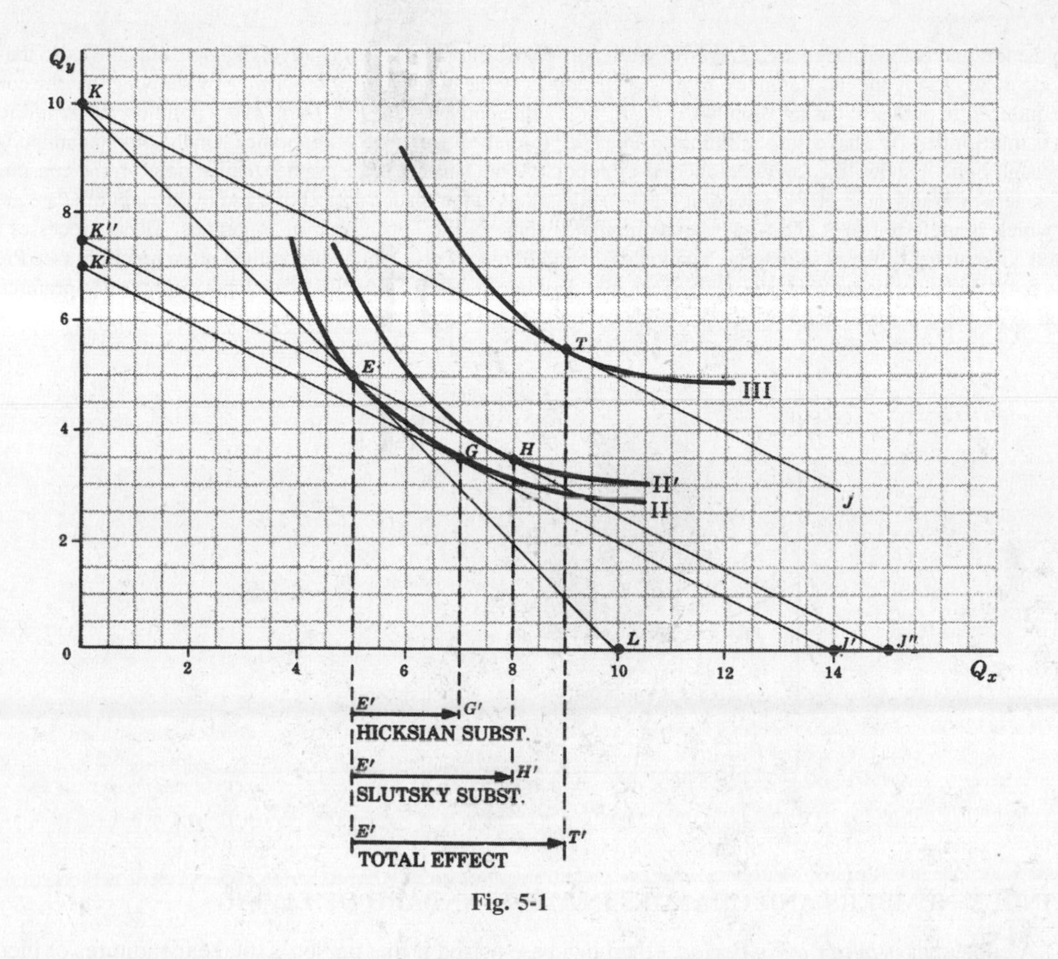

Fig. 5-1

5.2 THE THEORY OF REVEALED PREFERENCE

Up to now we assumed that indifference curves were derived by asking the consumer to choose among all possible baskets or combinations of commodities. However, consumers often cannot or will not give trustworthy answers to direct questions on their preferences. According to the *theory of revealed preference*, a consumer's preferences can be inferred (and indifference curve derived) from a sufficient number of observed choices or purchases in the marketplace, without any need to inquire directly into the individual's preferences. For example, if a consumer is observed to purchase basket A rather than basket B, and A is not cheaper than B, then for this consumer A must be superior to B.

The theory of revealed preference rests on the following assumptions:

(1) The individual's tastes do not change over the period considered.

(2) There is *consistency*; that is, if the consumer is observed to prefer basket A to basket B, then this consumer will never prefer B to A.

(3) There is *transitivity*; that is, if A is preferred to B and B to C, then A is preferred to C.

(4) Finally, the consumer can be induced to purchase any basket of goods if its price is made sufficiently attractive.

EXAMPLE 2. Figure 5-2 shows how a consumer's indifference curve can be derived from revealed preference. Suppose that the consumer is observed to be at point A on budget line NN (the same as point E on KL in Fig. 5-1). Then, A is preferred to any point on or below NN. On the other hand, points above and/or to the right of A are superior to A since they involve more of X and/or Y. Thus, the consumer's indifference curve must be above NN, except at point A where it is tangent to NN, and to the left and below shaded area *LAM*. Such an indifference curve must be negatively sloped and convex to the origin. To locate more closely the indifference curve, we can chip away the lower *zone of ignorance* by showing that the consumer can be induced to purchase basket B on *NN* if P_x/P_y falls sufficiently, say, to *PP*. Then, every point on *PP* is inferior to *B*, which is inferior to *A*. We have, thus, eliminated area *NBP* from the lower zone of ignorance. On the other hand, budget line *S′S′* through point *A* shows the same real income as at point *A*, but since P_x/P_y is higher than at point *A*, the consumer will purchase less of X and more of Y, as at point *G*. Then all baskets in the shaded area above and to the right of *G* are preferred to *G*, which is preferred to *A*. Thus, we have eliminated some of the upper zone of ignorance. These processes can be repeated any number of times so that the location of the indifference curve can be pinpointed more precisely (see Problems 5.3 and 5.4). While not being very practical for actually deriving an indifference curve, the theory of revealed preference can be used to derive a demand curve easily and without indifference curves (see Problem 5.5).

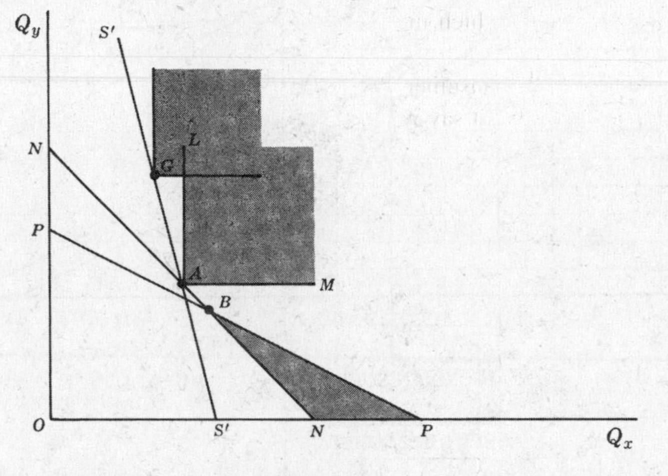

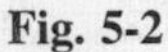
Fig. 5-2

5.3 INDEX NUMBERS AND CHANGES IN THE STANDARD OF LIVING

A consumer is *better off in period 1* than in a base period if that person's total expenditures or income in period 1 exceeds the cost of the base period basket of goods in terms of period 1 prices. That is, if

$$P_x^1X^1 + P_y^1Y^1 > P_x^1X^0 + P_y^1Y^0$$

or

$$\sum P^1q^1 > \sum P^1q^0$$

where *P* refers to price, *q* to quantity, the superscripts 1 and 0 refer to period 1 and the base period, respectively, while $\sum$ refers to "the sum of." By the same reasoning, the consumer is *better off in the base period* if

$$\sum P^0q^0 > \sum P^0q^1$$

This is because period 1 basket of X and Y was available in the base period but was not chosen.

Dividing both sides of the above inequality for an *increase* in the standard of living by $\sum P^0q^0$, we get

$$\frac{\sum P^1q^1}{\sum P^0q^0} > \frac{\sum P^1q^0}{\sum P^0q^0}$$

or

$$\mathscr{E} > \mathscr{L}$$

where $\mathscr{E}$ is the *expenditure index*, which measures the ratio of period 1 expenditures to base period expenditures, while $\mathscr{L}$ is the *Laspeyres price index*, which measures the cost of *base period quantities* at period 1 relative to base period prices. Thus, if $\mathscr{E} > \mathscr{L}$, the consumer's standard of living increased.

On the other hand, dividing both sides of the inequality for a *decrease* in the standard of living by $\sum P^1q^1$, we get

$$\frac{\sum P^0q^0}{\sum P^1q^1} > \frac{\sum P^0q^1}{\sum P^1q^1}$$

$$\frac{1}{\mathscr{E}} > \frac{1}{\mathscr{P}}$$

$$\mathscr{E} < \mathscr{P}$$

where $\mathscr{P}$ is the *Paasche price index*, which measures the cost of purchasing *period 1 quantities* at period 1 prices relative to base period prices.

Thus, if $\mathscr{E} > \mathscr{L}$ and $\mathscr{E} > \mathscr{P}$, the consumer's standard of living rose; if $\mathscr{E} < \mathscr{L}$ and $\mathscr{E} < \mathscr{P}$, it fell; and if $\mathscr{P} > \mathscr{E} > \mathscr{L}$ or $\mathscr{L} > \mathscr{E} > \mathscr{P}$, we cannot say whether it rose, fell, or stayed the same.

EXAMPLE 3. Using the data in Table 5.1,

Table 5.1

Period	P_x	X	P_y	Y
0 (base)	\$2	3	\$4	6
1	4	5	5	7

we find that

$$\mathscr{E} = \frac{\sum P^1q^1}{\sum P^0q^0} = \frac{P_x^1X^1 + P_y^1Y^1}{P_x^0X^0 + P_y^0Y^0} = \frac{(\$4)(5) + (\$5)(7)}{(\$2)(3) + (\$4)(6)} = \frac{\$55}{\$30} \cong 1.83$$

$$\mathscr{L} = \frac{\sum P^1q^0}{\sum P^0q^0} = \frac{P_x^1X^0 + P_y^1Y^0}{\$30} = \frac{(\$4)(3) + (\$5)(6)}{\$30} = \frac{\$42}{\$30} \cong 1.40$$

$$\mathscr{P} = \frac{\sum P^1q^1}{\sum P^0q^1} = \frac{\$55}{P_x^0X^1 + P_y^0Y^1} = \frac{\$55}{(\$2)(3) + (\$4)(7)} = \frac{\$55}{\$38} \cong 1.45$$

Since $\mathscr{E} > \mathscr{L}$ and $\mathscr{E} > \mathscr{P}$, the standard of living increased. The Laspeyres index ($\mathscr{L}$) gives an upward bias of the increase in the cost of living. The Paasche index ($\mathscr{P}$) gives a downward bias. Because $\mathscr{L}$ uses base period quantities, $\mathscr{L}$ becomes available sooner than $\mathscr{P}$. The consumer price index (CPI), published monthly by the Bureau of Labor Statistics is an $\mathscr{L}$ index for a "typical" urban family of four. CPI measures the change in the purchasing power of the dollar and is used for inflation adjustment in wage contracts, pensions, welfare payments, and so on. Consumer tastes and product quality are assumed to be constant. Other price indices are the wholesale price index (WPI) and the GNP deflator.

5.4 UTILITY THEORY UNDER UNCERTAINTY

Traditional economic theory implicitly assumed a riskless world. However, most economic choices involve risk or uncertainty. For example, an individual may decide to become a lawyer or to go into business, where incomes can be either very high or only modest. Similarly, a homeowner may purchase insurance against the small chance of a heavy loss through fire and also purchase a lottery ticket offering a small chance of a large win. Traditional economic theory could not explain choices involving risk because of its strict adherence to the principle of diminishing marginal utility. Such an apparently conflicting behavior as the same individual purchasing insurance and also gambling can be rationalized by a total utility curve that first rises at a decreasing rate (so that MU declines) and then at an increasing rate (so that MU rises).

EXAMPLE 4. Figure 5-3 gives a total utility curve which first faces down and then up, plotted against income. Suppose that the individual's income is OA with utility AA' without a fire, and OB with utility BB' with a fire.

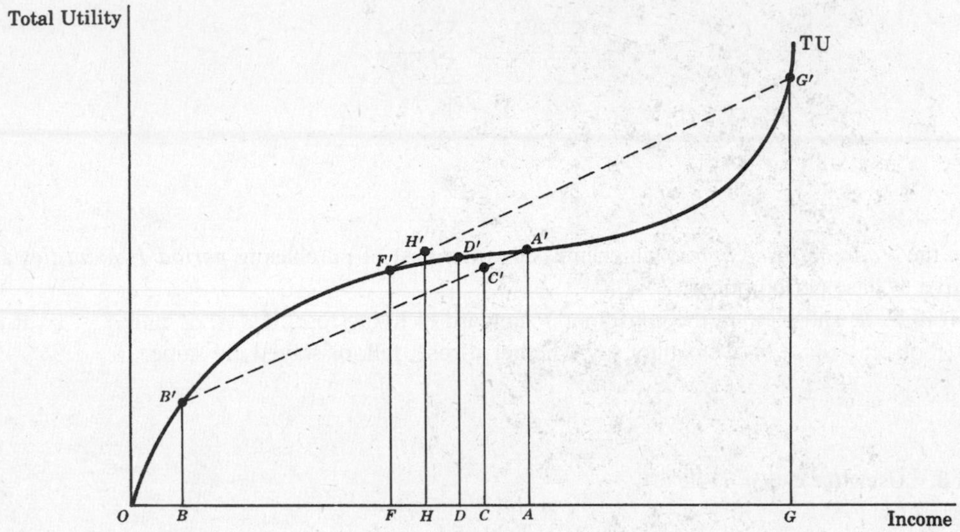

Fig. 5-3

If the probability of no fire is p, then the *expected income* ($\bar{I}$) of the individual is given by

$$\bar{I} = (p)OA + (1 - p)OB$$

If $\bar{I} = OC$, then the utility of $\bar{I}$ is CC' on dashed line $B'A'$. If, at the same time, the cost of insurance is AD, the individual's assured income with insurance is OD, with utility $DD' > CC'$. Thus, the individual should buy insurance. Furthermore, starting with income OD (with insurance), the same individual would also purchase a lottery ticket costing DF. Then the individual's income would be OF with probability p' of *not* winning, or OG with probability $(1 - p')$ of winning. Thus, the expected income ($\bar{I}'$) with insurance and the lottery ticket is:

$$\bar{I} = (p')(OF) + (1 - p')(OG)$$

If $\bar{I}' = OH$ with utility $HH' > DD'$, then the individual should also purchase the lottery ticket. (Problem 5.7 shows this with actual numbers, and Problem 5.8 shows a related method that was once believed to measure utility cardinally.)

5.5 A NEW APPROACH TO CONSUMER THEORY—THE DEMAND FOR CHARACTERISTICS

According to the *new approach to consumer theory* pioneered by Lancaster, a consumer demands a good because of the characteristics or properties of the good, and it is these characteristics and not the good itself that give rise to utility. For example, a consumer does not demand sugar as such but rather the characteristic of sweetness, which is the direct source of utility. In general, a good possesses more than one characteristic, and a given characteristic is present in more than one good. For example, sugar gives sweetness and calories and these characteristics are also present (but in a different proportion) in honey. This new approach is superior to traditional consumer theory because (1) substitute goods are explained in terms of possessing some common characteristic, (2) the introduction of new goods can be considered, and (3) the effect of changes in quality can be studied. Traditional consumer theory could not deal with these important considerations.

EXAMPLE 5. In panel A of Fig. 5-4, the horizontal axis measures the characteristic of sweetness and the vertical axis measures calories. One-dollar's worth of sugar gives the combination of sweetness and calories indicated by point A, and one-dollar's worth of honey gives point B. (It is assumed that two-dollar's worth of sugar gives a point twice as distant from the origin as point A along ray OA.) The consumer's budget constraint or frontier is then given by line AB. If the consumer's indifference curve in characteristic space is given by I, the consumer is in equilibrium at point C, where indifference curve I is tangent to budget frontier AB. The consumer reaches point C with OF characteristics from honey and FC (equals OG in length and direction) from sugar.

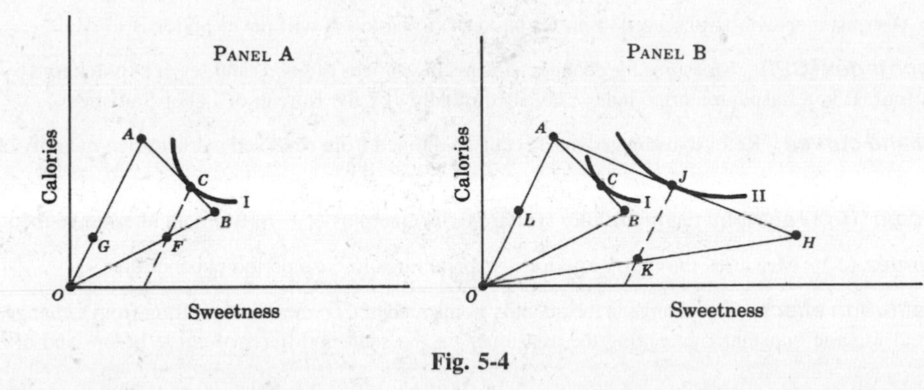

Fig. 5-4

Panel B shows that one-dollar's worth of a new good such as saccharin (with a much lower slope of calories to sweetness) gives point H, so that the budget constraint becomes AH. The consumer is in equilibrium at point J on indifference curve II by obtaining OK characteristics from saccharin and KJ (equals OL) from sugar, with no honey purchased. The new theory can also be used to show price, income, and quality changes (see Problems 5.10 to 5.12).

5.6 EMPIRICAL DEMAND CURVES

An actual or empirical market demand curve for a commodity can be estimated from market data on the quantities purchased of the commodity at various prices through time. But over time, consumers' tastes, income, and the price of related commodities change, causing the demand curve to shift. Similarly, changes in technology, factor prices, and weather conditions (for agricultural commodities) cause the supply curve to shift. Thus, the observed price-quantity relationships refer to equilibrium points on different demand and supply curves of the commodity. If the factors affecting *supply* are independent of and shift much more than the factors affecting demand and if tastes remain constant over the period of the analysis, then we can fit or derive a demand curve from the observed price-quantity observations. If, on the other hand, the factors affecting demand shift much more than the factors affecting supply, we get a supply curve.

EXAMPLE 6. The points in both panels of Fig. 5-5 refer to observed equilibrium points on shifting market demand and supply curves. If supply shifts much more than demand (as for agricultural commodities), we can derive the average market demand curve D in panel A by correcting for the factors causing the demand to shift. If demand shifts more than supply (as is usual for industrial commodities), we can derive the average market supply curve S in panel B. Assuming that supply shifts are much greater than demand shifts and making sure that tastes are constant, we can use regression analysis to separate the effects of price and income changes and fit or estimate an actual market demand curve from the price-quantity observations (see Problems 5.13 to 5.14).

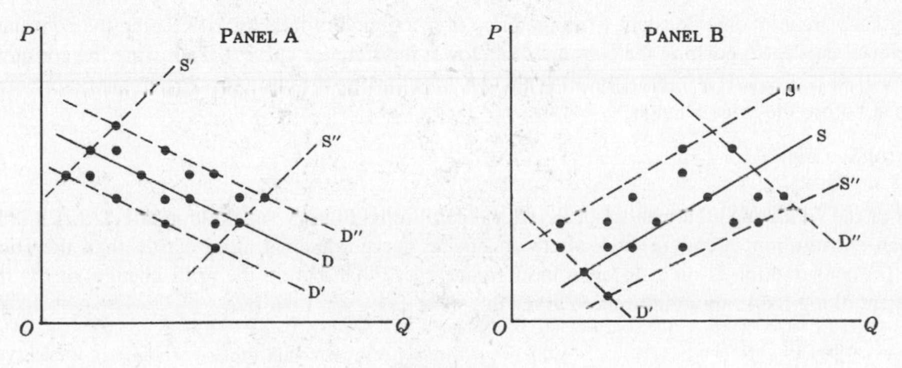

Fig. 5-5

Glossary

Consistency A consumer who is observed to prefer basket A to basket B will never prefer B to A.

Consumer price index (CPI) Measures the change in the average prices of goods and services purchased by a "typical" urban family of four. It is a Laspeyres price index published monthly by the Bureau of Labor Statistics.

Empirical demand curves Refer to estimated market curves derived from observed market price-quantity observations over time.

Expected income ($\bar{I}$) Is given by the probability (p) of one income plus $(1 - p)$ times an alternative income.

Expenditure index ($\mathscr{E}$) Measures the ratio of period 1 expenditures to base period expenditures.

Hicksian substitution effect The change in the quantity demanded of a commodity resulting from a change in its price, while holding real income constant by keeping the consumer on the same indifference curve before and after the price change.

Laspeyres price index ($\mathscr{L}$) Measures the cost of purchasing base period quantities at period 1 prices relative to base period prices.

New approach to consumer theory Postulates that a consumer demands a good because of the characteristics or properties of the good, and it is these characteristics and not the good itself that give rise to utility.

Paasche price index ($\mathscr{P}$) Measures the cost of purchasing period 1 quantities at period 1 prices relative to base period prices.

Price index numbers Measures the price of goods consumed over a particular period of time in relation to a base period.

Slutsky substitution effect The change in the quantity demanded of a commodity resulting from a change in its price, while keeping real income constant in the sense that the consumer could purchase the same basket of goods after the price change as that purchased prior to the price change.

Theory of revealed preference The theory according to which a consumer's preferences can be inferred (and indifference curve derived) from a sufficient number of observed choices or purchases in the marketplace.

Transitivity If A if preferred to B and B to C, then A is preferred to C.

Zone of ignorance The areas above the original budget line and to the right and to the left of the original point of consumer equilibrium within which we are uncertain of the exact location of the indifference curve.

Review Questions

1. Slutsky keeps real income constant when the price of a commodity falls by (*a*) keeping the consumer on the same indifference curve, (*b*) pushing the consumer to a lower indifference curve, (*c*) allowing the consumer to purchase the same basket of goods as before the price change, (*d*) allowing the consumer to purchase more of both commodities than before the price change.

Ans. (*c*) See Fig. 5-1.

2. Which of the following statements is *false* with regard to the Slutsky substitution effect? (*a*) It is larger than the Hicksian substitution effect, (*b*) it leads to a demand curve which is more elastic than the Hicksian demand curve, (*c*) consumption is on a different indifference curve than before the price change, or (*d*) it is given by a movement along the same indifference curve.

Ans. (*d*) See Fig. 5-1.

3. Which of the following is *not* an assumption of the theory of revealed preference? (*a*) A cardinal measure of utility; (*b*) consistency; (*c*) transitivity; (*d*) a consumer can be induced to purchase any basket of commodities if its price is made sufficiently attractive.

   Ans. (*a*) See Section 5.2.

4. Which of the following statements is correct with regard to the theory of revealed preference? (*a*) It infers a consumer's preferences from that person's market choices, (*b*) it can be used to derive a consumer's indifference curve, (*c*) it can be used to derive a consumer's demand curve, or (*d*) all of the above.

   Ans. (*d*) See Section 5.2.

5. The Laspeyres price index measures the cost of purchasing (*a*) period 1 quantities at period 1 prices relative to base period prices, (*b*) base period quantities at period 1 prices relative to base period prices, (*c*) base period quantities at base period prices, (*d*) period 1 quantities at period 1 prices.

   Ans. (*b*) See Section 5.3.

6. Which of the following statements is correct with regard to price indices? (*a*) $\mathscr{L}$ is biased upward, (*b*) $\mathscr{P}$ is biased downward, (*c*) $\mathscr{L}$ becomes available sooner than $\mathscr{P}$, or (*d*) all of the above.

   Ans. (*d*) See Section 5.3.

7. Traditional economic theory could not explain choices involving risk because it assumed that (*a*) MU always declines, (*b*) MU first declines and then rises, (*c*) MU first rises and then declines, or (*d*) MU always increases.

   Ans. (*a*) See Section 5.4.

8. If income is either \$10 with $p = 0.2$ or \$20, the expected income is (*a*) \$2, (*b*) \$16, (*c*) \$18, or (*d*) \$20.

   Ans. (*c*) See Example 4.

9. Which of the following is *incorrect* with respect to the new approach to consumer theory? (*a*) The characteristics of a good and not the good itself give rise to utility, (*b*) a consumer's equilibrium is shown in good or commodity space, (*c*) a good usually possesses more than one characteristic, or (*d*) a given characteristic is usually possessed by more than one good.

   Ans. (*b*) See Example 5.

10. Which of the following represent(s) an advance of the new approach to consumer theory over traditional consumer theory? (*a*) Substitute goods are explained in terms of possessing some common characteristics, (*b*) the introduction of new goods can be considered, (*c*) quality changes can be considered, or (*d*) all of the above.

    Ans. (*d*) See Section 5.5.

11. Empirical demand curves refer to demand curves estimated from (*a*) utility theory, (*b*) the new approach to consumer theory, (*c*) information provided by individual consumers, or (*d*) actual market price-quantities observations.

    Ans. (*d*) See Section 5.6.

12. Which of the following is *false* with regard to the derivation of empirical demand curves? (*a*) Supply shifts must be greater than demand shifts, (*b*) tastes must remain constant over the period of the analysis, (*c*) the price of related commodities must remain constant, or (*d*) market and not individual demand curves are derived.

    Ans. (*c*) See Example 6.

Solved Problems

THE SUBSTITUTION EFFECT ACCORDING TO HICKS AND SLUTSKY

5.1 Redraw Fig. 4-29 to show on that figure the Slutsky substitution and income effects and the Slutsky demand curve.

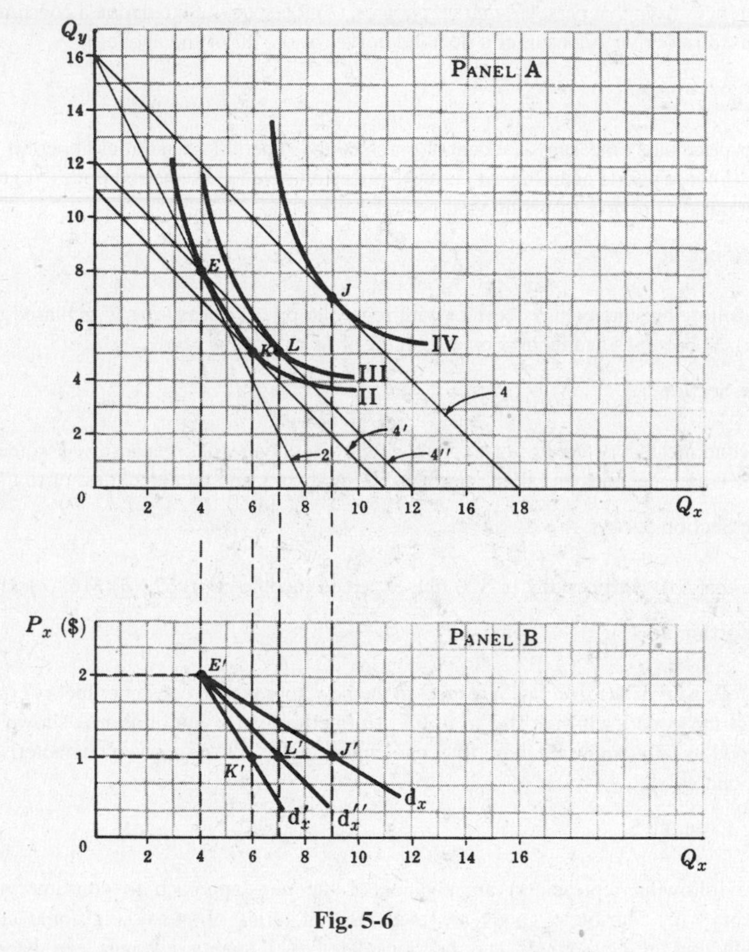

Fig. 5-6

In panel A of Fig. 5-6, the Slutsky budget line is 4″ and the substitution effect is 3X given by the movement from point E to point L. This gives the Slutsky demand curve d_x'' in panel B (sometimes referred to as the "compensated demand curve"), while d_x' is the Hicksian demand curve and d_x is the usual demand curve (as in panel B of Fig. 4-29).

5.2 With regard to the Slutsky and Hicksian substitution effects (*a*) which is a better measure? (*b*) As the magnitude of the price change declines, what happens to the magnitude of these two measures of the substitution effect?

(*a*) The Slutsky measure of the substitution effect is generally better because it puts the consumer on a different indifference curve, as does the income effect. More importantly, the Slutsky substitution effect can be measured from actual price-quantity observations before and after the price change, and without any knowledge of the exact shape of the indifference curve.

(*b*) As the magnitude of the change in P_x declines, the difference between the Slutsky and Hicksian substitution effects declines and approaches zero faster than the decline in the Slutsky and Hicksian substitution and income effects (see panel A of Fig. 5-6).

THE THEORY OF REVEALED PREFERENCE

5.3 Starting from Fig. 5-2, draw a figure showing haw we can derive the *entire* (*a*) lower boundary and (*b*) upper boundary of the indifference curve.

(*a*) The consumer can be induced to purchase basket C on *PP* in Fig. 5-7, if P_x/P_y is sufficiently low, as indicated by budget line *RR*. Thus, area *CPR* can also be removed from the lower zone of ignorance by reasoning analogous to that used in Example 2. Hence, the lower boundary for the indifference curve is *TFDABCR*.

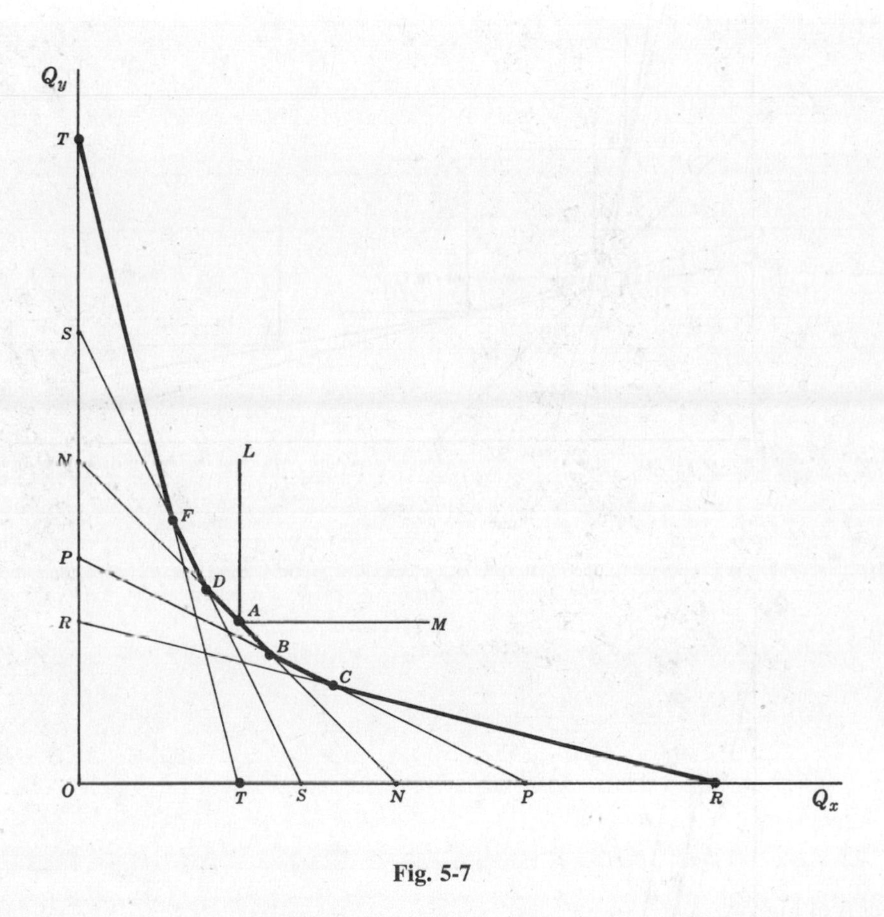

Fig. 5-7

(*b*) From Fig. 5-8, we can see that baskets above and to the right of *H* are preferred to *H*, which is preferred to *G*, which is preferred to *A*. Thus, we can remove the areas to the right of the boundary *AGH* from the upper zone of ignorance. By analogous reasoning, we know that the indifference curve must be below the *AJK* boundary. Thus, the upper boundary for the indifference curve is *HGAJK*.

5.4 Draw a figure showing the lower and upper boundaries found in Problem 5.3 and also showing indifference curve II from Fig. 5-1 that we seek to derive.

In Fig. 5-9, indifference curve II that we seek to derive must be above *TFDABCR* and below *HGAJK*. The exact location of indifference curve II can be pinpointed more closely by chipping away still more areas from the lower and upper zones of ignorance. While not very practical, the theory of revealed preference thus shows how a consumer's indifference curve can be derived from observed market choices and without direct questioning of the consumer about personal preferences.

5.5 Derive graphically the Slutsky and the usual demand curves, using the theory of revealed preference.

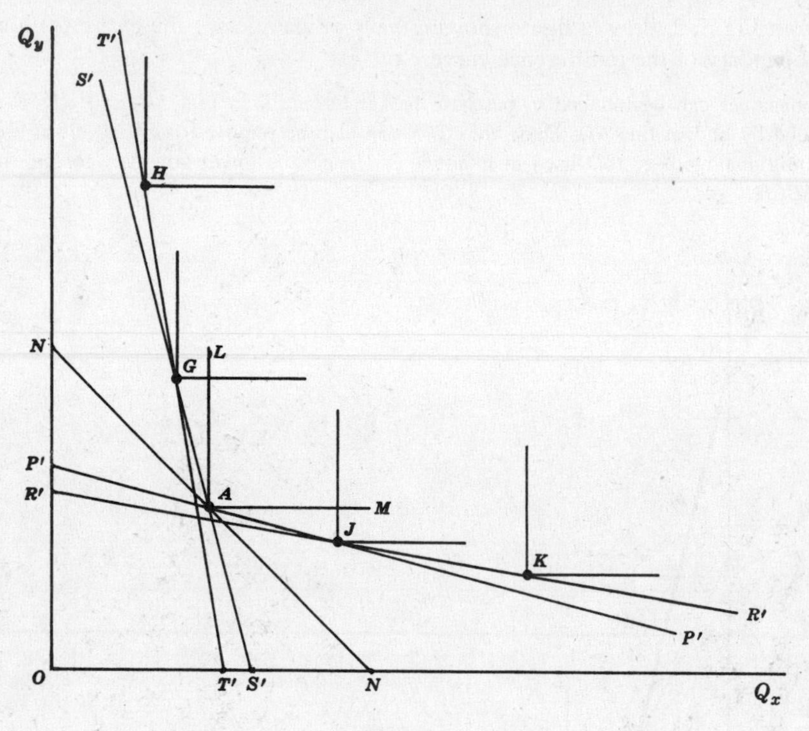

Fig. 5-8

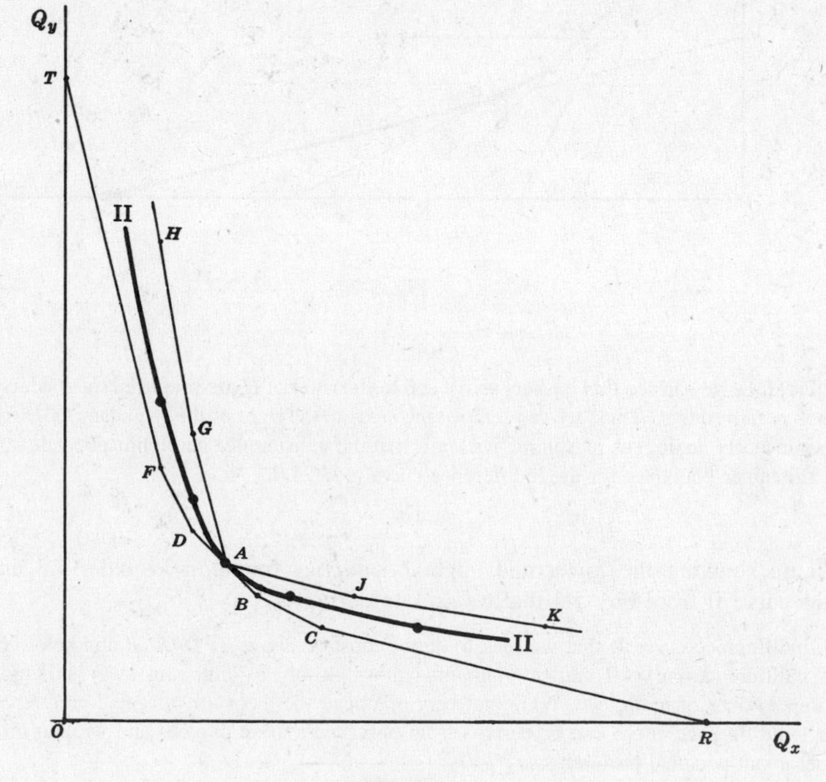

Fig. 5-9

Panel A of Fig. 5-10 is identical to Fig. 5-1, except for the omission of all indifference curves and the Hicksian budget line $K'J'$. The consumer is originally observed to be in equilibrium at point E on KL. When the price of X falls from $P_x = \$1.00$ to $P_x = \$0.50$, the budget line becomes KJ and the consumer's real income rises. To keep real income constant as at point E, KL is rotated through point E in a counterclockwise direction until it is parallel to KJ. The consumer will not consume along $K''E$ because it is below KE, and KE is inferior to E. The consumer will instead consume along EJ'', say, at point H. The movement from E to H (3X) is the substitution effect shown in the bottom panel by the Slutsky demand curve. If the consumer's real income is now allowed to rise with budget line KJ, the consumer will purchase more of commodity X if X is a normal good. If the consumer moves to point T, the movement from H to T (1X) is the income effect. The usual demand curve shown in panel B illustrates the total of the substitution and income effects resulting from the fall in P_x. Thus, the theory of revealed preference can be used to separate the (Slutsky) substitution from the income effect and derive the Slutsky and the usual demand curves *without any need for indifference curves*.

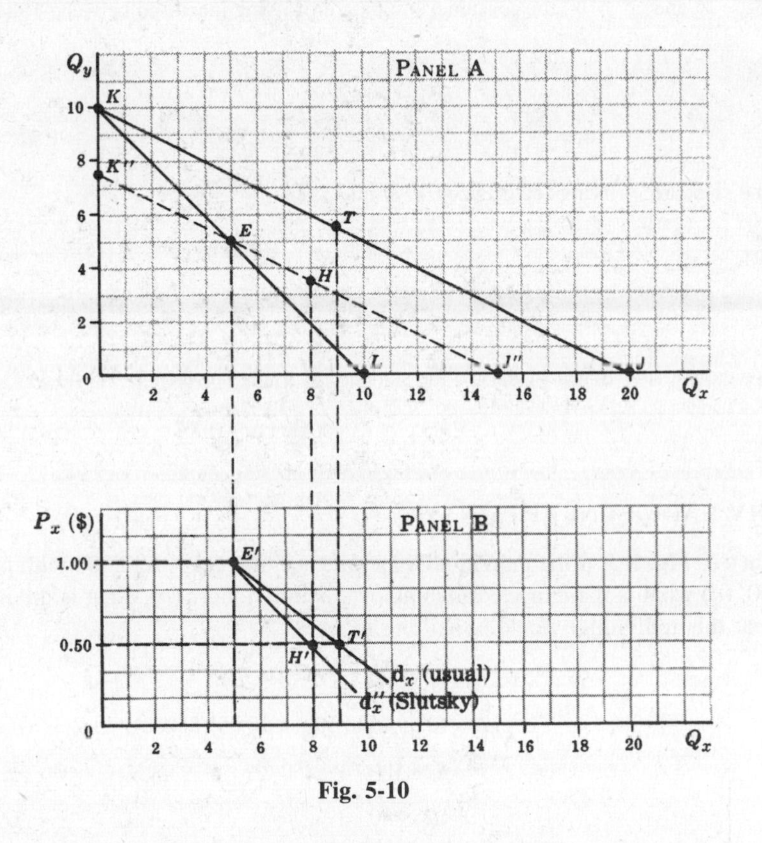

Fig. 5-10

PRICE INDEX NUMBERS AND CHANGES IN THE STANDARD OF LIVING

5.6 Given the hypothetical price and consumption data of Table 5.2 and using 1984 as the base year, find $\mathscr{E}$, $\mathscr{L}$, and $\mathscr{P}$ and indicate the change in the standard of living for (*a*) 1989, (*b*) 1990, and (*c*) 1991.

Table 5.2

Year	P_x	X	P_y	Y
1984 (base)	$4	5	$3	3
1989	5	6	4	6
1990	6	4	5	4
1991	6	4	7	4

(*a*) For 1989,

$$\mathscr{E} = \frac{\sum P^1 q^1}{\sum P^0 q^0} = \frac{P_x^1 X^1 + P_y^1 Y^1}{P_x^0 X^0 + P_y^0 Y^0} = \frac{(\$5)(6) + (\$4)(6)}{(\$4)(5) + (\$3)(3)} = \frac{\$54}{\$29} \cong 1.86 \text{ or } 186\%$$

$$\mathscr{L} = \frac{\sum P^1 q^0}{\sum P^0 q^0} = \frac{P_x^1 X^0 + P_y^1 Y^0}{\$29} = \frac{(\$5)(5) + (\$4)(3)}{\$29} = \frac{\$37}{\$29} \cong 1.28 \text{ or } 128\%$$

$$\mathscr{P} = \frac{\sum P^1 q^1}{\sum P^0 q^1} = \frac{\$54}{P_x^0 X^1 + P_y^0 Y^1} = \frac{\$54}{(\$4)(6) + (\$3)(6)} = \frac{\$54}{\$42} \cong 1.29 \text{ or } 129\%$$

Since $\mathscr{E} > \mathscr{L}$ and $\mathscr{L} > \mathscr{P}$, the consumer's standard of living increased between 1984 and 1989.

(*b*) For 1990,

$$\mathscr{E} = \frac{\$44}{\$29} \cong 1.52 \qquad \mathscr{L} = \frac{\$45}{\$29} \cong 1.55 \qquad \mathscr{P} = \frac{\$44}{\$28} \cong 1.57$$

Thus, the standard of living fell between 1977 and 1983.

(*c*) For 1991,

$$\mathscr{E} = \frac{\$52}{\$29} \cong 1.79 \qquad \mathscr{L} = \frac{\$51}{\$29} \cong 1.76 \qquad \mathscr{P} = \frac{\$52}{\$28} \cong 1.86$$

Thus, we cannot say what happened to the standard of living between 1984 and 1991.

UTILITY THEORY UNDER UNCERTAINTY

5.7 With reference to Fig. 5-3, if the individual's income is either OA = \$30,000 with probability of 0.95 or OB = \$5000, (*a*) what is the expected income of this individual? (*b*) What is the maximum amount of insurance that this individual would be willing to pay?

(*a*)

$$\bar{I} = (p)(OA) + (1 - p)(OB)$$

$$\bar{I} = (0.95)(\$30{,}000) + (0.05)(\$5000)$$

$$\bar{I} = \$28{,}5000 + \$250$$

$$\bar{I} = \$28{,}750$$

(*b*) We can answer this question by drawing a horizontal line from point C' to the left, until it crosses the TU curve in Fig. 5-3. The horizontal distance from the crossing point on the TU curve to the vertical line AA' represents the maximum amount of insurance that this individual is willing to pay. The reason for this is that the utility of the certain income with insurance given by the crossing point on the TU curve is the same (i.e., it is of the same height) as point C' (the expected income without insurance). Utility theory under uncertainty is associated with the names of Friedman and Savage—the original investigators.

5.8 Suppose that an individual is just willing to accept a gamble to win or lose \$1000 if the probability of winning is 0.6. Suppose that the utility gained if the individual wins is 100 utils. (*a*) Is this consumer an insurer or a gambler? Why? (*b*) How much utility does one lose if one loses the gamble?

(*a*) The individual is an insurer because this person required better-than-even odds of winning before being willing to gamble.

(*b*) Since the individual is just induced to accept the gamble when the probability of winning is 0.60 and would gain 100 utils upon winning, we can measure the utility lost in losing the gamble as follows:

$$\text{Expected gain in utility} = \text{expected loss in utility}$$
$$(0.6)(100\,\text{utils}) = (0.4)(\text{utils lost})$$
$$\text{utils lost} = \frac{(0.6)(100\,\text{utils})}{0.4} = 150\,\text{utils}$$

Since the individual would gain 100 utils upon winning $1000 and lose 150 utils on losing the $1000, the MU of money decreases, making the individual an insurer. Note that in choices involving risk, the consumer maximizes expected utility rather than utility. This general method of calculation is often referred to as *modern utility theory*.

5.9 Do the calculations in Problem 5.8(*b*) give a cardinal measure of utility? Why?

The calculations of Problem 5.8(*b*) (and modern utility theory) do not really give us a cardinal measure of utility, since the results obtained are arbitrary with regard to both origin and scale. For example, if we assigned 200 utils to the winning of $1000, the utility lost in losing the $1000 would have been 300 utils instead of 150 utils. Furthermore, 300 utils should only be taken to imply more utility than 150 utils, and not twice as much utility. Thus, modern utility theory only gives a method of *ordering* utility in conditions involving risk.

A NEW APPROACH TO CONSUMER THEORY—THE DEMAND FOR CHARACTERISTICS

5.10 Starting with panel A of Fig. 5-4, draw a figure that shows a hypothetical equilibrium with (*a*) 33% increase in the consumer's income and (*b*) 40% reduction in the price of honey (with no change in the price of sugar and in the consumer's income).

(*a*) A 33% increase in the consumer's income extends ray OA by 33% to OA' in Fig. 5-11 or OB to OB'. The budget frontier is then $A'B'$, and equilibrium may take place at C' on indifference curve III, with OB characteristics from honey and BC' (equals OG) from sugar. See Fig. 5-11.

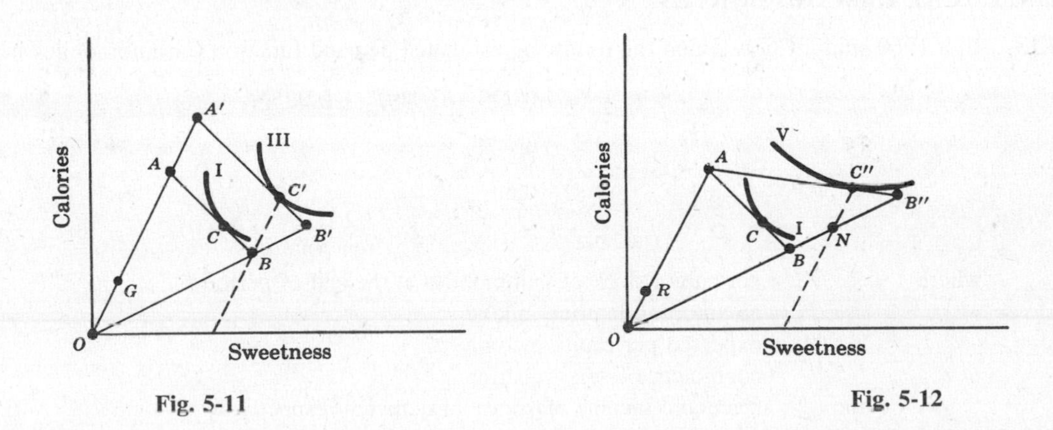

Fig. 5-11

Fig. 5-12

(*b*) A 40% reduction in the price of honey extends ray OB by 40% to OB'' in Fig. 5-12, so that the budget frontier becomes AB''. Equilibrium may then take place at point C'' on indifference curve V and is reached with ON characteristics from honey and NC'' (equals OR) from sugar. See Fig. 5-12.

5.11 Starting from panel B of Fig. 5-4, draw a figure showing a hypothetical consumer's equilibrium with a 40% reduction in the price of honey.

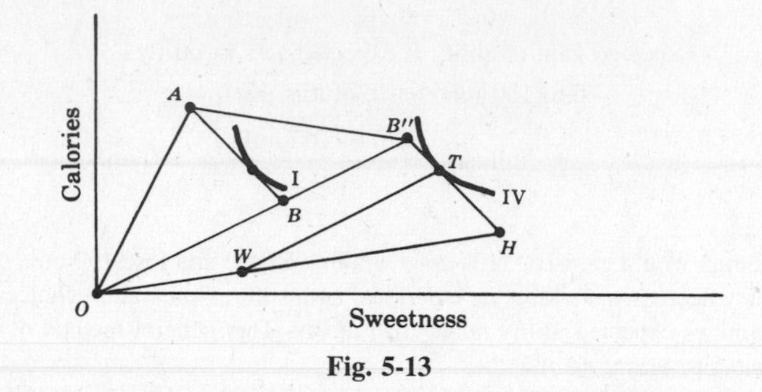

Fig. 5-13

When the price of honey falls by 40% ray OB extends to OB'' as in Fig. 5-12. As a result, the new production frontier becomes $AB''H$ in Fig. 5-13. A hypothetical equilibrium position is given by point T on indifference curve IV. Point T is reached with OW characteristics from saccharin and WT (equals OB) from honey, with no sugar purchased. Area $OAB''H$ is referred to as the *feasible region* and $AB''H$ as the *efficiency frontier.*

5.12 With regard to the new approach to consumer theory, (*a*) what can you conclude as to the number of goods purchased from the number of characteristics considered? (*b*) How could producers of sugar in Fig. 5-13 regain this market? (*c*) If saccharin is very profitable, what quality changes are producers of honey stimulated to introduce? How would these quality changes be reflected in Fig. 5-13?

(*a*) In Figs. 5-4, 5-11, 5-12, and 5-13, we have seen that the goods have two characteristics and the consumer purchases two goods when in equilibrium. In general, the number of goods consumed will never exceed the number of characteristics desired.

(*b*) Producers of sugar could regain the market they lost to honey if they succeed in reducing the price of sugar so as to extend ray OA sufficiently in length so that a line from its new end point to point H leaves point B'' inside such a line or budget frontier (see Fig. 5-13).

(*c*) If saccharin is very profitable, producers of honey are likely to attempt to reduce the caloric content of honey, thereby rotating ray OB'' clockwise toward ray OH in Fig. 5-13.

EMPIRICAL DEMAND CURVES

5.13 In a 1960 study, Chow found the following estimated demand function for automobiles in the U.S.:

$$X_t = -0.725 - 0.049P_t + 0.025M_t$$

$$R^2 = 0.90$$

$$e = -0.6$$

$$e_m = 1.5$$

where X_t = per capita stock of automobiles at the end of period t
P_t = an automobile price index
M_t = expected per capita income
R^2 = coefficient of determination
e and e_m = price and income elasticity of demand, respectively

With respect to the above results, what is the meaning of (*a*) the sign of the estimated coefficients, and (*b*) the size of the estimated coefficients? (*c*) How did Chow estimate e and e_m? (*d*) What does $R^2 = 0.90$ indicate?

(*a*) The negative sign of the estimated coefficient of P_t and the positive sign of the estimated coefficient of M_t indicate that X_t is inversely related to P_t and directly related to M_t. Note that tastes are implicitly assumed to be constant and no price of related goods (such as public transportation or gasoline) is included.

(*b*) The −0.049 coefficient of P_t indicates that a 100% increase in P_t reduces X_t by 4.9%. The 0.025 coefficient of M_t indicates that a 100% increase in M_t increases X_t *by* 2.5%.

(*c*) Since the coefficient of P_t refers to $\Delta X/\Delta P$, multiplying $\Delta X/\Delta P$ by P/X for 1960, we get

$$\frac{\Delta X}{\Delta P}\cdot\frac{P}{X} = e(= -0.6 \text{ in } 1960)$$

Similarly, since the coefficient of M_t refers to $\Delta X/\Delta M$, multiplying $\Delta X/\Delta M$ by M/X for 1960, we get

$$\frac{\Delta X}{\Delta M}\cdot\frac{M}{X} = e_m(= 1.5 \text{ in } 1960)$$

(*d*) $R^2 = 0.90$ indicates that 90% of the variation is explained or associated With the variation in P_t and M_t.

5.14 (*a*) Write the general form of the constant-elasticity demand function, (*b*) What is the meaning of the various coefficients?

(*a*) $$Q_x = aP_x^b P_0^c M^f u \quad \text{or} \quad \text{In } Q_x = \text{In } a + b \text{ In } P_x + c \text{ In } P_0 + f \text{ In } M + \text{ In } u$$

where Q_x = market quantity demanded of commodity X per unit of time
P_x = price of X
P_0 = price of unrelated commodities
M = money income
u = error term
In = natural logarithm (to base *e*)

(*b*)
a = constant or intercept
b = price elasticity of demand
c = cross elasticity of demand
f = income elasticity of demand

The constant-elasticity demand function is the most commonly used demand function in applied research because its coefficients give a direct estimate of the various elasticities.

CHAPTER 6

Theory of Production

6.1 PRODUCTION WITH ONE VARIABLE INPUT: TOTAL, AVERAGE, AND MARGINAL PRODUCT

The *production function* for any commodity is an equation, table, or graph showing the (maximum) quantity of the commodity that can be produced per unit of time for each of a set of alternative inputs, when the best production techniques available are used.

A simple agricultural production function is obtained by using various alternative quantities of labor per unit of time to farm a fixed amount of land and recording the resulting alternative outputs of the commodity per unit of time. [We refer to cases such as this, where at least one factor of production or input is fixed, as the *short run*.] The *average product of labor* (AP_L) is then defined as total product (TP) divided by the number of units of labor used. The *marginal product of labor* (MP_L) is given by the change in TP per unit change in the quantity of labor used.

EXAMPLE 1. The first three columns of Table 6.1 give a hypothetical short-run production function for wheat. Land is measured in acres, labor in worker-years, and total product (TP) in bushels per year. All units of land, labor, or wheat are assumed to be homogeneous or of the same quality. The average product of labor (AP_L) figures in column (4) are obtained by dividing each quantity in column (3) by the corresponding quantity in column (2). The marginal product of labor (MP_L) figures in column (5) are obtained by finding the differences between the successive quantities in column (3).

Table 6.1

(1) Land	(2) Labor	(3) TP	(4) AP_L	(5) MP_L
1	0	0	0	...
1	1	3	3	3
1	2	8	4	5
1	3	12	4	4
1	4	15	$3\frac{3}{4}$	3
1	5	17	$3\frac{2}{5}$	2
1	6	17	$2\frac{5}{6}$	0
1	7	16	$2\frac{2}{7}$	−1
1	8	13	$1\frac{5}{8}$	−3

The TP, AP_L, and MP_L schedules of Table 6.1 are plotted in Fig. 6-1. Since the MP_L has been defined as the *change* in TP per unit change in the quantity of labor used, each value of the MP_L has been recorded in panel B *halfway between* the quantities of labor used.

6.2 THE SHAPES OF THE AVERAGE AND MARGINAL PRODUCT CURVES

The shapes of the AP_L and MP_L curves are determined by the shape of the corresponding TP curve. The AP_L at any point on the TP_L curve is given by the slope of the straight line from the origin to that point on the TP curve. The AP_L curve usually rises at first, reaches a maximum, and then falls, but it remains positive as long as the TP is positive.

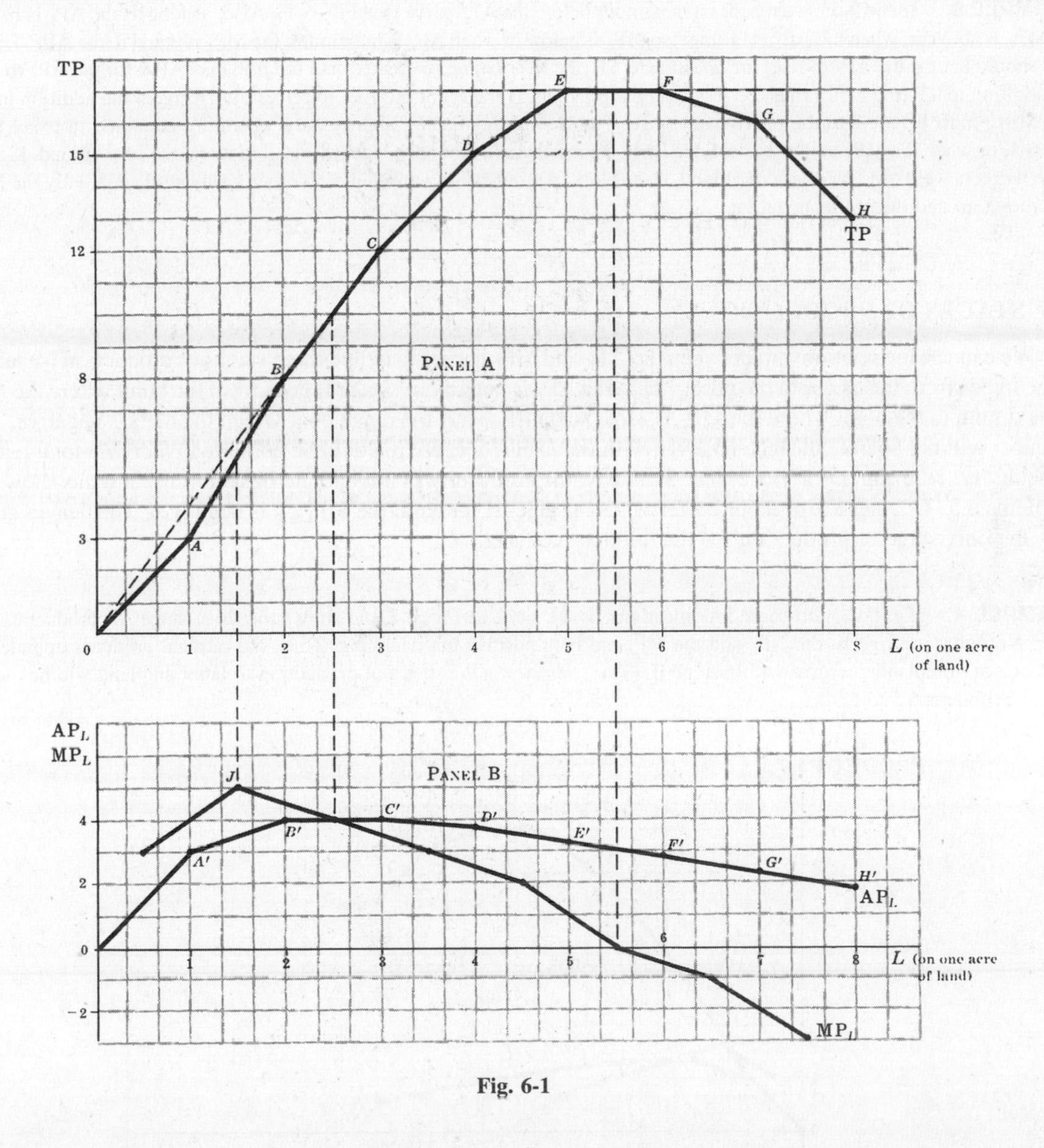

Fig. 6-1

The MP_L between two points on the TP curve is equal to the slope of the TP curve *between* the two points. The MP_L curve also rises at first, reaches a maximum (before the AP_L reaches its maximum), and then declines. The MP_L becomes zero when the TP is maximum and negative when the TP begins to decline. The falling portion of the MP_L curve illustrates *the law of diminishing returns*.

EXAMPLE 2. In Fig. 6-1, the AP_L at point A on the TP curve is equal to the slope of OA. This is equal to 3 and is recorded as point A' in panel B. Similarly, the AP_L at point B on the TP curve is equal to the slope of dashed line OB. This equals 4 and is recorded as point B' in panel B. At point C, the AP_L is again 4. This is the highest AP_L. Past point C, the AP_L declines but remains positive as long as the TP is positive.

The MP_L between the origin and point A on the TP curve is equal to the slope of OA. This slope is equal to 3 and is recorded halfway between 0 and 1, or at $\frac{1}{2}$, in panel B. Similarly, the MP_L between A and B is equal to the slope of AB. This is equal to 5 and is recorded at $\frac{1}{2}$, in panel B. The MP_L between B and C is equal to the slope of BC. This is 4 and is equal to the highest AP_L (the slope of OB and OC). Between E and F, the TP remains unchanged; therefore, the MP_L is zero. Past point F, the TP begins to decline and the MP_L becomes negative.

EXAMPLE 3. The MP_L curve reaches a maximum before the AP_L curve (see Fig. 6-1). Also, as long as the AP_L is rising, the MP_L is above it; when the AP_L is falling, the MP_L is below it; when AP_L is maximum, the MP_L is equal to the AP_L. This is as it should be: for the AP_L to rise, the *addition* to TP (the MP_L) must be greater than the *previous* AP_L; for the AP_L to fall, the addition to TP (the MP_L) must be less than the previous average; for the AP_L to remain unchanged, the addition to TP (the MP_L) must be equal to the previous average. The law of diminishing returns starts operating at point J in panel B of Fig. 6-1, or when the MP_L begins to decline. This occurs because "too much" labor is used to work one acre of land. If even more workers were used on one acre of land, these workers would start getting in each other's way until eventually the MP_L becomes zero and then turns negative.

6.3 STAGES OF PRODUCTION

We can use the relationship between the AP_L and MP_L curves to define three stages of production for labor. Stage I goes from the origin to the point where the AP_L is maximum. Stage II goes from the point where the AP_L is maximum to the point where the MP_L is zero. Stage III covers the range over which the MP_L is negative. The producer will not operate in stage III, even with free labor, because it would be possible to *increase* total output by using *less* labor on one acre of land. Similarly, the producer will not operate in stage I because, as shown in Problems 6.5–6.9, stage I for labor corresponds to stage III for land (the MP_{Land} is negative). This leaves stage II as the only stage of production for the rational producer.

EXAMPLE 4. Fig. 6-2, with some modifications, is the same as Fig. 6-1 and shows the three stages of production for labor. Note that in stage II, the AP_L and the MP_L are both positive but declining. Thus, the rational producer operates in the range of diminishing returns within stage II. (The *symmetry* in the stages of production of labor and land will be examined in Problems 6.5 to 6.9.)

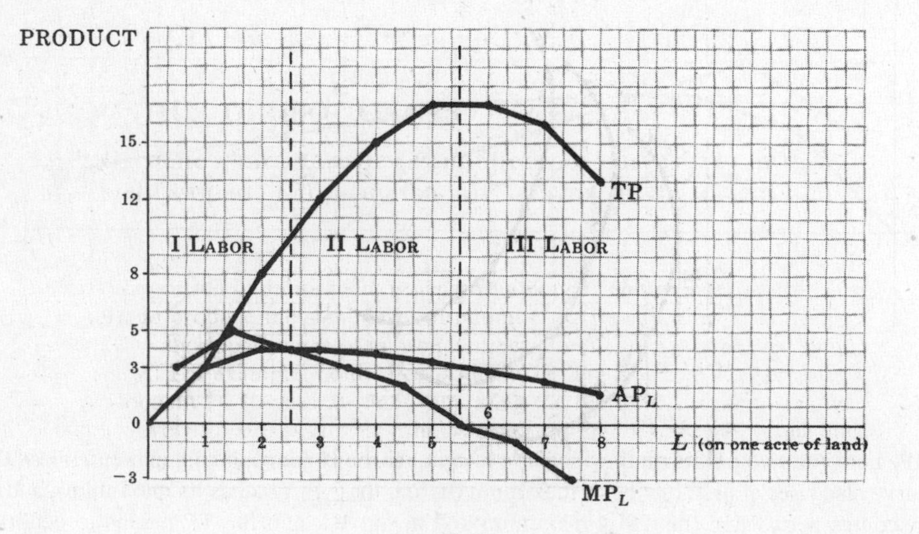

Fig. 6-2

6.4 PRODUCTION WITH TWO VARIABLE INPUTS: ISOQUANTS

We now turn to the case where the firm has only two factors of production, labor and capital, both of which are variable. Since all factors are variable, we are dealing with the *long run*.

An *isoquant* shows the different combinations of labor (L) and capital (K) with which a firm can produce a specific quantity of output. A higher isoquant refers to a greater quantity of output and a lower one, to a smaller quantity of output.

EXAMPLE 5. Table 6.2 gives points on three different isoquants.

Table 6.2

Isoquant I		Isoquant II		Isoquant III	
L	*K*	*L*	*K*	*L*	*K*
2	11	4	13	6	15
1	8	3	10	5	12
2	5	4	7	6	9
3	3	5	5	7	7
4	2.3	6	4.2	8	6.2
5	1.8	7	3.5	9	5.5
6	1.6	8	3.2	10	5.3
7	1.8	9	3.5	11	5.5

Plotting these points on the same set of axes and connecting them by smooth curves we get the three isoquants shown in Fig. 6-3. The firm can produce the output specified by isoquant I by using $8K$ and $1L$ (point B) or by using $5K$ and $2L$ (point C) or any other combination of L and K on isoquant I. Isoquants (as opposed to indifference curves) specify *cardinal* measures of output. For example, isoquant I might refer to 60 units of physical output; isoquant II to 100 units of output, etc.

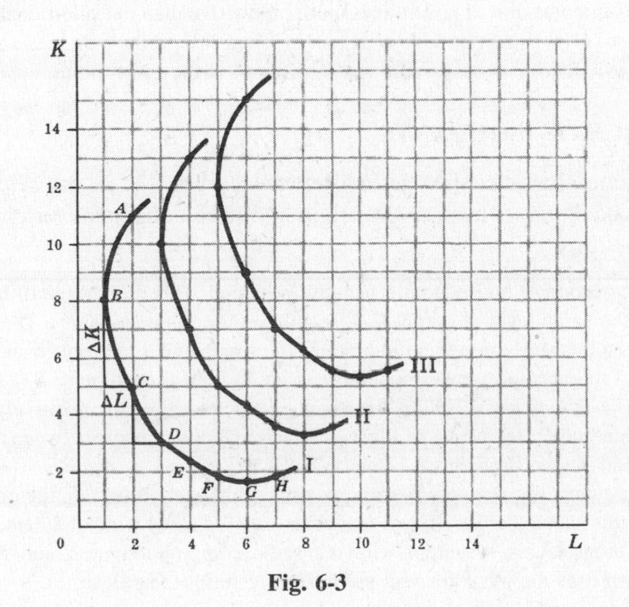

Fig. 6-3

6.5 THE MARGINAL RATE OF TECHNICAL SUBSTITUTION

The *marginal rate of technical substitution* of L for K ($MRTS_{LK}$) refers to the amount of K that a firm can give up by increasing the amount of L used by one unit and still remain on the same isoquant. The $MRTS_{LK}$ is also equal to MP_L/MP_K. As the firm moves down a isoquant, the $MRTS_{LK}$ diminishes.

EXAMPLE 6. In moving from point B to point C on isoquant I in Fig. 6-3, the firm gives up 3 units of K for one additional unit of L. Thus, the $MRTS_{LK} = 3$. Similarly, from point C to D on isoquant I, the $MRTS_{LK} = 2$. Thus, the $MRTS_{LK}$ diminishes as the firm moves down an isoquant. This is so because the less K and the more L the firm is using (i.e., the lower the point on the isoquant), the more difficult it becomes for the firm to substitute L for K in production.

EXAMPLE 7. Table 6.3 gives the $MRTS_{LK}$ between the various points on the negatively sloped portion of the isoquants in Table 6.2.

Table 6.3

Isoquant I			Isoquant II			Isoquant III		
L	K	$MRTS_{LK}$	L	K	$MRTS_{LK}$	L	K	$MRTS_{LK}$
2	11		4	13		6	15	
1	8		3	10		5	12	
2	5	3.0	4	7	3.0	6	9	3.0
3	3	2.0	5	5	2.0	7	7	2.0
4	2.3	.7	6	4.2	.8	8	6.2	.8
5	1.8	.5	7	3.5	.7	9	5.5	.7
6	1.6	.2	8	3.2	.3	10	5.3	.2
7	1.8		9	3.5		11	5.5	

Note that the $MRTS_{LK}$ between two points on the same isoquant is given by the absolute (or positive value of the) slope of the chord between the two points, while the $MRTS_{LK}$ at a point on the isoquant is given by the absolute slope of the isoquant at that point. The $MRTS_{LK}$ is also equal to the MP_L/MP_K. For example, if the MP_K is $\frac{1}{2}$ at a particular point on an isoquant while the MP_L is 2, this means that one unit of L is 4 times more productive than one additional unit of K at this point. Thus, the firm can give up four units of K by using one additional unit of L and still produce the same level of output (remain on the same isoquant). Therefore, the $MRTS_{LK} = MP_L/MP_K = 2/(1/2) = 4$ at the given point.

6.6 CHARACTERISTICS OF ISOQUANTS

Isoquants have the same characteristics as indifference curves: (1) in the relevant range isoquants are negatively sloped, (2) isoquants are convex to the origin and (3) isoquants never cross.

EXAMPLE 8. The relevant portion of an isoquant is negatively sloped. This means that if the firm wants to use less K, it must use more L to produce the same level of output (i.e., remain on the same isoquant). The firm will not operate on the positively sloped range of an isoquant because it could produce the same level of output by using less of both L and K. For example, point A on isoquant I in Fig. 6-4 involves both more L and more K than at point B (also on isoquant I). If we draw lines separating the relevant (i.e., the negatively sloped) from the irrelevant (i.e., the positively sloped) portions of the isoquants in Fig. 6-3, we get "ridge lines" OY and OX of Fig. 6-4. The range of isoquants between the ridge lines corresponds to stage II of production for L and K (see Problems 6.13 and 6.14).

In the relevant range, isoquants are not only negatively sloped but also convex to the origin because of diminishing $MRTS_{LK}$. In addition, isoquants cannot cross. If two isoquants crossed, the point of intersection would imply that the firm could produce two different levels of output with the same combination of L and K. This is impossible if we assume, as we do, that the firm uses the most efficient production techniques at all times.

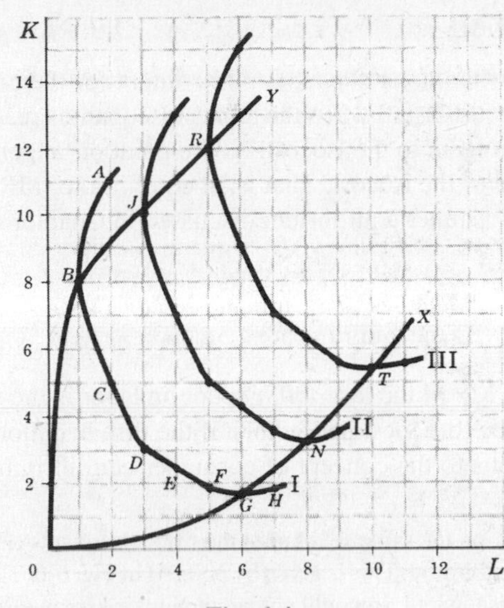

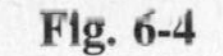
Fig. 6-4

6.7 ISOCOSTS

An *isocost* shows all the different combinations of labor and capital that a firm can purchase, given the total outlay (TO) of the firm and factor prices. The slope of an isocost is given by $-P_L/P_K$, where P_L refers to the price of labor and P_K to the price of capital.

EXAMPLE 9. If the firm spent all of its tolal outlay on capital, it could purchase TO/P_K units of capital. If the firm spent all of its total outlay on labor, it could purchase TO/P_L units of labor. Joining these two points by a straight line, we get the isocost of the firm. The firm can purchase any combination of labor and capital shown on its isocost. The slope of the isocost is given by

$$\frac{\mathrm{TO}/P_K}{\mathrm{TO}/P_L} = -\frac{\cancel{\mathrm{TO}}}{P_K} \cdot \frac{P_L}{\cancel{\mathrm{TO}}} = -\frac{P_L}{P_K}$$

For example, if $P_L = P_K = \$1$ and TO = \$10, we get the isocost of Fig. 6-5, with slope = -1.

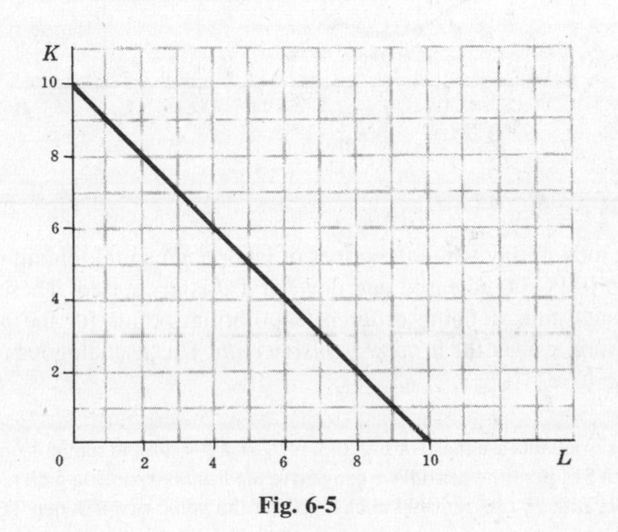

Fig. 6-5

6.8 PRODUCER EQUILIBRIUM

A producer is in *equilibrium* when he or she maximizes output for the given total outlay. Another-way of saying this is that a producer is in equilibrium when the highest isoquant is reached, given the particular isocost. This occurs where an isoquant is tangent to the isocost. At the point of tangency, the absolute slope of the isoquant is equal to the absolute slope of the isocost. That is, at equilibrium, $\text{MRTS}_{LK} = P_L/P_K$. (This is completely analogous to the concept of consumer equilibrium discussed in Chapter 4.) Since $\text{MRTS}_{LK} = \text{MP}_L/\text{MP}_K$, at equilibrium,

$$\frac{\text{MP}_L}{\text{MP}_K} = \frac{P_L}{P_K} \quad \text{or} \quad \frac{\text{MP}_L}{P_L} = \frac{\text{MP}_K}{P_K}$$

This means that at equilibrium the MP of the last *dollar* spent on labor is the same as the MP of the last *dollar* spent on capital. The same would be true for other factors, if the firm had more than two factors of production. (Again, this is completely analogous to the concept of consumer equilibrium.)

EXAMPLE 10. By bringing together on the same set of axes the firm's isoquants (Fig. 6-3) and its isocost (Fig. 6-5), we can determine the point of producer equilibrium. This is given by point *M* in Fig. 6-6. The firm cannot reach isoquant III with its isocost. If the firm produced along isoquant I, it would not be maximizing output. Isoquant II is the highest isoquant the firm can reach with its isocost. Thus, in order to reach equilibrium, the firm should spend \$5 of its TO to purchase 5*K* and its remaining \$5 to purchase 5*L*. At the equilibrium point (*M*),

$$\text{MRTS}_{LK} = \frac{\text{MP}_L}{\text{MP}_K} = \frac{P_L}{P_K} = 1$$

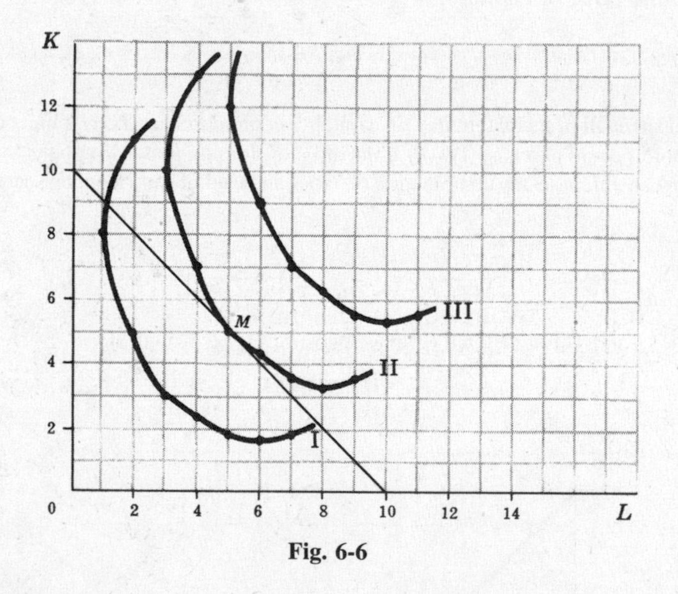

Fig. 6-6

6.9 EXPANSION PATH

If the firm changes its total outlay while the prices of labor and capital remain constant, the firm's isocost shifts parallel to itself—up if TO is increased and down if TO is decreased. These different isocosts will be tangent to different isoquants, thus defining different equilibrium points for the producer. By joining these points of producer equilibrium, we get the firm's *expansion path*. This is analogous to the income-consumption curve discussed in Chapter 4.

EXAMPLE 11. If the firm's isoquants are those of Fig. 6-3, if $P_L = P_K = \$1$ and remains unchanged, and if the firm's TO rises from \$6 to \$10 and then to \$14 per time period, we can derive the firm's expansion path (see Fig. 6-7). Isocosts 1, 2, and 3 are parallel to each other because P_L/P_K remains unchanged (at the value of 1). When TO = \$6, the producer reaches equilibrium at point D on isoquant I by purchasing $3K$ and $3L$. When TO = \$10, the producer attains equilibrium at point M on isoquant II by buying $5K$ and $5L$. When TO = \$14, the producer reaches equilibrium at point P on isoquant III by purchasing $7K$ and $7L$.

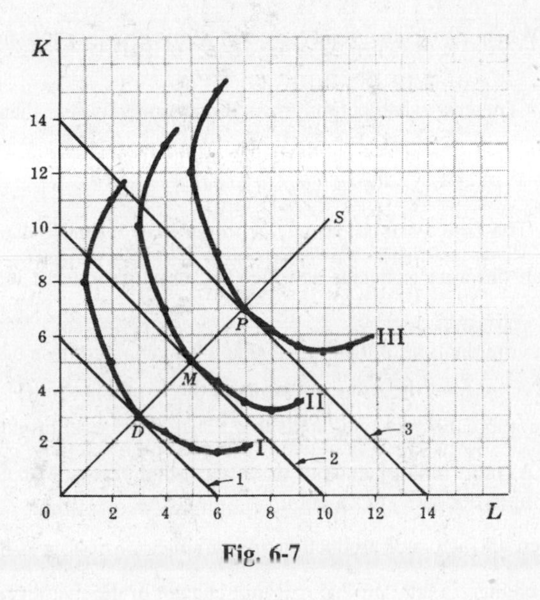

Fig. 6-7

Line OS joining the origin with equilibrium points D, M, and P is the expansion path for this firm. Note that in this case, the expansion path is a straight line through the origin. This means that as output is expanded, the K/L ratio (the slope of the expansion path) remains the same. (When the expansion path is a straight line through the origin, the ridge lines will also be straight lines through the origin, rather than as drawn in Fig. 6-5.)

The line joining points on different isoquants at which the MRTS (slope) is constant is called an *isocline*. Thus, an expansion path is the particular isocline along which output expands with factor prices remaining constant.

6.10 FACTOR SUBSTITUTION

If, starting from a position of producer equilibrium, the price of a factor falls, the equilibrium position will be disturbed. In the process of reestablishing equilibrium, the producer will substitute in production this (now relatively) cheaper factor for the other factor, until equilibrium is reestablished. The *degree* of substitutability of factor L for factor K, resulting *exclusively* from the change in *relative* factor prices, is called the *elasticity of technical substitution* and is measured by

$$(e\text{ subst.})_{LK} = \frac{\Delta\left(\frac{K}{L}\right)\left(\frac{K}{L}\right)}{\Delta(\text{MRTS}_{LK})/\text{MRTS}_{LK}}$$

(See Problems 6.19–6.23.)

6.11 CONSTANT, INCREASING, AND DECREASING RETURNS TO SCALE

We have *constant, increasing, or decreasing returns to scale* if, when all inputs are increased in a given proportion, the output of the commodity increases in *the same, in a greater, or in a smaller proportion*, respectively (see Problems 6.24 to 6.26).

Glossary

Average product (AP) Total product divided by the number of units of the input used.

Constant returns to scale When all inputs are increased in a given proportion and the output produced increases exactly in the same proportion.

Decreasing returns to scale The case when output grows proportionately less than inputs.

Expansion path The locus of points of producer equilibrium resulting from changes in total outlays while keeping factor prices constant.

Increasing returns to scale The case when output grows proportionately more than inputs.

Isocline The locus of points on different isoquants at which the marginal rate of technical substitution of factors of production or slope is constant.

Isocost Shows all the different combinations of two inputs that a firm can purchase or hire, given the total outlay of the firm and input prices.

Isoquant Shows the different combinations of two inputs that a firm can use to produce a specific quantity of output.

Law of diminishing returns As more units of an input are used per unit of time with fixed amounts of another input, the marginal product of the variable input declines after a point.

Long run The time period when all factors of production are variable.

Marginal product (MP) The change in total product per unit change in the quantity used of one input.

Marginal rate of technical substitution (MRTS) The amount of an input that a firm can give up by increasing the amount of the other input by one unit and still remain on the same isoquant.

Producer equilibrium The point where a producer maximizes output for the given total outlay.

Production function An equation, table, or graph showing the (maximum) quantity of a commodity that can be produced per unit of time for each of a set of alternative inputs, when the best production techniques available are used.

Short run The time period when at least one factor of production or input is fixed.

Review Questions

1. When the TP falls, (*a*) the AP_{Labor} is zero, (*b*) the MP_{Labor} is zero, (*c*) the AP_{Labor} is negative, or (*d*) the AP_{Labor} is declining.

   Ans. (*d*) See Fig. 6-1.

2. When the AP_{Labor} is positive but declining, the MP_{Labor} could be (*a*) declining, (*b*) zero, (*c*) negative, or (*d*) any of the above.

   Ans. (*d*) See Fig. 6-1.

3. Stage II of production begins where the AP_{Labor} begins to decline. (*a*) Always, (*b*) never, (*c*) sometimes, or (*d*) often.

   Ans. (*a*) See Example 4.

4. When the MP_{Land} is negative, we are in (*a*) stage I for land, (*b*) stage III for labor, (*c*) stage II for land, or (*d*) none of the above.

   Ans. (*d*) When the MP_{Land} is negative, we are in stage III for land and stage I for labor (see Section 6.3).

5. If, by increasing the quantity of labor used by one unit, the firm can give up 2 units of capital and still produce the same output, then the MRTS_{LK} is (*a*) $\frac{1}{2}$, (*b*) 2, (*c*) 1, or (*d*) 4.

   Ans. (*b*) See Section 6.5.

6. If the MRTS_{LK} equals 2, then the MP_K/MP_L is (*a*) 2, (*b*) 1, (*c*) $\frac{1}{2}$, or (*d*) 4.

   Ans. (*c*) See Section 6.5.

7. Within the relavant range, isoquants (*a*) are negatively sloped, (*b*) are convex to the origin, (*c*) cannot cross, or (*d*) are all of the above.

   Ans. (*d*) See Section 6.6.

8. If we plot capital on the vertical axis and labor on the horizontal axis, the slope of a straight-line isocost drawn on such a graph is (*a*) P_L/P_K, (*b*) P_K/P_L, (*c*) $-P_L/P_K$, or (*d*) $-P_K/P_L$.

   Ans. (*c*) See Section 6.7.

9. At the point of producer equilibrium, (*a*) the isoquant is tangent to the isocost, (*b*) the MRTS_{LK} equals P_L/P_K, (*c*) $\text{MP}_L/P_L = \text{MP}_K/P_K$, or (*d*) all of the above.

   Ans. (*d*) See Section 6.8.

10. The expansion path of production theory is analogous in consumption theory to the (*a*) price-consumption line, (*b*) Engle curve, (*c*) income-consumption line, or (*d*) budget constraint line.

    Ans. (*c*) Compare Fig. 6-7 in this chapter to Fig. 4-6 in Chapter 4.

11. The elasticity of technical substitution is measured by (*a*) the slope of the isoquant, (*b*) the change in the slope of the isoquant, (*c*) the ratio of factor inputs, or (*d*) none of the above.

    Ans. (*d*) The MRTS_{LK}, the change in the MRTS_{LK}, the K/L ratio, and the change in the K/L ratio are all components of the coefficient of elasticity of technical substitution but cannot individually give us that coefficient. (Two exceptions to this are discussed in Problem 6.23.)

12. If we have constant returns to scale and we increase the quantity of labor used per unit of time by 10% but keep the amount of capital constant, output will (*a*) increase by 10%, (*b*) decrease by 10%, (*c*) increase by more than 10%, or (*d*) increase by less than 10%.

    Ans. (*d*) Under constant returns to scale, if we increase both labor and capital by 10%, output will also increase by 10%. Since we are increasing only labor by 10%, output will increase by less than 10% (if we are operating *within* stage II of production).

Solved Problems

PRODUCTION WITH ONE VARIABLE INPUT

6.1 From Table 6.4, (*a*) find the AP and the MP of labor and (*b*) plot the TP, and the AP and MP of labor curves.

Table 6.4

Land	1	1	1	1	1	1	1	1	1	1
Labor	0	1	2	3	4	5	6	7	8	9
TP	0	2	5	9	12	14	15	15	14	12

(*a*)

Table 6.5

Land	Labor	TP	AP_L	MP_L
1	0	0	0	...
1	1	2	2	2
1	2	5	$2\frac{1}{2}$	3
1	3	9	3	4
1	4	12	3	3
1	5	14	$2\frac{4}{5}$	2
1	6	15	$2\frac{1}{2}$	1
1	7	15	$2\frac{1}{7}$	0
1	8	14	$1\frac{3}{4}$	−1
1	9	12	$1\frac{1}{3}$	−2

Note that the numbers in this table refer to *physical quantities* rather than monetary values.

(*b*)

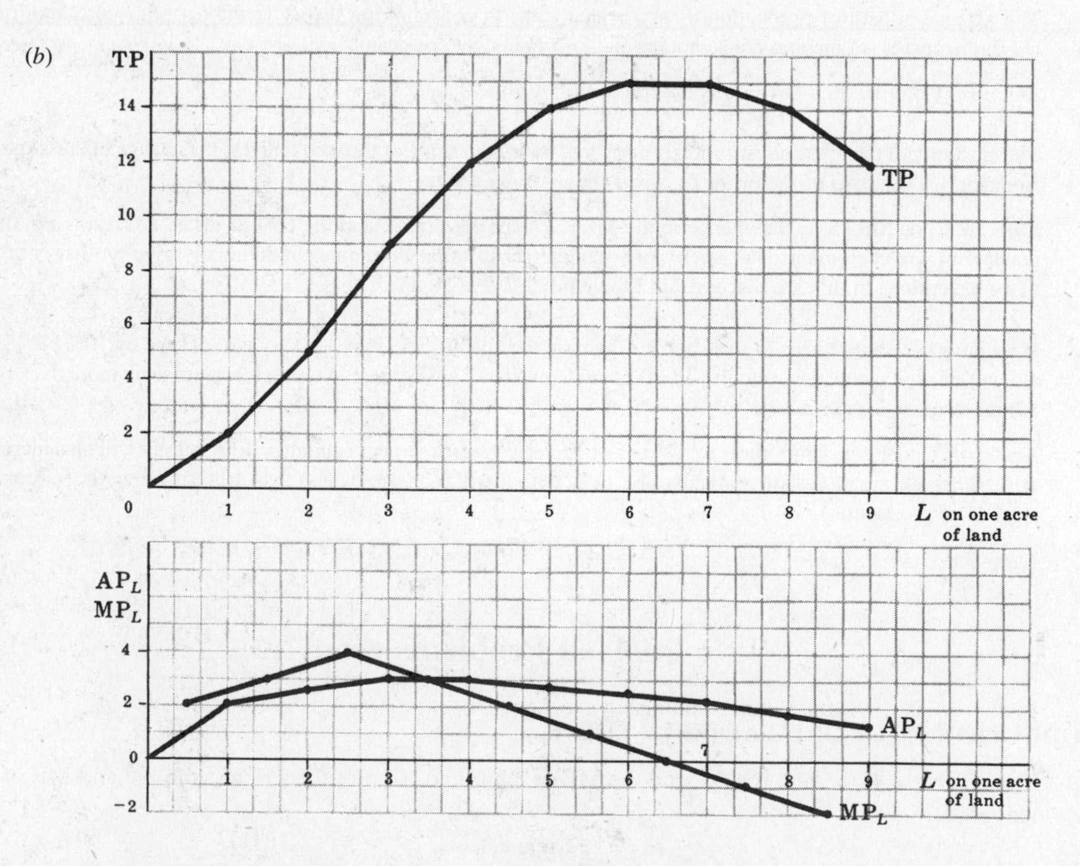

Fig. 6-8

6.2 (*a*) On the same set of axes, draw the TP, AP_L, and MP_L curves of Problem 6.1 as *smooth curves* (*b*) Explain the shape of the AP_L and MP_L curves in part (*a*) in terms of the shape of the TP curve.

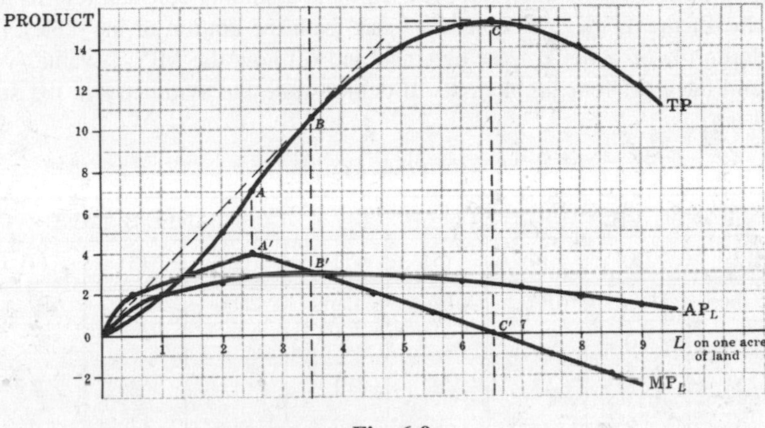

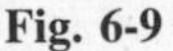

Fig. 6-9

(*a*) See Fig. 6-9. These smooth curves are the typical textbook TP, AP, and MP curves and are based on the assumption that inputs are perfectly divisible.

(*b*) The slope of a line from the origin to a point on the TP curve rises up to point *B* and declines afterward. Thus, the AP_L curve rises up to point B' and declines thereafter. Starting from the origin, the slope of the TP curve (the MP_L) rises up to point *A* (the point of inflection), then declines but remains positive up to point *C*. At point *C* (the maximum point of the TP curve), the slope of the TP curve (the MP_L) is zero. Past point *C*, the slope of the TP curve (the MP_L) is negative. At point *B*, the slope of the TP curve (the MP_L) is equal to the slope of a line from the origin to the TP curve (the AP_L).

6.3 (*a*) In terms of "labor" and "land," what does the law of diminishing returns state?
(*b*) Determine where the law of diminishing returns starts operating in Fig. 6-9.

(*a*) As more units of labor per unit of time are used to cultivate a fixed amount of land, after a point the MP_L will *necessarily* decline. This is one of the most important laws of economics and is referred to as *the law of diminishing returns.* Note that to observe the law of diminishing returns, one input (either land or labor) must be kept fixed while the other input is varied. Technology is also assumed to remain constant.

(*b*) The law of diminishing returns begins to operate at point A' in Fig. 6-9, where the MP_L starts declining. To the left of point A', labor is used too sparsely on one acre of land, and so we get increasing rather than diminishing returns to labor (the variable factor). (Do not confuse "increasing returns," which is a short-run concept, with "increasing returns to *scale*," which is a long-run concept.)

6.4 Define the three stages of production for labor shown in Fig. 6-9.

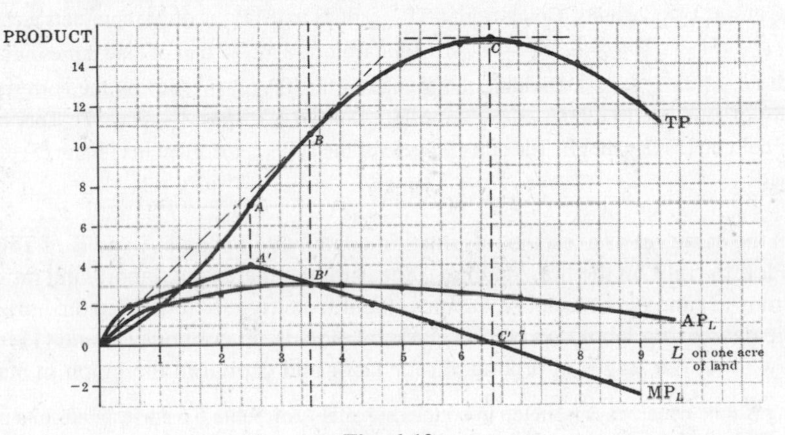

Fig. 6-10

6.5 Panel A of Table 6.6 is the same as Table 6.1. The TP_{Land} (column 3 in panel B of this table) is derived directly from panel A, by keeping labor fixed at one unit per time period and using alternative quantities of land, ranging from 1/8 of a unit (acre) to 1 unit and assuming constant returns to scale. Explain (*a*) how each value of the TP_{Land} was obtained (start from the bottom of the table), (*b*) how the AP_{Land} values in column (4) of panel B were obtained and (*c*) how the MP_{Land} values were obtained. (The aim of this and the next four problems is to demonstrate the symmetry in the stages of production for labor and land.)

Table 6.6

PANEL A: LABOR					PANEL B: LAND				
(1)	(2)	(3)	(4)	(5)	(1)	(2)	(3)	(4)	(5)
Land	Labor	TP_{Labor}	AP_{Labor}	MP_{Labor}	Land	Labor	TP_{Land}	AP_{Land}	MP_{Land}
1	0	0	0	...					
1	1	3	3	3	1	1	3	3	...
1	2	8	4	5	$\frac{1}{2}$	1	4	8	−2
1	3	12	4	4	$\frac{1}{3}$	1	4	12	0
1	4	15	$3\frac{3}{4}$	3	$\frac{1}{4}$	1	$3\frac{3}{4}$	15	3
1	5	17	$3\frac{2}{5}$	2	$\frac{1}{5}$	1	$3\frac{2}{5}$	17	7
1	6	17	$2\frac{5}{6}$	0	$\frac{1}{6}$	1	$2\frac{5}{6}$	17	17
1	7	16	$2\frac{2}{7}$	−1	$\frac{1}{7}$	1	$2\frac{2}{7}$	16	23
1	8	13	$1\frac{5}{8}$	−3	$\frac{1}{8}$	1	$1\frac{5}{8}$	13	37

(*a*) Starting from the bottom of panel A, we see that 8 units of labor on 1 unit of land produces 13 units of output; therefore, using 1/8 of the quantity of labor and land should result in 1/8 of 13 units of output, because of constant returns to scale. Thus, 1 unit of labor used on 1/8 unit of land produces 1/8 of 13 or 1 5/8 units of output [see the last row of column (3) in panel B]. The other figures of column (3) in panel B are obtained by following the same procedure. *Note that the* TP_{Land} *[column (3) in panel B] is identical with the* AP_{Labor} *[column (4) in panel A]*.

(*b*) From the TP_{Land} we can derive the AP_{Land} and the MP_{Land}. The AP_{Land} schedule [column (4)] is obtained by dividing the TP_{Land} [column (3)] by the corresponding quantities of land used [column (1)]. Starting at the bottom of panel B, we divide the TP_{Land} of $1\frac{5}{8}$ by $\frac{1}{8}$ unit of land to obtain 13 as the corresponding AP_{Land} ($1\frac{5}{8} \div \frac{1}{8} = \frac{13}{8} \div \frac{1}{8} = \frac{13}{8} \cdot \frac{8}{1} = 13$). The other figures for the AP_{Land} are obtained in a similar fashion. *Note that the* AP_{Land} *[column (4) in panel B] is identical with the* TP_{Labor} *[column (3) in panel A]*.

(*c*) The MP_{Land} is given by the *change* in the TP_{Land} divided by the *change* in the quantity of land used. Starting at the bottom of panel B, we see that when we change the amount of land used from $\frac{1}{8}$ unit to $\frac{1}{7}$ unit, the TP_{Land} changes from $1\frac{5}{8}$ to $2\frac{2}{7}$ units. Going from a TP_{Land} of $1\frac{5}{8}$ to a TP_{Land} of $2\frac{2}{7}$ represents a change of 37/56 unit of output ($2\frac{2}{7} - 1\frac{5}{8} = \frac{16}{7} - \frac{13}{8} = \frac{128-91}{56} = \frac{37}{56}$). Going from 1/8 to 1/7 unit of land represents a change of 1/56 unit of land ($\frac{1}{7} - \frac{1}{8} = \frac{8-7}{56} = \frac{1}{56}$). Dividing the change in the TP_{Land} (37/56) by the corresponding change in the quantity of land used (1/56), we get the MP_{Land} of 37($\frac{37}{56} \div \frac{1}{56} = \frac{37}{56} \cdot \frac{56}{1} = 37$). This is recorded in the *last* row of column (5) in panel B. The other figures for the MP_{Land} recorded in column (5) of panel B are similarly obtained.

6.6 (*a*) Plot, on the same set of axes, the information contained in panels A and B of Table 6.6. Let a movement from left to right on the horizontal axis measure the increasing labor/land ratios given by moving down columns (2) and (1) in panel A; the movement from right to left along the horizontal axis will then measure the decreasing labor/land ratios given by *moving* up columns (2) and (1) in panel B. (*b*) What can you say about the stages of production for labor and capital in the graph in part (*a*)?

(*a*) Moving (in the usual way) from top to bottom in panel A of Table 6.6 corresponds to a movement from left to right in Fig. 6-11, and we get the familiar TP_{Labor}, the AP_{Labor}, and the MP_{Labor} (as in Fig. 6-2). On the other hand, a movement from *bottom* to *top* in panel B of Table 6.6 corresponds to a movement from *right* to *left* in Fig. 6-11, and we get the TP_{Land}, the AP_{Land}, and the MP_{Land}. This movement from right to left along the horizontal axis of the figure refers to a *decline* in the labor/land ratio (i.e., from 8/1 to 7/1, 6/1, ..., 1/1). This is the same thing as an *increase* in the land/labor ratio (i.e., 1/8 to 1/7, 1/6, ..., 1/1). The arrows in the figure represent the direction of movements.

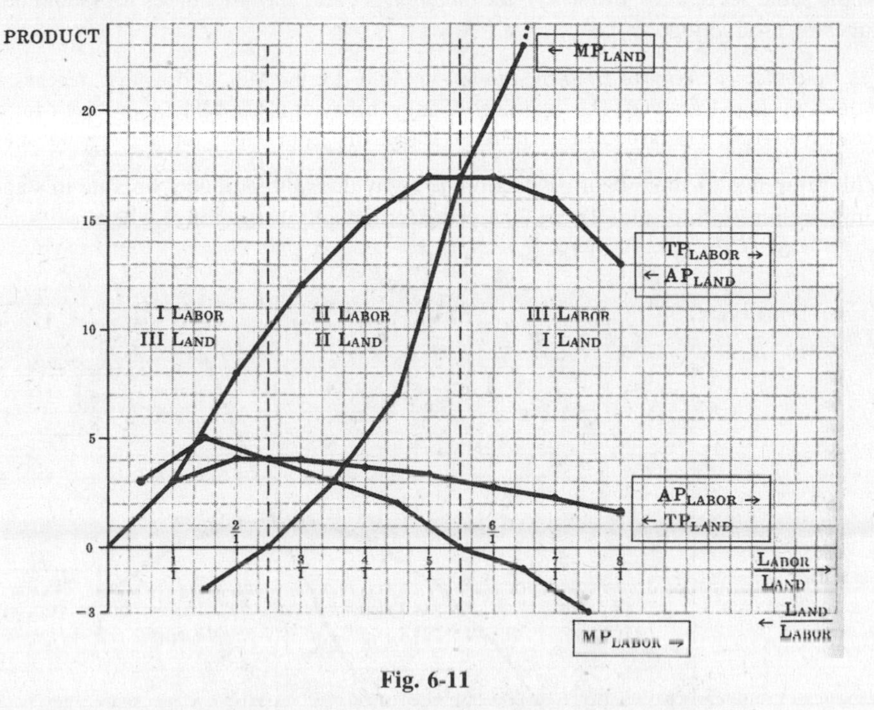

Fig. 6-11

(*b*) From Fig. 6-11, we see that the TP_{Land}, coincides precisely with the AP_{Labor} and the AP_{Land} coincides with the TP_{Labor}. Because of this, stage I for labor corresponds to stage III for land, stage II for labor covers the same range as stage II for land, and stage III for labor corresponds to stage I for land. *Thus there is perfect symmetry between the stages of production for labor and land under constant returns to scale.*

6.7 Assuming (1) constant returns to scale, (2) labor constant at one unit per time period, and (3) alternative quantities of land used, ranging from 1/9 to 1 acre of land per time period, (*a*) find the TP of land from Table 6.4; from this TP_{Land} find the AP and the MP of land. (*b*) Plot on the same set of axes (as in Problem 6.6) the TP_{Labor}, the AP_{Labor}, and the MP_{Labor} of Problem 6.1, and the TP_{Land}, the AP_{Land}, and the MP_{Land} found in part (*a*) of this problem, and define stages of production I, II, and III for labor and land.

(*a*) The values of the TP, the AP, and the MP of land are obtained as explained in Problem 6.5.

Table 6.7

Land	Labor	TP_{Land}	AP_{Land}	MP_{Land}
1	1	2	2	...
$\frac{1}{2}$	1	$2\frac{1}{2}$	5	−1
$\frac{1}{3}$	1	3	9	−3
$\frac{1}{4}$	1	3	12	0
$\frac{1}{5}$	1	$2\frac{4}{5}$	14	4
$\frac{1}{6}$	1	$2\frac{1}{2}$	15	9
$\frac{1}{7}$	1	$2\frac{1}{7}$	15	15
$\frac{1}{8}$	1	$1\frac{3}{4}$	14	22
$\frac{1}{9}$	1	$1\frac{1}{3}$	12	30

(*b*) (See Fig. 6-12).

Remember that for the relations shown in Fig. 6-12 to hold, the fixed factor must be unity and we must assume constant returns to scale.

6.8 On the same set of axes, draw "typical" *smooth* TP, AP, and MP curves for labor and land, and define the stages of production.

Note that as we move from right to left in Fig. 6-13, the MP_{Land} rises first, reaches a maximum, and then declines in stage I for land. This is analogous to the behavior of the MP_{Labor} in stage I for labor, for a movement from left to right. This aspect of the behavior of the MP_{Land} in stage I for land was not shown in Fig. 6-12.

6.9 With reference to stage II of production, (*a*) why does the producer operate in stage II, (*b*) what factor combination (within stage II) will the producer actually use, and (*c*) where will the producer operate if $P_{Labor} = 0$? If $P_{Land} = 0$? If $P_{Labor} = P_{Land}$?

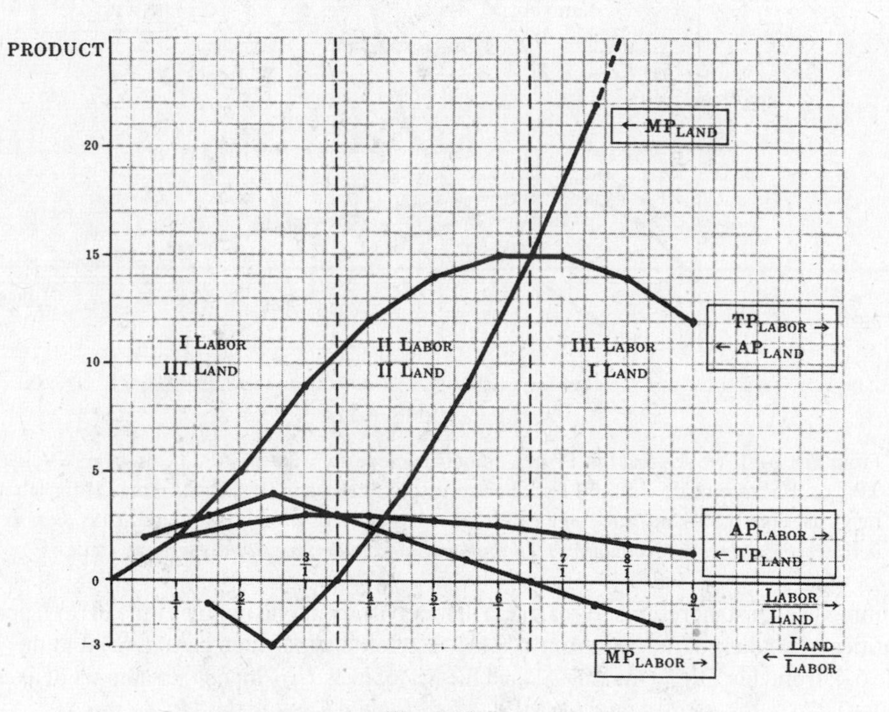

Fig. 6-12

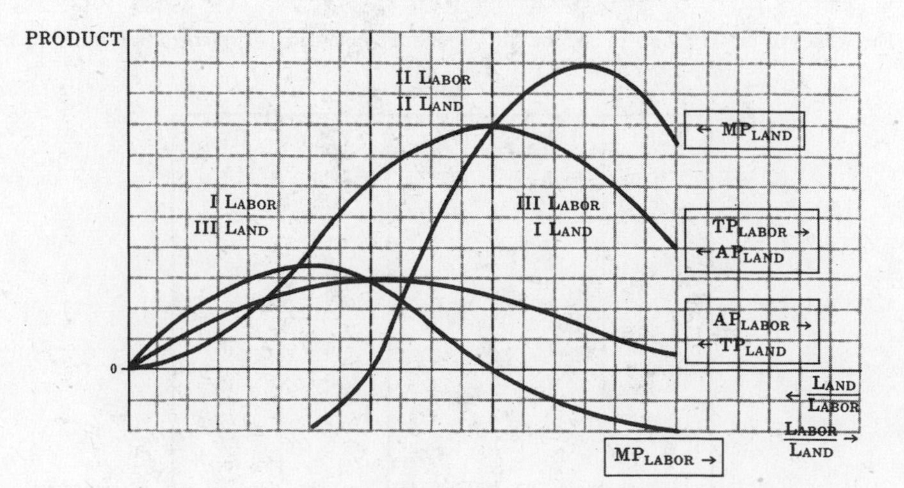

Fig. 6-13

(*a*) The producer will not operate in stage I for labor (=stage III for land) because the MP_{Land} is negative. The producer will not operate in stage III for labor because the MP_{Labor} is negative. The producer will produce in stage II because the MP of labor and land are both positive (even if declining).

(*b*) Within stage II, the producer will produce at the point where $MP_{Labor}/P_{Labor} = MP_{Land}/P_{Land}$.

(*c*) If $P_{Land} = 0$, the producer will want to produce at the point of greatest average efficiency for *labor*, and so he or she will produce at the beginning of stage II for labor (where the AP_{Labor} is maximum and the $MP_{Land} = 0$). If the $P_{Labor} = 0$, the producer will produce at the end of stage II for labor (where the $MP_{Labor} = 0$ and the AP_{Land} is maximum). If $P_{Labor} = P_{Land}$, the producer will produce at the point (within stage II) where the MP_{Labor} and the MP_{Land} curves intersect. The higher the price of labor in relation to the price of land, the closer to the beginning of stage II for labor will the producer operate. The higher the price of land in relation to the price of labor, the closer to the beginning of stage II for land (which is the end of stage II for labor) will the producer operate.

6.10 From Table 6.8, (*a*) find the AP and the MP of labor and (*b*) plot the TP, the AP, and the MP of labor, (*c*) How is the graph different from Fig. 6-12?

Table 6.8

Land	1	1	1	1	1
Labor	1	2	3	4	5
TP_{Labor}	10	18	24	28	30

(*a*)

Table 6.9

Land	Labor	TP_{Labor}	AP_{Labor}	MP_{Labor}
1	1	10	10	...
1	2	18	9	8
1	3	24	8	6
1	4	28	7	4
1	5	30	6	2

(*b*)

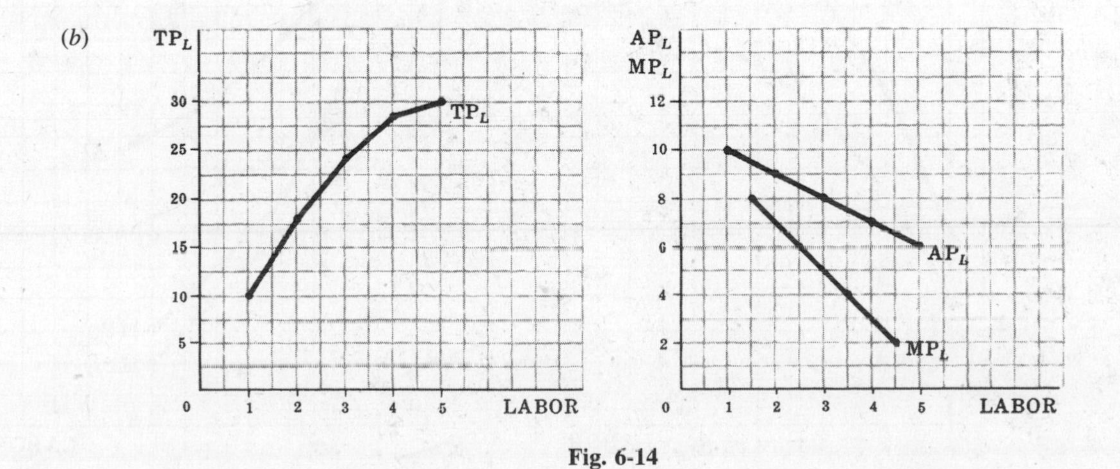

Fig. 6-14

(*c*) Fig. 6-14 shows only stage II. Stages I and III are missing. This may sometimes occur in the real world and if often assumed in empirical work.

6.11 From Table 6.10, (*a*) find the AP and the MP of labor and (*b*) plot the TP, the AP, and the MP of labor, (*c*) Why is this graph different from Fig. 6-14?

Table 6.10

Land	2	2	2	2	2
Labor	1	2	3	4	5
TP_{Labor}	15	26	33	38	41

(*a*)

Table 6.11

Land	Labor	TP_{Labor}	AP_{Labor}	MP_{Labor}
2	1	15	15	...
2	2	26	13	11
2	3	33	11	7
2	4	38	9.5	5
2	5	41	8.2	3

(*b*) See Fig. 6-15. The dashed curves in Fig. 6-15 are the functions of Problem 6.10 and are reproduced here for ease of reference.

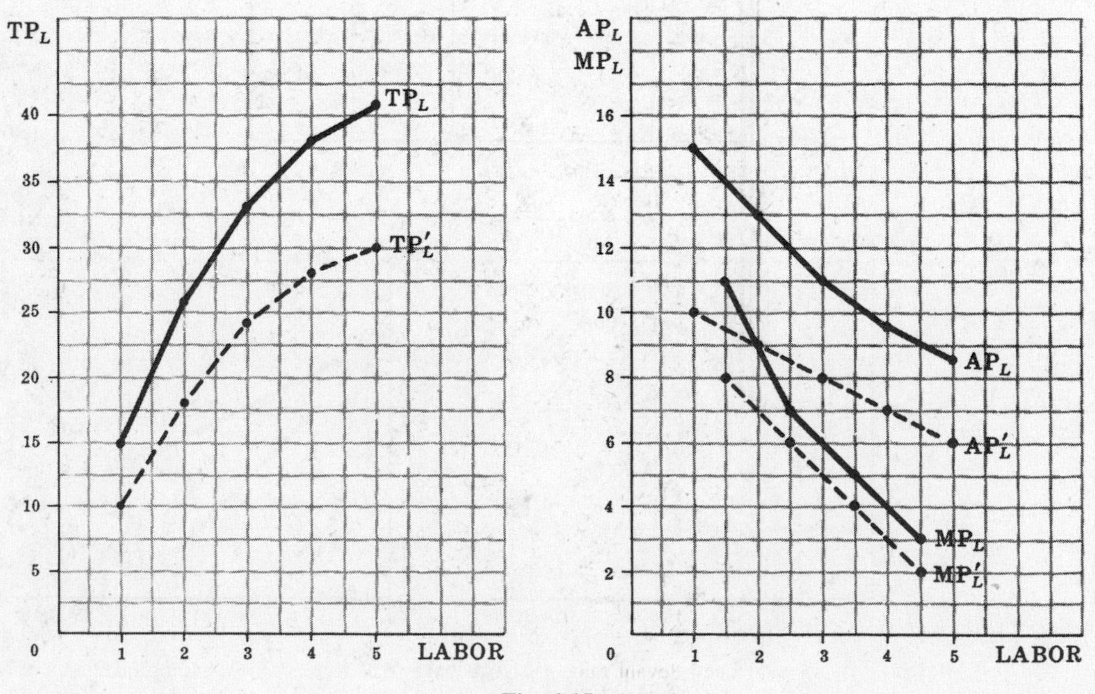

Fig. 6-15

(c) When the amount of land is kept fixed at 2 units rather than 1 unit, all the curves shift up (the solid curves as compared to the corresponding dashed ones). This is generally the case (in stage II) and results because each unit of the variable factor has more of the fixed factor to work with. Note that the horizontal axes in Fig. 6-15 refer to the number of units of labor used per unit of time on 2 units of land for the solid lines and on 1 unit of land for the dashed lines.

PRODUCTION WITH TWO VARIABLE INPUTS

6.12 Table 6.12 gives points on four different isoquants. (*a*) Find the $MRTS_{LK}$ between successive points within the relevant range of each isoquant. (*b*) Plot the four isoquants on the same set of axes and draw in the ridge lines.

Table 6.12

I		II		III		IV	
L	K	L	K	L	K	L	K
3	14	4	14	5.5	15	8	16
2	10	3	11	5	12	7	12.5
3	6	4	8	5.5	9	8	9
4	4.5	5	6.3	6	8.3	9	7
5	3.5	6	5	7	7	10	6.4
6	3	7	4.4	8	6	11	7
7	2.7	8	4	9	5.6		
8	3	9	4.4	10	6		

(*a*)

Table 6.13

I			II			III			IV		
L	K	$MRTS_{LK}$	L	K	$MRTS_{LK}$	L	K	$MRTS_{LK}$	L	K	$MRTS_{LK}$
3	14		4	14		5.5	15		8	16	
2	10		3	11		5	12		7	12.5	
3	6	4.0	4	8	3.0	5.5	9	6.0	8	9	3.5
4	4.5	1.5	5	6.3	1.7	6	8.3	1.4	9	7	2.0
5	3.5	1.0	6	5	1.3	7	7	1.3	10	6.4	0.6
6	3	0.5	7	4.4	0.6	8	6	1.0	11	7	
7	2.7	0.3	8	4	0.4	9	5.6	0.4			
8	3		9	4.4		10	6				

The $MRTS_{LK} = -\Delta K/\Delta L$. The relevant range of isoquants is that where corresponding quantities of labor and capital move in opposite directions. These correspond to the negatively sloped portions of isoquants.

(*b*)

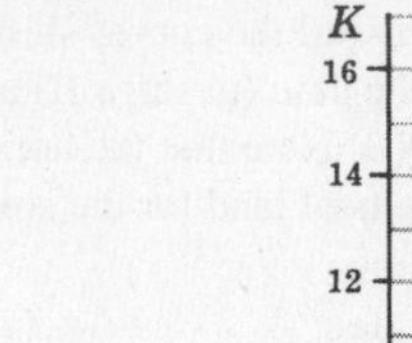
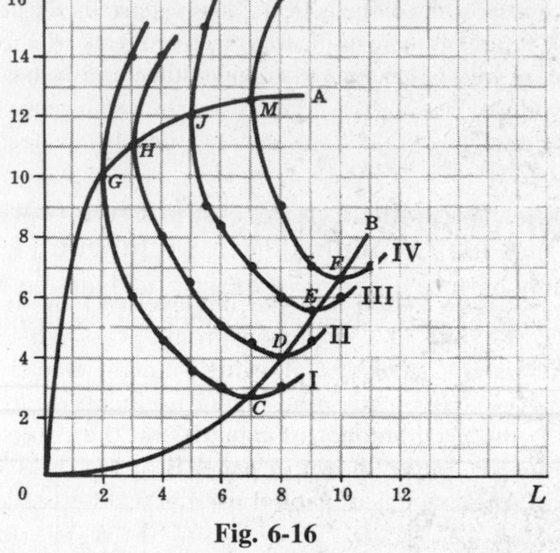

Fig. 6-16

Ridge lines separate the positively from the negatively sloped portions of isoquants. As we move down an isoquant (within the ridge lines), the $MRTS_{LK}$ diminishes. This diminishing $MRTS_{LK}$ is reflected in the isoquant being convex to the origin. If labor and capital are the only two factors, a movement down an isoquant refers to the long run. The actual length of time involved in the long run varies from industry to industry. In some industries, it is a few months; in others, it may be several years. It all depends on how long it takes for the firm to vary *all* of its inputs.

6.13 Explain (*a*) why to the right of ridge line *OB* in Fig. 6-16 we have stage III for labor and (*b*) why above ridge line *OA* in this figure we have stage III for capital.

(*a*) Ridge line *OB* joins points *C*, *D*, *E*, and *F* at which isoquants I, II, III, and IV have zero slope (and thus zero $MRTS_{LK}$). To the left of *OB*, the isoquants are negatively sloped. To the right of *OB*, the isoquants are positively sloped. This means that starting from point *C* on isoquant I, if the firm used more labor, it would also have to use more capital in order to remain on isoquant I. If it used more labor with the same amount of capital, the level of output would fall. The same is true at points *D*, *E*, and *F*. Therefore, the MP_L must be negative to the right of ridge line *OB*. This corresponds to stage III for labor. (Note that the quantities of capital indicated by points *C*, *D*, *E*, and *F* are the minimum amounts of capital to produce the output indicated by isoquants I, II, III, and IV. Also, at points *C*, *D*, *E*, and *F*, the $MRTS_{LK} = MP_L/MP_K = 0/MP_K = 0$.)

(*b*) Ridge line *OA* joins *G*, *H*, *J*, and *M* at which isoquants I, II, III, and IV have infinite slope (and thus infinite $MRTS_{LK}$). Above ridge line *OA*, the isoquants are positively sloped. Thus, starting at point *G* on isoquant I, if the firm used more capital, it would also have to use more labor in order to remain on isoquant I. If it used more capital with the same amount of labor, the level of output would fall. The same is true at points *H*, *J*, and *M*. Therefore, the MP_K must be negative above ridge line *OA*. This corresponds to stage III for capital. (Note that the quantities of labor indicated by points *G*, *H*, *J*, and *M* are the minimum amounts of labor to produce the output indicated by isoquants I, II, III, and IV. Also, at points *G*, *H*, *J*, and *M*, the $MRTS_{LK} = MP_L/MP_K = MP_L/0 =$ infinity.)

6.14 (*a*) Assuming that Fig. 6-16 shows constant returns to scale, define stages of production I, II, and III for labor and capital. (*b*) Explain why a movement down an isoquant (within the ridge lines) implies that the MP_L is declining.

(*a*) We saw in Problem 6.13(*b*) that above ridge line *OA* we have stage III for capital. With constant returns to scale, stage III for capital corresponds lo stage I for labor. To the right of ridge line *OB*, we have stage III for labor [see Problem 6.13(*a*)]. This corresponds to stage I for capital. Then the range of the isoquants within the ridge lines *OA* and *OB* corresponds to stage II for labor and capital.

(*b*) A movement down an isoquant (within the ridge lines) corresponds *both* to a downward *movement along* a MP_L curve (since we are in stage II, and we are increasing the amount of labor used) *and* to a downward *shift* in the MP_L curve (since we are reducing the amount of capital used with each quantity of labor employed). Thus as we move down an isoquant (within the ridge lines), the value of the MP_L falls for both reasons. We could use the same reasoning to explain why a movement *up* an isoquant (within the ridge lines) implies that the MP_K is declining.

6.15 Explain how, from an isoquant map, we can derive (*a*) the TP_L and (*b*) the TP_K. (*c*) What type of isoquant map is implied by a TP function like the one in Problem 6.10?

(*a*) Fixing the amount of capital used at a specific level ($\bar{K}$) and increasing the amount of labor used per unit of time corresponds to a movement from left to right along the line parallel to and above the horizontal axis in panel A of the following isoquant map (Fig. 6-17). As we move from left to right along this line, we cross higher and higher isoquants up to a point. By recording the quantity of labor used (with the fixed amount of capital) and the corresponding quantities of total output, we can generate the TP_L curve shown in panel B of Fig. 6-17. This brings us back to a short-run analysis. If we fixed the amount of capital used at a different level, we would get a different TP_L curve.

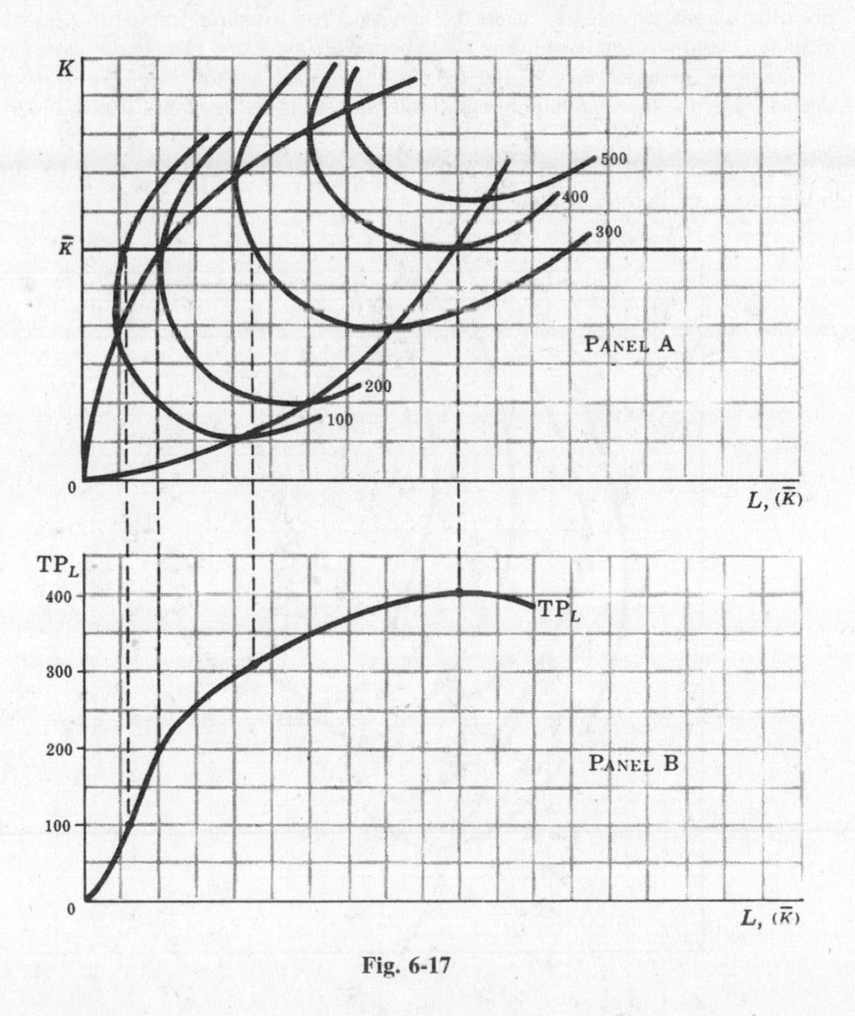

Fig. 6-17

(*b*) We could similarly derive the TP_K curve by drawing a vertical line at which the amount of labor is fixed, changing the amount of capital used per unit of time, and recording the output levels.

(*c*) A TP curve like the one in Problem 6.10 implies an isoquant map in which isoquants are defined only for their negatively sloped range.

6.16 Suppose that $P_K = \$1$, $P_L = \$2$, and TO = \$16. (*a*) What is the slope of the isocost? (*b*) Write the equation for the isocost. (*c*) What do we means by P_L? P_K?

(*a*) If we plot labor along the horizontal axis and capital along the vertical axis, the slope of the isocost is equal to $-P_L/P_K = -2$.

(*b*) The equation of the straight-line isocost is given by

$$\text{TO} = P_K K + P_L L \quad \text{or} \quad \$16 = K + 2L$$

where L and K stand for the quantity of labor and capital, respectively. Solving for K, we get

$$K = \frac{\text{TO}}{P_K} - \frac{P_L}{P_K} L \quad \text{or} \quad K = 16 - 2L$$

This means that the firm can buy $0L$ and $16K$, or $1L$ and $14K$, or $2L$ and $12K$, or ... $8L$ and $0K$. For each two units of capital the firm gives up, it can purchase one additional unit of labor. Thus, the rate of substitution of L for *K in the marketplace* is 2 (the absolute slope of the isocost) and remains constant.

(*c*) P_L refers to the *wage* that the firm must pay in order to *hire* labor or to purchase *labor time* for a specific period of time. It can be expressed in dollars per labor-hour, dollars per worker-year, etc. Roughly speaking, P_K is given by the market rate of interest the firm must pay to borrow capital (for investmment purposes). For example, the firm might have to pay 8% to borrow \$100 for one year. In this case, $P_K = \$8$. In our analysis, we implicitly assumed that P_L and P_K remain constant, regardless of the quantity of labor and capital demanded by the firm per unit of time. (Factor pricing is discussed in Chapter 13.)

6.17 Using the isoquants of Problem 6.12 and the isocost defined in Problem 6.16, determine the point at which the producer is in equilibrium.

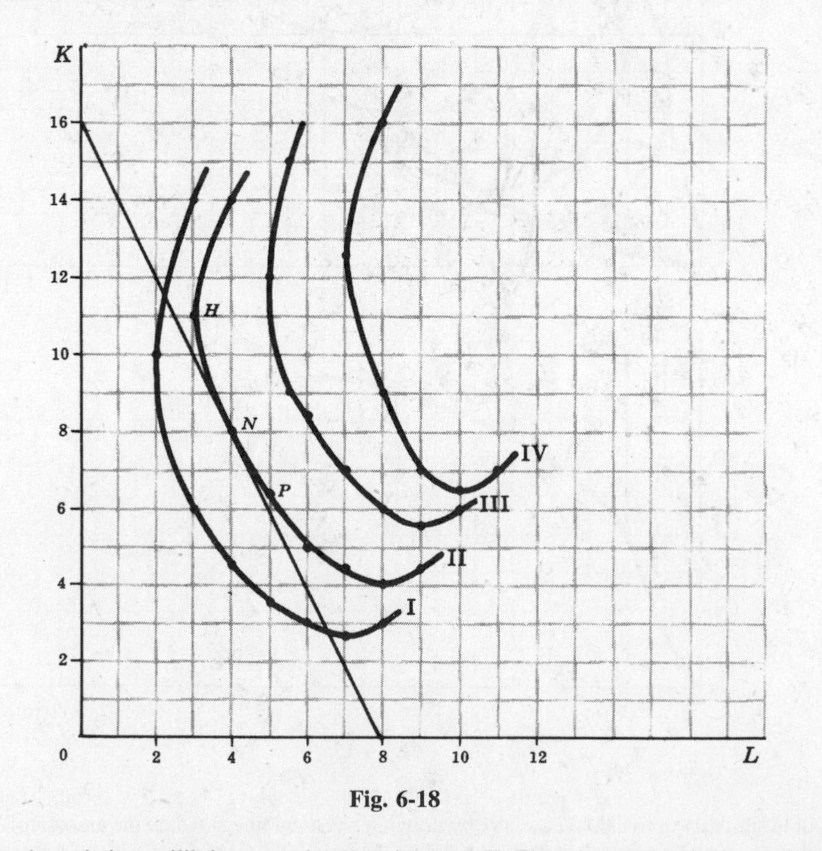

Fig. 6-18

The producer is in equilibrium at point N on isoquant II. Thus, in order to be in equilibrium, the producer should spend \$8 of its TO to purchase $8K$ and the remaining \$8 to purchase $4L$. At equilibrium, $\text{MRTS}_{LK} = \text{MP}_L/\text{MP}_K = P_L/P_K = 2$. At point H, the MRTS_{LK} exceeds the rate at which labor can be substituted for capital *in the market.* Therefore, it pays for the firm to substitute labor for capital until it reaches point *N*. The opposite is true at point *P*.

As an alternative to maximizing output for a given TO, the firm might want to minimize the cost of producing a specified level of output. This corresponds to finding the lowest isocost (TO) necessary to reach the specified isoquant (level of output).

6.18 Assume that (1) the firm has isoquants I, II, and III of Problem 6.12, (2) P_K and P_L are \$1 and \$2, respectively, and they remain constant, and (3) the TO of the firm rises from \$12 to \$16 and then to \$20 per time period. Derive the firm's expansion path.

With isocost 1, the producer is in equilibrium at point *R* on isoquant I; with isocost 2, the producer is in equilibrium at point *N* on isoquant II; with isocost 3, the producer is in equilibrium at point *S* on isoquant III. The line joining equilibrium points *R*, *N*, and *S* is the expansion path of this firm. Notice that in this case as output rises, the slope of the expansion path (the $\Delta K/\Delta L$ ratio) falls. Isocosts 1, 2, and 3 are parallel because P_K and P_L remain constant. Since the absolute slope of all three isocosts is equal to 2, the MRTS_{LK} at equilibrium points *R*, *N*, and *S*, is also equal to 2. That is, at equilibrium points *R*, *N*, and *S*,

$$\text{MRTS}_{LK} = \text{MP}_L/\text{MP}_K = P_L/P_K = 2$$

Thus, expansion path *ORNS* is an isocline.

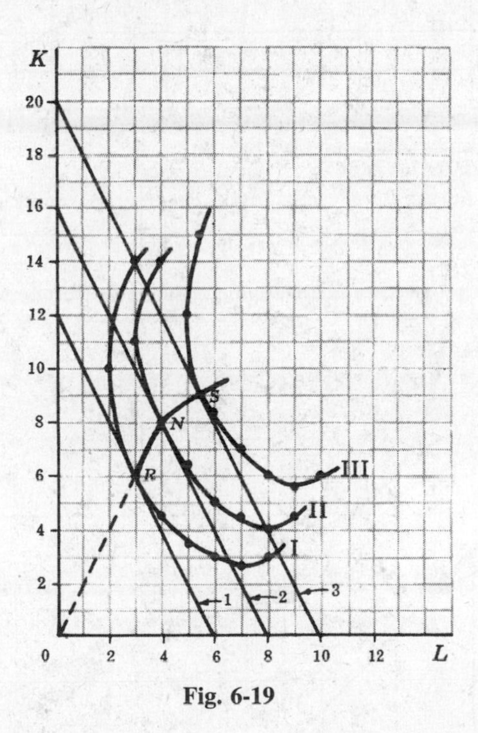

Fig. 6-19

FACTOR SUBSTITUTION

6.19 Starting from equilibrium position *M* in Fig. 6-6, find the new equilibrium point if P_L falls to \$0.50 (while P_K and TO remain unchanged at \$1 and \$10, respectively).

When P_L falls to \$0.50 (while P_K and TO remain unchanged) the isocost rotates counterclockwise from isocost 2 to isocost 4 (see Fig. 6-20). With this new isocost, the producer is in equilibrium at point *W* where isocost 4 is tangent to isoquant III. Thus when P_L falls from \$1 to \$0.50 (*ceteris paribus*), the quality of labor purchased by this producer increases from 5 to 9 units per time period. This total effect is the combined result of an *output effect* and a *substitution effect*. These are analogous to the income and substitution effects of demand theory (Chapter 4). The output effect results because when P_L falls, the producer could produce a greater output (isoquant III as opposed to isoquant II) with a given TO. This means that the producer could produce the output level indicated by isoquant II with a smaller TO, after P_L has fallen.

6.20 Separate the output effect from the total effect of the factor price change in Problem 6.19. What is the size of the substitution effect? What does this substitution effect measure?

We can separate the output effect from the total effect of the price change by shifting isocost 4 *down* and *parallel* to itself until it is tangent to isoquant II. What we get is isocost 4′. (The downward shift refers to a reduction in TO; the parallel shift is necessary so as to retain the *new* set of *relative* factor prices.)

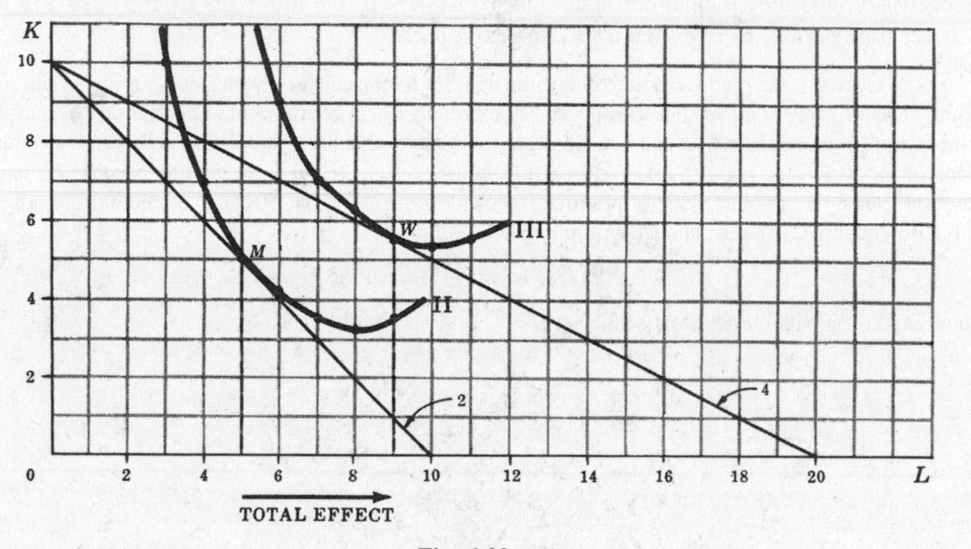

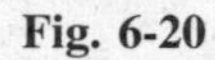
Fig. 6-20

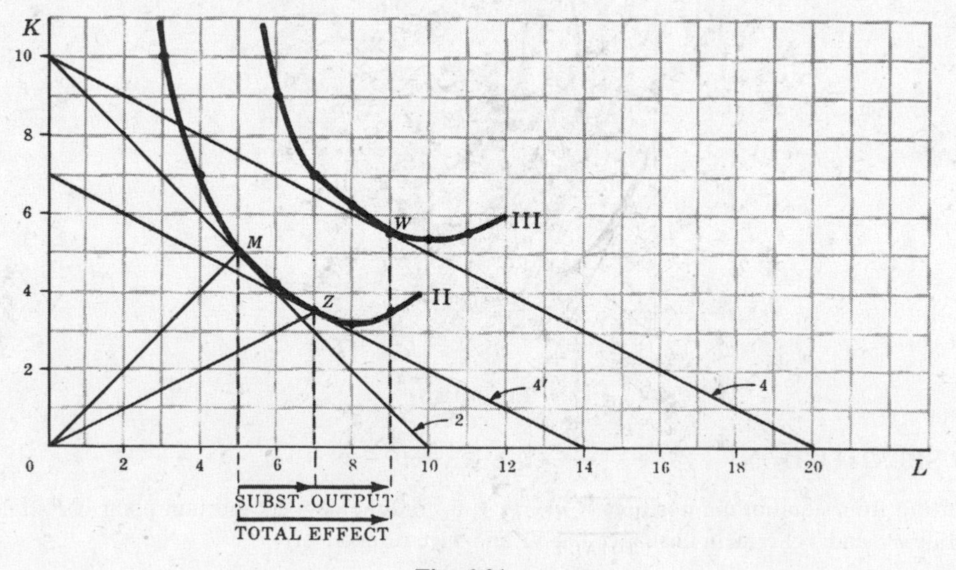

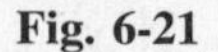
Fig. 6-21

Thus,

Total effect	=	Substitution effect	+	Output effect
MW	=	MZ	+	ZW

Note that the substitution effect is given by a movement along the same isoquant and measures the degree of substitutability of labor for capital in production, resulting exclusively from the change in relative factor prices.

6.21 Find the elasticity of substitution of L for K for the factor price change of Problems 6.19 and 6.20.

The degree of substitutability of L for K depends on the curvature of the isoquant and is measured by the coefficient of elasticity of technical substitutions. In Fig. 6-21, K/L at point M is 1 (the slope of ray OM), and K/L at point Z is 0.5 (the slope of ray OZ). Thus, $\Delta(K/L)$ from M to Z is 0.5. The MRTS_{LK} at point M equals $10/10$ or 1 (the absolute slope of isocost 2). The MRTS_{LK} at point Z equals $3.5/7$ or 0.5 (the absolute slope of isocost 4′). Thus ΔMRTS_{LK} from M to Z is 0.5. Substituting these values into the formula for the coefficient of elasticity of technical substitution, we get

$$(e\text{ subt.})_{LK} = \frac{\Delta\left(\dfrac{K}{L}\right) \Big/ \left(\dfrac{K}{L}\right)}{\Delta(\text{MRTS}_{LK})/\text{MRTS}_{LK}} = \frac{0.5/1}{0.5/1} = 1$$

6.22 If, starting from the equilibrium position of Problem 6.17, P_L falls to \$1 while P_K and TO remain unchanged, (*a*) separate geometrically the output effect from the substitution effect resulting from the change in P_L and (*b*) find the coefficient of elasticity of technical substitution for the change in P_L.

(*a*)

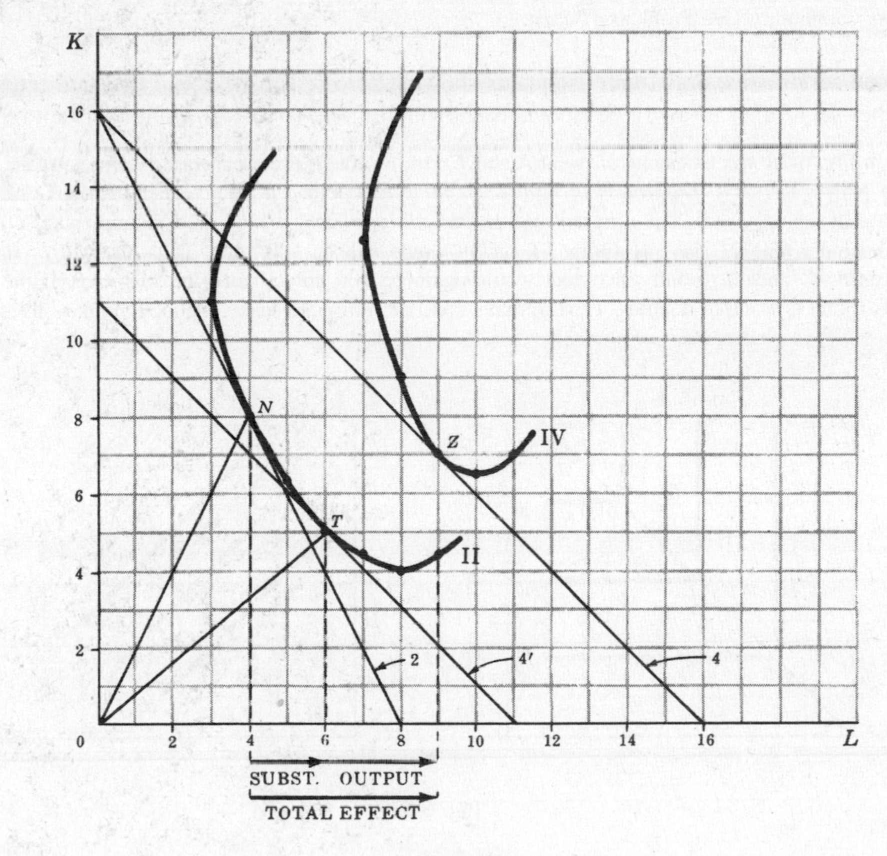

Fig. 6-22

When P_L falls from \$2 to \$1, we move from equilibrium point N on isocost 2 and isoquant II to equilibrium point Z on isocost 4 and isoquant IV. This firm would produce the *old* output level (i.e., the output level indicated by isoquant II) at the *new* input prices (the slope of isocost 4) with \$5 less of TO. This gives the new equilibrium point T on isoquant II and isocost 4′. Thus,

$$\begin{array}{ccccc}\text{Total effect} & = & \text{Substitution effect} & + & \text{Output effect} \\ NZ & = & NT & + & TZ\end{array}$$

(b) The movement along isoquant II from N to T is the substitution effect and results exclusively from the change in relative factor prices. Thus, as P_L falls in relation to P_K, the firm substitutes 2 units of labor for 3 units of capital to produce the same level of output. Substituting the values from this problem into the formula, we get the coefficient of elasticity of substitution of labor for capital between points N and T, as follows:

$$(e\,\text{subt.})_{LK} = \frac{\Delta\left(\frac{K}{L}\right) \Big/ \left(\frac{K}{L}\right)}{\frac{\Delta(MRTS_{LK})}{MRTS_{LK}}} = \frac{\left(\frac{7}{6}\right) \Big/ \left(\frac{2}{1}\right)}{\left(\frac{1}{2}\right)} = \frac{\left(\frac{7}{12}\right)}{\left(\frac{1}{2}\right)} = \frac{7}{6} \cong 1.17$$

To separate the substitution from the output effect for an *increase* in the price of a factor, we proceed in a manner analogous to that followed to separate the substitution from the income effect of a rise in the price of a commodity [see Problem 4.34(*a*)].

6.23 On one set of axes, draw three isoquants showing zero $(e\text{ subst.})_{LK}$ and constant returns to scale. On another set of axes, draw three isoquants showing infinite $(e\text{ subst.})_{LK}$ and constant returns to scale.

In Fig. 6-23, the isoquants of panel A show zero $(e\text{ subst.})_{LK}$ and constant returns to scale. Production takes place with a $K/L = 1$, *regardless of relative factor prices*. Thus, if relative factor prices change, $\Delta(K/L) = 0$, and the $(e\text{ subst.})_{LK} = 0$. The firm will use $2K$ and $2L$ to produce 100 units of output (point D). If the firm used $2K$ and more than $2L$, say, $4L$ (point F), output would still be 100 units. Thus, the $MP_L = 0$. Similarly, if the firm used $4K$ and $2L$ (point E), output would again be 100 units. Thus, the $MP_k = 0$. If the firm doubles all inputs (point G), output doubles. Thus we have constant returns to scale. Production takes place along ray OC.

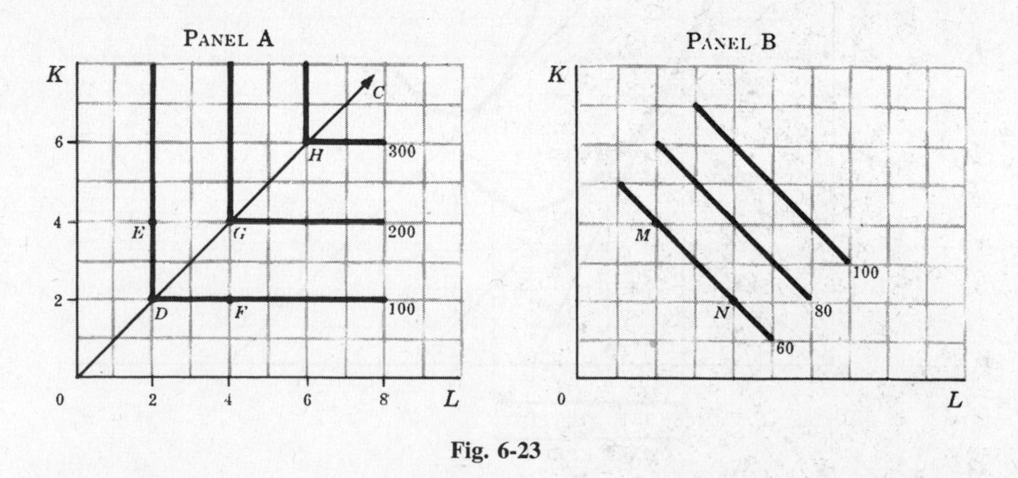

Fig. 6-23

The isoquants of panel B show infinite $(e\text{ subst.})_{LK}$ and constant returns to scale. Since the slope of the isoquants $(MRTS_{LK})$ remains unchanged, $\Delta MRTS_{LK} = 0$ and $(e\text{ subst.})_{LK} = \infty$. In addition, since output increases proportionately to the increase in both inputs, we have constant returns to scale.

The usual isoquane is convex to the origin and has an $(e\text{ subst.})_{LK}$ between zero and infinity (depending on the location and the curvature of the isoquant). In drawing continuous isoquants which are convex to the origin, we are implicitly assuming that inputs are available in continuously variable quantities.

RETURNS TO SCALE

6.24 Explain what is meant by (*a*) constant returns to scale, (*b*) increasing returns to scale, and (*c*) decreasing returns to scale. Explain briefly how each of these might arise.

(*a*) *Constant returns to scale* means that if all factors of production are increased in a given proportion, the output produced would increase in exactly the *same* proportion. Thus, if the quantities of labor and capital used per unit of time are both increased by 10%, output increases by 10% also; if labor and capital are doubled, output doubles. This makes sense; if we use two workers of the same type and two identical machines, we normally expect twice as much output as with one worker with one machine. Similarly, if all inputs are *reduced* by a given proportion, output is *reduced* by the same proportion.

(*b*) *Increasing returns to scale* refers to the case when all factors are increased in a given proportion, output increases in a *greater* proportion. Thus if labor and capital are increased by 10%, output rises by more than 10%; if labor and captial are doubled, output more than doubles. Increasing returns to scale may occur because by increasing the scale of operation, greater division of labor and specialization becomes possible. That is, each worker can specialize in performing a simple repetitive task rather than many different tasks. As a result, labor productivity increases. In addition, a larger scale of operation may permit the use of more productive specialized machinery which was not feasible at a lower scale of operation.

(*c*) If output increases in a *smaller* proportion than the increase in all inputs there are *decreasing returns to scale.* This may result because as the scale of operation increases, communications difficulties may make it more and more difficult for the entrepreneur to run a business effectively. It is generally believed that at very small scales of operation, the firm faces increasing returns to scale. As the scale of operation rises, increasing returns to scale give way to constant returns to scale and eventually to decreasing returns to scale. Whether this is the case in a particular situation is an empirical question.

6.25 Which set of isoquants in Fig. 6-24 shows (*a*) constant returns to scale, (*b*) increasing returns to scale, and (*c*) decreasing returns to scale?

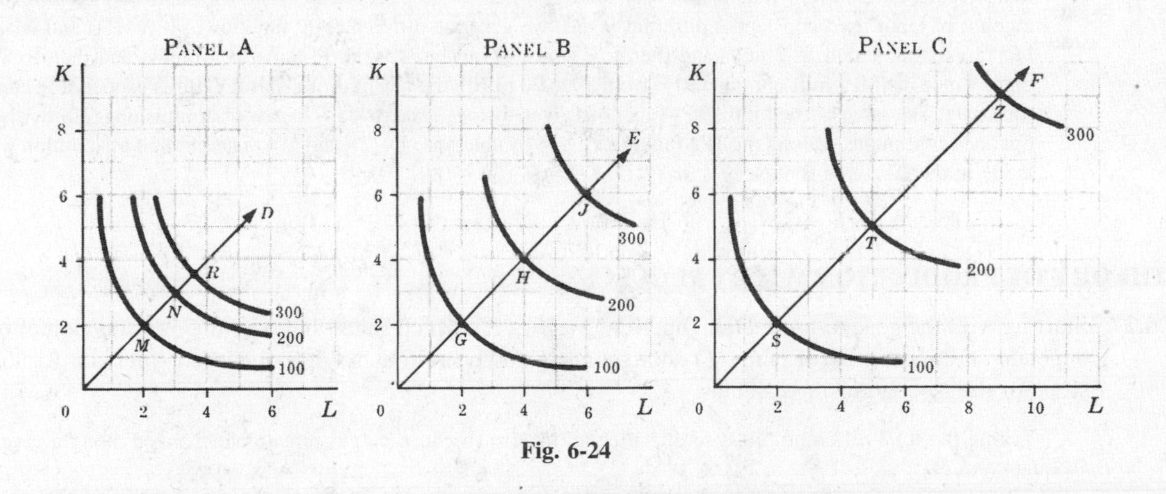

Fig. 6-24

(*a*) Panel B shows constant returns to scale. It shows that when we double both inputs, we double output; if we triple all inputs, we triple the level of output. Thus, $OG = GH = HJ$ (and similarly for any other ray from the origin). Note that output expands along ray OE (and the K/L ratio remains unchanged), *as long as relative factor prices remain unchanged.* (Compare panel B with panel A of Fig. 6-23, where the K/L ratio was *technologically* fixed.)

(*b*) The case of increasing returns to scale is shown in panel A, where an increase in both inputs in a given proportion causes a more than proportionate increase in output. Thus, $OM > MN > NR$. Once again, if relative factor prices remain unchanged, output expands along ray OD.

(*c*) Panel C shows decreasing returns to scale. Here, to double output per unit of time, the firm must more than double the quantity of both inputs used per unit of time. Thus, $OS < ST < TZ$.

6.26 With respect to the production function in Table 6.14, (*a*) indicate whether we have increasing, decreasing, or constant returns to scale. (*b*) Which of these points are on the same isoquant? (*c*) Is the law of diminishing returns operating?

(*a*) Table 6.14 indicates that $Q = f(L, K)$. This reads: The quantity of output produced per unit of time is a function of (depends on) the quantity of labor and capital used per time period. With $1L$ and $1K$, $Q = 50$; with $2L$ and $2K$, $Q = 100$; with $3L$ and $3K$, $Q = 150$. Thus we have constant returns to scale.

Table 6.14

$3K$	80	120	150
$2K$	70	100	120
$1K$	50	70	80
	$1L$	$2L$	$3L$

(*b*) The general equation for an isoquant is given by $Q = f(L, K)$ and refers to the different combinations of labor and capital needed to produce a *given* level of output of a good or *service*. It can be seen from Table 6.14 that an output of 70 units can be produced with either $1L$ and $2K$ or $2L$ and $1K$. These are two points on the isoquant, representing 70 units of output. Similarly, the firm can produce 80 units of output (and thus remain on the same isoquant) by using either $1L$ and $3K$ or $1K$ and $3L$. Finally, 120 units of output can be produced with either $2L$ and $3K$ or $3L$ and $2K$. These are two points on a higher isoquant.

(*c*) The law of diminishing returns is a short-run law. In the short run, we look at how the level of output varies, either by changing labor and keeping capital constant, or vice versa. This can be written in functional form as $Q = f(L, \bar{K})$ or $Q = f(\bar{L}, K)$. By doing this we get the TP_L function and the TP_K function, respectively. Note that we get a different TP_L function for each level at which we keep capital constant. (Similarly, by keeping the amount of labor used constant at different levels, we generate different TP_K functions.) If $\bar{K} = 1$, and labor increases from 1 unit to 2 units and then to 3 units, Q increases from 50 units to 70 units and then to 80 units. Since the MP_L falls continuously (from 50 to 20 to 10), the law of diminishimg returns is operating continuously. The same is true for the TP_L functions given by row 2 and row 3. The law of diminishing returns also operates continuously along the TP_K functions given by columns (1), (2), and (3). (The implicit assumption we made in the last three sentences is that $f(O, K) = f(L, O) = 0$.)

THEORY OF PRODUCTION WITH CALCULUS

***6.27** Starting with the general production function $Q = f(L, K)$, which states that output Q is a function of or depends on the quantity of labor (L) and capital (K) used in production, derive the expression for the slope of the isoquant using calculus.

Taking the total differential and setting it equal to zero (because output remains unchanged along a given isoquant) we get

$$dQ = \frac{\partial f}{\partial L} dL + \frac{\partial f}{\partial K} dK = 0$$

Thus, the expression for the absolute slope of the isoquant is

$$-\frac{dK}{dL} = \frac{\partial f/\partial L}{\partial f/\partial K} = \frac{MP_L}{MP_K} = MRTS_{LK}$$

***6.28** A firm faces the general production function of $Q = f(L, K)$ and given cost outlay of $C^* = wL + rK$, where w is the wage of labor and r is the rental price of capital. Determine by using calculus the amount of labor and capital that the firm should use in order to maximize output.

Forming function Z, which incorporates the production function to be maximized subject to the given cost outlay set equal to zero, and get

$$Z = f(L, K) + \lambda^*(C^* - wL - rK)$$

where λ^* is the Lagrangian multiplier. Taking the first partial derivative of Z with respect to L and K, we get

$$\frac{\partial Z}{\partial L} = \frac{\partial f}{\partial L} - \lambda^* w = 0 \qquad \text{and} \qquad \frac{\partial Z}{\partial K} = \frac{\partial f}{\partial K} - \lambda^* r = 0$$

Dividing the first equation by the second, we get

$$\frac{MP_L}{MP_K} = \frac{w}{r} \qquad \text{or} \qquad \frac{MP_L}{w} = \frac{MP_K}{r}$$

CHAPTER 7

Costs of Production

7.1 SHORT-RUN TOTAL COST CURVES

Cost curves show the *minimum* cost of producing various levels of output. Both explicit and implicit costs are included. *Explicit costs* refer to the *actual* expenditures of the firm to purchase or hire the inputs it need. *Implicit costs* refer to the value of the inputs owned by the firm and used by the firm in its own production processes. The value of these owned inputs should be imputed or *estimated* form what they could earn in their *best alternative use* (see Problem 7.1).

In the short run, one or more (but not all) factor of production are fixed in quantity. *Total fixed costs* (TFC) refer to the total obligations incurred by the firm per unit of time for all fixed inputs. *Total variable costs* (TVC) are the total obligations incurred by the firm per unit of time for all the variable inputs it uses. *Total costs* (TC) equal TFC plus TVC.

EXAMPLE 1. Table 7.1 presents hypothetical TFC, TVC, and TC schedules. These schedules are plotted in Fig. 7-1

Table 7.1

Q	TFC ($)	TVC ($)	TC ($)
0	60	0	60
1	60	30	90
2	60	40	100
3	60	45	105
4	60	55	115
5	60	75	135
6	60	120	180

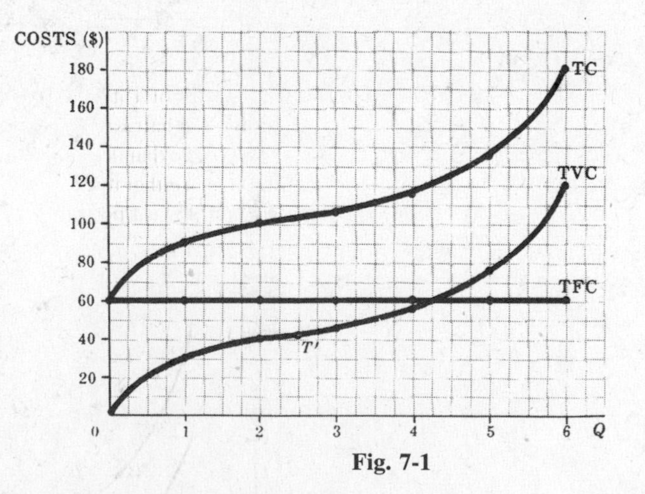

Fig. 7-1

From Table 7.1, we see that TFC are $60 regardless of the level of output. This is reflected in Fig. 7-1 in a TFC curve which is parallel to the quantity axis and $60 above it. TVC are zero when output is zero and rise as output rises. The particular shape of the TVC curve follows directly from the law of diminishing returns. Up to point T' (the point of inflection), the firm is using so few of the variable inputs together with its fixed inputs that the law of diminishing returns is not yet operating. So the TVC curve is concave downward and TVC increase at a decreasing rate. At point T', the law of diminishing returns beings to operate, so to the right of point T', the TVC curve is concave upward and TVC increase at an increasing rate. At every output level, TC equal TFC plus TVC. Thus the TC curve has the same shape as the TVC curve but is everywhere $60 above it.

7.2 SHORT-RUN PER-UNIT COST CURVES

Although total cost curves are very important, per-unit cost curves are even more important in the short-run analysis of the firm. The short-run per-unit cost curves that we will consider are the average fixed cost, the average variable cost, the average cost, and the marginal cost curves.

Average fixed cost (AFC) equals total fixed costs divided by output. *Average variable cost* (AVC) equals total variable costs divided by output. *Average cost* (AC) equals total costs divided by output; AC also equals AFC plus AVC. *Marginal cost* (MC) equals the change in TC or the change in TVC per unit change in output.

EXAMPLE 2. Table 7.2 presents the AFC, AVC, AC, and MC schedules derived from the TFC, TVC, and TC schedules of Table 7.1. The AFC schedule [columns (5) and (1)] is obtained by dividing TFC [column (2)] by the corresponding quantities of output produced [Q, in column (1)]. The AVC schedule [columns (6) and (1)] is obtained by dividing TVC [column (3)] by Q. The AC schedule [columns (7) and (1)] is obtained by dividing TC [column (4)] by Q. AC at every output level also equals AFC [column (5)] plus AVC [column (6)]. The MC schedule [columns (8) and (1)] is obtained by subtracting successive values of TC [column (4)] or TVC [column (5)]. Thus MC does not depend on the level of TFC.

Table 7.2

(1)	(2)	(3)	(4)	(5)	(6)	(7)	(8)
Q	TFC ($)	TVC ($)	TC ($)	AFC ($)	AVC ($)	AC ($)	MC ($)
1	60	30	90	60	30.00	90.00	..
2	60	40	100	30	20.00	50.00	10
3	60	45	105	20	15.00	35.00	5
4	60	55	115	15	13.75	28.75	10
5	60	75	135	12	15.00	27.00	20
6	60	120	180	10	20.00	30.00	45

The AFC, AVC, AC, and MC schedules of Table 7.2 are plotted in Fig. 7-2. Note that the values of the MC schedule [columns (8) and (1) in Table 7.2] are plotted halfway between successive levels of output in Fig. 7-2. Also note that while the AFC curve falls continuously as output is expanded, the AVC, AC, and MC curves are U-shaped. The MC curve reaches its lowest point at a lower level of output than either the AVC curve or the AC curve. Also, the rising portion of the MC curve intersects the AVC and AC curves at their lowest point.

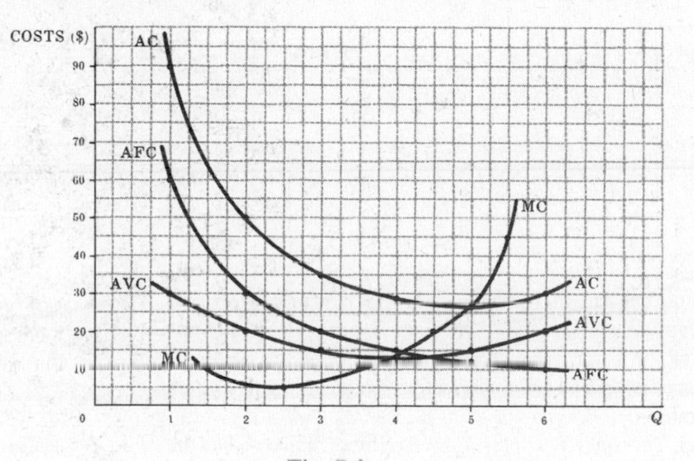

Fig. 7-2

7.3 THE GEOMETRY OF SHORT-RUN PER-UNIT COST CURVES

Short-run per-unit cost curves can be derived geometrically from the corresponding short-run total cost curves in exactly the same way as the AP_L, and the MP_L curves were derived (in Chapter 6) from the TP curve. Thus, the AFC for any level of output is given by the slope of the straight line from the origin to the corresponding point on the TFC curve. AVC is given by the slope of the line from the origin to various points on the TVC curve. Similarly, AC is given by the slope of the line from the origin to various points on the TC curve. On the other hand, the MC at any level of output is given by the slope of either the TC curve or the TVC curve at that level of output.

EXAMPLE 3. In the panels of Fig. 7-3(*a*) and (*b*), we see how the AFC, AVC, AC, and MC curves of Fig. 7-2 are derived geometrically from the TFC, TVC, and TC curves of Fig. 7-1.

In panel A of Fig. 7-3(*a*), the AFC at one unit of output is given by the slope of line *OE*. This equals TFC/1 = \$60/1 = \$60 and is plotted as point *E'* on the AFC curve, Point *F'* on the AFC curve is given by the slope of *OF* which equals \$60/3 = \$20. Other points on the AFC curve can be similarly obtained. Note that as output expands, the slope of the line from the origin to the TFC curve (which equals AFC) declines continuously.

In panel B, the AVC at two and six units of output is given by the slope of line *OH* or *OM*, which is \$20. This gives points *H'* and *M'* on the AVC curve. Note that the slope of a line from the origin to the TVC curve declines up to point *J* and then rises. So the AVC curve falls until point *J'* and then rises.

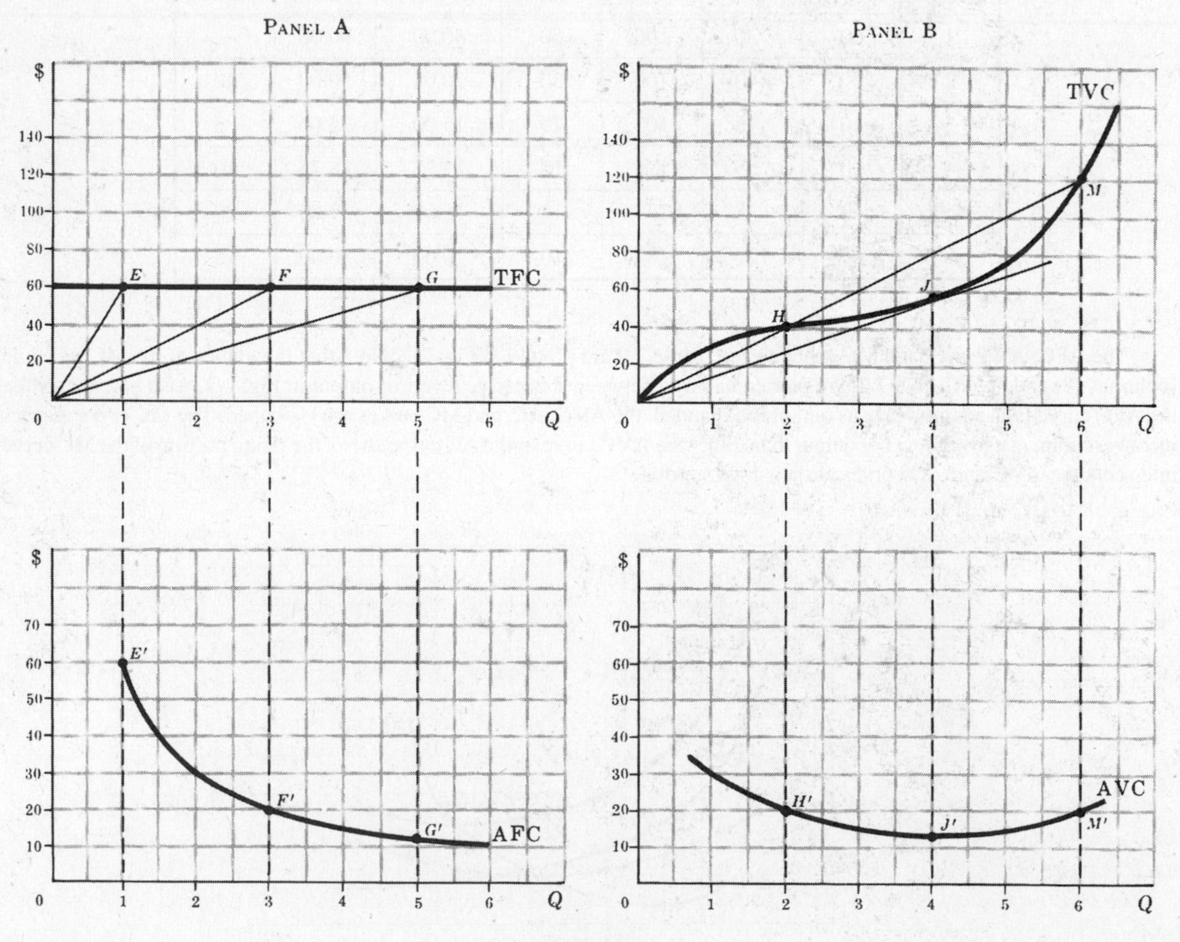

Fig. 7-3(*a*)

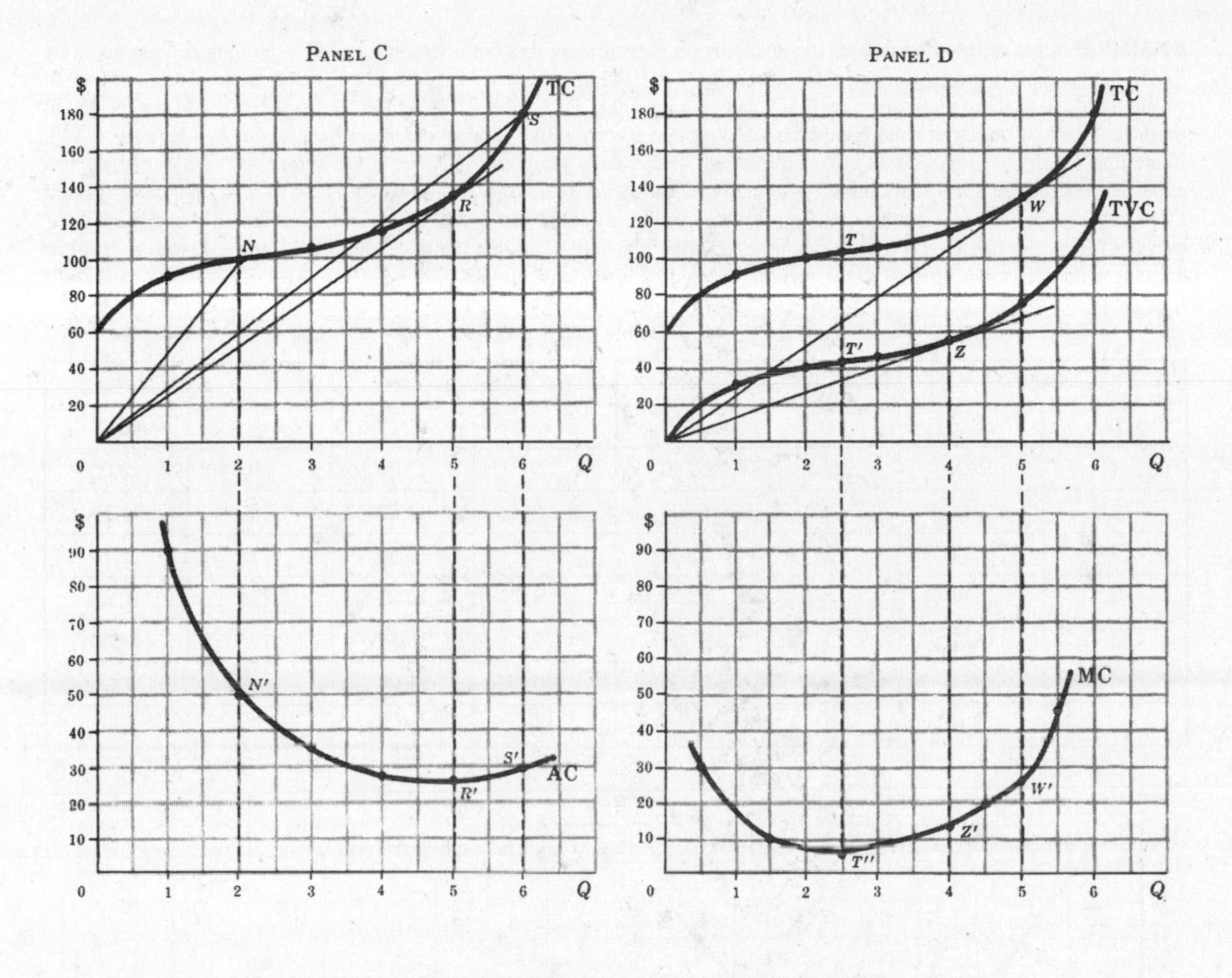

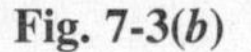

Fig. 7-3(*b*)

In panel C, the AC at 2 units of output is given by the slope of *ON*, which is \$50. This gives point *N′* on the AC curve. The AC at 6 units of output is given by the slope of *OS*, which is \$30. This is plotted as point *S′* on the AC curve. Note that as output expands, the slope of the line from the origin to the TC curve falls up to point *R* and rises thereafter. Thus, the AC curve falls up to point *R′* and rises thereafter.

In panel D, the slope of the TVC curve and the slope of the TC curve are the same at any level of output. Thus, MC is given either by the slope of the TVC curve or by the slope of the TC curve. As output expands, these slopes fall continuously until points *T* and *T′* (the points of inflection), and rise thereafter. Thus, the MC curve falls up to 2.5 units of output (point *T″*) and then rises. At 4 units of output, MC is given by the slope of the TVC curve at point *Z*. This is \$55/4 or \$13.75 and equals the lowest AVC. At 5 units of output, MC is given by the slope of the TC curve at point *W*. This is \$135/5 or \$27 and equals the lowest AC.

7.4 THE LONG-RUN AVERAGE COST CURVE

In Chapter 6 we defined the long run as the time period long enough to enable the firm to vary the quantity used of all inputs. Thus in the long run there are no fixed factors and no fixed costs, and the firm can build any size or scale of plant.

The *long-run average cost* (LAC) curve shows the minimum per-unit cost of producing each level of output when any desired scale of plant can be built. LAC is given by a curve tangent to all the short-run average cost (SAC) curves representing all the alternative plant sizes that the firm could build in the long run. Mathematically, the LAC curve is the *envelope* of the SAC curves.

EXAMPLE 4. Suppose that four of the alternative scales of plant that the firm could build in the long run are given by SAC_1, SAC_2, SAC_3, and SAC_4, of Table 7.3 and Fig. 7-4. If the firm expected to produce 2 units of output per unit of time, it would build the scale of plant given by SAC_1 and operate it at point *A*, where SAC is $17. If, however, the firm expected to produce 4 units of output, it would build the scale of plant given by SAC_2 and would operate it at point *B*, where AC is $13. (Note that 4 units of output could also be produced at the lowest point on SAC_1 but at the higher AC of $15.) If the firm expected to produce 8 units of output, it would build the larger scale of plant indicated by SAC_3 and operate it at point *C*. Finally, for 12 units of output, the firm would operate at point *D* on SAC_4. We could have drawn many more SAC curves in Fig. 7-4, one for each of the many alternative scales of plant that the firm could build in the long run. By then drawing a tangent to all of these SAC curves, we would get the LAC curve.

Table 7.3

SAC_1		SAC_2		SAC_3		SAC_4	
Q	AC ($)	*Q*	AC ($)	*Q*	AC ($)	*Q*	AC ($)
1	20.00	3	16.00	5	13.00	9	12.00
2	17.00	4	13.00	6	11.50	10	11.50
3	15.50	5	12.20	7	10.50	11	11.70
4	15.00	6	12.00	8	10.00	12	12.00
5	16.00	7	13.00	9	10.50	13	13.50
6	18.00	8	15.00	10	11.00		
				11	12.00		

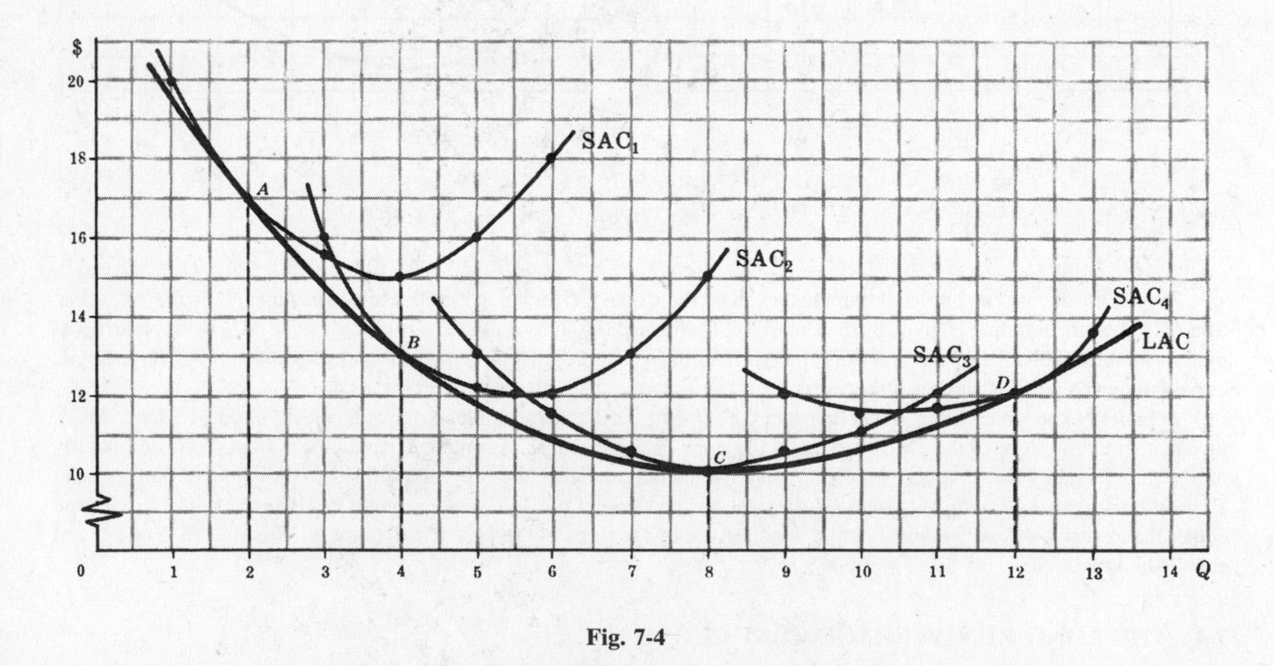

Fig. 7-4

7.5 THE SHAPE OF THE LONG-RUN AVERAGE COST CURVE

While the SAC curves and the LAC curve in Fig. 7-4 have been drawn as U-shaped, the reason for their shapes is quite different. The SAC curves decline at first, but eventually rise because of the operation of the law of diminishing returns (resulting from the existence of fixed inputs in the short run). In the long run there are no fixed inputs, and the shape of the LAC curve is determined by economies and diseconomies of scale. That is, as output expands from very low levels, increasing returns to scale cause the LAC, curve to decline initially. But as output becomes greater and greater, diseconomies of scale may become prevalent, causing the LAC curve to start rising.

Empirical studies seem to indicate that for some firms the LAC curve is either U-shaped and has a flat bottom (implying constant returns to scale over a wide range of outputs) or is L-shaped (indicating that over the observed levels of outputs there are no diseconomies of scale) (see Problem 7.14).

7.6 THE LONG-RUN MARGINAL COST CURVE

Long-run marginal cost (LMC) measures the change in *long-run total cost* (LTC) per unit change in output. The LTC for any level of output can be obtained by multiplying output by the LAC for that level of output. By plotting the LMC values midway between successive levels of output and joining these points, we get the LMC curve. The LMC curve is U-shaped and reaches its minimum point before the LAC curve reaches its minimum point. Also, the rising portion of the LMC curve goes through the lowest point of the LAC curve.

EXAMPLE 5. The LAC schedule given by columns (2) and (1) of Table 7.4 are read off or estimated from the LAC curve of Fig. 7-4. The (minimum) LTC to produce various levels of output [column (3)] is obtained by multiplying output by the corresponding LAC. The LMC values of column (4) are then obtained by finding the difference between successive LTC values. The resulting LMC schedule is plotted (together with its corresponding LAC schedule) in Fig. 7-5.

Table 7.4

(1)	(2)	(3)	(4)
Q	LAC ($)	LTC ($)	LMC ($)
1	19.60	19.60	..
2	17.00	34.00	14.40
3	14.90	44.70	10.70
4	13.00	52.00	7.30
5	11.70	58.50	6.50
6	10.80	64.80	6.30
7	10.20	71.40	6.60
8	10.00	80.00	8.60
9	10.20	91.80	11.80
10	10.60	106.00	14.20

Note that when the LAC curve is declining, the LMC curve is below it; when the LAC is rising, the LMC curve is above it, and when the LAC curve is at its minimum point, LMC = LAC. The reason for this is that for the LAC to fall, the *addition* to the LTC to produce one more unit of output (i.e., the LMC) must be less than or below the previous LAC. Similarly, for the LAC to rise, the addition to LTC to produce one more unit of output (i.e., the LMC) must be greater than or above the previous LAC. For the LAC to remain unchanged, the LMC must equal the LAC.

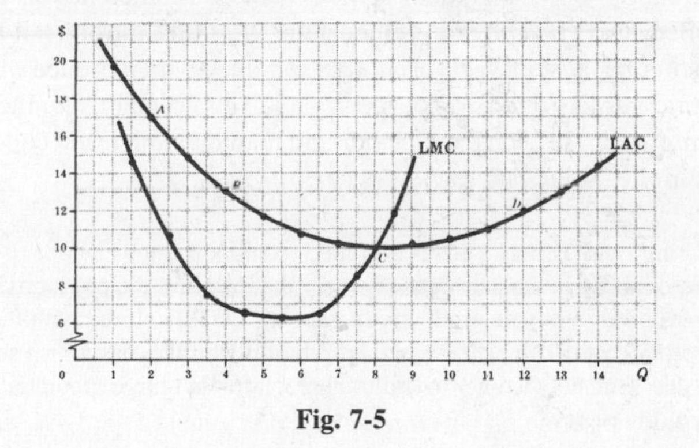

Fig. 7-5

7.7 THE LONG-RUN TOTAL COST CURVE

In Section 7.6 and Example 5 we saw that the LTC for any level of output can be obtained by multiplying output by the LAC for that level of output. By plotting the LTC values for various levels of output and joining these points, we get the LTC curve. The LTC curve shows the minimum total costs of producing each level of output when any desired scale of plant can be built. The LTC curve is also given by a curve tangent to all the *short-run total cost* (STC) curves representing all the alternative plant sizes that the firm could build in the long run. Mathematically, the LTC curve is the envelope to the STC curves (see Problem 7.17).

The LAC and the LMC curves and the relationship between them could also be derived from the LTC curve—just as the SAC and the SMC curves and the relationship between them were derived from the STC curve in Example 3 (see Problem 7.18). In addition, from the relationship between the STC curves and the LTC curve derived from them, we can explain the relationship between the SAC curves and the corresponding LAC curve, and between the SMC curves and the corresponding LMC curve (see Problem 7.19).

Finally, Problems 7.20 to 7.24 show the relationship between production functions and cost curves.

7.8 THE COBB-DOUGLAS PRODUCTION FUNCTION

The *Cobb-Douglas* is the most widely used production function in empirical work. The function is expressed by

$$Q = AL^{\alpha}K^{\beta}$$

where Q is output and L and K are inputs of labor and capital, respectively. A, α (alpha) and β (beta) are positive parameters determined in each case by the data. The greater the value of A, the more advanced is the technology. The parameter α measures the percentage increase in Q resulting from a 1% increase in L while holding K constant. Similarly, β measures the percentage increase in Q resulting from a one-percent increase in K while holding L constant. Thus, α and β are the *output elasticity* of L and K, respectively. If $\alpha + \beta = 1$, there are constant returns to scale; if $\alpha + \beta > 1$, there are increasing returns to scale; and if $\alpha + \beta < 1$, there are decreasing returns to scale. For the Cobb-Douglas function, $e_{LK} = 1$.

EXAMPLE 6. If $A = 10$ and $\alpha = \beta = 1/2$, we have

$$Q = 10L^{1/2}K^{1/2}$$

Since $\alpha + \beta = 1$, this Cobb-Douglas exhibits constant returns to scale, so that its isoquants are equally spaced and parallel along an expansion path that is a straight line from the origin. By holding K constant and by varying L, we generate the total product of labor (TP_L) and, from it, the AP_L and MP_L. These curves exhibit only stage II of production (as in Fig. 6-14). Furthermore, the AP_L and MP_L are functions of or depend only on K/L. (See Problems 7.25 to 7.28.) The same is true for K.

7.9 X-INEFFICIENCY

In Section 6.1, we defined production function as the technological relationship that shows the maximum quantity of a commodity that can be produced per unit of time for each input combination. However, in many real-world situations, neither labor nor management work as hard or as efficiently as they could, so that output is not maximum. This was called *X-inefficiency* by Leibenstein, who first introduced the concept.

X-inefficiency often occurs because of lack of motivation due to the absence of incentives or competitive pressures. For example, labor contracts often do not specify a job completely, leaving the amount and quality of effort required open to interpretation. In such cases, labor and management often choose not to exert themselves as much as they could, leading to X-inefficiency.

EXAMPLE 7. Considerable empirical evidence has been found to support the existence of X-inefficiency. For example, Leibenstein pointed out the case of an Egyptian petroleum refinery that had half the productivity of another similar installation. When new management was brought in, the productivity gap was quickly closed with the same labor force. For many years business has known that productivity can be increased by providing employees with a sense of belonging and accomplishment, but only recently has business come to fully appreciate the large potential gain possible by reducing X-inefficiency (i.e., increasing X-efficiency).

7.10 TECHNOLOGICAL PROGRESS

Technological progress refers to an increase in. the productivity of inputs and can be represented by a shift toward the origin of the isoquant referring to any output level. This means that any level of output can be produced with fewer inputs, or more output can be produced with the same inputs. Hicks classified technological progress as *neutral, capital-using*, or *labor-using*, depending on whether MP_K increased in the same proportion, greater proportion, or lesser proportion than MP_L.

EXAMPLE 8. Figure 7-6 shows neutral technological progress in panel A, K-using in panel B, and L-using in panel C. Since neutral technological progress increases MP_K and MP_L, in the same proportion, $MRTS_{LK} = MP_L/MP_K =$ slope of isoquant remains constant at point E_1 and point E_2 along the original $K/L = 1$ ray (see panel A). All that happens is that $Q = 100$ can now be produced with $2L$ and $2K$ instead of $4L$ and $4K$. On the other hand, since K-using technological progress increases MP_K proportionately more than MP_L, the absolute slope of the isoquant declines as it shifts toward the origin along the $K/L = 1$ ray (see panel B). Finally, L-using technological progress is the opposite of L-using technological progress (see panel C). K-using technological progress is sometimes referred to as K-deepening or L-saving because it leads to more K and less L being used in production. Similarly, L-using is called L-deepening or K-saving technological progress. The type of technological progress taking place is an important determinant of the share of Net National Product (NNP) going to L and K over time (see Problem 7.31).

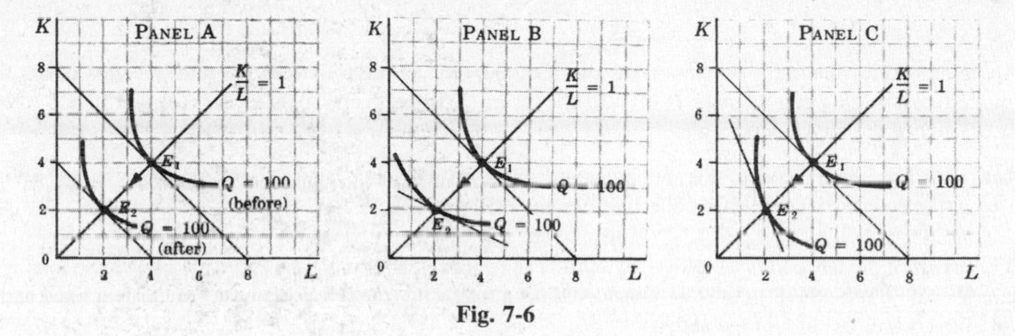

Fig. 7-6

Glossary

Average cost **(AC)** Equals total costs divided by output; AC also equals average fixed costs plus average variable costs.

Average fixed cost **(AFC)** Equals total fixed costs divided by output.

Average variable cost **(AVC)** Equals total variable costs divided by output.

Capital-using technological progress The greater proportionate increase in the marginal product of capital than the marginal product of labor, so that the slope of the isoquant declines as it shifts toward the origin at the original capital-labor ratio.

Cobb-Douglas production function This function is given by $Q = AL^{\alpha} K^{\beta}$, where Q is output and L and K are inputs. A, α, and β are the parameters, $\alpha =$ output elasticity of L, while $\beta =$ output elasticity of K. We have constant, increasing, or decreasing returns to scale when a $\alpha + \beta = 1$, >1 or <1, respectively.

Cost curves Show the minimum cost of producing various levels of output.

Explicit costs The actual expenditures of the firm to purchase or hire the inputs it needs.

Implicit costs The value of owned inputs used by the firm in its own production processes.

Labor-using technological progress The greater proportionate increase in the marginal product of labor than the marginal product of capital, so that the slope of the isoquant increases as it shifts toward the origin at the original capital-labor ratio.

Long-run average cost **(LAC)** Shows the minimum per-unit cost of producing each level of output when any desired scale of plant can be built.

Long-run marginal cost **(LMC)** Measures the change in long-run total cost per unit change in output.

***Long-run total cost* (LTC)** Shows the minimum total costs of producing each level of output when any desired scale of plant can be built.

***Marginal cost* (MC)** Equals the change in total costs or total variable costs per unit change in output.

Neutral technological progress The proportionate increase in the marginal product of capital and labor, so that the slope of the isoquant remains unchanged as it shifts toward the origin at the original capital-labor ratio.

Output elasticity Gives the percentage increase in output resulting from a given percentage increase in an input, while holding all other inputs constant.

***Total costs* (TC)** The sum of total fixed costs plus total variable costs.

***Total fixed costs* (TFC)** The total obligations incurred by the firm per unit of time for all fixed inputs.

***Total variable costs* (TVC)** The total obligations incurred by the firm per unit of time for all variable inputs it uses.

X-inefficiency The degree by which the output of a commodity falls short of the maximum possible (indicated by the production function) due to lack of adequate motivation of labor and management.

Review Questions

1. An entrepreneur running a business takes out \$20,000/year as "salary" from the total receipts of the firm. The implicit cost of this entrepreneur is (*a*) \$20,000/year, (*b*) more than \$20,000/year, (*c*) less than \$20,000/year, or (*d*) any of the above is possible.

Ans. (*d*) The implicit cost of this entrepreneur depends on how much labor and other factors that person owns and uses in the enterprise could earn collectively in their best alternative use.

2. If only part of the labor force employed by a firm can be dismissed at any time and without pay, the total wages and salaries paid out by the firm must be considered (*a*) a fixed cost, (*b*) a variable cost, (*c*) partly a fixed and partly a variable cost, or (*d*) any of the above.

Ans. (*c*) The wages paid out to the portion of the labor force which can be dismissed at any time and without pay is a variable cost. That part of the labor force which because of a labor contract cannot be dismissed without pay represents a fixed cost until the expiration of the contract.

3. When the law of diminishing returns begins to operate, the TVC curve begins to (*a*) fall at an increasing rate, (*b*) rise at a decreasing rate, (*c*) fall at a decreasing rate, or (*d*) rise at an increasing rate.

Ans. (*d*) See the TVC curve in Fig. 7-1, to the right of point T'.

4. MC is given by
(*a*) the slope of the TFC curve,
(*b*) the slope of the TVC curve but not by the slope of the TC curve,
(*c*) the slope of the TC curve but not by the slope of the TVC curve, or
(*d*) either the slope of the TVC curve or the slope of the TC curve.

Ans. (*d*) See panel D of Fig. 7-3 and the discussion relating to it in Example 3.

5. The MC curve reaches its minimum point before the AVC curve and the AC curve. In addition, the MC curve intersects the AVC curve and the AC curve at their lowest point. The above statements are both true. (*a*) Always, (*b*) never, (*c*) often, or (*d*) sometimes.

Ans. (*a*) See Figs. 7-2 and 7-3.

6. At the point where a straight line from the origin is tangent to the TC curve, AC (*a*) is minimum, (*b*) equals MC, (*c*) equals AVC plus AFC, or (*d*) is all of the above.

Ans. (*d*) For choices (*a*) and (*b*), see panels C and D of Fig. 7-3. Choice (*c*) is always true.

7. If the LAC curve falls as output expands, this is due to (*a*) economies of scale, (*b*) the law of diminishing returns, (*c*) diseconomies of scale, or (*d*) any of the above.

Ans. (*a*) See Section 7.5.

8. When $\alpha = 3/4$ and $\beta = 1/4$ for the Cobb-Douglas production function, returns to scale are (*a*) constant, (*b*) increasing, (*c*) decreasing, or (*d*) first increasing and then decreasing.

Ans. (*a*) Because $\alpha + \beta = 1$. See Section 8.1.

9. The output elasticity of labor measures (*a*) $(\Delta Q)/(\Delta L)$, (*b*) $(\%\Delta Q)/(\%\Delta L)$, (*c*) $(\Delta L)/(\Delta Q)$, or (*d*) $(\%\Delta L)/(\%\Delta Q)$.

Ans. (*b*) See Section 7.8.

10. Which of the following statements is *false* with regard to X-inefficiency? (*a*) It measures the degree by which the output of a commodity falls short of the maximum indicated by the production function; (*b*) it results from lack of adequate motivation; (*c*) it has been found to exist, according to several empirical studies; or (*d*) all of the above.

Ans. (*d*) See Section 7.9.

11. Technological progress refers to (*a*) an increase in MP_L and MP_K, (*b*) the reduction in L and K to produce any level of output, (*c*) a shift of the isoquants toward the origin, or (*d*) all of the above.

Ans. (*d*) See Section 7.10.

12. Labor-using technological progress (*a*) means L-deepening, (*b*) means K-saving, (*c*) reduces K/L, or (*d*) all of the above.

Ans. (*d*) See Example 8.

Solved Problems

SHORT-RUN COST CURVES

7.1 (*a*) What are some of the implicit costs incurred by an entrepreneur in running a firm? How are these implicit costs estimated? Why must they be included as part of costs of production? (*b*) What price does the firm pay to purchase or hire the factors it does not own?

(*a*) An entrepreneur must include as part of the costs of production not only what this person actually pays out to hire labor, purchase raw and semifinished materials, borrow money, and rent land and buildings (the explicit costs) but also the *maximum* salary that the entrepreneur could have earned working in a similar capacity for someone else (say, as the manager of another firm). Similarly, the entrepreneur must include as part of the costs of production the return in the best alternative use from the capital, land, and on any other factor of production that this person owns and uses in the enterprise. These resources owned and used by the firm itself are not "free" resources. The (implicit) cost to the firm involved in using them is equal to the (best) alternatives foregone (i.e., what these same resources would have earned in their best alternative use). Whenever we speak of costs in economics or draw cost curves, we always include both explicit *and* implicit costs.

(*b*) For the inputs which the firm purchases or hires, the firm must pay a price at least equal to what these same inputs could earn in their best alternative use. Otherwise, the firm could not purchase them or retain them for its use. Thus the cost to the firm involved in the use of any input, whether owned by the firm (implicit cost) or purchased (explicit cost), is equal to what the same input could earn in its best alternative use. This is *the alternative or opportunity cost doctrine*.

Throughout this chapter, we assume that factor prices remain constant, regardless of the quantity of each factor demanded by the firm per unit of time. That is, we assume that the firm is a perfect competitor in the factor market. (Changes in factor prices and their effect on cost curves are considered in Chapter 9. The discussion of how factor prices are actually determined is deferred to Chapter 13.)

7.2 (*a*) On the same set of axes, plot the TFC, TVC, and TC schedules in Table 7.5.
(*b*) Explain the reason for the shape of the curves.

Table 7.5

Q	TFC ($)	TVC ($)	TC ($)
0	120	0	120
1	120	60	180
2	120	80	200
3	120	90	210
4	120	105	225
5	120	140	260
6	120	210	330

(*a*)

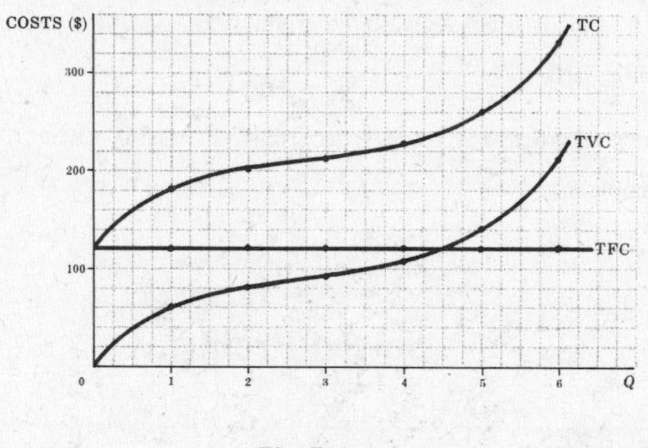

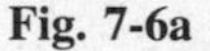

Fig. 7-6a

(*b*) Since TFC remain constant at $120 per time period regardless of the level of output, the TFC curve is parallel to the horizontal axis and $120 above it, TVC are zero when output is zero and rise as output rises. Before the law of diminishing returns begins to operate, TVC increase at a decreasing rate. After the law of diminishing returns begins to operate, TVC increases at an increasing rate. Thus the TVC curve begins at the origin and is positively sloped. It is concave downward up to the point of inflection and concave upward thereafter. Since TC equal TFC plus TVC, the TC curve has exactly the same shape as the TVC curve but is everywhere $120 above it. In drawing the TFC, TVC, and TC curves, all resources are valued according to their opportunity cost, which includes explicit and implicit costs. Also, the TFC, TVC, and TC curves indicate respectively the minimum TFC, TVC, and TC of producing various output levels per time period.

7.3 (*a*) Give some examples of fixed and variable factors in the short run. (*b*) What is the relationship between the quantity of fixed inputs used and the short-run level of output?

(*a*) Fixed factors in the short run include payments for renting land and buildings, at least part of depreciation and maintenance expenditures, most kinds of insurance, property taxes, and some salaries such as those of top management, which are fixed by contract and may have to be paid over the life of the contract whether the firm produces or not. Variable factors include raw materials, fuels, most types of labor, excise taxes, and interest on short-run loans.

(*b*) The quantity of fixed inputs used determines the size or the *scale of plant* which the firm operates in the short run. Within the limits imposed by its scale of plant, the firm can vary its output in the short run by varying the quantity of variable inputs used per unit of time.

7.4 From Table 7.5, (*a*) find the AFC, AVC, AC, and MC schedules and (*b*) plot the AFC, AVC, AC, and MC schedules of part (*a*) on one set of axes.

(*a*)

Table 7.6

Q	TFC ($)	TVC ($)	TC ($)	AFC ($)	AVC ($)	AC ($)	MC ($)
0	120	0	120				
1	120	60	180	120	60.00	180.00	60
2	120	80	200	60	40.00	100.00	20
3	120	90	210	40	30.00	70.00	10
4	120	105	225	30	26.25	56.25	15
5	120	140	260	24	28.00	52.00	35
6	120	210	330	20	35.00	55.00	70

AFC equals TFC divided by output. AVC equals TVC divided by output. AC equals TC divided by output. MC equals the change in either TVC or in TC per unit change in output.

(*b*) See Fig. 7-7.

7.5 From the TFC curve in Problem 7.2, derive the AFC curve geometrically and explain its shape.

See Fig. 7-8. AFC equals TFC divided by output. TFC equal $120. Thus, when output is 2, AFC equals $120 divided by 2, or $60. This is equal to the slope of ray *OA* and is plotted as point *A′* on the AFC curve. At point *B* on the TFC curve, the AFC is given by the slope of ray *OB*. This equals $30 per unit ($120/4 units) and is plotted as point *B′* on the AFC curve. At point *C* on the TFC curve, AFC equals the slope of ray *OC* which is $20, This gives point *C′* on the AFC curve. Other points on the AFC curve could be similarly obtained.

The AFC curve is *asymptotic* to both axes. That is, as we move further and further away from the origin along either axis, the AFC curve approaches but never quite touches the axis. Also, AFC times quantity always gives the same amount (i.e., the constant TFC). Thus, the AFC curve is a *rectangular hyperbola*.

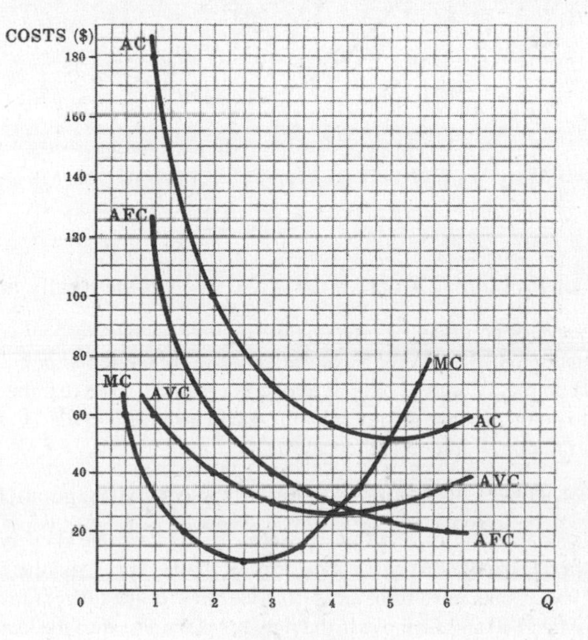

Fig. 7-7

7.6 From the TVC curve of Problem 7.2, derive the AVC curve geometrically and explain its shape.

See Fig. 7-9. AVC equals TVC divided by output. For example, at point D on the TVC curve, TVC equal \$60. Thus, AVC equals \$60 divided by 1, or \$60. This is equal to the slope of ray OD and is plotted as point D' on the AVC curve. At point E on the TVC curve, the AVC is given by the slope of ray OG. This equals \$26.50 (\$105/4) and is plotted as point E' on the AVC curve. At point F on the TVC curve, AVC equals the slope of ray OF which is \$35 (\$210/6). This gives point F' on the AVC curve. Other points on the AVC curve could be similarly obtained. Note that the slope of a ray from the origin to the TVC curve falls up to point E (where the ray from the origin is tangent to the TVC curve) and rises thereafter. Thus, the AVC curve falls up to point E' and rises afterward.

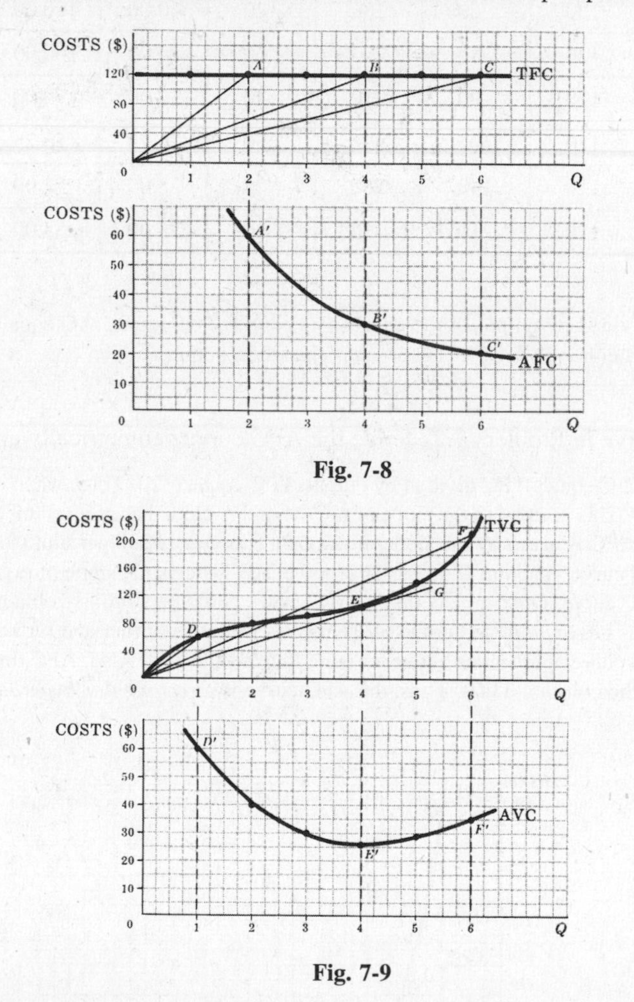

Fig. 7-8

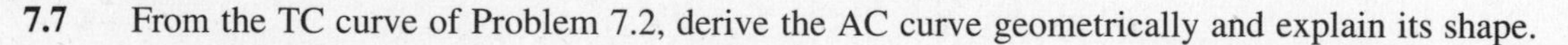

Fig. 7-9

7.7 From the TC curve of Problem 7.2, derive the AC curve geometrically and explain its shape.

See Fig. 7-10. The AC at points H, J, and N on the TC curve is given respectively by the slope of rays OH, OM, and ON. These are equal to \$70, \$52, and \$55, respectively and are plotted as points H', J', and N' on the AC curve. The AC at other points on the TC curve could be similarly obtained. Note that the slope of a ray from the origin to the TC curve falls up to point J (where the ray from the origin is tangent to the TC curve) and rises thereafter. Thus, the AC curve falls up to point J' and rises thereafter.

7.8 From the TC and TVC curves of Problem 7.2, derive the MC curve geometrically and explain its shape.

See Fig. 7-11. The slope of the TC and TVC curves is exactly the same at every output level. Thus, MC is given by the slope of either the TC or the TVC curve. The slope of the TC curve and the TVC curve (i.e., the MC) at point D is \$32. (The value of \$32 is obtained from measuring the slope of the tangent to the TC curve at point D. That is, moving from D to R we rise \$40 and we move to the right by 1.25 units; thus the slope of DR equals 40/1.25 or \$32.) This gives point D' on the MC curve. Point S is the point of inflection on the TC and TVC curves. At this point, the slope of the TC and TVC curves is at its lowest value. That value gives us the lowest point (i.e., point S') on the MC curve. Past point S and S', the law of diminishing returns is operating and the MC curve rises. The slope of (the tangent to) the TC and TVC curves (i.e., the MC) at point E equals the lowest AVC, which is \$26.25. This gives point E' on the MC curve. The slope of (the tangent to) the TC and TVC curves (i.e., the MC) at point J equals the lowest AC, which is \$52. This gives point J' on the MC curve.

7.9 (*a*) On the same set of axes, draw the TVC curve and the TC curve of Problem 7.2; on another set of axes directly below the first set draw the corresponding AVC, AC, and MC curves, (*b*) Explain briefly the relationship between the shape of the TC and the TVC curves and the shape of the AVC, AC, and MC curves, (*c*) Explain the relationship among the per-unit cost curves.

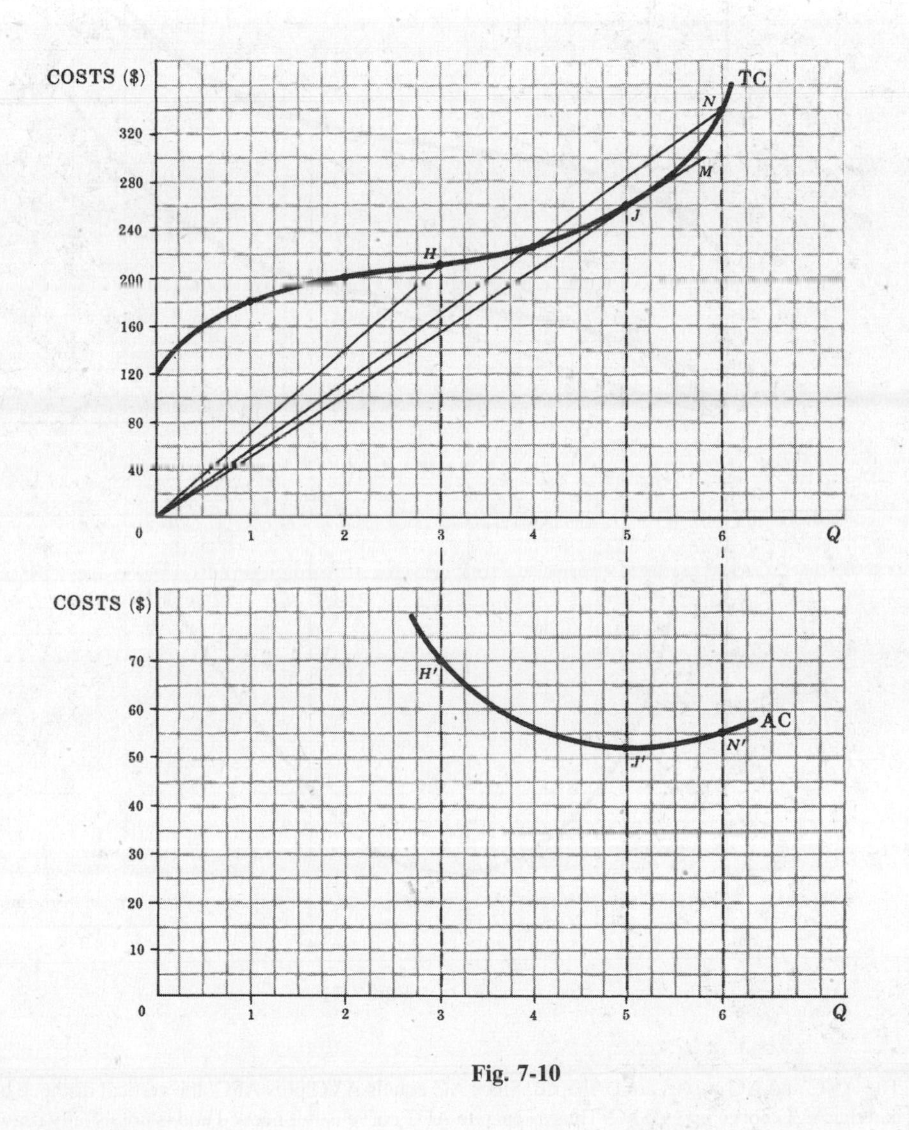

Fig. 7-10

(*a*) See Fig. 7-12.

(*b*) AVC equals TVC divided by output. AVC is given by the slope of a ray from the origin to the TVC curve. Up to point E (the point where a ray from the origin is tangent to the TVC curve), the AVC falls Past point E, it rises. AC equals TC divided by output. AC is given by the slope of a ray from the origin to the TC curve. Up to point J (the point of tangency), the slope of the ray from the origin to the TC curve (i.e., the AC) falls. Past point J, it rises. The MC curve can be obtained either from the slope of the TVC curve or from the slope of the TC curve. The slope of the TC and TVC curves (i.e., the MC) falls up to the point of inflection (point S) and rises afterward. Note that the MC between two points on the TC or TVC curve is given by the slope of the chord between the two points. This is the *average* MC. As the distance between the two points approaches zero in the limit, the value of the MC approaches the value of the slope of the TC or TVC curves at a point.

The AVC, AC, and MC curves include implicit and explicit costs and give the minimum per-unit costs of producing various levels of output. The shape of the AVC, AC, and MC can be explained by the law of diminishing returns. As we will see in Chapter 9, when factor prices change, the AVC, AC, and MC curves shift up if factor prices rise and down if factor prices fall.

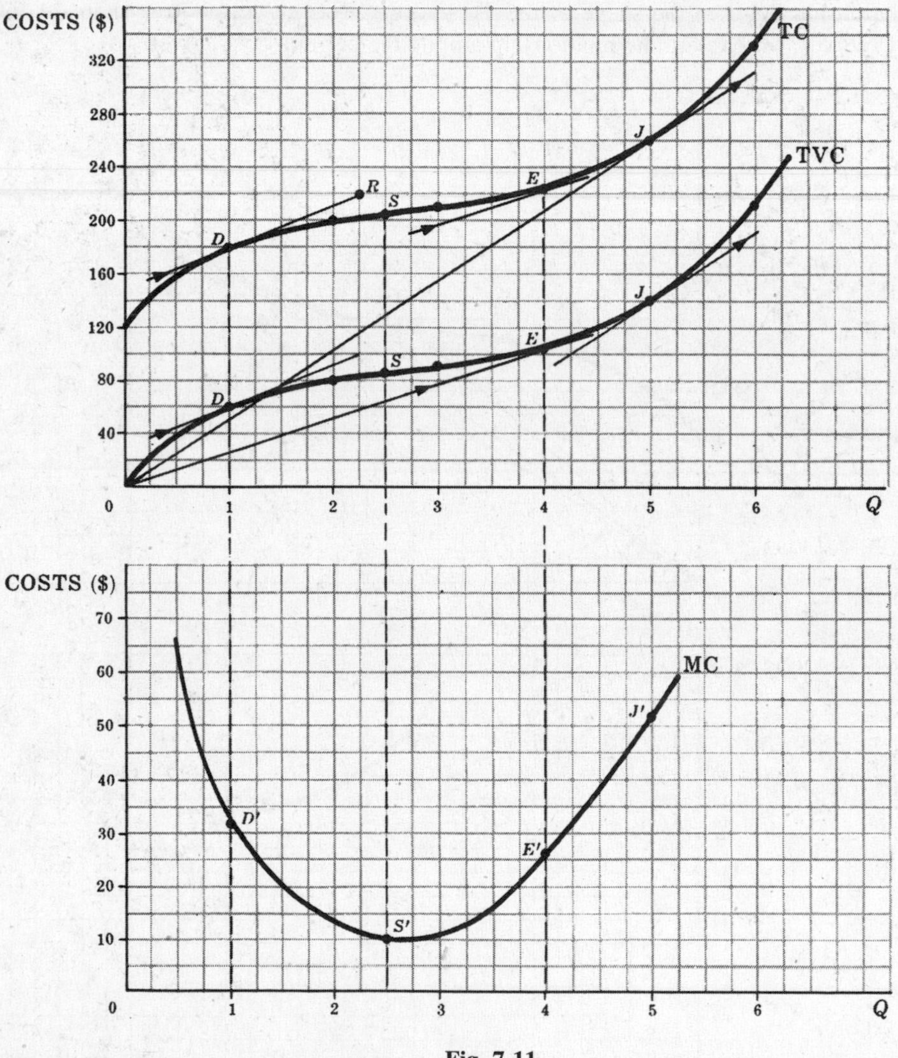

Fig. 7-11

(*c*) The AVC and AC curves are U-shaped. Since AC equals AVC plus AFC, the vertical distance between the AC and the AVC curve gives AFC. Thus a separate AFC curve is not needed and is not usually drawn. Note that as output expands, the vertical distance between the AC and the AVC curve (i.e., AFC) declines. This is always true.

The MC curve is also U-shaped, and it reaches its minimum point before the AVC and the AC curves. MC is below AVC when AVC is falling, equals AVC at the lowest point on the AVC curve, and is above AVC when AVC is rising. Exactly the same relationship exists between the MC and the AC curves, the AC curve reaches its minimum point after the AVC. This is due to the fact that, for a while, the falling AFC overwhelms the rising AVC.

A figure such as the one in this problem which shows the MC, the AVC, and the AC curves will be used a great deal in Chapters 9 to 12. What is important in the figure is the *relationship* between the various curves rather than the actual values used in drawing them.

7.10 Assuming for simplicity that labor is the only variable input in the short run and that the price of labor is constant, explain the U-shape of (*a*) the AVC curve and (*b*) the MC curve in terms of the shape of the AP_L and MP_L curves, respectively.

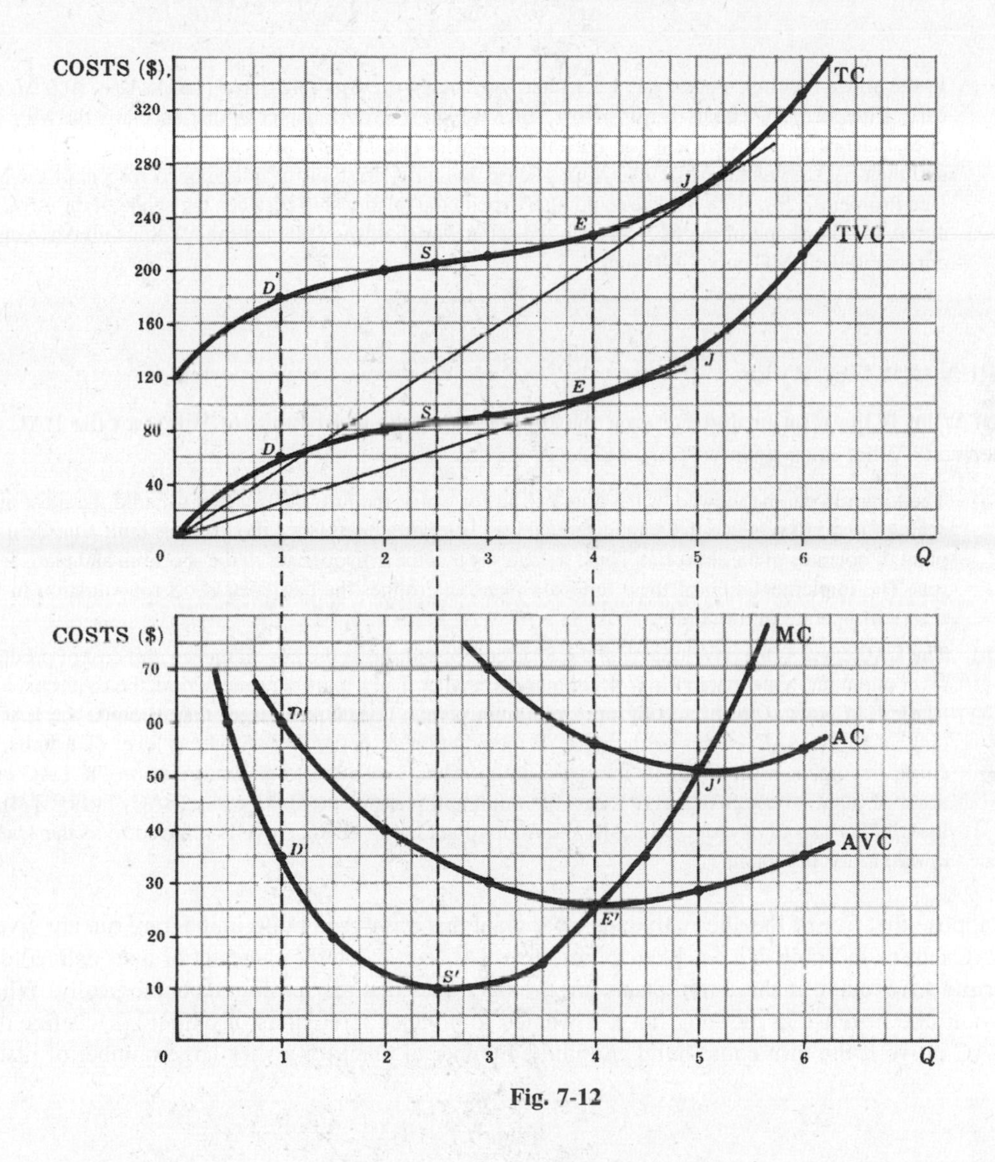

Fig. 7-12

(*a*) When labor is the only variable input, TVC equals the price of labor (P_L) times the number of units of labor used (L). Then

$$\text{AVC} = \frac{\text{TVC}}{Q} = \frac{(P_L)(L)}{Q} = \frac{P_L}{Q/L} = \frac{P_L}{AP_L}$$

Now, with a constant P_L (by assumption), and with our knowledge (from Chapter 6) that the AP_L *normally rises, reaches a maximum and then falls*, it follows that *the* AVC *normally falls, reaches a minimum, and then rises*. That is, the AVC curve is, in a sense, the monetized mirror image or reciprocal of the AP_L curve (see Problem 7.23).

(*b*) When labor is the only variable input and we let P_L equal the price of labor, L equal the quantity of labor used per unit of time, and "Δ" refer to "the change in," we have

$$\text{MC} = \frac{\Delta(\text{TVC})}{\Delta Q} = \frac{\Delta[(P_L)(L)]}{\Delta Q} = P_L\left(\frac{\Delta L}{\Delta Q}\right) = P_L\left(\frac{1}{MP_L}\right)$$

In the above identity, since P_L is a constant, we can rewrite $\Delta[(P_L)(L)]$ as $P_L(\Delta L)$. Also, $\Delta Q/\Delta L$ equals the MP_L. Thus, $\Delta L/\Delta Q$ equals $1/MP_L$. Now, since we know (from Chapter 6) that normally the MP_L curve first rises, reaches a maximum, and then falls, it follows that normally the MC curve falls first, reaches a minimum, and then rises. Thus the MC curve is, in a sense, the monetized mirror image or reciprocal of the MP_L curve (see Problem 7.23). Note that we could also explain the relationship between the shape of the AVC (and AC) curve and the shape of the MC curve in the same way that we explained the relationship between the LAC curve and the LMC curve in Example 5.

LONG-RUN COST CURVES

7.11 (*a*) What is the relationship between the long run and the short run? (*b*) How can the LAC curve be derived? What does it show?

(*a*) The long run can be viewed as the time period for which the firm plans ahead to build the most appropriate scale of plant to produce the anticipated (future) level of output. Once the firm has built a particular scale of plant, it operates in the short run. Thus, we can say that the firm operates in the short run and plans for the long run. The implementation of these long-run plans determines the particular short-run situation in which the firm will operate in the future.

(*b*) The LAC curve is the envelope of all the SAC curves and shows the minimum per-unit cost of producing each level of output. Note that in Fig. 7-4, for outputs smaller than 8 units per time period, the LAC curve is tangent to the SAC curves to the left of their minimum points. For outputs larger than 8 units, the LAC curve is tangent to the SAC curves to the right of their minimum points. At an output level of 8 units, the LAC curve is tangent to SAC_3 at its minimum point. This is also the minimum point on the LAC curve. The scale of plant whose SAC curve forms the minimum point of the LAC curve (SAC_3 in Fig. 7-4), is called the *optimum scale of plant*, while the minimum point on any SAC curve is referred to as the *optimum rate of output* for that plant.

7.12 Suppose that five of the alternative scales of plant that a firm can build in the long run are given by the SAC curves in Table 7.7. (*a*) Sketch these five SAC curves on the same set of axes and (*b*) define the firm's LAC curve if these five plants are the only ones that are feasible technologically. Which plant would the firm use in the long run if it wanted to produce three units of output? (*c*) Define the firm's LAC curve if the firm could build an infinite number of plant (or a very large number of plants).

Table 7.7

SAC_1		SAC_2		SAC_3		SAC_4		SAC_5	
Q	SAC ($)	Q	SAC ($)	Q	SAC ($)	Q	SAC ($)	Q	SAC ($)
1	15.50	2	15.50	5	10.00	8	10.00	9	12.00
2	13.00	3	12.00	6	8.50	9	9.50	10	11.00
3	12.00	4	10.00	7	8.00	10	10.00	11	11.50
4	11.75	5	9.50	8	8.50	11	12.00	12	13.00
5	13.00	6	11.00	9	10.00	12	15.00	13	16.00

(a)

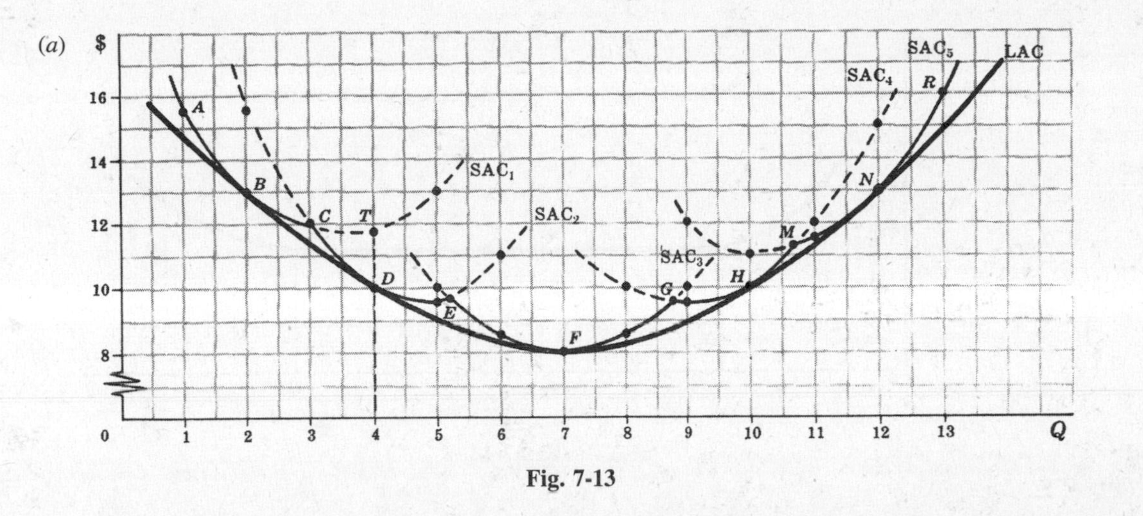

Fig. 7-13

(b) The firm's LAC curve is given by the solid portions of the SAC curves in Fig. 7-13. That is, the LAC curve for the firm is given by the solid line joining points *A*, *B*, *C*, *D*, *E*, *F*, *G*, *H*, *M*, *N*, and *R*. The dashed portions of the SAC curves are irrelevant since they represent higher-than-necessary AC for the firm in the long run. If the firm wanted to produce three units of output per time period, the firm would utilize either plant 1 or plant 2 and the firm would be at point *C* (see the previous figure). In either case the SAC for the firm would be the same.

(c) If the firm could build an infinite number of plants, or a very large number of alternative plants, in the long run, we have an infinite or very large number of SAC curves. By drawing a tangent to all these SAC curves we get the curve labeled LAC in the previous figure. This curve is the envelope of all the SAC curves and shows the minimum per-unit cost of producing each level of output when the firm can build any desired scale of plant.

7.13 With reference to Fig. 7-13, (*a*) indicate at what point on its LAC curve the firm is operating the optimum scale of plant at its optimum rate of output. (*b*) What type of plant would the firm operate and how would the firm utilize its plant for outputs smaller than seven units? (*c*) What about for outputs greater than seven units?

(a) At point *F* on the LAC curve, the firm would be operating its optimum scale of plant (indicated by SAC_3) at its optimum rate of output (point *F*).

(b) To produce outputs smaller than the seven units indicated by point *F*, the firm would *underutilize* (i.e., produce less than the optimum rate of output with) a *smaller* than the optimum scale of plant in the long run. For example, if the firm was utilizing the plant indicated by SAC_1 at point *B*, and wanted to increase its output from two to four units per time period, in the short run it would have to produce the optimum rate of output with plant 1 (point *T* in the figure). But in the long run the firm would build the larger scale of plant indicated by SAC_2 (or *convert* plant 1 to plant 2) and operate it at point *D*. Plant 2 is smaller than the optimum scale of plant (indicated in Fig. 7-13 by SAC_3) and is operated at less than its optimum rate of output.

(c) To produce more than seven units of output per time period, the firm would *overutilize* a *larger* than the optimum scale of plant in the long run (see Fig. 7-13).

The firm may know the approximate shape of the alternative SAC curves, either from experience or from engineering studies.

7.14 (*a*) Draw a LAC curve showing increasing returns to scale over a small range of outputs, constant returns to scale over a "large range" of outputs, and decreasing returns to scale thereafter. (*b*) What does a LAC curve like that in part (*a*) imply for the size of the firms in the same industry? Is there such a thing as an optimum scale of plant in this case?

(a)

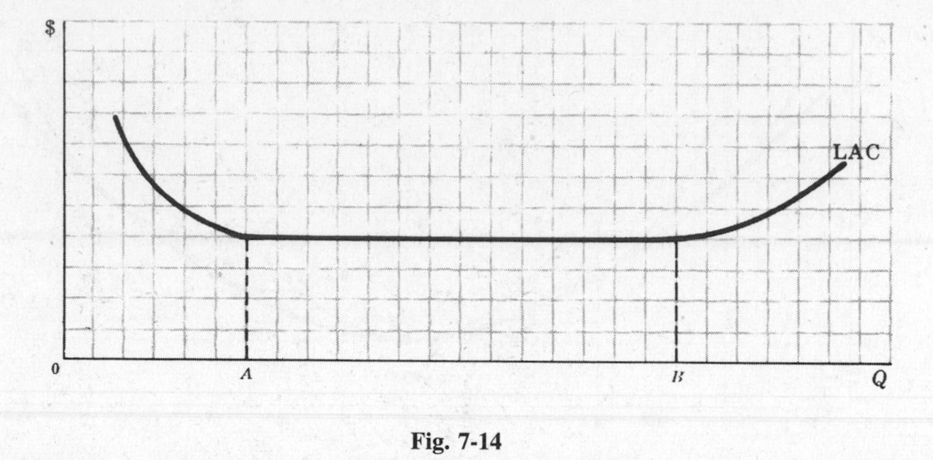

Fig. 7-14

In Fig. 7-14, we have increasing returns to scale or decreasing LAC up to output *OA*; we have constant returns to scale or constant LAC between the output levels *OA* and *OB*; and past output *OB*, we have decreasing returns to scale or increasing LAC. Thus LAC and returns to scale are opposite sides of the same coin. Note that economies and diseconomies of scale may both be operating over the same range of outputs. When economies of scale overwhelm diseconomies of scale, the LAC curve falls, otherwise the LAC is either constant or rising. The actual output level at which the LAC stops falling or starts rising depends, of course, on the industry.

(b) A LAC curve with a flat bottom, showing constant returns to scale over a wide range of outputs, implies that small firms coexist side by side with much larger firms in the same industry. If increasing returns to scale operated over a very wide range of outputs, large firms (operating large plants) would have much lower LAC than small firms and would drive the latter out of business. Many economists and business experts believe (and some empirical studies indicate) that the LAC curve in many industries has a flat bottom as in Fig. 7-14. In such cases, there is not a single optimum scale of plant, but many. That is, the flat portion of the LAC curve is formed by the lowest point of many SAC curves.

7.15 The LAC schedule in Table 7.8 is read off or estimated from the LAC curve of Problem 7.12. (*a*) From this LAC schedule, find the LMC schedule, (*b*) On the same set of axes plot the LAC and LMC schedules, (*c*) What is the relationship between the LAC curve and the LMC curve? What would the LMC curve corresponding to the LAC curve of Problem 7.14(*a*) look like?

Table 7.8

Q	1	2	3	4	5	6	7	8	9	10	11	12
LAC ($)	15	13	11.30	10	9	8.30	8	8.20	8.90	10	11.30	13

(a)

Table 7.9

Q	1	2	3	4	5	6	7	8	9	10	11	12
LAC ($)	15	13	11.30	10.00	9	8.30	8.00	8.20	8.90	10	11.30	13.00
LTC ($)	15	26	33.90	40.00	45	49.80	56.00	65.60	80.10	100	124.30	156.00
LMC ($)	..	11	7.90	6.10	5	4.80	6.20	9.60	14.50	19.90	24.30	31.70

(*b*)

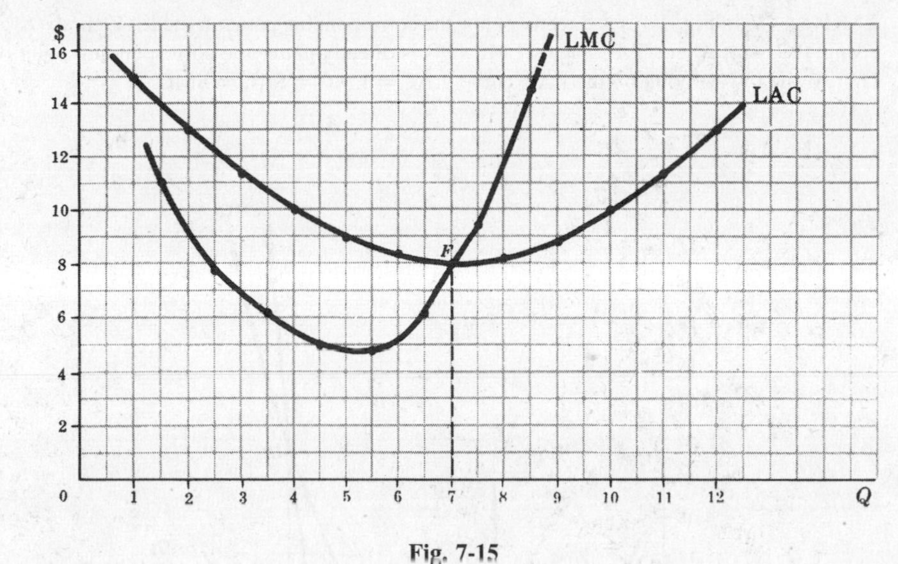

Fig. 7-15

(*c*) When the LAC curve is falling, the corresponding LMC curve is below the LAC curve; LMC = LAC when LAC is lowest; and when the LAC curve is rising the LMC curve is above the LAC curve. When the LAC curve has a flat bottom and looks like the LAC curve in Problem 7.14(*a*), the LMC curve will be below the LAC when the LAC curve is falling, *the* LMC *will coincide with the* LAC *when the* LAC *curve is horizontal*, and the LMC curve will be above the LAC when the LAC is rising.

7.16 (*a*) From SAC_1, SAC_3, and SAC_4 of Problem 7.12, find SMC_1, SMC_3, and SMC_4. (*b*) On the same set of axes, plot the LAC and LMC schedules of Problem 7.15, and the SAC_I, SAC_3, SAC_4, SMC_1, SMC_3, and SMC_4, schedules of part (*a*). (*c*) Describe the relationship between the AC curves and their respective MC curves and the relationship between the LMC curve and the SMC curves.

(*a*)

Table 7.10

Plant 1				Plant 3				Plant 4			
Q	SAC_1 ($)	STC_1 ($)	SMC_1 ($)	Q	SAC_3 ($)	STC_3 ($)	SMC_3 ($)	Q	SAC_4 ($)	STC_4 ($)	SMC_4 ($)
1	15.50	15.50	..	5	10.00	50.00	..	8	10.00	80.00	..
2	13.00	26.00	10.50	6	8.50	51.00	1.00	9	9.50	85.50	5.50
3	12.00	36.00	10.00	7	8.00	56.00	5.00	10	10.00	100.00	14.50
4	11.75	47.00	11.00	8	8.50	68.00	12.00	11	12.00	132.00	32.00
5	13.00	65.00	18.00	9	10.00	90.00	22.00	12	15.00	180.00	48.00

(*b*) See Fig. 7-16.

(*c*) Whether dealing with the short run or the long run, the MC curve is below the corresponding AC curve when the AC curve is falling; MC equals AC when AC is lowest; and the MC curve is above the AC curve when the AC curve is rising. At the output level where SAC equals LAC (i.e., at the output level where the SAC curve is tangent to the LAC curve), SMC equals LMC. When the LAC curve is declining, the point where SMC equals

LMC (e.g., B' in Fig. 7-16) is directly *below* the corresponding point on the LAC curve (B). When the LAC is rising, the point where SMC equals LMC (H') is directly *above* the corresponding point on the LAC curve (H): At the lowest point on the LAC curve, LAC = LMC = SAC = SMC.

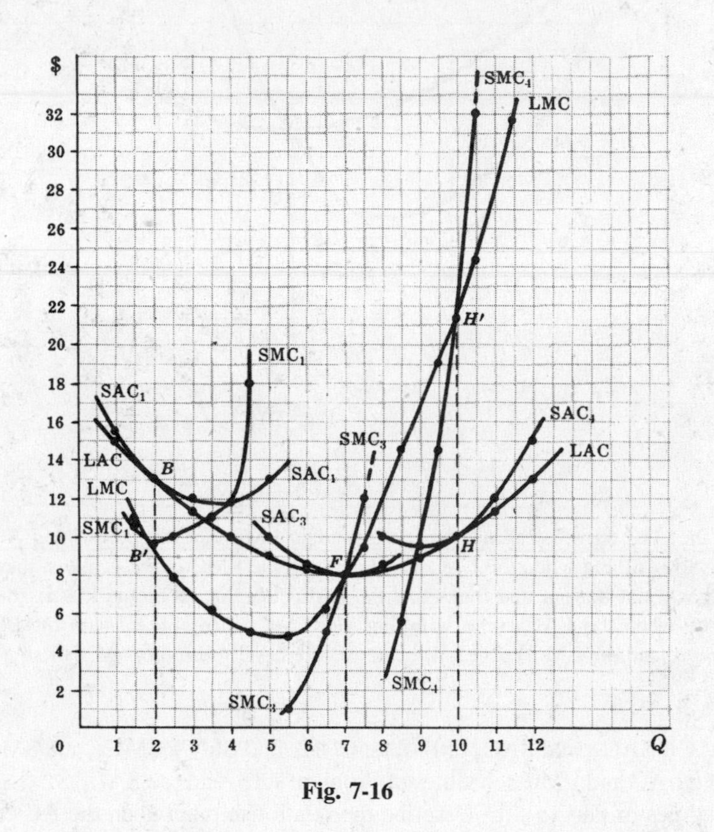

Fig. 7-16

7.17 From the SAC values in Table 7.7, (*a*) find the STC_1, STC_2, STC_3, STC_4, and STC_5 schedules [note that three of these schedules were already found in Problem 7.16(*a*)], (*b*) plot all five STC schedules on the same set of axes and derive the LTC curve, and (*c*) comment on the shape of the LTC curve of part (*b*).

(*a*)

Table 7.11

STC_1			STC_2			STC_3			STC_4			STC_5		
Q	AC($)	TC($)	Q	AC($)	TC($)	Q	AC($)	TC($)	Q	AC($)	TC($)	Q	AC($)	TC($)
1	15.50	15.50	2	15.50	31.00	5	10.00	50.00	8	10.00	80.00	9	12.00	108.00
2	13.00	26.00	3	12.00	36.00	6	8.50	51.00	9	9.50	85.50	10	11.00	110.00
3	12.00	36.00	4	10.00	40.00	7	8.00	56.00	10	10.00	100.00	11	11.50	126.50
4	11.75	47.00	5	9.50	47.50	8	8.50	68.00	11	12.00	132.00	12	13.00	156.00
5	13.00	65.00	6	11.00	66.00	9	10.00	90.00	12	15.00	180.00	13	16.00	208.00

(*b*)

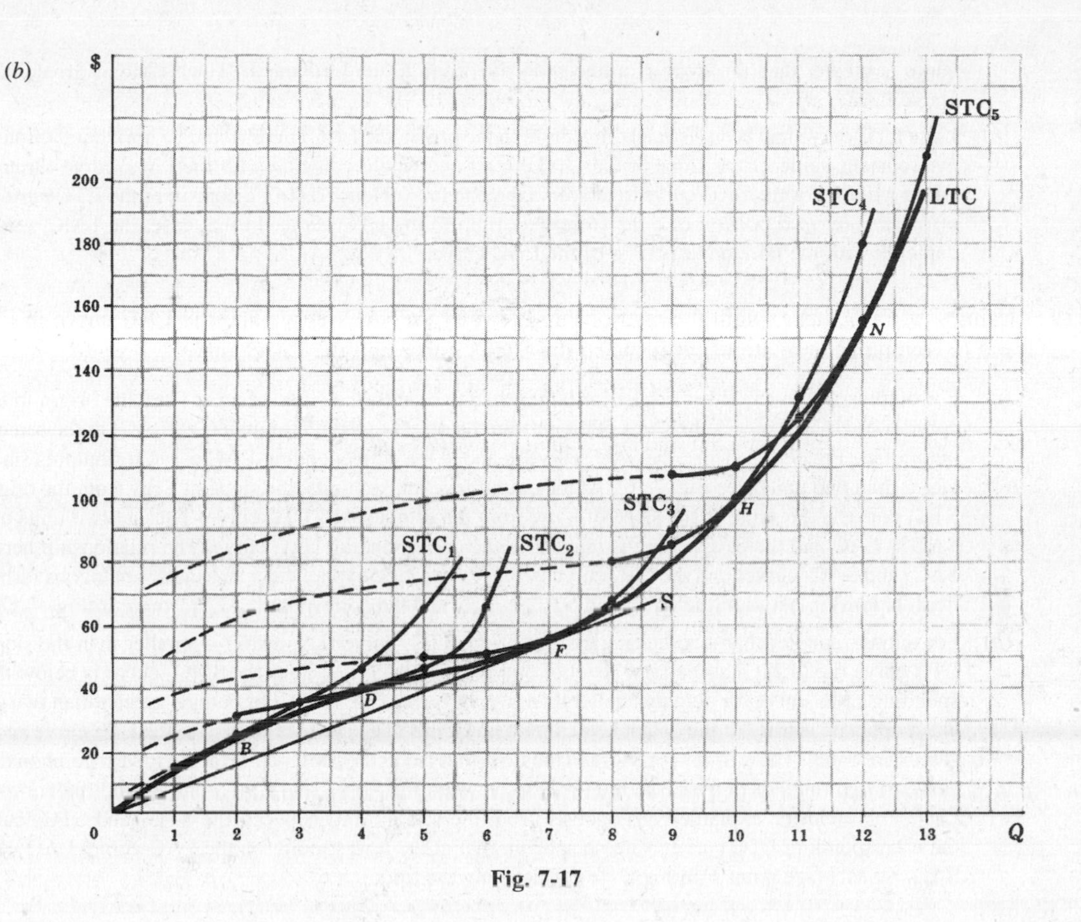

Fig. 7-17

(*c*) The LTC curve is the curve tangent to the STC curves. Note that, like the STC curves, the LTC curve is S-shaped; but it starts at the origin, since in the long run there are no fixed costs. STC curves representing larger scales of plant start higher on the vertical axis because of greater fixed costs. If instead of drawing only five STC curves, we had drawn many (each corresponding to one of the many alternative plants that the firm could build in the long run), then each point of the LTC curve would be formed by a point on the STC curve that represents the most appropriate plant to produce that output (i.e., the plant which gives the lowest possible cost to produce the *particular* level of output). Thus, no portion of the STC curves can ever be below the LTC curve derived from them. Hence the LTC curve gives the minimum LTC to produce any level of output. Also to be noted is that the LTC values for the various levels of output indicated by the LTC curve of part (*b*) correspond to the LTC values found (by multiplying output by the LAC at various levels of output) in Problem 7.15(*a*).

7.18 (*a*) Explain the shape of the LAC and LMC curves of Problem 7.15(*b*) and the relationship between them from the shape of the LTC curve of Problem 7.17(*b*). (*b*) What would be the shape of the LAC and LMC curves if the LTC curve were a straight line through the origin?

(*a*) LAC is given by the slope of a line from the origin to various points on the LTC curve. This slope declines up to point *F* (see Fig. 7-17) and rises thereafter. So the LAC curve Fig. 7-15 falls up to point *F* and then rises. On the other hand, the LMC for any level of output is given by the slope of the LTC curve at that level of output. The slope of the LTC curve of Fig. 7-17 falls continuously up to the output level of five units (the point of inflection) and rises thereafter. So the LMC curve of Fig. 7-15 falls up to the output level of five units and then rises. Finally, the slope of the LTC curve (i.e., the LMC) is less than the slope of a line from the origin to the LTC curve (i.e., the LAC), up to point *F* (see Fig. 7-17). Thus, LMC is less than or below LAC. At point *F*, the two slopes are the same, and LMC equals LAC. Past point *F*, the slope of the LTC curve is greater than the slope of a line from the origin to the LTC curve. Thus, LMC is greater than or is above LAC.

(*b*) If the LTC curve had been a straight line through the origin, the LAC curve would be horizontal throughout (at the constant value of the slope of the LTC curve) and would coincide with the LMC curve throughout its entire length. For the LAC curve to look like the one in Problem 7.14(*a*), a portion of the LTC *must coincide or be tangent to a portion* of a ray from the origin to the LTC curve. In that case, the LMC curve would coincide with the horizontal portion of the LAC curve.

7.19 Using Fig. 7-17, (*a*) explain the relationship between the SAC_1 curve and the LAC curve in Fig. 7-16 and (*b*) explain the relationship between the SMC_1 curve and the LMC curve.

(*a*) For outputs which are either smaller or larger than two units, the slope of a ray from the origin to the STC_1 curve (i.e., SAC) exceeds the slope of a ray from the origin to the LTC curve (i.e., LAC) at the same level of output (see Fig. 7-17). Thus, the SAC_1 curve is above the corresponding LAC curve for outputs smaller and larger than two units (see Fig. 7-16). At the output level of two units, the slope of a ray from the origin to the STC_1 curve is the same as the slope of a ray from the origin to the LTC curve. Thus, at two units of output, SAC = LAC and the SAC_1 curve is tangent to the corresponding LAC curve. The relationship between the SAC_3 and SAC_4 curves and the LAC curve in Fig. 7-16 can be explained in an exactly analogous fashion from the relationship between the STC_3 and STC_4 curves and the corresponding LTC curve in Fig. 7-17.

(*b*) For outputs smaller than two units, the slope of the STC_1 curve (i.e., SMC) is smaller than the slope of the LTC curve (i.e., LMC) at the same level of output (see Fig. 7-17). Thus the SMC_1 curve is below the corresponding LMC curve for outputs smaller than two units (see Fig. 7-16). For outputs greater than two units, the exact opposite is true. At the output level of two units, the STC_1 curve is tangent to the LTC curve and so their slopes are equal. Thus, SMC = LMC and the LMC intersects the SMC_1 curve at the lowest point on the SMC_1 curve at two units of output. The relationship between the SMC_3 and SMC_4 curves and the corresponding LMC curve can be explained analogously from the relationship between the STC_3 and STC_4 curves and the corresponding LTC curve. Note once again that at the lowest point on the LAC curve, LAC = LMC = SAC = SMC (see point *F* in Fig. 7-16). This is always true.

PRODUCTION FUNCTIONS AND COST CURVES

7.20 (*a*) State the relationship between production functions and cost curves. (*b*) Explain how we can derive the TP, AP, and MP curves for a factor of production from an isoquant diagram. (*c*) Explain how we derive the TVC curve from a TP curve. (*d*) State the relationship between the AVC and MC curves and the corresponding AP and MP curves.

(*a*) On Problem 6.17 we saw how a firm should combine inputs in order to minimize the cost of producing various levels of output. The production function of a firm together with the prices that the firm must pay for its factors of production or inputs determine the firm's cost curves.

(*b*) Suppose that we have only two factors of production, say labor and capital, and we keep the amount of capital used (per time period) fixed at a particular level (and are thus dealing with the short run). Then, by increasing the amount of labor used per time period, we reach higher and higher isoquants or levels of output (up to a maximum). If we plot the output that we get with different quantities of labor used per unit of time (with the fixed amounts of capital), we get the TP_L function or curve. From this TP_L curve we can derive the AP_L and the MP_L curves (see Problem 7.21).

(*c*) For each level of the TP_L, we can get the corresponding TVC by multiplying the price per unit of labor times the quantity of labor required to produce the specified level of output. Thus, from the TP_L curve we can get the corresponding TVC curve. Then from the TVC curve we can derive the AVC and the MC curves (see Problem 7.22).

(*d*) The AVC curve we get is the monetized reciprocal of the corresponding AP curve, and the MC curve is the monetized reciprocal of the corresponding MP curve (see Problem 7.23). Note that from an isoquant-isocost diagram we can also obtain the LTC and the LAC curves and show the relation between LTC and STC and between LAC and SAC (see Problem 7.24). Thus, Problems 7.21 to 7.24 summarize the relationship between production functions and cost curves.

7.21 From the isoquant diagram in Fig. 7-18, and assuming that the amount of capital is fixed at three units per time period (thus we are dealing with the short run), (*a*) derive the TP_L schedule and from it the AP_L and the MP_L schedules and (*b*) plot these curves.

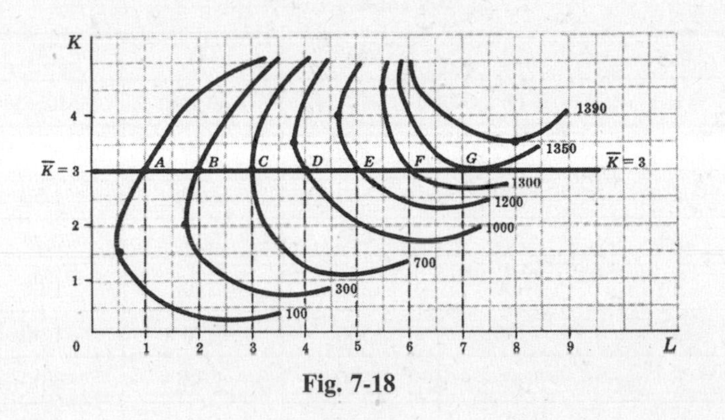

Fig. 7-18

(*a*)

Table 7.12

(1) L	1	2	3	4	5	6	7
(2) TP_L	100	300	700	1000	1200	1300	1350
(3) AP_L	100	150	233	250	240	217	194
(4) MP_L	..	200	400	300	200	100	50

(*b*)

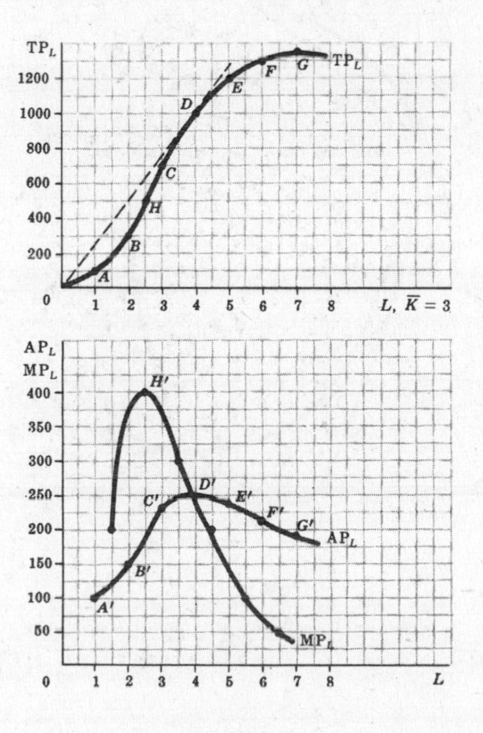

Fig. 7-19

7.22 From the TP_L schedule in Table 7.12, and assuming that the price of labor is \$300 per unit, (*a*) derive the TVC schedule and from it the AVC and MC schedules and (*b*) plot these curves.

(*a*)

Table 7.13

(1)	(2)	(3)	(4)	(5)
L	*Q*	TVC (\$)	AVC (\$)	MC (\$)
1	100	300	3.00	..
2	300	600	2.00	1.50
3	700	900	1.29	0.75
4	1000	1200	1.20	1.00
5	1200	1500	1.25	1.50
6	1300	1800	1.38	3.00
7	1350	2100	1.56	6.00

(*b*)

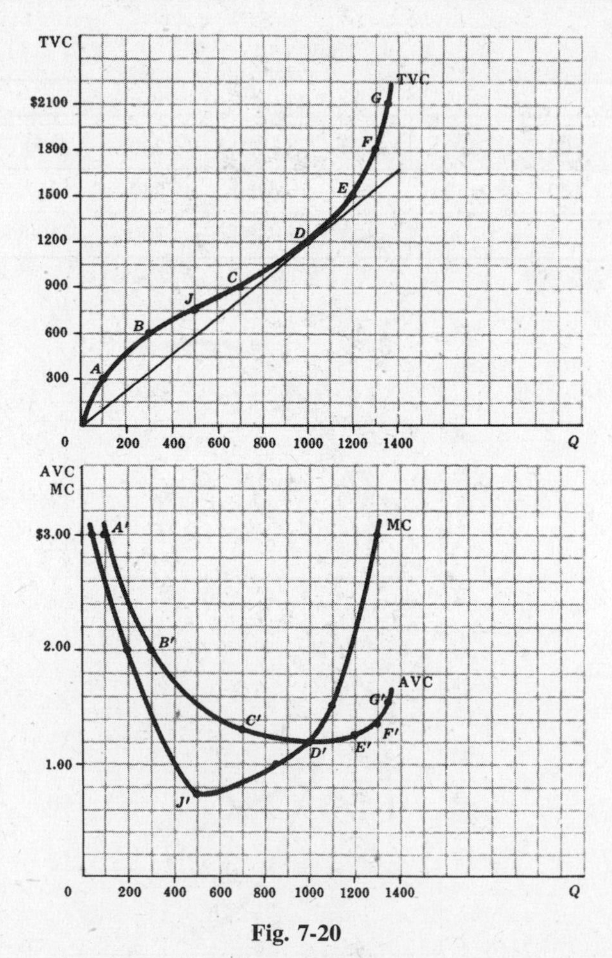

Fig. 7-20

7.23 (*a*) On the same set of axes, draw again the AVC curve and the MC curve of Fig. 7-20; on a second set of axes directly below the first, plot the AP_L and the MP_L schedules of Problem 7.21, *but with the* TP_L

(i.e., with Q), rather than L, on the horizontal axis. (*b*) On one set of axes, draw again the AP_L and the MP_L curves *exactly as they appear in Fig. 7-19* (i.e., with *L* on the horizontal axis); on a second set of axes directly below the first, plot the AVC and the MC schedules of Table 7.13, *but with L, rather than Q, on the horizontal axis*. (*c*) What is the relationship between the AP_L curve and the AVC curve? What is the relationship between the MP_L curve and the MC curve?

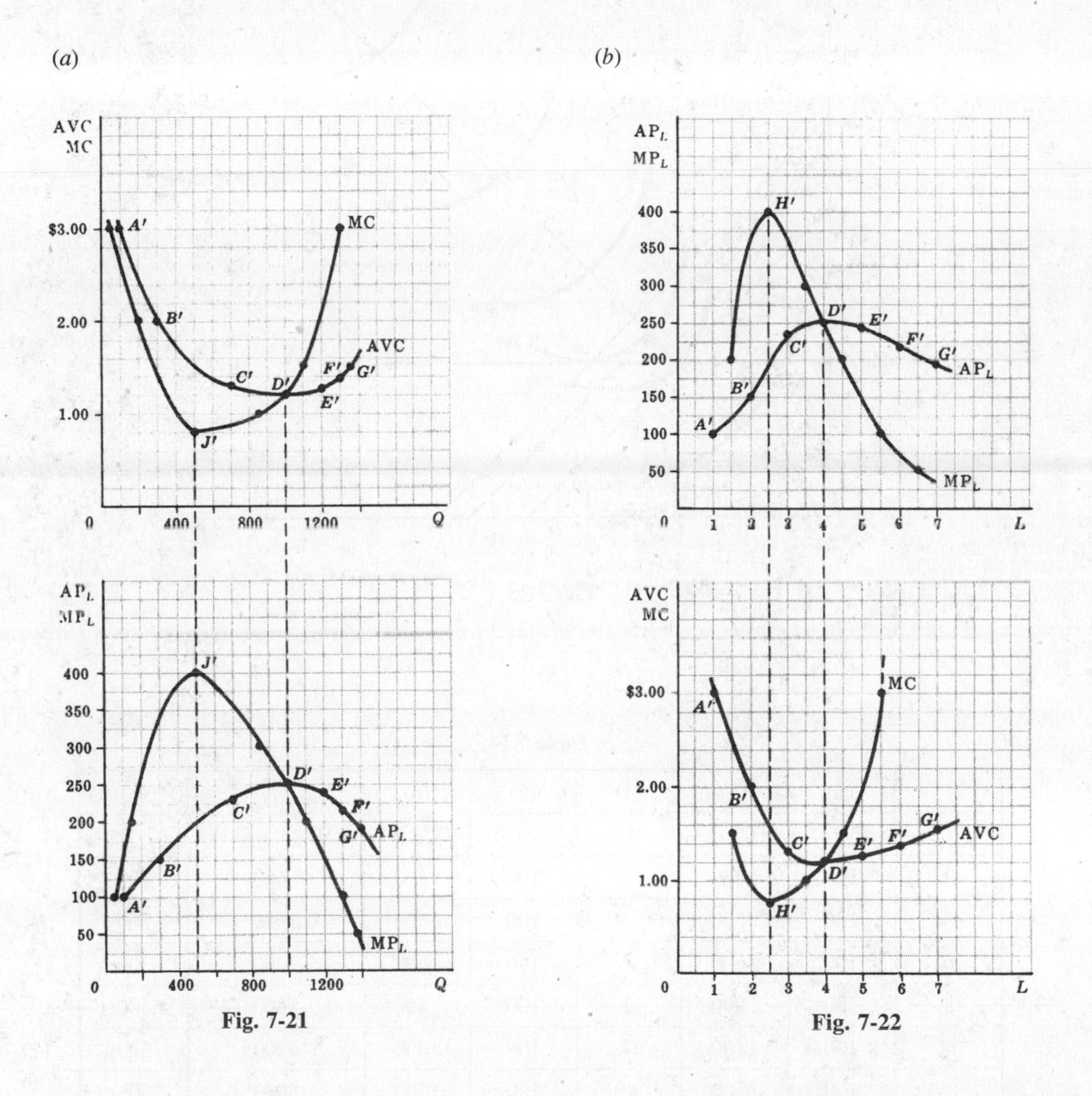

Fig. 7-21

Fig. 7-22

(*c*) Whether we measure *Q* [part (*a*)] or *L* [part (*b*)] on the horizontal axis, the AVC curve is the monetized mirror image or reciprocal of the AP_L curve, and the MC curve is the monetized mirror image or reciprocal of the MP_L curve. That is, when the AP_L curves rises, the AVC curve falls; when the AP_L is maximum, the AVC is minimum; when the AP_L curve falls, the AVC curve rises. The same relationship exists between the MP_L curve and the MC curve. Note that in Figs. 7-21 and 7-22, stage of production II for labor begins at point *D′* (i.e., where the AP_L curve begins to decline or where the AVC curve begins to rise).

7.24 In Fig. 7-23, line *OA* is the expansion path. If $P_L = P_K = \$100$, (*a*) find the LTC schedule and plot it and (*b*) with reference to the isoquant-isocost diagram in Fig. 7-23 and assuming that the amount of capital used per time period is kept fixed at five units, explain why STC can never be less than LTC.

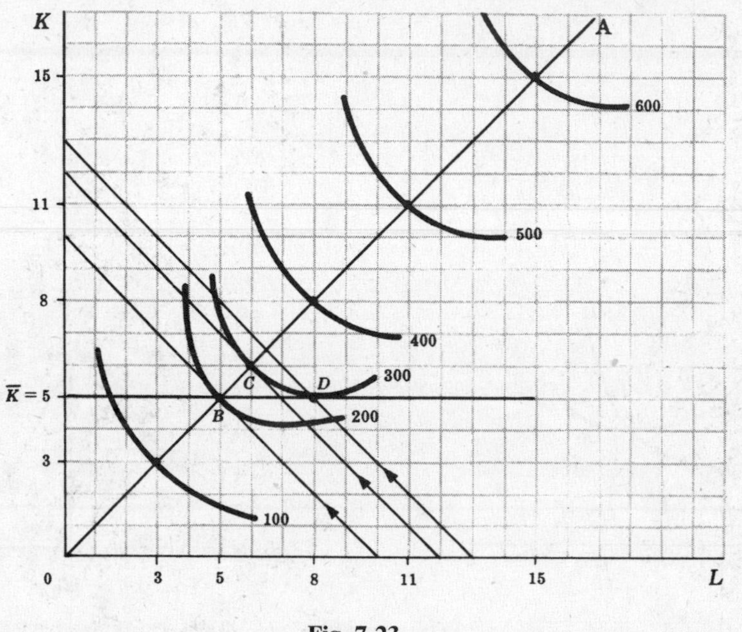

Fig. 7-23

(*a*)

Table 7.14

(1)	(2)	(3)	(4)	(5)	(6)	(7)	(8)
L	P_L (\$)	TC_L (\$)	K	P_K (\$)	TC_K (\$)	LTC $(3+6)$ (\$)	Q
3	100	300	3	100	300	600	100
5	100	500	5	100	500	1000	200
6	100	600	6	100	600	1200	300
8	100	800	8	100	800	1600	400
11	100	1100	11	100	1000	2200	500
15	100	1500	15	100	1500	3000	600

(*b*) When the firm employs five units of labor and five units of capital per time period, it produces 200 units of output at a cost of \$1000. This is given by point *B* in the isoquant-isocost diagram (Fig. 7-23). At point *B*, $MP_L/P_L = MP_K/P_K$. Suppose that now the firm wants to increase its output to 300 units per time period. With the amount of capital fixed at five units (we are thus dealing with the short run), the firm could produce 300 units of output by using eight units of labor (thus moving to point *D*). At point *D*, the firm incurs a TC of \$1300 and $MP_L/P_L < MP_K/P_K$. In the long run (i.e., when all factors are variable), the firm would produce 300 units of output by using six units of labor and six units of capital (point *C*) and incur a TC of only \$1200. At point *C*, MP_L/P_L is once again equal to MP_K/P_K.

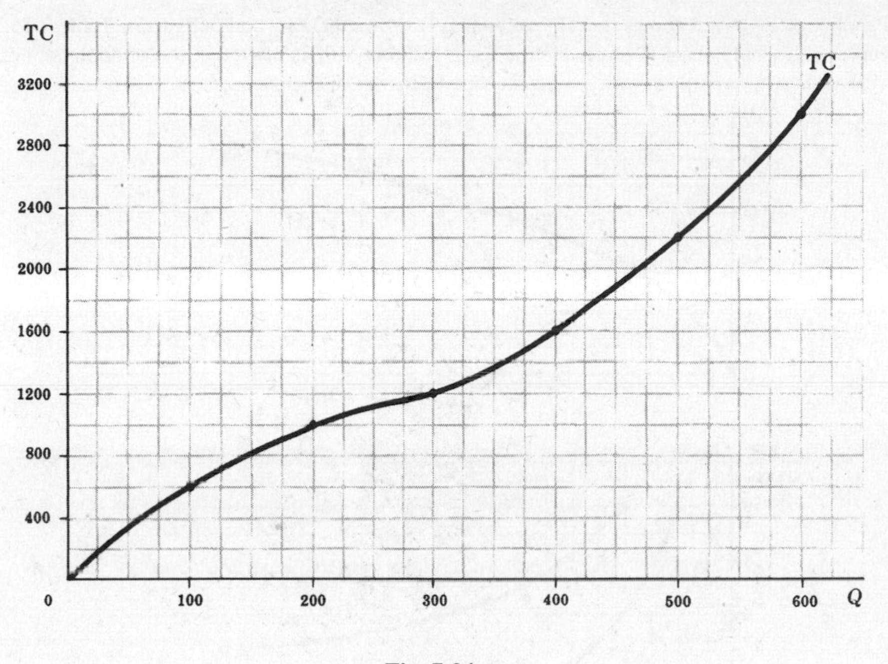

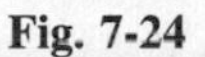
Fig. 7-24

Points along the expansion path correspond to the points of optimal adjustment. So STC equals LTC and the STC curve is tangent to the LTC curve. Points off the expansion path correspond to points of suboptimal adjustment. So STC exceeds LTC and the STC curve is above the LTC curve. Thus, STC is never less than LTC and the STC curve is never below the LTC curve. (Note that from the expansion path we can also derive directly the LAC schedule and show the relationship between LAC and SAC. Try to do that.)

THE COBB-DOUGLAS PRODUCTION FUNCTION

7.25 Assuming that K is constant at $\bar{K} = 1$ for the Cobb-Douglas production function of Example 1, (*a*) derive the TP_L, AP_L, MP_L and (*b*) plot the TP_L, AP_L, and MP_L.

(*a*) $\text{TP}_L = 10L^{1/2}1^{1/2} = 10L^{1/2} = 10\sqrt{L}$

Table 7.15

L	TP_L	AP_L	MP_L
0	0	...	...
1	10.00	10.00	10.00
2	14.14	7.07	4.14
3	17.32	5.77	3.18
4	20.00	5.00	2.68

(*b*) Panel A of Fig. 7.25 shows the TP_L and panel B shows the AP_L and MP_L from Table 7.15. Note that these curves show only stage II of production for L and that MP_L is plotted at the midpoints of L.

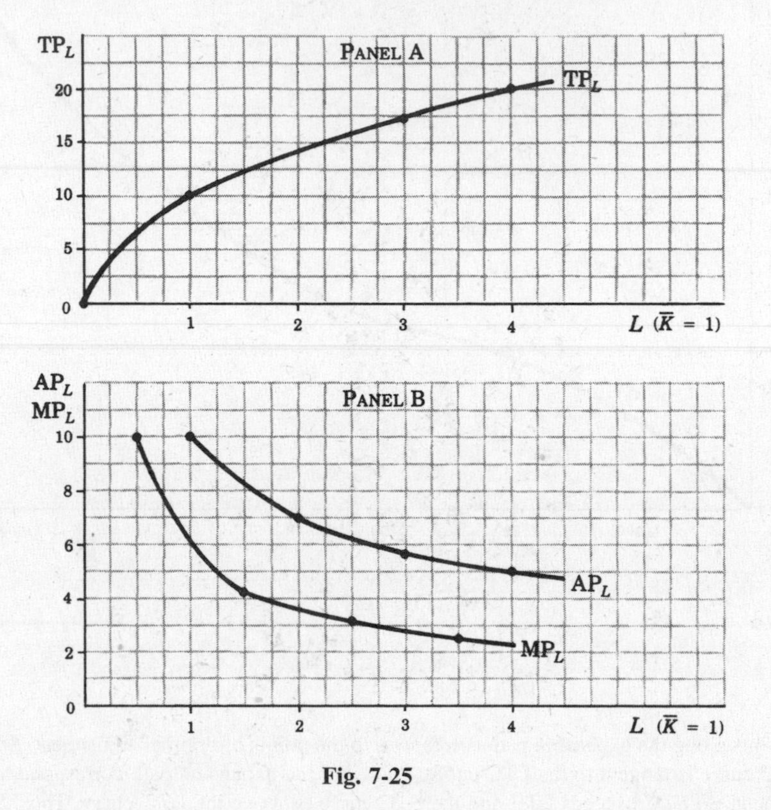

Fig. 7-25

7.26 For the Cobb-Douglas of Example 1, (*a*) derive the expansion path and (*b*) plot the expansion path, assuming $P_L = P_K = \$1$, and sketch on the same figure the isoquants for $Q = 10$, $Q = 20$, and $Q = 40$.

(*a*) The expansion path is the locus of producer equilibrium points resulting from increasing expenditures while holding factor prices constant. It is derived in Table 7.16 from $Q = 10L^{1/2}K^{1/2} = 10\sqrt{L}\sqrt{K}$ by varying both L and K proportionately.

Table 7.16

L	K	$10\sqrt{L}\sqrt{K}$	Q
0	0	$10\sqrt{0}\sqrt{0}$	0
1	1	$10\sqrt{1}\sqrt{1}$	10
2	2	$10\sqrt{2}\sqrt{2}$	20
3	3	$10\sqrt{3}\sqrt{3}$	30
4	4	$10\sqrt{4}\sqrt{4}$	40

(*b*) Fig. 7-26 shows the expansion path and hypothetical isoquants for $Q = 10$, $Q = 20$, and $Q = 40$. Note that the expansion path is a straight line through the origin and the isoquants are equally spaced and have equal slope along any ray or isocline from the origin.

7.27 For a Cobb-Douglas production function of the form $Q = AL^{\alpha}K^{1-\alpha}$ prove that (*a*) it shows constant returns to scale and (*b*) the AP_L is a function of K/L only.

(*a*) Since $\alpha + 1 - \alpha = 1$, this Cobb-Douglas production function exhibits constant returns to scale and is said to be homogeneous of degree one or linearly homogeneous. "Constant returns to scale," "homogeneous of degree one," and "linearly homogeneous" all mean the same thing and are used interchangeably.

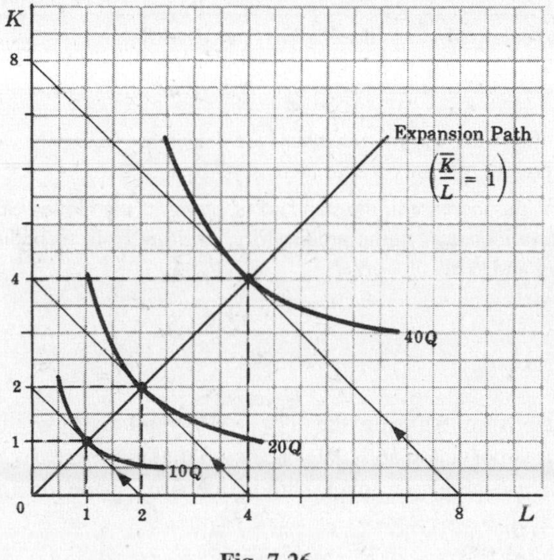

Fig. 7-26

(*b*)
$$AP_L = \frac{Q}{L} = \frac{AL^{\alpha}K^{1-\alpha}}{L} = AL^{\alpha-1}K^{1-\alpha} = A\left(\frac{K}{L}\right)^{1-\alpha}$$

Since for any Cobb-Douglas production function, A and α assume fixed values, $AP_L = f(K/L)$ only. That is, the AP_L remains the same regardless of amount of L and K used in production, as long as K/L remains constant (or along any expansion path or isocline). The same is true for $MP_L = \alpha A(K/L)^{1-\alpha} = f(K/L)$.

7.28 (*a*) If the actual estimated α and β are as given in Table. 7.17, what type of returns to scale does each industry exhibit? (*b*) By how much does output rise in the American food industry if L increases by 1%? If K increases by 1%? (*c*) It has been found that for the United States and other developed nations only about one-third of the increase in the standard of living over the years was due to the increase in the physical units of L and K used. What was the remainder due to?

Table 7.17

Industry	Country	α	β
1. Telphone	Canada	.70	.41
2. Gas	France	.83	.10
3. Chemicals	India	.80	.37
4. Electricity	India	.20	.67
5. Machinery and tools	United States	.71	.26
6. Food	United States	.72	.35
7. Communications	U.S.S.R	.80	.38

(*a*) The answer for each of the seven industries is given in Table 7.18, where i = increasing returns to scale and d = decreasing returns to scale.

Table 7.18

Industry	1	2	3	4	5	6	7
$\alpha + \beta$	1.11	0.93	1.17	0.87	0.96	1.07	1.18
Returns to scale	i	d	i	d	d	i	i

(*b*) Since $\alpha = 0.72$ in the American food industry, a 1% increase in L only would increase Q by 0.72%. Since $\beta = 0.35$, a 1% increase in K only would increase Q by 0.35%.

(*c*) About two-thirds of the increase in the standard of living of the United States and other developed nations over time was due to increases in the productivity resulting from technological advances and increases in the level of training and skills of workers.

X-INEFFICIENCY

7.29 (*a*) What is the relationship between the TP_L, AP_L, and MP_L of Table 7.15 and X-efficiency? (*b*) If additional worker supervision and better decision making increase X-efficiency, how much supervision should the firm use and how much should the firm spend on improving its decision-making process?

(*a*) The TP_L, AP_L, and MP_L schedules are based on the assumption of full X-efficiency. That is, they represent the maximum quantity of output per unit of time that can be obtained from a particular combination of inputs with the best technology available. They assume that labor and management put forth their best effort. In the real world, this is seldom the case, so that for each input combination, the TP_L, AP_L, and MP_L are usually less than indicated in Table 7.15 by the extent of the X-efficiency present.

(*b*) It is true that additional worker supervision and better decision making can often increase X-efficiency. However, they also have a cost. Therefore, a firm should implement more worker supervision and expend money to improve decision making if the extra return from these efforts exceeds their extra costs and until MR = MC. At present, the reduction of X-inefficiency by increasing motivation may represent a huge and largely untapped potential source of benefit.

TECHNOLOGICAL PROGRESS

7.30 Repeat Fig. 7-6 and show on it the effect of each type of technological progress on K/L at constant relative factor prices (w/r).

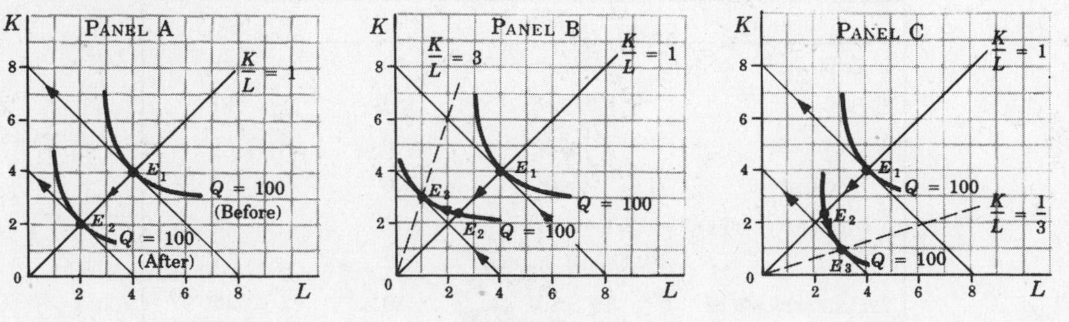

Fig. 7-27

Since with neutral technological progress the MP_L and MP_K increase in the same proportion, there is no substitution of L for K (or K for L) in production at unchanged w/r, so that K/L remains unchanged at $K/L = 1$ (see point E_2 in panel A of Fig. 7.27). Since with K-using technological progress MP_K increases proportionately more than MP_L, K is substituted for L in production at constant w/r so that K/L rises to $K/L = 3$ (see point E_3 in panel B). With L-using technological progress K/L falls to $K/L = 1/3$ at constant w/r (see point E_3 in panel C).

7.31 (*a*) What is the relative share of NNP going to L and K and the ratio of the relative shares going to L and K? (*b*) How do the different types of technological progress affect relative shares if w/r remains constant?

(*a*) Let w = average wave rate, r = average return on capital or interest rate, L = total amount of L employed in the economy, K = total amount of capital, P = general price index, and Q = general quantity index (so that PQ = NNP). Then, the relative share of NNP going to L is wL/PQ, the relative share going to $K = rK/PQ$, and the ratio of the relative share going to L and $K = (wL/PQ) \div (rK/P2) = wL/rK$.

(*b*) Since neutral technological progress leaves K/L unchanged, the ratio of the relative share going to L and K remains unchanged if w/r remains unchanged. Since K-using technological progress increases K/L (which means that L/K falls), wL/rK falls. Finally, since L-using technological progress reduces K/L, wL/rK increases.

COSTS OF PRODUCTION WITH CALCULUS

***7.32** A firm faces the general cost function of $C = wL + rK$ and production function of $Q = f(L, K)$. Derive by using calculus the condition to minimize the cost of producing a given level of output (Q^*).

Forming function Z', which incorporates the cost function to be minimized to produce output Q^*, we get

$$Z' = wL + rK + \lambda'[Q^* - f(L, K)]$$

where λ' is the Lagrangian multiplier. Taking the first partial derivative of Z' with respect to L and K and setting them equal to zero, we get

$$\frac{\partial Z'}{\partial L} = w - \lambda'\frac{\partial f}{\partial L} = 0 \quad \text{and} \quad \frac{\partial Z'}{\partial K} = r - \lambda'\frac{\partial Z'}{\partial K} = 0$$

Dividing the first equation by the second, we get

$$\frac{w}{r} = \frac{\partial f/\partial L}{\partial f/\partial K} = \frac{MP_L}{MP_K} = MRTS_{LK} \quad \text{or} \quad \frac{MP_L}{w} = \frac{MP_K}{r}$$

***7.33** Given $Q = 100K^{0.5}L^{0.5}$, $w = \$30$, and $r = \$40$. (*a*) Find the quantity of labor and capital that the firm should use in order to minimize the cost of producing 1444 units of output. (*b*) What is this minimum cost?

(*a*)
$$Z' = \$30L + \$40K + \lambda'[Q^* - 100L^{0.5}K^{0.5}]$$
$$\frac{\partial Z'}{\partial L} = \$30 - \lambda' 50L^{-0.5}K^{0.5} = 0$$
$$\frac{\partial Z'}{\partial K} = \$40 - \lambda' 50L^{0.5}K^{-0.5} = 0$$

Dividing the first partial derivative equation by the second, we have

$$\frac{3}{4} = \frac{K}{L} \quad \text{so that} \quad K = \left(\frac{3}{4}\right)(L)$$

By then substituting this value of K into the given production function for 1444 units of output, we get

$$1444 = 100L^{0.5}(0.75L)^{0.5} \quad \text{so that} \quad 1444 = 100L = \sqrt{0.75}$$

$$\text{and} \quad L = \frac{1444}{86.6} = 16.67$$

Substituting the value of $L = 16.67$ into $K = (3/4)L$, we then get

$$K = \left(\frac{3}{4}\right)16.67 = 12.51$$

(*b*) The minimum cost of producing 1444 units of output is

$$C = \$30(16.67) + \$40(12.51) = \$1000.50$$

***7.34** Given $Q = 100KL$, $w = \$30$, and $r = \$40$. (*a*) Find the quantity of labor and capital that the firm should use in order to maximize output. (*b*) What is this level of output?

(*a*)

$$Z = 100L^{0.5}K^{0.5} + \lambda(\$1000 - \$30L - \$40K)$$

$$\frac{\partial Z}{\partial L} = 50L^{-0.5}K^{0.5} - \lambda\$30 = 0$$

$$\frac{\partial Z}{\partial K} = 50^{0.5}K^{-0.5} - \lambda\$40 = 0$$

Dividing the second partial derivative by the first, we have

$$\frac{K}{L} = \frac{3}{4} \quad \text{so that} \quad K = \frac{3}{4}L$$

By then substituting this value of K into the cost or expenditure constraint on the firm, we get

$$\$1000 = \$30L + \$40 \times \frac{3}{4}L$$

$$\$1000 = \$60L$$

so that $L = 16.67$ units.

Substituting this value of L into $K = \frac{3}{4}L$, we have

$$K = \frac{3}{4} \times 16.67 = 12.50$$

(*b*) With $L = 16.67$ and $K = 12.50$, the output of the firm is

$$Q = 100\sqrt{16.67}\sqrt{12.50} = 1444$$

That is, the maximum output that the firm can produce is 1444 units of the commodity.

Midterm Examination

1. As a result of the 1979–1980 energy crisis, government policy makers originally estimated that American consumers would have to reduce their consumption of gasoline by about 30%. (*a*) What measures could be undertaken to reduce gasoline consumption? What are the pros and cons of each measure? (*b*) If by 1982 the quantity of gasoline consumed by each vehicle dropped by 8% in the face of a 40% increase in price, what is a rough measure of the coefficient of price elasticity of demand for gasoline? To achieve the needed 30% reduction in gasoline consumption, what increase in the price of gasoline does your estimate of the price elasticity of demand require? (*c*) How did the administration in Washington attempt to solve this problem?

2. Using indifference curve analysis, derive an elastic demand curve of commodity X for a reduction in P_x, while keeping constant the price of Y and the consumer's tastes and money income.

3. (*a*) Given the following TP_L, find the AP_L and MP_L.

L	1	2	3	4	5	6	7
TP	2	6	12	16	18	18	16

(*b*) On the same set of axes, plot the TP_L, AP_L, and MP_L schedules and indicate on the figure the stages of production for L and K; where does the law of the diminishing returns for L begin to operate? Where will a rational producer produce? Why? (*c*) If both L and K are variable, and TO = \$12, P_L = \$1, and P_K = \$2, plot the isocost. What is its slope? On the same graph, draw an isoquant which shows the equilibrium point where the producer uses $6L$ and $3K$. Express the condition for producer equilibrium in terms of the $MRTS_{LK}$, MP_L, MP_K, P_L, and P_K.

4. (*a*) Given the following TVC schedule and TFC = \$12, (*a*) find TC, AFC, AVC, AC, and MC for the various levels of output.

Q	1	2	3	4	5	6
TVC	\$6	8	9	10.5	14	21

(*b*) Plot on the same graph the AVC, AC, and MC schedules of part (*a*). What is the relationship between AVC, AC, and MC? (*c*) Draw a figure clearly showing the relationship between the typical SAC, SMC, LAC, LMC.

***5.** Redraw the figure of Problem 2 and show on it the Hicksian and Slutsky substitution and income effects and derive the Hicksian and the Slutsky demand curves. Which is a better measure of the substitution and income effects? Why?

***6.** For a Cobb-Douglas production function, (*a*) write its formula in terms of L and K, α and β, and indicate the economic meaning of each component of the formula. (*b*) Sketch the typical TP_L, AP_L, and MP_L curves. To which stage of production do they refer? (*c*) If $\alpha = 1.5$ and $\beta = 0.5$, sketch the expansion path with isoquants $Q = 100$ and $Q = 400$. What is the value of $(e \text{ subst.})_{LK}$?

*Optional

Answers

1. (*a*) One way to reduce gasoline consumption is rationing. Such a policy could cut gasoline consumption by the required 30% but would also lead to black markets and a huge bureaucracy to enforce rationing. As a result, rationing was not adopted but was reserved as a policy of last resort only. Another way to reduce gasoline consumption is by increasing the price of gasoline. The advantage of this policy is that it works through the price mechanism rather than replacing it (as in the case of rationing). The disadvantage is that because the coefficient of price elasticity of demand is very low, a huge price increase would be required to achieve the needed 30% cutback in the quantity of gasoline consumed.

(*b*) When the amount of gasoline demanded per vehicle dropped 8% in the face of a price increase of 40%, the coefficient of price elasticity of demand for gasoline was roughly

$$e = -\frac{\%\Delta Q}{\%\Delta P} = -\frac{(-8\%)}{(+40\%)} = 0.2$$

This is a very rough measure because it assumes that everything else remained constant, which was clearly not the case. To achieve the 30% reduction in gasoline consumption, the required price increase would have to be roughly

$$\%\Delta P = \frac{\%\Delta Q}{e} = \frac{30\%}{0.2} = 150\%$$

(*c*) The Administration in Washington, while stressing conservation, believed that deregulation and the resulting sharp increase in gasoline prices would stimulate new exploration which would lead to a large increase in domestic petroleum extraction. Thus the Administration stressed the supply side to attempt to solve this problem while previous efforts relied mostly on the demand side.

2. In the top panel of Fig. M-1, point A on budget line 1 and indifference curve I is the original consumer equilibrium point. When P_x falls, equilibrium is at point B, where indifference curve II is tangent to budget line 2. The movement from point A to point B (Q_1 Q_4) is the total of the substitution and income effects of the fall in P_x and gives d_x (the usual demand curve) in the bottom panel. Because the slope of the price consumption curve is negative between points A and B, d_x is price-elastic.

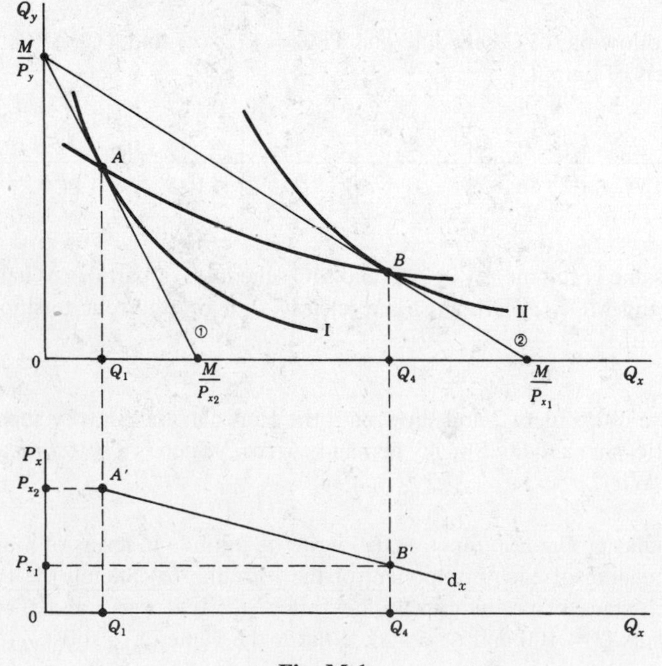

Fig. M-1

3. (*a*)

L	TP_L	AP_L	MP_L
0	0	0	—
1	2	2	2
2	6	3	4
3	12	4	6
4	16	4	4
5	18	3.6	2
6	18	3	0
7	16	2.29	−2

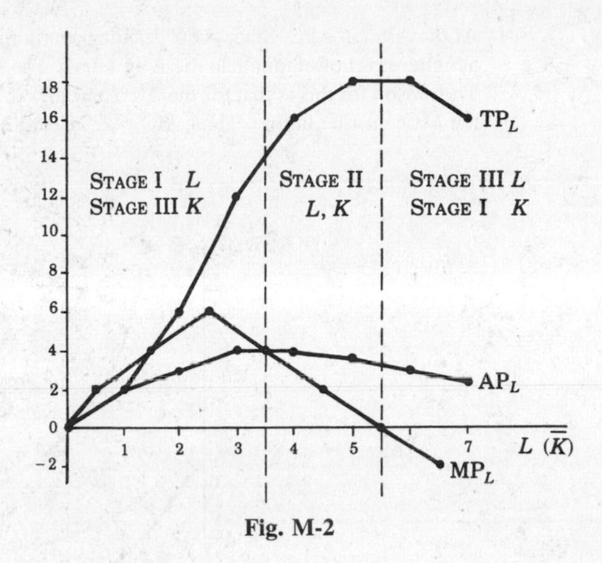

Fig. M-2

(*b*) The law of diminishing returns for L begins to operate where MP_L begins to decline. A rational producer will produce at stage II for L and K, where the AP and MP of L and K are both positive but declining. The producer will not produce in stage I for L because MP_K is negative. Similarly, the producer will not produce in stage III for L because MP_L is negative. See Fig. M-2.

(*c*) The slope of the isoquant is

$$(-)\frac{TO/P_K}{TO/P_L} = (-)\frac{\cancel{TO}}{P_K} \cdot \frac{P_L}{\cancel{TO}} = (-)\frac{P_L}{P_K} = (-)\frac{1}{2}$$

The condition for producer's equilibrium is

$$(+)MRTS_{LK} = (-)\frac{MP_L}{MP_K} = (-)\frac{P_L}{P_K}$$

That is, at equilibrium, the slope of the isoquant equals the slope of the isocost.

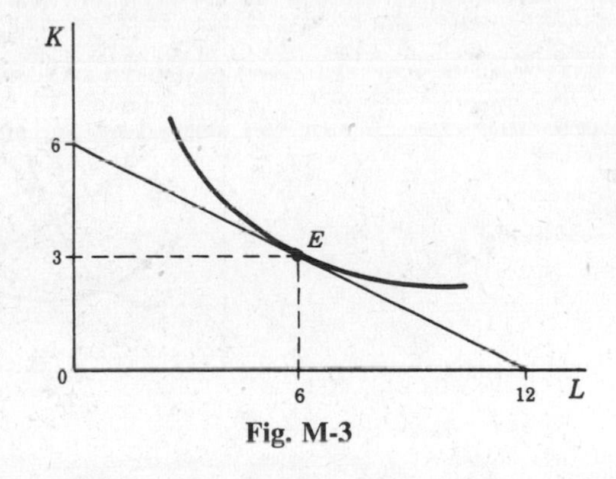

Fig. M-3

4. (*a*)

Q	TFC ($)	TVC ($)	TC ($)	AFC ($)	AVC ($)	AC ($)	MC ($)
0	12	0	12	—	—	—	—
1	12	6	18	12	6	18	6
2	12	8	20	6	4	10	2
3	12	9	21	4	3	7	1
4	12	10	22	3	2.50	5.50	1
5	12	14	26	2.40	2.80	5.20	4
6	12	21	23	2	3.50	5.50	7

(*b*) AC = AVC + AFC. Since AFC declines continuously as output expands, the AC curve reaches its lowest point at a higher level of output than the AVC curve. The MC curve crosses the AVC and AC curves at their lowest point. The reason for this is that for the AVC and the AC to fall, the MC must be lower, and for the AVC and AC to rise, the MC must be higher. Thus, MC = AVC and MC = AC at the lowest AVC and AC. See Fig. M-4.

(*c*) See Fig. M-5.

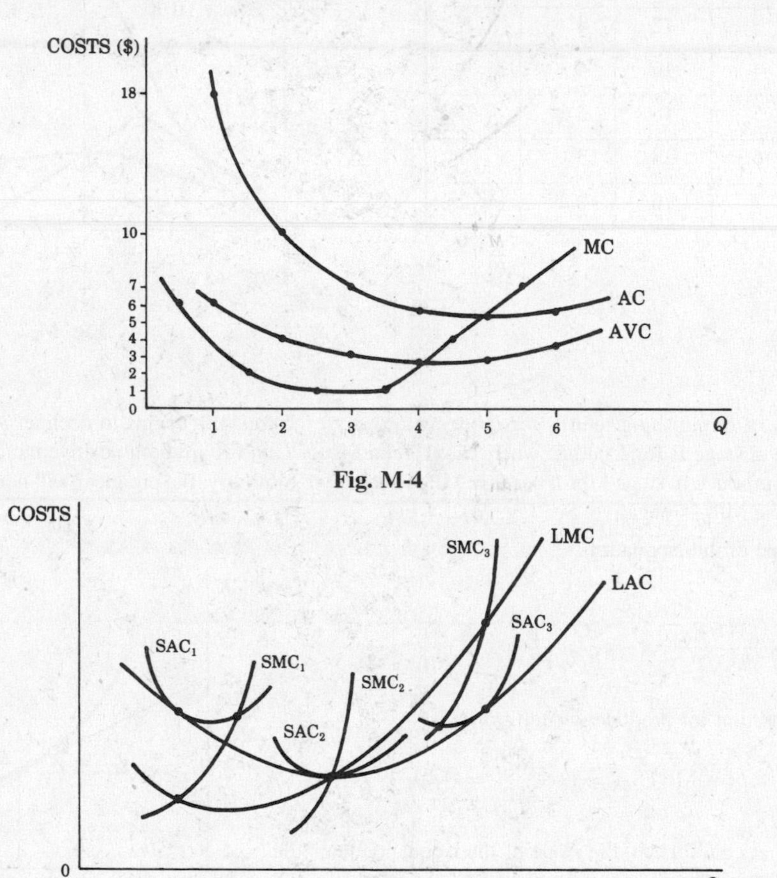

Fig. M-4

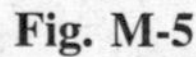

Fig. M-5

***5.** In the top panel of Fig. M-6, real income is kept constant according to Hicks by shifting budget line 2 down and parallel to itself (budget line 3) until it is tangent to the original indifference curve I at point *C*. The movement from *A* to *C* (Q_1 Q_2) is the Hicksian substitution effect shown on the Hicksian demand curve in the bottom panel. Q_2 Q_4 is then the Hicksian income effect. In the top panel, real income is kept constant according to Slutsky by rotating budget line 1 through point *A* until it is parallel to budget line 2. This gives budget line 4, which is tangent to indifference curve III at point *D*. The movement from *A* to *D* (Q_1 Q_3) is the Slutsky substitution effect shown on the Slutsky demand curve in the bottom panel. Q_3 Q_4 is then the Slutsky income effect. The Slutsky method is a better measure of the substitution effect because, as with the income effect, it puts the consumer on a higher indifference curve and because it can be obtained from observed prices and quantities without the need to know the exact shape of the indifference curve.

***6.** (*a*) $Q = AL^{\alpha}K^{\beta}$, where Q = output, and L and K = inputs. A, α, and β are positive parameters determined in each case by the data. The greater the value of A, the more advanced is the technology. α and β measure the output elasticity of L and K, respectively. There are constant, increasing, or decreasing returns to scale to the extent that $\alpha + \beta = 1$, $\alpha + \beta > 1$, or $\alpha + \beta < 1$, respectively.

(*b*) See Fig. M-7. The TP_L, AP_L, and MP_L refer only to stage II of production (i.e., the Cobb-Douglas production function is not defined for stage I or III of L and K).

(*c*) In Fig. M-8, doubling the inputs of L and K quadruples output. e subst.$_{LK} = 1$ for a Cobb-Douglas.

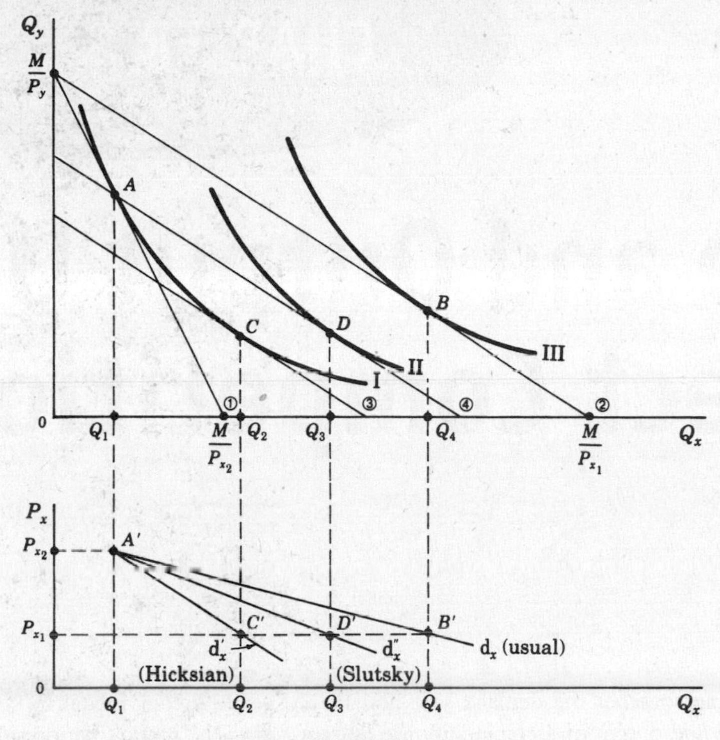

Fig. M-6

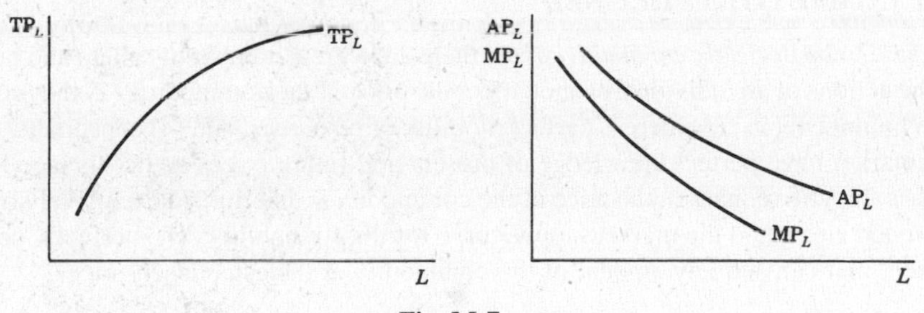

Fig. M-7

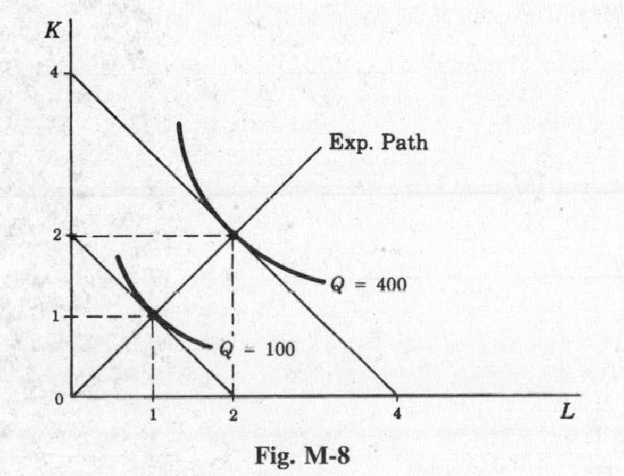

Fig. M-8

CHAPTER 8

Price and Output Under Perfect Competition

We will now bring together the demand side and the cost side of our model to see how, under perfect competition, the price and output of a commodity are determined in the market period, in the short run, and in the long run.

8.1 PERFECT COMPETITION DEFINED

A market is said to *be perfectly competitive* if (1) there are a great number of sellers and buyers of the commodity, so that the actions of an individual cannot affect the price of the commodity; (2) the products of all firms in the market are homogeneous; (3) there is perfect mobility of resources; and (4) consumers, resource owners, and firms in the market have perfect knowledge of present and future prices and costs (see Problem 8.1).

In a perfectly competitive market, the price of the commodity is determined exclusively by the intersection of the market demand curve and the market supply curve for the commodity. The perfectly competitive firm is then a "price taker" and can sell any amount of the commodity at the established price.

EXAMPLE 1. In Fig. 8-1, d is the demand curve facing a "representative" or average firm in a perfectly competitive market. Note that d is infinitely elastic or is given by a horizontal line at the equilibrium market price of $8 per unit. This means that the firm can sell any quantity of the commodity at that price.

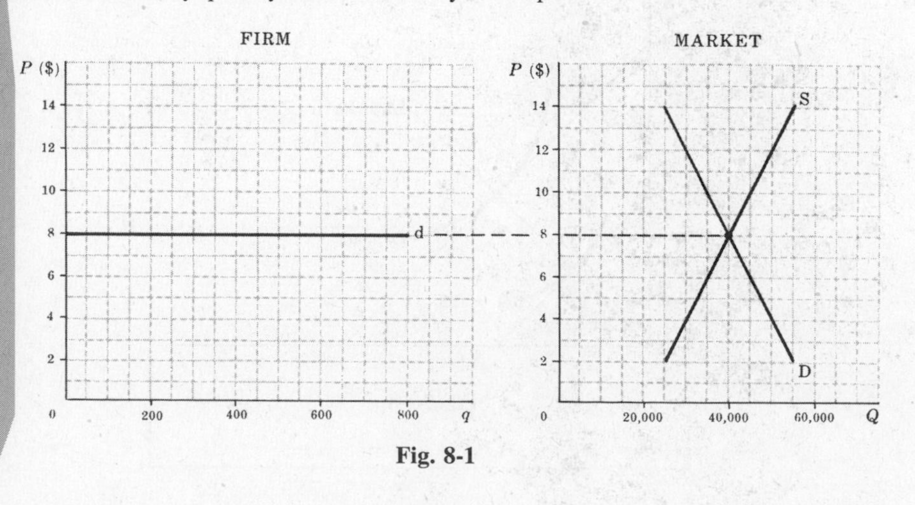

Fig. 8-1

8.2 PRICE DETERMINATION IN THE MARKET PERIOD

The *market period*, or the very short run, refers to the period of time in which the market supply of the commodity is completely fixed. When dealing with perishable commodities in the market period, costs of production are irrelevant in the determination of the market price and the entire supply of the commodity is offered for sale at whatever price it can fetch.

EXAMPLE 2. In Fig. 8-2, S represents the fixed market supply of a commodity in the market period. If the market demand curve for the commodity is given by D, the equilibrium market price is $8 per unit in the market period. If we had D' instead, the equilibrium price, would be $24.

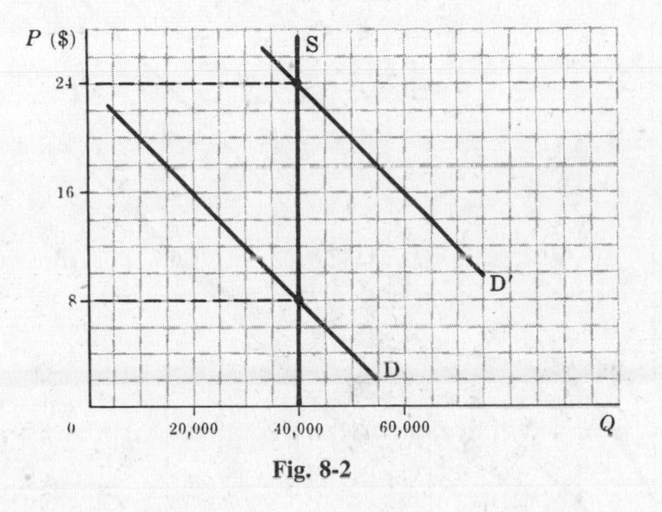

Fig. 8-2

8.3 SHORT-RUN EQUILIBRIUM OF THE FIRM: TOTAL APPROACH

Total profits equal total revenue (TR) minus total costs (TC). Thus, total profits are maximized when the positive difference between TR and TC is greatest. The equilibrium output of the firm is the output at which total profits are maximized.

EXAMPLE 3. In Table 8.1, quantity [column (1)] times price [column (2)] gives us TR [column (3)]. TR minus TC [column (4)] gives us total profits [column (5)]. Total profits are maximized (at $1690) when the firm produces and sells 650 units of the commodity per time period.

Table 8.1

(1) *Q*	(2) *P* ($)	(3) TR ($)	(4) TC ($)	(5) Total Profits ($)
0	8	0	800	−800
100	8	800	2000	−1200
200	8	1600	2300	−700
300	8	2400	2400	0
400	8	3200	2524	+676
500	8	4000	2775	+1225
600	8	4800	3200	+1600
*650	8	5200	3510	+1690
700	8	5600	4000	+1600
800	8	6400	6400	0

EXAMPLE 4. The profit-maximizing level of output for this firm can also be viewed from Fig. 8-3 (obtained by plotting the values of columns 1, 3, 4, and 5 of Table 8.1). In Fig. 8-3, the arrows indicate parallel lines. The TR curve is a positively sloped straight line through the origin because P remains constant at \$8. At 100 units output, this firm maximizes total *losses* or negative profits (points A and A'). At 300 units of output, TR equals TC (point B) and the firm *breaks even* (point B'). The firm maximizes its total profits (point D') when it produces and sells 650 units of output. At this output level, the TR curve and the TC curve have the same slope and so the vertical distance between them is greatest.

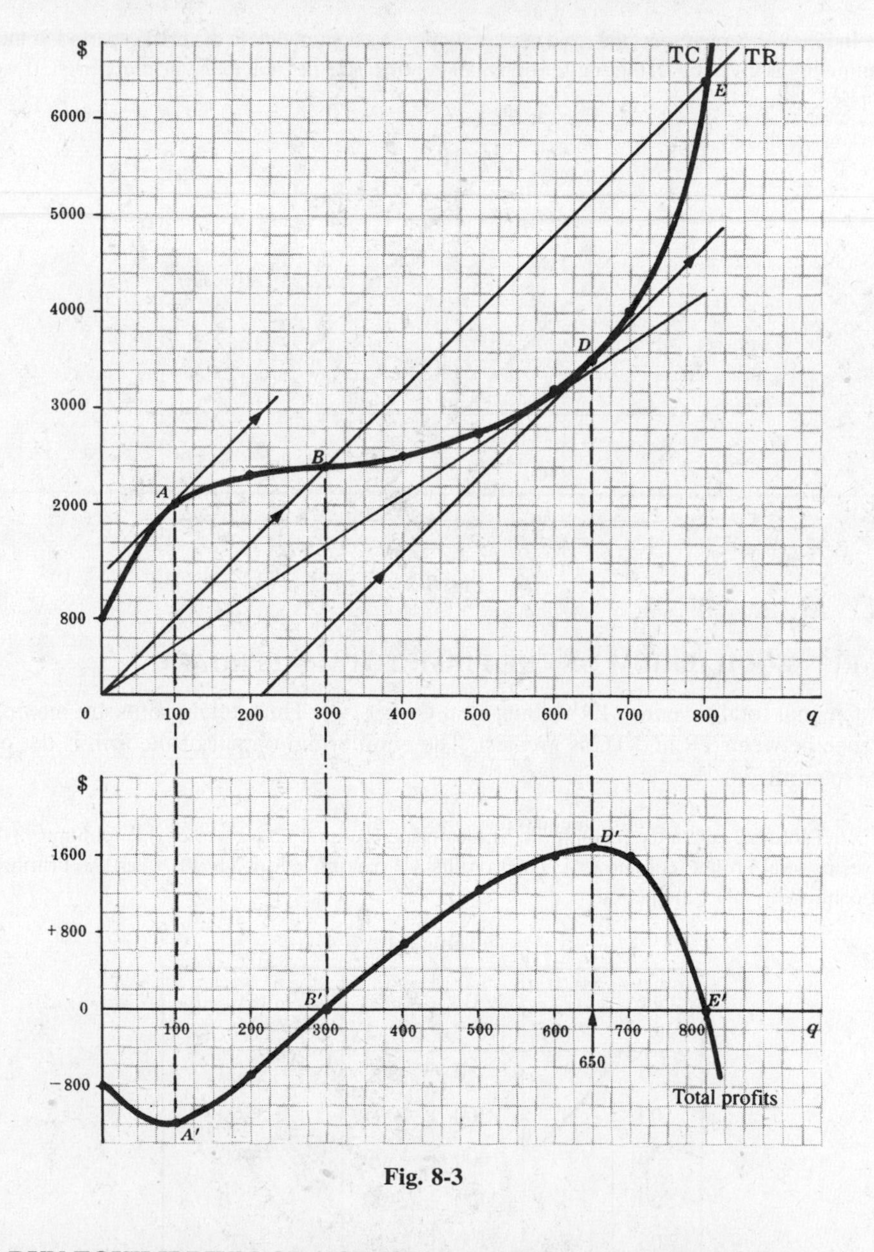

Fig. 8-3

8.4 SHORT-RUN EQUILIBRIUM OF THE FIRM: MARGINAL APPROACH

In general, it is more useful to analyze the short-run equilibrium of the firm with the marginal revenue–marginal cost approach. *Marginal revenue* (MR) is the change in TR for a one-unit change in the quantity sold. Thus, MR equals the slope of the TR curve. Since in perfect competition, P is constant for the firm, MR equals P. The marginal approach tells us that the perfectly competitive firm maximizes its short-run total profits at the output level, where MR *or P equals* marginal cost (MC) *and* MC *is rising*. The firm is in short-run equilibrium at this *best, or optimum, level of output*.

EXAMPLE 5. In Table 8.2, columns (1) and (2) are the same as in Table 8.1. Columns (3) and (4) of Table 8.2 are calculated directly from column (4) and column (1) of Table 8.1. (Since the MC values refer to the midpoints between successive levels of output, the MC *at* 650 units of output is $8 and is the same as the MC recorded alongside 700 units of output.) The values in column (5) are obtained by subtracting each value of column (4) from the corresponding value in column (2). The values of column (6) are then obtained by multiplying each value of column (5) by the values in column (1). Note that the values of total profits are the same as those in Table 8.1 (except for two very small rounding errors). The firm maximizes total profits when it produces 650 units of output. At that level of output, MR = MC and MC is rising.

Table 8.2

(1) Q	(2) $P = \text{MR}$ ($)	(3) MC ($)	(4) AC ($)	(5) Profits/Unit ($)	(6) Total Profits ($)
100	8	12.00	20.00	−12.00	−1200
200	8	3.00	11.50	−3.50	−700
300	8	1.00	8.00	0	0
400	8	1.25	6.31	+1.69	+676
500	8	2.50	5.55	+2.45	+1225
600	8	4.25	5.33	+2.67	+1602
*650	8	(8.00)	5.40	+2.60	+1690
700	8	8.00	5.71	+2.29	+1603
800	8	24.00	8.00	0	0

EXAMPLE 6. The profit-maximizing, or best, level of output for this firm can also be viewed from Fig. 8-4 (obtained by plotting the values of the first four columns of Table 8.2). As long as MR exceeds MC (from A' to D'), it pays for the firm to expand output. The firm would be adding more to its TR than to its TC and so its total profits would rise. It does not pay for the firm to produce past point D', since MC exceeds MR. The firm would be adding more to its TC than to its TR and so its total profits would fall. Thus, the firm maximizes its total profits at the output level of 650 units (given by point D', where P or MR equals MC and MC is rising). The profit per unit at this level of output is given by $D'D''$ or $2.60, while total profit is given by the area of rectangle $D'D''FG$, which equals $1690.

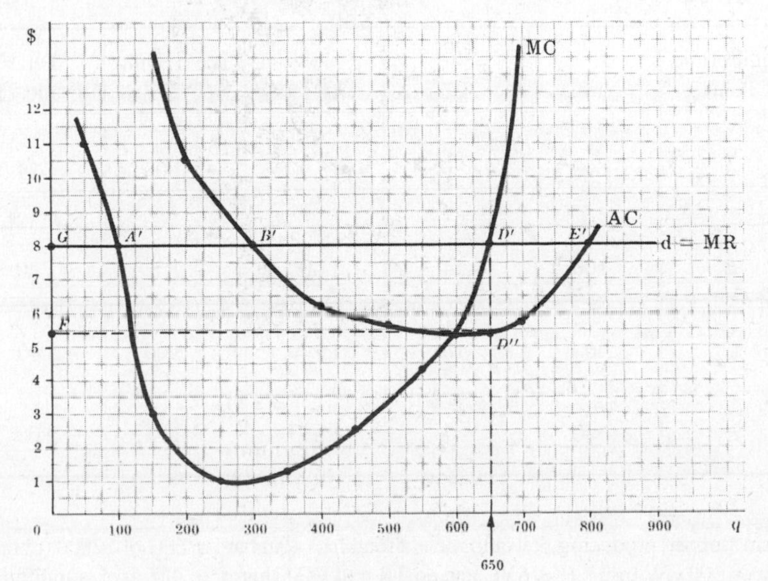

Fig. 8-4

8.5 SHORT-RUN PROFIT OR LOSS?

If, at the best, or optimum, level of output, *P* exceeds AC, the firm is maximizing total *profits*; if *P* is less than AC but greater than AVC, the firm is minimizing total losses; if *P* is less than AVC, the firm minimizes its total losses by shutting down.

EXAMPLE 7. Fig. 8-5 shows hypothetical MC, AC, and AVC curves for a "representative" firm; d_1 to d_4 (and MR_1 to MR_4) are *alternative* demand (and marginal revenue) curves that might face the perfect competitive firm. The results with each alternative demand curve are summarized in Table 8.3.

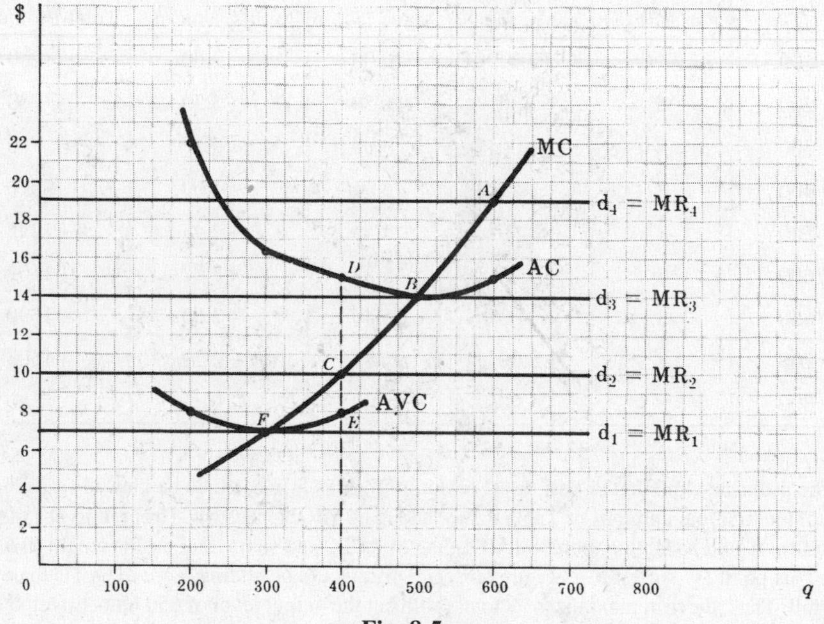

Fig. 8-5

Table 8.3

	Equilibrium Point	*q*	*P* ($)	AC ($)	Profit/Unit ($)	Total Profits ($)	Result
With d_4	*A*	600	19	15.00	4.00	24.00	Total profits maximized
With d_3	*B*	500	14	14.00	0	0	Break-even point
With d_2	*C*	400	10	15.00	−5.00	−2000	Total losses minimized
With d_1	*F*	300	7	16.33	−9.33	−2800	Shut-down point

With d_2, if the firm stopped producing, it would incur a total loss equal to its TFC of $2800 (obtained from the AFC of *DE*, or $7 per unit, times 400). With d_1, *P* = AVC and so TR = TVC. Therefore, the firm is indifferent to whether it produces or not (in either case it would incur total losses equal to its TFC). At prices below $7 per unit, AVC exceeds *P* and so

TVC exceeds TR. Therefore, the firm minimizes its total losses (at the level of its TFC of $2800) by shutting down altogether.

8.6 SHORT-RUN SUPPLY CURVE

Since, in a perfectly competitive market, we can read from the MC curve how much the firm will produce and sell at various prices, the firm's *short-run supply curve* is given by the rising portion of its MC curve (over and above its AVC curve). If factor prices remain constant, the competitive *industry* short-run supply curve is obtained by summing horizontally the SMC curves (over and above their respective AVC curves) of all the firms in the industry.

EXAMPLE 8. Panel A of Fig. 8-6 gives the short-run supply curve of the firm in Example 7 and Fig. 8-5. The industry or market short-run supply curve shown in panel B is obtained on the assumption that there are 100 *identical* firms in the industry and factor prices remain constant to this industry regardless of the amount of inputs it uses. (The "$\sum$" sign refers to the "summation of.") Note that no output of the commodity is produced at prices below $7 per unit.

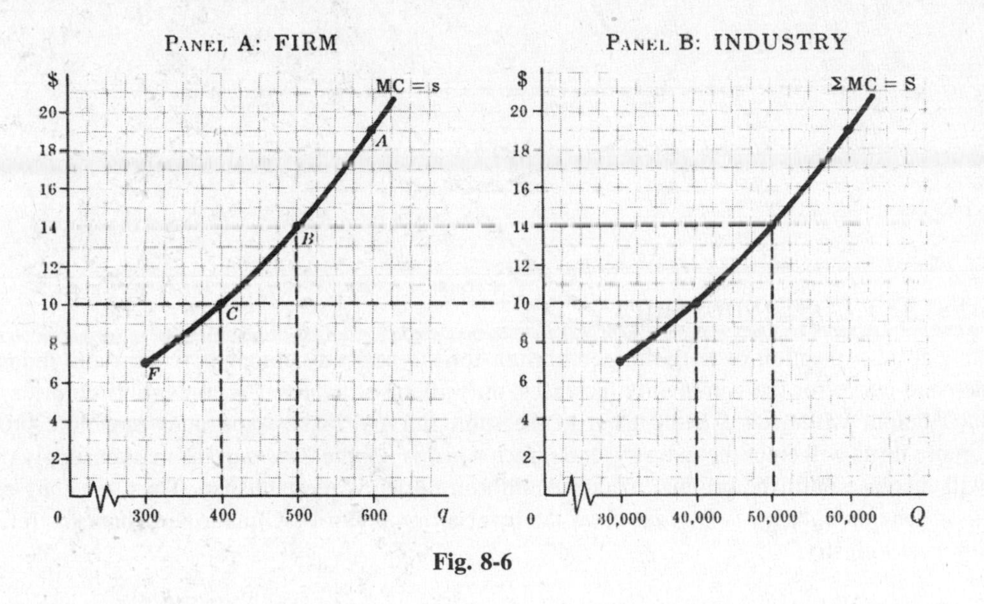

Fig. 8-6

8.7 LONG-RUN EQUILIBRIUM OF THE FIRM

In the long run, all factors of production and all costs are variable. Therefore, a firm will remain in business in the long run only if (by constructing the most appropriate plant to produce the best level of output) its TR equals or is greater than its TC. The best, or optimum, level of output for a perfectly competitive firm in the long run is given by the point where P or MR equals LMC and LMC is rising. If, at this level of output, the firm is making a profit, more firms will enter the perfectly competitive industry until all profits are squeezed out.

EXAMPLE 9. In Fig. 8-7, at the market price of $16, the perfectly competitive firm is in long-run equilibrium at point A, where P or MR $=$ SMC $=$ LMC $>$ SAC $=$ LAC. The firm produces and sells 700 units of output per time period, utilizing the most appropriate scale of plant (represented by SAC_2) at point B. The firm makes a profit of $5 per unit ($AB$) and a total profit of $3500.

EXAMPLE 10. Since the firm of Example 9 and Fig. 8-7 is making profits, in the long run more firms will enter the industry, attracted by those profits. The market supply of the commodity will increase, causing the market equilibrium price to fall. This will continue until all firms just break even. In Fig. 8-7, this occurs at point E, where $P = \text{MR} = \text{SMC} = \text{LMC} = \text{SAC} = \text{LAC} = \$8$. The firm will operate the optimum scale of plant (represented by SAC_1) at the optimum rate of output (400 units) and will make zero profits. All firms in the industry find themselves in the same situation (if all firms have identical cost curves), and so there is no incentive for any of them to leave the industry or for new firms to enter it.

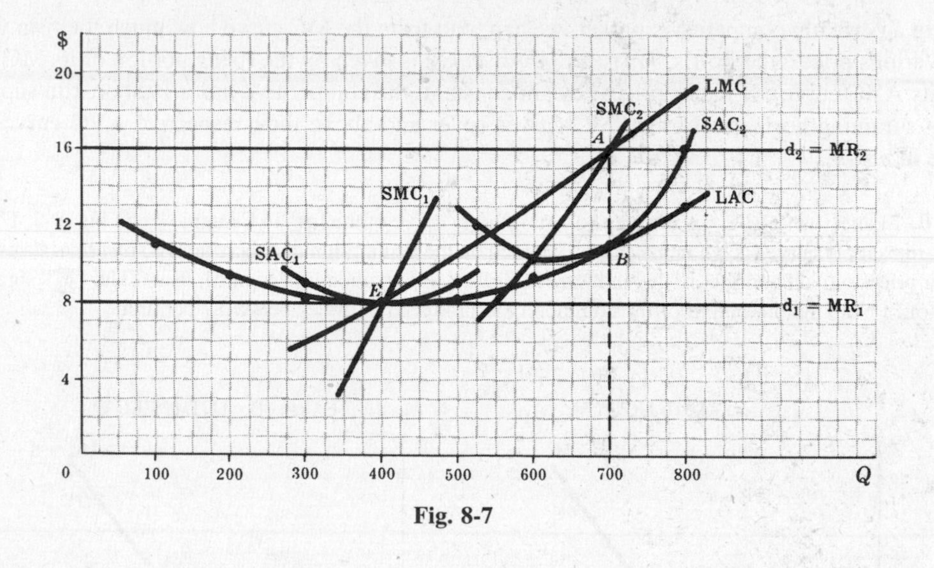

Fig. 8-7

8.8 CONSTANT COST INDUSTRIES

Starting from a position of long-run equilibrium for the perfectly competitive firm and industry, if the market demand curve for the commodity increases, thus giving a higher market equilibrium price, each firm will expand output within its existing plant in the short run and make some pure economic profit. In the long run, more firms will enter the industry, and *if factor prices remain constant*, the market supply of the commodity will increase until the original market equilibrium price is reestablished. Thus, *the long-run market supply curve for this industry is horizontal* (at the level of minimum LAC) and the industry is referred to as a "constant cost industry."

EXAMPLE 11. In panel B of Fig. 8-8, the original market equilibrium price of $8 is established by the intersection of the short-run industry or market demand curve (D) and supply curve (S) for the commodity (see point 1 in the figure). At this price, the perfectly competitive firm (panel A) is in long-run equilibrium at point E (as in Fig. 8-7). If all firms have identical cost curves, there will be 100 identical firms in the industry, each producing 400 units of the 40,000 units equilibrium output for the industry. If, for some reason, the short-run market demand curve shifts up to D′, the new market equilibrium price of this commodity becomes $16 (point 2 in panel B of Fig. 8-8). At this new price, each of the identical 100 firms will expand output within its existing scale of plant in the short run to 600 units (given by point C) and will make a profit of $5 per unit ($CF$) and $3000 in total.

EXAMPLE 12. Since all firms in Example 11 make profits, in the long run more firms will enter the industry. If factor prices remain constant, the short-run market supply curve will shift to S′, giving (at the intersection with D′) the original market equilibrium price of $8 per unit (see point 3 in panel B). At this price, each perfectly competitive firm will return to the original long-run equilibrium point (point E in panel A). There will now be 200 identical firms, each producing 400 units of the 80,000 units new equilibrium output for the industry. By joining equilibrium points 1 and 3, we get the long-run supply curve (LS) for this perfectly competitive industry. Since the LS curve is horizontal (at the level of minimum LAC), this is a constant cost industry.

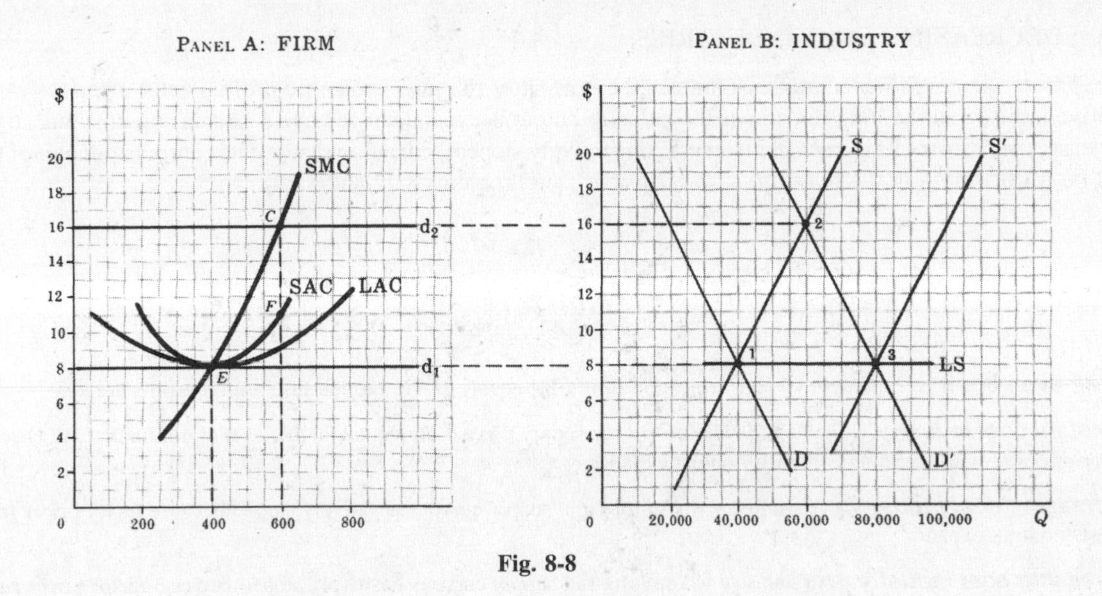

Fig. 8-8

8.9 INCREASING COST INDUSTRIES

If factor prices rise as more firms (attracted by pure economic profits in the short run) enter a perfectly competitive industry in the long run and as the industry output is expanded, we have an increasing cost industry. In this case, the industry long-run supply curve is positively sloped, indicating that greater outputs of the commodity per unit of time will be forthcoming in the long run only at higher prices.

EXAMPLE 13. In Fig. 8-9 the perfectly competitive industry and the firm are originally in long-run equilibrium at points 1 and *E*, respectively. If the short-run market demand curve shifts from D to D′ the new equilibrium price becomes \$16 (point 2) and each established firm will expand output in the short run to point *C* and make *CF* profits per unit (so far Example 13 is identical with Example 11). If factor prices *rise* as more firms enter this industry, the firm's entire set of cost curves will *shift up* (from LAC, SAC, and SMC to LAC′, SAC′, and SMC′). The firm and industry will return to long-run equilibrium when the short-run industry supply curve has shifted from S to S′, giving the new equilibrium price of \$12 (point 3) at which all firms just break even (point *E*′). We will now have 175 firms, each producing 400 units of the new equilibrium output of 70,000 units for the industry. Joining market equilibrium points 1 and 3, we get the rising industry LS curve.

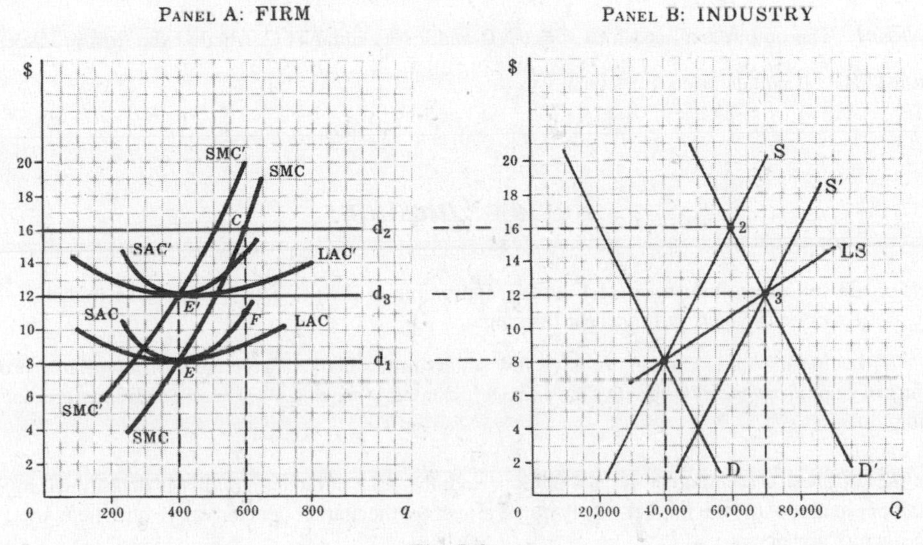

Fig. 8-9

8.10 DECREASING COST INDUSTRIES

If factor prices fall as more firms (attracted by the short-run pure economic profits) enter a perfectly competitive industry in the long run and as the industry output is expanded, we have a decreasing cost industry. In this case, the industry long-run supply curve is negatively sloped, indicating that greater outputs per unit of time will be forthcoming in the long run at *lower* prices (see Problems 8.22 and 8.23).

Glossary

Break-even point The output level at which the firm's TR equals its TC and the firm's total profits are zero.

Constant cost industry An industry whose long-run supply curve is horizontal (at the level of minimum LAC) because factor prices remain constant as industry output expands.

Decreasing cost industry An industry whose long-run supply curve is negatively sloped because factor prices fall as industry output expands.

Increasing cost Industry An industry whose long-run supply curve is positively sloped because factor prices rise as industry output expands.

Long-run equilibrium of the perfectly competitive firm The output level at which MR or P equals LMC and LMC is rising (provided that $P \geqslant$ LAC).

***Marginal revenue* (MR)** The change in TR for a one-unit change in the quantity sold.

Market period The very short run or time period in which the market supply of the commodity is completely fixed.

Perfect competition The form of market organization in which (1) there are a great number of sellers and buyers of the commodity, so that the actions of an individual cannot affect the price of the commodity, (2) the products of all firms in the market are homogeneous, (3) there is perfect mobility of resources, and (4) consumers, resource owners, and firms in the market have perfect knowledge of present and future prices and costs.

Profit The excess of P over AC and TR over TC.

Short-run equilibrium of the perfectly competitive firm The output level at which MR or P equals MC and MC is rising (provided that $P >$ AVC).

Short-run supply curve The rising portion of the perfectly competitive firm's marginal cost (MC) curve, over and above its AVC curve or shut-down point.

Shut-down point The output level at which $P =$ AVC and losses equal TFC, whether the firm produces or not.

***Total revenue* (TR)** It equals price times quantity.

Review Questions

1. Which of the following industries most closely approximates the perfectly competitive model? (*a*) Automobile, (*b*) cigarette, (*c*) newspaper, or (*d*) wheat farming.

Ans. (*d*) In the first three choices we have few sellers in the market; we have a differentiated product and vast amounts of capital are needed to enter the industry (among other things). These conditions are not true in wheat farming.

2. Given the supply of a commodity in the market period, the price of the commodity is determined by (*a*) the market demand curve alone, (*b*) the market supply curve alone, (*c*) the market demand curve and the market supply curve, or (*d*) none of the above.

Ans. (*a*) See Fig. 8-2.

3. Total profits are maximized where (*a*) TR equals TC, (*b*) the TR curve and the TC curve are parallel, (*c*) the TR curve and the TC curve are parallel and TC exceeds TR, or (*d*) the TR curve and the TC curve are parallel and TR exceeds TC.

Ans. (*d*) See points *A*, *B*, and *D* in Fig. 8-3.

4. The best, or optimum, level of output for a perfectly competitive firm is given by the point where (*a*) MR equals AC, (*b*) MR equals MC, (*c*) MR exceeds MC by the greatest amount, or (*d*) MR equals MC and MC is rising.

Ans. (*d*) See point D' in Fig. 8-4.

5. At the best, or optimum, short-run level of output, the firm will be (*a*) maximizing total profits, (*b*) minimizing total losses, (*c*) either maximizing total profits or minimizing total losses, or (*d*) maximizing profits per unit.

Ans. (*c*) Whether the firm is maximizing total profits or minimizing total losses in the short run depends on whether *P* exceeds AC or *P* falls short of AC at the best level of output.

6. If *P* exceeds AVC but is smaller than AC at the best level of output, the firm is (*a*) making a profit, (*b*) incurring a loss but should continue to produce in the short run, (*c*) incurring a loss and should stop producing immediately, or (*d*) breaking even.

Ans. (*b*) The firm minimizes losses in the short run (at a level smaller than its TFC) by continuing to produce at the best level of output (see point *C* in Fig. 8-5).

7. At the shut-down point, (*a*) $P = \text{AVC}$, (*b*) $\text{TR} = \text{TVC}$, (*c*) the total losses of the firm equal TFC, or (*d*) all of the above.

Ans. (*d*) See point *F* in Fig. 8-5.

8. The short-run supply curve of the perfectly competitive firm is given by

(*a*) the rising portion of its MC curve over and above the shut-down point,

(*b*) the rising portion of its MC curve over and above the break-even point,

(*c*) the rising portion of its MC curve over and above the AC curve, or

(*d*) the rising portion of its MC curve.

Ans. (*a*) See Fig. 8-5 and panel A of Fig. 8-6.

9. When the perfectly competitive firm and industry are both in long-run equilibrium

(*a*) $P = \text{MR} = \text{SMC} = \text{LMC}$, (*b*) $P = \text{MR} = \text{SAC} = \text{LAC}$,

(*c*) $P = \text{MR} =$ lowest point on the LAC curve, or (*d*) all of the above.

Ans. (*d*) See point *E* in Fig. 8-7.

10. When the perfectly competitive firm but not the industry is in long-run equilibrium,

(*a*) $P = \text{MR} = \text{SMC} = \text{SAC}$, (*b*) $P = \text{MR} = \text{LMC} = \text{LAC}$,

(*c*) $P = \text{MR} = \text{SMC} = \text{LMC} \neq \text{SAC} = \text{LAC}$, or

(*d*) $P = \text{MR} = \text{SMC} = \text{LMC} \neq \text{SAC} =$ lowest point on the LAC curve.

Ans. (*c*) See points *A* and *B* in Fig. 8-7.

11. An increase in output in a perfectly competitive and constant cost industry which is in long-run equilibrium will come (*a*) entirely from new firms, (*b*) entirely from existing firms, (*c*) either entirely from new firms or entirely from existing firms, or (*d*) partly from new firms and partly from existing firms.

Ans. (*a*) See equilibrium points 1, 3, and *E* in Fig. 8-8.

12. If factor prices and factor quantities move in the same direction, we have (*a*) a constant cost industry, (*b*) an increasing cost industry, (*c*) a decreasing cost industry, or (*d*) any of the above.

Ans. (*b*) In order to increase the industry output of a commodity, more factors are required. If factor prices rise as factor usage increases, the perfectly competitive industry LS curve will slope upward and we have an increasing cost industry. The opposite occurs for a decrease in the industry output (compare equilibrium point 3 to equilibrium point 1 in panel B of Fig. 8-9).

Solved Problems

PERFECT COMPETITION DEFINED

8.1 Explain in detail exactly what is meant by each of the four component parts of the definition of perfect competition given in the text.

(*a*) According to the first part of the definition, there are a great number of sellers and buyers of the commodity under perfect competition, each seller or buyer being too small (or behaving as though too small) in relation to the market to be able to affect the price of the commodity by one's own actions. This means that a change in the output of a single firm will not *perceptibly* affect the market price of the commodity. Similarly, each buyer of the commodity is too small to be able to extract from the seller such things as quantity discounts and special credit terms.

(*b*) The product of each firm in the market is homogeneous, identical, or perfectly standardized. As a result, the buyer cannot distinguish between the output of one firm and that of another, and so is indifferent as to the particular firm from which to buy. This refers not only to the physical characteristics of the commodity but also to the "environment" (such as the pleasantness of the seller, selling location, etc.) in which the purchase is made.

(*c*) There is perfect mobility of resources. That is, workers and other inputs can easily move geographically and from one job to another, and respond very quickly to monetary incentives. No input required in the production of the commodity is monopolized by its owners or producers. In the long run, firms can enter or leave the industry without much difficulty. That is, there are no patents or copyrights, "vast amounts" of capital are not necessary to enter the industry, and already established firms do not have any lasting cost advantage over new entrants because of experience or size.

(*d*) Consumers, resource owners, and firms in the market have perfect knowledge as to present and future prices, costs, and economic opportunities in general. Thus consumers will not pay a higher price than necessary for the commodity. Price differences are quickly eliminated and a single price will prevail throughout the market for the commodity. Resources are sold to the highest bidder. With perfect knowledge of present and future prices and costs, producers know exactly how much to produce.

8.2 (*a*) Does perfect competition as defined above exist in the real world? (*b*) Why do we study the perfectly competitive model?

(*a*) Perfect competition, as defined above, has never really existed. Perhaps the closest we may have come to satisfying the first three assumptions is in the market for such agricultural commodities as wheat and corn.

(*b*) The fact that perfect competition has never really existed in the real world does not reduce the great usefulness of the perfectly competitive model. As indicated in Chapter 1, a theory must be accepted or rejected on the basis of its ability to explain and to predict correctly, and not on the realism of its assumptions. And the perfectly competitive model does give us some very useful (even if at times rough) explanations and predictions of many real-world economic phenomena when the assumptions of the perfectly competitive model are only approximately (rather than exactly) satisfied. In addition, this model helps us evaluate and compare the *efficiency* with which resources are used under different forms of market organization.

8.3 A certain car manufacturer regards his business as highly competitive because he is keenly aware of his rivalry with the other few car manufacturers in the market. Like the other car manufacturers, he undertakes vigorous advertising campaigns seeking to convince potential buyers of the superior quality and better style of his automobiles and reacts very quickly to claims of superiority by rivals. Is this the meaning of perfect competition from the economist's point of view? Explain.

The above concept is diametrically opposed to the economist's view of perfect competition. It describes a competitive market, which stresses the *rivalry* among firms. The economist's view stresses the *impersonality* of a perfectly competitive market. That is, according to the economist, in a perfectly competitive market there are so many sellers and buyers of the commodity, each so small in relation to the market, as not to regard others as competitors or rivals at all. The products of all firms in the market are homogeneous, and so there is no rivalry among firms based on advertising and quality and style differences.

8.4 (*a*) What four different types of market organization do economists usually identify?
(*b*) Why do economists identify these four different types of market organization?
(*c*) Why do we study the two extreme forms of market organization first?

(*a*) The four different types of market organization that economists usually identify are perfect competition, monopolistic competition, oligopoly, and pure monopoly. The latter three forms of market organization fall into the realm of imperfect competition.

(*b*) Economists identify these four types of market organization in order to systematize and organize their analysis. However, in the real world, such a sharp distinction does not in fact exist. That is, in the real world, firms often exhibit elements of more than one market form and so it may be difficult to classify them into any one of the above market categories.

(*c*) We look first at the two extreme forms of market organization (i.e., perfect competition and pure monopoly) because historically, these are the models that were first developed. More importantly, these are the models that are more fully and satisfactorily developed. The monopolistic competition and oligopoly models, though more realistic in terms of actual forms of business organization in our economy (and, in general, in most other economies), are not very satisfactory and leave much to be desired from a theoretical point of view.

8.5 Suppose that the market demand in a perfectly competitive *industry* is given by $QD = 70{,}000 - 5000P$ and the market supply function is $QS = 40{,}000 + 2500P$, with P given in dollars, (*a*) Find the market equilibrium price, (*b*) find the market demand schedule and the market supply schedule at prices of \$9, \$8, \$7, \$6, \$5, \$4, \$3, \$2, and \$1, and (*c*) draw the market demand curve, the market supply curve and the demand curve of one of 100 identical, perfectly competitive firms in this industry. (*d*) What is the equation of the demand curve of the firm?

(*a*) In a perfectly competitive market (and in the absence of any interference with the operation of the forces of demand and supply such as government price controls), the price of the commodity is determined exclusively by the market demand curve and the market supply for the commodity.

$$QD = QS$$

$$70{,}000 - 5000P = 40{,}000 + 2500P$$

$$30{,}000 = 7500P$$

$$P = \$4 \text{ (equilibrium price)}$$

(*b*)

Table 8.4

P (\$)	QD	QS
9	25,000	62,500
8	30,000	60,000
7	35,000	57,500
6	40,000	55,000
5	45,000	52,000
4	50,000	50,000
3	55,000	47,500
2	60,000	45,000
1	65,000	42,500

(c)

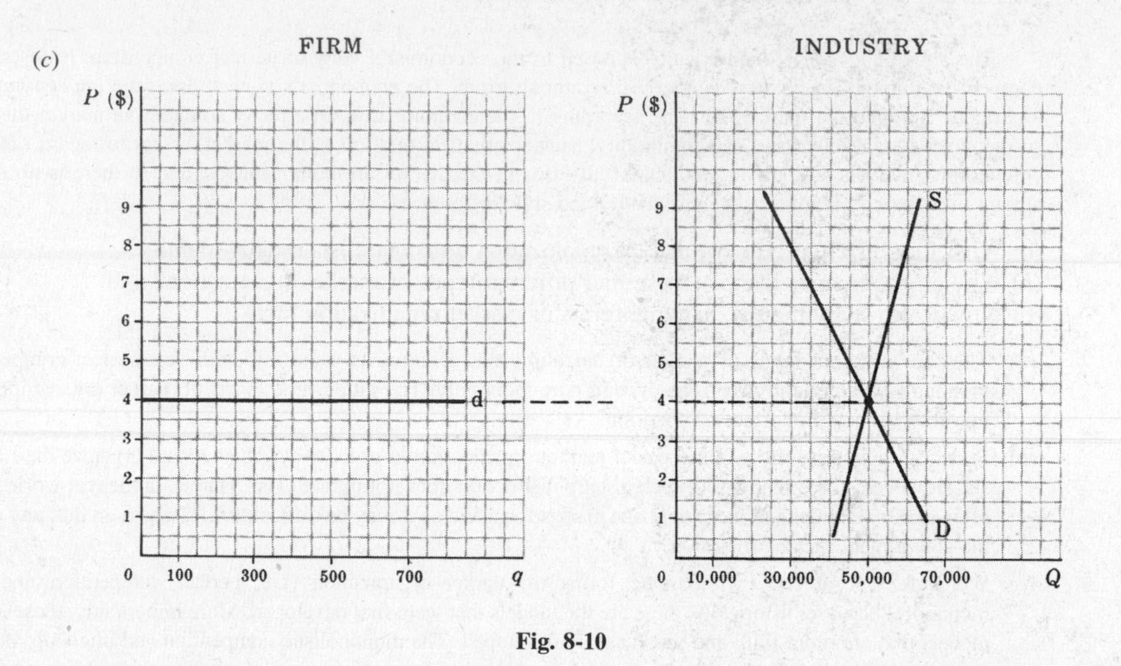

Fig. 8-10

(d) The equation of the demand curve for the perfectly competitive firm in this industry is given by $P = \$4$. That is, the firm can sell any quantity at that price. Note that if only one firm increases the quantity of the commodity produced and sold, the effect on the equilibrium market price will be imperceptible. If many or all firms increase output, the market supply curve will shift down and to the right, giving a lower market equilibrium price.

PRICE DETERMINATION IN THE MARKET PERIOD

8.6 If the market supply for a commodity is given by $QS = 50{,}000$, (a) are we dealing with the market period, the short run, or the long run? (b) If the market demand is given by $QD = 70{,}000 - 5000P$ and P is expressed in dollars, what is the market equilibrium price (P)? (c) If the market demand function changes to $QD' = 100{,}000 - 5000P$, what is the new market equilibrium price (P')? (d) If the market demand function changes to $QD'' = 60{,}000 - 5000P$, what is the new equilibrium price (P'')? (e) Draw a graph showing parts (b), (c), and (d) of this problem.

(a) The quantity supplied to the market is fixed at 50,000 units per time period regardless of the price of the commodity. That is, the market supply curve (and the supply curve of each producer) of the commodity has zero price elasticity. Thus we are dealing with the very short run or market period.

(b)

$$QD = QS$$
$$70{,}000 - 5000P = 50{,}000$$
$$20{,}000 = 5000P$$
$$P = \$4$$

(c)

$$QD' = QS$$
$$10{,}000 - 5000P = 50{,}000$$
$$50{,}000 = 5000P$$
$$P' = \$10$$

(d)

$$QD'' = QS$$
$$60{,}000 - 5000P = 50{,}000$$
$$10{,}000 = 5000P$$
$$P'' = \$2$$

(e)

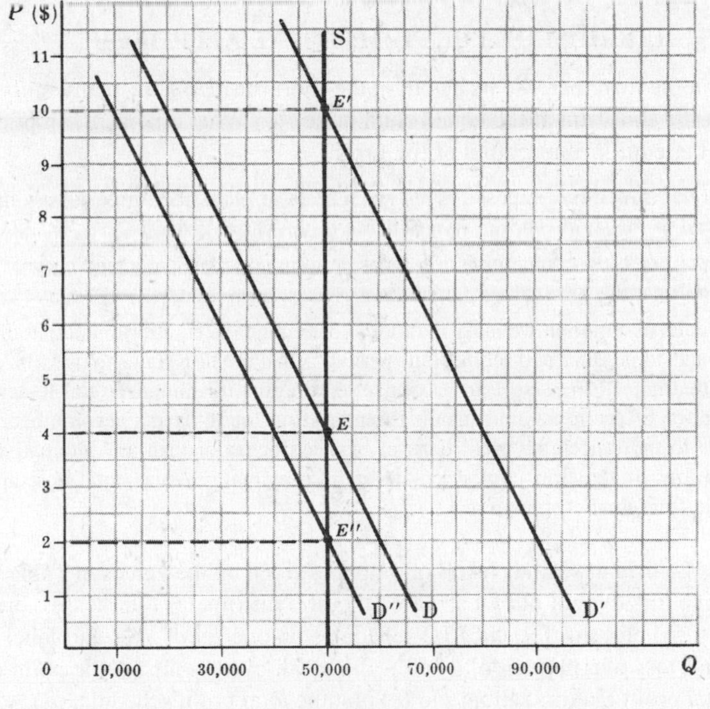

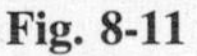
Fig. 8-11

Note that, given the fixed quantity of the commodity supplied, market demand alone determines the equilibrium market price of the commodity in the market period. Also, a vertical shift in the market demand curve causes an identical change in the equilibrium market price of the commodity.

8.7 (*a*) To what length of time does the market period refer? (*b*) Explain briefly how the price mechanism rations the existing market supply of a commodity, say, wheat, *over the time* of the market period. (*c*) On what does the price of wheat depend *over the time* of the market period?

(*a*) The market period refers to the period of time over which the market supply of a commodity is completely fixed. This may be one day, one month, one year, or more and depends on the industry involved. For example, if fresh strawberries are delivered to the New York market every Monday and no other deliveries can be made during the same week, then the market period for strawberries in New York is one week. For wheat, the market period extends from one harvest to the next or for one year. For Da Vinci's paintings, the market period refers to an infinite length of time.

(*b*) In general, the price of wheat is lowest just after harvest time and highest just before the next harvest. However, the price is usually not so low after harvest time that all the wheat available will be exhausted long before the next harvest. Or it is usually not so high during the year that large quantities of wheat are left unsold by the nest harvest or must be sold at very low prices. In a perfectly functioning market (including perfect knowledge of present and future conditions), the entire supply of wheat from one harvest will just be exhausted at the time of the next.

(*c*) The price of wheat between consecutive harvests (the span of the market period) is equal to the harvest price plus the opportunity cost of holding capital tied down in wheat and the cost of storage and insurance between harvest time and the time of sale. In the real world, speculators in wheat make sure (unless they make serious mistakes in their expectations) that this equality is approximately true.

SHORT-RUN EQUILIBRIUM OF THE FIRM: TOTAL APPROACH

8.8 (*a*) How can the firm increase its output in the short run? (*b*) How many units of the commodity can the firm sell in the short run at the equilibrium price? (*c*) What crucial assumption do we make in order to determine the equilibrium output of the firm?

(*a*) Within the limitations imposed by its given scale of plant, the firm can vary the amount of the commodity produced in the short run by varying its use of the variable inputs.

(*b*) Since the perfectly competitive firm faces an infinitely elastic demand curve, it can sell any amount of the commodity at the given market price.

(*c*) The crucial assumption we make in order to determine the equilibrium output of the firm (i.e., how much the firm wants to produce and sell per time period) is that the firm wants to maximize its total profits. It should be noted that not all firms seek to maximize total profits (or mininize total losses) at all times. However, the assumption of profit maximization is essential if we are to have a general theory of the firm, and in general it leads to more accurate predictions of business behavior than any alternative assumption. The short-run equilibrium of the firm can be looked at from a total revenue–total cost approach or from a marginal revenue–marginal cost approach.

8.9 If the STC of a firm at various levels of output is given by the values in Table 8.5 and TR $= PQ = \$4Q$, (*a*) determine the level of output at which the firm maximizes total losses, breaks even, and maximizes total profits; (*b*) plot the TR and STC schedules on one set of axes and label (on the STC curve) *A* the point of total loss maximization, *B* and *E* the break-even points, *C* the point of lowest SAC, and *D* the point of total profit maximization; and (*c*) plot the total profit schedule, (*d*) At which point is the firm in short-run equilibrium?

Table 8.5

Q	0	100	200	300	400	500	600	700	750	800	900
STC ($)	400	1000	1300	1500	1600	1700	1850	2100	2265	2500	3600

(*a*)

Table 8.6

(1) Q	(2) P (\$)	(3) TR (\$)	(4) TC (\$)	(5) Total Profit (\$)	
0	4	0	400	−400	
100	4	400	1000	−600	Total Losses Maximized
200	4	800	1300	−500	
300	4	1200	1500	−300	
400	4	1600	1600	0	Break-Even Point
500	4	2000	1700	+300	
600	4	2400	1850	+550	
700	4	2800	2100	+700	
750	4	3000	2265	+735	Total Profits Maximized
800	4	3200	2500	+700	
900	4	3600	3600	0	Break-Even Point

(*b*)

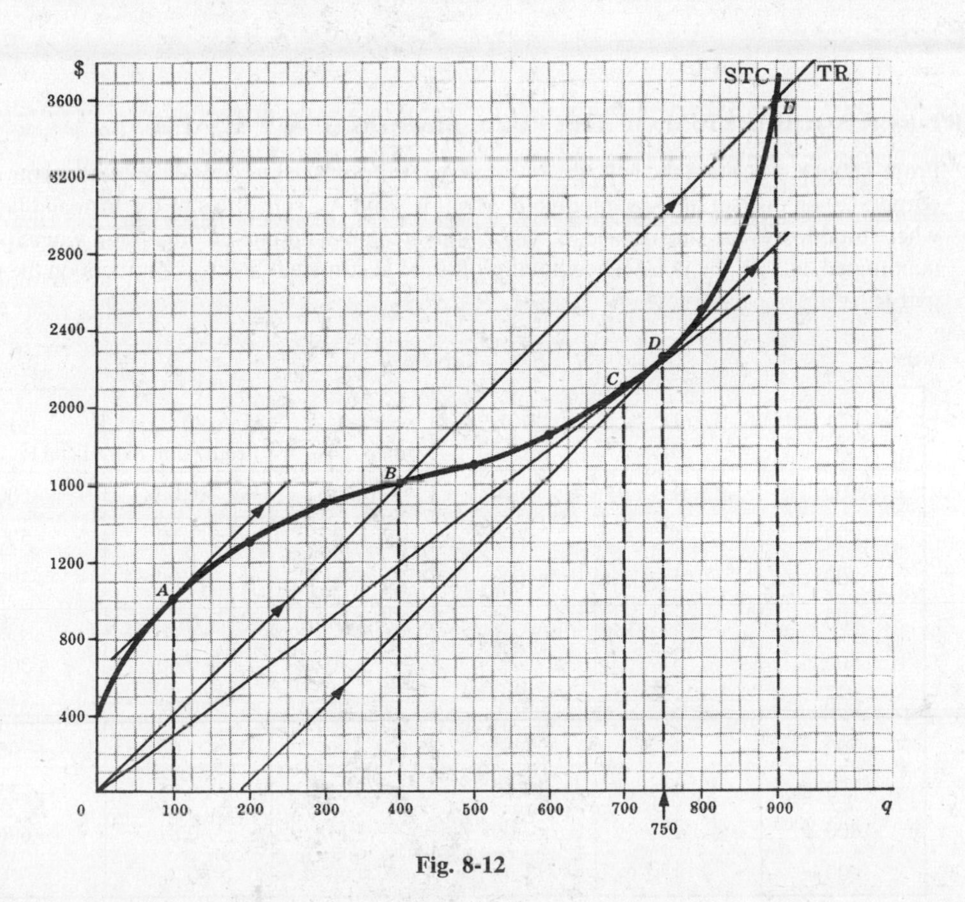

Fig. 8-12

(*c*)

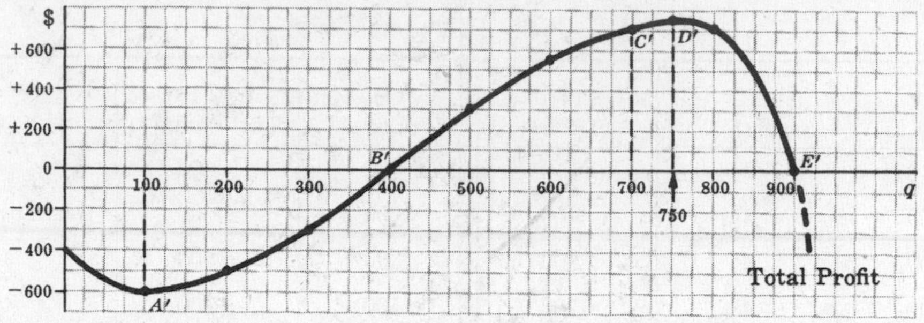

Fig. 8-13

(*d*) The firm is in short-run equilibrium at point *D* (and *D′*) where it maximizes short-run total profits. Note that at outputs slightly smaller than 750 units, the slope of the TR curve is greater than the slope of the STC curve; as a result the vertical distance between the TR curve and the STC curve (i.e., total profit) increases as output expands to 750 units. Similarly, for outputs slightly larger than 750 units, the slope of the STC curve is greater than the slope of the TR curve, and so total profit would increase as output is *reduced* to 750 units. If the STC curve was above the TR curve at every point, the firm would try to *minimize* total losses since it could not possibly make profits.

SHORT-RUN EQUILIBRIUM OF THE FIRM: MARGINAL APPROACH

8.10 From Table 8.6, (*a*) find the MR, the MC, the AC, the profit per unit, and the total profits at each level of output; (*b*) on one set of axes, plot the d, MR, MC, and AC schedules of the firm and label *A′* the point where total losses are maximized, *B′* and *E′* the break-even points, *C′* the point where profit per unit is maximized, and *D′* the point where total profits are maximized; and (*c*) comment on the graph drawn in part (*b*).

(*a*)

Table 8.7

(1) Q	(2) P = MR ($)	(3) MC ($)	(4) AC ($)	(5) Profit/Unit ($)	(6) Total Profit ($)
100	4	6.00	10.00	−6.00	−600
200	4	3.00	6.50	−2.50	−500
300	4	2.00	5.00	−1.00	−300
400	4	1.00	4.00	0	0
500	4	1.00	3.40	+0.60	+300
600	4	1.50	3.08	+0.92	+552
700	4	2.50	3.00	+1.00	+700
*750	4	(4.00)	3.02	+0.98	+735
800	4	4.00	3.13	+0.87	+696
900	4	11.00	4.00	0	0

The MC of $4.00 *at* 750 units of output was obtained by finding the change in TC per unit increase in output, when output is increased from 700 to 800 units. The total profits found above differ slightly (in two instances) from the figures of Table 8.6 because of rounding errors. Since $P = \text{MR}$, this firm is in a perfectly competitive market.

(*b*)

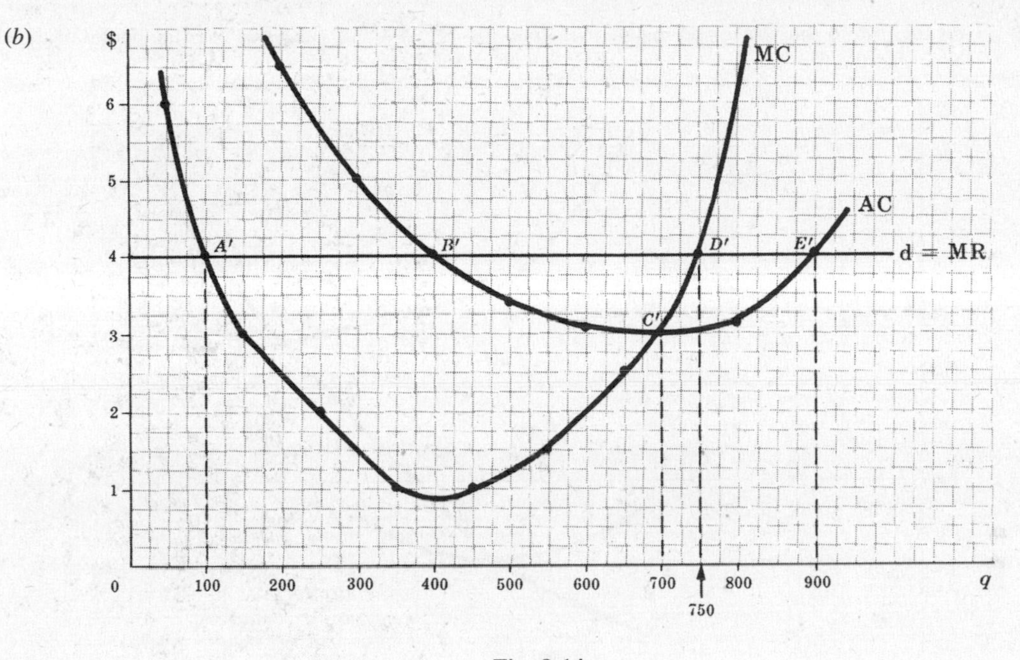

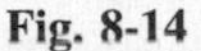
Fig. 8-14

(*c*) The best, or optimum, level of output of this perfectly competitive firm is given by point D', where MR = MC and MC is rising. At this point the firm is maximizing total profits (at \$735) and is in short-run equilibrium. If the firm raises its price, it will lose all its customers. If the firm lowers its price, it will reduce its TR unnecessarily, since it can sell any amount at the market price of \$4 per unit. Note that at the output level of 700 units, the *profit per unit* is maximum (\$1.00), but the firm wants to maximize *total* profits, not profits per unit. Note too that MR or P is also equal to MC (point A') at 100 units of output. At that level of output, however, the firm maximizes total *losses* (since the firm has produced all units of the commodity for which MC exceeds MR or P) and no units for which MR > MC.

8.11 Given the short-run cost curves (Fig. 8-15) for a firm in a perfectly competitive market, find the firm's best level of output and its total profits if the equilibrium market price is (*a*) \$18, (*b*) \$13, (*c*) \$9, (*d*) \$5, or (*e*) \$3.

(*a*) When $P = \$18$, the best, or optimum, level of output is 7000 units (given by point A). The firm makes \$4 of profit per unit (AN) and a total profit of \$28,000. This represents the maximum total profit that the firm can make at this price.

(*b*) When $P = \$13$, the best level of output is 6000 units (point B) and the firm breaks even.

(*c*) When $P = \$9$, the best level of output is 5000 units (point C). At this level of output, the firm incurs a loss of \$5 per unit (DC) and \$25,000 in total. However, if the firm went out of business, it would incur a total loss equal to its TFC of \$40,000 (obtained by multiplying the AFC of DE or \$8 per unit, times 5000 units). Thus, the firm would minimize its total losses in the short run by staying in business.

(*d*) When $P = \$5$, the best level of output is 4000 units (point F). However, since P = AVC and thus TR = TVC (=\$20,000), the firm is indifferent to whether it produces or not. In either case, the firm would incur a short-run total loss equal to its TFC of \$40,000. Point F is thus the shut-down point.

(*e*) When $P = \$3$, the best level of output is 3000 units (point G). However, since P is smaller than AVC, TR (\$9000) does not even cover TVC (\$18,000). Therefore, the firm would incur a total loss equal to its TFC (\$40,000) *plus the* \$9000 amount by which TVC exceeds TR (\$18,000 − \$9000 = \$9000). Thus, it pays for the firm to shut down and minimize its total losses at \$40,000 (its TFC) over the period of the short-run. Note that the firm produces its best short-run level of output

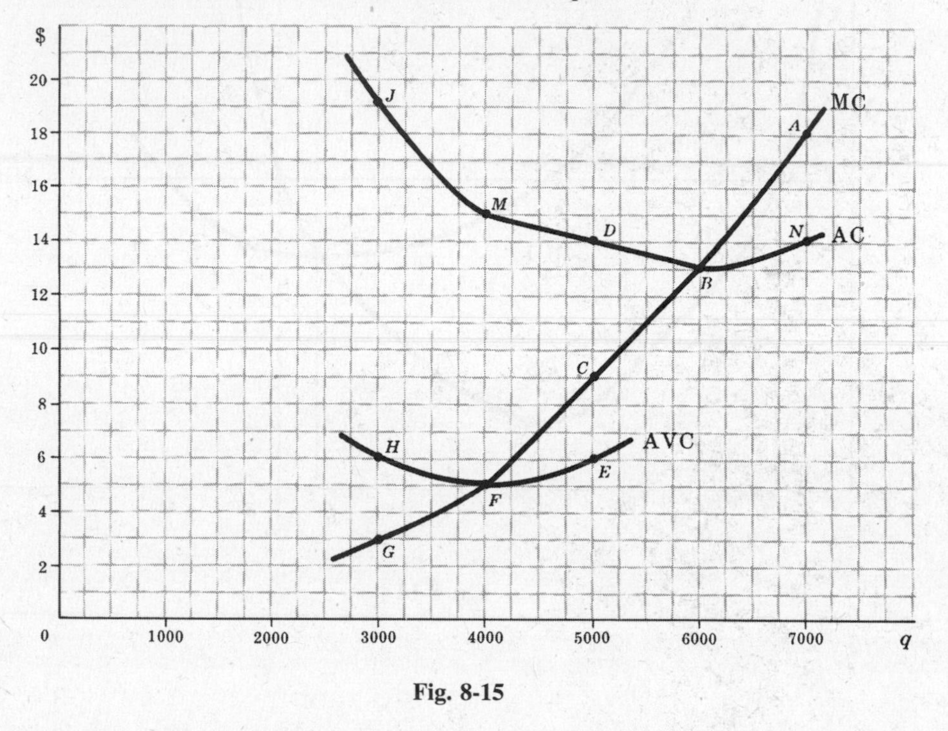

Fig. 8-15

provided $P \geq$ AVC (the symbol "$\geq$" means "equal to or larger than"). If $P \leq$ AVC, the firm shuts down rather than produce its best short-run level of output.

8.12 (*a*) Draw the short-run supply curve for the perfectly competitive firm of Problem 8.11. Also draw the industry short-run supply curve on the assumptions that there are 100 identical firms in the industry and that factor prices remain unchanged as industry output expands (and thus more factors are used) and (*b*) explain the graph of part (*a*). (*c*) What quantity of the commodity will be supplied by each firm and the industry at the commodity price of \$9? At \$18? At prices below \$5?

(*a*)

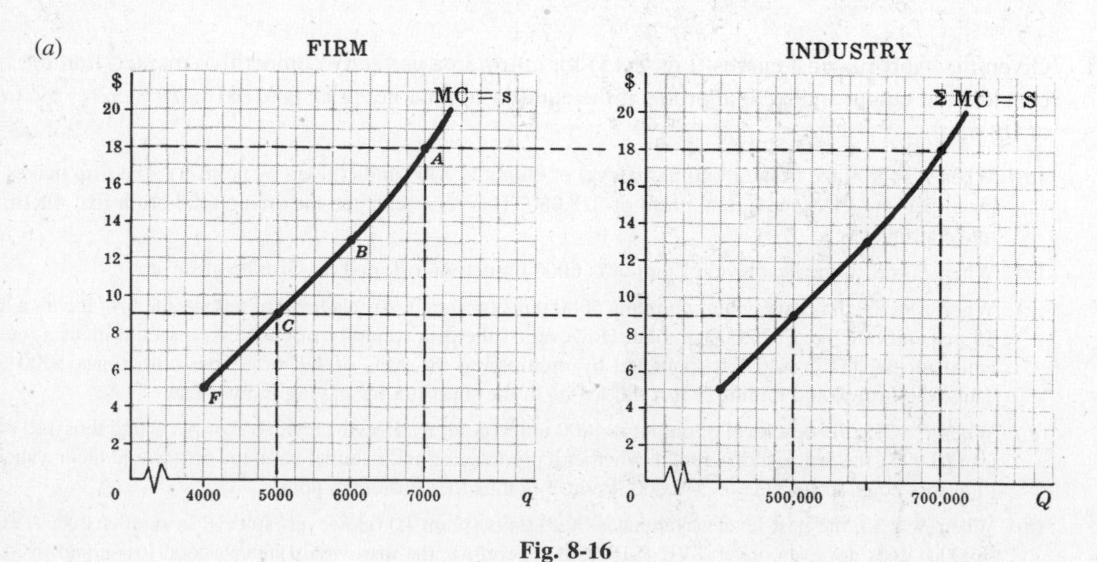

Fig. 8-16

(*b*) The firm's short-run supply curve is given by the rising portion of its MC curve over and above its AVC curve. If the supplies of inputs to the industry are perfectly elastic (that is, if the prices of factors of production remain the same regardless of the quantity of factors demanded per unit of time by the industry), then the market or industry short-run supply curve is obtained by the horizontal summation of the SMC curves (over and above their respective AVC curves) of all the firms in the industry. (See also Section 2.8.) To be noted is that when a single firm expands its output (and demands more factors), it is reasonable to expect that factor prices will remain unchanged. However, when all firms together expand output (and demand more factors), factor prices are likely to rise (see Problem 8.13).

(*c*) If the short-run equilibrium market price of the commodity is $9, each of the 100 identical firms in the industry will produce and sell 5000 units of output (point *C*) and the total for the industry will be 500,000 units. At the commodity price of $18, each firm produces and sells 7000 units. The industry total is 700,000 units. No output of the commodity is produced at prices below $5 per unit (i.e., below the shut-down point, the supply curves coincide with the price axis).

8.13 Suppose that as the commodity price increases from $9 to $18 in Problem 8.12, factor prices also rise, causing the MC curve of each firm to shift up, say, by a vertical distance of $5. (*a*) With the aid of a diagram, determine the quantity supplied by each firm and by the industry at the commodity price of $18 and (*b*) compare this result with that of Problem 8.12.

(*a*) As the industry output is expanded (and more inputs are needed), the prices of the variable inputs may rise. This would cause the MC curve of each firm in the industry to shift up and to the left. In this problem we are told that the MC curve of each firm shifts up from MC to MC′ (see Fig. 8-17). Thus when the commodity price rises from $9 to $18, the quantity supplied by each firm will rise from 5000 units (point *C* on MC) to 6000 units (point *B*′ on MC′) and the industry output rises from 500,000 units per time period (point *C*) to 600,000 units (point *B*′)

(*b*) For the same increase in the commodity price (from $9 to $18), the output of each firm, and the output of the industry rise *less* when factor prices rise than when they do not. (In Problem 8.12, we saw that when factor prices remain unchanged, the output of each firm rose from 5000 to 7000 units and the industry output rose from 500,000 to 700,000 units.)

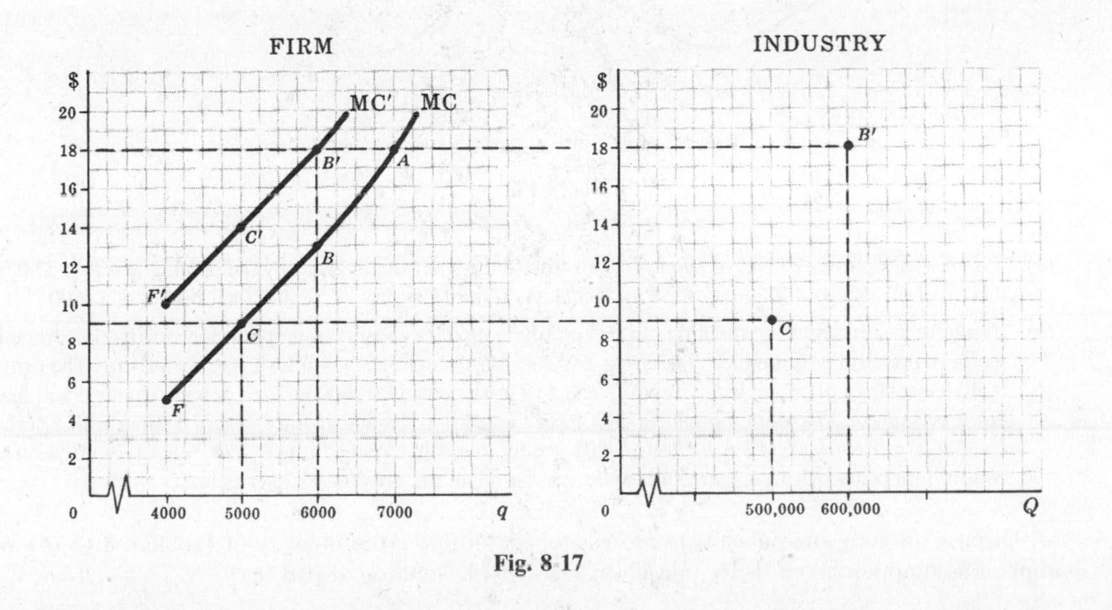

Fig. 8-17

8.14 (*a*) Explain the *sequence* of events leading to the expansion of output when the commodity price rises in Problem 8.13(*a*). (*b*) Must the output of each of the 100 identical firms producing the commodity rise? Why? (*c*) What different results do we get in times of cost-push inflation?

(a) The sequence of events when the commodity price rises in Problem 8.13(*a*) is as follows: As the commodity price rises, each firm (and the industry) expands output, the demands for factors increase, factor prices rise, and the MC curve of each firm shifts up and to the left so that the expansion in the output of each firm (and of the industry) is less than in the absence of the increases in factor prices.

(b) Since we are dealing with the short run and the number of firms cannot increase, in order for the industry output to rise (thus causing factor prices to rise), the output of each of the identical firms must rise (i.e., point B' in Fig. 8-17 must be to the right of point C). The exact opposite occurs if factor prices fall as the industry output is expanded. If some factor prices rise and some fall, the MC curve may shift up or down and the shape of the MC curve is also likely to change.

(c) In times of cost-push inflation, the higher prices of variable inputs lead to higher commodity prices, reduced commodity outputs, and the reduced employment of the variable inputs.

LONG-RUN EQUILIBRIUM OF THE FIRM

8.15 In Fig. 8-18, suppose that the perfectly competitive firm has a scale of plant indicated by SAC_1 and the short-run market equilibrium price is \$16. (*a*) What output will this firm produce and sell in the short run? Is the firm making a profit or a loss at this level of output? (*b*) Discuss the adjustment process for this firm in the long run, *if only this firm* and no other firm in the industry *adjusted to the long run*.

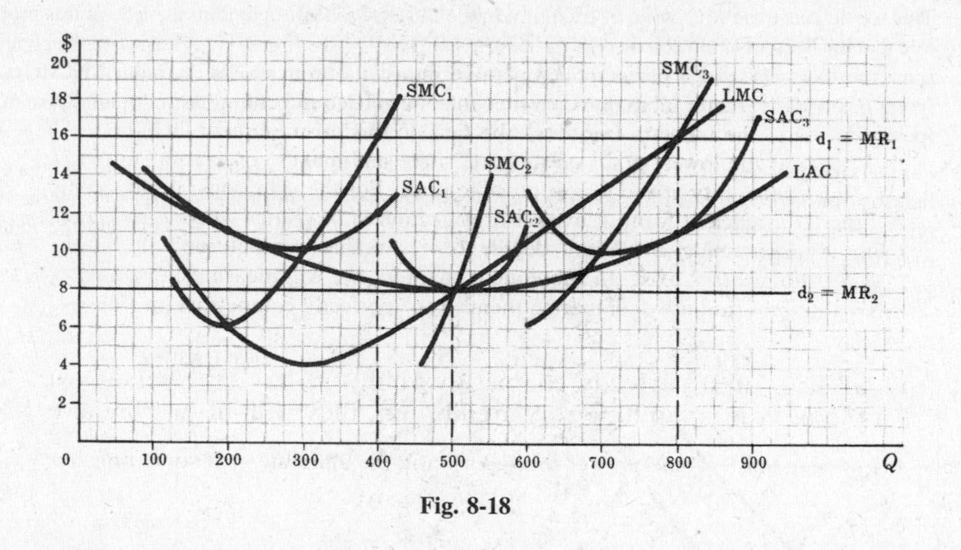

Fig. 8-18

(a) The best, or optimum, level of output for this firm in the short run is given by the point where $P = SMC_1$. At this level of output (400 units), the firm is making a profit per unit of \$4 and total profits of \$1600.

(b) If only this firm adjusts to the long run (a simplifying and unrealistic assumption for a perfectly competitive market), this firm will produce where $P = SMC_3 = LMC$, and SMC_3 and LMC are both rising. The firm will build the scale of plant indicated by SAC_3 and will produce and sell 800 units of output. The firm will make a profit per unit of \$5 and total profits of \$4000 per time period. Note that since we are dealing with a perfectly competitive firm, we can safely assume that if only this firm expanded its output, the effect on the market equilibrium price will be imperceptible and we can retain the price of \$16 per unit.

8.16 (*a*) Discuss the long-run adjustment process for the firm *and* the industry of Problem 8.15 (*b*) What implicit assumption about factor prices was made in the solution of part (*a*)?

(a) In the long run, all the firms in the industry will adjust their scale of plant and their level of output and more firms will enter the industry, attracted by the short-run pure economic profits. This will increase the industry supply of the commodity and thus cause a fall in the market equilibrium price to \$8 (see Fig. 8-18). At this price, $P = MR_2 = SMC = LMC = SAC = LAC$. Each firm produces 500 units of output (if they all have the same cost curves) and receives only a "normal return" (equal to the implicit opportunity cost) on its owned factors. If firms were making short-run losses to begin with, the exact opposite would occur. In any event, when all firms are in long-run equilibrium, they all produce at the lowest point on their LAC curve, they all just break even, and they spend little if anything on sales promotion.

(*b*) In the solution to part (*a*), the implicit assumption was made that factor prices remained unchanged as more firms entered the industry and industry output was expanded.

8.17 (*a*) If each firm is in long-run equilibrium, need the industry also be in long-run equilibrium? (*b*) If the firm and the industry are in long-run equilibrium, need they also be in short-run equilibrium? (*c*) Discuss some of the efficiency implications of a perfectly competitive industry when in long-run equilibrium.

(*a*) *If* the industry is in long-run equilibrium, *then* each firm in the industry must also be in long-run equilibrium. However, the reverse is not true [compare the answer to Problem 8.15(*b*) with the answer to Problem 8.16(*a*)].

(*b*) If the firm and the industry are in long-run equilibrium, they must also be in short-run equilibrium. However, the reverse is not true [compare the answer to Problem 8.16(*a*) with the answer to Problem 8.15(*a*)].

(*c*) Since each firm in a perfectly competitive industry produces where $P = \text{LMC}$ (provided that P is equal to or greater than LAC) when in long-run equilibrium, there is an optimal allocation of resources to the industry (more will be said on this in subsequent chapters). Also, since each firm produces at the lowest point on its LAC curve and makes zero profits in the long run, consumers get this commodity at the lowest possible price. For these reasons, perfect competition is regarded as the most efficient form of market organization *in industries where it can exist*. Our antitrust laws aim at maintaining a healthy degree of "workable competition" in industries where perfect competition cannot exist. In subsequent chapters, we will measure the efficiency of other forms of market organization by comparing them to the perfectly competitive model.

8.18 Must all firms in a perfectly competitive industry have the same cost curves so that when the industry is in long-run equilibrium, they will all just break even? Explain.

Most economists would answer this question in the affirmative. If some firms *appear* to have lower costs than other firms, this is due to the fact that they use *superior resources or inputs* such as more fertile land or superior management. These superior resources, under the threat of leaving to work for other firms, can extract from the firms using them the higher price or return commensurate with their greater productivity. In any event, the firm should price all resources it owns, and the forces of competition will force the firm to price all resources it does not own at their opportunity cost. So it is the owners of such superior resources who receive the benefit (in the form of higher prices or returns) from their greater productivity rather than the firms employing them (in the form of lower costs). This results in all firms having identical cost curves. Therefore, all firms just break even when the perfectly competitive industry is in long-run equilibrium.

CONSTANT, INCREASING, AND DECREASING COST INDUSTRIES

8.19 Assume that (1) the lowest point on the LAC curve of each of the many identical firms in a perfectly competitive industry is \$4 and it occurs at the output of 500 units, (2) when the optimum scale of plant is operated to produce 600 units of output per unit of time, the SAC of each firm is \$4.50, and (3) the market demand and supply functions are given respectively by $QD = 70{,}000 - 5000P$ and $QS = 40{,}000 + 2500P$. (*a*) Find the market equilibrium price. Is the industry in short-run or long-run equilibrium? Why? (*b*) How many firms are in this industry when in long-run equilibrium? (*c*) If the market demand function shifts to $QD' = 10{,}000 - 5000P$, find the new *short-run* equilibrium price and quantity for the industry and the firm. Are firms making profits or losses at this new equilibrium point?

(*a*) The market demand and supply functions are those of Problem 8.5. Thus the market equilibrium price is \$4 (see Problem 8.5). Since this price is equal to the lowest LAC for each firm in the industry (assumption 1 above), all firms in the industry, and the industry itself, are in long-run equilibrium at this price.

(*b*) In order to find the number of firms in this industry, we must find the market equilibrium quantity. This is obtained by substituting the equilibrium price of \$4 into either the market demand function or the market supply function:

$$QD = QS$$

$$70{,}000 - 5000(4) = 40{,}000 + 2500(4)$$

$$70{,}000 - 20{,}000 = 40{,}000 + 10{,}000$$

$$50{,}000 = 50{,}000 \text{ (equilibrium quantity 1)}$$

Since all firms are identical and each produces 500 units of output (assumption 1) when the industry is in long-run equilibrium, there will be 100 such firms in the industry.

(*c*) When the market demand function changes to QD', the new market equilibrium price and quantity are obtained by

$$QD' = QS$$

$$100{,}000 - 5000P = 40{,}000 + 2500P$$

$$60{,}000 = 7{,}500P$$

$$P = \$8 \text{ (equilibrium price 2)}$$

$$100{,}000 - 5000(8) = 40{,}000 + 2500(8)$$

$$60{,}000 = 60{,}000 \text{ (equilibrium quantity 2)}$$

In the short run, the number of firms in the industry is still 100 and each must still operate its optimum scale of plant. However, each firm now produces and sells 600 units of output. Since at this output, SAC = \$4.50 (assumption 2), each firm is making \$3.50 profit per unit and \$2100 in total.

8.20 (*a*) With reference to Problem 8.19, if *in the long run* the market demand function remains at $QD' = 100{,}000 - 5000P$ but the market supply function becomes $QS' - 70{,}000 + 2500P$, (*a*) what are the new long-run equilibrium price and quantity for this industry? (*b*) What type of industry is this? What does this imply for factor prices? (*c*) Draw a figure (similar to Fig. 8-8 in the text) showing the steps in parts (*a*) and (*b*) of Problem 8.19 and in part (*a*) of this problem.

(*a*) The new long-run equilibrium price and quantity become

$$QD' = QS'$$

$$100{,}000 - 5000P = 70{,}000 + 2500P$$

$$30{,}000 = 1{,}500P$$

$$P = \$4 \text{ (equilibrium price 3)}$$

$$100{,}000 - 5000(4) = 70{,}000 + 2500(4)$$

$$80{,}000 = 80{,}000 \text{ (equilibrium quantity 3)}$$

(*b*) Since this market equilibrium price is the same as equilibrium price 1 [see Problem 8.19(*a*)], the LS curve of the industry is horizontal and the industry is a constant cost industry. This means that as the industry output expands, either all factor prices remain unchanged or the increase in some factor prices are exactly balanced by the reduction of others. If all factor prices remain unchanged, then the cost curves of each firm remain completely unchanged (i.e., they will shift neither up nor down, nor sideways). Each firm will remain in exactly the same position as in part (*a*) of Problem 8.19, but now we have 160 firms in the industry (each producing 500 of the 80,000 units of the industry equilibrium output) rather than 100 firms as in part (*b*) of Problem 8.19.

(*c*) The steps in parts (*a*) and (*b*) of Problem 8.19 and in part (*a*) of this problem are shown in Fig. 8.19.

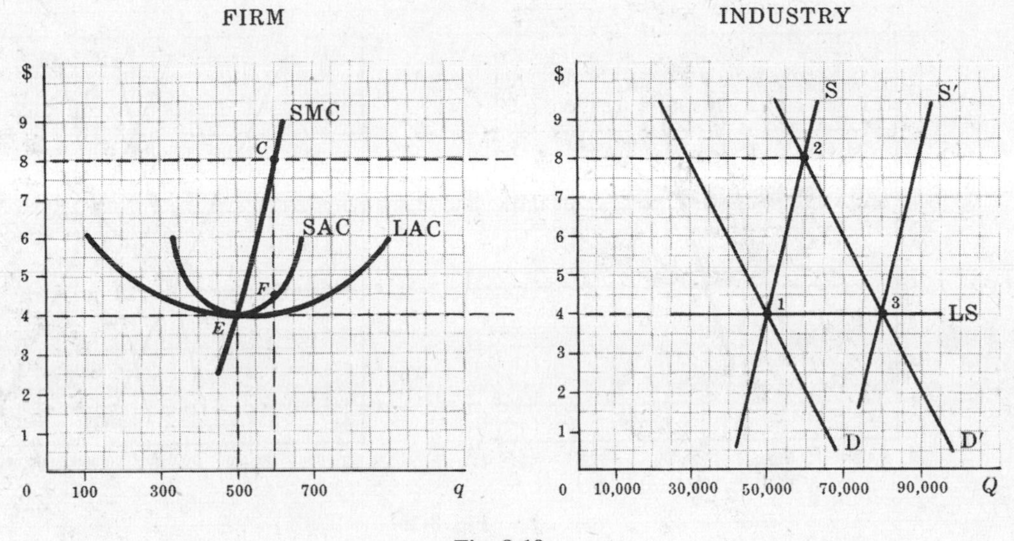

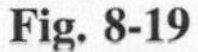
Fig. 8-19

8.21 Suppose that in Problem 8.20(*a*), the market supply function in the long run became instead $QS' = 55{,}000 - 2500P$. (*a*) What would the new industry long-run equilibrium price and quantity be? (*b*) Explain why this is an increasing cost industry, (*c*) If, as the result of a change in (relative) factor prices, each firm's entire set of cost curves shifts not only upward but also to the left, so that the lowest LAC occurs now at the output of 400 units, how many firms would there be in this industry? (*d*) Draw a figure similar to that in Problem 8.20(*c*) but reflecting the changes introduced in this problem.

(*a*) The new equilibrium price and quantity become

$$QD' = QS'$$

$$100{,}000 - 5000P = 55{,}000 + 2500P$$

$$45{,}000 = 7500P$$

$$P = \$6 \text{ (new equilibrium price 3)}$$

$$100{,}000 - 5000(6) = 70{,}000 \text{ (new equilibrium quantity 3)}$$

(*b*) Since this new long-run equilibrium price is greater than equilibrium price 1 [see Problem 8.19(*a*)], we have an increasing cost industry. That is, as industry output rises, there is a net *absolute* increase in factor prices so that the whole set of each firm's cost curves shifts up, and the lowest LAC of each firm now becomes \$6 [from \$4 at long-run equilibrium 1 in Problem 8.19(*a*)]. This increase in costs resulting from the expansion of the entire industry is called an "external diseconomy" and will be discussed in detail in Chapter 14.

(*c*) Since at the new long-run equilibrium point 3, each firm will produce 400 units of output, there will be 175 firms in the industry (to produce the new long-run industry equilibrium output of 70,000 units).

(*d*) Fig. 8-20 is similar to that in Problem 8.20(*c*) but reflects the changes introduced in this problem.

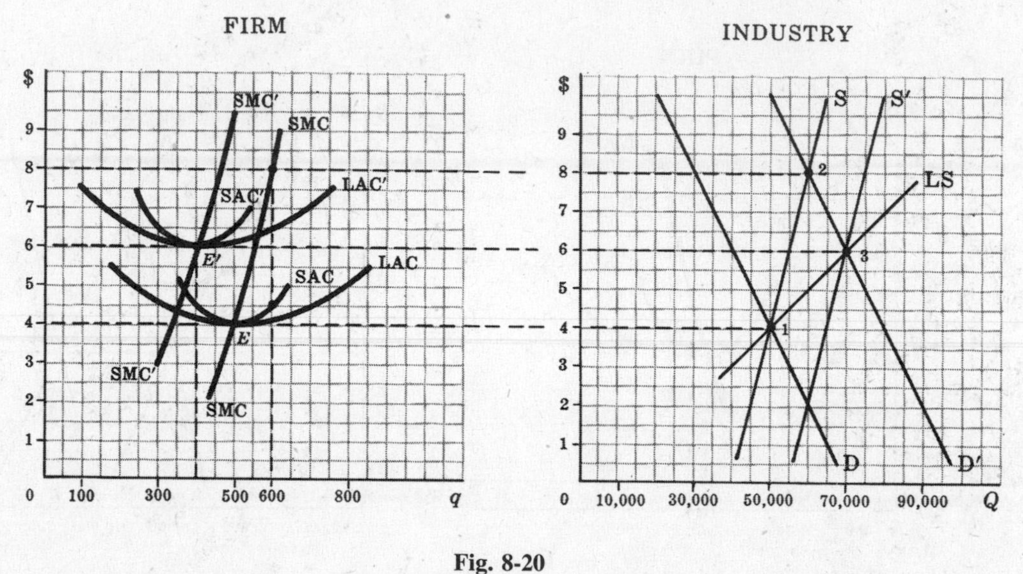

Fig. 8-20

8.22 Suppose that in Problem 8.20(*a*), the market supply function in the long run became instead $QS' = 85{,}000 + 2500P$. (*a*) What would the new industry long-run equilibrium price and quantity be? (*b*) Explain why this is a decreasing cost industry, (*c*) If, as a result of a change in relative factor prices, the entire set of cost curves of each firm shifted not only downward but also to the right so that the lowest point on the LAC curve occurs now at the output of 600 units, how many firms will there be in this industry? (*d*) Draw a figure similar to that in Problem 8.20(*c*) but reflecting the changes introduced in this problem.

(*a*) The new equilibrium price ad quantity become

$$QD' = QS'$$

$$100{,}000 - 5000p = 85{,}000 + 2500P$$

$$15{,}000 = 7500p$$

$$P = \$2 \text{ (new equilibrium price 3)}$$

$$100{,}00 - 5000(2) = 85{,}000 + 2500(2)$$

$$90{,}000 = 90{,}000 \text{ (new equilibrium quantity 3)}$$

(*b*) Since the new long-run equilibrium price 3 is lower than the long-run equilibrium price 1 [see Problem 8.19(*a*)], this is a decreasing cost industry. That is, as industry output rises, there is a new absolute reduction in factor prices so that the whole set of each firm's cost curves shifts down, and the lowest LAC becomes $2 [from $4 at long-run equilibrium 1 in Problem 8.19(*a*)]. This reduction in costs resulting from the expansion of the entire industry is called an "external economy" and will be discussed in detail in Chapter 14. It should be noted that decreasing cost industries are the least prevalent of the three cases discussed, while increasing cost industries are the most prevalent.

(*c*) The LAC curve not only shifts down but we are told that it also shifts to the right. At the new long-run equilibrium point 3, each firm will produce 600 units of output and there will then be 150 firms in the industry to produce the industry equilibrium output of 90,000 units.

(*d*) Figure 8-21 is similar to those in Problem 8.20(*c*) and Problem 8.21(*d*) but reflects the changes introduced in this problem. (The student should compare these three figures.)

Fig. 8-21

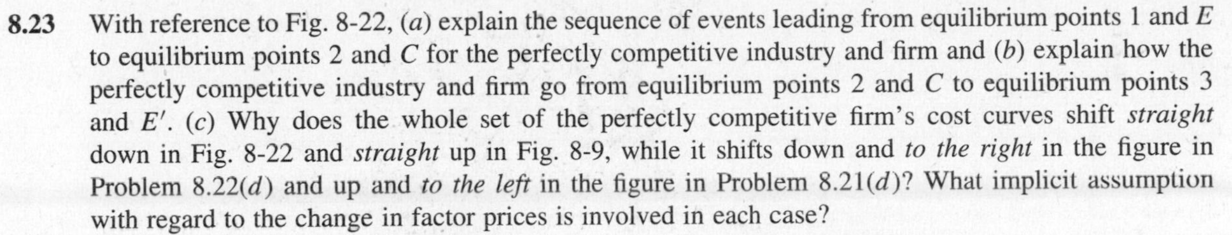

8.23 With reference to Fig. 8-22, (*a*) explain the sequence of events leading from equilibrium points 1 and *E* to equilibrium points 2 and *C* for the perfectly competitive industry and firm and (*b*) explain how the perfectly competitive industry and firm go from equilibrium points 2 and *C* to equilibrium points 3 and *E'*. (*c*) Why does the whole set of the perfectly competitive firm's cost curves shift *straight* down in Fig. 8-22 and *straight* up in Fig. 8-9, while it shifts down and *to the right* in the figure in Problem 8.22(*d*) and up and *to the left* in the figure in Problem 8.21(*d*)? What implicit assumption with regard to the change in factor prices is involved in each case?

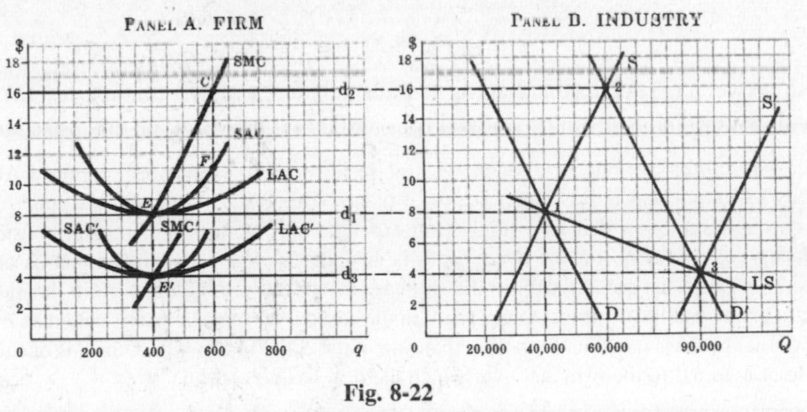

Fig. 8-22

(*a*) In Fig. 8-22, the perfectly competitive industry and firm are originally in long-run equilibrium at points 1 and *E*, respectively. If now the short-run market demand curve shifts from D to D′, the new equilibrium price becomes \$16 (point 2) and each established firm will expand output to point *C* and make *CF* profits per unit (so far, this is identical with Examples 11 and 13).

(*b*) Since established firms are making short-run profits, more firms enter this perfectly competitive industry in the long run. The short-run industry supply curve shifts from S to S′, giving the new equilibrium price of \$4 (point 3) at which all firms just break even (point *E′*). Joining market equilibrium points 1 and 3, we get the negatively sloped LS curve for this decreasing cost industry. The firm's entire set of cost curves shifted down (from LAC, SAC, and SMC to LAC′, SAC′, and SMC′) because factor prices fell as more firms entered the industry (attracted by the profits) and the industry output expanded. If all firms in this industry are identical in size, there will be 225 firms, each producing 400 units of the new equilibrium output of 90,000 units for the industry.

(*c*) Since the firm's entire set of cost curves has shifted *straight* down in panel A of Fig. 8-22 and *straight* up in panel A of Fig. 8-9, we have implicitly assumed that all factor prices changed (increased in Fig. 8-9 and decreased here) by *the same proportion*. In Fig. 8-20, on the other hand, the firm's LAC curve shifted not only up but also to the *left*. This means that *the price of fixed factors increased relative to the price of variable factors*, the firm economized on its use of fixed factors and built a smaller optimum scale of plant than before. In Fig. 8-21, the opposite occurred (from what happened in Fig. 8-20) and for the opposite reason.

8.24 Starting from a condition of long-run equilibrium in a perfectly competitive industry, if the market demand curve shifts, what is the relative adjustment burden on prices in relation to output in the market period, in the short run and in the long run?

In Fig. 8-23, D is the original market demand curve and E is the original equilibrium point. If the market demand curve now shifts up to D′, the new equilibrium point will be E_1 in the market period, E_2 in the short run, and E_3 in the long run (for an increasing cost industry). Thus, the burden of the adjustment falls exclusively on prices in the market period, only partially on prices in the short run, and less on prices in the long run than in the short run. (Of course, if the industry was a constant cost one, the entire adjustment would fall on output in the long run.)

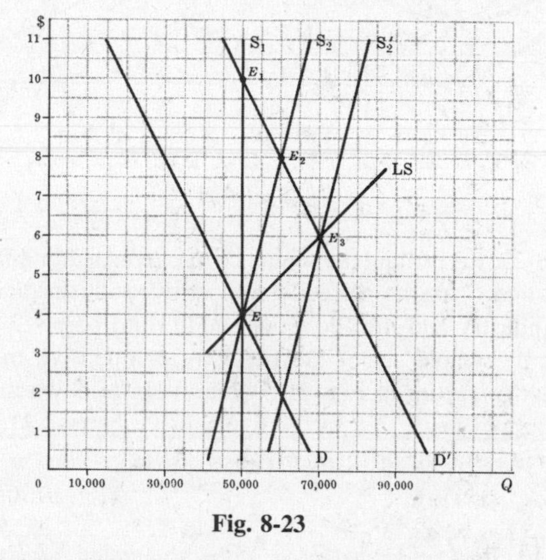

Fig. 8-23

8.25 Distinguish between (*a*) decreasing returns to scale and increasing cost industries, (*b*) increasing returns to scale and decreasing cost industries, and (*c*) constant returns to scale and constant cost industries.

(*a*) Decreasing returns to scale or diseconomies of scale refers to an upward sloping LAC curve as the firm expands its output and builds larger scales of plants. This results from factors purely *internal* to the firm (and on the assumption that as a single firm expands, factor prices will remain constant to the firm). An increasing cost industry, on the other hand, is an industry where expansion causes an increase in factor prices. This causes an upward shift in the entire set of cost curves of each firm in the industry. This increase in factor prices and the resulting upward shift in the cost curves of each firm is called an *external* diseconomy. It is external because it results from the expansion of the entire industry and, thus, is due to factors completely outside or external to the firm and over which the firm has no control.

(*b*) The opposite is true for increasing returns to scale and decreasing cost industries. Note that increasing returns to scale over a sufficiently large range of outputs is inconsistent with the existence of perfect competition. This is because the best level of output for the firm may be so large as to require only a few firms to produce the equilibrium industry output (more will be said on this in the chapters that follow).

(*c*) Constant returns to scale refers to a horizontal LAC curve or to the horizontal portion of the LAC curve. This refers to a single firm. A constant cost industry refers to an industry with a horizontal LS curve; this occurs because factor prices remain constant (or the rise in some factors is neutralized by the fall in the price of others) as industry output expands. Note that under constant returns to scale, there is no such thing as a *single or optimum scale of plant*. That is, there are many plants of different sizes, each represented by a SAC curve which is tangent to the LAC curve of the firm at the lowest point of the SAC curve.

PRICE AND OUTPUT UNDER PERFECT COMPETITION WITH CALCULUS

***8.26** Derive with the use of calculus the first- and second-order conditions for the output that a perfectly competitive firm must produce in order to maximize total profits.

Total profits (π) are equal to total revenue (TR) minus total costs (TC). That is,

$$\pi = \text{TR} - \text{TC}$$

where π, TR, and TC are all functions of output (Q).

Taking the first derivative of π with respect to Q and setting it equal to zero gives

$$\frac{d\pi}{dQ} = \frac{d(\text{TR})}{dQ} - \frac{d(\text{TC})}{dQ} = 0$$

so that

$$\frac{d(\text{TR})}{dQ} = \frac{d(\text{TC})}{dQ} \quad \text{and} \quad \text{MR} = \text{MC}$$

Since under perfect competition MR $= P$, the first-order condition for profit maximization for a perfectly competitive firm becomes

$$P = \text{MR} = \text{MC}$$

The above is only the first-order condition for maximization (and minimization). The second-order condition for profit maximization requires that the second derivative of π with respect to Q be negative. That is,

$$\frac{d^2\pi}{dQ^2} = \frac{d^2(\text{TR})}{dQ^2} - \frac{d^2(\text{TC})}{dQ^2} < 0$$

so that

$$\frac{d^2(\text{TR})}{dQ^2} < \frac{d^2(\text{TC})}{dQ^2}$$

Since under perfect competition the MR curve is horizontal, this means that the MC curve must be rising at the point where MR $=$ MC for the firm to maximize its total profits (or minimize its total losses).

***8.27** A perfectly competitive firm faces $P = \$4$ and TC $= Q^3 - 7Q^2 + 12Q + 5$. (*a*) Determine by using calculus the best level of output of the firm by the marginal approach and (*b*) find the total profit of the firm at this level of output.

(*a*)

$$\text{TR} = PQ = \$4Q \quad \text{so that} \quad MR = \frac{d(\text{TR})}{dQ} = \$4 = P$$

and

$$\text{MC} = \frac{d(\text{TC})}{dQ} = 3Q^2 - 14Q + 12$$

Setting MR $=$ MC and solving for Q, we get

$$4 = 3Q^2 - 14Q + 12$$

or

$$3Q^2 - 14Q + 8 = 0$$
$$(3Q - 2)(Q - 4) = 0$$

so that

$$Q = \frac{2}{3} \quad \text{and} \quad Q = 4$$

Thus, MR $=$ MC at $Q = 1$ and $Q = 4$.

But in order for profits to be maximized rather than minimized, the MC curve must be rising (i.e., its slope must be positive) at the point where MR $=$ MC. The equation for the slope of the MC curve is

$$\frac{d(\text{MC})}{dQ} = 6Q - 14$$

At $Q = \frac{2}{3}$, the slope of the MC curve is -10 (and so the firm minimizes total profits). At $Q = 4$, the slope of the MC curve is 10 so that the firm maximizes its total profits.

(*b*)

$$\begin{aligned}\pi &= \text{TR} - \text{TC} \\ &= 4Q - Q^3 + 7Q^2 - 12Q - 5 \\ &= -Q^3 + 7Q^2 - 8Q - 5 \\ &= -64 + 112 - 32 - 5 \\ &= \$11\end{aligned}$$

CHAPTER 9

Price and Output Under Pure Monopoly

9.1 PURE MONOPOLY DEFINED

Pure monopoly is the form of market organization in which there is a single firm selling a commodity for which there are no close substitutes. Thus the firm *is* the industry and faces the negatively sloped industry demand curve for the commodity. As a result, in order to sell more of the commodity, the monopolist must lower its price. Thus for a monopolist, MR $< P$ and the MR curve lies below the D curve.

EXAMPLE 1. In Table 9.1, columns (1) and (2) give the demand schedule faced by the monopolist. The TR values of column (3) are obtained by multiplying each value of column (1) by the corresponding value in column (2). The MR values of column (4) are obtained from the difference between successive TR values. Because of this, the MR values of column (4) should have been recorded half way *between* successive levels of TR and sales. However, this was not done

Table 9.1

(1) P (\$)	(2) Q	(3) TR (\$)	(4) MR (\$)
8.00	0	0	..
7.00	1	7.00	7
6.00	2	12.00	5
*5.50	2.5	13.75	(3)
5.50	3	15.00	3
4.00	4	16.00	1
3.00	5	15.00	−1
2.00	6	12.00	−3
1.00	7	7.00	−5
0	8	0	−7

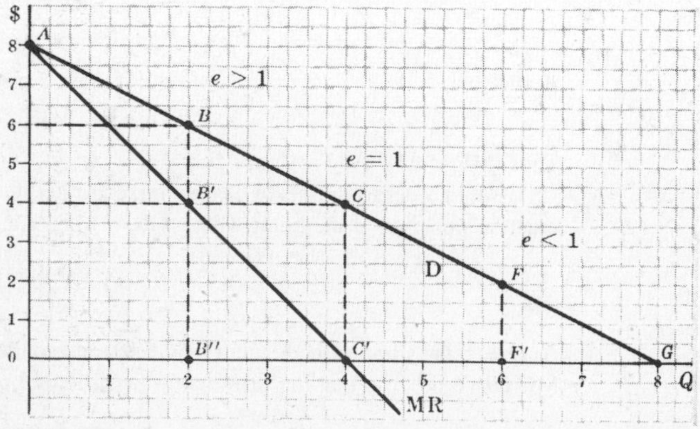

Fig. 9-1

so as not to unduly complicate the table. The MR of \$3 recorded *at* the sales level of 2.5 units is obtained from the change in TR resulting from the increase in sales from 2 to 3 units; it will be needed later to show the equilibrium level of output for the monopolist.

The D and MR schedules of Table 9.1 facing the monopolist are plotted in Fig. 9-1. Note that MR is positive as long as the demand curve is elastic, is zero when $e = 1$, and is negative when $e < 1$. This is because when D is elastic, a reduction in the commodity price will cause TR to increase, so MR (which is given by $\Delta TR/\Delta Q$) is positive. When D has unitary elasticity, a fall in price leaves TR unchanged, and so MR is zero. When D is inelastic, a reduction in price will result in a reduction in TR, and so MR is negative.

9.2 THE MR CURVE AND ELASTICITY

The MR curve for any straight-line demand curve is a straight line which starts at the same point on the vertical axis as the demand curve but falls at twice the rate as (i.e., it has twice the absolute slope of) the D curve. Also, the MR at any level of sales is related to the price at the level of sales by the formula $MR = P(1 - 1/e)$, where e stands for the absolute value of the coefficient of price elasticity of demand at that level of sales.

EXAMPLE 2. From point A to point B, the D curve of Fig. 9-1 falls by two units and has an absolute slope of 1. To locate the MR corresponding to point B on the D curve, we drop four units from point A, or twice the drop from A to B, to get point B' on the MR curve. Similarly, from A to C, the D curve falls by four units; thus, the MR corresponding to point C (i.e., point C') is obtained by dropping another four units from point C (or 8 units from point A). A straight line from point A through any one of such MR points (as B' or C') will give us the MR curve.

For the demand curve in Fig. 9-1, at point B,

$$e = \frac{B''G}{OB''} = \frac{6}{2} = 3$$

therefore,

$$MR = \$6\left(1 - \frac{1}{3}\right) = \$6\left(\frac{2}{3}\right) = \$4 \text{ (point } B'\text{)}$$

at point C,

$$e = \frac{C'G}{OC'} = \frac{4}{4} = 1$$

therefore,

$$MR = \$4\left(1 - \frac{1}{1}\right) = \$4(0) = 0 \text{ (point } C'\text{)}$$

at point F,

$$e = \frac{F'G}{OF'} = \frac{2}{6} = \frac{1}{3}$$

therefore,

$$MR = \$2\left(1 - \frac{1}{1/3}\right) = \$2(-2) = -\$4 \text{ (not shown in the figure)}$$

Note that in the case of perfect competition, $e = \infty$ (infinity). Therefore, $MR = P(1 - 1/\infty) = P(1 - 0) = P$. Thus, the marginal revenue curve and the demand curve of the perfectly competitive firm coincide.

9.3 SHORT-RUN EQUILIBRIUM UNDER PURE MONOPOLY: TOTAL APPROACH

The short-run equilibrium output of the monopolist is the output at which either total profits are maximized or total losses minimized (provided TR > TVC; see Section 8.5).

EXAMPLE 3. In Table 9.2, TR [column (3)] minus STC [column (4)] gives total profits [column (5)]. Total profits are maximized (at \$3.75) and the monopolist is in short-run equilibrium when producing and selling 2.5 units of the commodity per time period at the price of \$5.50.

Table 9.2

(1) P (\$)	(2) Q	(3) TR (\$)	(4) STC (\$)	(5) Total Profits (\$)
8.00	0	0	6	−6.00
7.00	1	7.00	8	−1.00
6.00	2	12.00	9	+3.00
*5.50	2.5	13.75	10	+3.75
5.00	3	15.00	12	+3.00
4.00	4	16.00	20	−4.00
3.00	5	15.00	35	−20.00

The short-run equilibrium output of the monopolist can also be viewed geometrically by plotting the value of columns (2), (3), (4), and (5) of Table 9.2. Note that while the TR curve for the perfectly competitive firm was given by a straight line through the origin (because the commodity price remained constant), the TR curve of the monopolist takes the shape of an inverted U. Note also that in Fig. 9-2, the level of output at which the monopolist's total profits are maximized is smaller than the output at which TR is maximum.

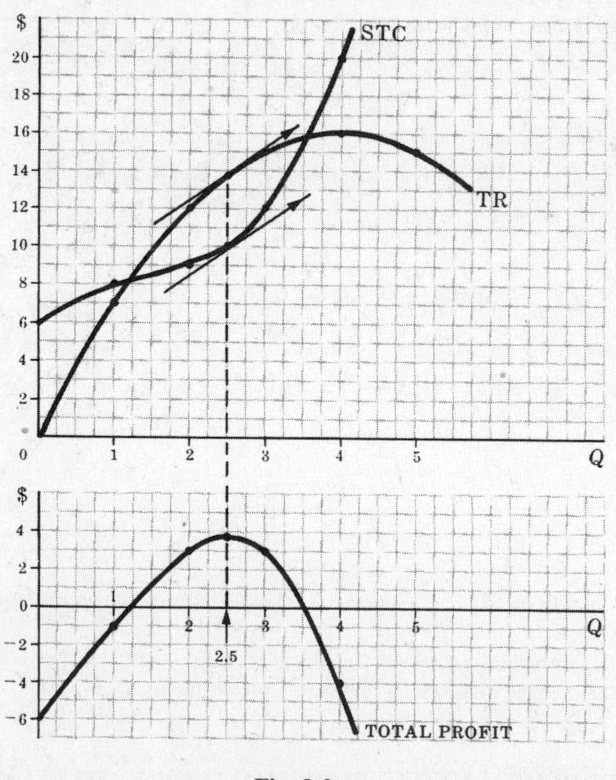

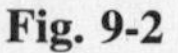
Fig. 9-2

9.4 SHORT-RUN EQUILIBRIUM UNDER PURE MONOPOLY: MARGINAL APPROACH

As in the case of perfect competition, it is more useful to analyze the short-run equilibrium of the pure monopolist with the marginal approach. This tells us that the short-run equilibrium level of output for the monopolist is the output at which MR = SMC *and the slope of the* MR *curve is smaller than the slope of the* SMC *curve* (provided that at this output $P \geqslant$ AVC).

EXAMPLE 4. The values in columns (1) through (5) of Table 9.3 come from Tables 9.1 and 9.2. The other values in Table 9.3 are derived from the values given in columns (1), (2), (3), and (5). The monopolist maximizes total profits (at \$3.75) when producing and selling 2.5 units of output at the price of \$5.50. At this level of output, MR = SMC (=\$3); MR is falling and SMC is rising (so that the negative slope of the MR curve is smaller than the positive slope of the SMC curve). As long as MR > SMC, it pays for the monopolist to expand output and sales since doing so would add more to TR than to STC (so profits rise). The opposite is true when MR < SMC (see Table 9.3). Thus total profits are maximized where MR = SMC.

Table 9.3

(1) P (\$)	(2) Q	(3) TR (\$)	(4) MR (\$)	(5) STC (\$)	(6) SMC (\$)	(7) SAC (\$)	(8) Profit/ Unit (\$)	(9) Total Profit (\$)
8.00	0	0	..	6	..	..	..	−6.00
7.00	1	7.00	7	8	2	8.00	−1.00	−1.00
6.00	2	12.00	5	9	1	4.50	+1.50	+3.00
*5.50	2.5	13.75	(3)	10	(3)	4.00	+1.50	+3.75
5.00	3	15.00	3	12	3	4.00	+1.00	+3.00
4.00	4	16.00	1	20	8	5.00	−1.00	−4.00
3.00	5	15.00	−1	35	15	7.00	−4.00	−20.00

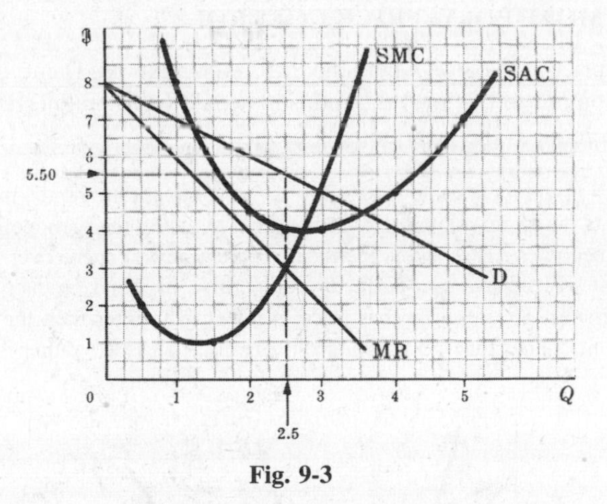

Fig. 9-3

The profit-maximizing or best level of output for this monopolist can also be viewed in Fig. 9-3 [obtained by plotting the values of columns (1), (2), (4), (6), and (7) of Table 9.3].

In Fig. 9-3, the best, or optimum, level of output for the monopolist is given by the point where *the* SMC *curve intersects the* MR *curve from below* (so that at the intersection point, the slope of the MR curve, which is always negative, is smaller than the slope of the SMC curve, which is usually positive). At this best output level of 2.5 units, the monopolist makes a profit of \$1.50 per unit (the vertical distance between D and SAC at 2.5 units of output) and \$3.75 in total (2.5 units of output times the \$1.50 profit per unit). Note that the best level of output is smaller than that associated with minimum SAC and smaller than the output level at which $P =$ SMC.

9.5 LONG-RUN EQUILIBRIUM UNDER PURE MONOPOLY

In the long run, a monopolist will remain in business only if he or she can make a profit (or at least break even) by producing the best level of output with the most appropriate scale of plant. The best level of output in the long run is given by the point where the LMC curve intersects the MR curve from below. The most appropriate scale of plant is the one whose SAC curve is tangent to the LAC curve at the best level of output.

EXAMPLE 5. In Fig. 9-4, D, MR, SMC_1, and SAC_1 are those of Fig. 9-3. As we saw in Example 4, the best level of output in the short run for this monopolist is 2.5 units per time period.

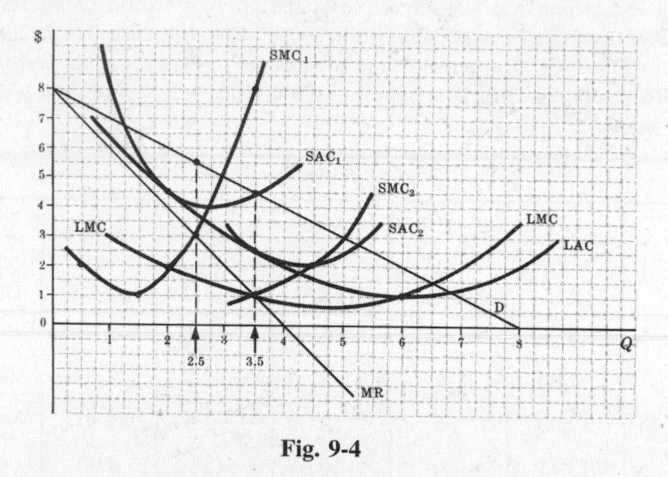

Fig. 9-4

In the long run, the best level of output is 3.5 units and is given by the point where the LMC curve intersects the MR curve from below (i.e., at the point of intersection, the slope of the MR curve has a larger negative value than the slope of the LMC curve). The most appropriate scale of plant is given by the SAC_2 curve (which is tangent to the LAC curve at 3.5 units of output). Thus at long-run equilibrium, $SMC_2 = LMC = MR$, $P = \$4.50$, $SAC_2 = \$2.50$, and profit is \$2 per unit and \$7 in total.

9.6 REGULATION OF MONOPOLY: PRICE CONTROL

By setting a maximum price at the level where the SMC curve cuts the D curve, the government can induce the monopolist to increase output to the level the industry would have produced if organized along perfectly competitive lines. This also reduces the monopolist's profits.

EXAMPLE 6. Starting with a figure identical to Fig. 9-3, if the government imposed a maximum price of \$5 (i.e., at the level where the SMC curve cuts the D curve), the new demand curve facing the monopolist becomes *ABK* (see Fig.9-5). The corresponding MR curve becomes *ABCL* and is identical with the new D curve over the infinitely elastic range, *AB*. Thus, the regulated monopolist will behave as a perfectly competitive firm and produce at point *B*, where *P* or MR = SMC and the SMC curve is rising. The result is that price is lower (\$5 rather than the \$5.50 in the absence of price control), output is greater (3 units rather than 2.5 units), profit per unit is less (\$1 rather than \$1.50), and total profits are reduced (from \$3.75 to \$3).

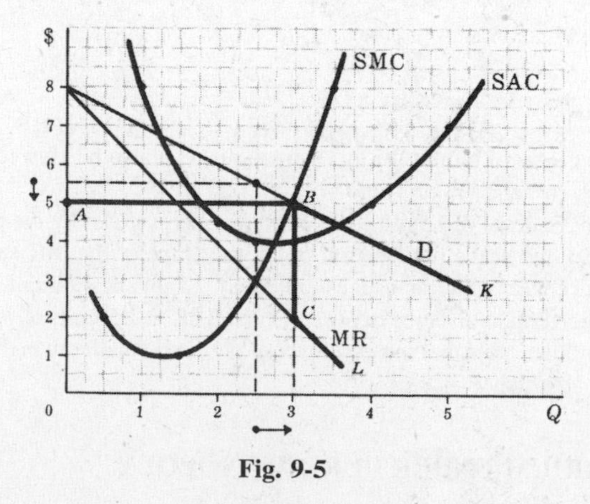

Fig. 9-5

9.7 REGULATION OF MONOPOLY: LUMP-SUM TAX

By imposing a *lump-sum tax* (such as a license fee or a profit tax), the government can reduce or even eliminate the monopolist's profits without affecting either the commodity price or output.

EXAMPLE 7. Starting from the equilibrium condition of the monopolist in Table 9.3 and Fig. 9-3, if the government imposed a lump-sum tax of $3.75, all of the monopolist's profits would be eliminated. Note that the values of column (5) of Table 9.4 are obtained by adding the lump-sum tax of $3.75 to the STC values of column (2). Since a lump-sum tax is like a fixed cost, it does not affect SMC [compare column (5) to column (2)]. With his or her MR and SMC curves unchanged, the monopolist's best level of output remains at 2.5 units and the monopolist continues to charge a price of $5.50. But now, since SAC′ at 2.5 units of output is also $5.50, the monopolist breaks even (see Fig. 9-6).

Table 9.4

(1) Q	(2) STC ($)	(3) SMC ($)	(4) SAC ($)	(5) STC′ ($)	(6) SAC′ ($)
0	6	..	..	9.75	..
1	8	2	8.00	11.75	11.75
2	9	1	4.50	12.75	6.38
*2.5	10	(3)	4.00	13.75	5.50
3	12	3	4.00	15.75	5.25
4	20	8	5.00	23.75	5.94

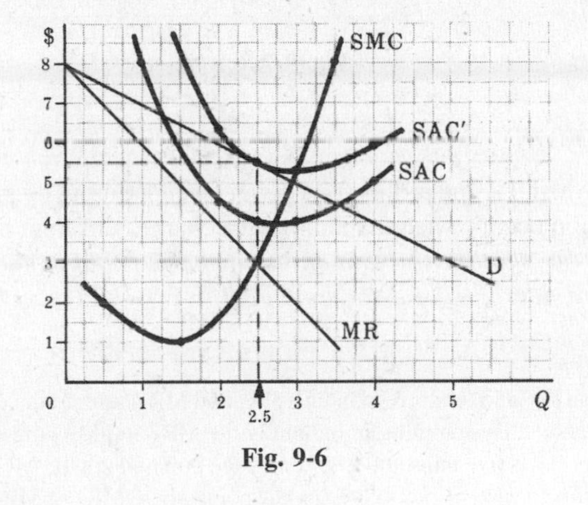

Fig. 9-6

9.8 REGULATION OF MONOPOLY: PER-UNIT TAX

The government can also reduce the monopolist's profit by imposing a *per-unit tax*. However, in this case the monopolist will be able to shift part of the burden of the per-unit tax to consumers, in the form of a higher price and a smaller output of the commodity.

EXAMPLE 8. Suppose that the government imposes a tax of $2 per unit of output on the monopolist of Table 9.3 and Fig. 9-3. Then the values of column (5) of Table 9.5 are obtained by adding the tax of $2 on each unit of output to the STC values of column (2).

Table 9.5

(1) Q	(2) STC ($)	(3) SMC ($)	(4) SAC ($)	(5) STC′ ($)	(6) SMC′ ($)	(7) SAC′ ($)
1	8	..	8.00	10	..	10.00
2	9	1	4.50	13	3	6.50
3	12	3	4.00	18	5	6.00
4	20	8	5.00	28	10	7.00

Note that the per-unit tax is like a variable cost and thus causes an upward shift in both the monopolist's SAC and SMC curves (to SAC′ and SMC′). The new equilibrium output is 2 units (and is given by the point where the SMC′ intersects the unchanged MR curve from below); $P = \$6$, $SAC' = \$6.50$, and the monopolist now incurs a short-run loss of \$0.50 per unit and \$1 in total (see Fig. 10-7). If TR > TVC at this new best level of output, the monopolist stays in business in the short run, but will produce 0.5 unit less than without the per-unit tax and will charge \$0.50 more for each of the 2 units sold.

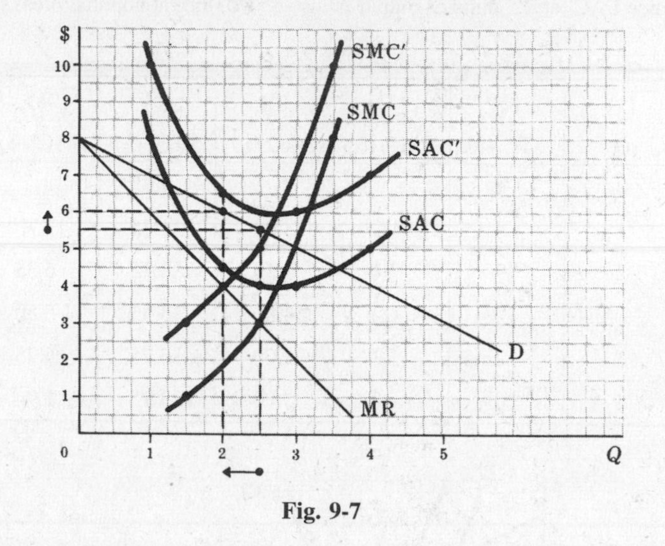

Fig. 9-7

9.9 PRICE DISCRIMINATION

Monopolists can increase their TR and profits for a given level of output by practicing price discrimination. One form of price discrimination occurs when the monopolist charges different prices for the same commodity in different markets *in such a way that the last unit of the commodity sold in each market gives the same* MR. This is often referred to as *third-degree price discrimination* (for first- and second-degree price discrimination; see Problems 9.21 to 9.24).

EXAMPLE 9. In Fig. 9-8, D_1 and D_2 (and the corresponding MR_1 and MR_2) refer to the demand (and MR) curves faced by the monopolist in two separate markets. By summing horizontally the MR_1 and MR_2 curves, we get the $\sum MR$ curve. The best level of output for this monopolist is five units and is given by the point where the MC curve intersects the $\sum MR$ from below. The monopolist sells 2.5 units in each market (given by the point where $MR_1 = MR_2 = MC$) and charges the price P_1 in the first market and P_2 in the second market. As long as the MR of the last unit of the commodity sold in market 1 is smaller or larger than the MR of the last unit sold in market 2, the monopolist could increase TR and total profits by redistributing sales among the two markets until $MR_1 = MR_2$. However, when MR_1 equals MR_2, P_2 exceeds P_1 (see Fig. 9-8).

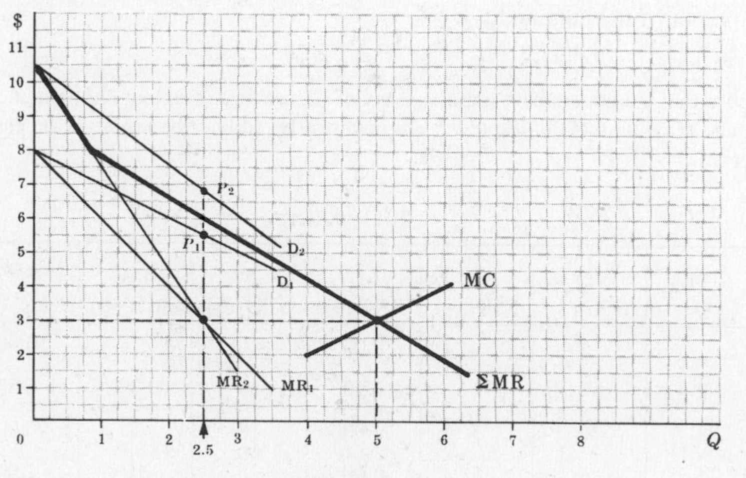

Fig. 9-8

Glossary

Long-run equilibrium of the pure monopolist The output level at which the LMC curve intersects the MR curve from below (provided that $P \geqslant LAC$).

Lump-sum tax A tax, such as a profit tax or a license fee, which is imposed on a firm regardless of its level of output.

Per-unit tax A tax on each unit produced.

Price control The setting of a maximum price on a commodity at or close to where the perfectly competitive industry would produce.

Pure monopoly The form of market organization in which there is a single firm selling a commodity for which there are no close substitutes.

Short-run equilibrium of the pure monopolist The output level at which MR = SMC and the slope of the MR curve is smaller than the slope of the SMC curve (provided that at this output $P \geqslant$ AVC).

Third-degree price discrimination The practice of charging different prices in different markets in such a way that the last unit of the commodity sold in each market gives the same MR.

Review Questions

1. When the D curve is elastic, MR is (*a*) 1, (*b*) 0, (*c*) positive, or (*d*) negative.

Ans. (*c*) See Fig. 9-1.

2. If $P = \$10$ at the point on the D curve where $e = 0.5$, MR is (*a*) \$5, (*b*) \$0, (*c*) −\$1, or (*d*) −\$10.

Ans. (*d*) See Section 9.2.

3. The best, or optimum, level of output for the pure monopolist occurs at the point where (*a*) STC is minimum, (*b*) TR = STC, (*c*) TR is maximum, or (*d*) the TR and STC curves are parallel.

Ans. (*d*) See Fig. 9-2.

4. At the best, or optimum, level of output for the pure monopolist, (*a*) MR = SMC, (*b*) P = SMC, (*c*) P = lowest SAC, or (*d*) P is highest.

Ans. (*a*) See Fig. 9-3.

5. In the short run, the monopolist (*a*) breaks even, (*b*) incurs a loss, (*c*) makes a profit, or (*d*) any of the above.

Ans. (*d*) Whether the monopolist makes a profit, breaks even, or incurs a loss in the short run depends on whether $P >$ SAC, P = SAC, or $P <$ SAC at the best level of output. If at the best level of output $P <$ AVC, the monopolist will discontinue production.

6. If the monopolist incurs losses in the short run, then in the long run (*a*) the monopolist will go out of business, (*b*) the monopolist will stay in business, (*c*) the monopolist will break even, or (*d*) any of the above is possible.

Ans. (*d*) See Section 9.5.

7. The monopolist who is in

(*a*) short-run equilibrium will also be in a long-run equilibrium,

(*b*) long-run equilibrium will also be in short-run equilibrium,

(*c*) long-run equilibrium may or may not be in short-run equilibrium, or

(*d*) none of the above.

Ans. (*b*) For example, in Fig. 9-4, at the output level of 3.5 units, LMC $= \text{SMC}_2 = $ MR, and both the SMC_2 and LMC curves intersect the MR curve from below. So the monopolist is both in long-run and in short-run equilibrium. At the output level of 2.5 units, $\text{SMC}_1 = \text{MR} > \text{LMC}$, so the monopolist is in short-run but not long-run equilibrium.

8. In long-run equilibrium, the pure monopolist (as opposed to the perfectly competitive firm) can make pure profits because of (*a*) blocked entry, (*b*) high selling prices, (*c*) low LAC costs, or (*d*) advertising.

Ans. (*a*) If entry into the monopolized market were not blocked, more firms would enter the industry until all profits in the industry disappeared.

9. The imposition of a maximum price at the point where the monopolist's SMC curve intersects the D curve causes the monopolist to (*a*) break even, (*b*) incur losses, (*c*) make profits, or (*d*) any of the above.

Ans. (*d*) The imposition of a maximum price at the point where the monopolist's SMC curve intersects the D curve induces the monopolist to behave as a perfect competitor. In the short run, a perfect competitor can make profits, break even, or incur losses.

10. The imposition of a per-unit tax causes the monopolist's (*a*) SAC curve alone to shift up; (*b*) SAC and SMC curves to shift up, because the per-unit tax is like a fixed cost; (*c*) SAC and SMC curves to shift up, because the per-unit tax is like a variable cost; or (*d*) none of the above.

Ans. (*c*) See Fig. 9-7. Note that the monopolist's AVC curve (not shown in Fig. 9-7) also shifts up when the per-unit tax is imposed.

11. Which form of monopoly regulation is most advantageous for the consumer? (*a*) Price control, (*b*) lump-sum tax, (*c*) per-unit tax, or (*d*) all of the above three forms are equally advantageous.

Ans. (*a*) With price control (as seen in Fig. 9-5), the consumer can buy a larger output at a lower price than with a lump-sum tax or a per-unit tax (compare Fig. 9-5 to Figs 9-6 and 9-7).

12. If the demand curves for a monopolist's commodity are identical in two separate markets, then, by practicing third-degree price discrimination, the monopolist (*a*) will increase TR and total profits, (*b*) can increase TR and total profits, (*c*) cannot increase TR and total profits, or (*d*) will charge a different price in different markets.

Ans. (*c*) If the demand curves in the two markets are identical, then the marginal revenue curves are also identical. Therefore, at the point where $\text{MR}_1 = \text{MR}_2 = \text{MC}$, $P_1 = P_2$ and so it will not be profitable for the monopolist to practice third-degree price discrimination (i.e., charge a different price in each market).

Solved Problems

PURE MONOPOLY DEFINED

9.1 Define pure monopoly in a way analogous to the definition of perfect competition given in Problem 8.1. What is the difference between pure monopoly and perfect monopoly?

Pure monopoly refers to the case where (1) there is a single firm selling the commodity, (2) there are no close substitutes for the commodity, and (3) entry into the industry is very difficult or impossible (see Problem 9.2). If we further assume that the monopolist has perfect knowledge of present and future prices and costs, we have *perfect* monopoly. In the rest of this book, as in most other microeconomics books, we will not make such a distinction and will use the term "pure monopoly" to refer to both pure and perfect monopoly.

9.2 What are the conditions that might give rise to monopoly?

The firm may control the entire supply of raw materials required to produce the commodity. For example, up to World War II, Alcoa owned or controlled almost every source of bauxite (the raw material necessary to produce aluminum) in the U.S. and thus had a complete monopoly over the production of aluminum in the U.S.

The firm may own a patent which precludes other firms from producing the same commodity. For example, when cellophane was first introduced, DuPont had monopoly power in its production based on patents.

A monopoly may be established by a government franchise. In this case, the firm is set up as the sole producer and distributor of a good or service but is subjected to governmental control in certain aspects of its operation.

In some industries, increasing returns to scale may operate over a sufficiently large range of outputs as to leave only one firm to produce the equilibrium industry output. These are called "natural monopolies" and are fairly common in the areas of public utilities and transportation. What the government usually does in these cases is to allow the monopolist to operate but subjects the monopoly to government control. For example, electricity rates in New York City are set so as to leave Con Edison with only a "normal rate of return" (say, 10 to 15%) on its investment.

9.3 (*a*) Are cases of pure monopoly common in the U.S. today? (*b*) What forces limit the pure monopolist's market power?

(*a*) Aside from regulated monopolies, cases of pure monopoly have been rare in the past and are forbidden today by United States antitrust laws. Even so, the pure monopoly model is often useful in explaining observed business behavior in cases approximating pure monopoly, and also gives us insights into the operation of other types of imperfectly competitive markets.

(*b*) A pure monopolist does not have unlimited market power. The monopolist faces indirect competition for the consumer's dollar from all other commodities. Although there are no *close* substitutes for the commodity sold by the monopolist, substitutes may nevertheless exist. Fear of government prosecution and the threat of potential competition also act as a check on the monopolist's market power.

DEMAND, MARGINAL REVENUE, AND ELASTICITY

9.4 Given the D function $QD = 12 - P$, (*a*) find the D and MR schedules, (*b*) plot the D and MR schedules, and (*c*) find MR when $P = \$10$, \$6, and \$2.

(*a*)

Table 9.6

P ($)	12	11	10	9	8	7	6	5	4	3	2	1	0
Q	0	1	2	3	4	5	6	7	8	9	10	11	12
TR ($)	0	11	20	27	32	35	36	35	32	27	20	11	0
MR ($)	..	11	9	7	5	3	1	−1	−3	−5	−7	−9	−11

(*b*)

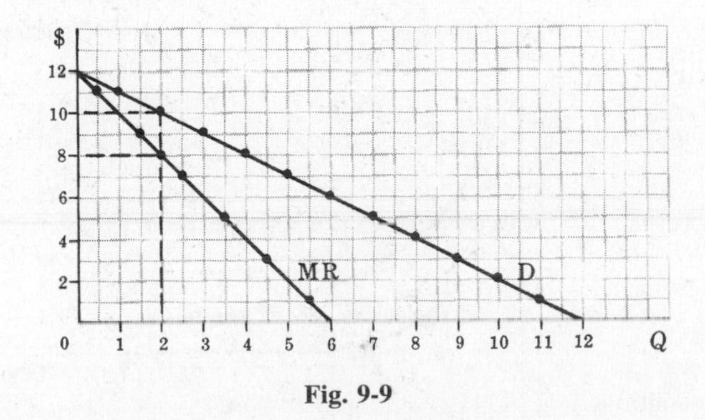

Fig. 9-9

Note that when the D curve is a straight line, the MR curve bisects the distance between the D curve and the price axis.

(*c*) From Fig. 9-9, we see that when $P = \$10$,

$$e = \frac{10}{2} = 5$$

therefore $$\text{MR} = \$10\left(1 - \frac{1}{5}\right) = \$10\left(\frac{4}{5}\right) = \$8$$

When $P = \$6$, $$e = \frac{6}{6} = 1$$

therefore $$\text{MR} = \$6(1 - 1) = \$0$$

When $P = \$2$, $$e = \frac{2}{10} = 0.2$$

therefore $$\text{MR} = \$2\left(1 - \frac{1}{0.2}\right) = \$2(1 - 5) = -\$8$$

Note that when TR is maximum (in this problem, \$36), $e = 1$ and MR = \$0.

9.5 (*a*) Sketch the curvilinear demand curve given by the points in Table 9.7. Derive *geometrically* the MR curve by drawing tangents to the given D curve at various points and then proceeding in exactly the same way as with a straight-line D curve. (*b*) What is the justification for this procedure?

Table 9.7

P (\$)	11	8	5	4
Q	1	2	6	10

(*a*) In Fig. 9-10, the MR corresponding to point *A* on the curvilinear D curve is given by point *A*′. To get point *A*′, we draw a tangent to the D curve at point *A*, extend this tangent to the price axis, and treat this tangent as a straight-line D curve. Since this (straight-line) tangent falls by three units from the point where it crosses the price axis to point *A*, we get point *A*′ by dropping three units directly below point *A*. We get the MR corresponding to points *B* and *C* on the curvilinear D curve in exactly the same way. This will give us points *B*′ and *C*′. By joining points *A*′, *B*′, and *C*′ we get the MR curve shown in Fig. 9-10.‘

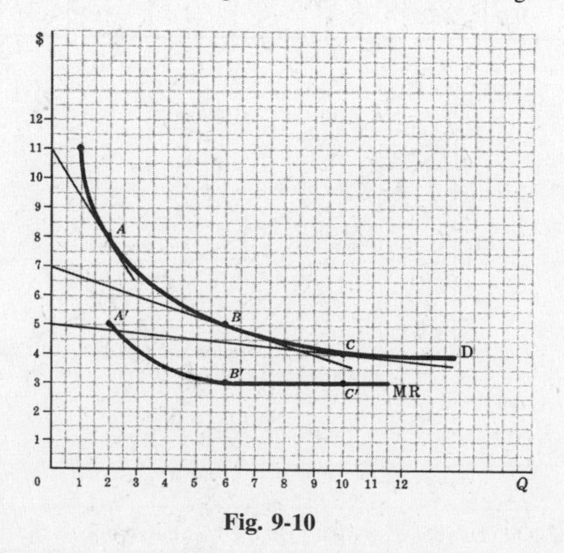

Fig. 9-10

(*b*) The justification for this procedure is as follows. If we treat the tangent to the curvilinear D curve as a straight-line D curve, then at the point of tangency these two D curves will have the same *e* and will indicate the same

P. Therefore, since $MR = P(1 - 1/e)$, the MR corresponding to the point of tangency of these two D curves must also be the same. Thus by finding the MR corresponding to the point of tangency (say point A) on the straight-line D curve, we will also have found the MR corresponding to point A on the curvilinear D curve.

9.6 From Fig. 9-11, derive the formula $MR = P(1 - 1/e)$.

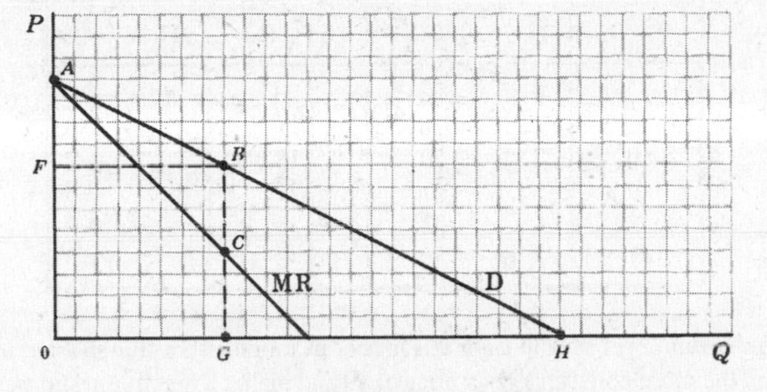

Fig. 9-11

From Fig. 9-11,

$$e = \frac{GH}{OG} = \frac{BH}{AB} = \frac{FO}{AF}$$

But $FO = BG$ and, by congruent triangles, $AF = BC$. Hence,

$$e = \frac{BG}{BC} = \frac{BG}{BG - GC} = \frac{P}{P - MR}$$

Since $e = P/(P - MR)$, $e(P - MR) = P$; $P - MR = P/e$; $-MR = -P + P/e$; $MR = P - P/e$; $MR = P(1 - 1/e)$.

SHORT-RUN EQUILIBRIUM UNDER PURE MONOPOLY: TOTAL APPROACH

9.7 (*a*) What is the basic difference between the pure monopolist and the perfectly competitive firm, if the monopolist does not affect factor prices? (*b*) What basic assumption do we make in order to determine the short-run equilibrium output of the pure monopolist?

(*a*) If the monopolist does not affect factor prices (i.e., if the monopolist is a perfect competitor in the factor markets), then short-run cost curves will be similar to those developed in Chapter 7 and need not be different from those used in Chapter 8 for the analysis of perfect competition. Thus, the basic difference between the perfectly competitive firm and the monopolist lies on the selling or demand side rather than on the production or cost side.

(*b*) In order to determine the short-run equilibrium output of the pure monopolist, we assume (as in the case of perfect competition) that the monopolist wants to maximize total profits. This equilibrium condition can be looked at either from the total revenue and total cost approach or from the marginal revenue and marginal cost approach.

9.8 If the D function facing a pure monopolist is given by $QD = 12 - P$ and the STC schedule by the figures in Table 9.8, (*a*) using the TR and STC approach, find the monopolist's best level of output in the short run and (*b*) show the solution geometrically.

Table 9.8

Q	0	1	2	3	4	5
STC ($)	10	17	18	21	30	48

(*a*)

Table 9.9

P ($)	Q	TR ($)	STC ($)	Total Profits ($)
12	0	0	10	−10
11	1	11	17	−6
10	2	20	18	+2
*9	3	27	21	+6
8	4	32	30	+2
7	5	35	48	−13

The best, or optimum, level of output for this monopolist in the short run is three units per time period. At this level of output, the monopolist charges a price of $9 and makes a maximum short-run total profit of $6 per time period.

(*b*) See Fig. 9.12. Note that the monopolist's TR curve takes the shape of an inverted U except when the D curve facing the monopolist is a rectangular hyperbola. In that case the TR curve is a horizontal line. At the best level of output, the slope of the TR curve is equal to the slope of the STC curve, or MR = SMC.

SHORT-RUN EQUILIBRIUM UNDER PURE MONOPOLY: MARGINAL APPROACH

9.9 Show with the marginal approach (*a*) numerically and (*b*) geometrically the best short-run level of output for the pure monopolist of Problem 9.8 (*c*) Comment on the graph of part (*b*).

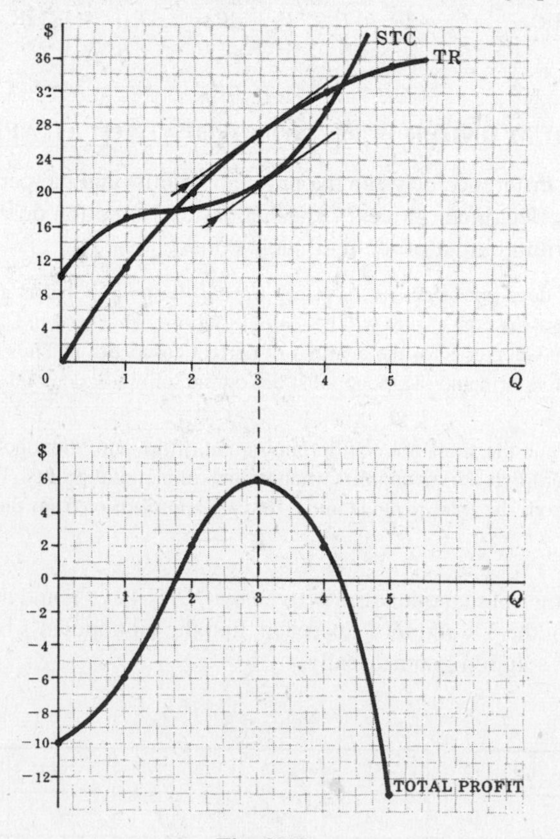

Fig. 9-12

(*a*)

Table 9.10

P ($)	Q	TR ($)	MR ($)	STC ($)	SMC ($)	SAC ($)	Profit/ Unit ($)	Total Profit ($)
12	0	0	..	10	..	..	..	−10
11	1	11	11	17	7	17.00	−6.00	−6
10	2	20	9	18	1	9.00	+1.00	+2
*9	3	27	7	21	3	7.00	+2.00	+6
8	4	32	5	30	9	7.50	+0.50	+2
7	5	35	3	48	18	9.60	−2.60	−13

(*b*) See Fig. 9-13.

(*c*) The best short-run level of output for this monopolist is three units per time period and is given by the point where the SMC curve intersects the MR curve from below. At this level of output, the monopolist charges a price of $9 and makes a profit per unit of $2 and a total profit of $6 per time period. Note that the best level of output for the monopolist is smaller than the best level of output for the perfectly competitive firm, which is determined by $P = \text{SMC}$. Note also that at the best level of output, $\text{SMC} = \text{MR} > 0$. Since D is elastic when $\text{MR} > 0$, the pure monopolist will always produce in the elastic portion of the D curve. (If at the best level of output $\text{SMC} = 0$, the monopolist will produce where $e = 1$.)

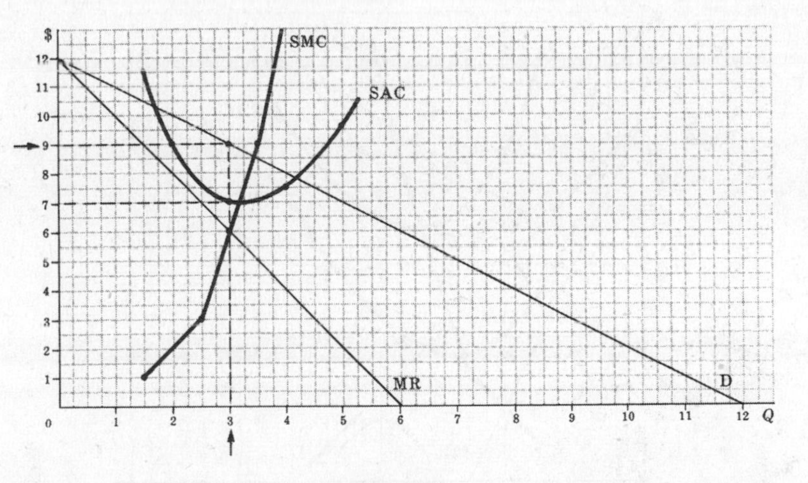

Fig. 9-13

9.10 (*a*) Will the monopolist continue to produce in the short run if a loss is incurred at the best short-run level of output? (*b*) What happens in the long run?

(*a*) If at best level of output $\text{AVC} < P < \text{SAC}$, the monopolist will continue to produce in the short run in order to minimize short-run total losses. On the other hand, if at the best level of output $P < \text{AVC}$, the monopolist minimizes short-run total losses (equal to the TFC) by shutting down. Thus, the point where $P = \text{AVC}$ is also the short-run shut-down point for the monopolist.

(*b*) In the long run, this monopolist could build the most appropriate scale of plant to produce the best long-run level of output. The monopolist could also advertise in an attempt to cause an upward shift in the D curve (this, however, will also shift up the cost curves). If still incurring a loss after having considered all of these long-run possibilities, this monopolist would stop producing the commodity in the long run.

9.11 If there is no change in the cost curves of the pure monopolist of Problems 9.8 and 9.9 but the D curve shifts down to $QD = 5 - 1/2P$, determine by the marginal approach (*a*) numerically and (*b*) geometrically whether or not the monopolist will continue to produce in the short run.

(*a*)

Table 9.11

(1) P ($)	(2) Q ($)	(3) TR ($)	(4) MR ($)	(5) STC ($)	(6) TFC ($)	(7) TVC ($)	(8) SMC ($)	(9) SAC ($)	(10) AVC ($)	(11) Profit/ Units ($)	(12) Total Profit ($)
10	0	0	..	10	10	0	..	..	..	..	−10
8	1	8	8	17	10	7	7	17.00	7.00	−9.00	−9
*6	2	12	4	18	10	8	1	9.00	4.00	−3.00	−6*
4	3	12	0	21	10	11	3	7.00	3.67	−3.00	−9
2	4	8	−4	30	10	20	9	7.50	5.00	−5.50	−22
0	5	0	−8	48	10	38	18	9.60	7.60	−9.60	−48

The new D function will give us the new D schedule of columns (1) and (2). The STC values of column (5) are the same as those in Problems 9.8 and 9.9. Since STC = $10 when output is zero, TFC = $10. By subtracting $10 from the STC values of column (5), we get the TVC values of column (7). The values in the other columns are obtained as before.

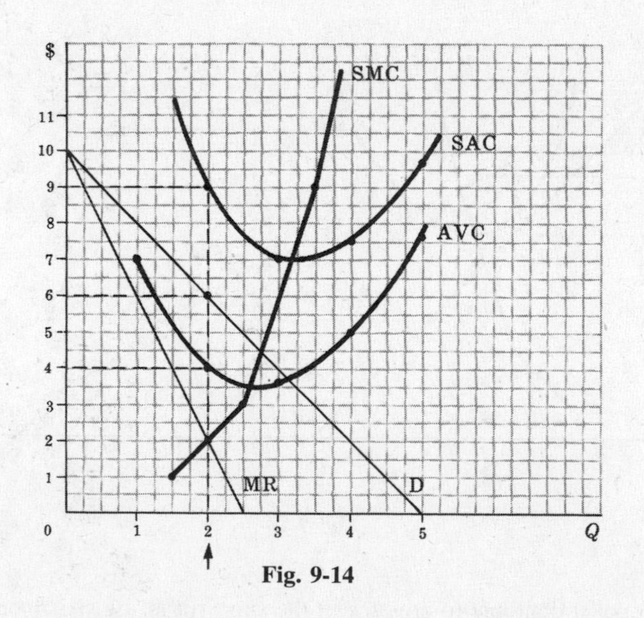

Fig. 9-14

(*b*) The best short-run level of output for this pure monopolist is two units. At this level of output, SAC > *P* > AVC. Since SAC = $9 and *P* = $6, the monopolist takes a loss of $3 pet unit and $6 in total. Since *P* exceeds AVC by $2, it pays for the monopolist to remain in business in the short run. If going out of business in the short run, the monopolist would incur the greater loss of $10 (the TFC).

9.12 The D function faced by a monopolist is $QD = 17 - P$. The monopolist operates two plants (plant 1 and plant 2) with SMC *at* various levels of output given in Table 9.12. (*a*) Determine (both numerically and geometrically) the best level of output for this monopolist, (*b*) How much of this output should the monopolist produce in each plant? Why?

Table 9.12

Q	1	2	3	4	5
SMC_1 (\$)	3	4	7	11	15
SMC_2 (\$)	5	7	9	13	17

(*a*)

Table 9.13

P (\$)	Q	TR (\$)	MR (\$)	SMC_1 (\$)	SMC_2 (\$)	Σ SMC (\$)
17	0	0	..	..	..	..
16	1	16	16	3	5	3
15	2	30	14	4	7	4
14	3	42	12	7	9	5
13	4	52	10	11	13	7
*12	5	60	8	15	17	7
11	6	66	6	..	..	9
10	7	70	4	..	..	11
9	8	72	2	..	..	13

To be noted is that the SMC_1 and SMC_2 values are given in this problem (and are plotted in Fig. 9-15) *at* various levels of output, while the MR values as usual refer to (and thus are plotted at) the midpoint *between* consecutive levels of output.

In Fig. 9-15, the $\sum$ SMC curve is obtained by summing *horizontally* the SMC_1, and the SMC_2 curves. The $\sum$ SMC curve shows the monopolist's minimum SMC for producing each additional unit of the commodity. Thus the monopolist should produce the first and second units in plant 1 (at an SMC of \$3 and \$4, respectively), the third unit in plant 2 (at an SMC of \$5), the fourth and fifth units in plant 1 and plant 2 (one unit in each plant, at a SMC of \$7), etc. The best level of output for this monopolist is five units and is given by the point where the $\sum$ SMC curve intersects the MR curve from below.

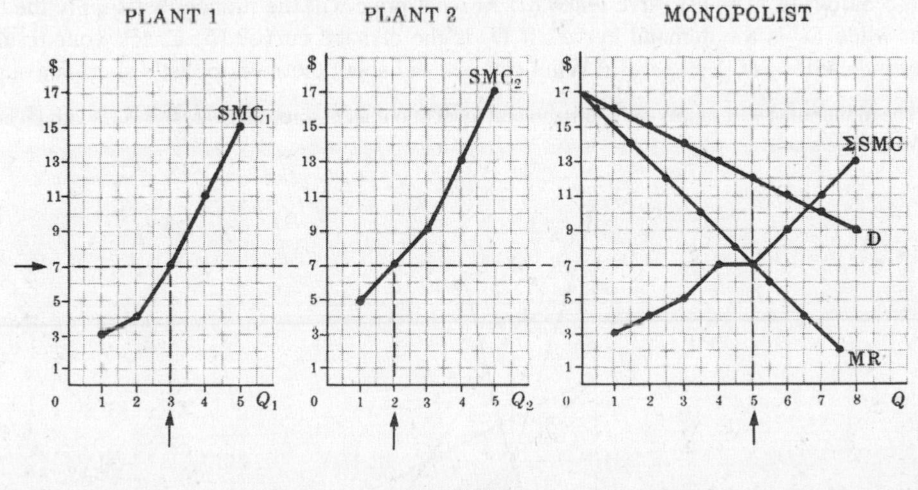

Fig. 9-15

(*b*) The multiplant monopolist minimizes STC at the best level of output when the last unit produced in each plant has the same SMC. In the present case, the monopolist should distribute the best level of output between the two plants in such a way that $SMC_1 = SMC_2 = \sum SMC = MR$. Thus the monopolist should produce three of the five units in plant 1 and the remaining two units in plant 2 (see Table 9.13 and Fig. 9-15). Any other distribution of the five units of production between the two plants makes the monopolist's STC greater and profits smaller.

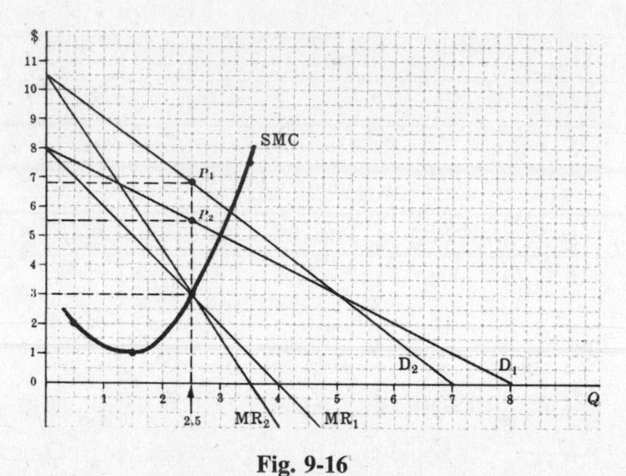

Fig. 9-16

9.13 In Fig. 9-16, D_1 and D_2 are two *alternative* D curves facing a monopolist. (*a*) Determine the monopolist's short-run equilibrium output and price with each alternative D curve. (*b*) Can you define the short-run supply curve of this monopolist? Explain.

(*a*) The SMC curve intersects from below the MR_1 curve and the MR_2 curve *at the same point*, so that with either D curve the best level of output for the monopolist is 2.5 units per time period. However, if the D curve facing the monopolist is D_1, this best level of output will be supplied at $P_1 = \$5.50$; with D_2, the same (best) level of output will be supplied at $P_2 = \$6.75$.

(*b*) Since the same best level of output will be supplied at different prices, depending on the price elasticity and the level of D, there is no unique relationship between quantity supplied and price. So we cannot define the short-run supply curve of the monopolist.

9.14 Two alternative D functions facing the monopolist are $QD_1 = 12 - P$ and $QD_2 = 8 - P/3$. The monopolist incurs an SMC of \$1 to increase output from one to two units, an SMC of \$3 to increase output from two to three units, an SMC of \$9 to increase output from three to four units, and an SMC of \$18 to increase output from four to five units, (*a*) At what price will the monopolist supply the best level of output when D_1 is the demand curve? If D_2 is the demand curve? (*b*) Check your results by using the formula $MR = P(1 - 1/e)$. (*c*) What can you say about the monopolist's short-run supply curve?

(*a*) The monopolist will supply the short-run best level of output of three units at $P_2 = \$15$ with D_2 and at $P_1 = \$9$ with D_1.

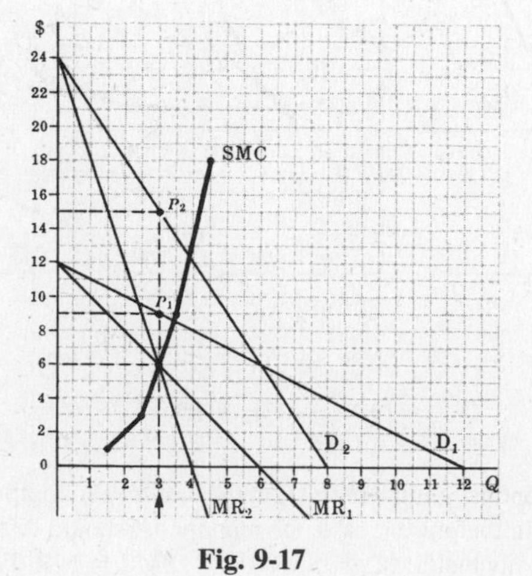

Fig. 9-17

(*b*) At P_2, $e_2 = 5/3$; at P_1, $e_1 = 3$. Therefore,

$$\text{MR}_2 = P_2\left(1 - \frac{1}{e_2}\right) \quad \$6 = P_2\left(1 - \frac{1}{5/3}\right) \quad \$6 = P_2\left(\frac{6}{15}\right)$$

thus $P_2 = \$15$.

$$\text{MR}_1 = P_1\left(1 - \frac{1}{e_1}\right) \quad \$6 = P_1\left(1 - \frac{1}{3}\right) \quad \$6 = P_1\left(\frac{2}{3}\right)$$

thus $P_1 = \$9$.

(*c*) The short-run supply curve of the monopolist is undefined. (As we will see in the next chapter, the same is true for all other imperfectly competitive firms.)

LONG-RUN EQUILIBRIUM UNDER PURE MONOPOLY

9.15 With reference to Fig. 9-18, (*a*) explain why the monopolist is not in long-run equilibrium when utilizing plant 1. (*b*) At what point is this monopolist in long-run equilibrium? (*c*) Find the monopolist's total profit when the monopolist is in long-run equilibrium, and compare this with the maximum total profit this monopolist can make when operating plant 1.

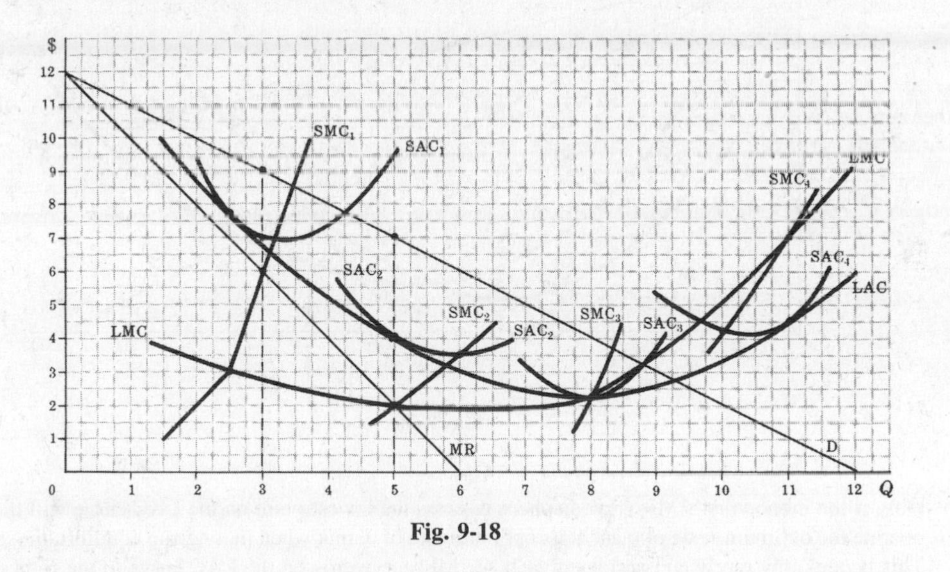

Fig. 9-18

(*a*) This monopolist is not in long-run equilibrium when operating plant 1 because at the point where SAC_1 is tangent to the LAC curve, MR > LMC = SMC_1.

(*b*) The monopolist's long-run equilibrium output is five units and is given by the point where the LMC curve intersects the MR curve from below. Thus, MR = LMC = SMC_2.

(*c*) At the long-run equilibrium level of output of five units, $P = \$7$ and SAC = LAC = \$4. Thus, the monopolist makes a profit \$3 per unit and a maximum long-run total profit of \$15. This compares with a maximum short-run total profit of \$6 at the best short-run output of three units. Note that this monopolist *underutilizes a plant smaller than the optimum scale of plant* when in long-run equilibrium.

9.16 (*a*) Draw a figure showing a pure monopolist operating the optimum scale of plant at its optimum rate of output when in long-run equilibrium. (*b*) Draw another figure showing a pure monopolist overutilizing a larger-than-the-optimum scale of plant when in long-run equilibrium, (*c*) State the general condition which determines whether a monopolist will operate scale of plant, a larger-than-the-optimum scale of plant, or a smaller-than-the-optimum scale of plant, when in long-run equilibrium.

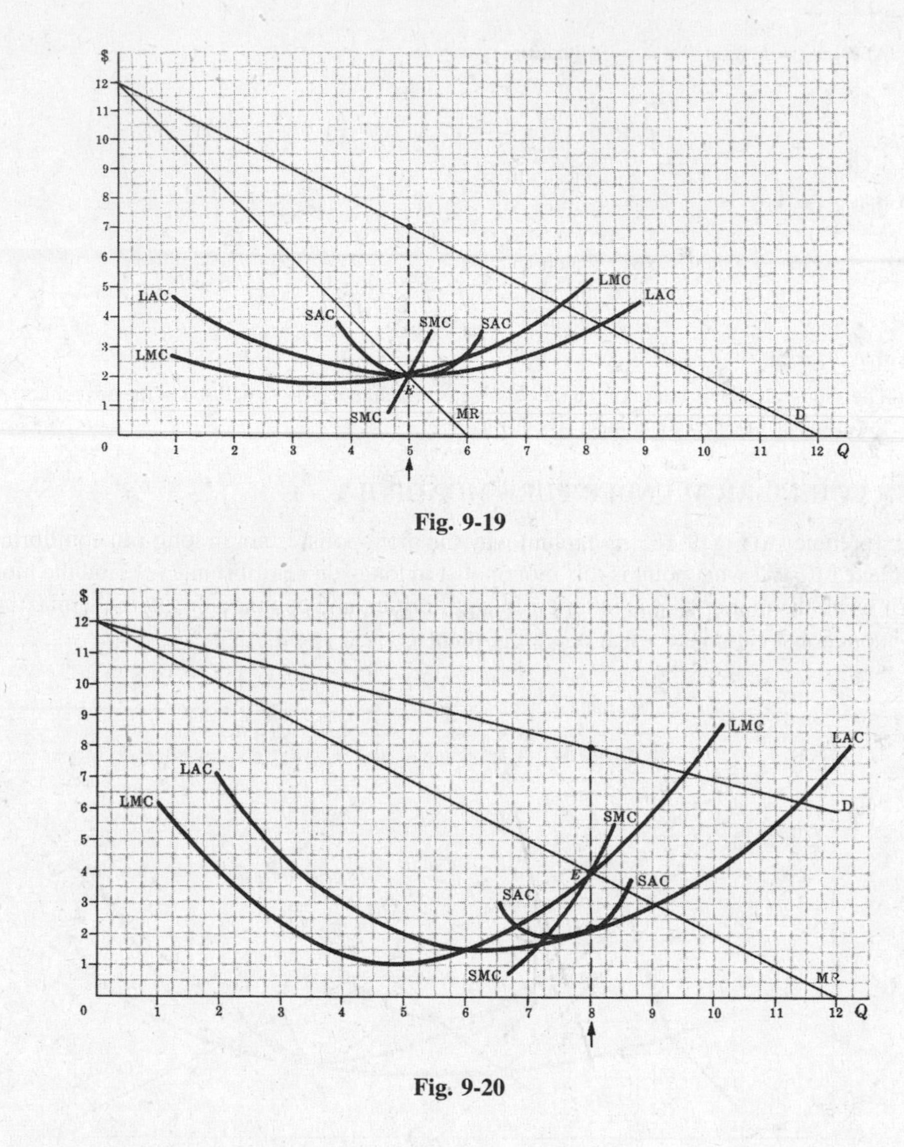

Fig. 9-19

Fig. 9-20

(c) Only if the monopolist's MR curve happens to cross the lowest point on the LAC curve will the monopolist operate the optimum scale of plant at its optimum rate of output when in long-run equilibrium (see Fig. 9-19). This occurs only rarely and accidentally. If the MR curve crossed the LAC curve to the right of the lowest point on the LAC curve, the monopolist would overutilize a larger-than-the-optimum scale of plant when in long-run equilibrium (see Fig. 9-20). Finally, if the MR curve crossed the LAC curve to the left of the lowest point on the LAC curve, the monopolist would underutilize a smaller-than-the-optimum scale of plant when in long-run equilibrium (see Fig. 9-4).

9.17 (*a*) Compare the long-run equilibrium point of a pure monopolist with that of a perfectly competitive firm and industry. (*b*) Should the government break up a monopoly into a great number of perfectly competitive firms?

(*a*) Because of blocked entry into the industry, the pure monopolist can make profits when in long-run equilibrium, while the perfect competitor breaks even. In addition, a monopolist usually does not operate at the lowest point on the LAC curve, while the perfect competitor must when in long-run equilibrium. Finally, while each perfectly competitive firm produces where $P = \text{LMC}$ when in long-run equilibrium (and so there is an optimal allocation of resources in the industry), the pure monopolist produces where $P > \text{LMC}$

(and so there is an underallocation of resources to the industry and a misallocation of resources in the economy).

(b) *In industries operating under cost and technological conditions (such as constant returns to scale) that make the existence of perfect competition feasible*, the breaking up of a monopoly (by government antitrust action) into a great number of perfectly competitive firms will result in a greater long-run equilibrium output for the industry, a lower commodity price, and usually a lower LAC than under monopoly. However, because of cost and technological considerations, it is not feasible to break up *natural* monopolies into a great number of perfectly competitive firms. In such cases, comparison of the long-run equilibrium position of the monopolist with that of the perfectly competitive industry is meaningless. In dealing with natural monopolies, the government usually chooses to regulate them rather than break them up. (We will return to this general topic in Sections 14.12 and 14.13.)

REGULATION OF MONOPOLY

9.18 (*a*) What maximum price should the government impose on the monopolist of Problem 9.9 to induce this monopolist to produce the competitive industry output level? (*b*) Compare the equilibrium point of the regulated with that of the unregulated monopolist.

(*a*) By imposing a maximum price at the point where $P = \text{SMC}$, the government can induce the monopolist to produce the perfectly competitive industry output level. This is given by point *B* in Fig. 9-21, where the market D curve intersects the SMC curve (which could be taken as the perfectly competitive industry short-run supply curve if we assume, among other things, that factor prices are constant).

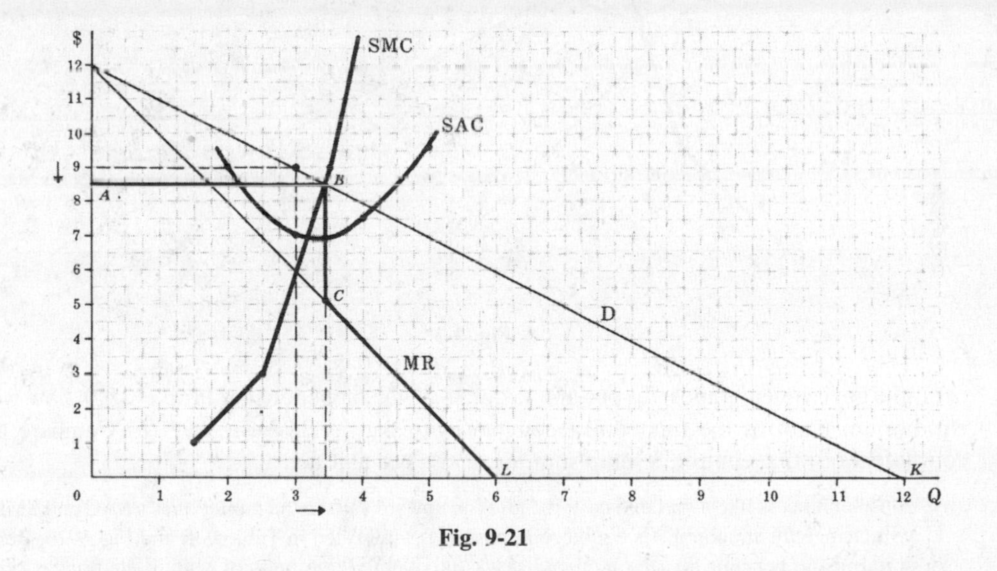

Fig. 9-21

(*b*) In Fig. 9-21, the D curve of the regulated monopolist is *ABK*, while his MR curve becomes *ABCL*. Thus, the regulated monopolist would behave as a perfectly competitive firm and produce where *P* or $\text{MR} = \text{SMC}$. The result is that price is lower (about \$8.50 rather than \$9), output is greater (a little less than 3.5 units rather than 3 units), profit per unit is less (about \$1.50 rather than \$2), and total profits are reduced (from \$6 to about \$5.25). Thus the consumer is now better off (being able to buy more of the commodity at a lower price) and the monopolist is worse off (total profit is now less).

9.19 (*a*) What lump-sum tax should the government impose on the monopolist of Problem 10.9 in order to eliminate all of that monopolist's profits? (*b*) Compare the equilibrium point of the regulated with that of the unregulated monopolist.

(*a*) Since the unregulated monopolist makes a maximum total profit of \$6 in the short run, the government should impose a lump-sum tax of \$6 to eliminate all of the monopolist's profits.

(*b*) Since the imposition of a lump-sum tax is like a fixed cost, it will not affect the monopolist's SMC curve. Thus, the monopolist will produce the same level of output and charge the same price as before the imposition of the tax, but now the monopolist breaks even after paying the tax. These things are reflected in Table 9.14 and Fig. 9-22.

Table 9.14

Q	STC ($)	SAC ($)	STC′ ($)	SAC′ ($)	SMC ($)
1	17	17.00	23	23.00	. .
2	18	9.00	24	12.00	1
*3	21	7.00	27	9.00	3
4	30	7.50	36	9.00	9
5	48	9.60	54	10.80	18

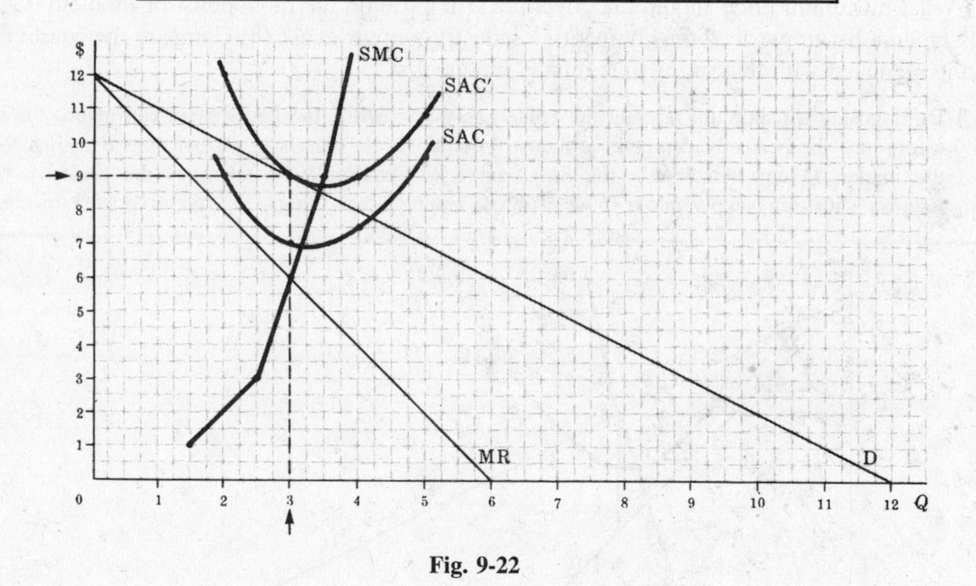

Fig. 9-22

9.20 (*a*) If the government imposed a per-unit tax of $1 on the monopolist of Problem 9.9, how would the new equilibrium point of the monopolist compare with that in Problem 9.9? (*b*) Compare the effect on consumers of price control, a lump-sum tax, and a per-unit tax.

(*a*) A per-unit tax is like a variable cost; it causes an upward shift in the monopolist's SAC and SMC curves. This will change the monopolist's equilibrium position as indicated in Table 9.15 and Fig. 9-23. Before the imposition of the per-unit tax, the monopolist was producing three units of output, charging a price of $9, and making a profit of $2 per unit and $6 in total. After the imposition of the per-unit tax, the same monopolist will produce a little less than three units, charge a price a little higher than $9, and make a profit of about $1 per unit and $3 in total.

Table 9.15

Q	STC ($)	SMC ($)	SAC ($)	STC′ ($)	SMC′ ($)	SAC′ ($)
1	17	. .	17.00	18	. .	18.00
2	18	1	9.00	20	2	10.00
3	21	3	7.00	24	4	8.00
4	30	9	7.50	34	10	8.50
5	48	18	9.60	53	19	10.60

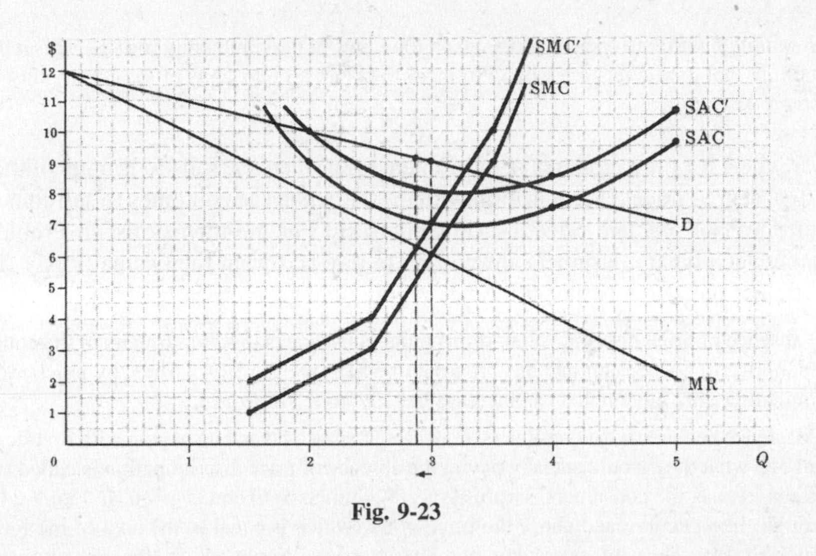

Fig. 9-23

(*b*) Consumers benefit from the imposition of price control as in Problem 9.18 since they can buy a greater output at a lower price. Consumers do not benefit directly from the imposition of a lump-sum tax on the monopolist as in Problem 9.19 since output and price are not affected. Consumers are worse off with the imposition of a per-unit tax on the monopolist since output is less and the price is higher. That is, the monopolist is able to shift part of the per-unit tax to consumers. In all cases, the monopolist's per-unit and total profits decline.

PRICE DISCRIMINATION

9.21 In *first-degree price discrimination*, the monopolist behaves as if each unit of the commodity were sold separately to consumers and charges the highest price obtainable for each unit of the commodity. If the D function facing a certain monopolist is $QD = 8 - P$, (*a*) draw a figure and show on it the price she charges for each of four units of the commodity when she practices first-degree discrimination, and (*b*) explain your answer to part (*a*).

(*a*)

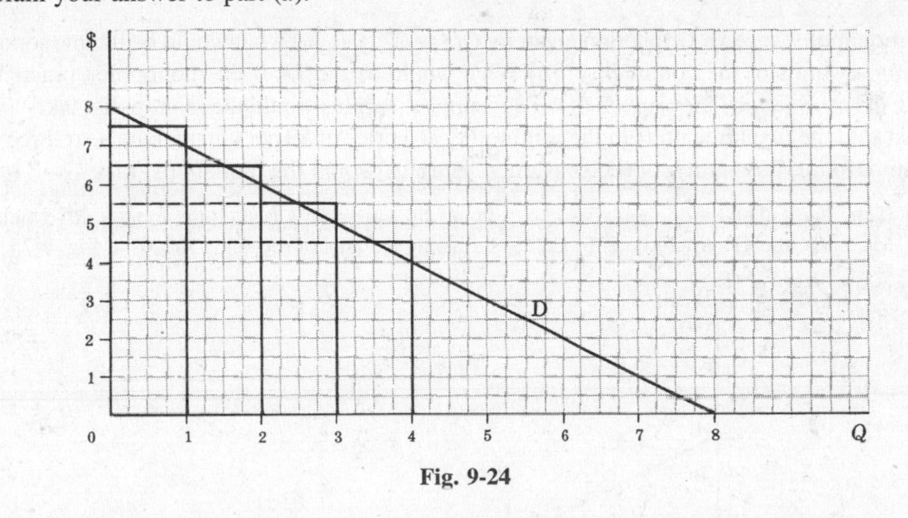

Fig. 9-24

(*b*) By practicing first degree price discrimination, this monopolist behaves as if each of the four units of the commodity were sold separately to consumers, and she charges \$7.50 for the first unit, \$6.50 for the second unit, \$5.50 for the third, and \$4.50 for the fourth unit. These represent respectively the highest price the monopolist can receive for each of the four units sold and correspond to the areas of the four rectangles in Fig. 10-24. The monopolist actually achieves the same result (i.e., a TR of $\$24 = \$7.50 + \$6.50 + \$5.50 + \$4.50$) by making an *all-or-nothing* offer to consumers to sell all four units of the commodity for \$24. This represents the greatest expenditure that consumers are willing to incur to obtain all four units of the commodity rather than give up this commodity entirely.

9.22 (*a*) Compare the TR of the monopolist in Problem 9.21 when she sells four units of the commodity and practices first-degree price discrimination with the TR when she continues to sell four units of the commodity but does not practice price discrimination. (*b*) For the monopolist in Problem 9.21, find the difference between what consumers are willing to pay and what they actually pay (in the absence of price discrimination). How is this difference represented geometrically?

(*a*) In the absence of price discrimination, if this monopolist wants to sell four units of the commodity, she would charge a price of \$4 per unit and the TR would be \$16 (see Fig.9-24). Thus, by practicing first-degree price discrimination, this monopolist can increase her TR from \$16 to \$24.

(*b*) The difference between what consumers are willing to pay (and end up paying with first-degree price discrimination) and what they would actually pay in the absence of price discrimination is called *consumers' surplus.* In the above case, the consumers' surplus is \$8 (\$24 minus \$16) and is given (in Fig. 9-24) by the area under the straight-line D curve and above the price of \$4 (which is equal to the area of the four rectangles above the price of \$4). Thus, by practicing first-degree price discrimination, the monopolist is able to extract from consumers all of the consumers' surplus.

9.23 In *second-degree price discrimination*, the monopolist sets a uniform price per unit for a specific quantity of the commodity, a lower price per unit for a specific additional batch of the commodity, and so on. (*a*) If the monopolist in Problem 9.21 sets a price of \$6.50 on each of the first two units and a price of \$4.50 on each of the next two units of the commodity, what proportion of the consumers' surplus would this monopolist be extracting from consumers? (*b*) What if the monopolist set the price at \$6 for the first two units and \$4 for the next two units?

(*a*) The monopolist's TR would be \$22(\$13 + \$9), and the monopolist would thus be extracting from consumers three-fourths of the consumer's surplus (see Fig. 9-24).

(*b*) The TR would be \$20 and the monopolist would be extracting from consumers half of the consumers' surplus (see Fig. 9-24).

9.24 If a monopolist faced a D function given by $QD = 12 - P$, (*a*) what would be the monopolist's TR upon selling six units of the commodity? (*b*) What would be the TR if the monopolist practiced first-degree price discrimination? How much of the consumers' surplus would the monopolist take? (*c*) If the monopolist sold the first three units of the commodity at a price of \$9 per unit and the next three units at a price of \$6 per unit, how much of the consumers' surplus would the monopolist take?

(*a*) If the unregulated monopolist sold six units of the commodity (which the monopolist would do only if the MC = 0), the TR would be \$36. This is shown by the area of rectangle *BCOF* in Fig. 9-25.

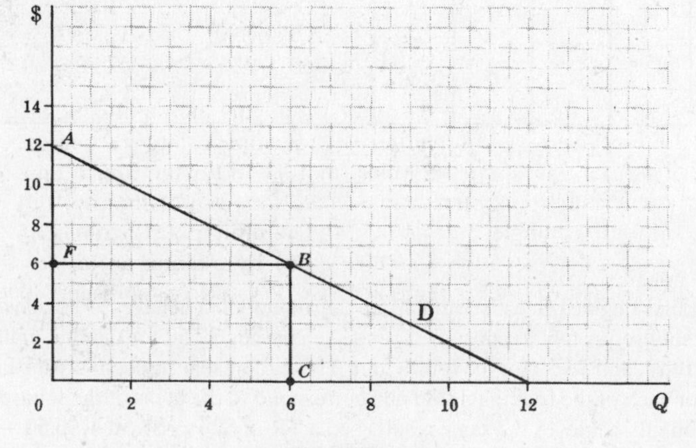

Fig. 9-25

(*b*) With first-degree price discrimination, this monopolist's TR would be \$54 as given by area *ABCO* in Fig. 9-25. This represents the maximum total expenditure that consumers (faced with an all-or-nothing offer) are willing to make to get six units of this commodity rather than forgo entirely the consumption of this commodity. If we assume that the MU of money is constant, the consumers' surplus is \$18 and is given by the area of triangle *ABF* in Fig. 9-25. Thus, by practicing first-degree price discrimination, the monopolist can extract from consumers the entire consumers' surplus. First-degree price discrimination is rare in the real world. To practice it, a monopolist must have exact knowledge of the D curve he or she faces and charge exactly the maximum amount that consumers are willing to pay for the quantity the monopolist wants to sell.

(*c*) The monopolist's TR would be \$45 and he or she would take one half of the consumers' surplus. This is one way of practicing second-degree price discrimination. Second-degree price discrimination is fairly common in the real world. For example, a telephone company may charge 7¢ per call for the first 50 calls and 5¢ per call for the next 25 calls, and so on. Usually, companies supplying electricity, water, and gas also practice second-degree price discrimination.

9.25 In order for the monopolist to find it profitable to practice third-degree price discrimination, two conditions are necessary. What are these conditions?

Third-degree price discrimination occurs when the monopolist charges different prices for the same commodity in different markets. One condition necessary for its occurrence is that *there must be two or more markets which can be separated and can be kept separate*. If the markets cannot be kept separate, some people would purchase the commodity in the lower-priced market and undersell the monopolist in the higher-priced market, until the prices of the commodity in the two markets were equalized. They would thus undermine the monopolist's attempts to set different prices in different markets.

Another condition required in order for third-degree price discrimination to be profitable is that *the coefficients of price elasticity of demand* (e) *in these two or more markets must be different*. (If the coefficient of price elasticity of demand is the same in all markets, then the best price to charge is the same in all markets.) When these two conditions hold, then by distributing the best level of output among the various markets in such a way that the last unit sold in each market will give the same MR (and charging the prices indicated by the demand curves in the various markets), the monopolist will increase TR and total profits (over what they would be in the absence of price discrimination).

9.26 A monopolist, selling in two separate markets (market 1 and market 2), faces the following D functions: $QD_1 = 24 - 2P$ and $QD_2 = 16 - P$. The monopolist operates a single plant with LTC as in Table 10.16. (*a*) Find the LMC and the LAC schedules for this monopolist. (*b*) On the same set of axes, plot D_1, MR_1, D_2, MR_2, $\sum MR$, LMC, and LAC. (*c*) Find the best level of output for the monopolist; how much of this output should the monopolist sell in market 1 and in market 2? (*d*) At what price should the monopolist sell in each market? Check your results by using the formula. (*e*) How much profit will the monopolist make in market 1, in market 2, and in total?

Table 9.16

Q	10	11	12	13	14	15
LTC (\$)	82.50	88	94.50	104	119	142.50

(*a*)

Table 9.17

Q	LTC (\$)	LMC (\$)	LAC (\$)
10	82.50	..	8.25
11	88.00	5.50	8.00
12	94.50	6.50	7.875
13	104.00	9.50	8.00
14	119.00	15.00	8.50
15	142.50	23.50	9.50

(*b*) See Fig. 9-26.

(*c*) This monopolist's best long-run level of output is 11 units and is given by the point where the LMC curve intersects the $\sum$MR curve from below. The best way to distribute this total output between the two markets occurs when LMC $= \sum \text{MR} = \text{MR}_1 = \text{MR}_2 = \$6$. Thus the monopolist should sell six units in market 1 and the remaining five units in market 2 (see Fig. 9-26).

(*d*) From Fig. 9-26, we see that the monopolist should charge a price of \$9 per unit in market 1 and \$11 per unit in market 2. At these points, $e_1 = 3$ and $e_2 = 11/5$. From $\text{MR}_1 = P_1, (1 - 1/e)$, we get $\$6 = P_1(1 - 1/3)$; thus $P_1 = \$9$. From $\text{MR}_2 = P_2(1 - 1/e_2)$, we get $\$6 = P_2[1 - 1/(11/5)]$; thus $P_2 = \$11$. Note that the monopolist should charge a higher price in the market with the more inelastic D curve. This is always the case.

(*e*) The LAC to produce 11 units of output is \$8. Thus, the monopolist makes a profit of \$1 per unit and \$6 in total in market 1 and a profit of \$3 per unit and \$15 in total in market 2. The total profit of \$21 represents the maximum total profit this monopolist can make per unit of lime in the long run.

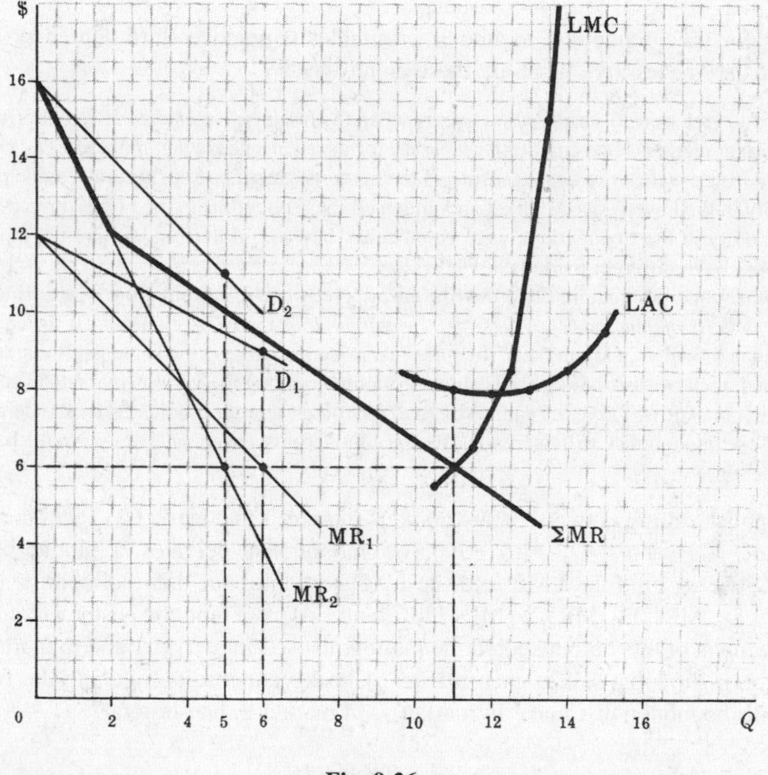

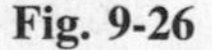

Fig. 9-26

9.27 Give two real-world examples of third-degree price discrimination.

Third-degree price discrimination is fairly common in the real world. For example, electric power companies charge a lower rate to industrial users of electricity than to households because the former have a more elastic D curve for electricity since there are more substitutes, such as generating their own electricity, available to them. The markets are kept separate by different meters. If the two markets were not separate, industrial users of electricity would buy more electricity than they need and would undersell the monopolist in supplying electricity to households and other private users until the price of electricity in the two markets were completely equalized. Note also that if the D curves in the two markets have the same price elasticity, the monopolist would maximize total profits by selling the commodity at the same price in the two markets.

A second example of third-degree price discrimination occurs in international trade when a nation sells a commodity abroad at a lower price than in its home market. This is referred to as "dumping." The reason for dumping is that the D curve for the monopolist's product is more elastic abroad (because substitutes are available from other nations) than in the domestic market (where imports from other nations are kept out and the market kept separate by import restrictions).

PRICE AND OUTPUT UNDER PURE MONOPOLY

***9.28** Derive, with the use of calculus, the formula relating marginal revenue to price and the price elasticity of demand.

Let P equal the price and Q equal the quantity of a commodity. The total revenue (TR) of the seller of the commodity is then

$$\text{TR} = PQ$$

and the marginal revenue is

$$\text{MR} = \frac{d(\text{TR})}{dQ} = P + Q\frac{dP}{dQ}$$

Manipulating the above equation algebraically, we get

$$\text{MR} = P\left(1 + \frac{Q}{P}\frac{dP}{dQ}\right) = P\left(1 - \frac{1}{e}\right)$$

where e equals -1 times the price elasticity of demand.

***9.29** Derive using calculus the condition for a monopolist to maximize profits in selling the commodity in two different markets (third-degree price discrimination).

The total profits of the monopolist (π) are equal to the sum of the total revenue the monopolist receives from selling the commodity in the two markets (that is, $\text{TR}_1 + \text{TR}_2$) minus the total cost (TC) of producing the total output. That is,

$$\pi = \text{TR}_1 + \text{TR}_2 - \text{TC}$$

Taking the first partial derivative of π with respect to Q_1, (the quantity sold in the first market) and Q_2 (the amount sold in the second market) and setting them equal to zero, we get

$$\frac{\partial \pi}{\partial Q_1} = \frac{\partial \text{TR}_1}{\partial Q_1} - \frac{\partial \text{TC}}{\partial Q_1} = 0 \quad \text{and} \quad \frac{\partial \pi}{\partial Q_2} = \frac{\partial \text{TR}_2}{\partial Q_2} - \frac{\partial \text{TC}}{\partial Q_2} = 0$$

or

$$\text{MR}_1 = \text{MR}_2 = \text{MC}$$

That is, in order to maximize the total profits π, the monopolist must distribute sales between the two markets in such a way that the marginal revenue is the same in both markets and equals the common marginal cost.

The above represents the first-order condition for profit maximization. The second-order condition is that

$$\frac{\partial^2 \pi}{\partial Q_1^2} < 0 \quad \text{and} \quad \frac{\partial^2 \pi}{\partial Q_2^2} < 0$$

CHAPTER 10

Price and Output Under Monopolistic Competition and Oligopoly

10.1 MONOPOLISTIC COMPETITION DEFINED

Monopolistic competition refers to the market organization in which there are many firms selling closely related but not identical commodities. An example is given by the many cigarette brands available (e.g., Marlboro, Winston, Kent). Another example is given by the many different detergents on the market (e.g., All, Cheer, Tide). Because of this product differentiation, sellers have some degree of control over the prices they charge and thus face a negatively sloped demand curve. However, the existence of many close substitutes severely limits the sellers "monopoly" power and results in a highly elastic demand curve.

10.2 SHORT-RUN EQUILIBRIUM UNDER MONOPOLISTIC COMPETITION

Since a firm in a monopolistically competitive industry faces a highly elastic but negatively sloped demand curve for the differentiated product it sells, its MR curve will lie below its demand curve. The short-run equilibrium level of output for the firm is given by the point where its SMC curve intersects its MR curve from below (provided that at this output level $P \geqslant \text{AVC}$).

EXAMPLE 1. In Fig. 10-1, d is the highly price-elastic demand curve faced by a typical monopolistic competitor and MR is the corresponding MR curve. The best level of output of the firm in the short run is 6 units and is given by point E, at which MR = SMC. At $Q = 6$, $P = \$9$ (point A on the demand curve) and SAC = \$7 (point B), so that the monopolistic competitor maximizes profits at $AB = \$2$ per unit and $ABCF = \$12$ in total. The monopolistic competitor would break even if $P = \text{SAC}$ and would minimize losses if $P < \text{SAC}$, as long as $P \geqslant \text{AVC}$ at the best level of output (see Problem 10.3).

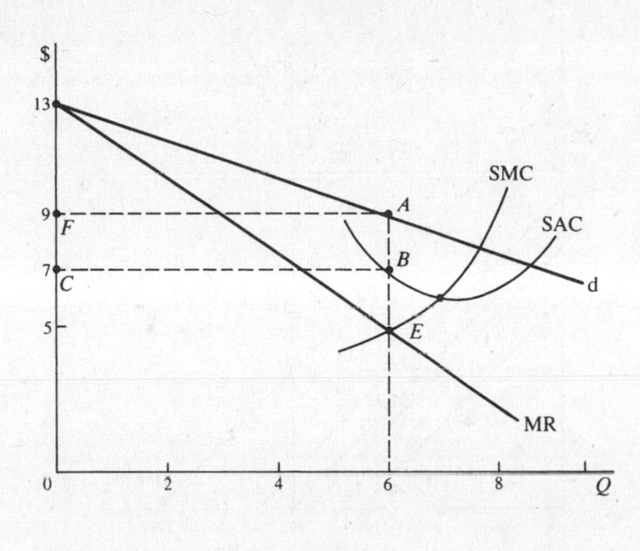

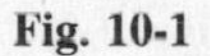
Fig. 10-1

10.3 LONG-RUN EQUILIBRIUM UNDER MONOPOLISTIC COMPETITION

If the firms in a monopolistically competitive industry earned economic profits in the short run, firms will enter the industry in the long run. This shifts each firm's demand curve down (since each firm now has a smaller share of the market) until all profit are squeezed out. The opposite occurs if firms suffered losses in the short run.

EXAMPLE 2. If the typical or representative monopolistically competitive firm earns a profit in the short run, more firms enter the market in the long run. This causes the demand curve of the typical firm (say, d in Fig. 10-1) to shift down to d′ in Fig. 10-2 (as the firm's market share declines), so as to be tangent to the LAC curve at the output level of 4 units, at which $\text{MR}' = \text{LMC}$ (point E'). At $Q = 4, P = \text{LAC} = \text{SAC}' = \$6$ (point A') and the firm breaks even in the long run.

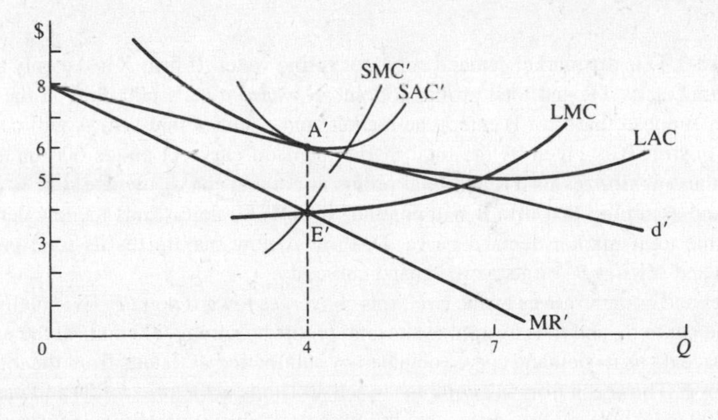

Fig. 10-2

10.4 OLIGOPOLY DEFINED

Oligopoly is the market organization in which there are few sellers of a commodity. So, the actions of each seller will affect the other sellers. As a result, unless we make some specific assumptions about the reactions of other firms to the actions of the firms under study, we cannot construct the demand curve for that oligopolist, and we will have an indeterminate solution. For each specific behavioral assumption we make, we get a different solution. Thus, we have no general theory of oligopoly. All we have are many different models, most of which are more or less satisfactory.

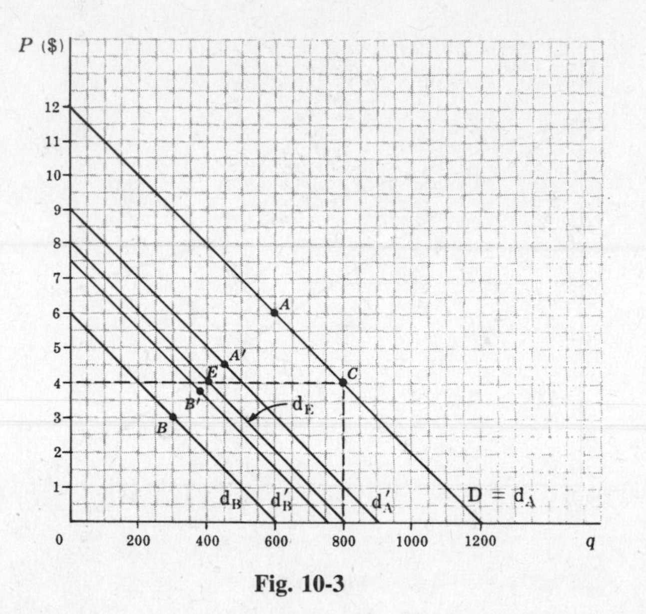

Fig. 10-3

10.5 THE COURNOT MODEL

In the *Cournot model*, we begin by assuming (with Cournot) that there are two firms selling spring water under conditions of zero costs of production. Therefore, the profit-maximizing level of sales of each firm occurs at the midpoint of its negatively sloped straight-line demand curve, where $e = 1$ and TR is maximum [see Example 1 and Problems 9.4(*c*) and 9.9(*c*) in Chapter 9]. The basic behavioral assumption made by Cournot is that each firm, in attempting to maximize its total profits or TR, assumes that the other firm will hold its *output* constant. Faced with this assumption, there will be a number of converging moves and countermoves by the two firms until each of them sells exactly 1/3 of the total amount of spring water that would be sold if the market had been perfectly competitive.

EXAMPLE 3. In Fig. 10-3, D is the market demand curve for spring water. If firm A is the only seller in the market, then $D = d_A$ and firm A maximizes its TR and total profits at point *A*, where it sells 600 units at the price of $6. This is the monopoly solution. Next, suppose that firm B enters the market, and assumes that firm A will continue to sell 600 units. Then the demand curve of firm B is given by the total market demand curve D minus 600 units, and is represented by d_B in Fig. 10-3. Firm B thus maximizes its TR and total profits at point *B* (on d_B) where it sells 300 units at the price of $3. Firm A now reacts, and assuming that firm B will continue to sell 300 units, finds its new demand curve, d'_A, by subtracting 300 units from the total market demand curve, D. Firm A now maximizes its total profits at point A' on d'_A. Firm B now reacts again and sells at B' on its new demand curve, d'_B.

The process of moves and countermoves by the two firms converges toward point *E*. Eventually, either firm A or firm B will be faced with demand curve d_E and thus maximizes its total profits by selling 400 units at the price of $4 (point *E*). The other firm will then also face d_E as its demand curve (obtained by subtracting 400 units from the total market demand curve D) and will also be at point *E*. Thus each firm will continue to sell 400 units at the price of $4 and make a TR and total profits of $1600, The output of 400 units by each firm represents 1/3 of the perfectly competitive industry output of 1200 (given by the condition $P = MC = 0$).

If, in determining its best level of output, each firm assumes that the other holds its *price* (rather than its output) constant, we have a *Bertrand model* (see Problem 10.11).

10.6 THE EDGEWORTH MODEL

In the *Edgeworth model*, as in the Cournot model, we assume that there are two firms, A and B, selling a homogeneous commodity produced at zero cost. In addition, in the Edgeworth model, the following further assumptions are made: (1) each firm faces an identical straight-line demand curve for its product, (2) each firm has limited production capacity and cannot supply the entire market by itself, and (3) each firm, in attempting to maximize its TR or total profit, assumes that the other firm holds its *price* constant. The result of these assumptions is that there will be a continuous oscillation of the product price between the monopoly price and the maximum output price of each firm (see Problems 10.2 and 10.4). Price oscillations are sometimes observed in oligopolistic markets.

10.7 THE CHAMBERLIN MODEL

Both the Cournot and Edgeworth models are based on the extremely naive assumption that the two oligopolists (duopolists) never recognize their interdependence. We nevertheless study these models because they give us some indication of the nature of oligopolistic interdependence and also because they are the forerunners of more realistic models. One such more realistic model is the *Chamberlin model.* Chamberlin starts with the same basic assumptions as Cournot. However, Chamberlin further assumes that the duopolists do recognize their interdependence. The result is that without any form of agreement or collusion, the duopolists set identical prices, sell identical quantities, and maximize their *joint* profits.

EXAMPLE 4. In Fig. 10-4, D is the total market demand curve for the combined output of duopolists A and B. If firm A is the first one to enter the market, it will choose to be at point *A* on D (= d_A), thus making the monopoly profit of $3600. Firm B, taking A's output as given, faces demand curve d_B and thus decides to sell 300 units at point *B*. (So far the Chamberlin model is exactly the same as the Cournot model.) However, duopolists A and B *now* realize that the best thing they can do is to share equally the monopoly profits of $3600. Thus each duopolist sells 300 units or half of the monopoly output at the monopoly price of $6 and makes a profit of $1800. To be noted is that this solution is stable, is reached without collusion, and results in $200 more profits for each firm than under the Cournot solution.

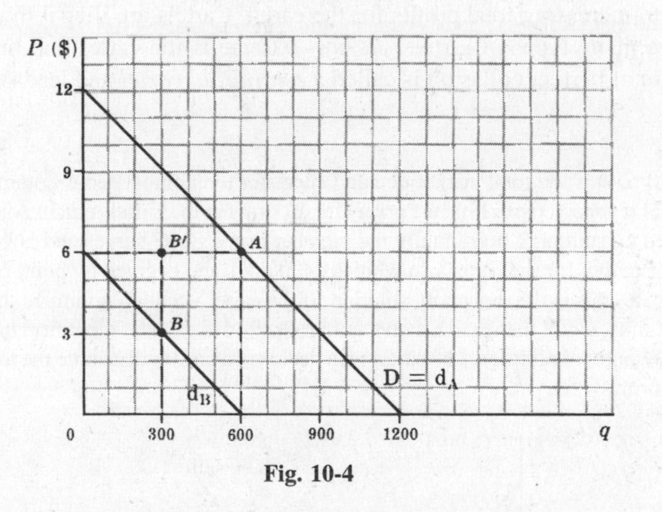

Fig. 10-4

10.8 THE KINKED DEMAND CURVE MODEL

As a further development toward more realistic models, we have the *kinked demand curve* or *Sweezy model.* This tries to explain the price rigidity often observed in oligopolistic markets. Sweezy postulates that if an oligopolistic firm increases its price, others in the industry will not raise theirs and so the firm would lose most of its customers. On the other hand, an oligopolistic firm cannot increase its share of the market by lowering its price since the other oligopolists in the industry will match the price cut. Thus there is a strong compulsion for the oligopolist not to change the prevailing price but rather to compete for a greater share of the market on the basis of quality, product design, advertisement, and service.

EXAMPLE 5. In Fig. 10-5, the demand curve facing the oligopolist is *CEJ* and has a "kink" at the prevailing sales level of 200 units and \$4 price. Note that demand curve *CEJ* is much more elastic above the kink than below, because of the assumption that other oligopolists will not match price increases but will match price cuts. The corresponding marginal revenue curve is given by *CFGN*; *CF* is the segment corresponding to the *CE* portion of the demand curve; *GN* corresponds to the *EJ* portion of the demand curve. The kink at point *E* on the demand curve causes the *FG* discontinuity in the marginal revenue curve. The oligopolist's marginal cost curve can rise or fall anywhere within the discontinuous portion of the MR curve (from SMC to SMC′, in Fig. 10-5) without inducing the oligopolist to change sales level and the prevailing price (\$4).

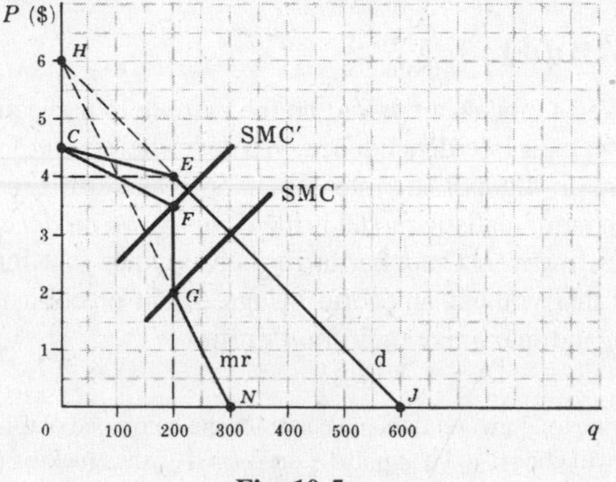

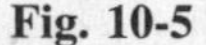
Fig. 10-5

10.9 THE CENTRALIZED CARTEL MODEL

A *cartel* is a formal organization of producers within an industry that determines policies for all the firms in the cartel, with a view to increasing total profits for the cartel. Cartels are illegal in the U.S., but not in many other nations. There are many types of cartels. At one extreme is the cartel that makes all decisions for all member firms. This form of perfect collusion is called a *centralized cartel* and leads to the monopoly solution.

EXAMPLE 6. In Fig. 10-6, D is the total market demand curve for the homogeneous commodity facing the centralized cartel and MR the marginal revenue curve. If factor prices for all firms in the cartel remain constant, then the cartel's marginal cost curve is obtained by summing horizontally the member firms' SMC curves and is given by the $\sum$ MC curve in Fig. 10.6. The best level of output for the cartel as a whole is 400 units and is given by point *E*, where MR $= \sum$ MC. The cartel will set the price of \$8. This is the monopoly solution. If the cartel wants to minimize the total cost of producing its best level of output of 400 units, it will then assign a quota of production to each member firm in such a way that the SMC of the last unit produced is the same for all firms. The cartel then decides on how to distribute the total cartel profits in a manner agreeable to the member firms.

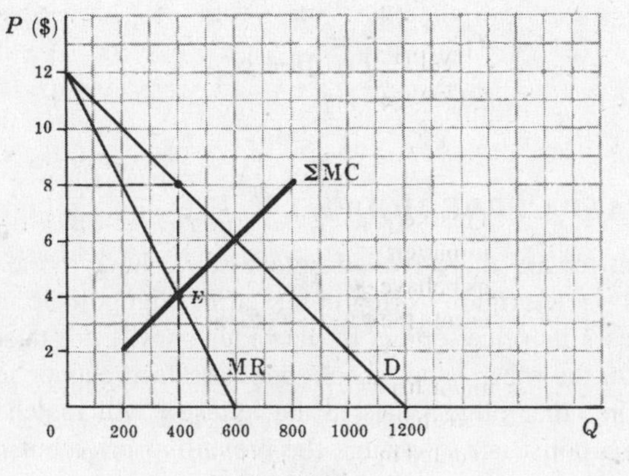

Fig. 10-6

10.10 THE MARKET-SHARING CARTEL MODEL

Another type of cartel, somewhat looser than the centralized one, is the *market-sharing cartel*, in which the member firms agree upon the share of the market each is to have. Under certain conditions, the market-sharing cartel can also result in the monopoly solution.

EXAMPLE 7. Suppose that there are only two firms selling a homogeneous commodity and they decide to share the market equally. If D in Fig. 10-7 is the total market demand curve for the commodity, then d is the half-share curve for each firm, and mr is the corresponding marginal revenue. If we further assume for simplicity that each firm has the identical SMC curve shown in the figure, then each duopolist will sell 200 units (given by point *E*, where mr = SMC) at the price of \$8. Thus, the two firms together will sell the monopoly output of 400 units at the monopoly price of \$8 (see Example 6). However, this monopoly solution depends on the assumption of identical SMC curves for the two firms and on agreement to share the market equally.

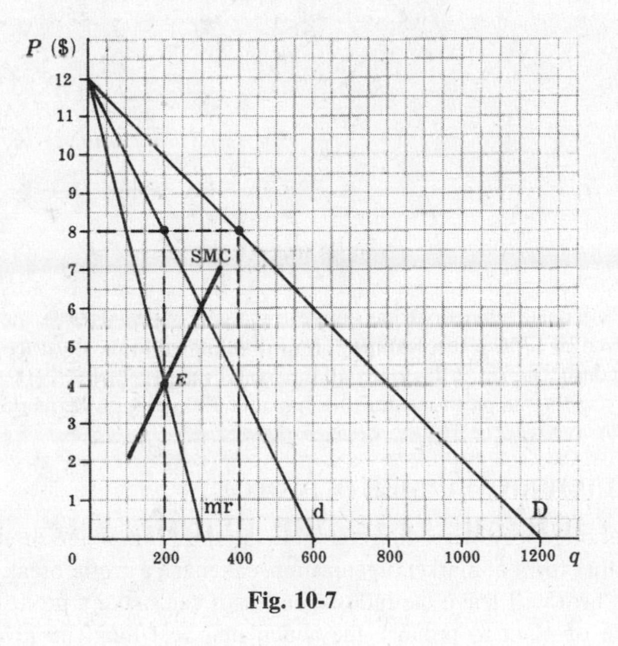

Fig. 10-7

10.11 PRICE LEADERSHIP MODEL

Price leadership is the form of imperfect collusion in which the firms in an oligopolistic industry tacitly (i.e., without formal agreement) decide to set the same price as the price leader for the industry. The price leader may be the low-cost firm, or more likely, the dominant or largest firm in the industry. In the latter case, the dominant firm sets the industry price, allows the other firms in the industry to sell all they want at that price, and then the dominant firm comes in to fill the market. (For price leadership by the low-cost firm, see Problems 10.19 and 10.20.)

EXAMPLE 8. In Fig. 10-8, D is the total market demand curve for the homogeneous commodity in an oligopolistic industry, the $\sum MC_s$ curve is the horizontal summation of the SMC curves of all the (small) firms in the industry other than the dominant firm itself. Since these small firms behave as perfect competitors (i.e., they can sell all they want at the price set by the dominant firm), the $\sum MC_s$ curve represents the short-run supply curve for all the small firms together (if we assume that factor prices remain constant).

The demand curve faced by the dominant firm, d, is then obtained by subtracting horizontally the $\sum MC_s$ from the D curve, at each possible price. For example, if the dominant firm sets the price of \$7, the quantity supplied by all the small firms together equals the total quantity demanded in the market at that price (point *B*). Thus we get the price intercept (point *F*) on d. At the market price of \$6, the total market quantity demanded of 600 units (point *C*) minus the total quantity of

400 units supplied by all the small firms at this price (point G) gives the quantity of 200 units that the dominant firm can sell at the price of \$6 (point H on the d curve). Other points on the d curve can be obtained in the same way.

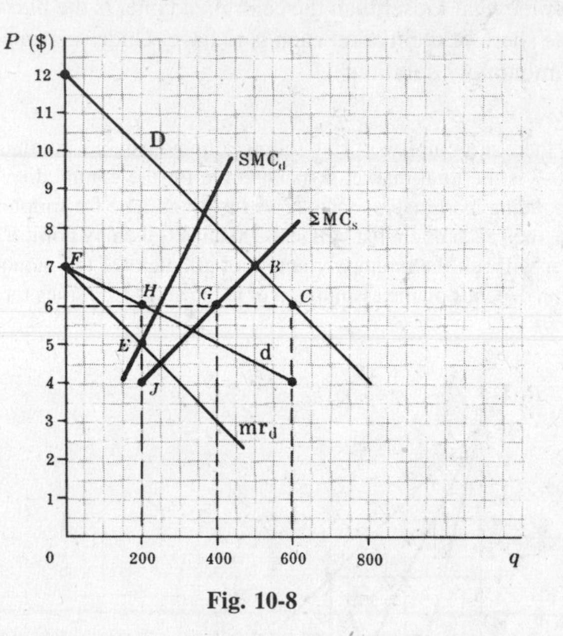

Fig. 10-8

From the dominant firm's demand curve d, we can derive its marginal revenue curve, mr_d. If the dominant firm's short-run marginal cost curve is given by SMC_d, the dominant firm will set its profit-maximizing price of \$6 (given by point E, where $mr_d = SMC_d$) as the industry price. At this price, all the small firms together sell 400 units. Then the dominant firm comes in to fill the market by selling its profit-maximizing output of 200 units, at the market price of \$6 that it set.

10.12 LONG-RUN EQUILIBRIUM UNDER OLIGOPOLY

Most of our analysis of oligopoly has so far referred to the short run. In the short run, an oligopolist, just as any other firm under any other form of market organization, can make a profit, break even, or incur a loss. In the long run, the oligopolistic firm will leave the industry unless it can make a profit (or at least break even) by constructing the best scale of plant to produce the anticipated best long-run level of output. If profits are being made, firms may seek to enter the oligopolistic industry in the long run, and unless entry is blocked or at least restricted, the industry may not remain oligopolistic in the long run. (For the long-run efficiency implications of oligopoly, see Problems 10.22 and 10.23.)

Glossary

Bertrand model The premise of this model of oligopoly is that each oligopolistic firm, in attempting to maximize its profits (or TR if TC = 0), assumes that the other firm holds its *price* constant.

Cartel A formal organization of producers within an oligopolistic industry that determines policies for all firms in the cartel, with a view to increasing total profits for the cartel.

Centralized cartel A cartel that makes all decisions for the member firms, leading to the monopoly solution.

Chamberlin model It is similar to the Cournot model except that the two oligopolists recognize their interdependence and maximize their *joint* profits.

Cournot model The premise of this model of oligopoly is that each oligopolistic firm, in attempting to maximize its total profits (or TR if TC = 0), assumes that the other firm holds its *output* constant.

Edgeworth model It is similar to the Bertrand model but results in continuous oscillations of the product price between the monopoly price and the maximum output price of each firm.

Kinked demand curve, or Sweezy model It attempts to explain price rigidity of oligopolistic market by postulating that oligopolists will match price decreases, but not price increases.

Market-sharing cartel A cartel in which all member firms agree on the share of the market each is to have.

Monopolistic competition The market organization in which there are many firms selling a differentiated product.

Oligopoly The market organization in which there are few sellers of a homogeneous or a differentiated product.

Price leadership A form of tacit collusion in which oligopolists decide to set the same price as the leader of the industry.

Review Questions

1. In monopolistic competition, we have (*a*) few firms selling a differentiated product, (*b*) many firms selling a homogeneous product, (*c*) few firms selling a homogeneous product, or (*d*) many firms selling a differentiated product.

   Ans. (*d*) See Section 10.1.

2. The short-run equilibrium level of output for a monopolistic competitor is given by the point where (*a*) $P = \text{SMC}$, (*b*) $P = \text{SAC}$, (*c*) the MR curve intersects the SMC curve, or (*d*) the MR curve intersects the SMC curve from below and $P \geqslant \text{AVC}$.

   Ans. (*d*) See Fig. 10-1 and Section 10.2.

3. The short-run supply curve of the monopolistic competitor (*a*) cannot be defined, (*b*) is given by the rising portion of monopolistic competitor's SMC curve, (*c*) is given by the rising portion of monopolistic competitor's SMC curve over and above AVC, or (*d*) can be defined only if factor prices remain constant.

   Ans. (*a*) As in the case of pure monopoly, $P > \text{MR}$ for the monopolistic competitor; thus there is no unique relationship between P and output in monopolistic competition, either. See Fig. 10-1 and Problems 9.13 and 9.14. The same is true in oligopoly.

4. When the industry is in long-run equilibrium, the monopolistic competitor will produce at the lowest point on its LAC curve, (*a*) Always, (*b*) never, (*c*) sometimes, or (*d*) cannot say.

   Ans. (*b*) When entry into the industry is open and the industry is in long-run equilibrium, the monopolistic competitor produces where the demand curve is tangent to the LAC curve. Since d is negatively sloped, the point of tangency can never occur at the lowest point on the competitor's LAC curve (see Fig. 10-2).

5. Which of the following most closely approximates our definition of oligopoly? (*a*) The cigarette industry,(*b*) the barber shops in a city, (*c*) the gasoline stations in a city, or (*d*) wheat farmers in the midwest.

   Ans. (*a*) See Section 10.4.

6. With reference to the Cournot model, determine which of the following statements *is false*.

   (*a*) The duopolists do not recognize their interdependence.

   (*b*) Each duopolist assumes the other will keep its quantity constant.

   (*c*) Each duopolist assumes the other will keep its price constant.

   (*d*) The solution is stable.

   Ans. (*c*) See Sections 10.4 and 10.5.

7. With reference to the Edgeworth model, determine which of the following statements is *correct*.

(*a*) The duopolists recognize their interdependence.

(*b*) It explains price rigidity.

(*c*) Each duopolist assumes the other keeps its price constant.

(*d*) Each duopolist assumes the other keeps its quantity constant.

Ans. (*c*) See Section 10.6.

8. In both the Chamberlin and the kinked demand curve models, the oligopolists (*a*) recognize their interdependence, (*b*) do not collude, (*c*) tend to keep prices constant, or (*d*) all of the above.

Ans. (*d*) See Sections 10.7 and 10.8.

9. The centralized cartel (*a*) leads to the monopoly solution, (*b*) behaves as the multiplant monopolist if it wants to minimize the total costs of production, (*c*) is illegal in the U.S., or (*d*) all of the above.

Ans. (*d*) For choice (a), see Fig. 10-6; for choice (*b*), see Problem 9.12.

10. A market-sharing cartel will reach the monopoly solution (*a*) sometimes, (*b*) always when the product is homogeneous, (*c*) always when the product is differentiated, or (*d*) never.

Ans. (*a*) This statement is true only when the duopolists agree to share equally the market for a homogeneous commodity and have identical SMC curves (see Fig. 10.7). It is not true when the product is differentiated, the markets are not shared equally, or the duopolists do not have identical SMC curves.

11. In the case of price leadership by the dominant firm, all the firms in the purely oligopolistic industry will produce their best level of output. (*a*) Always, (*b*) never, (*c*) sometimes, or (*d*) often.

Ans. (*a*) This is so because the dominant firm will set the industry price at which it maximizes its total profits and all the other firms in the industry will behave as perfect competitors and produce where $P = \text{SMC}$, and the SMC curve is rising.

12. If an oligopolist incurs losses in the short run, then in the long run, (*a*) the oligopolist will go out of business, (*b*) the oligopolist will stay in business, (*c*) the oligopolist will break even, or (*d*) any of the above is possible.

Ans. (*d*) See Section 10.12.

Solved Problems

MONOPOLISTIC COMPETITION DEFINED

10.1 (*a*) Define monopolistic competition and give a few examples of it. (*b*) Identify the competitive and monopolistic elements in monopolistic competiton. (*c*) Why is it difficult or impossible to define the market demand curve, the market supply curve, and the equilibrium price under monopolistic competition?

(*a*) Monopolistic competition refers to the market organization in which there are many sellers of a differentiated product. Monopolistic competition is very common in the retail and service sectors of our economy. Examples of monopolistic competition are the numerous barber shops, gasoline stations, grocery stores, liquor stores, and drug stores located close to one another.

(*b*) The competitive element results from the presence in a monopolistically competitive market (as in a perfectly competitive market) of so many firms that the activities of each have no perceptible effect on the other firms in the market. Furthermore, firms can enter or leave the market without much difficulty in the long run. The monopolistic element results because the many firms in the market sell a differentiated rather than a homogeneous product.

(c) Since, under monopolistic competition, each firm produces a somewhat different product, we cannot define the market demand curve and the market supply curve of the product, and we do not have a single equilibrium price but rather a cluster of prices, each for the different product produced by each firm. Thus, the graphical analysis of monopolistic competition must be confined to the typical or representative firm.

SHORT-RUN EQUILIBRIUM UNDER MONOPOLISTIC COMPETITION

10.2 (a) Draw a figure for a monopolistically competitive firm which faces a demand curve showing $Q = 0$ at $P = \$12$ and $Q = 8$ at $P = \$8$, a SMC curve which intersects the MR curve at $Q = 8$, and for which SAC = \$6 at $Q = 8$. (b) What is the best level of output for this firm? How much profit or loss per unit and in total would this firm make or incur?

(a)

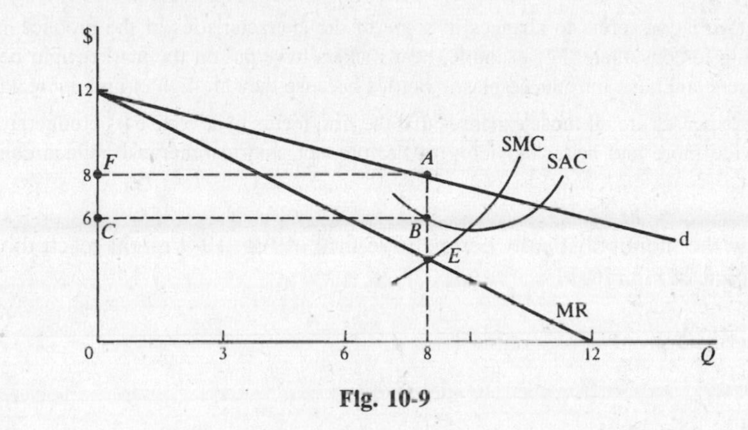

Fig. 10-9

(b) In Fig. 10-9, d is the highly price-elastic demand curve faced by the monopolistically competitive firm and MR is the corresponding MR curve. The best level of output of the firm in the short run is 8 units and is given by point E, at which MR = SMC. At $Q = 8$, $P = \$8$ (point A on the demand curve), and SAC = \$6 (point B), so that the firm maximizes profits at $AB = \$2$ per unit and $ABCF = \$16$ in total.

10.3 (a) On the demand and marginal revenue curves in Fig. 10-9, draw an alternative ATC curve showing that at the best level of output of 8 units, the monopolistically competitive firm incurs a loss of \$2 per unit, but $P > \text{AVC}$ by \$2. (b) What is the total profit or loss of the firm at the best level of output? Will the firm produce or not? Why?

(a) See Fig. 10-10.

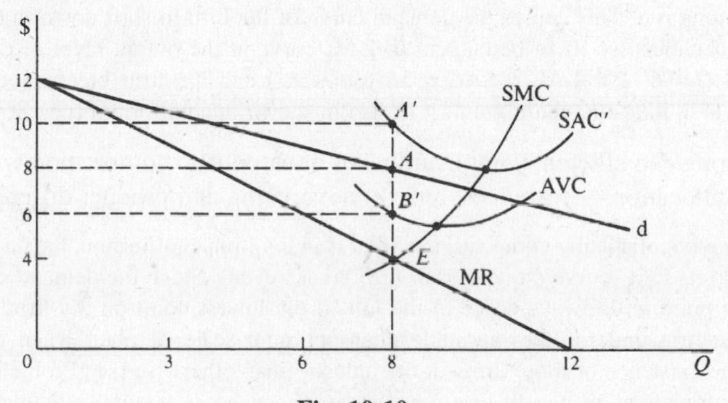

Fig. 10-10

(*b*) At the best level of output of 8 units, the firm incurs a total loss of \$16 per time period. However, since $P >$ AVC, the firm minimizes its total losses by continuing to produce in the short run. Specifically, if the firm stopped producing it would incur a total loss of \$32 (equal to the \$4 average fixed cost at $Q = 8$ units times the output of 8 units) as compared to a total loss of \$16 by continuing to produce.

10.4 (*a*) What are the choice-related variables for a firm under monopolistic competition? (*b*) What is nonprice competition? (*c*) Product variation? (*d*) What are selling expenses?

(*a*) The choice-related variables for a monopolistically competitive firm are price, product variation, and selling expenses. That is, in order to maximize short-run profits, the firm can charge the price at which MR = MC. The firm can also undertake product variation and increase selling expenses until the *MR* from these efforts equals the MC. This is to be contrasted to the case under perfect competition where the firm only determines the best level of output to produce.

(*b*) Nonprice competition refers to all the efforts on the part of firms to increase sales or make the demand curves that they face less elastic through product variation and selling expenses.

(*c*) Product variation refers to changes in some of the characteristics of the product in order to make it more appealing to consumers. For example, beer makers have put on the market light beer for weight-conscious consumers and have introduced plastic bottles because they are lighter and unbreakable.

(*d*) Selling expenses are all those expenses that the firm incurs to advertise its product, to increase its sales force, to provide more and better servicing of the product, and to otherwise induce consumers to purchase the product.

10.5 Explain how the monopolistically competitive firm of Fig. 10-9 might reach the long-run equilibrium position shown in Fig. 10-11.

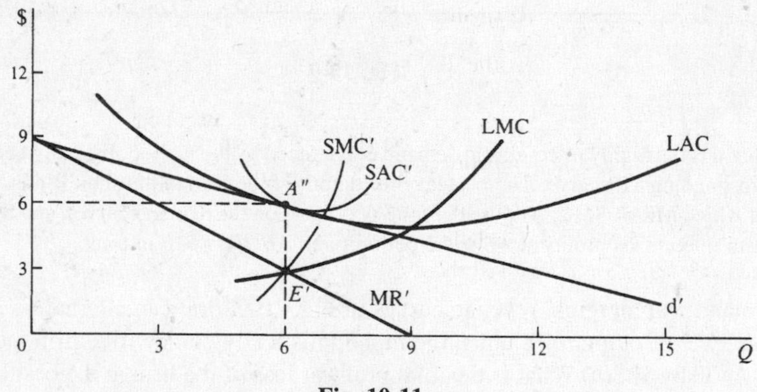

Fig. 10-11

Since the monopolistically competitive firm of Fig. 10-9 earns a profit in the short run, more firms enter the market in the long run. This causes the demand curve of the firm to shift down to d′ in Fig. 10-11 (as this firm's market share declines), so as to be tangent to LAC curve at the output level of 6 units, at which MR′ = LMC (point E'). At $Q = 6$, $P =$ LAC = SAC = \$6 (point A'') and the firm breaks even in the long run. Note that since the firm is in long-run equilibrium, it is also in short-run equilibrium (i.e., at $Q = 6$, MR′ = SMC′).

10.6 Discuss the long-run efficiency implications of monopolistic competition with respect to (*a*) utilization of plant, (*b*) allocation of resources, and (*c*) advertising and product differentiation.

(*a*) When a monopolistically competitive market is in long-run equilibrium, the demand curve facing each firm is tangent to its LAC curve (so that each firm breaks even). Since the demand curve is negatively sloped, the tangency point will always occur to the left of the lowest point on the firm's LAC curve (see Fig. 10-1). Thus, the firm underutilizes a smaller-than-optimum scale of plant when in long-run equilibrium. This allows the existence of more firms in the industry than otherwise (see Problem 10.7). An example of this is the "overcrowding" of gasoline stations, barber shops, grocery stores, etc., with each business idle much of the time.

(*b*) When the monopolistically competitive market is in long-run equilibrium, the price charged by each firm exceeds the LMC of the last unit produced. Therefore, resources are underallocated to the firms in the market and misallocated in the economy. This misallocation of resources is not large, however, because the demand curve facing the monopolistically competitive firm, although negatively sloped, is highly elastic.

(*c*) Though some advertising is useful (since it informs consumers), the amount of advertising undertaken by monopolistically competitive firms may be excessive. This only adds to costs and prices. Similarly, some product differentiation is beneficial since it gives the consumer a greater range of choices. However, an excessive number of brands, styles, designs, etc., only serves to confuse the consumer and adds to costs and prices.

10.7 Compare the long-run equilibrium point of the firm in Problem 10.5 to the long-run equilibrium point of a perfectly competitive firm with the same LAC curve.

In Fig. 10-12, A″ is the long-run equilibrium point for the monopolistically competitive firm of Problem 10.5. If this had been a perfectly competitive firm instead (with the same LAC curve), it would have produced at point E^* when the industry is in long-run equilibrium. Thus, the cost of production and price of the monopolistically competitive firm is $6 rather than $5 and its output is 6 rather than 9 units. As a result, there is an underallocation of resources to the monopolistically competitive firm. The higher cost of production and price under monopolistic competition results from product differentiation, some of which, at least, has economic value since it gives the consumer a greater range of choices. The smaller output of each firm under monopolistic competition allows more firms to exist and results in excessive capacity and overcrowding.

Since d′ is tangent to LAC at point A'', the monopolistic competitor breaks even, does not produce at the lowest point on its LAC curve, and underutilizes a smaller-than-optimum scale of plant when the industry is in long-run equilibrium.

Some waste from excessive advertising and model changes is likely to take place in monopolistic competition, but not under perfect competition (where the product is homogeneous and the firm can sell all it wants at the going market price). These effects become smaller as the elasticity of d′ increases.

10.8 Can you give the reasons why the theory of monopolistic competition has fallen somewhat into disrepute in recent years.

The theory of monopolistic competition has fallen somewhat into disrepute recently because:

(1) It may be difficult to define the market and determine the firms and products to include in it. For example, should moist paper tissues be included with other paper tissues or with soaps? Are toothpaste, dental floss, toothpicks, and water picks part of the same market or product group?

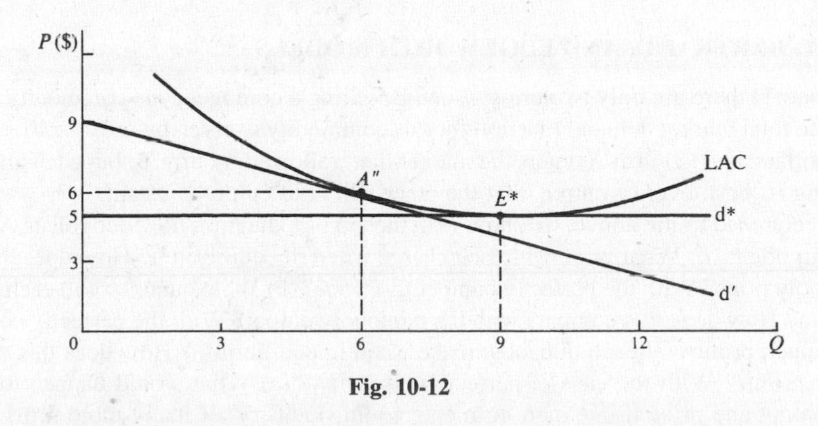

Fig. 10-12

(2) In markets in which there are many small sellers, the demand curve facing monopolistic competitors is nearly horizontal, so that the model of perfect competition is appropriate to use.

(3) In markets in which there are strong brand preferences, the product usually turns out to have only a few sellers, so that oligopoly is the relevant model.

(4) Even in markets in which there are many small sellers of a good or service (say, gasoline stations) a change in price by one of them affects nearby stations significantly and evokes a response. In such cases, the oligopoly model is the more appropriate model to use.

Despite these serious criticisms, however, the monopolistic competition model provides some important insights, such as its emphasis on product differentiation and selling expenses, that are applicable to oligopolistic markets.

OLIGOPOLY DEFINED

10.9 (*a*) Define oligopoly. (*b*) What is the single most important characteristic in oligopolistic markets and (*c*) to what problem does it lead? (*d*) What does oligopoly theory achieve?

(*a*) Oligopoly is the form of market organization in which there are few sellers of a commodity. If there are only two sellers, we have a duopoly. If the product is homogeneous (e.g., steel, cement, copper), we have a pure oligopoly. If the product is differentiated (e.g., cars, cigarettes), we have a differentiated oligopoly. For simplicity, in the text and in that which follows we deal mostly with a pure duopoly. Oligopoly is the most prevalent form of market organization in the manufacturing sector of modern economies and arises for the same general reasons as monopoly (i.e., economies of scale, control over the source of raw materials, patents, and government franchise).

(*b*) The interdependence among the firms in the industry is the single most important characteristic setting oligopoly apart from other market structures. This interdependence is the natural result of fewness. That is, since there are few firms in an oligopolistic industry, when one of them lowers its price, undertakes a successful advertising campaign, or introduces a better model, the demand curve faced by other oligopolists will shift down. So the other oligopolists react.

(*c*) There are many different reaction patterns of the other oligopolists to the actions of the first, and unless and until we assume a specific reaction pattern, we cannot define the demand curve faced by our oligopolist. So we have an indeterminate solution. But even if we assume a particular reaction pattern so that we may have a determinate solution, this is only one out of many possible solutions.

(*d*) Because of the situation outlined in (*c*), we do not now have a general theory of oligopoly. All we have are specific cases or models, a few of which are discussed in Sections 10.6 to 10.11. These few models, however, do accomplish three things: (1) they show clearly the nature of oligopolistic interdependence, (2) they point out the gaps that a satisfactory theory of oligopoly must fill, and (3) they give some indication as to how very difficult this branch of microeconomics really is and how long we may have to wait to get a general theory of oligopoly. In short, oligopoly theory is one of the least satisfactory segments of microeconomics.

THE COURNOT, BERTRAND, AND EDGEWORTH MODELS

10.10 Assume that (1) there are only two firms, A and B, selling a homogeneous commodity produced at zero cost, (2) the total market demand function for this commodity is given by $QD = 240 - 10P$, where P is given in dollars, and (3) firm A enters the market first, followed by firm B, but each always assumes, in determining its best level of output, that the other will hold output constant.

With reference to the above, (*a*) show with the aid of a diagram how duopolists A and B reach the equilibrium point. (*b*) What price will each charge when in equilibrium? How does this compare with the monopoly price? With the perfectly competitive price? (*c*) What quantity will each produce when in equilibrium? How does this compare with the monopoly output? With the perfectly competitive output (*d*) How much profit will each duopolist make when in equilibrium? How does this compare with the monopoly profits? With the case of perfect competition? (*e*) What would happen to the equilibrium industry output and price if one more firm entered this industry? If many more firms came in?

(*a*) Assumptions 1, 2, and 3 given in this problem define the Cournot model. The way duopolists A and B reach their equilibrium point is shown in Fig. 10-13. Before duopolist B enters the market, duopolist A will maximize total profits at point *A* on $D = d_A$. This is the monopoly solution. When duopolist B enters the industry, B will sell at point *B* on d_B. Duopolist A reacts by selling at point A' on d'_A. The process will continue until each duopolist will be in equilibrium at point *E* on d_E.

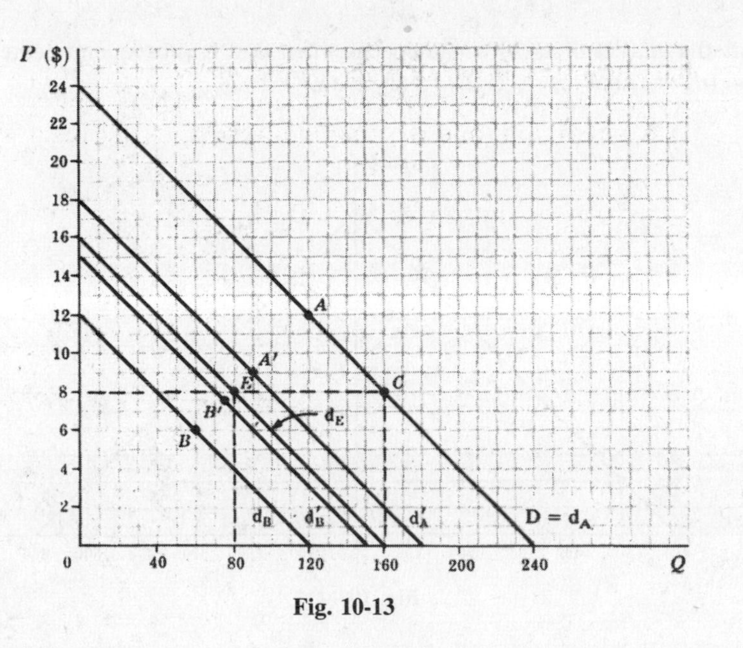

Fig. 10-13

(*b*) When in equilibrium, duopolists A and B will charge a price of \$8. The monopoly price is \$12 (given by point *A*). The perfectly competitive price is zero (so that for each firm in long-run equilibrium, $TR - TC = 0$).

(*c*) When in equilibrium, the duopolists will produce 80 units each, for a total of 160 units. This is 4/3 of the monopoly output of 120 units given by point *A*, and 2/3 of the perfectly competitive output of 240 units (when in long-run equilibrium).

(*d*) When in equilibrium, the duopolists will make \$640 of profit each, for a total of \$1280. This compares with a total profit of \$1440 under monopoly and zero profit under perfect competition.

(*e*) If one more firm entered the industry, each of the three firms will produce 60 units or 1/4 of the total perfectly competitive output when in long-run equilibrium (so all three of them together will produce 180 units or 3/4 of the total perfectly competitive output). The price would then fall to \$6 (see Fig. 10-13). As more and more firms enter the industry, the long-run equilibrium industry output and price approach the long-run perfectly competitive equilibrium output (of 240 units) and price (of zero dollars).

This entire analysis can be extended to cases where costs of production are not zero.

10.11 What would happen if, in determining the best level of output, each of the duopolists in Problem 10.10 assumes that the other holds *price* (rather than output) constant?

Prices will be undercut by each firm until they are driven down to the competitive level. For example, in Fig. 10-13, before duopolist B enters the market, duopolist A will maximize total profits at point *A* on $D = d_A$. If duopolist B enters the market and assumes that duopolist A will hold the *price* constant, duopolist B can capture the entire market by selling at a lower price, say at \$11 per unit (see Fig. 10-13). This is so because the product is homogeneous. Duopolist A, having lost all sales and on the assumption that duopolist B keeps the price at \$11, lowers its price, say to \$10, and will sell the entire quantity of 140 units in the market (see Fig. 10-13). Duopolist B now reacts and the process continues until the perfectly competitive price of \$0 and output of 240 units is established. *This is the Bertrand model.*

10.12 Suppose that (1) there are two firms, A and B, selling a homogeneous commodity produced at zero cost, (2) d_A and d_B in Fig. 10-14 are duopolist A's and duopolist B's demand curves respectively, (3) the maximum output of each firm is 500 units per time period, and (4) each firm in attempting to maximize its TR or total profit assumes that the other firm holds its *price* constant. Determine: (*a*) what happens if firm A enters the market first, (*b*) what happens when firm B subsequently enters the market, (*c*) A's reaction, and (*d*) the final result. Is the result stable? Why?

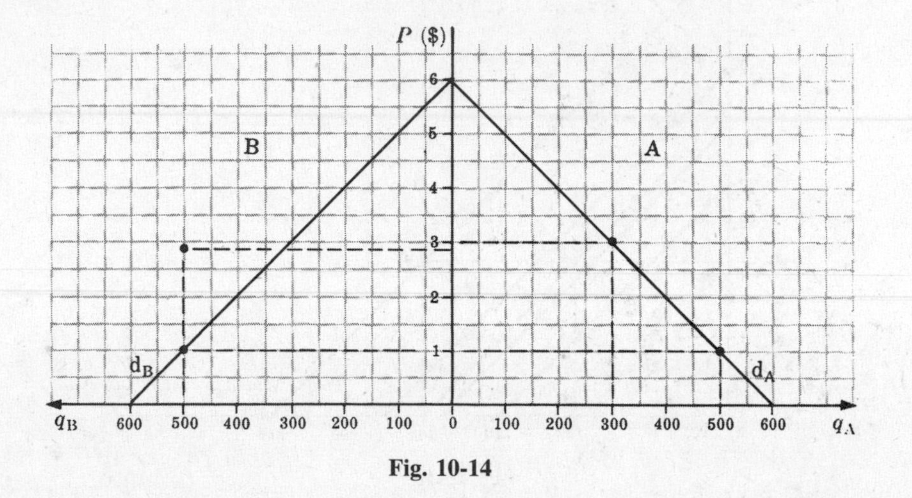

Fig. 10-14

(*a*) If *A* enters the market first, A will sell 300 units at the price of $3 and thus maximize its TR and total profits at the level of $900. This is the monopoly solution for duopolist A.

(*b*) Now B enters the market, and assumes that A will continue to charge the price of $3, Since we are dealing with a homogeneous product, by selling at a price slightly below $3, B can sell its maximum output of 500 units and thus capture most of A's market. Thus B's TR and total profits will be almost $1500 (see Fig. 10-14).

(*c*) Firm A now reacts, and assuming that B will keep its price constant, A can sell its maximum output of 500 units (and capture most of B's market) by setting its price slightly below B's price.

(*d*) This process will continue until each firm will sell its maximum output of 500 units at the price of $1 (and thus make $500 of profit). The above result is not stable, however. For example, suppose firm A is the first to take stock of the situation and notes that if firm B maintains the price of $1, A could increase its total profits to $900 by selling 300 units of output at the price of $3 (the original monopoly solution for firm A). But then firm B realizes that by raising its price from $1 to slightly below $3, it can sell its maximum output of 500 units and thus increase its total profits to almost $1500. Having lost most of its market, A reacts by lowering its price, and the process goes on indefinitely with the price fluctuating between the monopoly price of $3 and the maximum output price of $1 for each firm. *The above is an illustration of the Edgeworth model.*

10.13 Assume that (1) there are only two firms, A and B, selling a homogeneous commodity produced at zero cost; (2) the total market demand function is $QD = 240 - 10P$ and is divided equally between A and B; (3) each firm can produce no more than 100 units of output; and (4) firm A enters the market first, followed by B, but each always assumes, in determining its best level of output, that the other holds its *price* constant. (*a*) With the aid of a figure, explain what happens when A enters the market first; when B enters the market; and A's and B's reaction pattern and (*b*) explain why and how the price of the commodity will fluctuate indefinitely. (*c*) What do the Cournot, the Bertrand and the Edgeworth models have in common?

(*a*) The assumption above define the Edgeworth model. From Fig. 10-15, we see that if A enters the market first, A will sell 60 units at $6 each and make the monopoly profit of $360. Since the commodity is homogeneous, by selling at a price slightly below $6, B can enter the market, capture 2/3 of A's market, and sell its maximum output of 100 units. A reacts and the process will continue until A and B both sell their maximum output of 100 units at the price of $2, and so each makes a profit of $200.

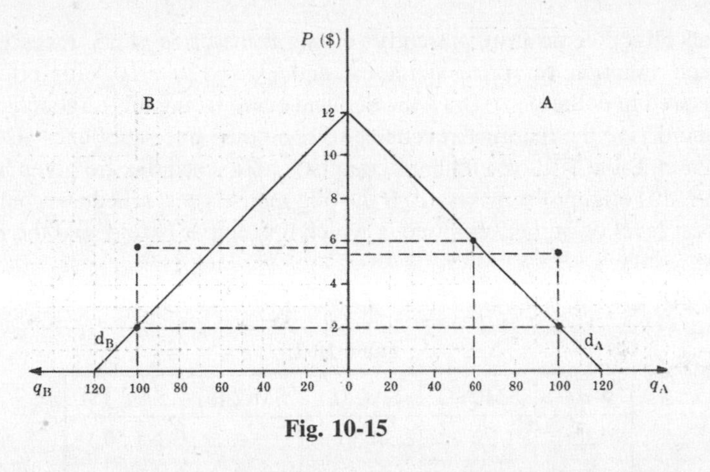

Fig. 10-15

(b) But now either firm, say firm A, realizes that by raising its price back to \$6, A can sell 60 units and thus increase its profits once again to \$360. (When A does this, A will lose only those customers who are not willing to pay the high price of \$6; it does not lose any customers to B since B is already selling its maximum output of 100 units.) B now realizes that by raising its price from \$2 to slightly below \$6, B can capture 2/3 of A's market, sell its maximum output of 100 units, and make almost \$600 of profit. A reacts and so the price oscillates continuously between \$6 and \$2.

(c) The Cournot, the Bertrand, and the Edgeworth models are all based on the extremely naive assumption that the duopolists act independently and that they never recognize their interdependence. In addition, the Edgeworth model assumes that the duopolists have maximum output levels, whereas we know that output can be increased in the long run. Thus these models are very unsatisfactory.

THE CHAMBERLIN AND THE KINKED DEMAND CURVE MODELS

10.14 Starting with the same assumptions as those in Problem 10.10, show step by step what happens if the duopolists recognize their interdependence.

This is the Chamberlin model. In Fig. 10-16, when firm A enters the market, it will choose the monopoly solution indicated by point *A*. Firm B, taking firm A's output as given, will choose point *B* on d_B. But now the Chamberlin model breaks away from the Cournot model. That is, firm A, recognizing its interdependence with firm B, will voluntarily and without collusion choose to sell 60 units at the price of \$12. Firm B also recognizes its interdependence with firm A and will continue voluntarily to sell 60 units, but at the new price of \$12. Thus, the final (stable) result of the Chamberlin model is that each firm shares equally in the monopoly profits of \$1440. This compares with the (stable) equilibrium profit of \$640 for each firm and (\$1280 in total) achieved without the recognition of interdependence in the Cournot solution (see point *E* in Fig. 10-13). It is difficult to know how often in the real world sophisticated but noncollusive behavior of this sort occurs.

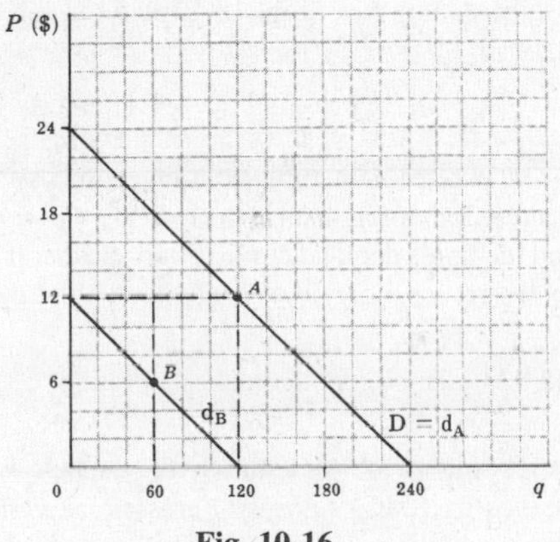

Fig. 10-16

10.15 Assume that an oligopolistic firm, presently selling at the price of \$8, faces $Qd = 360 - 40P$ as its relevant demand function for price increases, and $Qd = 120 - 10P$ for price reductions (in both cases P is measured in dollars). (*a*) Draw the demand curve facing this oligopolist, given an explanation for its shape and derive the marginal revenue curve; on the same set of axes also sketch the set of cost schedules given in Table 10.1. (*b*) If the oligopolist's cost schedules are given by SMC and SAC, find how much profit this oligopolist makes, (*c*) If the oligopolist's cost schedules change to SMC′ and SAC′, find the new best level of output, the price at which this output is sold, and the new level of profits for this oligopolist.

Table 10-1

q	SMC (\$)	SAC (\$)	SMC′ (\$)	SAC′ (\$)
20	3	4.50	4	5.50
30	4	4.00	5	5.00
40	5	4.50	6	5.50

(*a*)

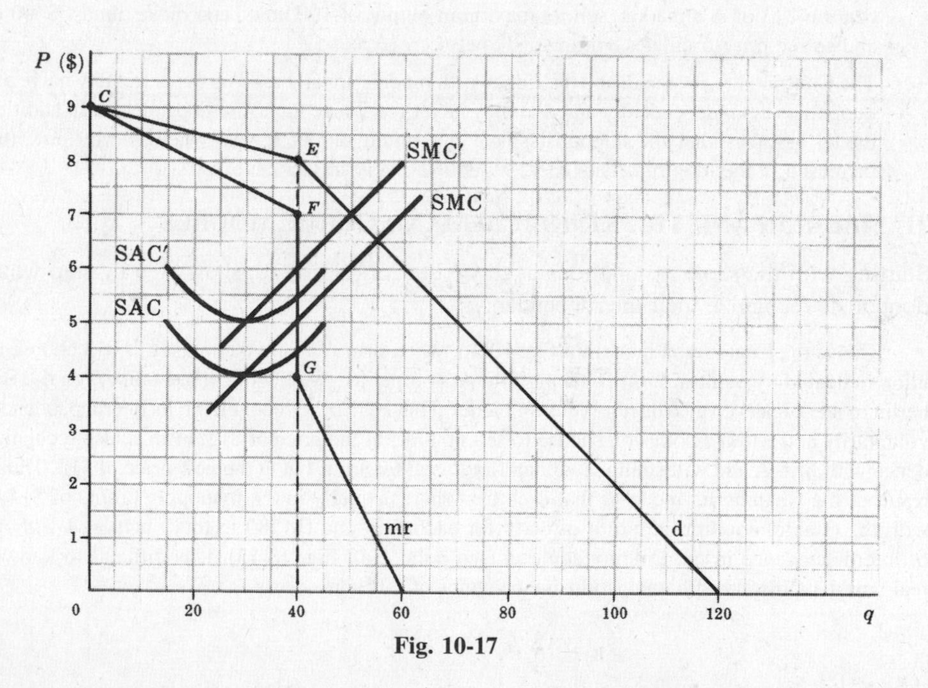

Fig. 10-17

The shape of d in Fig. 10-17 can be explained by assuming that if this oligopolistic firm raises its price (from the prevailing level of \$8), the other oligopolists in the industry will *not* raise theirs, so the firm will lose a great deal of its sales to rivals and the firm's demand curve is very elastic. If the firm lowers its price, others will also lower theirs, so our oligopolist retains more or less only its share of the market and its demand curve becomes less elastic.

(*b*) With cost curves SMC and SAC, the oligopolist makes a profit of \$3.50 per unit on each of the 40 units sold (and thus \$140 in total).

(*c*) If the oligopolist's cost curves shift up to SMC′ and SAC′, the best level of output of this oligopolist remains 40 units per time period (since the SMC′ curve still crosses the vertical or discontinuous section of the mr curve) and the firm continues to sell at the price of \$8. But now the oligopolist's profit is only \$2.50 per unit and \$100 in total. (Note that there is also a wide range over which the oligopolist's demand curve, with its kink at the same price level, can shift and result only in a change in the oligopolist's equilibrium quantity but not in the equilibrium price.)

10.16 (*a*) What does the kinked demand curve or Sweezy model accomplish? (*b*) What would happen if the new and higher SMC curve (e.g., the SMC′ curve in Fig. 10-17) intersects the mr curve to the left of and above its vertical or discontinuous portion? (*c*) Why is the oligopolist in general reluctant to lower price even when justified by demand and cost considerations? (*d*) What do the Chamberlin and the kinked demand curve models have in common?

(*a*) It can *rationalize* the price rigidity in oligopolistic markets, in the face of widespread changes in cost conditions. It is of no use, however, in *explaining* how the prevailing prices were determined in the first place.

(*b*) This and other firms would want to increase prices. An orderly price increase might then occur through price leadership.

(*c*) The oligopolistic firm fears it would star a price war. So the firm prefers to compete on the basis of quality, product design, advertising, and service. Thus, to a great extent, the decision context in oligopoly resembles military warfare and poker playing. This is studied in *game theory*.

(*d*) In both these models, the oligopolists do recognize their mutual dependence (which makes these models better than the Cournot, Bertrand, and Edgeworth models) but act without collusion.

CARTEL AND PRICE LEADERSHIP MODELS

10.17 Assume that (1) the 10 identical firms in a purely oligopolistic industry form a centralized cartel, (2) the total market demand function facing the cartel is $QD = 240 - 10P$ and P is given in dollars, and (3) each firm's SMC is given by \$1q for $q > 4$ units, and factor prices remain constant. Find (*a*) the best level of output and price for this cartel, (*b*) how much each firm should produce if the cartel wants to minimize costs of production, and (*c*) how much profits the cartel will make if the SAC of each firm at its best level of output is \$12. (*d*) Why do we study cartel models if cartels are illegal in the U.S. today?

(*a*) From Fig. 10-18, we see that the best level of output for this cartel is 80 units and is given by the point where $\text{MR} = \sum \text{MC}$. The cartel will set a price of \$16. This is the monopoly solution.

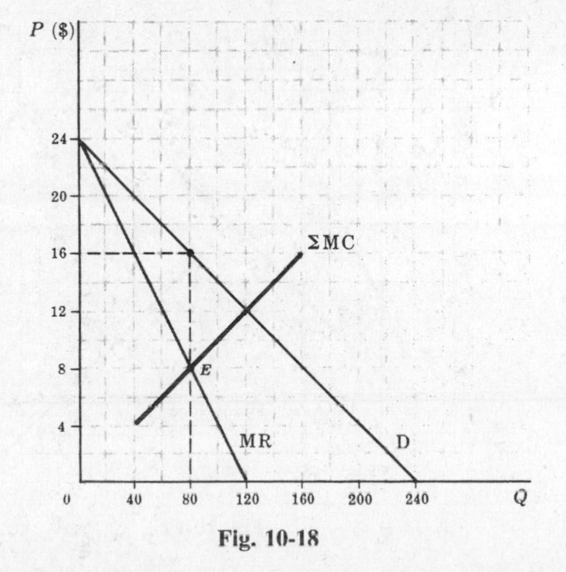

Fig. 10-18

(*b*) If the cartel wants to minimize costs of production, it will set a quota of eight units of production for each firm (given by the condition $\text{SMC}_1 = \text{SMC}_2 = \cdots = \text{SMC}_{10} = \text{MR} = \$8$, where the subscripts refer to the firms in the cartel). This is the same as for the multiplant monopolist.

(*c*) If $\text{SAC} = \$12$ at $Q = 8$ for each firm, each firm will make a profit of \$4 per unit and \$32 in total. The cartel as a whole will make \$320 of profit. In this case, each firm will very likely share equally in the cartel's profits.

In other more complicated and realistic cases, it may not be so easy to decide on how the cartel's profits should be shared. The bargaining strength of each firm then becomes important.

(*d*) Even if cartels are illegal in the U.S., cartel models give some indication of how a tightly organized oligopolistic industry might operate. The best known *international* cartel today is OPEC (Organization of Petroleum Exporting Countries). Note that the greater the number of firms in the cartel, the easier it is for members to "cheat" on others and thus cause the collapse of the collusive agreement.

10.18 Assume that (1) the two identical firms in a purely oligopolistic industry agree to share the market equally, (2) the total market demand function for the commodity is $QD = 240 - 10P$ and P is given in dollars, and (3) the cost schedules of each firm are as given by the figures in Table 10.2 and factor prices remain constant. Show that this market-sharing cartel also reaches the monopoly solution. What are the total profits of the cartel? Is this solution likely to occur in the real world?

Table 10.2

q	40	60	80
SMC ($)	8	12	16
SAC ($)	13	12	13

In Fig. 10-19, each duopolist is in equilibrium at point C (where mr = SMC) and sells 40 units of output at the price of $16 on d, the half-share demand curve. The market as a whole will produce 80 units (given by point E, where MR = $\sum$ MC) and the price is $16 on D. This is the monopoly solution. Each duopolist makes a profit of $3 per unit and $120 in total. So this market-sharing cartel as a whole will make profits of $240. However, in the real world, the market need not be shared equally and we may have more than two firms, each facing different cost curves. So the solution is not likely to be the neat monopoly solution found in Fig. 10-19.

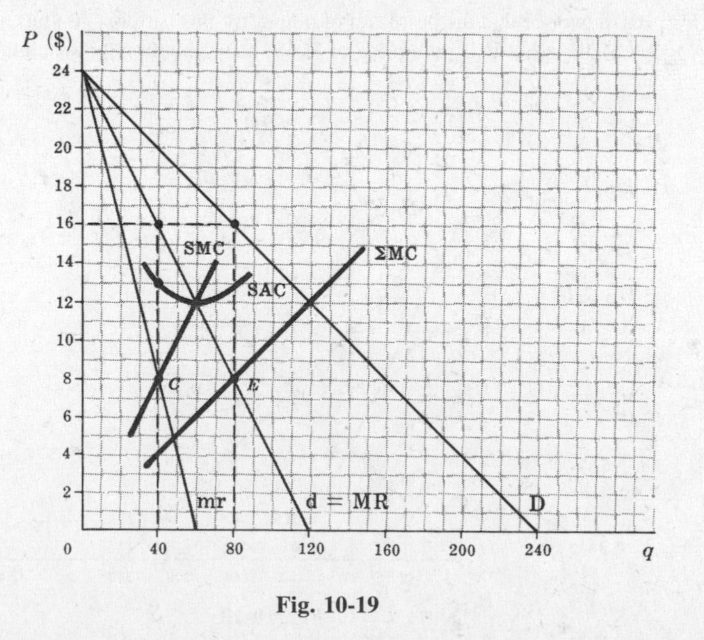

Fig. 10-19

10.19 Suppose that there are only one low-cost firm and one high-cost firm selling a homogeneous commodity, and they tacitly agree to share the market equally. If D in Fig. 10-20 is the total market demand curve for the commodity, then d is the half-share curve for each firm and mr is the corresponding marginal revenue curve. If the subscripts 2 and 1 refer, respectively, to the low-cost and the high-cost firms, determine what each firm *would like* to do and what it actually does.

In Fig. 10-20, we see that firm 2 wants to sell 200 units at the price of \$8 (given by point E_2, where mr = SMC_2) while firm 1 would like to sell 150 units at the price of \$9 (given by E_1 where mr = SMC_1). Since the commodity is homogeneous, firm 1 will usually have to follow firm 2 and also sell at the price of \$8. Thus only firm 2 (i.e., the price leader) will usually be producing and selling its best level of output.

10.20 Assume that (1) two firms selling a homogeneous commodity share the market equally, (2) the total market demand schedule facing them is the same as in Problem 10.18, and (3) the cost schedules of each firm are as given in Tables 10.3 and 10.4. (*a*) What would be the total profit of each firm if each were producing its best level of output? (*b*) What is the most likely result? (*c*) What other result is possible?

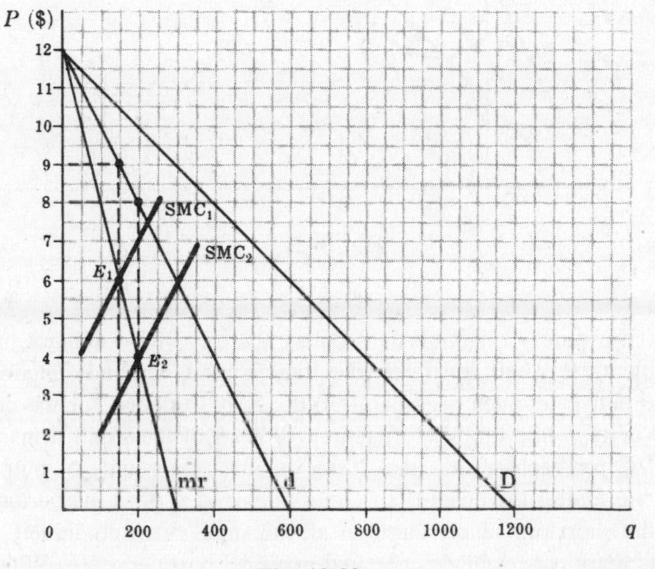

Fig. 10-20

Table 10.3

q_1	40	50	60	80
SMC_1 (\$)	8	10.00	12	16
SAC_1 (\$)	13	12.30	12	13

Table 10.4

q_2	50	70	100
SMC_2 (\$)	4	6	9
SAC_2 (\$)	7	6	7

(*a*) From Fig. 10-21, we see that firm 1 would like to sell 40 units at the price of \$16 (given by point E_1), thereby maximizing its total profits at \$120. Firm 2 maximizes its total profits (at \$350) by selling 50 units at the price of \$14 (given by point E_2).

(*b*) Since the commodity is homogeneous, it must sell at the single price of \$14. That is, the high-cost firm (firm 1) will have to follow the price leadership of the low-cost firm (firm 2). Thus, only firm 2 will produce its best level of output (given by E_2) and maximize its total profits (at \$350). Firm 1 will now also have to charge the price of \$14 and sell 50 units, and so it will now make only \$85 of profits (\$1.70 per unit times 50 units).

(*c*) In some cases, the price that the low-cost firm would set at its best level of output is so low that it would drive the high-cost firm(s) out of business. When this is true, the low-cost firm might want to forgo profit maximization and set a (higher) price that would allow other firms to remain in business. By doing so, it would avoid becoming a monopoly and facing possible prosecution under U.S. antitrust laws.

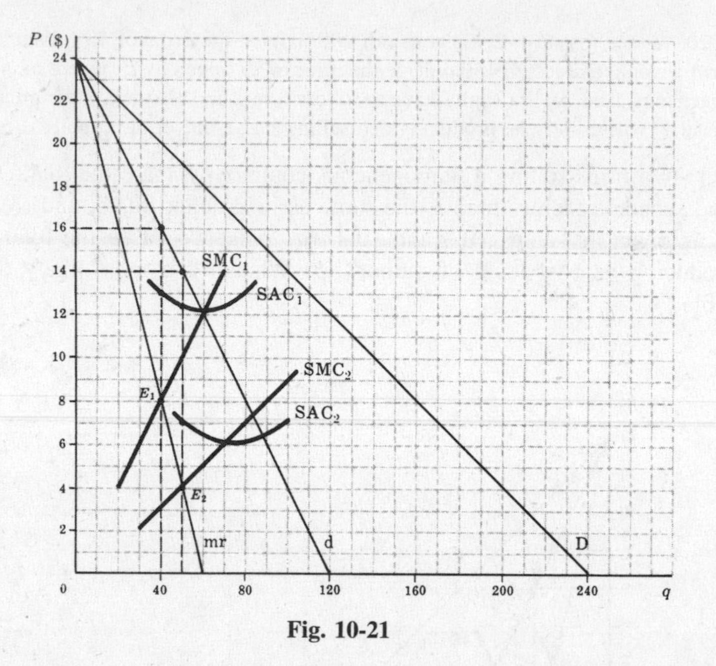

Fig. 10-21

10.21 Assume that (1) in a purely oligopolistic industry there is one dominant firm that acts as the price leader and ten identical small firms, (2) the total market demand function for the commodity is $QD = 240 - 10P$ and P is given in dollars, (3) the SMC function for the dominant firm is given by $q/\$5$ for $q > 10$ units, while the SMC function for *each* of the small firms is given by \$1 for $q > 4$ units and the AVC for each of the small firms is \$4 at four units of output, and (4) factor prices remain constant, no matter the quantity of factors demanded per time period. (*a*) On the same set of axes, sketch D, the short-run supply curve of all the small firms combined, the demand curve of the dominant firm, its marginal revenue curve, and marginal cost curve. (*b*) What price will the dominant firm set? How much will all the small firms together and the dominant firm sell at that price? (*c*) What do the cartel and price leadership models have in common?

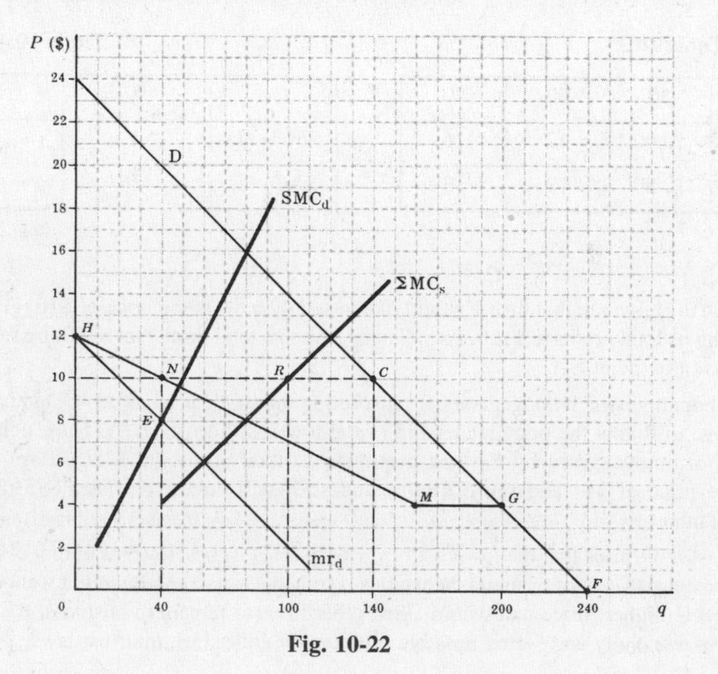

Fig. 10-22

(a) In Fig. 10-22, the $\sum MC_s$ curve represents the short-run supply curve of all the small firms together. This is so because the small firms, in following the price leader, behave as perfect competitors, and factor prices remain constant. Since the AVC for each of the small firms is \$4 at four units of output, they will supply nothing at prices below \$4 per unit. By subtracting $\sum MC_s$ from D at each price, we get the demand curve faced by the dominant firm. This is given by *HNMGF*. Note that since the small firms supply nothing at prices below \$4, the demand curve of the dominant firm coincides with the market demand curve over segment *GF*.

(b) The dominant firm will set the price of \$10, at which it can sell its best level of output of 40 units (given by point *E*, where $mr_d = SMC_d$). Since each of the small firms can sell all it wants at this price, each faces an infinitely elastic demand curve (which coincides with its marginal revenue curve) at the price of \$10. Each of the small firms produces where $P = MR = SMC = \$10$, and all of them together produce 100 units (point *R* on the $\sum MC_s$ curve), leaving 40 units (*RC*) to be sold by the dominant firm (shown by point *N* on its demand curve). To find the amount of profit, we need the SAC at the best level of output for each firm.

(c) In the cartel and price leadership models, the oligopolists recognize their mutual dependence and act collusively. The collusion is perfect in the cartel models and imperfect in the price leadership models.

LONG-RUN EFFICIENCY IMPLICATIONS

10.22 (a) What are some of the natural and artificial barriers to entry into certain oligopolistic industries? (b) What are the possible harmful effects of oligopoly? (c) What are the possible beneficial effects of oligopoly?

(a) The natural barriers to entry into such oligopolistic industries as the car, aluminum, and steel industries are the smallness of the market in relation to efficient operation and the huge amounts of capital and specialized inputs required to start efficient operation. Some of the artificial barriers to entry are control over sources of raw materials, patents, and government franchise. When entry is blocked or at least restricted (the usual case), the firms in an oligopolistic industry can earn long run profits.

(b) In the long run, oligopoly may lead to the following harmful effects: (1) as in monopoly, price usually exceeds LAC in oligopolistic markets, (2) the oligopolist usually does not produce at the lowest point on his LAC curve, (3) $P < LMC$, so there is an underallocation of the economy's resources to the firms in the oligopolistic industry, and (4) when oligopolists produce a differentiated product, too much may be spent on advertising and model changes.

(c) For technological reasons (economies of scale), many products (such as cars, steel, aluminum, etc.) cannot possibly be produced under conditions of perfect competition (or their cost of production would be prohibitive). In addition, oligopolists spend a great deal of their profits on research and development, and many economists believe that this leads to much faster technological advance and higher standards of living than if the industry were organized along perfectly competitive lines. Finally, some advertising is useful since it informs consumers, and some product differentiation has the economic value of satisfying the different tastes of different consumers.

10.23 Compare the efficiency implications of long-run equilibria under different forms of market organization, with respect to (a) total profits, (b) the point of production on the LAC curve, (c) allocation of resources, and (d) sales promotion.

(a) It is difficult to interpret and answer this question since cost curves probably differ under various forms of market organization. A few generalizations can nevertheless be made, if they are interpreted with caution. First, the perfectly competitive firm and the monopolistically competitive firm break even when the industry is in long-run equilibrium. Thus, consumers get the commodity at cost of production. On the other hand, the monopolist and the oligopolist can and usually do make profits in the long run. These profits, however, may lead to more research and development and therefore to faster technological progress and rising standard of living in the long run.

(b) While the perfectly competitive firm produces at the lowest point on its LAC curve when the industry is in long-run equilibrium, the monopolist and the oligopolist are very unlikely to do so, and the monopolistic competitor never does so when the industry is in long-run equilibrium. However, the size of efficient operation is often so large in relation to the market as to leave only a few firms in the industry. Perfect competition under such circumstances would either be impossible or lead to prohibitive costs.

(*c*) While the perfectly competitive firm, when in long-run equilibrium, produces where $P = \text{LMC}$, for the imperfectly competitive firm $P > \text{LMC}$ and so there is an underallocation of resources to the firms in imperfectly competitive industries and a misallocation of resources in the economy. That is, under all forms of imperfect competition, the firm is likely to produce less, and charge a higher price, than under perfect competition. This difference is greater under pure monopoly and oligopoly than under monopolistic, competition because of the greater elasticity of demand in monopolistic competition.

(*d*) Finally, waste resulting from excessive sales promotion is likely to be zero in perfect competition and greatest in oligopoly and monopolistic competition.

10.24 It is often asserted that businesspeople often have no knowledge of the exact shape of the demand curve and cost curves that they face and so cannot determine their best level of output and price to charge. Therefore, most of microeconomics is "academic" and irrelevant. How would you counter such charges?

It is true that businesspeople often have no knowledge of the shape of the demand curve and cost curves that they face. In the real world many businesspeople in imperfectly competitive markets set prices at the level of their estimated average cost plus a certain percentage, or "markup," of costs (see Section 11.5). However, those firms who constantly set their prices at levels far different from those consistent with the $\text{MR} = \text{MC}$ condition are likely to go out of business in the long run. On the other hand, those firms which, by a process of trial and error, correctly estimate the "best" price to charge are more likely to make profits, to remain in business in the long run, and to expand.

The study of the general principles of demand, production, and cost can be very useful as guidelines in this estimation process. They also introduce a rational and logical way of thinking for the firm to follow in its production and pricing policies. In addition, they will surely stimulate the alert entrepreneur to collect more pertinent data. Note, however, that sometimes the firm may purposely not want to charge the price that would lead to profit maximization, even if it knew exactly what that price should be. One reason for this was given in Problem 10.20(*c*). Another reason to limit profits might be to discourage potential entrants into the oligopolistic or monopolistic industry. This is called *limit pricing.*

PRICE AND OUTPUT UNDER MONOPOLISTIC COMPETITION AND OLIGOPOLY WITH CALCULUS

***10.25** Suppose that the market demand function for a two-firm equal market sharing cartel is

$$Q = 120 - 10P$$

and that the total cost function of each duopolist is

$$\text{TC}' = 0.1Q^2$$

Determine, using calculus, the best level of output of each duopolist, the price at which each will sell the commodity, and the total profits of each.

The half-share market faced by each duopolist is

$$Q' = 60 - 5P \qquad \text{or} \qquad P' = 12 - 0.2Q$$

so that

$$TR' = P'Q' = (12 - 0.2Q')Q' = 12Q' - 0.2Q'^2$$

and

$$MR' = \frac{d(\text{TR})'}{dQ'} = 12 - 0.4Q'$$

The marginal and average total cast of each duopolist is

$$MC' = \frac{d(\text{TC}')}{dQ'} = 0.2Q' \qquad \text{and} \qquad \text{ATC}' = \frac{\text{TC}'}{Q'} = \frac{0.1Q'^2}{Q'} = 0.1Q'$$

Setting MC′ equal to MR′, we get

$$0.2Q' = 12 - 0.4Q'$$
$$0.6Q' = 12$$
$$Q' = 20$$

and $$P' = 12 - 0.2(20) = \$8$$

Therefore, $$\text{TR}' = 12(20) - 0.2(20)^2 = 240 - 80 = \$160$$

and $$\pi' = \text{TC}' - 160 - 0.1(20)^2 = 160 - 40 = \$120$$

CHAPTER 11

Recent and Advanced Topics in Market Structure

11.1 THE LERNER INDEX AS A MEASURE OF A FIRM'S MONOPOLY POWER

The *Lerner index* (L) measures the degree of a firm's monopoly power. L is given by the ratio of the difference between price (P) and marginal cost (MC) to price, or by one over the absolute value of the price elasticity of demand e. The value of L can range from zero (for a perfectly competitive firm) to one (for a monopolist).

EXAMPLE 1. If $P = \$8$ and $\text{MC} = \$6$ or $e = 4$, then $L = (\$8 - \$6)/\$8 = 0.25$ or $1/e = 1/4 = 0.25$. On the other hand, if $P = \$8$ and $\text{MC} = \$4$ or $e = 2$, $L = 0.50$ and the firm has double the monopoly power of the firm in the previous case. For a perfectly competitive firm, $P = \text{MC}$ and $e = \infty$, and so $L = 0$. On the other hand, the smaller is MC in relation to P and the smaller is e, the largest is L and the degree of the firm's monopoly power.

11.2 THE HERFINDAHL INDEX AS MEASURE OF MONOPOLY POWER IN AN INDUSTRY

The *Herfindahl index* (H) is a measure of the monopoly power *in an industry as a whole.* H is given by the sum of the squared values of the market sales shares of all the firms in the industry. That is,

$$H = S_1^2 + S_2^2 + \cdots + S_N^2$$

Where S_1 is the market sales share of the largest firm in the industry, S_2 is the market sales share of the second largest firm in the industry, and so on, for all the N firms in the industry. In general, the greater is the value of H, the greater is the degree of monopoly power in the industry.

EXAMPLE 2. With monopoly or a single firm in the industry, so that its market share is 100%, $H = (100)^2 = 10{,}000$. On the other hand, if there are 100 equal-sized firms in the (competitive) industry, each with 1% of the market, $H = 100$. For an industry with 10 equal-sized firms, each with 10% market share, $H = 1000$. For an industry with 11 firms, one with 50% market share and the other 10 firms with 5% market share each, $H = 2{,}750$.

11.3 CONTESTABLE-MARKET THEORY

According to the *contestable-market theory*, even if an industry has a single firm (monopoly) or only a few firms (oligopoly), it would still operate as if it were perfectly competitive if entry is "absolutely free" (i.e., if other firms can enter the industry and face exactly the same costs as existing firms) and exit is "entirely costless" (i.e., if there are no sunk costs so that the firm can exit the industry without any loss of capital) in this case, the market is said to be contestable. Actual competition is then less important than potential competition and the firm or firms will charge a price that only covers average cost (and earn zero economic profit).

EXAMPLE 3 In Fig 11-1, D is the market demand curve and SAC and SMC are the short-run average and marginal cost curves, respectively, of each of two identical firms in a contestable market. Each firm will sell 60 units of output at $P = \text{SAC} = \text{SMC} = \$6$ (point E in the figure) and behave as a perfect competitor facing horizontal demand curve AEE' and earn zero economic profit. Any higher price invites "hit-and-run" entrants that would quickly eliminate all profits.

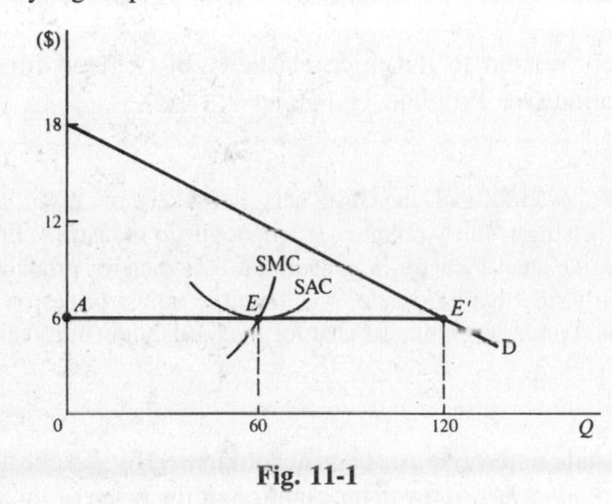

Fig. 11-1

11.4 PEAK-LOAD PRICING

The demand for some services, such as electricity, is higher during some periods (such as in the evening and in the summer) than at other times. Electricity is also a nonstorable service (i.e., it must be generated when needed). In order to satisfy peak demand, electrical power companies must bring into operation older and less efficient equipment and thus incur higher costs during peak periods. According to *peak-load pricing*, consumer welfare will be higher if power companies charge a price equal to short-run marginal cost, both during peak periods when demand and marginal cost are higher and during off-peak periods when demand and marginal cost are lower, rather than charging a constant price equal to the average cost for both periods combined.

EXAMPLE 4. Figure 11-2 shows that at the constant price of 4¢ kilowatt-hour, the public utility sells 4 million kilowatt-hours (kWh) of electricity (point A_1 on D_1) during the off-peak period and 8 million kWh during the peak period (point A_2 on D_2). But at A_1, $P > \text{SMC}$, while at A_2, $P < \text{SMC}$. With peak-load pricing, $P = \text{SMC} = 3$¢ (point E_1) in the off-peak period and $P = \text{SMC} = 5$¢ (point E_2) in the peak period. The gain in consumer welfare is thus given by the sum of the two shaded triangles.

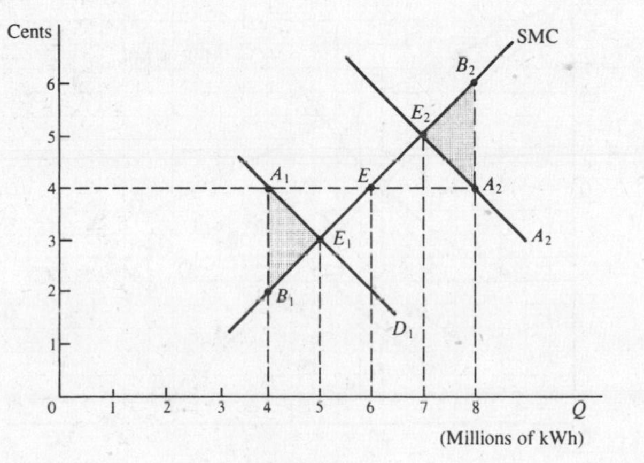

Fig. 11-2

11.5 COST-PLUS PRICING

When a firm lacks information to set price according to the MR = SMC profit-maximizing rule, it usually adopts *cost-plus pricing*. Here, the firm estimates the average variable cost for a "normal" level of output (usually between 70 and 80% of capacity) and then adds a *markup m* over average variable cost to determine the price of the commodity. The markup is set sufficiently high to cover average variable and fixed costs, and also to provide a profit margin for the firm. That is,

$$m = \frac{P - \text{AVC}}{\text{AVC}} \quad \text{so that} \quad P = \text{AVC}(1 + m)$$

The markup is usually inversely related to the price elasticity of demand for the commodity and so it is consistent with profit maximization (see Problem 11.14).

EXAMPLE 5. If a firm's AVC = \$100 and the firm sets $m = 0.20$ or 20%, the firm would then set $P =$ \$100(1 + 0.20) = \$120. Cost-plus pricing is fairly common in oligopolistic industries. Empirical studies have found that the markup is about 0.2 or 20% in the steel industry in general but is higher for products facing less elastic demand or in periods of high demand. Similarly, the retailing sector was found to adjust prices on the basis of feedback from the market and to reduce the markup and price when the demand for the product declines and becomes more elastic.

11.6 TRANSFER PRICING

The rapid rise of the large-scale enterprise has been accompanied by decentralized operations and the need for transfer pricing. *Transfer pricing* refers to the determination of the price of the intermediate products sold by one semiautonomous division of a firm to another semiautonomous division of the same enterprise. Appropriate transfer pricing is essential in determining the optimal level of output of each division and of the firm as a whole. In the absence of an external market for the intermediate product, the transfer price of the intermediate product is given by the marginal cost of production of the production division at the best level of output of the intermediate product.

EXAMPLE 6. In Figure 11-3, we assume that there is no external market for the intermediate product and that one unit of the intermediate product is required to produce each unit of the final product. The marginal cost of the firm, MC, is equal to the vertical summation of MC_p and MC_m, the marginal cost curves of the firm's production and marketing divisions. D_m is the external demand for the final product faced by the firm, and MR_m is the corresponding marginal revenue curve. The firm's best level of output is 40 units and is given by point E_m, at which $MR_m = MC$, so that $P_m = \$14$. Since each unit of the final product requires one unit of the intermediate product, the transfer price for the intermediate product, P_t, is set equal to MC_p at $Q_p = 40$ (point E_p). Thus, $P_t = \$6$.

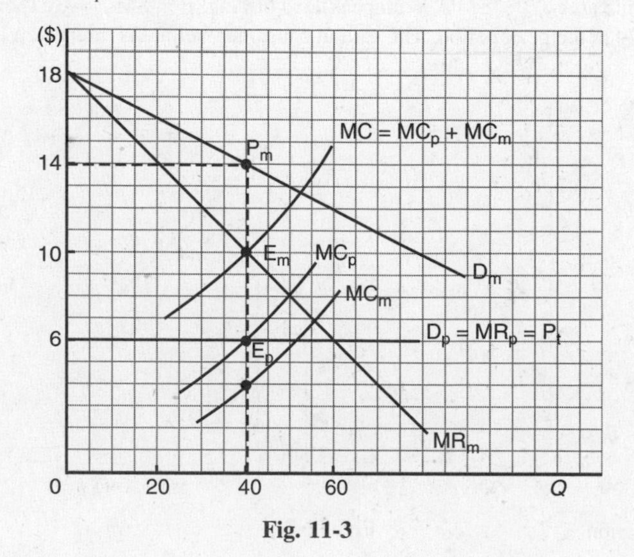

Fig. 11-3

Glossary

Contestable-market theory The theory that postulates that even if an industry has only one or a few firms, it could still operate as if it were perfectly competitive if entry is absolutely free and if exit is entirely costless.

Cost-plus pricing The setting of a price equal to average cost plus a markup.

Herfindahl index A measure of the monopoly power in an industry, which is given by the sum of the squared values of the market sales shares of all the firms in the industry.

Lerner index A measure of the degree of a firm's monopoly power, which is given by the ratio of the difference between price and marginal cost to price or by one over the absolute value of the price elasticity of demand.

Markup The ratio or percentage over average variable cost in cost-plus pricing.

Peak-load pricing The charging of a price equal to short-run marginal cost, both in the peak period when demand and marginal cost are higher and in the off-peak period when both are lower.

Transfer pricing The price of the intermediate products sold by one semiautonomous division of a firm to another semiautonomous division of the same enterprise.

Review Questions

1. The Lerner Index equals (*a*) $(MC - P)/MC$, (*b*) $(P - MC)/P$, (*c*) $P/(MC - P)$, or (*d*) $MC/(MC - P)$.

   Ans. (*b*) See Section 11.1.

2. An alternative way of calculating the Lerner index is (*a*) $1/e$, (*b*) e, (*c*) $e - 1$, or (*d*) $1 - e$.

   Ans. (*a*) See Section 11.1.

3. The Lerner index for a firm increases when (*a*) the number of substitutes for the firm's product increases, (*b*) better substitutes for the firm's product are introduced, (*c*) more competitors enter the market, or (*d*) the price elasticity of demand for the firm's product decreases.

   Ans. (*d*) When e falls, $1/e = L$ increases.

4. The smallest value that the Herfindahl index can assume is (*a*) 10,000, (*b*) 1000, (*c*) 100, or (*d*) smaller than 100.

   Ans. (*d*) This would arise if there are more than 100 equal-sized firms in the industry.

5. An industry for which the Herfindahl index is 1000 or less is (*a*) oligopolistic, (*b*) monopolistic, (*c*) highly concentrated, or (*d*) relatively unconcentrated.

   Ans. (*d*) See Section 11.2. This might be an industry with 10 or more firms with 10% or less market sales share.

6. According to the theory of contestable markets, perfect competition can occur (*a*) only if there are a large number of firms in the industry, (*b*) if entry into the industry is absolutely free and exit from the industry is entirely costless, (*c*) only in the absence of government regulation, or (*d*) only in the presence of foreign competition.

   Ans. (*b*) See Section 11.3.

7. Peak-load pricing refers to the charging of (*a*) different prices for different customers in different markets, (*b*) different prices for different quantities of a commodity, (*c*) a higher price during periods of peak demand and a lower price during periods of off-peak demand, or (*d*) a lower price during periods of peak demand and a higher price during periods of off-peak demand.

   Ans. (*c*) See Section 11.4.

8. Which of the following is true with regard to peak-load pricing? (*a*) It is applicable only for electrical public utilities. (*b*) It leads to some substitution in consumption from the period of peak demand to the period of low demand. (*c*) It leads to a reduction in customer welfare. (*d*) All of the above.

Ans. (*b*) See Problem 11.3.

9. Cost-plus pricing (*a*) is used when firms do not have knowledge of MR and SMC, (*b*) is fairly common in oligopolistic industries, (*c*) is usually consistent with profit maximization, or (*d*) all of the above.

Ans. (*d*) See Section 11.5.

10. Transfer pricing refers to the price (*a*) that a firm pays for the intermediate products of another firm, (*b*) that a foreign firm pays for the final products of a domestic firm, (*c*) of the intermediate products sold by one semiautonomous division of a firm to another semiautonomous division of the same enterprise, (*d*) of the final products sold by one semiautonomous division of a firm to another semiautonomous division of the same enterprise.

Ans. (*c*) See Section 11.6.

11. When there is no external market for an intermediate product and one unit of the intermediate product is required to produce a unit of the final product of the firm, the appropriate transfer price of the inter-mediate product is the (*a*) marginal cost of production of the intermediate product, (*b*) marginal cost of production of the final product, (*c*) price of the final product, (*d*) marginal revenue of the final product.

Ans. (*a*) See Section 11.6 and Fig. 11-3.

12. Appropriate transfer pricing is essential in determining (*a*) the optimal output of each division of the firm, (*b*) the optimal output of the firm, (*c*) evaluating divisional performance, (*d*) all of the above.

Ans. (*d*) See Section 11.6.

Solved Problems

THE LERNER INDEX AS A MEASURE OF A FIRM'S MONOPOLY POWER

11.1 What is the value of the Lerner index when (*a*) $e = 5$? $e = 3$? (*b*) $P = \$10$ and $\mathrm{MR} = \$5$?

(*a*) When $e = 5$, $L = 1/e = 1/5 = 0.20$.
When $e = 3$, $L = 1/3 = 0.33$.

(*b*) Since at the best level of output MR = MC, we can substitute MR for MC in the formula for the Lerner index and get

$$L = \frac{P - \mathrm{MC}}{P} = \frac{P - \mathrm{MR}}{P} = \frac{\$10 - \$5}{\$10} = 0.50$$

11.2 Derive the formula for $L = 1/e$ from $L = (P - \mathrm{MC})/P$.

Since at the best level of output MR = MC, we can substitute MR for MC into the formula and get $L = (P - \mathrm{MR})/\mathrm{P}$. But from Section 9.2, we know that $\mathrm{MR} = P(1 - 1/e)$. Substituting this value for MR into the above formula for L, we get

$$L = \frac{P - P(1 - 1/e)}{P} = 1 - 1\left(\frac{1 - 1}{e}\right) = 1 - 1 + \frac{1}{e} = \frac{1}{e}$$

11.3 Explain why the value of the Lerner index can seldom, if ever, be equal to one (i.e., the value of L usually ranges from zero to smaller than one).

Given that $L = 1/e$, for L to be equal to 1, e has to have a value of 1. But at $e = 1$, MR = 0. For this to be the best level of output of the firm, MC must also be equal to zero. This is seldom, if ever, the case.

11.4 What are the major shortcomings in using the Lerner index as a measure of the firm's monopoly power?

One shortcoming is that a firm with a great deal of monopoly power might keep its price low in order to avoid legal scrutiny or to deter entry into the industry. In that case, the value of L would be low even though the firm has a great deal of monopoly power.

Another shortcoming is that the Lerner index is applicable in a static context, but it is not very useful in a dynamic context when the firm's demand and cost functions shift over time.

THE HERFINDAHL INDEX AS A MEASURE OF MONOPOLY POWER IN AN INDUSTRY

11.5 Find the value of the Herfindahl index for (*a*) duopoly of one firm having 60% of the market and (*b*) an industry with 1000 equal-sized firms.

(*a*) $H = (60)^2 + (40)^2 = 3600 + 1600 = 5200.$

(*b*) $H =$ sum of $(0.1)^2$ for all 100 firms. Thus, $H = 1000(0.01) = 10.$

11.6 Sometimes in measuring the Herfindahl index the market share of each firm in the industry is expressed in ratio form rather than in percentages. Find the Herfindahl index if the market share of each firm is expressed as a ratio when (*a*) there is a single firm in the industry, (*b*) there is duopoly with one firm having 0.6 of the total industry sales, (*c*) there is one firm with sales equal to 0.5 of total industry sales and 10 other equal-sized firms, (*d*) there are 10 equal-sized firms, (*e*) there are 100 equal-sized firms in the industry, and (*f*) there are 1000 equal-sized firms in the industry.

(*a*) $H = (1)^2 = 1.$

(*b*) $H = (0.6)^2 + (0.4)^2 = 0.36 + 0.16 = 0.52.$

(*c*) $H = (0.5)^2 + 10(0.05)^2 = 0.25 + 10(0.0025) = 0.25 + 0.025 = 0.275.$

(*d*) $H = 10(0.1)^2 = 10(0.01) = 0.1.$

(*e*) $H = 100(0.01)^2 = 100(0.0001) = 0.01.$

(*f*) $H = 1000(0.001)^2 = 1000(0.000001) = 0.0001.$

11.7 According to Justice Department guidelines, a merger is likely to be challenged if the postmerger Herfindahl index is a greater than 1800. Determine whether a merger of four firms in an industry of 10 equal-sized firms is likely to be challenged.

Before the merger, the Herfindahl index for the 10 equal-sized firms is 1000. After the merger, $H = 2200$ for the 7 remaining firms. Thus, the Justice Department is likely to challenge the merger. For the complete set of Justice Department guidelines for challenging mergers, see Section 13.4 of D Salvatore, *Microeconomics: Theory and Applications*, 4th ed. (New York: Oxford University Press, 2003).

11.8 What are the major shortcomings in using the Herfindahl index as a measure of monopoly power in an industry?

The major shortcomings are:

(1) In industry (such as automobiles) where imports are significant, the Herfindahl index greatly overestimates the relative important of concentration in the industry.

(2) The Herfindahl index for the nation as a whole may not be relevant when the market is local (as in the case of cement where transportation costs are very high).

(3) The Herfindahl index depends on how broadly or narrowly a product is defined.

(4) The Herfindahl index does not give any indication of potential entrants into the market and of the degree of actual and potential competition in the industry.

CONTESTABLE-MARKET THEORY

11.9 With regard to the theory of contestable markets (*a*) give an example from the airline industry, (*b*) indicate how it differs from limit pricing, and (*c*) identify a possible shortcoming.

(*a*) An airline market is contestable if an airline establishes a service between two cities already served by other airlines if the new entrant faces the same costs as existing airlines and could subsequently leave the market by simply reassigning its planes to other routes without incurring any loss of capital.

(*b*) With limit pricing a firm charges lower than the profit-maximizing price in order to discourage potential entrants into the market. But while profits can still be earned (even though they are not maximized) with limit pricing (because entry is not absolutely free and sunk costs do exist in the industry), economic profits are zero in a contestable market because entry is absolutely free and exit is entirely costless. Even purely transitory profits will not be disregarded by potential entrants into the industry.

(*c*) One possible criticism of the contestable-market theory is that entry is seldom, if ever, absolutely free and exit is seldom if ever entirely costless. The theory, however, can still be acceptable and useful even if entry into and exit from the industry are only reasonably easy rather than absolutely free and costless.

11.10 Starting with demand curve D in Fig. 11-1, draw a figure showing three identical firms in the contestable market.

In the Fig. 11-4 SAC and SMC refer, respectively, to the short-run average and marginal cost curves of each of the three identical firms in a contestable market. Each firm will sell 40 units of output at $P = \text{SAC} = \text{SMC} = \$6$ (point E) and behave as a perfect competitor facing horizontal demand curve AEE^*E' and earning zero profit. Any higher price invites hit-and-run entrants that will quickly bring profits to zero.

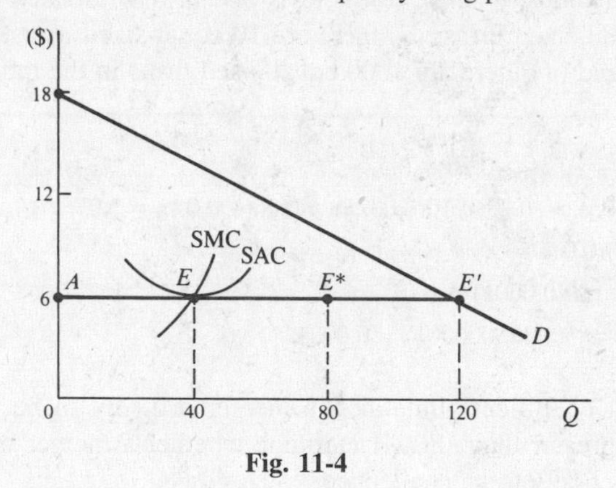

Fig. 11-4

PEAK-LOAD PRICING

11.11 With regard to peak-load pricing indicate (*a*) whether it can be regarded as an application of the marginal principle, (*b*) in which private enterprises it might be applicable, and (*c*) why regulatory commissions have been slow in allowing peak-load pricing for electricity.

(*a*) By equating price to marginal cost, both during peak periods when demand and marginal cost are higher and during off-peak periods when demand and marginal cost are lower, peak-load pricing is an excellent example of the marginal principle.

(*b*) Peak-load pricing is applicable to hotels, restaurants, airlines, movie theaters, and other private enterprises that face a demand that fluctuates sharply and in a predictable way during peak and off-peak periods. These enterprises usually charge lower rates during off-season or in periods of naturally low demand (when marginal costs are lower) than during high season or periods of high demand (when marginal costs are higher).

(*c*) Regulatory commissions have been slow in allowing peak-load pricing for electricity possibly because of inertia or lack of knowledge and because it requires meters to measure consumption at different times of the day, week, or year, and these can be quite expensive to install.

11.12 From the following figure indicate (*a*) how much electricity would be purchased at the uniform price of 3¢ per kilowatt-hour during off-peak and during peak periods, (*b*) how much benefit arises from charging instead the price equal to the marginal cost during the off-peak period, and (*c*) during the peak period.

(*a*) In Fig. 11-5 D_o is the market demand curve for electricity during the off-peak period, while D_p is the higher market demand curve for electricity during the peak period. The short-run marginal cost curve of the firm is given by SMC. At the uniform price of 3¢/kWh at all times (to cover the short-run average cost of both periods together) the firm public utility sells 1 million kWh during the off-peak period (A_o on D_o) and 5 million kWh during peak periods (A_p on D_p).

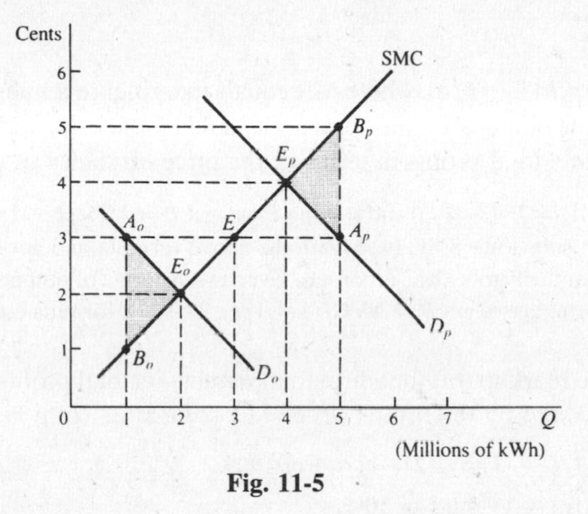

Fig. 11-5

(*b*) At A_o the marginal benefit to consumers from one additional kilowatt-hour (given by the price of 3¢/kWh) exceeds the marginal cost of 1¢ for generating the last kilowatt-hour of electricity produced (given by point B_o on the SMC curve). From the society viewpoint, it would be profitable if the public utility supplied more electricity until $P = \text{SMC} = 2$¢ (point E_o, at which D_o and SMC intersect). The social benefit gained would thus be equal to the shaded triangle $A_oB_oE_o$.

(*c*) At point A_p, the marginal benefit to consumers from one additional kilowatt-hour (given by the price of 3¢/kWh) is smaller than the marginal cost of 5¢ for generating the last kilowatt-hour of electricity produced (point B_p on the SMC curve). From society's point of view, it would pay if the firm supplied less electricity until $P = \text{SMC} = 4$¢ (point E_p, at which D_p and SMC intersect). The social benefit gained (by using the same resources to produce some other service that society values more) would thus be equal to the shaded triangle $B_pA_pE_p$.

11.13 (*a*) Starting from Fig. 11-6 draw a figure showing peak-load pricing when substitution in consumption is taken into consideration. (*b*) Is the benefit of peak-load pricing greater or smaller when substitution in consumption is taken into consideration than when it is not? Why?

(*a*) When substitution in consumption is taken into account, with peak-load pricing, the off-peak demand will be higher and the peak demand will be lower as compared with the case where substitution in consumption is not taken into account. This is shown by D'_o and D'_p, respectively, in Fig. 11-5.

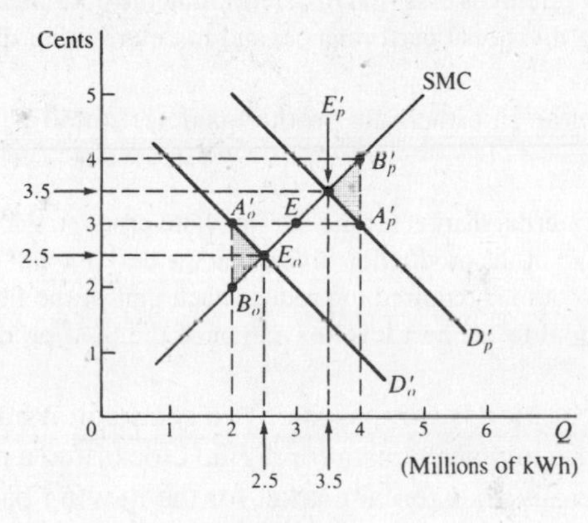

Fig. 11-6

(*b*) The gain in shifting from constant pricing to peak-load pricing (shown by the sum of the two shaded triangles in Fig. 11-6) is smaller when substitution in consumption is taken into account than when it is not. The reason is that the demand curves differ less with peak-load pricing when substitution in consumption is taken into account than when it is not.

COST-PLUS PRICING

11.14 Starting with $\text{MR} = P(1 - 1/e)$, where MR equals marginal revenue, P is commodity price, and e is the price elasticity of the demand for the commodity sold by the firm, derive the formula for the markup that maximizes the firm's total profits in terms of the price elasticity of demand.

Starting from $\text{MR} = P(1 - 1/e)$ and solving P, we get $P = \text{MR}/(1 - 1/e)$. Since profits are maximized where $\text{MR} = \text{SMC}$, we can substitute SMC for MR in the above formula and get $P = \text{SMC}/(1 - 1/e)$.

To the extent that the firm's SMC is constant over a wide range of outputs, $\text{SMC} = \text{AVC}$. Substituting AVC for SMC in the above formula, we get $P = \text{AVC}/(1 - 1/e)$. This last formula equal $P = \text{AVC}(1 + m)$ if $m = 1(e - 1)$.

11.15 What should be the markup (m) for a firm to maximize its total profits if the price elasticity e of demand for the commodity sold by the firm is (*a*) $e = 2$? (*b*) $e = 3$? (*c*) $e = 4$? (*d*) $e = 5$?

(*a*) If $e = 2$, $m = 1/(e - 1) = 1(2 - 1) = 1$ or 100%.

(*b*) If $e = 3$, $m = 1(3 - 1) = 0.5$ or 50%.

(*c*) If $e = 4$, $m = 1/(4 - 1) = 0.33$ or 33%.

(*d*) If $e = 5$, $m = 1/(5 - 1) = 0.25$ or 25%.

TRANSFER PRICING

11.16 (*a*) Explain what has stimulated the growth of the large scale-modern enterprise. (*b*) Indicate what organizational development was introduced in order to contain the tendency toward rising costs. (*c*) Indicate the problem to which this has led. (*d*) Explain why it is important to solve this problem.

(*a*) The growth of the large-scale modern enterprise has been stimulated by economies of scale in production (i.e., by the opportunity of taking advantage of very large cost reductions with large-scale or mass production) and by the tremendous improvements in communications.

(*b*) The rapid rise of the large-scale enterprise has been accompanied by decentralized operations and the establishment of semi-autonomous profit centers in order to contain the tendency toward rising communications and organizational costs.

(*c*) Decentralization and the establishment of semi-autonomous profit centers also led to the transfer pricing problem. Transfer pricing refers to the pricing of intermediate products sold by a semi-autonomous division of the firm and purchased by another semi-autonomous division of the firm.

(*d*) Appropriate transfer pricing is essential in determining the optimal output of each division and of the firm as a whole, in evaluating divisional performance, and in determining divisional rewards.

11.17 Explain how the price of an intermediate product is determined when there is no external market for the product.

In the absence of an external market for the intermediate product, the transfer price for the intermediate product is given by the marginal cost of the production division at the best level of output for the intermediate product. If one unit of the intermediate product is required to produce each unit of the final product, the best level of output of the intermediate product is equal to the best level of output of the final product.

11.18 The Digital Clock Corporation is composed of two semi-autonomous divisions—a production division that manufactures the moving mechanism for digital clocks and a marketing division that assembles and markets the clocks. There is no external market for the moving parts of the clocks manufactured by the production division. The external demand and marginal revenue functions for the finished product (i.e., the clock) sold by the marketing division of the firm are, respectively,

$$Qm = 160 - 10Pm \quad \text{or}$$
$$Pm = 16 - 0.1Qm \quad \text{and}$$
$$MRm = 16 - 0.2Qm$$

The marginal cost functions of the production and marketing divisions of the firm are, respectively

$$MCp = 3 + 0.1Qp \quad \text{and}$$
$$MCm = 1 + 0.1Qm$$

Draw a figure showing (1) the firm's best level of output and price for the finished product (the clock) and (2) the transfer price and output of the intermediate product (the moving parts of the clock).

See Figure 11-7.

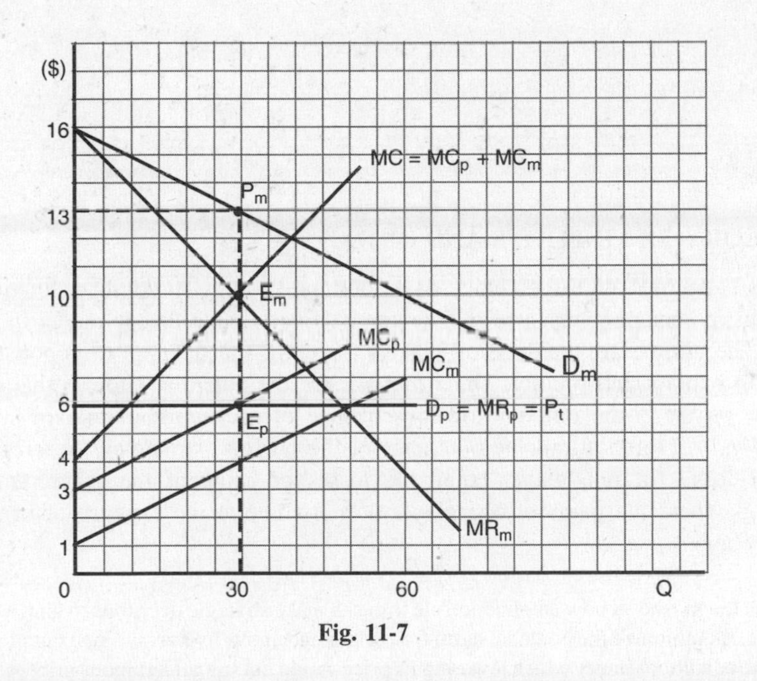

Fig. 11-7

In the figure, MC, the marginal cost of the firm, is equal to the vertical summation of MCp and MCm, the marginal cost curves of the production and the marketing divisions of the firm, respectively. Dm is the external demand for the final product faced by the marketing division of the firm, and MRm is the corresponding marginal revenue curve.

The firm's best level of output of the final product is 30 units and is given by point Em, at which MRm = MC, so that Pm = \$13. Since the production of each unit of the final product requires one unit of the intermediate product, the transfer price for the intermediate product, Pt, is set equal to MCp at Qp = 30. Thus, Pt = \$6. With Dp = MRp = Pt = MCp = \$6 at Qp = 30 (see point Ep), Qp = 30 is the best level of output of the intermediate product for the production division.

CHAPTER 12

Game Theory and Oligopolistic Behavior

12.1 GAME THEORY: DEFINITIONS AND OBJECTIVES

Game theory is concerned with the choice of an optimal strategy in conflict situations and extends the analysis of oligopolistic behavior presented in Chapter 10. Every game theory model includes players, strategies, and payoffs. The *players* are the decision-makers (here, the managers of oligopolist firms) whose behavior we are trying to explain and predict. The *strategies* are the potential choices that can be made by the players (firms). The *payoff* is the outcome or consequence of each combination of strategies by the two players. The *payoff matrix* refers to all the outcomes of the players' strategies. A *zero-sum game* is one in which the gains or losses of one player equal the losses or gains of the other. On the other hand, a *nonzero-sum game* is where the gains of one player do not come at the expense of or are not equal to the losses of the other player.

EXAMPLE 1. Game theory shows how an oligopolistic firm can make strategic decisions to gain a competitive advantage over its rivals or how it can minimize the potential harm from a strategic move by a rival. For example, game theory can help a firm determine (1) the conditions under which lowering its price would not trigger a ruinous price war; (2) whether the firm should build excess capacity to discourage entry into the industry, even though this lowers the firm's short-run profits; and (3) why cheating in a cartel usually leads to its collapse.

12.2 DOMINANT STRATEGY

The *dominant strategy* is the optimal choice for a player, no matter what the opponent does.

EXAMPLE 2. In the payoff matrix in Table 12.1, the first number in each of the four cells refers to the payoff (profit) for firm A, while the second is the payoff (profit) for firm B, if each firm advertises or does not advertise. If firm B does advertise (i.e., moving down the left column of the table), we see that firm A will earn a profit of 4 if it also advertises and 2 if it doesn't. Thus, firm A should advertise if firm B advertises. If firm B doesn't advertise, (i.e., moving down the right column in the table), firm A would earn a profit of 5 if it advertises and 3 if it doesn't. Thus, firm A should advertise whether firm B advertises or not. Advertising is then the dominant strategy for firm A. Moving across each row of the table shows that advertising is also the dominant strategy for firm B.

Table 12.1

		Firm B	
		Advertise	Don't Advertise
Firm A	Advertise	4, 3	5, 1
	Don't Advertise	2, 5	3, 2

12.3 NASH EQUILIBRIUM

The *Nash equilibrium* occurs when each player has chosen his or her optimal strategy, given the strategy chosen by the other player.

EXAMPLE 2. The payoff matrix in Table 12.2 is same as the payoff matrix in Table 12.1, except that the first number in the bottom right cell was changed from 3 to 6. Now firm B has a dominant strategy (as in Example 1) but firm A does not. Thus, if firm B advertises, firm A should also advertise. If firm B does not advertise, firm A earns a profit of 5 if it advertises and 6 if it does not. This might occur, for example, if advertising adds more to firm's A costs than to its revenue. The high-advertising strategy for firm A and firm B is the Nash equilibrium, because given that firm B chooses its dominant strategy of advertising, the optimal strategy for firm A is also to advertise. Not all games have a Nash equilibrium, and some games can have more than one Nash equilibrium (see Problem 12.7).

Table 12.2

		Firm B	
		Advertise	Don't Advertise
Firm A	Advertise	4, 3	5, 1
	Don't Advertise	2, 5	6, 2

12.4 THE PRISONERS' DILEMMA

Prisoners' dilemma refers to the situation where each player adopts his or her dominant strategy but could do better by cooperating. The name comes from the case where two individuals arrested on suspicion of having committed a crime adopt their dominant strategy of confessing and receiving more jail time than if they cooperated (i.e., did not confess). Oligopolistic firms often face an analogous prisoners' dilemma problem in deciding their best business strategy.

EXAMPLE 3. Two suspects are arrested for armed robbery and, if convicted, each could receive a maximum sentence of 10 years imprisonment. Unless one or both suspects confess, however, there is only evidence to convicted them for possessing stolen goods, which carries a maximum sentence of 1 year in prison. Each suspect is interrogated separately and no communication is allowed between them. The district attorney promises each suspect that by confessing, he or she will go free while the other suspect (who does not confess) will receive the full 10-year sentence. If both suspects confess, each gets a reduced sentence of 5 years imprisonment. The (negative) payoff matrix in terms of years of detention is given in Table 12.3.

Table 12.3

		Suspect B	
		Confess	Don't Confess
Suspect A	Confess	5, 5	0, 10
	Don't Confess	10, 0	1, 1

From the table, we see that confessing is the best or dominant strategy for suspect A. The reason is that if suspect B confesses, suspect A revives a 5-year jail sentence if he also confesses and a 10-year sentence if he does not. Similarly, if suspect B does not confess, suspect A goes free if he confesses and receives a 1-year sentence if he does not. Similarly, confessing is also the best or dominant strategy for suspect B. With each suspect adopting his or her dominant strategy of confessing, each ends up receiving a 5-year jail sentence, instead of only a 1-year jail sentence by not confessing. Each suspect, however, is afraid that if he or she does not confess, the other will confess, and so he or she would end up receiving a 10-year jail sentence.

12.5 PRICE AND NONPRICE COMPETITION AND CARTEL CHEATING

Oligopolistic firms often face a prisoners' dilemma problem in deciding on their pricing and advertising strategy, or on whether or not to cheat in a cartel. In these cases, each adopts its dominant strategy but could do better (i.e., earn larger profit) by cooperating (colluding).

EXAMPLE 4. The payoff matrix of Table 12.4 shows that if firm B charged a low price (say, $6), firm A would earn a profit of 2 if it also charged the low price ($6) and 1 if it charged a high price (say, $8). Similarly, if firm B charged a high price ($8), firm A would earn a profit of 5 if it charged the low price and 3 if it charged the high price. Thus, firm A should adopt its dominant strategy of charging the low price. From the payoff matrix of Table 12.4, we see that firm B should also adopt its dominant strategy of charging the low price. However, both firms could do better (i.e., earn the higher profit of 3) if they cooperated and both charged the high price (the bottom right cell). Thus, the firms are in a prisoners' dilemma: each firm will charge the low price and earn a smaller profit because if it charges the high price, it cannot trust its rival to also charge the high price.

Table 12.4

		Firm B	
		Low Price	High Price
Firm A	Low Price	2, 2	5, 1
	High Price	1, 5	3, 3

12.6 REPEATED GAMES AND TIT-FOR-TAT STRATEGY

The best strategy for repeated or multiple-move prisoners' dilemma games is tit-for-tat. This strategy postulates that each firm should start by cooperating and continue to do so as long as the rival cooperates, but stop cooperating once the rival stops cooperating.

12.7 STRATEGIC BEHAVIOR

Oligopolists often make strategic moves. A strategic move is one in which a player constrains its own behavior in order to make a threat credible so as to gain a competitive advantage over a rival. The firm making the threat must be committed to carrying it out for the threat to be credible. This may involve accepting lower profits or building excess capacity. Most real-world business decisions are made in the face of risk or uncertainty and this greatly complicates the development and conduct of a business strategy by the firm.

Glossary

Dominant strategy The optimal strategy for a player no matter what the other player does.

Game theory The theory that examines the choice of optimal strategies in conflict situations.

Nash equilibrium The situation when each player has chosen his or her optimal strategy, *given the strategy chosen by the other player.*

Nonzero-sum game A game where the gains of one a player does not come at the expense of or are not equal to the losses of the other.

Payoff The outcome or consequence of each combination of strategies by the players in game theory.

Payoff matrix The table of all the outcomes of the players' strategies.

Players The decision-makers in the theory of games (here the oligopolistic firms or its managers) whose behavior we are trying to explain and predict.

Prisoners' dilemma The situation where each player adopts his or her dominant strategy but could do better by cooperating.

Repeated games Prisoners' dilemma games of more than one move.

Strategic move A player's strategy of constraining his or her own behavior to make a threat credible so as to gain a competitive advantage.

Strategies The potential choices that can be made by the players (firms) in the theory of games.

Tit-for-tat The best strategy in repeated prisoners' dilemma games which postulates "do to your opponent what he or she has just done to you".

Zero-sum game A game where the gains of one player equals the losses of the other (so that total gains plus total losses sum to zero).

Review Questions

1. Game theory (*a*) examines the choice of optimal strategies in conflict situations, (*b*) seeks to predict the behavior of players, (*c*) can be used to analyze oligopolistic interdependence, (*d*) all of the above.

   Ans. (*d*) See Section 12.1.

2. A dominant strategy refers to the strategy that a player in a game chooses (*a*) independently of the strategy of the other player, (*b*) given the strategy of the other player, (*c*) in Nash equilibrium, (*d*) in a cartel.

   Ans. (*a*) See Section 12.2.

3. Which of the following statements is correct? (*a*) a dominant strategy equilibrium is always a Nash equilibrium, (*b*) a dominant strategy equilibrium can be a Nash equilibrium, (*c*) a Nash equilibrium is also a dominant strategy equilibrium, (*d*) a Nash equilibrium cannot be a dominant strategy equilibrium.

   Ans. (*a*) See Sections 12.2 and 12.3.

4. All games always have (*a*) a single dominant strategy, (*b*) multiple dominant strategies, (*c*) a single Nash equilibrium, (*d*) none of the above.

   Ans. (*d*) See Sections 12.2 and 12.3.

5. In a prisoners' dilemma (*a*) each player has a dominant strategy, (*b*) the players are not in Nash equilibrium, (*c*) the players cannot do better by cooperating, (*d*) none of the above.

   Ans. (*a*) See Section 12.4.

6. The prisoners' dilemma can be used to analyze (*a*) price competition, (*b*) advertising expenditures by rival firms, (*c*) product style changes, and (*d*) all of the above.

   Ans. (*d*) See Section 12.5.

7. For a prisoners' dilemma to occur it is sufficient (*a*) for each player to have a dominant strategy, (*b*) for both players to be in Nash equilibrium, (*c*) for each player to adopt its dominant strategy but to be able to do better by cooperation, (*d*) all of the above.

Ans. (*c*) See Sections 12.4 and 12.5.

8. One disadvantage of the analysis of the prisoners' dilemma is that it (*a*) refers to a one-move game only, (*b*) does not lead the players to maximize gains, (*c*) only applies to economics, (*d*) cannot be overcome by cooperation.

Ans. (*a*) See Section 12.6.

9. The best strategy for repeated prisoners' dilemma games is (*a*) tit-for-tat, (*b*) the dominant strategy, (*c*) the Nash equilibrium, (*d*) the Cournot solution.

Ans. (*a*) See Section 12.6.

10. Tit-for-tat refers to the game theory rule that (*a*) you should cooperate as long as your rival cooperates, (*b*) you should not cooperate when your rival does not cooperate, (*c*) is best to follow in repeated games, (*d*) all of the above.

Ans. (*d*) See Section 12.6.

11. The following condition is required for tit-for-tat to be the best strategy in repeated prisoners' dilemma games: (*a*) there must be a reasonably stable set of players, preferably two, (*b*) each firm must be able to quickly detect cheating by other firms, (*c*) demand and cost conditions must be relatively stable (*d*) the number of moves must be infinite, or at least a very large and uncertain, (*e*) all of the above.

Ans. (*e*) See Section 12.6.

12. A strategic move refers to all the following except (*a*) a Nash equilibrium, (*b*) making a credible threat, (*c*) adopting policies to deter entrance into the market, (*d*) making a preventive investment.

Ans. (*a*) See Section 12.7.

Solved Problems

GAME THEORY

12.1 Explain in what way game theory extends the analysis of oligopolistic behavior presented in Chapter 10.

Game theory offers many insights into oligopolistic interdependence and the strategic behavior of oligopolistic firms that could not be examined with the traditional tools of analysis presented in Chapter 10. Specifically, game theory is used to identify all the possible responses of a competitor to the actions of an oligopolist and on how the oligopolist can choose the best strategy or choice open to it.

12.2 Indicate (*a*) whether game theory can be used only for oligopolistic interdependence and (*b*) in what way game theory is similar to playing chess.

(*a*) Game theory is a general theory that can be used to analyze the choice of optimal strategies in any conflict situation, not just oligopolistic interdependence. For example, it can be used in deciding the optimal amount of defense expenditures in the face of the nation's desire for defense and in light of the possible responses that its defense expenditures elicit in the defense expenditures of other nations.

(*b*) Game theory is similar to playing chess in the sense that both involve players, strategies, and payoffs. Specifically, they both involve the choice of optimal strategies in conflict situations.

DOMINANT STRATEGY AND NASH EQUILIBRIUM

12.3 From the payoff matrix in Table 12.5, where the payoffs are the profits or losses of the two firms, determine (*a*) whether firm A has a dominant strategy, (*b*) whether firm B has a dominant strategy (*c*) the optimal strategy for each firm.

Table 12.5

		Firm B	
		Low Price	High Price
Firm A	Low Price	1, 1	3, −1
	High Price	−1, 3	2, 2

(*a*) When firm B charges a low price, firm A will earn a profit of 1 when it also charges a low price and a profit of −1 (i.e., a loss of 1) when it charges a high price. Similarly, when firm B charges a high price, firm A earns a profit of 3 when it charges a low price and a profit of 2 when it charges a high price. Therefore, charging a low price is the dominant strategy for firm A.

(*b*) When firm A charges a low price, firm B earns a profit of 1 when it also charges a low price and a profit of −1 when it charges a high price. Similarly, when firm A charges a high price, firm B earns a profit of 3 when it charges a low price and a profit of 2 when it charges a high price. Therefore, charging a low price is also the dominant strategy for firm B.

(*c*) The optimal strategy for each firm is to adopt its dominant strategy of charging a low price.

12.4 Explain whether or not there is a Nash equilibrium when each firm chooses its dominant strategy.

When each firm chooses its dominant strategy (assuming they have one), we automatically have a Nash equilibrium without even the need for each firm to consider the strategy of its rival.

12.5 (*a*) Indicate whether the Cournot equilibrium is a Nash equilibrium and (*b*) in what way the Cournot equilibrium differs from the Nash equilibrium given in Table 12.2.

(*a*) The Cournot equilibrium is a Nash equilibrium because each firm has adopted its optimal output given its rival's output.

(*b*) The Cournot equilibrium differs from the Nash equilibrium given in Table 12.2 because in the Cournot equilibrium neither firm has a dominant strategy, while in Table 12.2, firm B has a dominant strategy, but firm A does not.

12.6 From the payoff matrix in Table 12.6, where the payoffs are the profits or losses of the two firms, determine (*a*) whether firm A has a dominant strategy, (*b*) whether firm B has a dominant strategy, (*c*) the optimal strategy for each firm, and the Nash equilibrium, if there is one.

Table 12.6

		Firm B	
		Low Price	High Price
Firm A	Low Price	1, 1	3, −1
	High Price	1, 3	4, 2

(*a*) When firm B charges a low price, firm A will earn a profit of 1 when it also charges a low price and a profit of −1 (i.e., a loss of 1) when it charges a high price. When firm B charges a high price, firm A earns a profit of 3 when it charges a low price and a profit of 4 when it charges a high price. Therefore, firm A does not have a dominant strategy.

(*b*) When firm A charges a low price, firm B earns a profit of 1 when it also charges a low price and a profit of -1 when it charges a high price. Similarly, when firm A charges a high price, firm B earns a profit of 3 when it charges a low price and a profit of 2 when it charges a high price. Therefore, charging a low price is the dominant strategy for firm B.

(*c*) The optimal strategy for firm B is its dominant strategy of charging a low price. The optimal strategy for firm A is a low price, *given that firm B will charge a low price.*

(*d*) The Nash equilibrium occurs when each firm charges a low price.

12.7 From the payoff matrix of Table 12.7, where the payoffs are the profits or losses of the two firms, determine (*a*) whether firm A has a dominant strategy, (*b*) whether firm B has a dominant strategy, (*c*) the optimal strategy for each firm, and (*d*) the Nash equilibrium. (*e*) Under what conditions is the situation indicated in the payoff matrix likely to occur?

Table 12.7

		Firm B	
		Small Cars	Large Cars
Firm A	Small Cars	4, 4	−2, −2
	Large Cars	−2, −2	4, 4

(*a*) If firm B produces small cars, firm A will earn a profit of 4 if it produces small cars and has a payoff of -2 (i.e., incurs a loss of 2) if it produces large cars. If firm B produces large cars, firm A will incur a loss of 2 if its also produces small cars and it earns of profit of 4 if it produces small cars. Therefore, firm A does not have a dominant strategy.

(*b*) If firm A produces small cars, firm B will earn a profit of 4 if it also produces small cars and has a payoff of -2 (i.e., incurs a loss of 2) if it produces large cars. If firm A produces large cars, firm B will incur a loss of 2 if it produces small cars and it earns a profit of 4 if it produces large cars. Therefore, firm B does not have a dominant strategy.

(*c*) The optimal strategy is for both firms to produce either small cars or large cars. In that case, each firm earns a profit of 4. If one firm produces small cars and the other produces large cars, both will incur a loss of 2.

(*d*) In this case we have two Nash equilibria: both firms either produce small cars (the top left cell in the given payoff matrix) or both firms produce large cars (the bottom right cell in the payoff matrix).

(*e*) A situation such as that indicated in the payoff matrix of this problem might arise if each firm does not have the resources to invest in the plant and equipment necessary to produce both large and small cars, and the demand for either small or large cars is not sufficient to justify the production of small or large cars by both firms.

THE PRISONERS' DILEMMA

12.8 Explain in what way the prisoners' dilemma is related to the choice of dominant strategies by the players in a game and to the concept of Nash equilibrium.

In the prisoners' dilemma, each prisoner (player or firm) has a dominant strategy and chooses that dominant strategy. When each player chooses his optimal strategy, we automatically have a Nash equilibrium, but the players could do better by cooperating.

12.9 Explain (*a*) how the concept of the prisoners' dilemma can be used to analyze price competition, (*b*) how introducing yearly style changes can lead to a prisoners' dilemma for automakers, (*c*) what is the incentive for the members of a cartel to cheat on the cartel.

(*a*) The concept of the prisoners' dilemma is useful in explaining the type of price competition in which each firm adopts its dominant strategy of charging a high or low price but could do better by cooperating and doing the opposite (i.e., charging a low or high price, respectively).

(*b*) Auto makers face a prisoners' dilemma in introducing yearly style changes if each auto maker introduces yearly style changes only to avoid losing a great deal of sales, but introducing yearly style changes reduces every auto maker's profit.

(*c*) Each member of a cartel has an incentive to cheat because by cheating it can increase its profits over and above those that it would receive without cheating. However, when every cartel member cheats, each will earn less profit than if no member cheated.

12.10 Explain whether or not the duopolists in a Cournot equilibrium face a prisoners' dilemma.

The duopolists in a Cournot equilibrium do face a prisoners' dilemma because each adopts its dominant strategy but could do better by coordination (i.e., by choosing to jointly produce the monopoly output and share equally in the higher profits).

12.11 Explain how the 1971 law that banned cigarette advertising on television solved the prisoners' dilemma for cigarette producers.

Before the 1971 law that banned cigarette advertising on television, each producer spent too much on advertising and this cut into its profits. Yet, no producer would unilaterally reduce its advertising because others would then have an incentive to continue advertising heavily to increase their market share and profits. While the 1971 law that banned TV cigarette advertising was intended to discourage smoking (and to some extent the law achieved its purpose), it also had the unintended effect of solving the prisoners' dilemma for cigarette producers. Specifically, by being forced to reduce TV advertising, cigarette producers were able to reduce costs and increase profits—something that they had been unable to do on their own.

12.12 From the payoff matrix of Table 12.8, where the payoffs (the negative values) are the years of possible imprisonment for individuals A and B, determine (*a*) whether individual A has a dominant strategy, (*b*) whether individual B has a dominant strategy, (*c*) the optimal strategy for each individual. (*d*) Do individuals A and B face a prisoners' dilemma?

Table 12.8

		Individual B	
		Confess	Don't Confess
Individual A	Confess	−5, −5	−1, −10
	Don't Confess	−10, −1	−2, −2

(*a*) Individual A has the dominant strategy of confessing because if individual B confesses, individual A gets a 5-year sentence if he also confesses and a 10-year sentence if he does not. Similarly, if individual B does not confess, individual A gets a 1-year sentence if he confesses and a 2-year sentence if he does not confess.

(*b*) For individual B the dominant strategy is also to confess because if individual A confesses, individual B gets a 5-year sentence if he also confesses and a 10-year sentence if he does not. Similarly, if individual A does not confess, individual B gets a 1-year sentence if he confesses and a 2-year sentence if he does not confess.

(*c*) The optimal strategy for each individual is to adopt his dominant strategy, which is to confess.

(*d*) Individuals A and B face the prisoners' dilemma. That is, when each individual adopts his dominant strategy of confessing, each gets a 5-year sentence. However, if each did not confess, each would get a 2-year sentence only.

PRICE AND NONPRICE COMPETITION AND CARTEL CHEATING

12.13 Explain why the payoff matrix in Problem 12.3 indicates that firms A and B face the prisoners' dilemma.

We have seen in the answer to Problem 12.3(c) that each firm adopts its dominant strategy of charging the low price and earns a profit of 1 (see the top left cell of the payoff matrix in Problem 12.3(c). Each firm, however, would earn a profit of 2 if each charged a high price (see the bottom right cell). But that could only be achieved through cooperation. Thus, firms A and B face the prisoners' dilemma.

12.14 Do firms A and B in Problem 12.6 face the prisoners' dilemma? Why?

Even though the payoff matrix in Problem 12.6 shows that firm B has a dominant strategy while firm A does not, both firms still face the prisoners' dilemma. As we have seen in the answer to Problem 12.6, firm B adopts its dominant strategy of charging a low price. The optimal strategy for firm A is then also to charge a low price. When each firm charges a low price, each earns a profit of 1 (the top left cell of the payoff matrix of Problem 12.6). If both firms charged a high price, however, firm A could earn a profit of 4 and firm B a profit of 2. Thus, the firms face the prisoners' dilemma.

12.15 From the payoff matrix of Table 12.9, where the payoffs refer to the profits that firms A and B earn by cheating and not cheating in a cartel, (*a*) determine whether firms A and B face the prisoners' dilemma. (*b*) What would happen if we changed the payoff in bottom left cell to (5, 5)?

Table 12.9

		Firm B	
		Cheat	Don't Cheat
Firm A	Cheat	4, 3	8, 1
	Don't Cheat	2, 6	6, 5

(*a*) Each firm adopts its dominant strategy of cheating (the top left cell), but could do better by cooperating not to cheat (the bottom right cell). Thus the firms face the prisoners' dilemma.

(*b*) If the payoff in the bottom right cell were changed to (5, 5), the firms would still face the prisoners' dilemma by cheating.

REPEATED GAMES AND TIT-FOR-TAT STRATEGY

12.16 (*a*) What is the meaning of "tit-for-tat" in game theory? (*b*) What conditions are usually required for tit-for-tat strategy to be the best strategy?

(*a*) Tit-for-tat is the best strategy in repeated or multiple-move prisoners' dilemma games. It postulates that each firm should begin by cooperating and cooperate as long as the rival cooperates and refuse to cooperate when the rival does not cooperate.

(*b*) The following conditions are usually required for tit-for-tat to be the best strategy: (1) there must be a reasonably stable set of players; (2) the number of players must be small, preferably two; (3) each firm must be able to quickly detect (and be willing and able to quickly retaliate for) cheating by other firms; (4) demand and cost conditions must be relatively stable; (5) the number of moves must be infinite, or at least a very large and *uncertain*.

12.17 Starting with the payoff matrix of Problem 12.3, show what the tit-for-tat strategy would be for the first five of an infinite number of games, if firm A starts by cooperating but firm B does not cooperate in the next period.

The tit-for-tat strategy for the first 5 of an infinite number of games for the payoff matrix of Problem 12.3, when firm A begins by cooperating but firm B does not cooperate in the next period is given by Table 12.10:

Table 12.10

Period	Firm A	Firm B
1	2	2
2	−1	3
3	1	1
4	3	−1
5	2	2

Table 12.10 shows that in the first period, firm A sets a high price (i.e., cooperates) and so does firm B (so that each firm earns a profit of 2). If in the second period firm B does not cooperate and sets a low price while firm A is still cooperating and setting a high price, firm B earns a profit of 3 and firm A incurs a loss of 1. In the third period, firm A retaliates and also sets a low price. As a result, each firm earns a profit of only 1 in period 3. In period 4, firm B cooperates again by setting a high price. With firm A still setting a low price, firm A earns a profit of 3 while firm B incurs a loss of 1. In the fifth period, firm A also cooperates again and sets a high price. Since both firms are now setting a high price, each earns a profit of 2.

STRATEGIC BEHAVIOR

12.18 Given the payoff matrix of Table 12.11 (*a*) indicate the best strategy for each firm. (*b*) Why is the entry-deterrent threat by firm A to lower price not credible to firm B? (*c*) What could firm A do to make its threat credible without building excess capacity?

Table 12.11

		Firm B	
		Enter	Don't Enter
Firm A	Low Price	3, −1	3, 1
	High Price	4, 5	6, 3

(*a*) From the payoff matrix of the problem, we see that firm A adopts its dominant strategy of charging a high price and firm B enters the market and also charges a high price. Thus, firm A earns a profit of 4 and firm B earns a profit of 5.

(*b*) The threat by firm A to lower price should not discourage firm B from entering the market because the threat is not credible. The reason is that firm A earns a profit of 3 if it charges the low price and a profit of 4 if it charges the high price.

(*c*) Short of building excess capacity, firm A can make its threat credible by cultivating a reputation for aggressively fending off entry into the market by lowering price (and thus imposing a loss on the potential entrant), even if this means lower profits.

12.19 Show how the payoff matrix in the table of Problem 12.17 might change for firm A to make a credible threat to lower price by building excess capacity to deter firm B from entering the market.

Table 12.12 shows that by building excess capacity, firm A can make a credible threat to lower price, which would deter firm B from entering the market.

Table 12.12

		Firm B	
		Enter	Do Not Enter
Firm A	Low Price	3, 1	3, 1
	High Price	2, 5	5, 3

The payoff matrix of Table 12.12 is the same as in Problem 12.18, except that firm A's profits are now lower when it charges a high price because idle or excess capacity increases firm's A costs without increasing its sales. On the other hand, we assume that charging a low price would allow firm A to increase sales and utilize its newly built capacity so that costs and revenues increase leaving firm A's profits the same as in Problem 12.18 (i.e., the same as before firm A expanded capacity). Building excess capacity in anticipation of future need now becomes a credible threat because with excess capacity, firm A will charge a low price and earn a profit of 3 instead of a profit of 2 if it charged the high price. Firm B would then incur a loss of 1 if it entered the market and would thus stay out. Entry deterrence is now credible and effective.

12.20 (*a*) How is a strategic move differentiated from a Nash equilibrium? (*b*) What is a credible threat? When is a threat not credible? (*c*) What is the greatest difficulty in deciding and implementing a business strategy on the part of the firm?

(*a*) A Nash equilibrium refers to the situation when each player is adopting the best strategy, given what the other player is doing. On the other hand, a strategic move refers to a player's strategy of constraining his own behavior to make a threat credible so as to gain a competitive advantage. This means even accepting lower profits, which is not a Nash equilibrium.

(*b*) A threat is credible if it is believed. This occurs if the threat is backed by a commitment that the rival player believes the firm making the threat will carry out even if at the cost of lower profits.

(*c*) Most real-world business decisions are made in the face of risk or uncertainty. Specifically, a firms often does not know the exact payoff or outcome of the strategic moves open to it and this greatly complicates the development and conduct of a business strategy by the firm.

CHAPTER 13

Input Pricing and Employment

Broadly speaking, the price of an input is determined, just as the price of a final commodity, by the interaction of the market demand and supply. The first and crucial step in obtaining the market demand curve for an input is to derive the demand curve of a single firm for the input. The firm will use the amount of the input that will maximize its total profits. We shall consider three combinations of product and input market organizations.

Perfect Competition in the Product and Input Markets

13.1 PROFIT MAXIMIZATION AND LEAST-COST INPUT COMBINATIONS

In order for a firm to maximize its total profits, it must produce its best level of output with the best (least-cost) input combination. This double condition is satisfied when

$$\frac{\mathrm{MP}_a}{P_a} = \frac{\mathrm{MP}_b}{P_b} = \frac{1}{\mathrm{MC}_x} = \frac{1}{P_x}$$

where MP = marginal product, P = price, MC = marginal cost; A and B are inputs and X is the final commodity (see Problem 13.2).

13.2 THE DEMAND CURVE OF THE FIRM FOR ONE VARIABLE INPUT

A profit-maximizing firm will employ an input as long as the extra income from the sale of the output produced by the input is larger than the extra cost of hiring the input. If input A is the only variable input used by the firm to produce commodity X, the extra income or *marginal revenue product* of input A (MRP_a) is given by the marginal product of input A (MP_a) times the marginal revenue of the firm (MR_x). That is, $\mathrm{MRP}_a = \mathrm{MP}_a \cdot \mathrm{MR}_x$.

If the firm is a perfect competitor in the product market, $\mathrm{MR}_x = \mathrm{P}_x$ and $\mathrm{MRP}_a = \mathrm{VMP}_a$ (the *value of the marginal product* of input A). That is, $\mathrm{VMP}_a = \mathrm{MP}_a \cdot \mathrm{P}_x = \mathrm{MP}_a \cdot \mathrm{P}_x = \mathrm{MRP}_a$. As more units of input A are hired, the MP_a, and thus the MRP_a, eventually decline. The declining portion of the MRP_a schedule is the firm's demand schedule for input A.

EXAMPLE 1. In Table 13.1, column (1) shows the units of input A (the only variable input) used by the firm. Column (2) gives the total quantities of commodity X produced. Column (3) refers to the change in total output per unit change in the use of input A. The MP_a declines because we are in stage II of production (the only relevant stage), where the law of diminishing returns is operating. Column (4) gives MR_x; $MR_x = P_x$ and remains constant because of perfect competition in the commodity market. Column (5) is obtained by multiplying each value of column (3) by the value in column (4). The MRP_a declines because the MP_a declines. Column (6) gives the price at which the firm purchases input A; P_a remains constant because of perfect competition in the input market. In order to maximize profits, the firm will hire more units of input A as long as the $MRP_a > P_a$ and until $MRP_a = P_a$. Thus, this firm will hire seven units of input A. When columns (5) and (1) of Table 13.1 are plotted, we get this firm's MRP_a curve. This is the firm's demand curve for input A, d_a (see Problem 13.4).

Table 13.1

(1) q_a	(2) q_x	(3) MP_a	(4) $MR_x = P_x$	(5) $MRP_a = VMP_a$	(6) P_a
3	6	..	\$10	..	\$20
4	11	5	10	\$50	20
5	15	4	10	40	20
6	18	3	10	30	20
7	20	2	10	20	20
8	21	1	10	10	20

13.3 THE DEMAND CURVE OF THE FIRM FOR ONE OF SEVERAL VARIABLE INPUTS

When input A is only one of several variable inputs, the MRP_a no longer represents the firm's demand curve for input A. The reason for this is that, given the price of the other variable inputs, a change in the price of input A will bring about changes in the quantity used of these other variable inputs. These changes, in turn, cause the entire MRP_a curve of the firm to shift. The quantities of input A demanded by the firm at different prices of input A will then be given by points on *different* MRP_a curves.

EXAMPLE 2. Suppose that a firm is initially producing its best level of output with the least-cost combination of variable inputs and is using three units of input A at $P_a = \$8$ (point A on the MRP_a curve in Fig. 13-1). If, for some reason, P_a falls from \$8 to \$4 in the face of *constant prices* for other variable inputs, the firm will want to hire more units of input A, since the $MRP_a > P_a$ now. But as this occurs, the MP curve (and thus the MRP curve) of variable inputs *complementary* to input A will shift to the right, and the firm will hire more of these complementary inputs at their given prices. In addition, the MP curve (and thus the MRP curve) of variable inputs which are *substitutes* for input A will shift to the left, so the firm will purchase fewer of these inputs at their given prices. *Both of these effects will cause this firm's* MP_a *and* MRP_a *curves to shift to the right*, as the firm attempts to maximize profits and reestablish a least-cost combination of inputs. This shift in the firm's MRP_a curve as P_a changes is referred to as the *internal effect* (i.e., the effect internal to the firm) resulting from the change in P_a.

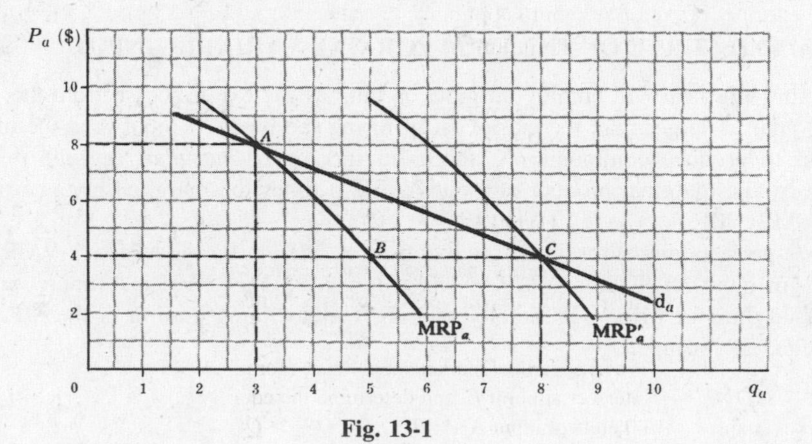

Fig. 13-1

Thus, if the firm's MRP_a curve shifts to MRP'_a as P_a falls from \$8 to \$4 (see Fig. 13-1), the firm will increase the quantity it uses of input A from three units (point A on the MRP_a curve) to eight units (point C on the MRP'_a curve). Point A and point C are then two points on this firm's demand curve for input A. Other points could be obtained in a similar way. Joining these points, we get this firm's demand curve for input A (d_a in Fig. 13-1).

13.4 THE MARKET DEMAND CURVE FOR AN INPUT

We cannot get the market demand curve for input A by simply summing horizontally the individual firms' demand curves for input A. A so-called *external effect* on the firm resulting from the reduction in the price of input A must also be considered. That is, d_a in Fig. 13-1 was drawn on the assumption that the price at which the firm sells commodity X remains constant. However, when P_a falls, all firms producing commodity X will increase their quantity of input A demanded, and produce more of commodity X. This will increase the market supply of commodity X, and given the market demand for X, will result in a fall in P_x. This fall in P_x will cause a leftward shift in the firm's MRP_a curves and thus in d_a. It is the quantity of input A demanded by each firm on this lower d_a that is summed to get the market quantity demanded of input A when P_a falls.

EXAMPLE 3. In Fig. 13-2, d_a is the same as in Fig. 13-1. When $P_a = \$8$, the firm demands three units of input A (point A on d_a). If there are 100 identical firms demanding input A, we get point A' on D_a. When P_a falls to \$4, each firm using input A will expand its use of input A. Thus, QS_x increases and P_x falls. This shifts d_a to the left, say to d'_a, and the firm demands six units of input A at $P_a = \$4$ (point E on d'_a). With 100 identical firms in the market, we get point E' on D_a. Other points can be similarly obtained. By joining these points, we get D_a.

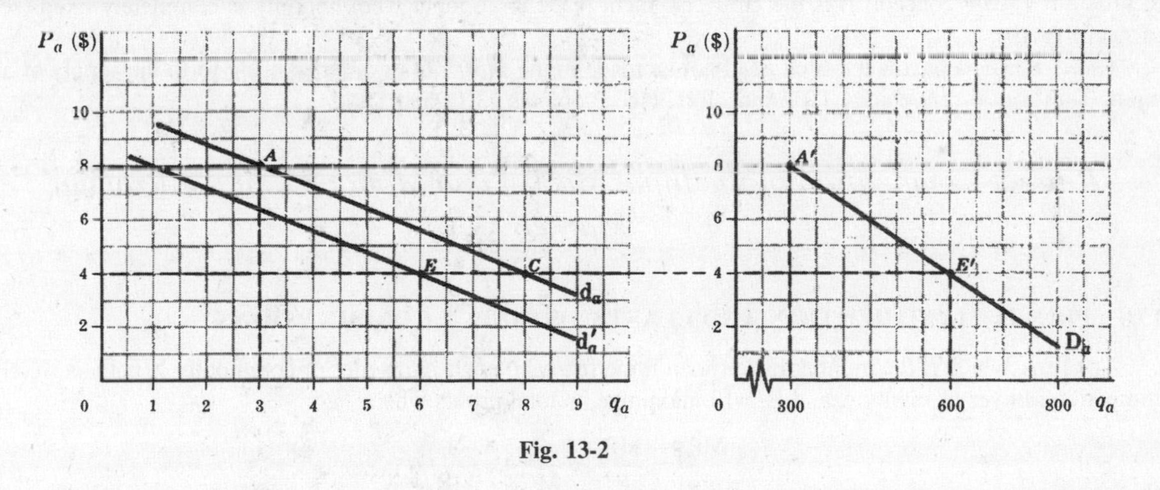

Fig. 13-2

13.5 THE MARKET SUPPLY CURVE FOR AN INPUT

The market supply curve of an input is obtained by the straightforward horizontal summation of the supply curve of the individual suppliers of the input. Thus, the supply curve of the input to an individual firm is infinitely elastic. The market supply curve of an input is usually positively sloped, however, indicating that greater quantities of the input will be placed on the market only at higher input prices. (For a discussion of a "backward-bending" supply curve of labor, see Problem 13.9.)

13.6 PRICING AND LEVEL OF EMPLOYMENT OF AN INPUT

Just as in the case of a final commodity, the equilibrium price of an input and the quantity of it employed are determined at the intersection of the market demand curve and the market supply curve for the input.

EXAMPLE 4. In Fig. 13-3, S_a is a hypothetical market supply curve for input A, while D_a is the market demand curve for input A of Fig. 13-2; D_a and S_a intersect at point E' and determine the equilibrium market price of \$4 for input A and the equilibrium market quantity of 600 units of input A. At $P_a > \$4$, $QS_a > QD_a$ and P_a falls. At $P_a < \$4$, $QD_a > QS_a$ and P_a

rises. If there are 100 identical and perfectly competitive firms purchasing input A, each buys six units of input A at $P_a = \$4$ (see point E on d'_a in Fig. 13-2).

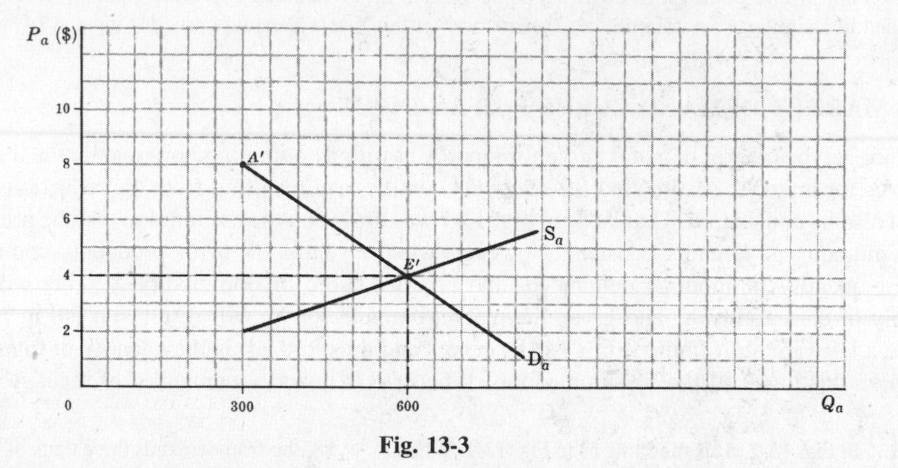

Fig. 13-3

13.7 RENT AND QUASI-RENT

Any payment for an input over and above the minimum amount needed to bring forth its supply is *rent*. Rent is a *long-run* concept; it is the entire payment made to an input whose supply is completely fixed (see Problem 13.10).

Quasi-rent is a payment which need not be made in the *short run* in order to bring forth the supply of an input. Thus, quasi-rent equals TR minus TVC (see Problems 13.11 and 13.12).

Perfect Competition in the Input Market and Monopoly in the Product Market

13.8 PROFIT MAXIMIZATION AND LEAST-COST INPUT COMBINATIONS

The firm, which is the monopolistic (or an imperfectly competitive) seller of commodity X but a perfectly competitive buyer of inputs A and B, will maximize its total profits when

$$\frac{\mathrm{MP}_a}{P_a} = \frac{\mathrm{MP}_b}{P_b} = \frac{1}{\mathrm{MC}_x} = \frac{1}{\mathrm{MR}_x}$$

(see Problems 13.13 and 13.14).

13.9 THE DEMAND CURVE OF THE FIRM FOR ONE VARIABLE INPUT

When input A is the only variable input for the monopolistic seller of commodity X, the firm's demand curve for input A is given by its MRP_a curve, which now lies below the VMP_a curve because MR_x is smaller than P_x. The $\mathrm{MRP}_a = \mathrm{MP}_a \cdot \mathrm{MR}_x$ and measures the change in the monopolist's TR in selling the output of commodity X that results from the employment of one additional unit of input A.

EXAMPLE 5. The first three columns of Table 13.2 are the same as in Table 13.1. Column (4) gives the declining prices at which the monopolist can sell increasing quantities of commodity X. The TR_x values of column (5) are obtained by multiplying Q_x by P_x. The MRP_a values of column (6) are then obtained from the difference between successive TR_x values of column (5). That is, the MRP_a measures the change in the monopolist's TR in selling the output of commodity X that results from the employment of one additional unit of input A (together with fixed quantities of other inputs). More briefly, $\mathrm{MRP}_a = \Delta\mathrm{TR}_x/\Delta q_a$. The MRP_a is also equal to the MP_a times the MR_x (see Problem 13.15). With monopoly (or imperfect competition) in the product market, $\mathrm{MR}_x < P_x$ and so $\mathrm{MRP}_a = \mathrm{MP}_a \cdot \mathrm{MR}_x < \mathrm{MP}_a \cdot P_x = \mathrm{VMP}_a$. The MRP_a values in column (6) fall because both the MP_a and the MR_x fall. *Columns* (6) *and* (1) *of Table 2 represent the demand schedule* *of* input A *for the monopolist seller of commodity* X, *when* input A *is the only variable* input. The P_a values of \$21 in column (7) remain constant because we are assuming here that the monopolist seller of commodity X is a perfectly competitive buyer of input A. In order to maximize its total profits, this firm will hire more units of input A as long as the $\text{MRP}_a > P_a$ and up to the point where the $\text{MRP}_a = P_a$. Thus, the firm will hire five units of input A.

Table 13.2

(1) q_a	(2) Q_x	(3) MP_a	(4) P_x (\$)	(5) TR_x (\$)	(6) MRP_a (\$)	(7) P_a (\$)
3	6		10	60		21
4	11	5	9	99	39	21
5	15	4	8	120	21	21
6	18	3	7	126	6	21
7	20	2	6	120	−6	21
8	21	1	5	105	−15	21

EXAMPLE 6. Fig. 13-4 shows the typical shape of a firm's MRP curve for input A. When input A is its only variable input, and the firm is a monopolist (or an imperfect competitor) in the product market, then the MRP_a curve is the firm's demand curve for input A. If the firm is a perfectly competitive buyer of input A, it will purchase two units of input A when $P_a = \$8$ (point *A* in Fig. 13-4). Thus at point *A*, $P_a = \$8 = \text{MRP}_a < \text{VMP}_a$. If P_a falls to \$4, the firm will increase the quantity it uses of input A from two to three units (point *B*). Thus at point *B*, $P_a = \$4 = \text{MRP}_a < \text{VMP}_a$. The excess of the VMP_a over the corresponding MRP_a when the firm is in equilibrium is sometimes referred to as *monopolistic exploitation* (see Problem 13.16).

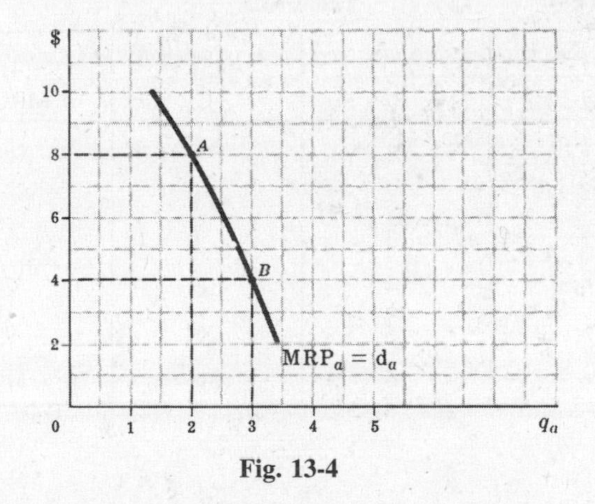

Fig. 13-4

13.10 THE DEMAND CURVE OF THE FIRM FOR ONE OF SEVERAL VARIABLE INPUTS

When input A is only one of several variable inputs, then the MRP_a curve no longer represents the firm's demand curve for input A. We can derive d_a by considering the *internal effect* on the firm that results from changes in P_a. This internal effect is the same as described in Example 2.

13.11 THE MARKET DEMAND CURVE AND INPUT PRICING

If all the firms demanding input A are monopolists in their respective commodity markets, then the market demand curve for input A (D_a) is obtained very simply by the straightforward horizontal summation of each monopolist's demand curve for input A (d_a). On the other hand, if the firms demanding input A are monopolistic competitors or oligopolists, in order to go from the firms' to the market demand curve for input A, we must consider the *external effect* on the firms resulting from changes in P_a. (See Section 13.14.)

The equilibrium market price and employment level of input A are determined at the intersection of the market demand curve and the market supply curve of input A, as described in Section 13.6 and Example 4. Each perfectly competitive buyer of input A will then hire input A as long as the MRP_a (on the firm's appropriate MRP_a and d_a curves) exceeds P_a and until $MRP_a = P_a$.

Monopsony

13.12 INPUT SUPPLY CURVE AND MARGINAL RESOURCE COSTS

Monopsony refers to the case where there is a single buyer of a particular input or resource. Thus, the monopsonist faces the (usually) positively sloped market supply curve for the input. This means that if the monopsonistic firm wants more of the input, it must pay a higher price not only for the additional units but for all the units of the input that it purchases. As a result, the *marginal* input or resource *cost* (MRC) exceeds the input or resource price, and the marginal resource cost curve faced by the monopsonist lies above the input or resource supply curve that the firm faces. (For the conditions giving rise to monopsony, see Problem 13.19.)

EXAMPLE 7 In Table 13.3, columns (1) and (2) give the market supply schedule of input A facing the monopsonist. Column (3) refers to the total cost of hiring various quantities of input A and is obtained by multiplying each quantity of input A used by the corresponding P_a. Column (4) is obtained by subtracting successive TC_a values of column (3) and measures the change in the monopsonist's TC per unit change in the quantity of input or resource A that the firm hires. That is, $MRC_a = \Delta TC_a/\Delta Q_a$. Note that the $MRC_a > P_a$ for the monopsonist. The values of columns (2) and (1) of Table 13.3 are plotted as the S_a curve and the values of columns (4) and (1) are plotted as the MRC_a curve in Fig. 13-5. Note that the values of the MRC_a are plotted midway between the values on the horizontal axis.

Table 13.3

(1) Q_a	(2) P_a	(3) TC_a	(4) MRC_a
1	\$1	\$1	. .
2	2	4	\$3
3	3	9	5
4	4	16	7
5	5	25	9
6	6	36	11

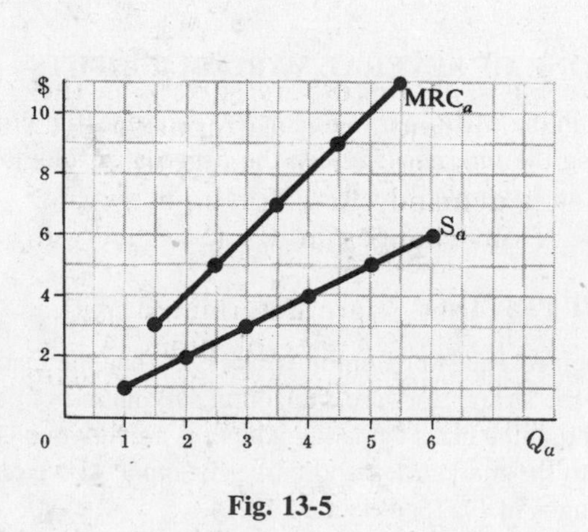

Fig. 13-5

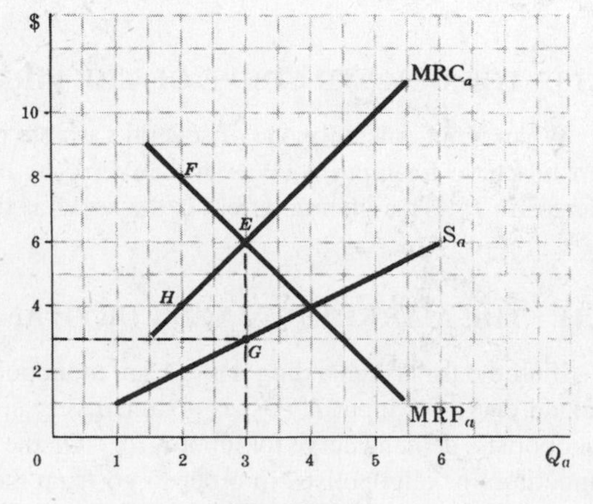

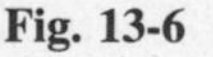
Fig. 13-6

13.13 PRICING AND EMPLOYMENT FOR ONE VARIABLE INPUT

When input A is the only variable input, in order to maximize total profits, the monopsonist will hire more units of input or resource A as long as the $MRP_a > MRC_a$ and until the $MRP_a = MRC_a$. The price of input A that the monopsonist pays is then given by the corresponding point on the S_a curve.

EXAMPLE 8. In Fig. 13-6, the monopsonistic firm maximizes total profits when it hires three units of input or resource A (given by point E, where the MRP_a curve intersects the MRC_a curve that the firm faces). Thus, $P_a = \$3$ (given by point G on the S_a curve). Note that the second unit of input A adds more to the monopsonist's TR (point F) than to the TC (point H), and so the monopsonist's total profits increase by hiring this second unit of input A. The monopsonist does not hire more than three units of input A because the $MRP_a < MRC_a$ and total profits would fall. The excess by which the $MRP_a > P_a$ when the monopsonist is in equilibrium (EG or \$3 in Fig. 13-6) is called *monopsonistic exploitation*. (For ways to counteract monopsonistic exploitation, see Problems 13.23 and 13.24.)

13.14 PRICING AND EMPLOYMENT OF SEVERAL VARIABLE INPUTS

The least-cost input combination to produce any level of output for the monopsonist using more than one variable input is that combination at which the MP per dollar's worth of an input is equal to the MP per dollar's worth of every other variable inputs. That is,

$$\frac{MP_a}{MRC_a} = \frac{MP_b}{MRC_b} = \cdots = \frac{MP_n}{MRC_n}$$

where A, B, ..., N, refer to the monopsonist's variable inputs.

However, in order for the monopsonist to maximize total profits, the firm must not only use the best or least-cost input combination, but it must also use the correct absolute amount of each variable input to produce the best level of output of commodity X. This occurs when

$$\frac{MP_a}{MRC_a} = \frac{MP_b}{MRC_b} = \cdots = \frac{1}{MC_x} = \frac{1}{MR_x}$$

(See Problem 13.22.)

It should be noted that *this is the general condition for profit maximization under any form of market organization in the input and product markets*. When we have perfect competition in the input market, $MRC_a = P_a$, $MRC_b = P_b, \ldots, MRC_n = P_n$ (see Sections 13.1 and 13.8). When we have perfect competition in the product market, $MR_x = P_x$ (see Section 13.1).

In the market situation where the monopsonistic buyer of a factor faces the monopolistic seller of the input (*bilateral monopoly*), the equilibrium price and quantity of the input are theoretically indeterminate (see Problems 13.26 and 13.27).

Problems 13.28 to 13.31 provide some important extensions and applications of input pricing and employment. Problem 13.28 deals with economic profit, 13.29 with investment in human capital, 13.30 with wage differences, and 13.31 with the effect of unions and minimum wage legislation on the level of wages and employment.

Glossary

Bilateral monopoly The market situation where the monopsonistic buyer of an input faces the monopolistic seller of the input.

***Marginal resource cost* (MRC)** The extra cost in hiring one extra unit of the input. MRC exceeds input price when the supply curve of the input is positively sloped.

***Marginal revenue product of an input* (MRP)** The marginal product of the input times the marginal revenue resulting from the sale of the marginal product. For input A and commodity X, $MRP_a = MP_a \cdot MR_x$.

Monopsony The case where there is a single buyer of an input.

Quasi-rent A payment which need not be made in the *short run* in order to bring forth the supply of an input.

Rent A payment which need not be made in the *long run* in order to bring forth the supply of an input.

***Value of the marginal product of an input* (VMP)** The marginal product of the input times the price of the final commodity. For input A and. commodity X, $\text{VMP}_a = \text{MP}_a \cdot P_x$.

Review Questions

1. A firm operating in perfectly competitive product and input markets maximizes its total profits when

(*a*) $P_x = \text{MC}_x$ and MC_x is rising,

(*b*) $\dfrac{\text{MP}_a}{P_a} = \dfrac{\text{MP}_b}{P_b}$,

(*c*) $\dfrac{\text{MP}_a}{P_a} = \dfrac{\text{MP}_b}{P_b} = \dfrac{1}{\text{MC}_x}$, or

(*d*) $\dfrac{\text{MP}_a}{P_a} = \dfrac{\text{MP}_b}{P_b} = \dfrac{1}{\text{MC}_x} = \dfrac{1}{P_x}$.

Ans. (*d*) See Section 13.1.

2. If input A is the only variable input for a perfectly competitive firm in the product market, the firm's demand curve for input A is given by its (*a*) VMP_a curve, (*b*) MP_a curve, (*c*) MRC_a curve, or (*d*) none of the above.

Ans. (*a*) See Section 13.2.

3. In order to get the demand curve for a firm for one of several variable inputs, we must consider (*a*) the internal effect of the change in the input price, (*b*) the external effect of the change in the input price, (*c*) monopolistic exploitation, or (*d*) monopolistic exploitation.

Ans. (*a*) See Example 2.

4. Consideration of the external effect of a fall in the input price will make the market demand curve of the input (*a*) vertical, (*b*) more elastic than otherwise, (*c*) less elastic than otherwise, or (*d*) will have no effect on the elasticity of the market demand curve for the input.

Ans. (*c*) For example, when we consider the external effect of the reduction in P_a from \$8 to \$4 per unit, the increase in QD_a in Fig. 13-2 is only 300 units rather than 500 units.

5. When the market supply curve of input A (S_a) is positively sloped, (*a*) QS_a is fixed regardless of P_a, (*b*) D_a alone determines the equilibrium P_a, (*c*) the intersection of D_a and S_a determines the equilibrium P_a but not the equilibrium Q_a, or (*d*) the intersection of D_a and S_a determines both the equilibrium P_a and Q_a.

Ans. (*d*) See Example 4.

6. When S_a has zero (price) elasticity, (*a*) QS_a is fixed regardless of P_a, (*b*) the D_a curve alone determines the equilibrium P_a (given the level at which QS_a is fixed), (*c*) the entire payment received by input A is a rent, or (*d*) all of the above are true.

Ans. (*d*) See Section 13.7.

7. Quasi-rent is (*a*) equal to the firm's total profit, (*b*) greater than the firm's total profits, (*c*) smaller than the firm's total profits, or (*d*) any of the above is possible.

Ans. (*b*) Quasi-rent equals TR less TVC; total profits equal TR less TC. In the short run, TC exceeds TVC by the TFC; therefore, quasi-rent exceeds total profits by an amount equal to the firm's TFC.

8. When input A is the only variable input for an imperfect competitor in the product market, the firm's demand for input A is given by its (*a*) VMP_a curve, (*b*) MRP_a curve, (*c*) MFC_a curve, or (*d*) none of the above.

Ans. (*b*) See Fig. 13-4 and Example 5.

9. When all firms using input A are monopolists in their respective product markets, D_a is obtained by a consideration of the firms' MRP_a curves and (*a*) the internal effects only of a change in P_a, (*b*) the external effects only of a change in P_a, (*c*) either the internal effects or the external effects, or (*d*) both the internal and the external effects.

Ans. (*a*) When all firms using input A are monopolists in their respective product markets, the effects of a change in P_a on P_x, P_y, $P_z, \ldots$ (i.e., the external effect of the change in P_a) have already been considered in their MRP_a curves. Therefore, only the internal effects need be considered in order to get D_a.

10. The $MRC_a > P_a$ when the firm is (*a*) a monopsonist, (*b*) an oligopsonist, (*c*) a monopsonistic competitor, or (*d*) all of the above.

Ans. (*d*) Choices (*a*), (*b*), and (*c*) represent different forms of imperfectly competitive input markets. All imperfect competitors in input markets must pay a higher P_a in order to get a greater quantity of input A. Thus, for all of them the $MRC_a > P_a$.

11. When $VMP_a > MRP_a > P_a$, we have (*a*) monopolistic exploitation, (*b*) monopsonistic exploitation, (*c*) both monopolistic and monopsonistic exploitation, or (*d*) neither type of exploitation.

Ans. (*c*) See Examples 6 and 8.

12. The general condition for profit maximization for a firm under any form of organization in the input and product markets is

(*a*) $\dfrac{MP_a}{P_a} = \dfrac{MP_b}{P_b} = \cdots = \dfrac{MP_n}{P_n} = \dfrac{1}{MC_x} = \dfrac{1}{P_x}$,

(*b*) $\dfrac{MP_a}{P_a} = \dfrac{MP_b}{P_b} = \cdots = \dfrac{MP_n}{P_n} = \dfrac{1}{MC_x} = \dfrac{1}{MR_x}$,

(*c*) $\dfrac{MP_a}{MRC_a} = \dfrac{MP_b}{MRC_b} = \cdots = \dfrac{MP_n}{MRC_n} = \dfrac{1}{MC_x} = \dfrac{1}{MR_x}$, or

(*d*) all of the above.

Ans. (*c*) See Section 13.14.

Solved Problems

INPUT PRICING AND EMPLOYMENT WITH PERFECT COMPETITION IN THE INPUT AND PRODUCT MARKETS

13.1 (*a*) What do we mean when we say that a firm is a perfect competitor in the product and input markets? (*b*) How does the firm decide whether or not to employ an additional unit of an input? (*c*) Why does the firm's VMP schedule for a factor decline after a point? Why are we interested in the declining portion of the VMP schedule of an input?

(*a*) With perfect competition in the product market, the firm can *sell* any quantity of the commodity at the given market price for the commodity. That is, the firm faces an infinitely elastic *demand curve* for the commodity at the given market price of the commodity. With perfect competition in the input market, the firm can *purchase* any quantity of the input at the given market price of the input. That is, the firm faces an infinitely elastic *supply curve* of the input at the given market price of the input.

Note that while commodities are supplied by firms, some inputs such as labor are supplied by individuals. Also, at least in the case of labor and capital, we want to determine the price of *using* the input for a specified period of time, not the price of *purchasing* the input.

(*b*) A profit-maximizing firm will employ an input as long as the extra income from the sale of the output produced by the input is larger than the extra cost of hiring the input. If the firm uses only one variable input, the extra income or marginal revenue product of the input (MRP) is given by the marginal product of the input (MP) times the marginal revenue of the firm (MR). If the firm is a perfect competitor in the product market, price $P = \text{MR}$ and MRP equals the value of the marginal product (VMP).

(*c*) Because the firm produces in stage II of production (where the law of diminishing returns operates), as more of the input is used together, with fixed quantities of the other input(s), the MP declines. This causes the MRP to decline as more units of the input are hired, even though MR remains constant. The declining portion of the firm's MRP schedule for the input is the firm's demand schedule for the input.

13.2 For a perfectly competitive seller of commodity X and a perfectly competitive buyer of variable inputs A and B, (*a*) indicate the profit-maximizing level of output of commodity X for the firm, (*b*) state the condition for minimizing the cost of producing any level of output, (*c*) explain why $\text{MP}_a/P_a = 1/\text{MC}_x$, and (*d*) state the condition for profit maximization for the firm.

(*a*) The profit-maximizing level of output of commodity X is given by MR_x or $P_x = \text{MC}_x$ and MC_x is rising, provided that at this level of output, $P_x \geqslant \text{AVC}_x$ (see Chapter 9).

(*b*) $\dfrac{\text{MP}_a}{P_a} = \dfrac{\text{MP}_b}{P_b}$ (See Chapter 8.)

(*c*) When P_a remains constant, an additional unit of input A will add P_a to the firm's total cost and contributes MP_a to the firm's total product. Thus, P_a/MP_a is the change in the firm's total costs per unit change in its total product or output. This is the definition of marginal cost. Thus, $P_a/\text{MP}_a = \text{MC}_x$. Similarly, $P_b/\text{MP}_b = \text{MC}_x$. So the best (least-cost) input combination to produce any level of output can be rewritten as

$$\frac{P_a}{\text{MP}_a} = \frac{P_a}{\text{MP}_b} = \text{MC}_x \qquad \text{or} \qquad \frac{\text{MP}_a}{P_a} = \frac{\text{MP}_b}{P_b} = \frac{1}{\text{MC}_x}$$

(*d*) In order for the firm to maximize its total profits, it must not only use the best (least-cost) input combination, but it must also use the correct absolute amount of each input to produce its best level of output of the final commodity. This occurs when

$$\frac{\text{MP}_a}{P_a} = \frac{\text{MP}_b}{P_b} = \frac{1}{\text{MC}_x} = \frac{1}{P_x}$$

13.3 With reference to Fig. 13-7, indicate whether the firm is using the least-cost input combination and producing its best level of output at points *H* and *E*.

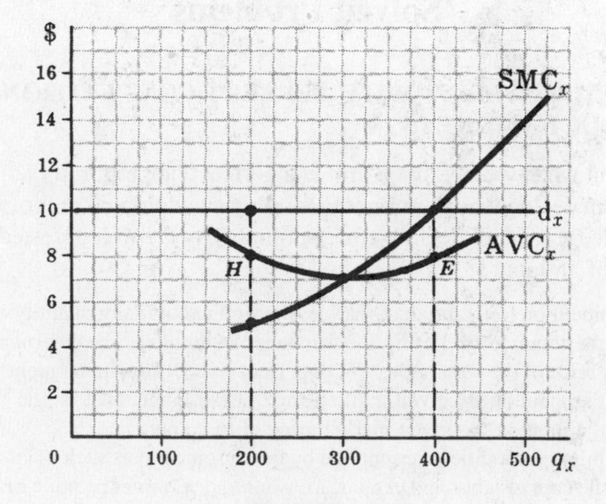

Fig. 13-7

At point H in the figure,

$$\frac{MP_a}{P_a} = \frac{MP_b}{P_b} = \frac{1}{MC_x} > \frac{1}{P_x}$$

That is, at point H, the firm is minimizing the cost of producing 200 units of output (since point H is on its AVC curve), but this is not its best level of output (since $MC_x < P_x$ or $1/MC_x > 1/P_x$). In order to maximize its short-run total profits or minimize its short-run total losses, this firm must expand its output of commodity X. To do this, the firm must use more of each of its variable inputs and make sure at the same time to combine inputs so as to minimize its TVC. As the firm expands its output of commodity X, the SMC_x increases (since we are in stage II of production) while P_x remains constant. The firm should continue to expand its output until its $SMC_x = P_x$ (i.e., until 400). At point E,

$$\frac{MP_a}{P_a} = \frac{MP_b}{P_b} = \frac{1}{MC_x} = \frac{1}{P_x}$$

and the firm is producing its best level of output of 400 units of X (since $MC_x = P_x$) with the best or least-cost input combination (since point E is on its AVC curve).

13.4 Assume that (1) factor A is the only variable input of a firm producing commodity X, (2) the firm is a perfect competitor in both the input and product markets and $P_a = \$8$ and $P_x = \$2$ and (3) the quantities of commodity X produced by the firm with various quantities of input A are those given in Table 13.4. (*a*) Construct a table showing this firm's MP_a, d_x, MRP_a and S_a schedules and (*b*) sketch the d_a and S_a curves for this firm. (*c*) How many units of input A should this firm hire in order to maximize its total profits?

Table 13.4

q_a	2	3	4	5	6	7
q_x	10	20	28	34	38	40

(*a*)

Table 13.5

(1) q_a	(2) q_x	(3) MP_a	(4) P_x	(5) $MRP_a = VMP_a$	(6) P_a
2	10	...	\$2	...	\$8
3	20	10	2	\$20	8
4	28	8	2	16	8
5	34	6	2	12	8
6	38	4	2	8	8
7	40	2	2	4	8

In Table 13.5, columns (3) and (1) give this firm's MP_a schedule. Columns (4) and (2) refer to the d_x schedule facing this firm; columns (5) and (1) give the firm's MRP_a schedule, and columns (6) and (1) refer to the S_a schedule facing this firm.

(*b*) Since this firm is a perfect competitor in the product market and input A is its only variable input, this firm's d_a curve. Note that just like the values of any other marginal schedule (and for the same reason), the figures of the MRP_a schedule are plotted between the values on the horizontal axis of Fig. 13-8. Also note that while commodities are demanded by consumers in order to satisfy their wants, inputs are demanded by firms in order to produce commodities. Thus d_a is a *derived-demand curve*—derived from P_x and the declining segment of the firm's MP_a curve in stage II.

(*c*) It pays for this firm to expand its use of input A as long as the MRP_a (i.e., the addition to its TR) exceeds P_a (i.e., the addition to its TC) and until the $\text{MRP}_a = P_a$. Thus, in order to maximize its total profits, this firm should hire six units of input A. Another way of stating this firm's profit-maximization point with respect to input A is

$$\frac{\text{MP}_a}{P_a} = \frac{1}{\text{MC}_x} = \frac{1}{P_x} \quad \text{or} \quad \frac{P_a}{\text{MP}_a} = P_x$$

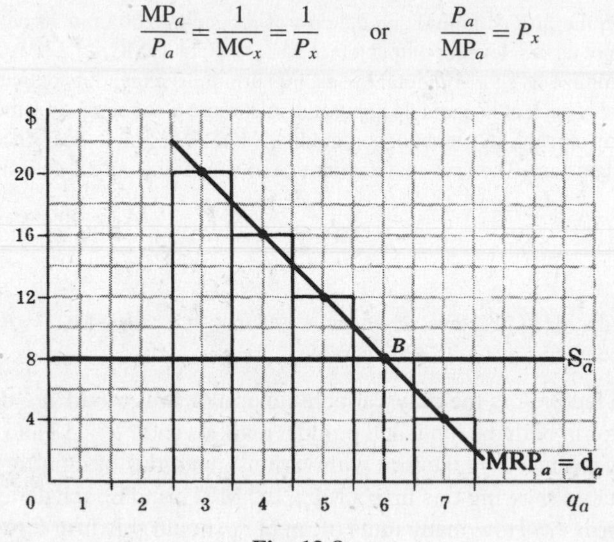

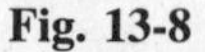
Fig. 13-8

Cross-multiplying, we get $P_a = \text{MP}_a \cdot P_x = \text{VMP}_a$. Note that in Fig. 13-8, input A is treated as a discrete variable, while in the text (and in the problems that follow), input A is treated as a continuous variable.

13.5 Assume that (1) the MRP_a of a firm is \$40 when $q_a = 4$ and \$20 when $q_a = 7$ and (2) in the long run, when all of the firm's inputs are variable, a fall in P_a from \$40 to \$20 per unit, with all the other input prices remaining constant, causes this firm's MRP_a curve to shift everywhere to the right by three units. (*a*) Derive geometrically this firm's d_a, (*b*) explain in detail the internal effect resulting from inputs which are *complementary* to input A in production, and (*c*) explain in detail the internal effect resulting from inputs which are *substitutes* for input A. (*d*) Until when will these internal effects operate?

(*a*)

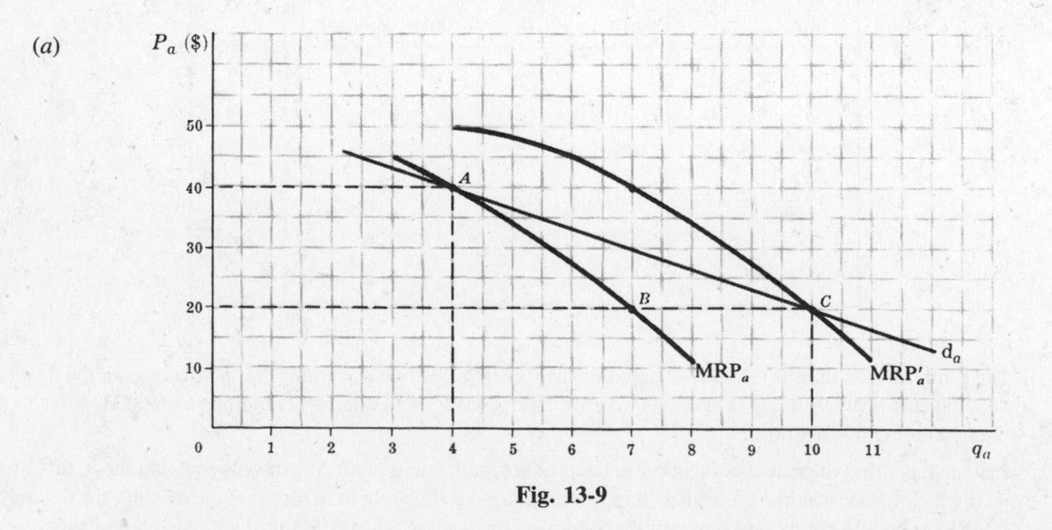

Fig. 13-9

The MRP_a curve is drawn on the assumption that the *quantity* of all inputs other than input A is fixed. It thus represents the firm's short-run d_a. In this problem, we are told that in the long run, when all inputs are variable and their prices other than P_a are constant, a fall in P_a from \$40 to \$20 per unit causes the firm's MRP_a curve to shift to the right to MRP'_a (see Fig. 13-9). Thus, point A and point C are two points on the firm's long-run d_a. (The movement from point B to point C is the internal effect of the change in P_a.)

(*b*) Starting from the profit-maximizing point A, a fall in P_a from \$40 per unit causes the MRP_a to exceed the new and lower P_a. Thus the firm, in its attempt to maximize its profits with respect to input A, expands its use of input A (a movement down its unchanged MRP_a curve). However, as the firm uses more of input A, the MP, and thus the MRP curve of inputs complementary to input A, shifts up and to the right. Thus, the new and higher MRP for these complementary inputs exceed their unchanged prices. So this profit-maximizing firm expands its use of these complementary inputs, but this causes its MP_a and thus its MRP_a curve to shift up and to the right.

(*c*) On the other hand, as the firm uses more of input A because of the fall in P_a, the MP and thus the MRP curve of each input which is a substitute for input A shifts down and to the left. Thus, the new and lower MRP for a substitute input is now smaller than its unchanged price. As a result the firm will reduce its use of these substitute inputs, but this causes the firm's MP_a and thus the MRP_a curve to shift *even further to the right*.

(*d*) These shifts in the firm's MRP curves (of input A, their complements and substitutes) and the corresponding changes in the firm's utilization of all of these inputs will continue until the firm has once again reestablished its profit-maximizing position with respect to all of its variable inputs. The more and better is the availability of inputs which are complementary and substitutes for input A, the further to the right the firm's MRP_a curve shifts and the more elastic is the firm's long-run d_a.

13.6 Suppose that the external effect of the fall in P_a from \$40 to \$20 per unit causes the d_a of each of 100 identical firms demanding input A to shift from the d_a in Fig. 13-9 everywhere to the left by two units. (*a*) Derive D_a geometrically and (*b*) explain how this external effect of the change in P_a operates on each firm. (*c*) What are the determinants of the price elasticity of D_a?

(*a*)

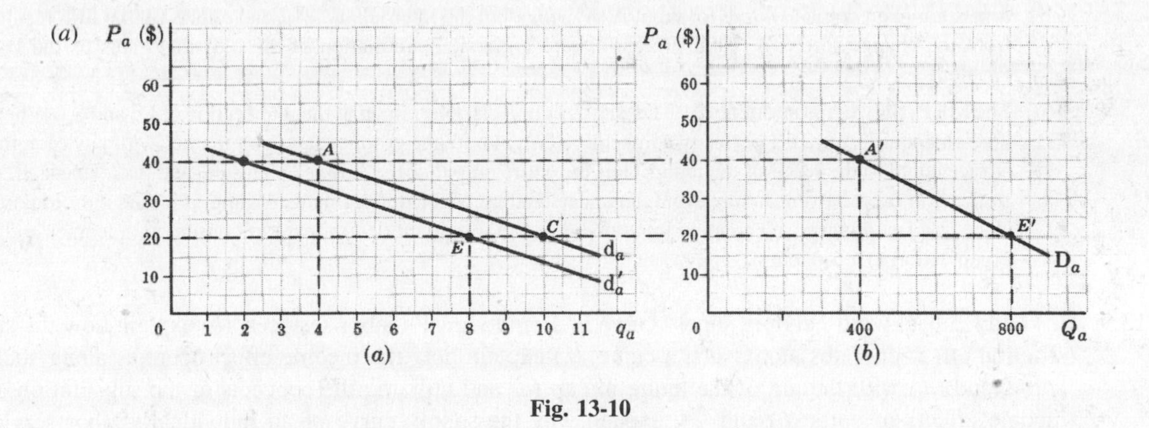

Fig. 13-10

(*b*) Starting from the profit-maximizing point A, if P_a falls (because, for example, S_a increases), the $MRP_a > P_a$ for each firm using input A. Thus, each firm expands its use of input A. But as all firms expand their use of input A, the S_x increases (i.e., shifts down and to the right). Given D_x, this causes a fall in P_x. Since the d_a of each firm was drawn on the assumption of a given and constant P_x, when P_x falls, the MRP_a curve of each firm shifts to the left and causes the d_a of each firm also to shift to the left (from d_a to d'_a in Fig. 13-10). It is the quantity demanded on these lower d'_a curves that are added in order to get a new QD_a (and thus another point on D_a) when P_a falls.

(*c*) D_a is more price-elastic, the more price-elastic D_x, the more and better the availability of substitutes and complements of input A, the more price-elastic the supply curve of these other related inputs, and the longer the period of time under consideration.

13.7 Given the D_a in Fig. 13-10(*b*) and $QS_a = 40P_a$ (with P_a given in dollars), determine geometrically the market equilibrium P_a and Q_a. How much of input A would each of 100 identical firms use?

D_a and S_a intersect at point E′. Therefore, the market equilibrium $P_a = \$20$ and $Q_a = 800$ units (see Fig. 13-11). At $P_a = \$20$, each of the 100 identical firms using input A will hire eight units of input A (point E on d_a^*).

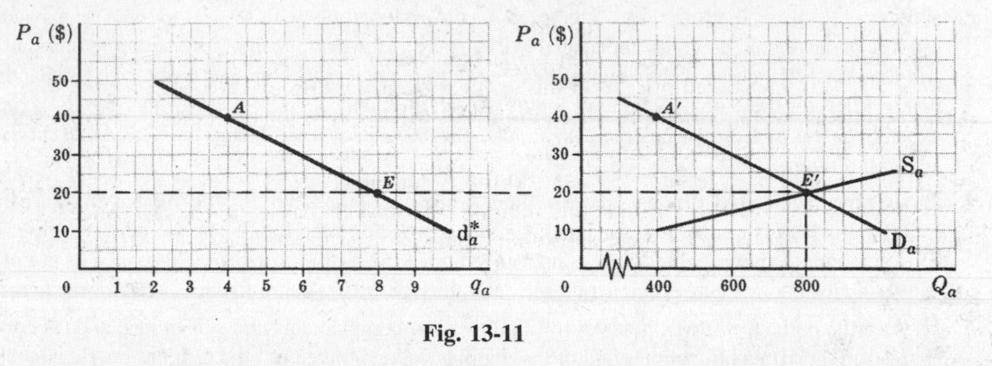

Fig. 13-11

13.8 (*a*) In Problems 13.4(*b*), 13.5(*a*), and 13.7, we have identified three different curves, each giving the firm's demand curve for input A under a specific set of circumstances. Explain under what condition each curve represents the firm's demand curve for input A. (*b*) Does the MRP_a determine the equilibrium P_a? What income do inputs receive when a perfectly competitive firm in both the product and input markets is in long-run equilibrium?

(*a*) The MRP_a curve of Problem 13.4(*b*) is the firm's short-run demand curve for input A when input A is the firm's only variable input and the firm is a perfect competitor in the product market; d_a in Problem 13.5(*a*) is the firm's long-run demand curve for input A when only the internal effect on the firm resulting from the change in P_a is considered; d_a^* in Problem 13.7 [derived from d_a and d_a' of Problem 13.6(*a*)] is the firm's long-run demand curve for input A showing both the internal and external effects on the firm resulting from the change in P_a. It is the straightforward horizontal summation of these d_a^* that gives us the D_a of Problem 13.7.

(*b*) The MRP_a only helps us define D_a. The equilibrium P_a is determined at the intersection of D_a and S_a. When in long-run equilibrium, the perfectly competitive firm in both the product and input markets will pay each input a price equal to the MRP of the input. Thus the entire output of the firm is exhausted, and just exhausted, and so the firm breaks even. In any event, an understanding of the determinants of input prices is very important since in a free-enterprise economy input prices are an important determinant of consumers' incomes and the organization of production.

13.9 (*a*) Draw a backward-bending supply curve of an individual's labor services, (*b*) explain how the substitution effect operates along such a curve, (*c*) explain how the income effect operates along such a curve, and (*d*) with the aid of the figure in part (*a*) and utilizing the concepts of the substitution and income effects of parts (*b*) and (*c*), explain why the supply curve of an individual's labor services might be backward-bending.

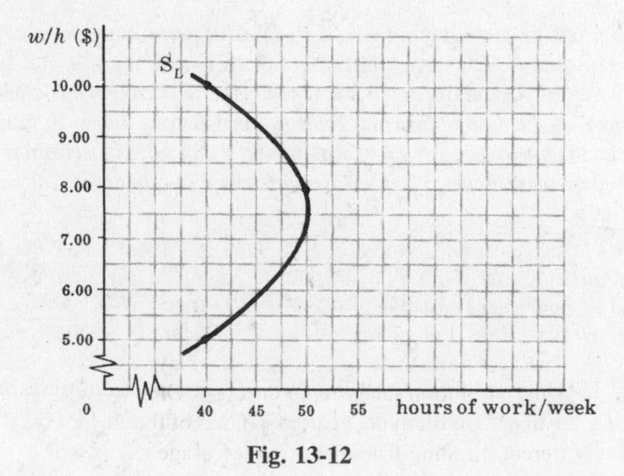

Fig. 13-12

(a) An individual's supply curve of his or her labor services is backward-bending if, after a point, higher wage rates result in a reduction in the number of hours the person offers to work per unit of time. For example, in Fig. 13-12, for higher and higher wage rates above \$8/hour, the individual will want to work fewer and fewer hours per week. See also Problem 4.40(b).

(b) When the wage rate rises, the individual tends to substitute more work for leisure since the price of leisure (the wage rate) has increased. So, by itself, the substitution effect tends to make the individual's S_L everywhere positively sloped.

(c) As one's wage rate rises, one's income rises, and when income rises, one tends to increase the quantity one demands of every normal commodity, including leisure (i.e., the person tends to work fewer hours). By itself, this income effect would tend to make the individual's S_L everywhere negatively sloped.

(d) With reference to Fig. 13-12 and taking the substitution and income effects together, we can say that, up to the wage rate of \$8/h, the substitution effect exceeds the income effect and so this individual's S_L is positively sloped. At the wage rate of \$8/h, the substitution effect exactly equals the income effect and so S_L is vertical. At wage rates above \$8/h, the income effect exceeds the substitution effect and so S_L becomes negatively sloped.

Note that, with the use of the tools of substitution and income effects, we can explain the existence of the bend on an individual's S_L, but we cannot predict at exactly what wage rate the bend might occur. As the general standard of living increases, an increasing number of individuals may have a backward-bending supply curve for their labor services. Thus, the market supply curve may also be backward-bending.

13.10 If $QS_a = 400$, regardless of P_a, (a) find the rent on input A when $QD_a = 800 - 100P_a$ and when $QD'_a = 600 - 100P_a$ (P_a is expressed in dollars). (b) If a tax of up to 100% is imposed on the returns to input A, how much of input A will be supplied? (c) If QS_a were not vertical but positively sloped, how much of the return to input A would be a rent?

(a) In Fig. 13-13, we see that with D_a, the equilibrium $P_a = \$4$ and the rent on input A equals \$1600. That is, given the fixed QS_a of 400 units, P_a is determined entirely by the height of D_a. Since QS_a is fixed and this quantity would be supplied regardless of P_a, the entire payment of \$1600 made to input A is a rent. It results entirely because of the perfect inelasticity of S_a. With D'_a, the equilibrium $P_a = \$2$ and the rent on input A equals \$800.

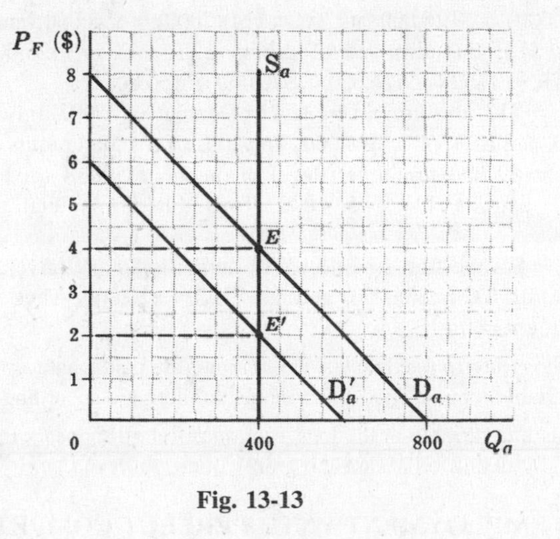

Fig. 13-13

(b) $QS_a = 400$ units, even if a tax of up to 100% of the rent on factor A is imposed. Thus, a tax on rent does not reduce the quantity of input A supplied to the market. In an important sense, a tax on rent is an ideal tax.

(c) If S_a were positively sloped, only that portion (if any) of the payment made to input A that is unnecessary to the supply of input A is a rent. For example, if a baseball star now earning \$1 million to play a certain number of games per year would continue to do so as long as the player's salary did not fall below \$200,000 per year, then \$800,000 out of the \$1 million salary represents rent. On the other hand, if the baseball player would not play baseball for less than \$1 million per year, no portion of the \$1 million salary is a rent. Note that "rent" in economics has a different meaning from the everyday usage of the word.

13.11 What is the firm's quasi-rent at the profit-maximizing level of output in Fig. 13-7?

At the best level of output of 400 units of commodity X, AVC = \$8. The TVC of \$3200 is a cost which the firm must pay in order to retain the use of its variable inputs. The difference of \$800 between the firm's TR of \$4000 and its TVC of \$3200 is a quasi-rent and represents a payment to the firm's fixed inputs, which the firm need not receive in order to produce commodity X in the short run. Note that the quasi-rent of this firm can be equal to, greater than, or less than the TFC of the firm.

13.12 Fig. 13-14 refers to a perfectly competitive firm in the product market. (*a*) What is the amount of total profit and quasi-rent for this firm, if P_x = \$18, \$13, \$9, \$5? (*b*) Are fixed inputs rewarded according to their MRP (*c*) What happens to quasi-rent in the long run?

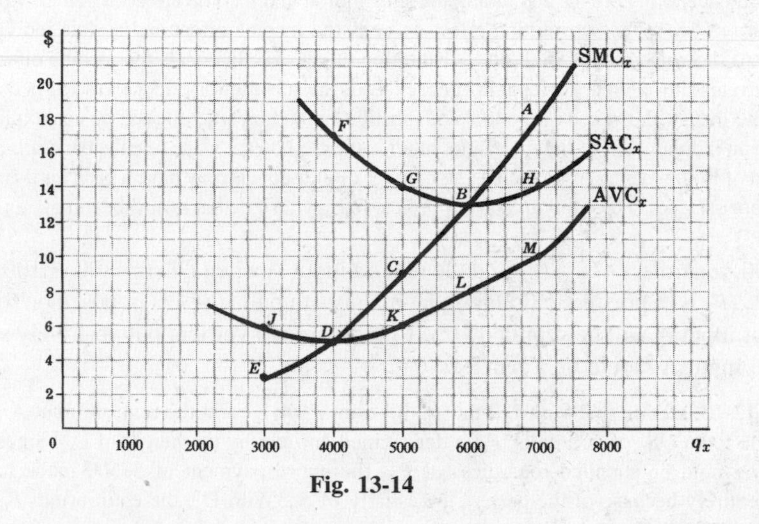

Fig. 13-14

(*a*) When P_x = \$18, the firm's best level of output is 7000X (given by point *A*), its TR = (\$18)(7,000) = \$126,000, its TC = (14)(7000) = \$98,000, and its TVC = (\$10)(7,000) = \$70,000. Thus at P_x = \$18, this firm's total profits = TR − TC = \$126,000 − \$98,000 = \$28,000. This firm's quasi-rent = TR − TVC = \$126,000 − \$70,000 = \$56,000.

When P_x = \$13, the firm's best level of output is 6000X (given by point *B*), its TR = \$78,000, its TC = \$78,000, and its TVC = \$48,000. Thus this firm's total profits = 0, while its quasi-rent = \$30,000.

When P_x = \$9, the firm's best level of output is 5000X (given by point *C*), its TR = \$45,000, its TC = \$70,000, and its TVC = \$30,000. Thus this firm's total profits = −\$25,000, while its quasi-rent = \$15,000.

When P_x = \$5, the firm's best level of output is 4000X (given by point *D*, the shut-down point), its TR = \$20,000, its TC = \$68,000, and its TVC = \$20,000. Thus this firm's total profits = −\$48,000, while its quasi-rent = 0.

(*b*) Quasi-rent is the return to fixed inputs. Fixed inputs are paid whatever is left from the firm's TR after the firm has paid its variable inputs. Thus, fixed inputs are not paid according to the MRP scheme.

(*c*) Since all inputs are variable in the long run, quasi-rent disappears in the long run. (Indeed, quasi-rent is a concept which by definition has meaning only in the short run.)

INPUT PRICING AND EMPLOYMENT WITH PERFECT COMPETITION IN THE INPUT MARKET AND MONOPOLY IN THE PRODUCT MARKET

13.13 (*a*) What is the profit-maximizing level of output for the monopolistic (or imperfectly competitive) seller of commodity X? (*b*) What is the best (least-cost) input combination to produce any level of output if the firm in part (*a*) is a perfect competitor in the input market? (*c*) State the condition for profit maximization for the firm in parts (*a*) and (*b*). (*d*) With reference to Fig. 13-15, indicate whether the firm is using the least-cost input combination and producing its best level of output at points *H* and *E*.

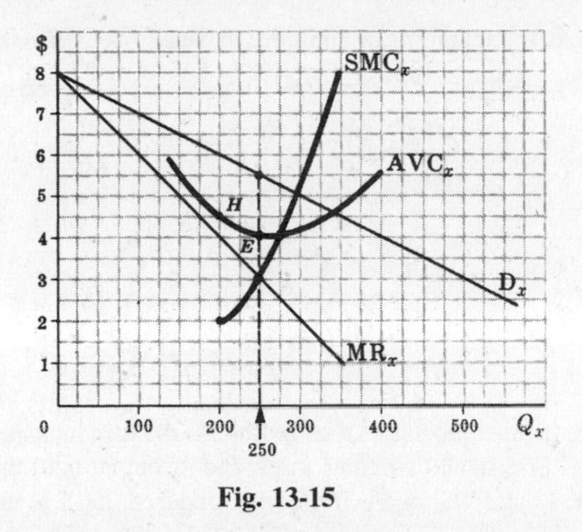

Fig. 13-15

(*a*) The profit-maximizing level of output for the firm is given by the point where $\text{MR}_x = \text{MC}_x$ and the MC_x curve intersects the MR_x curve from below, provided that at this level of output, $P_x \geq \text{AVC}_x$ (see Chapters 9 and 10).

(*b*) If the firm uses two variable inputs, say, input A and input B, the best (least-cost) input combination for the firm to produce any quantity of commodity X (or any other commodity) is given by $\text{MP}_a/P_a = \text{MP}_b/P_b$ (see Chapter 6). Also $\text{MP}_a/P_a = \text{MP}_b/P_b = 1/\text{MC}_x$ (see Problem 13.2).

(*c*)
$$\frac{\text{MP}_a}{P_a} = \frac{\text{MP}_b}{P_b} = \frac{1}{\text{MC}_x} = \frac{1}{\text{MR}_x}$$

(*d*) At point *H* in Fig. 13-15, the firm is not maximizing its total profits because

$$\frac{\text{MP}_a}{P_a} = \frac{\text{MP}_b}{P_b} = \frac{1}{\text{MC}_x} > \frac{1}{\text{MR}_x}$$

At point *E*, the firm is not only using the least-cost input combination (since point *E* is on its AVC curve), but is also using the correct absolute amounts of input A and B to produce the best level of output of 250 units of commodity X (given by the point where $\text{MR}_x = \text{SMC}_x$).

13.14 Fig. 13-16 refers to a firm which is the monopolistic seller of commodity X and is a perfect competitor in the market for inputs A, B, and C (the inputs required to produce commodity X). (*a*) What are the SMC_x, the AVC_x, and the P_x of this firm when it maximizes its total profits (or minimizes its total losses)? (*b*) How does this firm move from a nonprofit-maximizing but cost-minimizing position to the profit-maximizing point?

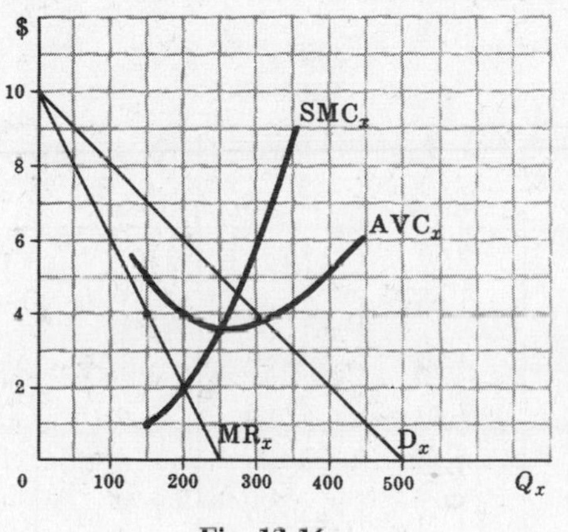

Fig. 13-16

(*a*) This firm will maximize its total profits or minimize its total losses when it produces 200X at a SMC of \$2 and an AVC of \$4, and sells commodity X at the price of \$6. At that point,

$$\frac{MP_a}{P_a} = \frac{MP_b}{P_b} = \frac{MP_c}{P_c} = \frac{1}{MC_x} = \frac{1}{MR_x} = 0.50$$

(see Fig. 13-16).

(*b*) If the firm produced 150X at an AVC of \$5,

$$\frac{MP_a}{P_a} = \frac{MP_b}{P_b} = \frac{MP_c}{P_c} = \frac{1}{1} > \frac{1}{4}$$

and the firm would not be maximizing its total profits. As the firm increases its output, its SMC increases and its MR decreases. This firm should continue to expand its output until the output of 200X is reached where $SMC_x = MR_x = \$2$ and the $AVC_x = \$4$. If the firm produced 250X at minimum cost,

$$\frac{MP_a}{P_a} = \frac{MP_b}{P_b} = \frac{MP_c}{P_c} = \frac{1}{3.5} < \frac{1}{0} \qquad \left(\text{or better, } \frac{P_a}{MP_a} = \frac{P_b}{MP_b} = \frac{P_c}{MP_c} = 3.5 > 0\right)$$

and the firm would not be maximizing its total profits. As the firm decreases its output, its SMC decreases and its MR increases. This firm should continue to reduce its output as long as its SMC > MR and until (at the output of 200X) they are equal (and the $AVC_x = \$4$).

13.15 Table 13.6 refers to the monopolistic seller of commodity X, when input A is the firm's only variable input. Find the firm's MP_a, TR_x, MR_x, VMP_a, and MRP_a schedules.

Table 13.6

q_a	2	3	4	5	6	7
Q_x	10	20	28	34	38	40
P_x (\$)	2.00	1.08	1.60	1.40	1.20	1.00
P_a (\$)	8.80	8.80	8.80	8.80	8.80	8.80

In Table 13.7, MP_a [column (3)] = $\Delta Q_x/\Delta q_a$; TR_x [column (5)] = $(Q_x)(P_x)$; MR_x [column (6)] = $\Delta TR_x/\Delta Q_x$; VMP_a [column (7)] = $(MP_a)(P_x)$; $MRP_a = \Delta TR_x/\Delta q_a = (MP_a)(MR_x)$. Note that if commodity X had been sold in a perfectly competitive market, $MR_x = P_x$ and the $VMP_a = MRP_a$. Since the monopolist must lower P_x in order to sell more of commodity X, $MR_x < P_x$ and declines. Thus, the MRP_x values in column (8) are less than the corresponding values of the VMP_a in column (7) and the MRP_a schedule falls both because the MP_a falls (since we are in stage II of production) and because the MR_x falls (since we have imperfect competition in the market for commodity X).

Table 13.7

(1) q_a	(2) Q_x	(3) MP_a	(4) P_x (\$)	(5) TR_x (\$)	(6) MR_x (\$)	(7) VMP_a (\$)	(8) MRP_a (\$)	(9) P_a (\$)
2	10	...	2.00	20.00	...	...	...	8.80
3	20	10	1.80	36.00	1.60	18.00	16.00	8.80
4	28	8	1.60	44.80	1.10	12.80	8.80	8.80
5	34	6	1.40	47.60	0.47	8.40	2.80	8.80
6	38	4	1.20	45.60	−0.50	4.80	−2.00	8.80
7	40	2	1.00	40.00	−2.80	2.00	−5.60	8.80

13.16 (*a*) Plot, on the same set of axes, the VMP_a, MRP_a, and S_a schedules for the firm in Problem 13.15. (*b*) How many units of input A should this firm use in order to maximize its total profits? (*c*) What is the amount of monopolistic exploitation when this firm is in equilibrium?

(*a*)

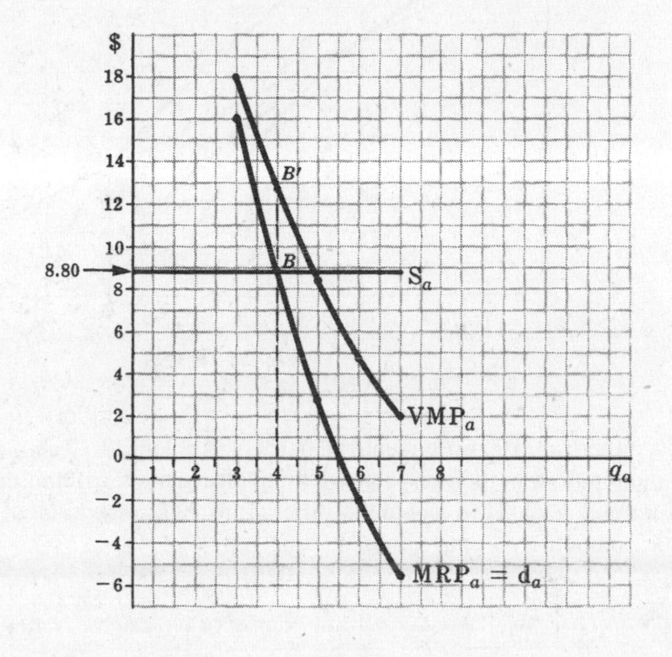

Fig. 13-17

Note that when we have monopoly or other forms of imperfect competition in the product market, the MRP_a curve represents the firm's short-run d_a, and the MRP_a curve or d_a lies below the corresponding VMP_a curve. Also, since this firm pays the same P_a for various quantities of input A it purchases, the firm behaves as a perfect competitor in the market for input A and thus the S_a it faces is infinitely elastic at $P_a = \$8.80$.

(*b*) This firm is in equilibrium (i.e., it maximizes its total profits with respect to input A) when $\text{MP}_a/P_a = 1/\text{MC}_x = 1/\text{MR}_x$ or $(\text{MP}_a)(\text{MR}_x) = \text{MRP}_a = P_a$. Thus, this firm should hire four units of input A (see point *B* in Fig. 13-17).

(*c*) Monopolistic exploitation in this case is \$4 (given by \$12.80 – \$8.80, or *BB'* in Fig. 13-17). The name "monopolistic exploitation" is somewhat misleading since the difference between the VMP_a and the corresponding MRP_a is not pocketed by the firm, and the input receives the entire increase that it contributes to the TR of the firm.

13.17 Assume that (1) the MRP_a for the monopolistic producer of commodity X is \$40 when $q_a = 3$ and \$20 when $q_a = 5$ and (2) a fall in P_a from \$40 to \$20 per unit, with the prices of all other inputs remaining constant in the long run, causes this firm's MRP_a curve to shift everywhere to the right by two units. (*a*) Why does this firm's MRP_a curve shift to the right when P_a falls? (*b*) Derive this firm's long-run d_a geometrically.

(*a*) Starting from the profit-maximizing point *A*, a fall in P_a will induce the firm to expand its use of input A (i.e., to move down its MRP_a curve). However, when this occurs, the MRP curve of factors complementary to input A shifts to the right and the firm uses more of them. This causes the firm's MRP_a curve to shift to the right. On the other hand, when the firm uses more of input A (because P_a has fallen), the MRP curve of factors which are substitutes for input A shifts to the left and the firm uses less of them. This causes the firm's MRP_a curve to shift even further to the right. However, as the MRP_a curve shifts to the right and more of input A is used, the MRP curves of complementary inputs again shift to the right and the MRP curves of substitute inputs again shift to the left. This in turn causes a further shift to the right in this firm's MRP_a curve, and the process is repeated until the firm reaches another profit-maximizing position [see Problem 13.13(*c*)]. The entire shift to the right of the firm's MRP_a curve is called the *internal* effect on the firm resulting from the change in P_a.

(*b*)

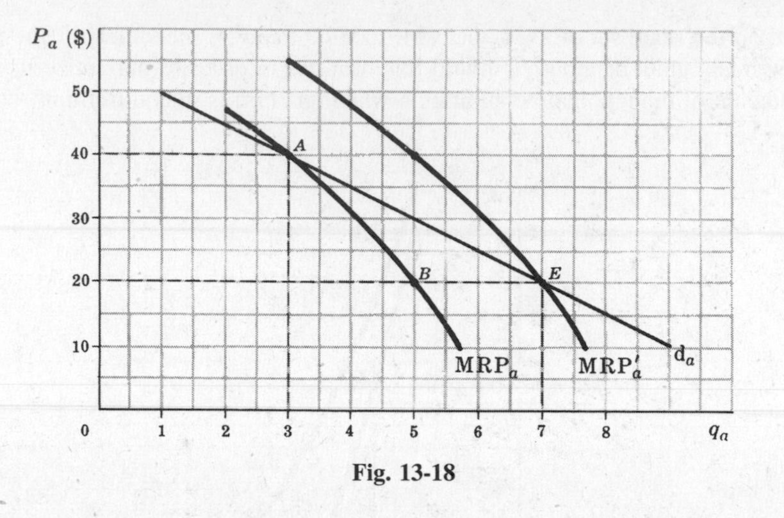

Fig. 13-18

13.18 If $QS_a = 35P_a$, if there are 100 firms identical to that of Problem 13.17 demanding input A, and all these 100 firms are monopolists in their respective commodity market, (*a*) find the equilibrium market price and quantity for input A. (*b*) How would this differ if, instead, some or all of the firms were oligopolists or monopolistic competitors in the commodity market(s)?

(*a*)

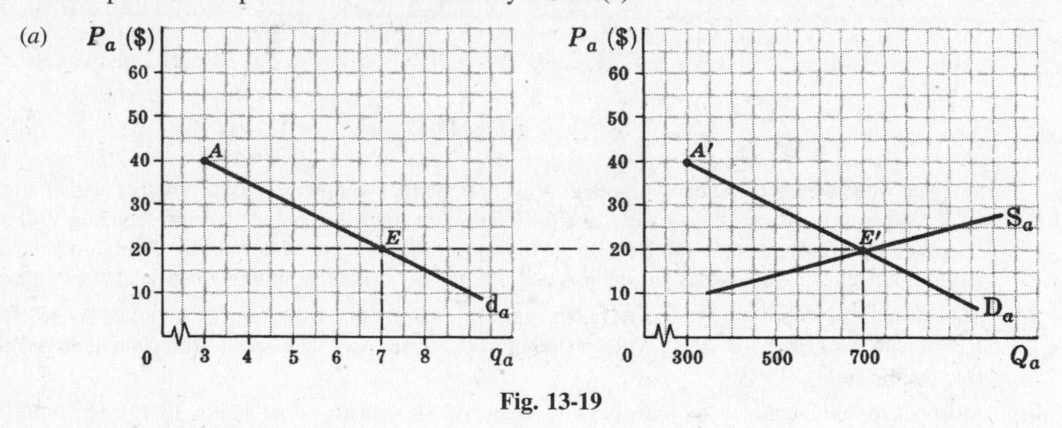

Fig. 13-19

The effects of changes in P_a on the price of the final commodities produced by the firms using input A have already been considered in deriving their d_a. Thus, there is no external effect to be considered, and D_a is obtained by the straightforward horizontal summation of each firm's d_a. The intersection of D_a and S_a gives the equilibrium $P_a = \$20$. At this price each firm will use seven units of input A for a total of 700 units (see Fig. 13-19).

(*b*) Before we can derive D_a we must consider the external effects of a change in P_a for each of the nonmonopolists. These external effects operate as described in Problem 13.6, except for the further complication introduced by oligopolistic uncertainty and product differentiation (see Sections 10.4 to 10.12).

MONOPSONY

13.19 (*a*) What is meant by monopsony? (*b*) How does monopsony arise? (*c*) What is meant by oligopsony and monopsonistic competition?

(*a*) Monopsony refers to the form of market organization where there is a single buyer of a particular input. An example of monopsony is given by the "mining towns" of yesteryear in the United States, where the mining company was the sole employer of labor in town (often these mining companies even owned and operated a single "company store" in town).

(*b*) Monopsony arises when an input is specialized and is thus much more productive to a particular firm than to any other firm or use. Because of the greater input productivity, this firm can pay a higher price for the input and so become a monopsonist. Monopsony also results from lack of geographical and occupational mobility of inputs.

(*c*) Oligopsony and monopsonistic competition refer to other forms of imperfect competition in input markets. An oligopsonist is one of few buyers of a homogeneous or differentiated input. A monopsonistic competitor is one of many buyers of a differentiated input.

13.20 $QS_a = -2 + P_a/5$ (with P_a given in dollars) is the market supply function for input A facing the monopsonist buyer of input A. (*a*) Find the monopsonist's supply and marginal input or resource cost schedules for input A and (*b*) plot these schedules. (*c*) How would these schedules look if we were dealing instead with an oligopsonist or monopsonistic competitor? A perfect competitor?

(*a*)

Table 13.8

(1) P_a ($)	10	15	20	25	30	35	40	45
(2) Q_a	0	1	2	3	4	5	6	7
(3) TC_a ($)	0	15	40	75	120	175	240	315
(4) MRC_a ($)	..	15	25	35	45	55	65	75

In Table 13.8, rows (1) and (2) give the supply schedule of input or resource A faced by this monopsonist. Rows (4) and (2) refer to the corresponding marginal cost schedule of input or resource A.

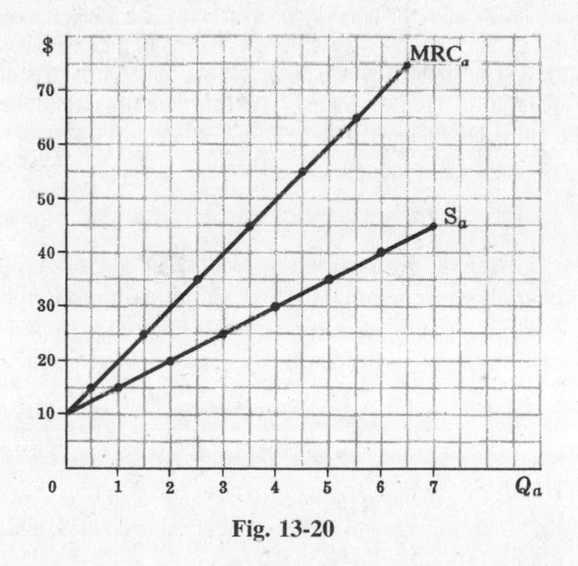

Fig. 13-20

(*b*) See page 304 or the next page.

(*c*) As imperfect competitors in input markets, oligopsonists and monopsonistic competitors also face a rising supply curve of the input (i.e., they must pay higher input prices for greater quantities of the input). Thus, the MRC > *P* of the input or resource and their MRC curve also lies above the input or resource supply curve that they face. This is to be contrasted with the case of perfect competition in the input market, where even though the market curve of the input is positively sloped, each buyer of the input is so small that the firm can purchase all it wants of the input at its given market price (i.e., the buyer faces an infinitely elastic supply curve of the input). Thus, for the perfectly competitive buyer of the input, the MRC curve coincides with the horizontal supply curve of the input or resource and MRC equals the given market equilibrium price of the input.

13.21 Given the S_a and the MRC_a curves of Fig. 13-20, if input A is the monopsonist's only variable input and if $MRP_a = \$60$ at $Q_a = 2$, \$50 at $Q_a = 4$, and \$40 at $Q_a = 6$, (*a*) determine how many units of input A this monopsonistic firm will employ if it wants to maximize total profits; what P_a will the firm pay? (*b*) What is the amount of monopsonistic exploitation?

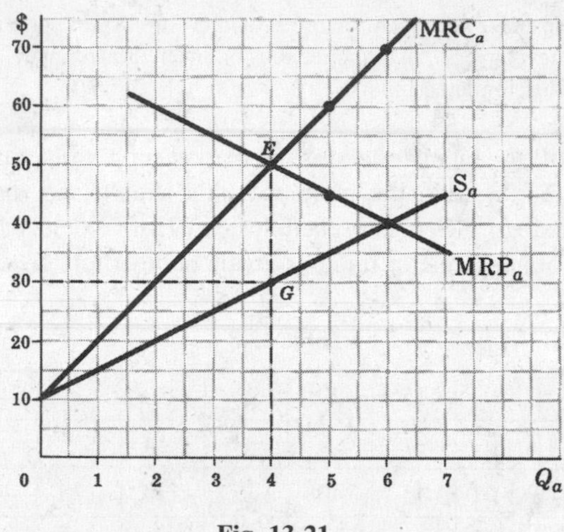

Fig. 13-21

(*a*) This monopsonist should use four units of input or resource A (given by point *E*, where the monopsonist's MRP_a curve intersects the MRC_a curve that this firm faces) and $P_a = \$30$ (given by point *G* on the S_a curve). Note that since the monopsonistic firm stops hiring input A when the $\text{MRP}_a = (\text{MP}_a)(\text{MR}_x) = \text{MRC}_a > P_a$, the firm hires fewer units of input A than if it were a perfect competitor in the input A market. If the monopsonist were to hire where the $\text{MRP}_a = P_a = \$40$, the firm would not be maximizing its total profits since the fifth unit of input A adds \$60 to TC but only \$45 to TR and the sixth unit of input A adds \$70 to TC but only \$40 to TR (see Fig. 13-21). Thus, the firm could increase its total profits by cutting back to four units on its use of input A.

(*b*) The amount of monopsonistic exploitation (i.e., the excess of the MRP_a over P_a at equilibrium) is \$20, or *EG*, in Fig. 13-21.

13.22 State (*a*) the least-cost input combination to produce any level of output for a monopsonist using more than one variable input or resource and (*b*) the condition for profit maximization for a monopsonist using more than one variable input or resource. (*c*) With reference to part (*b*), indicate how from a nonmaximizing profit position the monopsonist moves to a profit-maximizing position.

(*a*)
$$\frac{\text{MP}_a}{\text{MRC}_a} = \frac{\text{MP}_b}{\text{MRC}_b} = \cdots = \frac{\text{MP}_n}{\text{MRC}_n}$$

where A, B, . . . , *N* refer to the monopsonist's variable input or resource. But MRC_a/MP_a is the change in the monopsonist's TC per unit change in the output of commodity X, resulting from the use of an additional unit of input A. Thus,

$$\frac{\text{MRC}_a}{\text{MP}_a} = \text{MC}_x \quad \text{or} \quad \frac{\text{MP}_a}{\text{MRC}_a} = \frac{1}{\text{MC}_x}$$

This is true for every other variable input used by the monopsonist. Therefore, the best or least-cost input or resource combination to produce *any* output of commodity X (or any other commodity) can be rewritten as

$$\frac{\text{MP}_a}{\text{MRC}_a} = \frac{\text{MP}_b}{\text{MRC}_b} = \cdots = \frac{\text{MP}_n}{\text{MRC}_n} = \frac{1}{\text{MC}_x}$$

(*b*)
$$\frac{\text{MP}_a}{\text{MRC}_a} = \frac{\text{MP}_b}{\text{MRC}_b} = \cdots = \frac{\text{MP}_n}{\text{MRC}_n} = \frac{1}{\text{MC}_x} = \frac{1}{\text{MR}_x}$$

If the monopsonist is a perfectly competitive seller of commodity X, then $\text{MR}_x = P_x$.

(*c*) If initially $MP_a/MRC_a > MP_b/MRC_b$, the monopsonist can reduce costs of production by substituting input or resource A for input or resource B. As this takes place, the MP_a decreases while the MP_b, increases and the MRC_a increases while the MRC_b decreases. This should continue until $MP_a/MRC_a = MP_bMRC_b$; similarly when $MP_a/MRC_a < MP_b/MRC_b$. On the other hand, if $1/MC_x > 1/MR_x$, it pays for the firm to use more of each of its variable input or resource (in the least-cost combination) to produce more of commodity X. As this occurs, the MC_x increases and so $1/MC_x$ decreases. At the same time, if we have imperfect competition in the product market, the MR_x decreases and so $1/MR_x$ increases. This should continue until $1/MC_x = 1/MR_x$; similarly when $1/MC_x < 1/MR_x$.

13.23 What measures could be adopted to counteract monopsony and reduce or eliminate monopsonistic exploitation?

One way to counteract monopsony is to increase the mobility of the input or resource. If the input is a certain type of labor, this can be done through information of job opportunities elsewhere, training for other occupations, and subsidization of moving expenses. Another way to counteract monopsony is by a union wage contract or by the government imposing a minimum price for the input above the price that the monopsonist would pay for it. Indeed, by establishing a minimum price for the input, at the point where the monopsonist's MRP curve for the input intersects the S_a curve, the monopsonist can be made to behave as a perfectly competitive buyer of the input. In that case, monopsonistic exploitation is completely eliminated and more of the input or resource used (see Problems 13.24 and 13.25).

13.24 Fig. 13-22 is the same as Fig. 13-6. If the government sets a minimum P_a of \$4, (*a*) determine the new S_a and MRC_a curves by the monopsonist and (*b*) compare the result before and after the minimum P_a of \$4 is imposed.

(*a*) If the government sets the minimum $P_a = \$4$ (given by point *B*, where the MRP_a curve intersects the S_a curve), *ABH* becomes the new supply curve for input A facing the monopsonist. The new marginal resource cost curve for input A becomes *ABCF* and has a vertical or discontinuous section directly above (and caused by) the kink (at point *B*) on the new S_a curve.

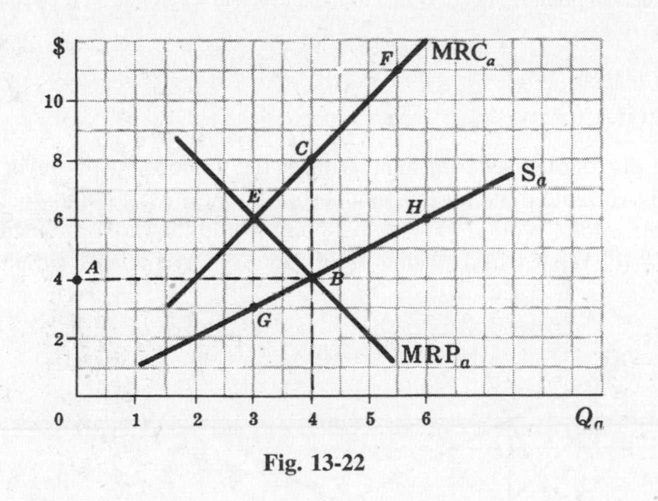

Fig. 13-22

(*b*) Before the establishment of the minimum price for input A, the monopsonist hired three units of input A (given by point *E*) and paid a price of \$3 per unit for input A (given by point *G*). Monopsonistic exploitation for each unit of input A hired thus equaled *EG*, or \$3. In order to maximize total profits when the minimum $P = \$4$ is imposed, the monopsonist will have to behave as a perfectly competitive buyer of input A and hire four units of input A (given by point *B*, where the $MRP_a = MRC_a = P_a$). Input A now receives a higher price (\$4 instead of \$3), more units of input A are hired (four units instead of three), and the monopsonistic exploitation of input A has been entirely eliminated (since $MRP_a = P_a$).

13.25 Starting with Fig. 13-21, explain what happens if the government establishes a minimum P_a of (*a*) \$40, (*b*) \$50, (*c*) \$60, or (*d*) \$35.

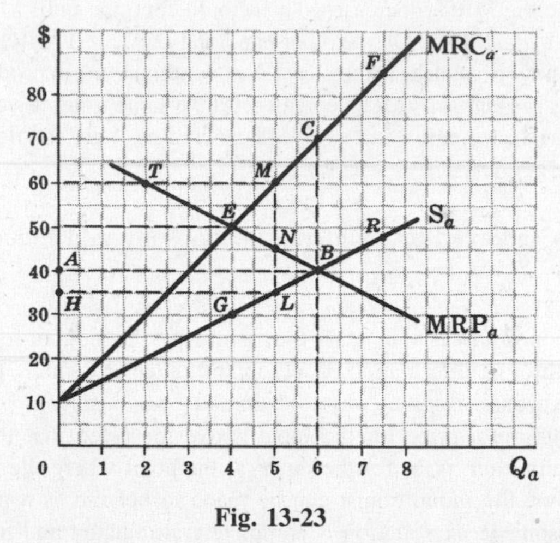

Fig. 13-23

(*a*) The monopsonist's S_a curve becomes *ABR* and the MRC_a curve becomes *ABCF*. The monopsonist will then behave as a perfect competitor in the input A market and hires six units of input A at $P_a = \$40$ (given by point *B*, where the $MRP_a = MRC_a = P_a$). Thus, monopsonistic exploitation is entirely eliminated and more of input A is used (compare point *B* to point *E* in Fig. 13-23). In the real world, it may be difficult to determine the precise P_a at which the $MRP_a = P_a$.

(*b*) The monopsonist will hire four units of input A but all monopsonistic exploitation is eliminated (see point *E*).

(*c*) Monopsonistic exploitation is completely eliminated but the firm hires only two units of input A (see point *T*).

(*d*) The monopsonist's S_a is given by *HLBR*, the new MRC_a curve is *HLMCF*, and the firm hires five units of input A (given by point *N*, where the MRP_a curve crosses the discontinuous or vertical segment *LM* of his MRC_a curve). Thus, the monopsonist hires one more unit of input A than in the absence of the minimum P_a of \$35 (compare point *N* to point *E*), but only half of monopsonistic exploitation is eliminated (compare $NL = \$10$ to $EG = \$20$).

BILATERAL MONOPOLY

13.26 In Fig. 13-24 the monopolist seller of input A faces the monopsonistic buyer of input A. Assume that input A is the only variable input for this monopsonist. (*a*) At what point would the monopolistic seller of input A maximize total profits? (*b*) At what point would the monopsonistic buyer of input A maximize total profits? (*c*) What will the actual result be? (*d*) Give some examples of bilateral monopoly.

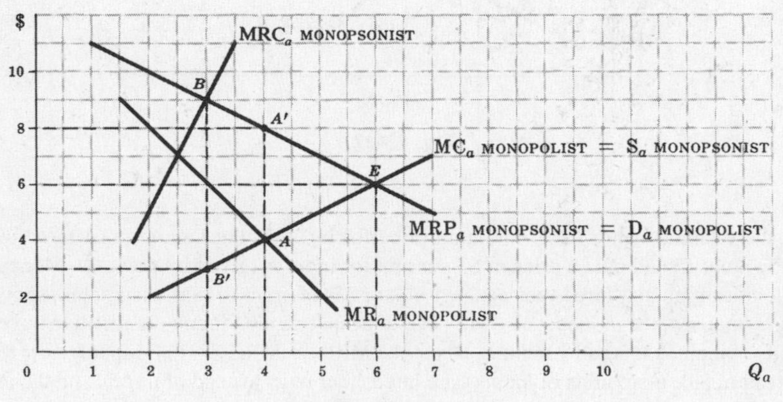

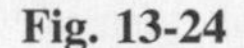

Fig. 13-24

(*a*) When input A is the only variable input, the monopsonist's d_a is given by the MRP_a curve. Since the monopsonist is the only buyer of input A, the monopsonist's MRP_a curve represents the D_a facing the monopolist seller of input A; MR_a is then the monopolist's marginal revenue curve in selling input A. If the monopolist's MC to supply various units of input A is given by the MC_a curve, the best level of sales of input A for the monopolist is four units (given by point *A*, where the monopolist's MR_a curve intersects the MC_a curve) and $P_a = \$8$ (given by point *A′* on the monopolist's D_a curve).

(*b*) The monopolist's MC_a curve represents the S_a curve facing the monopsonist. The monopsonist would thus maximize total profits upon hiring three units of input A (given by point *B*, where the monopsonist's MRP_a curve intersects the MRC_a curve that the monopsonist faces) and pays $P_a = \$3$ (given by point *B′* on the S_a curve facing the monopsonist).

(*c*) The results of (*a*) and (*b*) show that the monopolist's and the monopsonist's aims are in conflict. From a theoretical point of view, the result is indeterminate in this case. The actual quantity of input A sold and its price depends here on the relative bargaining strength of the two firms and will lie somewhere on or within the boundary *B′AA′B*.

(*d*) An example of bilateral monopoly occurs when the union representing the workers in an isolated locality faces the single employer in the area. Another example is when a shipowners' association faces the longshoremen's union. Note that we also have bilateral monopoly when the single seller of any *commodity* faces the single buyer of the commodity.

13.27 Assume that (1) the MRP of the sole buyer of input A is the same as that in Problems 13.20 and 13.25, (2) input A is the only variable input for this monopsonist and (3) the MC curve of the sole seller of input A is identical with the S_a curve of Problems 13.20, 13.21, and 13.25. For this bilateral monopoly, (*a*) draw a figure as in Problem 13.26 and label each curve. (*b*) What is the best level of output for this monopolist seller? At what price does the monopolist want to sell? (*c*) What quantity of input A should the monopsonist use in order to maximize total profits? What price is the monopsonist willing to pay for this quantity of input A? (*d*) How is this case of bilateral monopoly different from that in Problem 13.26? (*e*) What is the actual result of this bilateral monopoly? (*f*) If the two firms merged into a single firm, where would the merged firm maximize its total profits?

(*a*)

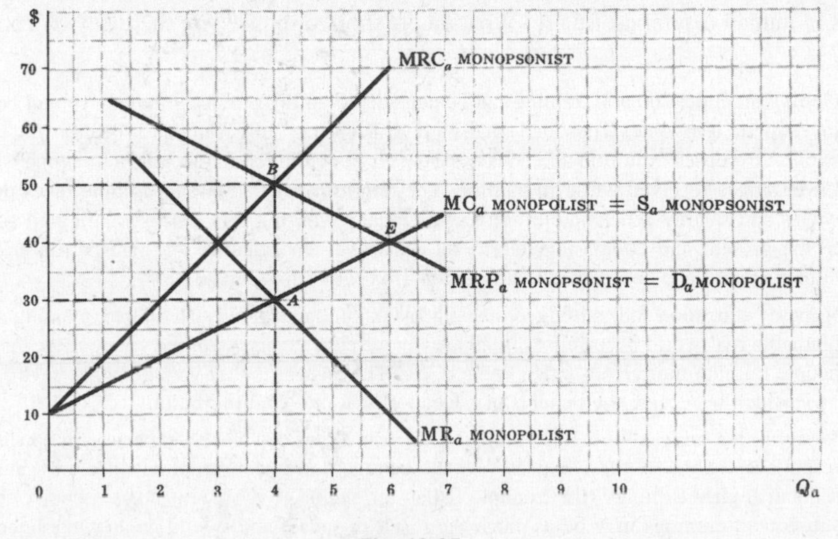

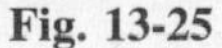

Fig. 13-25

(*b*) The best level of output for the monopolistic seller of input A is four units (given by point *A*) which the monopolist wants to sell at the price of \$50 (given by point *B*).

(c) In order to maximize total profits, the monopsonist should use four units of input A (given by point *B*) at the price of \$30 (given by point *A*).

(d) In Problem 13.26, there is disagreement between the monopolist and the monopsonist with respect to both the quantity and the price of the input. This is the typical case of bilateral monopoly. On the other hand, in Fig. 13-25, the monopolist and the monopsonist disagree on P_a but agree on the quantity of four units of input A. This is a special and less general case of bilateral monopoly.

(e) In the real world, the P_a will be somewhere between \$30 and \$50. The greater the relative bargaining strength of the monopolist, the closer will P_a be to \$50; the greater the relative bargaining strength of the monopsonist, the closer will P_a be to \$30.

(f) If the two firms merged into a single firm, the merged firm would maximize its total profits at point *E*, where its $\text{MRP}_a = \text{MC}_a$. That is, the merged firm would continue to supply input A *for its own use* until the extra revenue it receives from the use of one additional unit of input A exactly equals the extra cost of supplying that unit. The result is that the merged firm will supply and use six units of input A at the per-unit cost of \$40.

EXTENSIONS AND APPLICATIONS

13.28 From what do economic profits arise?

Profits can be regarded as the reward for a successful innovation, as a reward for bearing uncertainty, and as a result of monopoly power. We saw in Section 9.7, that in a long-run and perfectly competitive equilibrium, all firms make zero profit. In the short run, a firm may make profits by introducing a successful innovation such as a new product or a cost-reducing production technique. However, in the long run other firms will imitate the innovation until all profits are competed away. In the meantime, other innovations may be introduced. The expectation of higher profits is also necessary to induce investments in more uncertain ventures. For example, petroleum exploration and the introduction of new products face greater uncertainties and possibilities of losses than entering established industries to produce traditional products. Investments will flow into new ventures facing greater uncertainties only in the expectation of higher profits. Similarly, buying a stock may give a greater but more uncertain return than putting the money in a savings account. Finally, monopolists and oligopolists produce at a price which exceeds marginal cost, and by keeping competitors out, they can continue to make profits in the long run.

13.29 Getting an education and training is sometimes referred to as an "investment in human capital." (*a*) In what way is this similar to any other investment? (*b*) Why is treating education and training as investments in human capital useful? (*c*) What are its shortcomings? Are there any objections to this point of view?

(a) Getting an education and training can be considered an investment in human capital because, like any other investment, it involves a cost and entails a return. The cost of getting an education and training involves such explicit expenses as tuition and books; the cost is also implicit in the wages foregone while in school and the lower wages received while in training. The return on education and training takes the form of the higher wages and salaries received during the individual's working life. By discounting all costs and extra income to the present and comparing returns on costs, we can calculate the rate of return on the investment in human capital and compare it to the returns from other investments.

(b) Viewing education and training as investments in human capital is useful in explaining many otherwise unexplainable real-world occurrences, such as why we educate and train the young more than the old, why young people migrate more readily than the old, etc. The answer is that young people have a longer working time over which to receive the benefits of education, training, and migration.

(c) Some shortcomings of this line of thinking are as follows: (1) Not all expenses for education and training represent costs. Some of these expenses should be regarded as consumption since they do not contribute to subsequent higher earnings (for example, when an engineering student takes a course in poetry). (2) Higher subsequent earnings may be as much the result of innate ability and greater intelligence and effort as it is of training. (3) The antipoverty programs of the 1960s to improve the health of and to train low-income people failed to reduce income inequalities.

Besides these shortcomings, there is the objection that education and training deal with human beings and should not be compared or analyzed with the same tools used to analyze investment in machinery, factories, etc.

13.30 (*a*) What causes wage differences? (*b*) What are equalizing differences? How do these give rise to wage differences? (*c*) What are noncompeting groups? How do they give rise to wage differences? (*d*) What are imperfect labor markets? How do they give rise to wage differences?

(*a*) Wages differ among different categories of people and jobs because of (1) equalizing differences, (2) the existence of noncompeting occupational groups, and (3) imperfections in labor markets.

(*b*) Equalizing differences are wage differences that serve to compensate workers for nonmonetary differences among jobs. That is, jobs requiring equal qualifications may differ in attractiveness and higher wages must be paid to attract and retain workers in the more unpleasant jobs. For example, garbage collectors receive higher wages than porters.

(*c*) Noncompeting groups are occupations which require certain capacities, skills, training, and education and, therefore, receive different wages. That is, labor is not a single productive resource but many different resources, each not in direct competition with others. Thus, doctors form one group which is not in direct competition with other groups of workers. Lawyers, accountants, electricians, bus drivers, etc., belong to other separate, noncompeting groups. There is a particular wage rate structure for each of these noncompeting groups depending on the abilities, skills, and training required for each occupation. To be noted is that some job mobility among competing groups may be possible (for example, when an electrician becomes an electronics engineer by going to night school). However, mobility is generally limited.

(*d*) An imperfect labor market is one in which there is some lack of information on job opportunities and wages; where some workers are unwilling to move to other areas and jobs in order to take advantage of higher wages; and where union power, minimum wage laws, and monopsony power exist. Any of these circumstances causes some differences in wages for jobs which are exactly alike and require equal capacities and skills.

13.31 (*a*) Sketch a graph showing the three main methods that unions can use to raise wages. (*b*) To which of these methods is the imposition of a minimum wage by the government most similar? What are the pros and cons of having minimum wage laws? (*c*) Have unions raised wages in the United States?

(*a*) Panel A of Fig. 13-26 shows that a union can increase union wages from w to w' and employment from OA to OB by increasing D_L to D'_L (for example, by lobbying to restrict imports and advertising to buy the "union label"). This is the most desirable but also the least effective method. Panel B shows that a (craft) union can increase wages from w to w' by reducing S_L to S'_L (by forcing firms to hire only union members and then limiting the number of union members with high initiation fees, requirements of long apprenticeships, etc.). However, employment falls from OA to OC. Panel C shows that an industrial union might increase the wage from w to w' by direct bargaining with employers. However, employment falls from OA to OG and GH ($=E'F$) workers are unable to find jobs. The actual loss of employment resulting from a given rise in wages depends on the elasticity of D_L.

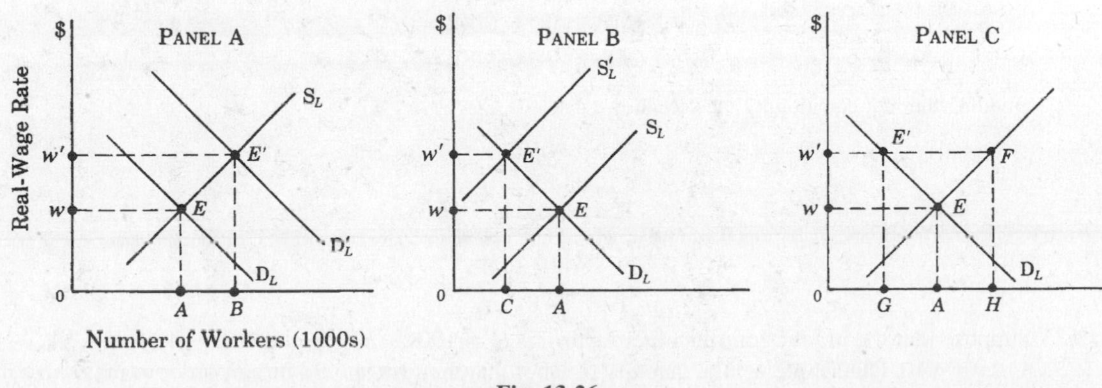

Fig. 13-26

(*b*) If government imposed a minimum wage of w', the result would be the same as the union negotiating a wage of w' shown in panel C. This is particularly beneficial to previously low paid workers near the poverty level. With higher wages and incomes, the health and vigor of these workers may increase and result in greater productivity. Imposing or raising a minimum wage can also have a "shock effect" on business and induce lethargic employers to institute more productive techniques. However, the imposition of a minimum wage also tends to reduce the level of employment. Therefore, while those remaining employed are better off, others find themselves jobless. Training programs for the unemployed might help them find jobs. However, this is not easy to accomplish. The United States has had a minimum wage since 1938. In April 1991, the minimum wage was raised to $4.25 per hour.

(*c*) The ability of unions to increase wages is a controversial subject. Union labor does receive wages that are 20% higher than nonunion labor wages in the United States today. However, unionized industries are generally large-scale industries that employ more skilled labor and that paid higher wages even before unionization. On the other hand, comparison of wage differences between unionized and nonunionized labor may lead to underestimating the effectiveness of unions in raising wages because nonunionized firms may more or less match union wages in order to retain their workers and to keep unions out. Most economists who have studied this question have tentatively concluded that unions in the United States have increased the wages of their members by about 10% to 15%.

PRICE AND EMPLOYMENT OF INPUTS

***13.32** Let P and Q equal the commodity price and output, w and r the wage rate of labor and the rental price of capital, and L and K the amounts of labor and capital used in production by a firm which is a perfect competitor in the product and input markets. Derive, using calculus, the condition for the amount of labor and capital that the firm should use in order to maximize its total profits.

Total profit (π) is

$$\pi = \text{TR} - \text{TC}$$
$$= PQ - wL - rK$$

Since $Q = f(L, K)$, we can rewrite the profit function as

$$\pi = Pf(L, K) - wL - rK$$

Taking the partial derivative of π with respect to L and K and setting them equal to zero, we get

$$\frac{\partial \pi}{\partial L} = \frac{P\,\partial f}{\partial L} - w = 0$$
$$\frac{\partial \pi}{\partial K} = \frac{P\,\partial f}{\partial K} - r = 0$$

Since $P = \text{MR}$, we can rewrite the above equations as

$$(\text{MP}_L)(\text{MR}) = \text{MRP} = w$$
$$(\text{MP}_K)(\text{MR}) = \text{MRP} = r$$

Dividing the first equation by the second, we get

$$\frac{\text{MP}_L}{\text{MP}_K} = \frac{w}{r}$$

Cross multiplying, we have

$$\frac{\text{MP}_L}{w} = \frac{\text{MP}_K}{r}$$

***13.33** Suppose that the production function of a firm is $Q = 100L^{0.5}K^{0.5}$ and that $K = 100$, $P = \$1$, $w = \$30$, and $r = \$40$. Determine (*a*) the quantity of labor that the firm should hire in order to maximize its total profits and (*b*) the maximum profit of this firm.

(*a*) Substituting $K = 100$ into the production function we get

$$Q = 100L^{0.5}100^{0.5}$$
$$= 1000L^{0.5}$$

Then we find the equation of the marginal product of labor (MP_L):

$$MP_L = \frac{\partial Q}{\partial L} = 500L^{-0.5}$$

To maximize profits the firm should hire labor until the $MRP_L = w$. Since $P = MR = \$1$,

$$MRP_L = (MR)(MP_L) = (\$1)(500L^{-0.5}) = \$50 = w$$

Thus

$$L = \left(\frac{\$500}{\$50}\right)^2 = 100$$

(*b*) With $L = 100$ and $K = 100$

$$Q = 100(100)^{0.5}(100)^{0.5} = 10{,}000$$

The total revenue and the total costs of the firm are

$$TR = (P)(Q) = (\$1)(10{,}000) = \$10{,}000$$
$$TC = wL + rK = \$50(100) + \$40(100) = \$9000$$

so that the total profit of the firm is

$$\pi = TR - TC = \$10{,}000 - \$9000 = \$1000$$

This represents the maximum profits that the firm can earn.

***13.34** A monopsonist hiring only labor faces the total cost function $TC = wL$. Derive, using calculus, the expression (*a*) for the marginal resource cost of labor (MRC_L) and (*b*) relating the MRC_L, the wage rate (w), and the wage elasticity of the supply of labor (e_L).

(*a*)
$$MRC_L = \frac{d(TC_L)}{dL} = w + L\frac{dw}{dL}$$

(*b*) Rearranging the above equation, we get

$$MRC_L = w\left(1 + \frac{L\,dw}{w\,dL}\right)$$

Therefore,
$$MRC_L = w\left(1 + \frac{1}{e_L}\right)$$

Graphically, this means that the MRC_L lies above the (positively sloped) S_L curve (see Fig. 13-5). If the firm were instead a perfect competitor in the labor market, $e_L = \infty$ and $MRC_L = w$ (i.e., the MRC_L curve would coincide with the horizontal S_L curve faced by the firm at the given level of w).

CHAPTER 14

General Equilibrium and Welfare Economics

General Equilibrium

14.1 PARTIAL AND GENERAL EQUILIBRIUM ANALYSIS

In Section 1.6, we defined partial equilibrium as the study of the behavior of individual decision-making units and of the workings of individual markets, viewed in isolation. In Chapters 2 through 13 of this book, we have dealt with partial equilibrium analysis. General equilibrium analysis, on the other hand, studies the behavior of all individual decision-making units and of all individual markets *simultaneously* (see Problems 14.1 to 14.4).

In this chapter, we look at a simple perfectly competitive economy composed of two individuals (A and B), two commodities (X and Y), and two factors (L and K) and present a graphical treatment of general equilibrium of exchange only, of production only, and then of production and exchange simultaneously. In the second part of the chapter we consider the welfare implications of this simple general equilibrium model.

14.2 GENERAL EQUILIBRIUM OF EXCHANGE

General equilibrium of exchange in the very simple economy of two individuals, two commodities, and *no production* was already presented in Section 4.8. There we concluded that the two individuals reached equilibrium in the exchange of the two commodities when the marginal rate of substitution (MRS) in consumption for the two commodities was the same for both individuals. Thus, the following example is in the way of a review (of Section 4.8 and Problems 4.24 to 4.27).

EXAMPLE 1. Fig. 14-1 refers to a very simple economy of two individuals (A and B), two commodities (X and Y), and no production. Every point in (or on) the box represents a particular distribution between individuals A and B of the 12X and 12Y available in the economy. Three of A's indifference curves (with origin at O_A) are A_1, A_2, and A_3; B's indifference curves (with origin at O_B) are B_1, B_2, and B_3. If the initial distribution of the 12X and 12Y between individuals A and B is given by point H in the figure, the slopes of A_1 and B_1 at point H differ (i.e., the MRS_{xy} for A is not equal to the MRS_{xy} for B) and there is a basis for exchange. Mutually advantageous exchange comes to an end at a point such as D (on A_2 and B_2) in the figure, where one of A's indifference curves is tangent to one of B's indifference curves. At that point, the MRS_{xy} for A equals the MRS_{xy} for B. Joining such points of tangency, we define the *consumption contract curve* O_ACDEO_B in the figure (for a more detailed discussion, see Problems 4.24 to 4.27). This simple exchange economy will thus be in equilibrium when on its contract curve (i.e., whenever the MRS_{xy} for A equals the MRS_{xy} for B). The above figure is usually referred to as an *Edgeworth box diagram.*

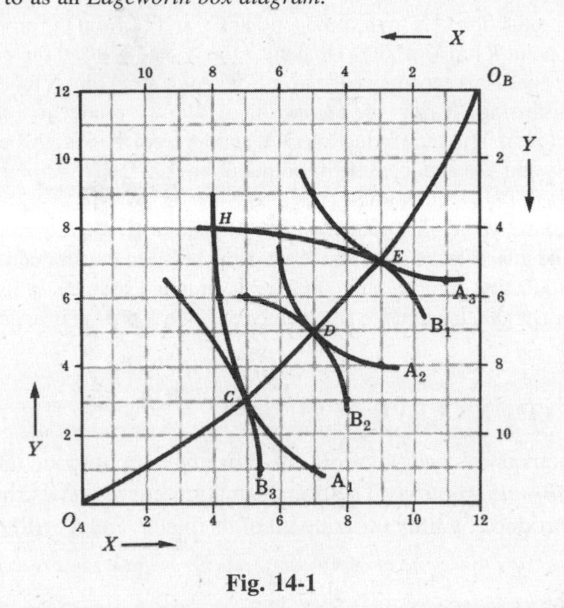

Fig. 14-1

14.3 GENERAL EQUILIBRIUM OF PRODUCTION

A producer of two commodities (X and Y) using two factors (L and K) reaches *general equilibrium of production* whenever the marginal rate of technical substitution between L and K ($MRTS_{LK}$) in the production of X is equal to the $MRTS_{LK}$ in the production of Y. We can show the general equilibrium of production for this economy by utilizing Edgeworth box diagram.

EXAMPLE 2. In Fig. 14-2, every point in (or on) the box represents a particular use of the 14 units of L and the 12 units of K available to this economy. For example, point R indicates that $3L$ and $10K$ are used to produce X_1 of commodity X and the remaining $11L$ and $2K$ to produce Y_1 of commodity Y. Three of X's isoquants (with origin at O_x) are X_1, X_2, and X_3; Y's isoquants (with origin at O_y) are Y_1, Y_2, and Y_3.

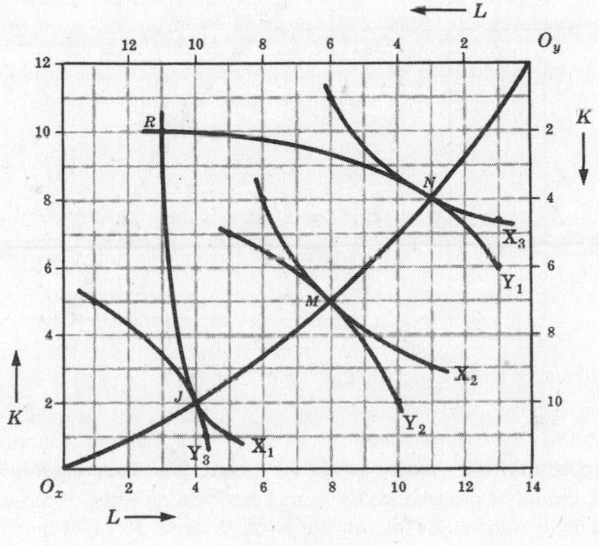

Fig. 14-2

If this economy were initially at point R, it would not be maximizing its output of X and Y, because at point R the slope of X_1 exceeds the slope of Y_1 (i.e., the $MRTS_{LK}$ in the production of X exceeds the $MRTS_{LK}$ in the production of Y). By simply transferring $8K$ from the production of X to the production of Y and $1L$ from the production of Y to the production of X, this economy can move from point R (on X_1 and Y_1) to point J (on X_1 and Y_3) and increase its output of Y without reducing its output of X. On the other hand, this economy can move from point R to point N (and increase its output of X without reducing its output of Y) by transferring $2K$ from the production of X to the production of Y and $8L$ from Y to X. Or, by transferring $5K$ from the production of X to the production of Y and $5L$ from Y to X, this economy can move from point R (on X_1 and Y_1) to point M (on X_2 and Y_2) and increase its output of both X and Y. At points J, M, and N, an X isoquant is tangent to a Y isoquant and so $(MRTS_{LK})_x = (MRTS_{LK})_y$.

If we join such tangency points, we get the *production contract curve* $O_x JMNO_y$ in Fig. 14-2. Thus, by simply transferring some of the given and fixed quantities of the L and K available between the production of X and Y, this economy can move from a point not on the production contract curve to a point on it and so increase its output. Once on its production contract curve, there is no further net gain in output to be obtained, and the economy is in general equilibrium of production.

14.4 THE TRANSFORMATION CURVE

By mapping the production contract curve of Fig. 14-2 from the input space into an output space, we get the corresponding *product transformation curve*. The transformation curve shows the various combinations of X and Y that this economy can produce by fully utilizing all of its fixed L and K with the best technology available.

EXAMPLE 3. If isoquant X_1 in Fig. 14-2 refers to 4 units of output of commodity X and Y_3 refers to 18Y, we can go from point J on the production contract curve (and input space) of Fig. 14-2 to point J' in the output space of Fig. 14-3. Similarly, if $X_2 = 12X$ and $Y_2 = 12Y$, we can go from point M in Fig. 14-2 to point M' in Fig. 14-3 and if $X_3 = 18X$ while $Y_1 = 4Y$, we can map point N of Fig. 14-2 as point N' in Fig. 14-3. By joining points J', M', and N', we derive the transformation curve for X and Y in Fig. 14-3.

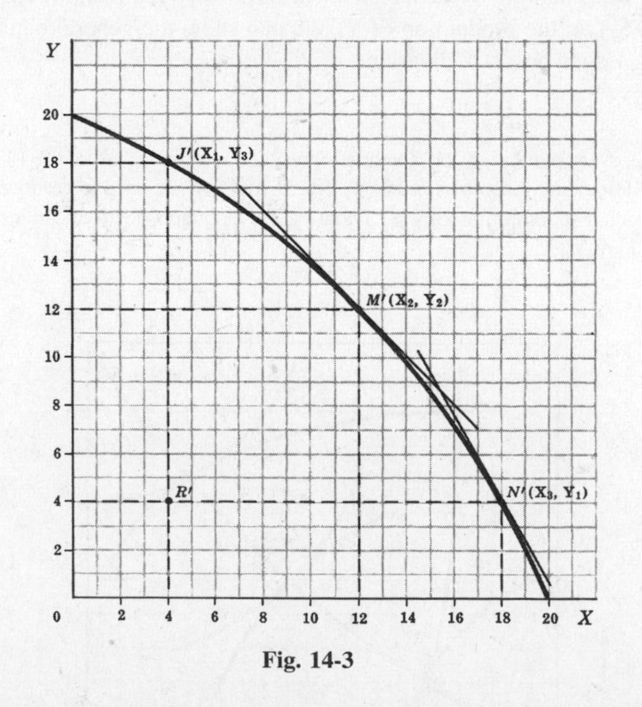

Fig. 14-3

The transformation curve shows the various combinations of X and Y that this economy can produce when in general equilibrium of production. Point R' inside the transformation curve corresponds to point R in Fig. 14-2 and indicates that the economy is not in general equilibrium of production. By simply reallocating some of the fixed L and K between the production of X and Y, this economy can increase either its output of Y (point J') or its output of X (point N') or its output of both X and Y (point M'). With the fixed L and K available and the technology existing at a particular point in time, this economy cannot currently achieve points above its transformation curve.

14.5 THE SLOPE OF THE TRANSFORMATION CURVE

The *slope of the transformation curve* at a particular point gives the marginal rate of transformation of X for Y (MRT_{xy}) at that point. It measures by how much this economy must reduce its output of Y in order to release enough L and K to produce exactly one more unit of X.

EXAMPLE 4. At point M' in Fig. 14-3, the slope of the transformation curve, or MRT_{xy}, is 1. This means that at point M', by reducing the amount of Y produced by one unit, enough L and K are released from the production of Y to allow exactly one additional unit of X to be produced. Note that as we move down the transformation curve, say from point M' to point N', its slope, or MRT_{xy}, increases. This means that we must give up more and more of Y to get each additional unit of X. That is, this economy incurs increasing costs (in terms of the amounts of Y it has to give up) to produce each additional unit of X. This is an instance of imperfect factor substitutability. Because of it, the transformation curve in Fig. 14-3 is concave to the origin rather than a straight line.

14.6 GENERAL EQUILIBRIUM OF PRODUCTION AND EXCHANGE

We now combine the results of Sections 14.2 to 14.5 and examine how our simple economy can achieve simultaneous general equilibrium of production and exchange.

If we take a particular point on the economy's production transformation curve, we specify a particular combination of X and Y produced. Given this particular combination of X and Y, we can construct an Edgeworth box diagram and derive the consumption contract curve. The economy will then be simultaneously in *general equilibrium of production and exchange* when $MRT_{xy} = (MRS_{xy})_A = (MRS_{xy})_B$.

EXAMPLE 5. The transformation curve in Fig. 14-4 is that of Fig. 14-3. Every point on such a transformation curve corresponds to a point of general equilibrium of production. Suppose that the output of X and Y produced by this economy is given by point M' (i.e., 12X and 12Y) on the transformation curve. By dropping perpendiculars from point M' to both axes, we can construct in Fig. 14-4 the Edgeworth box diagram of Fig. 14-1 for individuals A and B. Every point on consumption contract curve O_ACDEO_B is a point of general equilibrium of exchange. However, this simple economy will be simultaneously in general equilibrium of production and exchange at point D, where $(MRS_{xy})_A = (MRS_{xy})_B = MRT_{xy}$. If $(MRS_{xy})_A = (MRS_{xy})_B \neq MRT_{xy}$, the economy would not be in general equilibrium of production and exchange. For example, if the $(MRS_{xy})_A = (MRS_{xy})_B = 2$ while the $MRT_{xy} = 1$, individuals A and B would be willing (indifferent) to give up two units of Y of consumption for one additional unit of X, while in production only one unit of Y must be given up in order to get the additional unit of X. Thus more of X and less of Y should be produced until $(MRS_{xy})_A = (MRS_{xy})_B = MRT_{xy}$.

We conclude the following about this economy when in general equilibrium of production and exchange: (1) it produces 12X and 12Y (point M' in Fig. 14-4); exactly how this society decides on this level of production is discussed in Section 14.11; (2) individual A receives 7X and 5Y while individual B receives the remaining 5X and 7Y (point D in Fig. 14-4); (3) to produce the 12X, 8L and 5K are used while to produce the 12Y, the remaining 6L and 7K are used (see point M in Fig. 14-2). (For a discussion of equilibrium P_L, P_K, P_x, and P_y, see Problems 14.13 and 14.14; the conditions for general equilibrium of production, of exchange, and of production and exchange simultaneously, for an economy of many factors, commodities and individuals, are examined in Problem 14.15.)

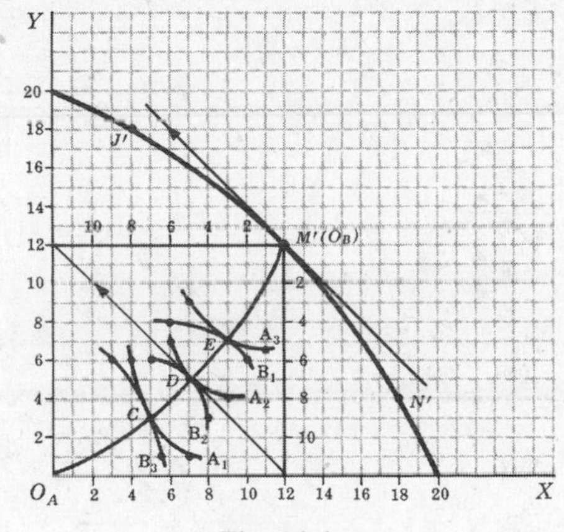

Fig. 14-4

Welfare Economics

14.7 WELFARE ECONOMICS DEFINED

Welfare economics studies the conditions under which the solution to a general equilibrium model can be said to be optimal. This requires, among other things, an optimal allocation of factors among commodities and an optimal allocation of commodities (i.e., distribution of income) among consumers.

An allocation of factors of production is said to be *Pareto optimal* if production cannot be reorganized to increase the output of one or more commodities without decreasing the output of some other commodity. Thus, in a two-commodity economy, the production contract curve is the locus of the Pareto optimal allocation of factors in the production of the two commodities. Similarly, an allocation of commodities can be said to be Pareto optimal if distribution cannot be reorganized to increase the utility of one or more individuals without decreasing the utility of some other individual. Thus, in a two-individual economy, the consumption contract curve is the locus of the Pareto optimal distribution of commodities between the two individuals.

14.8 THE UTILITY-POSSIBILITY CURVE

By mapping the consumption contract curve of Fig. 14-4 from the output space into a utility space, we get the corresponding *utility-possibility curve*. This shows the various combinations of utility received by individuals A and B (i.e., u_A and u_B) when the simple economy of Section 14.1 is in general equilibrium of exchange. The point on the consumption contract curve at which the MRS_{xy} for A and B equals the MRT_{xy} gives the point of Pareto optimum in production and consumption on the utility-possibility curve.

EXAMPLE 6. If indifference curve A_1 in Fig. 14-4 refers to 150 units of utility for individual A (i.e., $u_A = 150$ utils) and B_3 refers to $u_B = 450$ utils, we can go from point C on the consumption contract curve (and output space) of Fig. 14-4 to point C' in the utility space of Fig. 14-5. Similarly, if A_2 refers to $u_A = 300$ utils and B_2 refers to $u_B = 400$ utils, we can go from point D in Fig. 14-4 to point D' in Fig. 14-5. And if A_3 refers to $u_A = 400$ utils while B_1 refers to $u_B = 150$ utils, we can go from point E in Fig. 14-4 to point E' in Fig. 14-5. By joining points C', D', and E', we derive utility-possibility curve $F_{M'}$ (see Fig. 14-5). At point D' in this figure (which corresponds to point D in Fig. 14-4), this simple economy is simultaneously at Pareto optimum in both production and consumption.

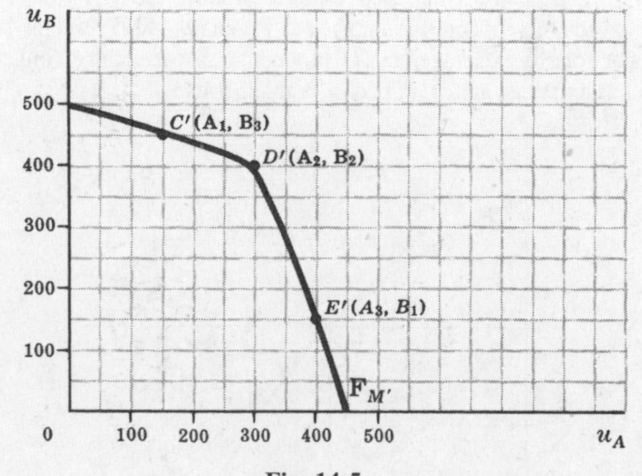

Fig. 14-5

14.9 GRAND UTILITY-POSSIBILITY CURVE

By taking another point on the transformation curve, we can construct a different Edgeworth box diagram and consumption contract curve. From this we can derive a different utility-possibility curve and another point of Pareto optimum in production and consumption. This process can be repeated any number of times. By then joining the resulting points of Pareto optimum in production and exchange, we can drive the *grand utility-possibility curve*.

EXAMPLE 7. Utility-possibility curve $F_{M'}$ in Fig. 14-5 was derived from the consumption contract curve drawn from point O_A to point M' on the transformation curve of Fig. 14-4. If we pick another point on the transformation curve of Fig. 14-4, say point N', we can construct another Edgeworth box diagram and get another consumption contract curve, this one drawn from point O_A to point N' in Fig. 14-4. From this different consumption contract curve (not shown in Fig. 14-4), we can derive another utility-possibility curve ($F_{N'}$ in Fig. 14-6) and get another Pareto optimum point in both production and exchange (point T' in Fig. 14-6). By then joining points D', T' and other points similarly obtained, we can-derive grand utility-possibility curve G in Fig. 14-6. Thus, the grand utility-possibility curve is the locus of Pareto optimum points of production and exchange. That is, no reorganization of the production-distribution process can make someone better off without at the same time making someone else worse off.

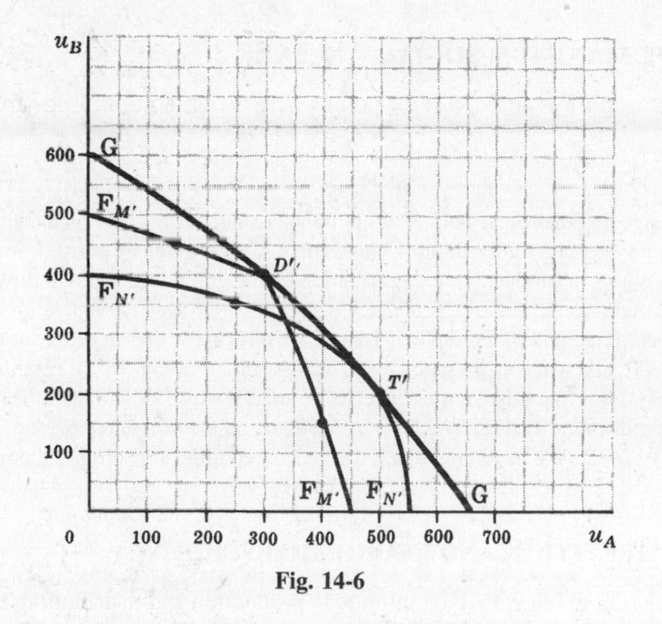

Fig. 14-6

14.10 THE SOCIAL WELFARE FUNCTION

The only way we can decide which of the Pareto optimum points on the grand utility-possibility curve represents the maximum social welfare is to accept the notion of interpersonal comparison of utility. We would then be able to draw *social welfare functions*. A social welfare function shows the various combinations of u_A and u_B that give society the same level of satisfaction or welfare.

EXAMPLE 8. In Fig. 14-7, W_1, W_2, and W_3 are three social welfare functions or social indifference curves from this society's dense welfare map. All points on a given curve give society the same level of satisfaction or welfare. Society prefers any point on a higher to any point on a lower social welfare function. Note, however, that a movement along a social welfare curve makes one individual better off and the other worse off. Thus, in order to construct a social welfare function, society must make an ethical or value judgment (interpersonal comparison of utility).

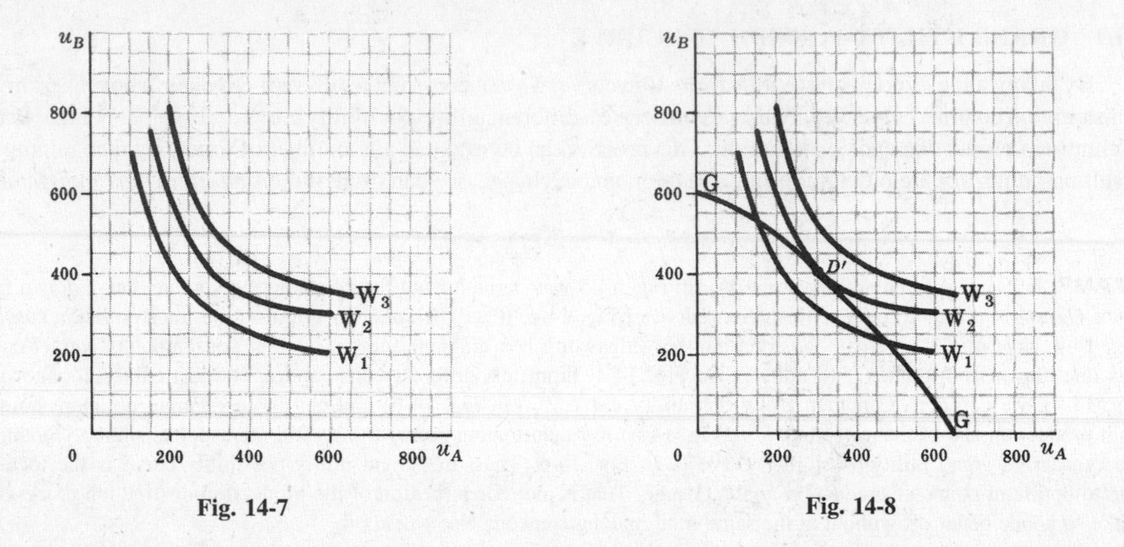

Fig. 14-7

Fig. 14-8

14.11 THE POINT OF MAXIMUM SOCIAL WELFARE

The *maximum social welfare* is attained at the point where the grand utility-possibility curve is tangent to a social welfare curve.

EXAMPLE 9. By superimposing the social welfare or indifference map of Fig. 14-7 on the grand utility-possibility curve of Fig. 14-6, we can determine the point of maximum social welfare. This is given by point D' in Fig. 14-8. Of all the infinite number of Pareto optimum points of production and distribution on the grand utility-possibility curve, we have chosen the one that represents the maximum social welfare. Note that we have now removed the indeterminacy (how much of X and Y to produce) that we discussed at the end of Example 5. That is, we now know that in order for this society to maximize its welfare: (1) u_A must equal 300 utils while u_B must equal 400 utils (point D' in Fig. 14-8); (2) this society must produce 12X and 12Y (point M' in Fig. 14-4); (3) individual A must receive 7X and 5Y while individual B the remaining 5X and 7Y (point D in Fig. 14-4); and (4) to produce the 12X, 8L and 5K must be used and the remaining 6L and 7K must be used to produce the 12Y (see point M in Fig. 14-2). We have thus found the general equilibrium solution that maximizes social welfare.

14.12 PERFECT COMPETITION AND ECONOMIC EFFICIENCY

We have seen that in order to reach Pareto optimum in production and distribution, the following three sets of conditions must be satisfied simultaneously: (1) $(\text{MRTS}_{LK})_x = (\text{MRTS}_{LK})_y$; (2) $(\text{MRS}_{xy})_A = (\text{MRS}_{xy})_B$; and (3) $(\text{MRS}_{xy})_A = (\text{MRS}_{xy})_B = \text{MRT}_{xy}$. All three conditions will be satisfied when all markets in the economy are perfectly competitive. (For a proof, see Problem 14.20.) *This is the basic argument in favor of perfect competition.*

14.13 EXTERNALITIES AND MARKET FAILURE

An *externality* is a divergence either between private costs and social costs or between private gains and social gains. In such cases of "*market failure*," the pursuit of private gains does not lead to maximum social welfare, even if perfect competition exists in all markets.

EXAMPLE 10. We saw in Chapter 8 that the best level of output for a perfectly competitive firm is given by the point where $P = \text{MC}$ and MC is rising. But if the firm pollutes the air, its marginal *private* cost is smaller than the marginal *social* cost and so too much of this commodity is produced for maximum social welfare. On the other hand, by resulting in a more responsible citizenry, the marginal social benefits of education exceed the marginal private (i.e., to the individual) benefit. If individuals pay for their own education, there will be underinvestment in education from society's point of view.

14.14 PUBLIC GOODS

Market failures also arise from the existence of public goods. *Public goods* are those that are *nonrival in consumption.* That is the use of the good or service by someone does not reduce its availability to others. For example, if one individual watches regular television there is no interference with the reception of the same TV program by others. Some public goods (such as cable TV) are exclusive (i.e., the service can be confined to those paying for it), while others, such as national defense are *nonexclusive* (i.e., it is impossible to limit the benefit to only those paying for it).

Public goods that are nonexclusive lead to a *free-rider problem*, i.e., the unwillingness of people to help pay for the public goods in the belief that the goods would be provided anyway. Less than the optimal amount of these goods would then be provided without the government's raising money to pay for them through general taxation. Even this does not entirely eliminate the problem because individuals have no incentive to accurately reveal their preferences, or demand, for the public good. Since a given amount of a public good can be consumed by more than one individual at the same time, the aggregate or total demand for the public good is obtained by the vertical summation of the demand curves for all of those who consume the public good.

EXAMPLE 11. In Fig. 14-9, d_A and d_B are, respectively, the demand curves for public good *X* of individuals *A* and *B*. If *A* and *B* are the only individuals in the market, the aggregate demand curve for public good *X*, D_T, is obtained by the *vertical* summation of d_A and d_B. The reason is that each unit of the good can be consumed by both individuals at the same time. Given market supply curve S_x for public good X, the optimal amount of X is 4 units per time period (indicated by the intersection of D_T and S_x at point *E*). At point *E*, the sum of the individual's marginal benefits equals the marginal cost of producing the 4 units of the public good (i.e., $AB + BC = AE$).

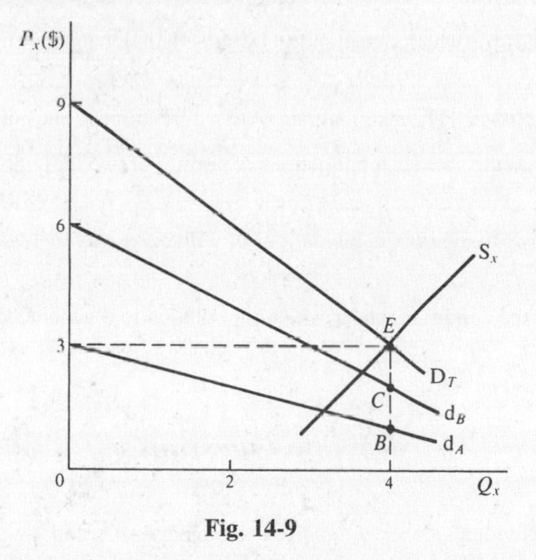

Fig. 14-9

Glossary

Consumption contract curve The locus of points where one individual's indifference curve is tangent to the other individual's indifference curve.

Externality and market failure Refers to a divergence either between private costs and social costs or between private gains and social gains.

Free-rider problem The unwillingness of people to help pay for an optimal amount of a public good in the belief that it will be provided anyway.

General equilibrium analysis Studies the behavior of all individual decision-making units and of all individual markets simultaneously.

General equilibrium of exchange The condition when the marginal rate of substitution (MRS) in consumption for the two commodities is the same for both individuals.

General equilibrium of production The condition when the marginal rate of technical substitution (MRTS) of one factor for another is the same in the production of both commodities.

General equilibrium of production and exchange The condition when the marginal rate of transformation between two commodities is equal to the marginal rate of substitution consumption between the two commodities for each individual.

Grand utility-possibility curve The locus of points of Pareto optimum in production and exchange.

Maximum social welfare Is attained at the point where the grand utility-possibility curve is tangent to a social welfare curve.

Nonexclusion The situation in which it is impossible or prohibitively expensive to confine the benefit or the consumption of a public good to only those people paying for it.

Nonrival consumption The distinguishing characteristic of a public good, whereby its consumption by some individuals does not reduce the amount available to others.

Pareto optimal The condition when production and distribution cannot be reorganized to increase the output of one commodity or the utility of one individual without reducing the production of the other commodity or the utility of the other individual.

Product transformation curve Shows the various combinations of two commodities that an economy can produce by fully utilizing all its resources with the best technology available.

Production contract curve The locus of points where one producer's isoquant is tangent to the other producer's isoquant.

Public good Goods and services for which consumption by some individuals does not reduce the amount available for others.

Slope of the transformation curve The marginal rate of transformation of one commodity for another in production.

Social welfare function Shows the various combinations of utilities of two individuals that give society the same level of satisfaction or welfare.

Utility-possibility curve Shows the various combinations of utility received by two individuals in general equilibrium of exchange.

Welfare economics Studies the conditions under which the solution to a general equilibrium model can be said to be optimal.

Review Questions

1. In an economy of two individuals (*A* and *B*) and two commodities (X and Y), general equilibrium of exchange is reached when (*a*) $\text{MRT}_{xy} = \text{MRS}_{xy}$ for *A* and *B*, (*b*) $\text{MRS}_{xy} = P_x/P_y$, (*c*) $(\text{MRS}_{xy})_A = (\text{MRS}_{xy})_B$, or (*d*) all of the above.

   Ans. (*c*) See Section 14.2.

2. The locus of general equilibrium points of exchange in a two-individual, two-commodity economy is called (*a*) the consumption contract curve, (*b*) the production contract curve, (*c*) the social welfare function, or (*d*) the transformation curve.

   Ans. (*a*) See Example 1 and Fig. 14-1.

3. In an economy of two commodities (X and Y) and two factors (*L* and *K*), general equilibrium of production is reached when (*a*) $\text{MRTS}_{LK} = P_L/P_K$, (*b*) $\text{MRTS}_{LK} = \text{MRS}_{xy}$, (*c*) $\text{MRT}_{xy} = \text{MRS}_{xy}$, or (*d*) $(\text{MRTS}_{LK})_x = (\text{MRTS}_{LK})_y$.

   Ans. (*d*) See Section 14.3.

4. The transformation curve is derived from (*a*) the consumption curve, (*b*) the utility-possibility curve, (*c*) the social welfare function, or (*d*) the production contract curve.

Ans. (*d*) See Section 14.4.

5. The slope of the transformation curve is given by (*a*) MRT_{xy}, (*b*) MRS_{xy}, (*c*) $MRTS_{LK}$, or (*d*) all of the above.

Ans. (*a*) See Section 14.5.

6. In an economy of two individuals (*A* and *B*) and two commodities (X and Y), general equilibrium of production and exchange occurs when (*a*) $MRT_{xy} = P_x/P_y$, (*b*) MRS_{xy} for *A* and $B = P_x/P_y$, (*c*) $(MRS_{xy})_A = (MRS_{xy})_B$, or (*d*) $MRT_{xy} = (MRS_{xy})_A = (MRS_{xy})_B$.

Ans. (*d*) See Section 14.6.

7. The distribution of two commodities between two individuals is said to be Pareto optimal if

(*a*) one individual cannot be made better off without making the other worse off,
(*b*) the individuals are on their consumption contract curve,
(*c*) the individuals are on their utility-possibility curve, or
(*d*) all of the above.

Ans. (*d*) Choice (*a*) is the definition of the Pareto optimal distribution of the two commodities between the two individuals. The consumption contract curve is the locus of Pareto optimal points in consumption while the utility-possibility curve is derived from the consumption contract curve and thus it is also the locus of Pareto optimal points of consumption.

8. In deriving the utility-possibility curve, we make interpersonal comparisons of utility. (*a*) Always, (*b*) never, (*c*) sometimes, or (*d*) often.

Ans. (*b*) In drawing a utility-possibility curve, the u_A scale is entirely independent from the u_B scale. More specifically, $u_A = 200$ is not necessarily greater than $u_B = 100$, although $u_A = 200 > u_A = 100$.

9. The locus of Pareto optimality in production and consumption is given by (*a*) the social welfare function, (*b*) the utility-possibility curve, (*c*) the transformation curve, or (*d*) the grand utility-possibility curve.

Ans. (*d*) See Section 14.9.

10. An ethical or value judgment must be made in order to derive (*a*) the transformation curve, (*b*) the consumption contract curve, (*c*) the grand utility-possibility curve, or (*d*) the social welfare function.

Ans. (*d*) See Section 14.10.

11. In a two-commodity (X and Y) and two-individual (*A* and *B*) economy, the maximum social welfare is reached at (*a*) any point on the grand utility-possibility curve, (*b*) any point on the social welfare function, (*c*) the point where the $MRT_{xy} = MRS_{xy}$ for *A* and *B*, or (*d*) the point of tangency of the grand utility-possibility curve with a social welfare function.

Ans. (*d*) See point D′ in Fig. 14-8.

12. Perfect competition leads to a point on the grand utility-possibility curve. (*a*) Always, (*b*) never, (*c*) sometimes, or (*d*) we cannot say.

Ans. (*c*) Perfect competition leads to a point on the grand utility-possibility curve except when externalities are present.

Solved Problems

GENERAL EQUILIBRIUM

14.1 (*a*) What is partial equilibrium analysis? Why is it used or employed? (*b*) What is the relationship of partial equilibrium to general equilibrium analysis? What does general equilibrium analysis accomplish? (*c*) When can we say that the entire economy is in general equilibrium?

(*a*) In partial equilibrium analysis, we study specific decision-making units and markets by abstracting from the interconnections that exist between them and the rest of the economy. Thus, we examine in detail the behavior of individual people acting as consumers, managers, and owners of factors of production; we also study the workings of individual markets. The justification for doing this is that partial equilibrium analysis reduces the problem under study to manageable proportions, while at the same time giving us, in most instances, a sufficiently close approximation to the results sought.

(*b*) The actions of each decision-making unit and the workings of each market affect, to a greater or lesser degree, every other decision-making unit and every other market in the economy. It is such interrelationships that general equilibrium analysis studies. Stated differently, general equilibrium analysis examines the interrelations among the various decision-making units and the various markets in the economy in an attempt to give a complete, explicit, and simultaneous answer to the basic economic questions of what, how, and for whom.

(*c*) The entire economy is in general equilibrium when each decision-making unit and market in the economy is individually and simultaneously in equilibrium.

14.2 Starting from a position of general equilibrium for the entire economy, if for any reason the market supply for commodity X (S_x) increases, examine what happens (*a*) in the markets for commodity X, its substitutes and complements, (*b*) in the factor markets, and (*c*) to the distribution of income.

(*a*) If S_x increases, P_x falls and QS_x increases. With partial equilibrium analysis, we stop at this point. However, the greater the effect of changes in the commodity X market on the rest of the economy, the less appropriate partial analysis is. The fall in P_x increases the demand of complementary commodities and reduces the demand for substitute commodities. Thus, the price and quantity of complementary commodities rise, and the price and quantity of substitutes fall (if supply curves are positively sloped).

(*b*) The above changes in the commodity markets affect the factor markets. The derived demand and thus the price, quantity, and income of factors used in the production of commodity X and its complementary commodities rise; the derived demand and thus the price, quantity, and income of factors used in the production of substitute commodities fall. These changes in the factor markets are dampened by the substitution of factors in production induced by the relative factor price changes.

(*c*) Because of the changes detailed in (*b*), the income of various factors of production and the distribution of income change. These changes, in turn, affect to a greater or lesser degree the demand of all final commodities, including the demand for commodity X. The derived demand of all factors of production is then affected and the process continues until all commodity and factor markets are once again simultaneously cleared and the economy is once again in general equilibrium.

14.3 Assume: (1) a simple economy that is initially in general, long-run, perfectly competitive equilibrium, (2) L and K are the only two factors of production and we have a fixed amount of each, (3) there are only two commodities, X and Y, and X is the more L-intensive (i.e., it is produced with a higher L/K ratio) than Y, (4) commodities X and Y are substitutes, and (5) industries X and Y are increasing-cost industries. (*a*) Discuss, from a partial equilibrium point of view, what happens if D_x rises. (*b*) What happens in the market for commodity Y? (*c*) What happens in the labor and capital markets? (*d*) How do the changes introduced in the labor and capital markets in turn affect the entire economy?

(*a*) When D_x increases, P_x rises. Firms producing commodity X now make profits, and so they expand their output of commodity X within existing plants. In the long run, they build larger plants and new firms enter the industry until all profits are squeezed out. Since industry X is an increasing-cost industry, the new long-run equilibrium price and quantity are higher than at the original equilibrium point. With partial equilibrium analysis we make the *ceteris paribus* (i.e., other things being equal) assumption, and we stop here.

(*b*) But clearly, "other things" will not be equal. Since X and Y are substitutes, the increase in D_x and P_x decreases D_y and thus P_y falls. The firms producing Y now suffer short-run losses, and so they reduce their output. In the long run, some firms leave the industry until all remaining firms just break even. Since industry Y is also an increasing-cost industry, its new long-run equilibrium price and output are lower than at the original equilibrium point.

(*c*) To produce more of X and less of Y, some L and K must shift from the production of Y to the production of X. However, since the L/K ratio is higher in the production of X than in the production of Y, P_L must rise relative to P_K in order for all of the available L and K to remain fully employed in the short run. This rise in P_L relative to P_K is moderated by the price-induced substitution of K for L in the production of both X and Y.

(*d*) The labor income of people rises relative to the income resulting from their ownership of capital. Thus, the income of people and its distribution change. This causes income-induced shifts in D_x and D_y and results in changes in P_x and P_y. The change in P_x causes a further shift of D_y and the change in P causes a further shift in D_x. These shifts in D_x and D_y cause changes in D_L, D_K, P_L, and P_K, and the process continues until the economy is once again in general equilibrium.

14.4 Can an economy ever reach general equilibrium in the real world?

Since in the real world, tastes, technology, and the supply of labor and capital are continuously changing, the economy will always be gravitating toward a general equilibrium point, never quite realizing it. That is, before the economy adjusts completely to a specific change and reaches general equilibrium, "other things" will usually change, keeping the economy always in the process of adjustment.

If, from the above discussion, the feeling comes across that general equilibrium analysis is very complicated, the reader is right, indeed. Imagine the degree of complexity of a truly (but impossibly) general equilibrium model (where everything affects everything else) for an economy such as ours, composed of hundreds of factors, thousands of commodities, millions of firms, and tens of millions of households or consuming units. The simple general equilibrium model in subsequent problems does show the interrelations between the various sectors of the system, however, and gives at least a flavor of (truly) general equilibrium analysis.

14.5 Suppose that the isoquants for commodities X and Y are given by X_1, X_2, X_3 and Y_1, Y_2, Y_3, respectively. Suppose also that only $18L$ and $12K$ are available for the production of X and Y. (*a*) Draw the Edgeworth box diagram for X and Y. (*b*) Starting at the point where X_1 crosses Y_1, show that the output of X, Y, or both can be increased with the given amounts of $18L$ and $12K$. (*c*) How do we get the contract curve? What does it show?

Table 14.1

X's Isoquants						Y's Isoquants					
X_1		X_2		X_3		Y_1		Y_2		Y_3	
L	K	L	K	L	K	L	K	L	K	L	K
3	10	7	9	9	10	3	6	9	9	13	10
4	5	8	7	12	8	6	4	10	5	14	7
6	2	11	4	15	7	15	2	13	3	16	5

(*a*) The Edgeworth box diagram for X and Y is shown in Fig. 14-10.

(*b*) At point R (where X_1 crosses Y_1), $3L$ and $10K$ are used to produce X_1 of X and the remaining $15L$ and $2K$ to produce Y_1 of Y. At point R, the $(MRTS_{LK})_x > (MRTS_{LK})_y$. A movement down isoquant X_1 from point R to point J results in the same amount of X being produced (X_1) but much more of Y (Y_3). On the other hand, a movement from point R to point N along isoquant Y_1 results in the same amount of Y being produced (Y_1) but much more of X (X_3). Or, we could have a movement from point R (on isoquant X_1 and Y_1) to point M (on isoquant X_2 and Y_2) and thus increase the output of both X and Y. Note that once an X isoquant is tangent to a Y isoquant (and so the $MRTS_{LK}$ for X and Y is the same) the output of one of the commodities cannot be

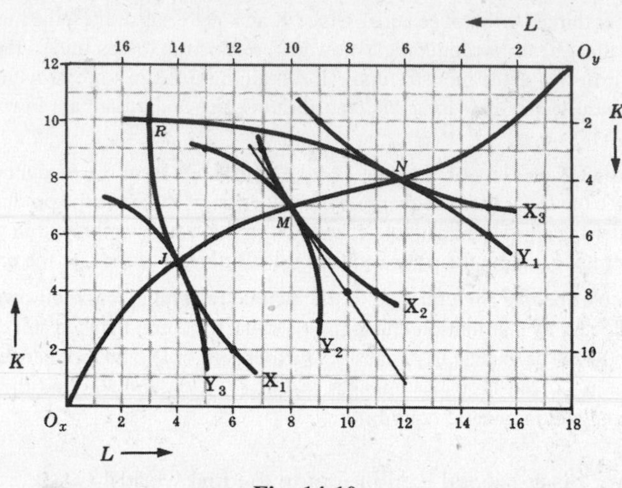

Fig. 14-10

increased without reducing the output of the other. Such points of tangency are assured by convexity and because the fields of isoquants are dense.

(c) The line joining point J to points M and N gives a portion of the production contract curve. By sketching many more isoquants for X and Y and joining all the points of tangency, we could obtain the entire production contract curve. Such a curve would extend from O_x to O_y (see Fig. 14-10). A movement from a point not on the production contract curve to a point on it results in an increase in the output of X, Y, or both, *without using more L or K*. Thus, the production contract curve is the locus of general equilibrium and Pareto optimal points of production.

14.6 (*a*) Give the equilibrium condition that holds along the production contract curve and (*b*) express in marginal productivity terms the equilibrium condition that holds along the production contract curve, (*c*) What is the value of the MRTS_{LK} at point M in Fig. 14-10?

(*a*)

$$(\text{MRTS}_{LK})_x = (\text{MRTS}_{LK})_y$$

(*b*) Since $\text{MRTS}_{LK} = \text{MP}_L/\text{MP}_K$ (see Section 6.8), the equilibrium condition that holds along the production contract curve can be restated in productivity terms as

$$\left(\frac{\text{MP}_L}{\text{MP}_K}\right)_x = \left(\frac{\text{MP}_L}{\text{MP}_K}\right)_y$$

(*c*) The value of the MRTS_{LK} at point M is given by the common absolute slope of isoquants X_2 and Y_2 at point M; this value is $3/2$ (see Fig. 14-9).

14.7 If, in Fig. 14-10, $X_1 = 30X$, $X_2 = 60X$, $X_3 = 90X$ and $Y_1 = 50Y$, $Y_2 = 70Y$, $Y_3 = 80Y$; (*a*) derive the transformation curve corresponding to the production contract curve of Problem 14.5(*a*). (*b*) What does a point inside the transformation curve stand for? A point outside?

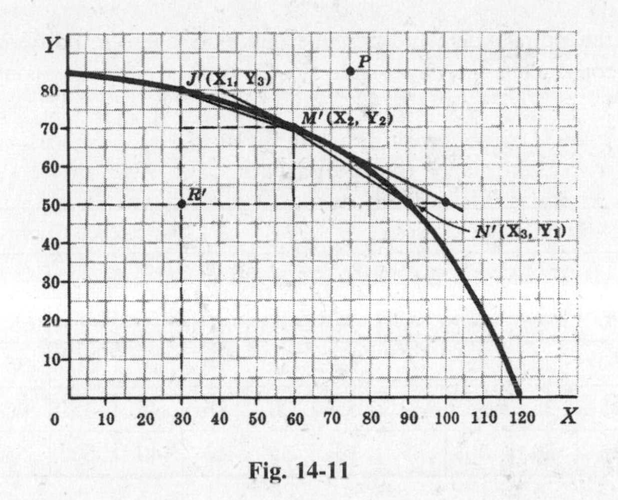

Fig. 14-11

(*a*) Point J' in Fig. 14-11 corresponds to point J (on X_1 and Y_3) in Fig. 14-10; point M' corresponds to point M (on X_2 and Y_2), and point N' corresponds to point N (on X_3 and Y_1). Other points could be similarly obtained; Joining these points, we get the transformation curve shown here. Thus, the transformation curve is obtained from mapping the production contract curve from the input space into the output space. The transformation curve is the locus of points of the maximum output of one commodity for a given output of the other. So it is the locus of general equilibrium and Pareto optimally in production. Another name for the transformation curve is the *production-possibility curve or frontier.*

(*b*) A point inside the transformation curve, say point R' (which corresponds to point R in Fig. 14-10), represents a nonoptimal allocation of resources. A point such as P in Fig. 14-11 cannot currently be achieved with the available L and K and technology. It can be reached only if there is an increase in the amounts of L *or* K available to this economy, if there is an improvement in technology, or both.

14.8 (*a*) Interpret the slope of the transformation curve. Evaluate the slope of the transformation curve of Fig. 14-11 at point M'. (*b*) Why is the transformation curve concave to the origin? (*c*) What would a straight-line transformation curve indicate?

(*a*) The slope of the transformation curve gives the MRT_{xy}, or the amount by which the output of Y must be reduced in order to release just enough L and K to be able to increase the output of X by one unit. Note that $\text{MRT}_{xy} = \text{MC}_x/\text{MC}_y$ also. For example, if $\text{MRT}_{xy} = 1/2$, this means that by giving up one unit of Y, we can produce two additional units of X. Thus, $\text{MC}_x = (1/2)\text{MC}_y$ and so $\text{MRT}_{xy} = \text{MC}_x/\text{MC}_y$. Specifically, *between points* J' and M' in Fig. 14-11, the average MRT_{xy} equals the absolute slope of chord $J'M' = \Delta Y/\Delta X = 10/30$ or $1/3$. Similarly, between points M' and N', the average MRT_{xy} equals the slope of chord $M'N'$, which is $2/3$. As the distance between two points on the transformation curve decreases and approaches zero in the limit, the MRT_{xy} approaches the slope of the transformation curve at a point. Thus, *at* point M', $\text{MRT}_{xy} = 1/2$ (see Fig. 14-11).

(*b*) The transformation curve of Fig. 14-11 is concave to the origin (i.e., its absolute slope, or MRT_{xy}, increases as we move downward along it) because of imperfect factor substitutability. That is, as this economy reduces its output of Y, it releases L and K in combinations which become less and less suitable for the production of more X. Thus, the economy incurs increasing MC_x in terms of Y.

(*c*) A straight-line transformation curve has a constant slope of MRT_{xy} and thus refers to the case of constant, rather than increasing, costs.

14.9 Suppose that there are only two individuals (A and B) in the economy of Problems 14.5 and 14.7 and they choose the combination of X and Y indicated by point M' (60X, 70Y) on the transformation curve of Fig. 14-11. Suppose also that the indifference curves of individuals A and B are given by A_1, A_2, A_3 and B_1, B_2, B_3, respectively. (*a*) Draw the Edgeworth box diagram for individuals A and

B. (*b*) Starting at the point where indifference curve A_1 crosses indifference curve B_1, show that mutually advantageous exchange is possible (*c*) How do we get the consumption contract curve? What does it show?

Table 14.2

A's Indifference Curves						B's Indifference Curves					
A_1		A_2		A_3		B_1		B_2		B_3	
X	Y	X	Y	X	Y	X	Y	X	Y	X	Y
5	60	25	45	15	65	5	20	10	50	35	60
15	25	35	35	40	55	20	15	25	35	45	45
30	15	50	30	55	53	55	10	40	33	55	40

(*a*) The Edgeworth box diagram for individuals *A* and *B* is given in Fig. 14-12. Every point in (or on) the Edgeworth box represents a particular distribution between individuals *A* and *B* of the 60X and 70Y produced (at point *M*′ on the transformation curve of Fig 14-11). For example, point *H* indicates that *A* has 5X and 60Y, while *B* has the remaining 55X and 10Y. *A*'s indifference curves (i.e., A_1, A_2, and A_3) have origin at O_A, while *B*'s indifference curves (i.e., B_1, B_2, and B_3) have origin at O_B.

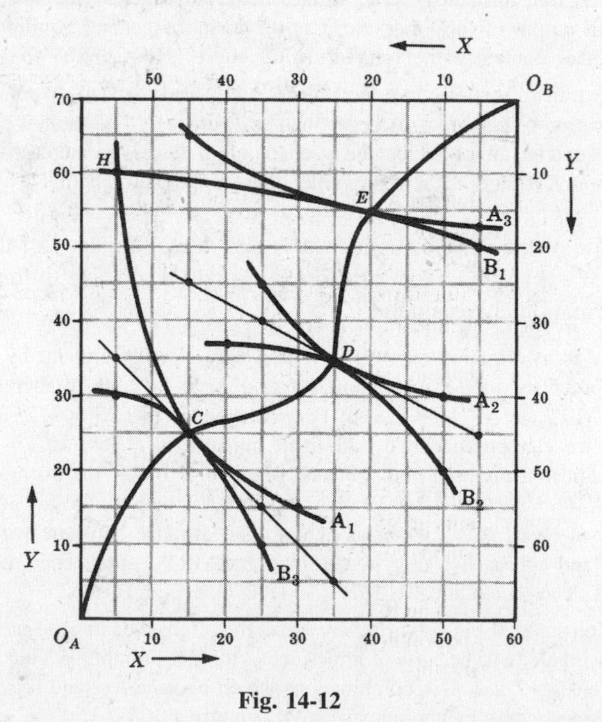

Fig. 14-12

(*b*) At point *H* (where A_1 crosses B_1), the slope of A_1 (i.e., the MRS_{xy} for *A*) exceeds the slope of B_1 (i.e., the MRS_{xy} for *B*), and so there is a basis for mutually advantageous exchange. For example, starting-at point *H* (on A_1 and B_1) if *A* gives up 25Y in exchange for 30X from *B, A* and *B* move to point *D* (on A_2 and B_1), and so both are better off. At point *D*, A_2 is tangent to B_2; that is, the $(MRS_{xy})_A$ is equal to the $(MRS_{xy})_B$, and so there is no further basis for mutually advantageous exchange. The greater *A*'s bargaining strength, the closer the final equilibrium point of exchange will be to point *E* (see Fig. 14-12) and the more *A*'s gain from the exchange relative to *B*'s. The greater *B*'s bargaining strength, the closer the final equilibrium point of exchange will be to point *C* and the more *B*'s gain from the exchange relative to *A*'s.

(*c*) By joining the points of tangency of A's to B's indifference curves, we get consumption contract curve O_ACDEO_B (see Fig. 14-12). Such points of tangency are assured because indifference curves are convex and dense. A movement from a point not on the consumption contract curve to a point on it benefits A, B, or both. Once on the consumption contract curve, one of the two individuals cannot be made better off without making the other worse off. Thus, the consumption contract curve is the locus of points of general equilibrium and Pareto optimality of consumption. Different points on the consumption contract curve refer to different distributions of real income (i.e., of X and Y) between individuals A and B.

14.10 (*a*) Give the equilibrium condition that holds along the consumption contract curve, and (*b*) express the equilibrium condition that holds along the consumption contract curve in utility terms. (*c*) What is the value of the MRS_{xy} at point D and at point C in Fig. 14-12?

(*a*)
$$(\text{MRS}_{xy})_A = (\text{MRS}_{xy})_B$$

(*b*) Since $\text{MRS}_{xy} = \text{MU}_x/\text{MU}_y$ (see Problem 4.28), the conditions that hold along the consumption contract curve can be restated in utility terms as

$$\left(\frac{\text{MU}_x}{\text{MU}_y}\right)_A = \left(\frac{\text{MU}_x}{\text{MU}_y}\right)_B$$

(*c*) The value of the MRS_{xy} at point D is given by the common absolute slope of indifference curves A_2 and B_2 at point D. Thus, at point D, the slope of A_2 (or the MRS_{xy} for A) = the slope of B_2 (or the MRS_{xy} for B) $= 1/2$ (see Fig. 14-12). At point C, the MRS_{xy} for A and $B = 1$.

14.11 Superimpose the Edgeworth box diagram of Fig. 14-12 on the transformation curve of Fig. 14-11, and determine the general equilibrium and Pareto optimal point of production and distribution.

This simple economy will be simultaneously in general equilibrium of (and at Pareto optimum in) production *and* distribution at point D, where $(\text{MRS}_{xy})_A = (\text{MRS}_{xy})_B = \text{MRT}_{xy} = 1/2$. We can verify this solution by showing that, *with output at point M'*, point C and point E cannot be points of general equilibria of production and distribution. For example, at point C, $(\text{MRS}_x)_A = (\text{MRS}_{xy})_B = 1 > 1/2 = \text{MRT}_{xy}$ (see Fig. 14-13). This means that individuals A and B would be willing (indifferent) to give up one unit of Y of consumption for one additional unit of X, while in production, two additional units of X can be obtained by giving up one unit of Y. If this were the case, this society would not have chosen the combination of X and Y given by point M', but rather a point further down on its transformation curve (involving more X and less Y). At point E, the exact opposite is true. Thus, with the output of X and Y given by point M', individuals A and B will have to be at point D, so that $(\text{MRS}_{xy})_A = (\text{MRS}_{xy})_B = \text{MRT}_{xy}$, in order for this simple economy to be simultaneously in general equilibrium of (and at Pareto optimum in) production and distribution. [Exactly how this society chooses to produce at point M' will be discussed in Problem 14.19(*a*).]

14.12 Given that the society of Problems 14.5, 14.7, 14.9, and 14.11 decides to produce at point M' on its transformation curve, determine (*a*) how much X and Y it produces, (*b*) how this X and Y is distributed between individuals A and B, and (*c*) how much L and K is used to produce X and how much to produce Y. (*d*) What questions have been left unanswered m this general equilibrium model?

(*a*) This society produces 60X and 70Y (given by point M' on the transformation curve of Fig. 14-13).

(*b*) Individual A receives 35X and 35Y, while individual B receives the remaining 25X and 35Y (given by point D in Fig. 14-13).

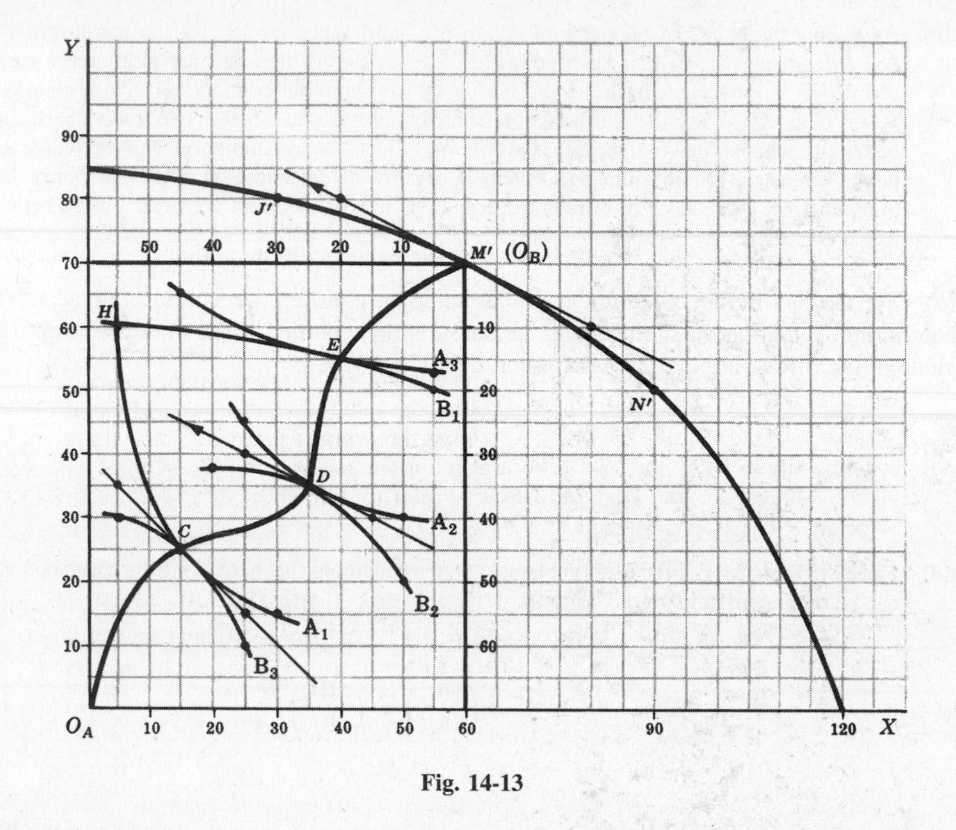

Fig. 14-13

(*c*) This society uses 8*L* and 7*K* to produce 60X, while the remaining 10*L* and 5*K* are used to produce 70Y (given by point *M* in Fig. 14-10).

(*d*) We still have not discussed how this society decides to produce 60X and 70Y [this question will be answered in Problem 14.19(*b*)], and we have not yet said anything about the equilibrium P_x, P_y, P_L, and P_K (see the next two problems).

14.13 Suppose that our simple economy of Problem 14.11 produces 60X and 70Y when in general equilibrium of (and at Pareto optimum in) production and exchange (*a*) what is the value of P_x/P_y at equilibrium? (*b*) What is the value of P_L/P_K equilibrium? (*c*) What can you say about the P_x, P_y, P_L, and P_K at equilibrium?

(*a*) We saw in Problem 14.11(*a*) that with output of 60X and 70Y, our simple economy is in general equilibrium of (and at Pareto optimum in) production and exchange when $(\text{MRS}_{xy})_A = (\text{MRS}_{xy})_B = \text{MRT}_{xy}$. This occurs at point *D* in Fig. 14-13, where the common absolute slope of indifference curves A_2 and B_2 equals the slope of the transformation curve (at point *M'*) This is equal to 1/2. But in Problem 4.20 we saw that consumers choose the quantity of X and Y such that $\text{MRS}_{xy} = P_x/P_y$ when in equilibrium. Thus, when our simple economy is in general equilibrium, $P_x/P_y = 1/2$, or $P_x = (1/2)\ P_y$.

(*b*) Turning to the factor markets, we see that point *M'* on the transformation curve corresponds to point *M* on the production contract curve. The common absolute slope of isoquants X_2 and Y_2 at point *M* equals $2/3 = (\text{MRTS}_{LK})_x = (\text{MRTS}_{LK})_y$ [see Problem 14.6(*c*)]. But in Section 6.8 we saw that producers choose the quantity of *L* and *K* such that $\text{MRTS}_{LK} = P_L/P_K$ when in equilibrium. It follows that when our simple economy is in general equilibrium, $P_L/P_K = 2/3$, or $P_L = (2/3)\ P_K$. Thus, we are able to determine the equilibrium output and input price *ratios* for the economy.

(*c*) Since we have dealt only with *real* (i.e., nonmonetary) variables, we cannot determine *unique* absolute equilibrium values for P_x, P_y, P_L, and P_K. All we can do is to assign an arbitrary dollar price to any one commodity or factor and then express the dollar price of all other commodities and factors in terms of this "*numéraire*" (see the next problem). In order to get unique absolute P_x, P_y, P_L, and P_K, we would have to add to our model a monetary equation, such as Fisher's "equation of exchange." This is introduced in a course in *macroeconomics* and is not really needed in an introduction to general equilibrium and welfare economics. All that we need here is the equilibrium output and input *relative prices or price ratios*—and those we have.

14.14 If we let $P_x = \$10$ when the economy of Problem 14.11 is in general equilibrium of production and exchange, (*a*) find P_y and (*b*) find P_L if the $(MP_L)_x = 4$ at perfectly competitive equilibrium; what is the $(MP_L)_y$? (*c*) Find P_K. (*d*) If we had set $P_x = \$20$, what would P_y, P_L, and P_K be?

(*a*) Since $P_x = (1/2)/P_y$ at equilibrium [see Problem 14.13(*a*)], if we let $P_x = \$10$, $P_y = \$20$.

(*b*) With perfect competition, each profit-maximizing entrepreneur employs each factor up to the point where the value of the marginal product of the factor in each use equals the factor price. Thus, $P_L = (VMP_L)_x = (P_x)(MP_L)_x = (\$10)(4) = \$40$. At equilibrium $P_L = (VMP_L)_x = (VMP_L)_y = \$40$. Since $(VMP_L)_y = (P_y)(MP_L)_y$ and $P_y = \$20$, $(MP_L)_y = \$2$.

(*c*) Since $P_L = 2/3P_K$ at equilibrium [see Problem 14.13(*b*)] and $P_L = \$40$, $P_K = \$60$.

(*d*) If we had set (arbitrarily) $P_x = \$20$, all other prices would have been double those found in parts (*a*), (*b*), and (*c*). Thus, specifying an arbitrary absolute price for P_x (the *numéraire*), we can find the corresponding price of the other commodity and factors. Specifying a different P_x will make all other prices proportionately different. Note that we could have used one of the factor prices as the *numéraire*. In that case, our knowledge of the equilibrium MP of the factor in the production of one of the commodities would have allowed us to find all the other prices. Thus, we see how in a general equilibrium model all prices form an integrated system—a change in the price of any commodity or factor affecting every other price (and quantity) in the system (see also Problems 14.2 and 14.3).

WELFARE ECONOMICS

14.15 For an economy of many factors, many commodities and many individuals, state the condition for Pareto optimum (*a*) in production, (*b*) in exchange, and (*c*) in production and exchange simultaneously.

(*a*) The condition for Pareto optimum production in an economy of many factors and many commodities is that the marginal rate of technical substitution between any pair of inputs be the same in the production of all commodities that use both inputs. If this condition did not hold, the economy could increase its output of one or more commodities without reducing the output of any other commodity. And a greater aggregate output is better than a smaller output.

(*b*) The condition for Pareto optimum in exchange in an economy of many commodities and many individuals is that the marginal rate of substitution between any pair of commodities be the same for all individuals who consume both commodities. If this condition did not hold, the satisfaction or welfare of one or more individuals could be increased without reducing the satisfaction or welfare of any other individual. This represents an unequivocal increase in social welfare.

(*c*) The condition for Pareto optimum in both production and exchange simultaneously, in an economy of many factors, many commodities, and many individuals, is that marginal rate of transformation in production be the same as the marginal rate of substitution in consumption for every pair of commodities and for every individual who consumes both commodities. If this condition did not hold, a reorganization of the production-distribution process until this Pareto optimality condition holds would represent an unequivocal increase in social welfare. Once we reach Pareto optimum, no one can be made better off without causing someone else to be made worse off at the same time. Note, however, that though the Pareto optimality conditions carry us a long way toward defining policy recommendations for increasing social welfare, they do not help us in deciding whether one particular distribution of income is better than another. In order to do that, we must make some ethical or value judgment about the relative "deservedness" of different individuals in the society.

14.16 If, in Fig. 14-13, A_1 refers to 150 utils, $A_2 = 300$ utils, $A_3 = 450$ utils and $B_1 = 300$ utils, $B_2 = 600$ utils, $B_3 = 750$ utils, (*a*) derive the utility-possibility curve corresponding to the consumption contract curve in Fig. 14-13. (*b*) What do points on, inside, and outside the utility-possibility curve stand for? (*c*) At what point is this economy simultaneously at Pareto optimum in production and exchange?

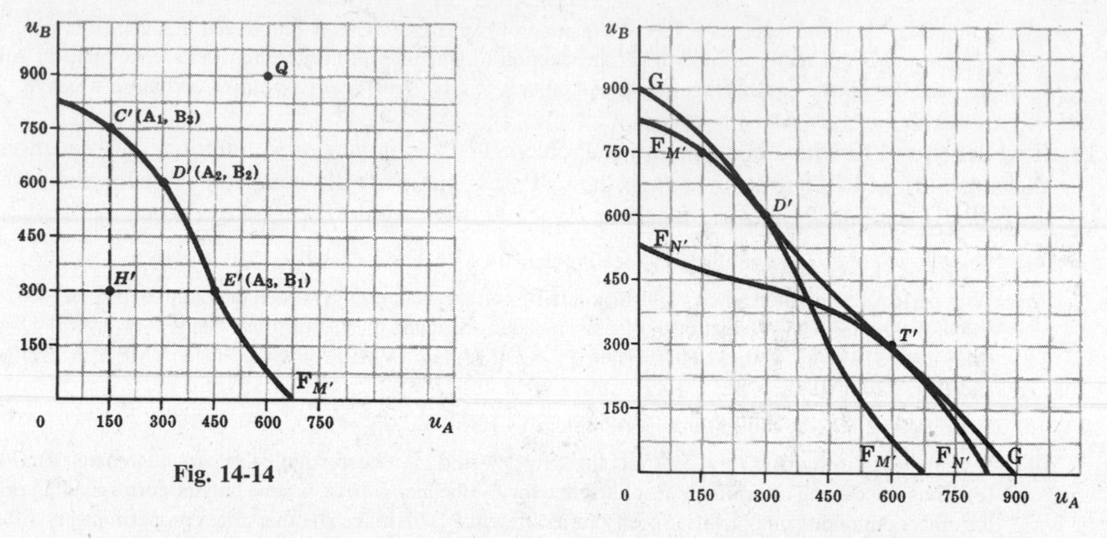

Fig. 14-14

Fig. 14-15

(*a*) Point C' in Fig. 14-14 corresponds to point C (on A_1 and B_3) in Fig. 14-13, point D' corresponds to point D (on A_2 and B_2), and point E' corresponds to point N (on A_3 and B_1). Other points could be similarly obtained. Joining these points, we get utility-possibility curve ($F_{M'}$) shown here. Thus, the utility-possibility curve is obtained from mapping the consumption contract curve from the output space into a utility space.

Notice that the scale along the horizontal axis refers only to individual *A*, while the scale along the vertical axis refers only to *B*. That is, the numbers along the axes are purely arbitrary as far as interpersonal comparisons of utility are concerned. For example, $u_A = 450$ utils is not necessarily greater than $u_B = 300$ utils, though $u_A = 450 > u_A = 300$. Also note that the utility-possibility curve need not be as regularly shaped as shown in Figs. 14-14 and 14-15.

(*b*) The utility-possibility curve, or frontier, is the locus of points of maximum utility for one individual for any level of utility for the other individual. So it is the locus of general equilibrium and Pareto optimality in exchange or consumption. A point inside the utility-possibility curve, say, point H' (which corresponds to point H in Fig. 14-13), represents a nonoptimal distribution of commodities. A point such as Q in Fig. 14-13 cannot currently be achieved with the available X and Y.

(*c*) Of all the points of Pareto optimality of exchange along the utility-possibility curve of Fig. 14-14, only point D' (which corresponds to point D in Fig. 14-13) is also a point of Pareto optimality in production. That is, at point D', $(MRS_{xy})_A = (\text{MRS}_{xy})_B = \text{MRT}_{xy}$.

14.17 From Fig. 14-13, (*a*) derive the grand utility-possibility curve. (*b*) What do points on the grand utility-possibility curve represent?

(*a*) $F_{M'}$ in Fig. 14-15 is the utility-possibility curve of Fig. 14-14 and point D' is the point of Pareto optimality in production and exchange. If we picked another point, say N', on the transformation curve of Fig. 14-13, we can construct a different Edgeworth box diagram (from point N') and get a different consumption contract curve, this one drawn from point O_A to point N' in Fig. 14-12. From this different consumption contract curve, we can derive another utility-possibility curve (F'_N in Fig. 14-15) and get another Pareto optimum point of production and exchange (point T' here). This process can be repeated any number of times. By then joining the resulting points (such as D' and T') of Pareto optimum in production and exchange, we can derive grand utility-possibility curve G of Fig. 14-15. This is an envelope of the utility-possibility curves associated with each point on the transformation curve.

(*b*) The grand utility-possibility curve or frontier is the locus of Pareto optimum points of production and exchange. Thus, the marginal conditions for Pareto optimality do not give us a unique solution for maximum social welfare. Each point on the grand utility-possibility frontier refers to: (1) a particular point on the transformation curve (i.e., combination of X and Y produced), (2) a particular point on the relevant consumption contract curve (i.e., distribution of X and Y or real income between individuals *A* and *B*), and (3) a particular point on the relevant production contract curve (i.e., allocation of *L* and *K* between X and Y). The aim of society is to choose among this infinity of Pareto optimum points along the grand utility-possibility frontier, the one point that leads to the maximum social welfare.

14.18 Suppose that three social welfare functions from the social welfare map of the economy of Problem 14.17 are given by the figures in Table 14.3. (*a*) Plot these social welfare functions; what do they show? (*b*) What assumption must we make in order to construct a social welfare function? How can a society gets its social welfare map?

Table 14.3

W_1		W_2		W_3	
u_A	u_B	u_A	u_B	u_A	u_B
75	900	150	900	225	975
225	525	300	600	375	675
450	375	525	450	600	525
900	225	900	375	900	450

(*a*) A social welfare function or social indifference curve shows the various combinations of u_A and u_B that give society the same level of satisfaction or welfare. For example, point S and D' on W_2 result in the same social welfare. However, at point *S*, individual *B* is better off than at point D', while individual *A* is better off at point D' than at point *S*. On the other hand, points on a higher social welfare function involve a greater social welfare than points on a lower social welfare function. For example, u_A and u_B are both greater at point D' than at point *D*, while u_A and u_B at point D' are both smaller than at point D''.

(*b*) In order to construct a social welfare function, society must make value or ethical judgments (interpersonal comparisons of utility). That is, since a movement along a social welfare curve makes one individual better off while the other worse off, in order to get a social welfare function, society must compare the two individuals in "deservingness". A social welfare function may be constructed by (and thus reflect the value judgment of) a dictator, if one exists. In a democracy, a social welfare function could be developed by voting, but only under certain circumstances. In any event, the construction of a social welfare function is very difficult. What we do here is simply *assume* that social welfare functions exist for our society and are given by W_1, W_2, and W_3 in Fig. 14-16.

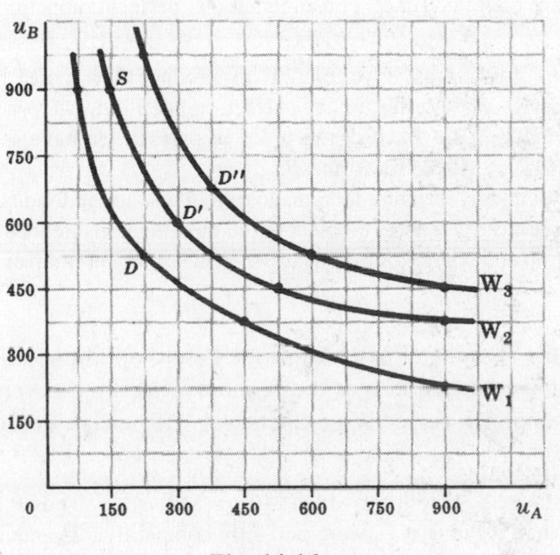

Fig. 14-16

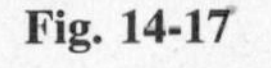
Fig. 14-17

14.19 For the economy of Problems 14.17 and 14.18, determine (*a*) the point of maximum social welfare and (*b*) how much of X and Y is produced, how this X and Y is distributed between A and B (i.e., X_A, X_B, Y_A, Y_B), the value of u_A and u_B, how much of L and K is used to produce X and Y (i.e., L_x, L_y, K_x, K_y), and the value of P_x/P_y and P_L/P_K when the economy reaches its maximum social welfare.

(*a*) By superimposing the social welfare or indifference map of Fig. 14-16 on the grand utility frontier of Fig. 14-15, we can determine the point of maximum social welfare, or "point of constrained bliss." In Fig. 14-17 this is given by point D', where the grand utility frontier is tangent to W_2, the highest attainable social welfare function. The choice of a point on the grand utility frontier is basically the choice of a particular income distribution. A movement away from point D' along the grand utility frontier will increase the welfare of one individual but reduce the total social welfare. Remember that the Pareto optimality conditions with which we started our discussion of welfare economics are necessary but insufficient to determine the point of maximum social welfare, since they simply define the grand utility frontier. This is as far as *positive economics* will take us. To find the point of constrained bliss we need *normative* information on the values of the society, so that we can construct a social welfare or indifference map.

(*b*) Point D' (i.e., the point of maximum social welfare) on the grand utility frontier corresponds to point D on the consumption contract curve and point M' on the transformation curve of Fig. 14-13. Thus, we now know how much of X and Y this economy must produce in order to maximize its social welfare, and so we have removed the indeterminancy that we talked about at the end of Problem 14.11. That is, having found the point of maximum social welfare, we can now *reverse the order* of Problems 14.5 to 14.18 and find that this society should produce 60X and 70Y [see Problem 14.12(*a*)]; $X_A = 35$, $X_B = 25$, $Y_A = 35$, $Y_B = 35$ [see Problem 14.12(*b*)]. With $X_A = 35$ and $Y_A = 35$, $u_A = 300$ utils; with $X_B = 25$ and $Y_B = 35$, $u_B = 600$ utils (see point D' in Fig. 14-17); $L_x = 8$, $L_y = 10$, $K_x = 7$, $K_y = 5$ [see Problem 14.12(*c*)], $P_x/P_y = 1/2$ and $P_L/P_K = 2/3$ (see Problem 14.13).

Note that we have now obtained the *complete* solution to the simple general equilibrium model we have set up, and in the process we have combined the theories of production, distribution, and consumption and the value system of the society. Our simple model also shows that a change in one sector will bring changes in every other sector of the economy, as indicated in our discussion of the circular flow in Chapter 1.

14.20 Prove that when all markets in our simple economy are perfectly competitive, the following conditions hold: (*a*) $(\text{MRTS}_{LK})_x = (\text{MRTS}_{LK})_y$, (*b*) $(\text{MRS}_{xy})_A = (\text{MRS}_{xy})_B$, (*c*) $(\text{MRS}_{xy})_A = (\text{MRS}_{xy})_B = \text{MRT}_{xy}$.

(*a*) We saw in Section 6.8 that under perfect competition, producers choose the quantity of L and K such that $\text{MRTS}_{LK} = P_L/P_K$. Since P_L and P_K and thus P_L/P_K are the same in all uses under perfect competition, $(\text{MRTS}_{LK})_x = (\text{MRTS}_{LK})_y$.

(*b*) We saw in Section 4.7 that under perfect competition, consumers choose the quantity of X and Y such that $\text{MRS}_{xy} = P_x/P_y$. Since P_x and P_y and thus P_x/P_y are the same for all consumers under perfect competition, $(\text{MRS}x_y)_A = (\text{MRS}_{xy})_B$.

(*c*) The $\text{MRT}_{xy} = \Delta y/\Delta x = \text{MC}_x/\text{MC}_y$. For example, if we must give up 2Y to produce 1X more, the $\text{MC}_x = 2\text{MC}_y$ and the $\text{MRT}_{xy} = 2$. But in Chapter 10 we saw that under perfect competition, $\text{MC}_x = P_x$ and $\text{MC}_y = P_y$. Therefore, $\text{MC}_x/\text{MC}_y = P_x/P_y = \text{MRT}_{xy}$. But since in the proof of part (*b*) we have seen that the MRS_{xy} for A and B also equals P_x/P_y, $\text{MRT}_{xy} = \text{MRS}_{xy}$ for A and B.

Similar results hold in a perfectly competitive economy of many factors, commodities, and individuals. Thus perfect competition in every market in the economy guarantees (subject to the qualifications in Section 14.13) the attainment of Pareto optimum in production and distribution. This is the basic argument in favor of perfect competition.

14.21 (*a*) Explain why with constant returns to scale and the absence of externalities, a Pareto optimum point will *not* be attained if there is *im*perfect competition in some markets of the economy. (*b*) If the government can make more but not all markets in the economy perfectly competitive, will social welfare increase?

(*a*) If industry X is imperfectly competitive, it will produce the output for which $\text{MC}_x = \text{MR}_x < P_x$. Thus P_x is higher, Q_x is lower, and fewer resources are used than if industry X were perfectly competitive. If another industry, say industry Y, is perfectly competitive, it will produce where $MC_y = MR_y = P_y$. Thus, $MRT_{xy} = MC_x/MC_y < P_x/P_y$, and so this economy does not reach Pareto optimum.

Similarly, if the labor market is perfectly competitive while the capital market is imperfectly competitive, the least-cost input or resource combination in production is given by

$$\frac{MP_L}{MRC_L} = \frac{MP_K}{P_K} \quad \text{or} \quad \frac{MP_L}{MP_K} = \frac{MRC_L}{P_K} > \frac{P_L}{P_K}$$

Thus, $MRTS_{LK} = MP_L/MP_K > P_L/P_K$ and so this economy does not reach Pareto optimum.

(*b*) The attempt on the part of the government to make as many markets in the economy as possible behave competitively when it cannot make *all* markets in the economy behave competitively may not increase social welfare. This is the conclusion of the "theory of the second best" which is studied in a more advanced course. Of course, even if the government were successful in making all markets behave competitively, this is not likely to lead to the particular Pareto optimum point associated with the maximum social welfare. Theoretically, an appropriate combination of lump-sum taxes and subsidies (that does not affect incentives) could then be used in order to reach the point of constrained bliss.

14.22 Explain why the existence of increasing returns to scale may not ensure maximum social welfare in a society.

As we saw in Chapters 9 and 10 increasing returns to scale over a sufficiently large range of outputs may lead to the breaking down of perfect competition and the formation of oligopoly or monopoly. Since imperfect competitors produce where $MR = MC > P$, too little of the commodity is being produced for maximum social welfare. Note, however, that the conditions for maximum social welfare were all expressed in terms of static efficiency. And what is most efficient at one time may not be most efficient through time in a dynamic world. For example, monopolists and oligopolists may use their long-run profits for research and development and bring about greater technological advance and a higher standard of living through time than perfect competition.

14.23 Define and give an example of each of the following: (*a*) external economy of production, (*b*) external economy of consumption, (*c*) external diseconomy of production, (*d*) external diseconomy of consumption, (*e*) technical externality, and (*f*) public good.

(*a*) An *external economy of production* is an unpaid for benefit received by some producers because of the expansion of output of some other producer. An example of this occurs when some producers, in the process of expanding their output, train more workers, some of whom end up working for other producers.

(*b*) An *external economy of consumption* is an unpaid for benefit received by some consumers because of an increase in the consumption expenditures of some other consumer. For example, when some consumers increase their expenditures on education, in addition to increasing their own salaries, they also confer uncompensated benefits to the rest of the community (by usually becoming more responsible citizens).

(*c*) An *external diseconomy of production* is an uncompensated cost imposed on some producers resulting from the expansion of output of some other producer. An example of this occurs when some of the producers in a locality, in the course of expanding their output, cause so much more pollution as to result in pollution-control legislation which increases the cost of disposing waste materials for all the producers in the locality.

(*d*) An *external diseconomy of consumption* is an uncompensated cost imposed on society from the increased consumption expenditures of some individuals. For example, as more and more people go camping, more beer cans, cigarette butts, and other junk is left in the wilderness, thus imposing either a monetary cost on society (for the cleaning up) or a psychic cost on others (for the reduced satisfaction of going camping).

(*e*) *Technical externalities* refer to increasing returns of scale. These can occur under perfectly competitive conditions. Wheat farming is usually given as an example of a perfectly competitive market with increasing returns to scale. Because of this, large wheat farmers are driving the small independent wheat farmers out of business.

(*f*) A good is called a *public good* if each unit of it can be used at the same time by more than one individual. Examples of public goods are public concerts, Niagara Falls, public schools, etc.

14.24 (*a*) State the conditions for Pareto optimum in terms of social and private benefits and costs, (*b*) explain why we cannot reach Pareto optimum with an external economy of production or consumption, with an external *diseconomy* of production or consumption, or with technical externality, (*c*) explain why when there are public goods, we cannot reach Pareto optimum even if we have perfect competition throughout the economy.

(*a*) The *marginal social benefit* (MSB) must be equal to the *marginal social cost* (MSC), the marginal social benefit must be equal to the *marginal private benefit* (MPB), and the marginal social cost must be equal to the *marginal private cost* (MPC). The existence of externalities and public goods will cause some of these conditions not to hold and so the economy cannot reach Pareto optimum, even if perfect competition exists in every market.

(*b*) With only an external economy of production, MSC $<$ MPC $= P =$ MPB $=$ MSB, and so too little of the commodity is produced by the economy for it to achieve a point of Pareto optimum. With only an external economy of consumption, MSB $>$ MPB $=$ MPC $=$ MSC, and too little of the commodity is consumed to achieve a point of Pareto optimum. With only an external diseconomy of production, MSC $>$ MPC $= P =$ MPB $=$ MSB, and too much of the commodity is produced. With only an external diseconomy of consumption, MSB $<$ MPB $=$ MPC $=$ MSC and too much of the commodity is consumed.

The existence of technical externalities in a perfectly competitive market either leads (*a*) to economic warfare and to oligopoly or monopoly, or (*b*) to a case where $P =$ AC $>$ MC. In either case a Pareto optimum point is not achieved (unless the government pays the perfectly competitive firm a subsidy such that the firm's MC plus the subsidy equals the firm's AC, so that the firm can produce where $P =$ MC).

(*c*) Finally, even with perfect competition throughout the economy, the economy will not reach a point of Pareto optimum when there are public goods. The reason for this is that if X is a public good in a two-commodity, two-individual economy, the economy is in equilibrium when $\text{MRT}_{xy} = (\text{MRS}_{xy})_A = (\text{MRS}_{xy})_B$. However, since individuals A and B can both use each unit of public good X at the same time, the equilibrium condition for maximum welfare is $\text{MRT}_{xy} = (\text{MRS}_{xy})_A + (\text{MRS}_{xy})_B$. Thus, perfect competition leads to the underproduction and the underconsumption of public goods and does not lead to a Pareto optimum point.

14.25 Given the following information, draw a figure showing the aggregate or total demand curve for good Y and its equilibrium price and quantity (*a*) if it is public good and (*b*) if it is not.

$$QD_A = 18 - 3P_y; \qquad qD_B = 15 - \tfrac{3}{2}P_y; \qquad QS_y = 1 + \tfrac{3}{2}P_y,$$

where P_y is in dollars.

(*a*) See Fig. 14-18. The figure shows that the market demand curve for good *Y* when it is a public good is obtained by the *vertical* summation of the demand curves of individuals A and B for good Y. This is given by D_T in the figure. With D_T and S_y, the equilibrium price for good Y is \$6 and the equilibrium quantity is 10. This is given

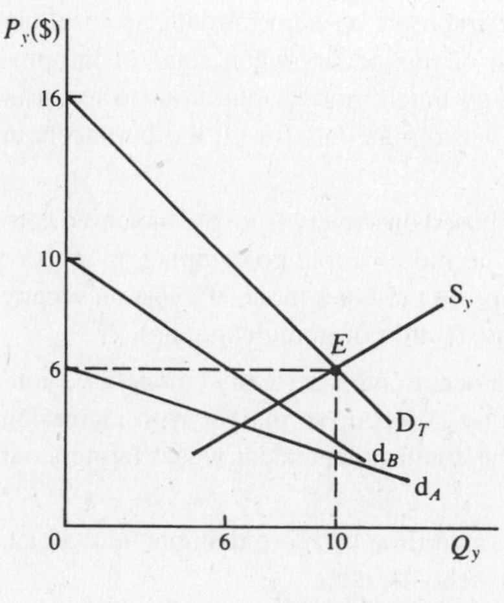

Fig. 14-18

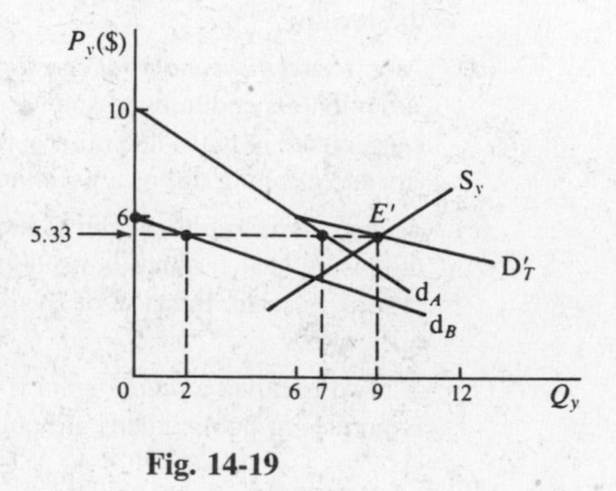

Fig. 14-19

by the intersection of D_T and S_y, at point *E*. From Fig. 14-18 we can see that when good Y is a public good, individuals A and B each consume 10 units of it.

(*b*) See Fig. 14-19. The figure shows that the market demand curve for good Y when it is a private rather than a public good is obtained by the *horizontal* summation of the demand curves of individuals A and B for the good. This is given by D'_T in the figure. With D_T and S_y, the equilibrium price for good Y is $5.33 and the equilibrium quantity is 9. This is given by the intersection of D'_T and S_y at point E'. These compare with $PY = \$6$ and $QY = 10$ when good Y is a public good (see Fig. 14-18). From Fig. 14-18 we can see that when good Y is a private good, individual A consumes 2 units and individual B consumes 7 units of the good (compared with 10 units of the good by each individual when good Y is a public good).

14.26 (*a*) Explain the distinction between public goods and good supplied by the government, and give some examples (*b*) What type of public goods can be provided only by the government? (*c*) Explain why public goods give rise to a free-rider problem.

(*a*) All goods and services provided by the government are public goods (i.e., are nonrival in consumption), but not all public goods are, or need be, provided by the government. Those public goods that exhibit nonexclusion (i.e., those for which each user can be charged) can be, and in fact often are, provided by the private sector. An example of a public good that is provided by the government and exhibits nonexclusion is national defense. An example of a public good that does not exhibit nonexclusion and is provided by private firms is a cable TV program. An example of a public good that does not exhibit nonexclusion (so that it could be provided by private firms but is often provided by the government) is garbage collection.

(*b*) Public goods that exhibit nonexclusion can be provided only by the government. Private firms will not provide these goods because they cannot exclude nonpaying users of these goods. The government generally raises the funds needed to pay for the public goods it provides by taxing the general public. The government can then either produce the goods itself or (more likely in the United States) it can pay private firms to produce those goods (as, for example, most items of national defense).

(*c*) Public goods give rise to a free-rider problem because each individual believes that the same amount of the public good will be supplied whether or not he or she shares in the cost of providing it. This leads to the undersupply of the public good, which prevents the attainment of Pareto optimum and requires government intervention.

CHAPTER 15

The Economics of Information

15.1 THE ECONOMICS OF SEARCH

Search costs refer to the time and money we spend seeking information about a product. The general rule is to continue the search for lower prices, higher quality, and so on until the marginal benefit from the search equals the marginal cost. In most instances, advertising provides a great deal of information and greatly reduces consumers' search costs, especially for *search goods*. These are goods whose quality can be evaluated by inspection at the time of purchase (as opposed to *experience goods*, which can only be judged after using them).

EXAMPLE 1. Information available to individuals, consumers and firms is increasing by leaps and bounds as a result of the development of the Internet. The *Internet* or simply "the Net" is a collection of more than 100,000 computers throughout the world linked together in a service called the World Wide Web (www). In 2005, about 200 million people scattered throughout the world were connected through the Web, with hundreds of thousands of new individuals joining each week. Half of the on-line community is now outside the United States. In a few years, more than 1 billion people and 300 million PCs are expected to be connected to the Internet. In short, the entire globe is very rapidly becoming a single unified *information superhighway* through the Internet. An individual can now use the Internet to browse through a firm's catalogue, click on a "buy" button, and fill in an electronic order form, including shipping and credit-card information.

15.2 SEARCHING FOR THE LOWEST PRICE

At any time, there will be a dispersion of prices in the market even for a homogeneous product. A consumer can accept the price quoted by the first seller of the product he or she approaches, or can continue the search for lower prices. The consumer should continue the search for lower prices as long as the marginal benefit from continuing the search exceeds the marginal cost of additional search. In general, the marginal benefit from searching declines as the time spent searching for lower prices continues. Even if the marginal cost of additional search is constant, a point is reached where $MB = MC$. At that point, the consumer should end the search. The approximate lowest price that expected with each additional search is:

$$\text{Expected Price} = \text{Lowest Price} + \frac{\text{Range of Prices}}{\text{Number of Searches} + 1}$$

EXAMPLE 2. Suppose that the price range for a small portable TV of a given brand is between \$80 to \$120. All sellers are identical in location, service, and so on, so that price is the only consideration. Suppose also that sellers are equally divided into five price classifications: Sellers of type I charge a price of \$80 for the TV, type II sellers charge \$90, type III charge \$100, type IV charge \$110, and type V charge \$120. For a single search, the probability of each price is 1/5, and the expected price is the weighted average of all prices, or \$100 [(\$80)(0,2) + (\$90)(0,2) + (\$100)(0,2) + (\$110)(0,2) + (\$120)(0,2) = \$100]. The consumer can now purchase the TV at the price of \$100, or she can continue the search for lower prices. With each additional search the consumer will find a lower price, until the lowest price of \$80 is found. The reduction in price with each search gives the marginal benefit of the search. The consumer will end the search when the marginal benefit from the search equals the marginal cost.

EXAMPLE 3. The lowest TV price expected from one search for the case in Example 2 is:

$$\text{Expected Price} = \$80 + \frac{\$40}{1+1} = \$100 \text{ (as found in Example 1)}$$

The approximate lowest expected price from two searches is \$80 + (\$40/3) = \$93.33. Thus, the approximate marginal benefit from the second search is \$100 − \$93.33 = \$6.67. The lowest expected price with three searches is \$80 + (\$40/4) = \$90, so that MB = \$3.33. For four searches it is \$80 + (\$40/5) = \$88, so that MB = \$2. For five searches it is \$80 + (\$40/6) = \$86.67, so that MB = \$1.33. If the marginal cost of each additional search for the consumer is \$2, the consumer should, therefore, conduct four searches. The higher is the price of the commodity, and the greater is the range of product prices, the more searches a consumer will undertake (see Problem 15.5). Because consumers face different marginal costs of search, they will end the search at different points and end up paying different prices for the product.

15.3 ASYMMETRIC INFORMATION: THE MARKET FOR LEMONS AND ADVERSE SELECTION

When one party to a transaction has more information than the other on the quality of the product (i.e., with *asymmetric information*), the low-quality product or "lemon" will drive the high-quality product out of the market. One way to overcome such a problem of *adverse selection* is for the buyer to get, or the seller to provide, more information on the quality of the product or service. Such is the function of brand names, chain retailers, professional licensing, and guarantees.

EXAMPLE 4. Insurance companies try to overcome the problem of adverse selection by requiring medical checkups, charging different premiums for different age groups and occupations, and offering different rates of coinsurance, amounts of deductibility, and length of contracts. The only way to avoid the problem entirely is with universal compulsory health insurance. Credit companies reduce the adverse selection process that they face by sharing "credit histories" with other insurance companies.

15.4 MARKET SIGNALING

The problem of adverse selection resulting from asymmetric information can be resolved or greatly reduced by *market signaling*. Brand names, guarantees, and warranties are used as signals for higher-quality products, for which consumers are willing to pay higher prices. The willingness to accept coinsurance and deductibles signals low-risk individuals to whom insurance companies can charge lower premiums. Credit companies use good credit histories to make more credit available to good-quality borrowers, and firms use educational certificates to identify more-productive potential employees to receive higher salaries.

15.5 THE PROBLEM OF MORAL HAZARD

The insurance market faces also the problem of *moral hazard*, or the increase in the probability of an illness, fire, or other accident when an individual is insured than when he or she is not. The reason is that with insurance, the loss is shifted from the individual to the insurance company. If not contained, this could lead to unacceptably high insurance costs. Insurance companies try to overcome the problem of moral hazard by specifying the precautions that an individual or firm must take as a condition of insurance, and by *coinsurance* (i.e., insuring only part of the possible loss).

EXAMPLE 5. With medical insurance, an individual may spend less on preventive health care (thus increasing the probability of getting ill); and if she does become ill, she will tend to spend more on treatment than would be the case if she had no insurance. With auto insurance, an individual may drive more recklessly (thus increasing the probability of a car accident) and then is likely to exaggerate the injury and inflate the property damage that he suffers if he does get into an accident. Similarly, with fire insurance, a firm may take fewer reasonable precautions (such as the installation of a fire-detector system, thereby increasing the probability of a fire) than in the absence of fire insurance; and then the firm is likely to inflate the property damage suffered if a fire does occur. Indeed, the probability of a fire is high if the property is insured for an amount greater than the real value of the property.

15.6 THE PRINCIPAL-AGENT PROBLEM

Because ownership is divorced from control in the modern corporation, a *principal-agent problem* arises. This refers to the fact that managers seek to maximize their own benefits rather than the owners' or principals' interests, which are to maximize the total profits or value of the firm. The firm may use *golden parachutes* (large financial payments to managers if they are forced out or choose to leave if the firm is taken over by another firm) to overcome the managers' objections to a takeover bid that sharply increases the value of the firm. The firm may also set up generous deferred-compensation schemes for its managers to reconcile their long-term interests to those of the firm.

15.7 THE EFFICIENCY WAGE THEORY

According to the *efficiency wage theory*, firms willingly pay higher than equilibrium wages to induce workers to avoid shirking or slacking off on the job. The no-shirk constraint curve is positively sloped and shows that the efficiency or minimum wage that the firm must pay to avoid shirking is higher the smaller is the level of unemployment. The equilibrium efficiency wage is the one given by the intersection of the firm's demand curve for labor and the no-shirking constraint curve.

EXAMPLE 6. In 1914, Henry Ford reduced the length of the working day from nine to eight hours while increasing the minimum daily wage from \$2.34 to \$5 for assembly-line workers. Ford did this in order to overcome the problem of low productivity and very high turnover of assembly line workers, which sharply increased costs and reduced profits. By paying of a wage much higher than the going wage, Ford was able to attract more productive and loyal workers, cut absenteeism in half, and increase productivity by more than 50 percent. In short, what Ford did in 1914 was to pay the efficiency wage—and it took 70 years for economists to develop the theory to fit the facts!

Glossary

Adverse selection The situation where low-quality products drive high-quality products out of the market as a result of the existence of asymmetric information between buyers and sellers.

Asymmetric information The situation where one party to a transaction has more information on the quality of the product or service offered for sale than the other party.

Coinsurance Insurance that covers only a portion of a possible loss.

Efficiency wage theory The higher than equilibrium wages that firms are willing to pay to induce workers to avoid shirking or slacking off on the job.

Experience goods Goods whose quality can only be judged after using them.

Golden parachute A large financial settlement paid out by a firm to its managers if they are forced or choose to leave as a result of a takeover that greatly increases the value of the firm.

Information superhighway The ability of researchers, firms, and consumers to hook up with libraries, databases, and marketing information through a national high-speed computer network and to have at their fingertips a vast amount of information as never before.

Internet A collection of thousands of computers, businesses, and millions of people throughout the world linked together in a service called World Wide Web.

Market signaling Signals that convey product quality, good insurance or credit risks, and high productivity.

Moral hazard The increased probability of a loss when an economic agent can shift some of its costs to others.

Principal-agent problem The fact that the agents (managers and workers) of a firm seek to maximize their own benefits (such as salaries) rather than the total profits or value of the firm, which is the owners' or principals' interest.

Search costs The time and money spent seeking information about a product.

Search goods Goods whose quality can be evaluated by inspection at the time of purchase.

Review Questions

1. The cost of search may include (*a*) time spent to learn the properties of the product, (*b*) time spent to compare the product to possible substitutes, (*c*) time spent to find lower-price sellers of the product, (*d*) money spent to purchase information on the product, (*e*) all of the above.

Ans. (*e*) See Section 15.1.

2. With each additional search, the marginal benefit from more search (*a*) increases, (*b*) declines, (*c*) first increases and then decreases, (*d*) does not change.

Ans. (*b*) See Section 15.2.

3. With a greater range of product prices, the marginal benefit from search (*a*) increases, (*b*) decreases, (*c*) does not change, (*d*) can increase or decrease.

Ans. (*a*) See Section 15.2.

4. Asymmetric information refers to the case where (*a*) the seller of a product or service has more information than the buyer, (*b*) the buyer of a product has more information than the seller, (*c*) the seller or the buyer of a product or service has more information than the other, (*d*) information is irrelevant to the transaction,

Ans. (*c*) See Section 15.3.

5. Which of the following statements is correct? (*a*) Asymmetric information leads to adverse selection, (*b*) adverse selection leads to asymmetric information, (*c*) adverse selection leads to an insurance problem, (*d*) moral hazard leads to asymmetric information.

Ans. (*a*) See Section 15.3.

6. How can the problem of adverse selection be overcome? (*a*) By buyers getting more information about the quality or the good or service, (*b*) by sellers providing more information of the quality of the good or service, (*c*) by brand names and chain retailers, (*d*) by professional licensing, (*e*) all of the above.

Ans. (*e*) See Section 15.3.

7. Credit companies reduce the adverse selection problem that they face by (*a*) sharing borrowers' credit histories with other credit companies, (*b*) asking borrowers to purchase health insurance, (*c*) asking borrowers for a medical checkup, (*d*) all of the above.

Ans. (*a*) See Section 15.3.

8. Which of the following is not a market signaling device? (*a*) Guarantees and warranties, (*b*) coinsurance and deductibles, (*c*) hedging, (*d*) a college education.

Ans. (*c*) See Section 15.4.

9. Which of the following is not related to moral hazard? (*a*) The probability of an illness, (*b*) the probability of a flood, (*c*) the probability of a car accident, (*d*) the probability of a fire.

Ans. (*b*) See Section 15.5.

10. The problem of moral hazard can be reduced by (*a*) requiring certain precautions from buyers of insurance, (*b*) co-insurance, (*c*) deductibles, (*d*) all of the above.

Ans. (*d*) See Section 15.5.

11. All of the following are examples of a principal-agent problem, except: (*a*) managers seeking to maximize their own interests rather than the total benefits of the firm, (*b*) workers seeking to maximize their salaries rather than the interests of the firm, (*c*) the owners of the firm seeking to maximize the value of the firm, (*d*) the manager of a hospital resisting a merger with another hospital.

Ans. (*c*) See Section 15.6.

12. A principal-agent problem can be overcome by the firm (*a*) offering golden parachutes to its top managers, (*b*) setting up generous deferred-compensation schemes for its top managers, (*c*) setting up profit-sharing schemes for its workers, (*d*) all of the above.

Ans. (*d*) See Section 15.6.

Solved Problems

THE ECONOMICS OF SEARCH

15.1 (*a*) In which market structure was perfect information assumed on the part of all economic agents? (*b*) If all consumers have perfect information, can a price dispersion for a given homogeneous product exist in the market if all conditions of the sale are identical? Why?

(*a*) Of the four types of market structure discussed (perfect competition, monopoly, monopolistic competition, and oligopoly), only the perfectly competitive model assumed perfect information on the part of all economic agents.

(*b*) If a product is homogeneous, the conditions of the sale are identical, and consumers have identical information, then each consumer will know the lowest-price seller and will not purchase the product at any higher price. Then no firm can sell the product at any higher price. A price dispersion for the product can only arise if one or more of the above assumptions do not hold.

15.2 (*a*) On which do you think consumers spend more time shopping for lower prices, sugar or coffee? Why? (*b*) Can you explain why the price dispersion for salt is much greater than the price dispersion for sugar?

(*a*) Since the price of coffee is so much higher than the price of sugar and consumers spend much more on coffee than on sugar, the marginal benefit from comparative shopping is likely to be much greater for coffee than for sugar. As a result, we would expect consumers to spend much more time shopping for lower prices for coffee than for sugar.

(*b*) Since consumers spend much more on sugar than on salt, it does not pay for them to spend as much time shopping for lower prices for salt than for sugar. With less search and information, a greater dispersion of prices is possible in the market for salt than in the market for sugar.

15.3 Frozen vegetables are search goods because they are purchased frequently by consumers. True or false? Explain.

False. It is true that frozen vegetables may be purchased frequently and would not be purchased again if consumers found their quality to be too low in relation to their price, but their quality can only be determined after eating them. Because of this, frozen vegetables are experience, not search goods.

15.4 Most advertising is manipulative and provides very little information to consumers. True or false? Explain.

False. Most advertising, especially advertising for search goods, provides a great deal of very useful information to consumers on the availability of products, their use and properties, the firms selling particular products, retail outlets that carry the product, and product prices, and it greatly reduces consumers' search costs.

Even advertising for experience goods provides indirect but still very useful information to consumers because of the seller's willingness to spend a great deal of money to induce consumers to try the product. A seller's profit and even ability to stay in business depends a great deal on repeated purchases of its products. If the products are not good or do not have the properties and quality advertised, consumers would not purchase the product again, even if advertising induces them to try the product once.

SEARCHING FOR THE LOWEST PRICE

15.5 Suppose that type I sellers charged the price of \$60 for the portable TV, type II sellers charged \$80, type III sellers charged \$100, type IV sellers charged \$120, and type V sellers charged \$140. Determine (*a*) the expected lowest price for the TV from one, two, three, four, and five searches and (*b*) the marginal benefit from each additional search.

(*a*) The lowest expected price with one search is $\$60 + \frac{\$80}{1+1} = \$100.00$.

With two searches, the lowest expected price is $\$60 + \frac{\$80}{3} = \$86.67$.

With three searches, the lowest expected price is $\$60 + \frac{\$80}{4} = \$80.00$.

With four searches, the lowest expected price is $\$60 + \frac{\$80}{5} = \$76.00$.

With five searches, the lowest expected price is $\$60 + \frac{\$80}{6} = \$73.33$.

(*b*) The marginal benefit from each search is measured by the reduction in the expected price resulting from the search. Thus, for the second search the marginal benefit (MB) is $\$100 - \$86.67 = \$13.37$.

For the third search, $\text{MB} = \$86.67 - \$80.00 = \$6.67$.
For the fourth search, $\text{MB} = \$80.00 - \$76.00 = \$4.00$.
For the fifth search, $\text{MB} = \$76.00 - \$73.33 = \$2.67$.

Note that the marginal benefits of each additional search are now twice as large as found in Example 3 where the range of prices was half what they are in this problem.

15.6 Using the data of Problem 15.5 indicate (*a*) How many searches should a consumer undertake if the marginal cost of each additional search is \$4 and (*b*) if it is \$2. (*c*) How many searches should a consumer undertake if the marginal cost of each additional search is \$5.34 and the consumer plans to purchase two TV sets?

(*a*) A consumer should continue searching for lower prices until the marginal benefit from the search equals the marginal cost. If $\text{MC} = \$4$, the consumer should undertake four searches because only then $\text{MB} = \text{MC} = \$4$.

(*b*) If $\text{MC} = \$2$, then the consumer should undertake five searches for which $\text{MP} = \$2.67$. The consumer should not undertake the sixth search because $\text{MB} = \$1.90$ for the sixth search.

(*c*) If a consumer plans to purchase two TV sets rather than one, the MB from each additional search is double that received from the purchase of only one set. With $\text{MC} = \$5.34$, the consumer should conduct five searches because then $\text{MB} = (2)(\$2.67) = \$5.34 = \text{MC}$.

15.7 Suppose that type I sellers charged the price of \$96 for the portable TV, type II sellers charged \$98, type III sellers charged \$100, type IV sellers charged \$102, and type V sellers charged \$104. Determine (*a*) the expected lowest price for the TV from one, two, three, four, and five searches and (*b*) the marginal benefit from each additional search. (*c*) How many searches should a consumer undertake if the marginal cost of each additional search is \$1.00?

(*a*) The lowest expected price with one search is $\$96 + \frac{\$8}{1+1} = \$100.00$.

With two searches, the lowest expected price is $\$96 + \frac{\$8}{3} = \$98.67$.

With three searches, the lowest expected price is $\$96 + \frac{\$8}{4} = \$98.00$,

With four searches, the lowest expected price is $\$96 + \frac{\$8}{5} = \$97.60$.

With five searches, the lowest expected price is $\$96 + \frac{\$8}{6} = \$97.33$.

(*b*) For the second search, MB = \$100 − \$98.67 = \$1.37.
For the third search, MB = \$98.67 − \$98.00 = \$0.67.
For the fourth search, MB = \$98.00 − \$97.60 = \$0.40.
For the fifth search, MB = \$76.00 − \$73.33 = \$0.27.

Note that the marginal benefit of each additional search is now much smaller than those found in the previous problem where the range of prices was much greater.

(*c*) If MC = \$1, then the consumer should undertake only two searches, for which MB = \$1.37. The consumer should not undertake the third search because MB = \$0.67 for the second search and thus exceeds the MC of the search.

ASYMMETRIC INFORMATION: THE MARKET FOR LEMONS AND ADVERSE SELECTION

15.8 Adverse selection is the direct result of asymmetric information. (*a*) True or false? Explain. (*b*) How can the problem of adverse selection be overcome?

(*a*) True. Adverse selection refers to the driving of high-quality products out of the market by the availability of low-quality products. This results because buyers are unable to determine the quality of the product and thus offers a price appropriate only for average-quality products. Since sellers do know the quality of their products (i.e., information is asymmetric), sellers of high-quality products refuse to sell their products at the average price, and so only low-quality products will be offered for sale (adverse selection).

(*b*) The problem of adverse selection can be overcome by buyers getting more information and/or sellers providing more information about the quality of the product or service. With more information on the quality of the product, buyers would be willing to pay an appropriately higher price for higher-quality goods and services, and thus avoid their withdrawal from the market. This is the purpose of brand names, national retail chains, and professional licensing.

15.9 Suppose that there are only two types of used cars in the market: high-quality and low-quality, and all the high-quality cars are identical and all the low-quality cars are identical. With perfect information, the quantity demanded of high-quality used cars is zero at \$16,000 and 100,000 at \$12,000, while the quantity demanded of low-quality cars is zero at \$8,000 and 100,000 at \$4,000. Suppose also that the supply curve for high-quality cars is horizontal at \$12,000, while the supply curve of low-quality used cars is horizontal at \$4,000 in the relevant range. (*a*) Draw a figure showing that with asymmetric information, no high-quality cars will be sold and 100,000 low-quality cars will be sold at the price of \$4,000 each. (*b*) Explain the precise sequence of events that leads to this result.

(*a*) See Fig. 15-1.

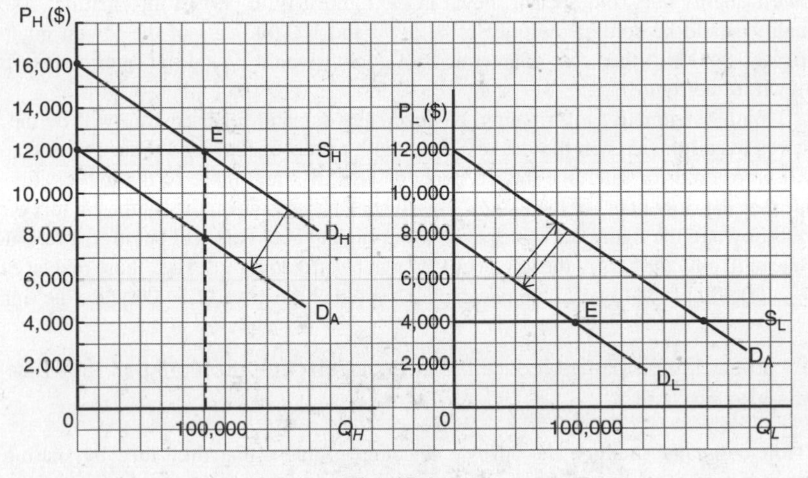

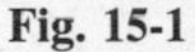
Fig. 15-1

(*b*) In Fig. 15-1, the subscripts H, L, and A refer, respectively, to high quality, low quality, and average quality. In the absence of perfect information (i.e., with asymmetric information), the demand for used cars will be the average of the demand curves for the high-quality and the low-quality used cars that would prevail in the market if all potential buyers had perfect information. As a result, the left panel of Fig. 15-1 shows that no high-quality cars will be offered for sale at the price of \$12,000. But with all the high-quality cars withdrawn from the market, only the low quality cars will be offered for sale. Thus, D_A will fall to D_L in the right panel and only the 100,000 low-quality cars will be sold in the market at $P_L = \$4{,}000$.

15.10 (*a*) Draw another figure similar to the figure in the answer to Problem 15.9 but with the supply curves of high-quality and low-quality cars positively sloped rather than horizontal. Assume further that used cars are of many different qualities rather than being simply of high-quality and low-quality. (*b*) With reference to the figure, explain the precise sequence of events that leads to only cars of the lowest quality being sold.

(*a*) See Fig. 15-2.

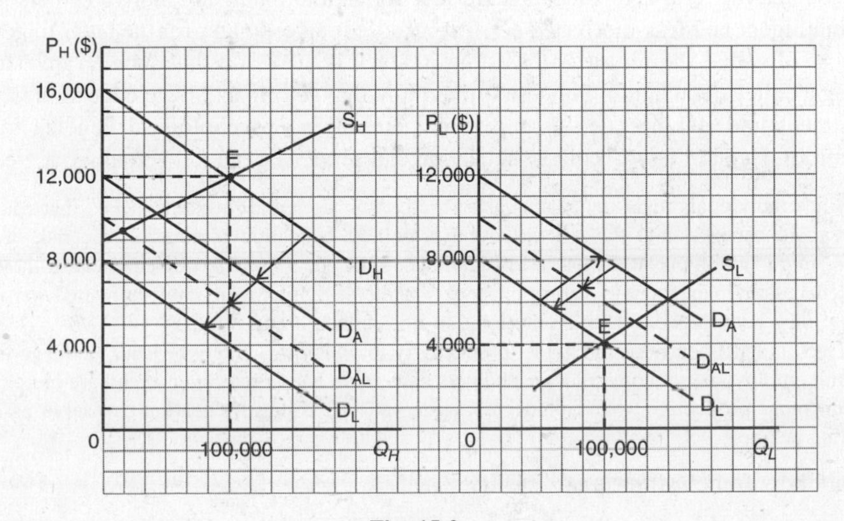

Fig. 15-2

(*b*) In Fig. 15-2 D_H and D_L refer, respectively, to the demand curve for the highest- and the lowest-quality used cars on the market. The demand curve for other used cars are between the demand curve for the highest- and lowest-quality cars (but are not shown in the future). With perfect information, 100,000 cars of the highest quality would be sold at the price of $12,000 and 100,000 cars of the lowest quality would be sold at the price of $4,000 (other cars of intermediate quality would be sold at intermediate prices, but these are not shown in the figure).

With asymmetric information, however, the demand for used cars will be the average of the demand curves for all the cars on the market, D_A in both panels of Fig. 15-2. Faced with D_A, fewer high-quality cars will be offered for sale (see the left panel of Fig. 15-2 and more of the low-quality cars will be offered for sale (see the right panel of the figure). This lowers the average quality of the car mix offered for sale to, say, D'_A (not shown in the figure), at which even fewer high quality cars will be offered for sale. The process will continue until only the cars of the lowest quality will be offered for sale (i.e., those that face demand curve D_L). With D_L, 100,000 of the lowest quality cars will be sold at the price of $4,000 (see the right panel of Fig. 15-2).

15.11 (*a*) How do credit companies reduce the adverse selection problem that they face? (*b*) What complaint does this give rise to?

(*a*) Credit companies reduce the adverse selection problem that they face by sharing the credit histories of borrowers with other credit companies.

(*b*) The sharing of borrowers' credit histories by credit companies in order to reduce the adverse selection problem that they face gives rise to complaints of invasion of privacy. This is true, but without sharing credit histories, credit companies would have to charge much higher credit rates, which might be unacceptable to most borrowers.

MARKET SIGNALING

15.12 Should education be viewed as an investment in human capital or a market signaling device? Explain.

Education should be viewed both as an investment in human capital and a market signaling device. As an investment in human capital, education increases labor productivity and justifies higher salaries. As a market signaling device, the level of educational achievement is used by firms to identify higher-productivity individuals to whom the firm can pay higher salaries. The idea is that less efficient individuals either are unable to get much of an education or it costs so much more (because it takes longer) that it does not pay for them. In either case, the holding of an educational certificate can be used as a market signal or indication of higher productivity.

15.13 Suppose that the returns to education are 12% for an intelligent and motivated person but only 8% for a less-intelligent and less-motivated person (because it takes longer for the latter to get a college degree). Suppose also that the return on investing in stock is 10% and that such an investment is as risky as getting a college education. Suppose furthermore that getting a college education is viewed as a strictly investment undertaking (i.e., assume that there are no psychological benefits to getting a college education). Explain how a college education can serve as a market signaling device in this case.

Since individuals regard education as a strictly human-capital investment (i.e., that education does not have any psychic benefits) and the risk in getting a college education is equal to the risk of investing in human capital, more intelligent and motivated individuals will get a college degree because they get a higher return from education than from investing in stocks, while less intelligent and motivated persons invest in stocks because they get a higher return on investing in stocks than in education.

Thus, independently of the higher productivity to which it is likely to lead, a college degree also signals to potential employers that college-degree holders have more native intelligence and are more motivated, and therefore are more productive, than non-degree holders. Thus, college education can serve as an important market signaling device.

15.14 Explain how franchising signals quality.

Franchising refers to the selling of the right to use the franchise chain's name (such as McDonald) and the ability of purchasing food and supplies at discounts from the parent company or its designated distributors as well as benefiting from the franchise good will and advertisements in return for a franchise fee, a fraction of the outlet's revenues, and the responsibility to abide by the franchise rules on quality, cleanliness, operating hours, etc. By enforcing these rules, the franchise ensures quality in all of its outlets.

Thus, while an area resident could conceivably find a better buy at a local retailer because of his knowledge of the area, a traveler who is not familiar with the area is happy to pay a little more at a national franchise outlet to ensure consistent quality wherever he happens to be. If the franchise were unable or unwilling to regularly inspect its outlets and close those that do not uphold its standard of quality, it would soon lose its value. Thus, a franchise provides a signal of quality.

THE PROBLEM OF MORAL HAZARD

15.15 (*a*) What problem can arise for General Motors by providing a 50,000-mile guarantee for its new automobiles sold? (*b*) How can GM reduce this problem?

(*a*) The problem that can arise for GM by providing a 50,000 miles guarantee for its new automobiles sold is that of moral hazard. That is, since GM pays for any breakdown on the new automobiles sold, buyers will not be as careful to avoid costly breakdowns.

(*b*) GM could try to reduce the moral hazard problem by demanding regular tune ups and requiring the buyer to bring their automobiles to a GM dealer as soon as any sign of problem arises.

15.16 An insurance company is considering providing fire insurance for $120,000, $100,000, or $80,000 to the owner of a house with a market value of $100,000. (*a*) How much insurance is the company likely to sell for the house? Why? (*b*) If the probability of a fire is 1 in 1000, what would be the premium charged by the company?

(*a*) The insurance company is likely to provide only $80,000 insurance to the owner of the house in order to reduce the problem of moral hazard. In fact, if the insurance company allowed the owner of the house to purchase insurance for $120,000, it would actually encourage that the house will go up in smoke because in that case the owner would collect more than the value of the house from the insurance company.

(*b*) If the probability of a fire is one in one thousand, the insurance premium would (1/1000)($80,000) = $80 per year plus the cost of operation (including the opportunity costs) of the insurance company for an insurance policy for $80,000.

15.17 What is the relationship between moral hazard and externalities?

Moral hazard arises whenever there is an externality (i.e., whenever an economic agent can shift some of its costs to others). Then the economic agent will not be as careful to avoid a possible loss. This increases the probability of a loss and the amount claimed for reimbursement from the insurance company.

PRINCIPAL-AGENT PROBLEM

15.18 From your school library, get the September 11, 2000 issue of *BusinessWeek* and read Dean Foust's article on "CEO's Pay: Nothing Succeeds like Failure" on p. 46 and indicate some of the abuses in the use of golden parachutes discussed in the article.

In his article, Dean Foust remarked "failure has never looked more lucrative". For example, in August 2000, Proctor & Gamble gave Durk Jager, its just-ousted CEO, a $9.5 million bonus even though he had been at P&G less than one-and-half years and P&G stock had fallen by 50% during his tenure. Also in 2000, Conseco Inc. gave a $49.3 million going-away gift to CEO Stephen Hilbert, who practically bankrupted the company with his ill-fated move into sub-prime lending. Similarly, Mattel gave a parachute package worth nearly $50 million in severance pay to Jill Barard, its departing CEO.

EFFICIENCY WAGE THEORY

15.19 (*a*) What is meant by the efficiency wage? (*b*) What problem is this intended to solve?

(*a*) The efficiency wage is the wage at which workers are induced to avoid shirking or slacking off on the job. This is higher than the equilibrium wage obtained by the intersection of the firm's demand and supply curves for labor and involves some unemployment. It is only the fear of unemployment that keeps workers from shirking at the efficiency wage. The efficiency wage will be higher the smaller the level of unemployment (and fear of workers losing their job because of shirking).

(*b*) The efficiency wage is intended to solve the problem of shirking which arises because managers cannot properly monitor workers' efforts. Thus, the efficiency wage is intended to solve the principal (manager) agent (worker) problem which arises from asymmetric information.

15.20 Draw a figure showing that a firm's demand and supply curves of labor (assuming for simplicity that the supply curve of labor is vertical) intersect at the wage rate of $10 per hour at which the firm employs 600 workers. On the same figure show a positively-sloped no-skirting efficiency constraint (NSC) or supply curve of labor that intersects the demand for labor at the no-skirting efficiency wage of $20 per hour, at which the firm hires 400 workers and leaves 200 other unemployed. What you now have is the efficiency wage and unemployment model presented in Section 15.7.

(*a*) See Fig. 15-3.

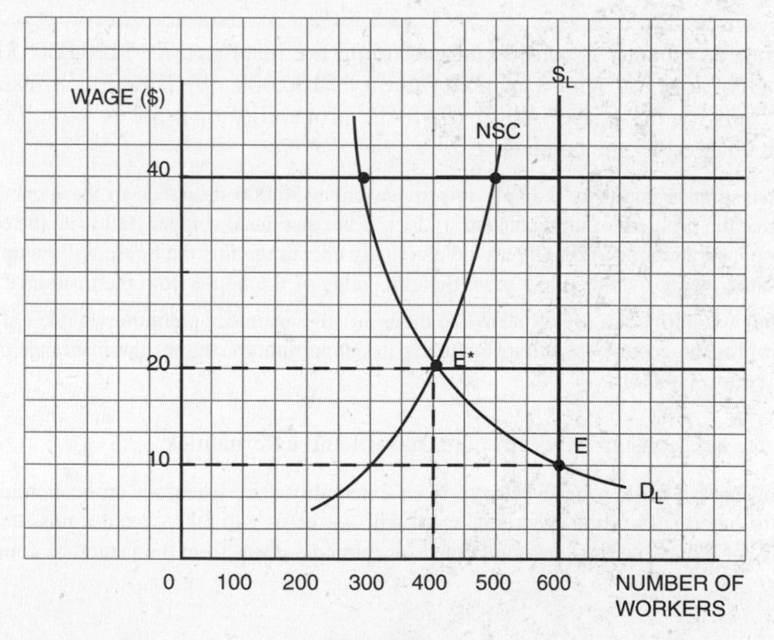

Fig. 15-3

Final Examination

1. Given Fig. F-l for a perfectly competitive firm, (*a*) determine the firm's best, or optimum, level of output, and P_x, AC, AVC, AFC, and profits per unit of output in total. What happens in the long run? (*b*) Which is the shut-down point? What is the firm's short-run supply curve? How can you get the industry short-run supply curve in the absence of external economies or diseconomies?

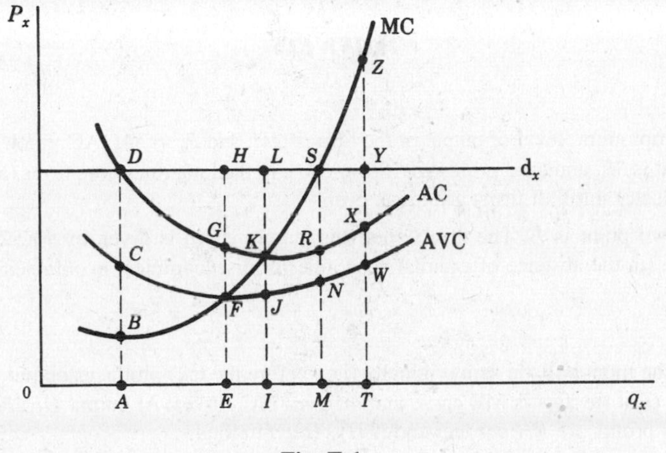

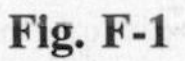

Fig. F-1

2. Draw a figure showing how the government can reduce a monopolist's profits by imposing a per-unit tax. Will the monopolist bare the entire burden of the tax? Why?

3. Compare the efficiency implications of long-run equilibria under different forms of market organization, with respect to (*a*) total profits, (*b*) the point of production on the LAC curve, (*c*) allocation of resources, and (*d*) sales promotion.

***4.** The following payoff matrix indicates that firm A has a choice of two possible strategies (A1 and A2), while firm B has the choice of three strategies (B1, B2, and B3). The payoffs payoffs refer to the percentage gain (+) or loss (−) in market share by firm A (and loss or gain in market share, respectively, by firm B). Determine (a) Firm A's optimal strategy and (b) Firm B's optimal strategy.

Table F-1

Matrix of Firm A's Gain (+) Loss (−) of Market Share in Percentages

		Firm B		
		B1	B2	B3
	A1	1	0	2
Firm A	A2	−2	−1	0

5. Show how to derive (*a*) the demand curve for labor of a firm that is a perfect competitor in the input market, (*b*) when labor is the only variable input, and (*c*) when labor is one of several variable inputs.

***5.** For an economy of two factors (*L* and *K*), two commodities (X and Y) and two individuals (A and B), (*a*) state the condition for Pareto optimum in production, in exchange, and in production and exchange simultaneously. Is Pareto optimum sufficient to define the maximum social welfare for this society? (*b*) Explain why with constant returns to scale and the absence of externalities and public goods a Pareto optimum point will not be attained if there is imperfect competiton in some product or factor market. (*c*) Why would.the existence of externalities and public good prevent the achievement of Pareto optimum?

*Optional

Answers

1. (*a*) The best, or optimum, level of output of the firm is *OM*, and $P_x = SM$, AC = *RM*, AVC = *NM*, AFC = *RN*, profit per unit is *SR*, and total profits are (*SR*) · (*OM*). In the long run, more firms (attracted by the profits) will enter the industry until all firms just break even.

(*b*) The shut-down point is *F*. The firm's short-run supply curve is given by *FKSZ*. The industry's short-run supply curve (in the absence of external economies or diseconomies) is obtained by the horizontal addition of all firms.

2. (*a*) In Fig. F-2, the monopolistic firm originally (i.e., before the tax) produces output *OF* (given by the intersection at point *G* of the firm's MR curve and *original* MC curve). At output *OF*, *P* = *EF*, AC = *HF*, and the monopolist's profits are *EH* per unit and (*EH*) · (*OF*) in total.

A per-unit tax is like a variable cost, and as such, it causes the monopolist's MC and AC curves to shift up by the amount of the per-unit tax. Suppose that the marginal and average cost curves shift up from MC and AC to MC′ and AC′, respectively, in the figure. Then the monopolist will produce only *OF*′ (given by the intersection at point *G*′ of the monopolist's MR curve and new or MC′ curve). At output *OF*′ *P*′ = *E*′*F*′, *AC*′ = *H*′*F*′, and the monopolist's new profits are *E*′*H*′ per unit and (*E*′*H*′) · (*OF*′) in total. Thus, profits per unit are reduced from *EH* to *E*′*H*′, and total profits are reduced from (*EH*) · (*OF*) to (*E*′*H*′) · (*OF*′). However, the monopolist is able to shift part of the burden of the tax to consumers in the form of higher prices and lower output. That is, part of the vertical shift (which represents the size of the per-unit tax) in the monopolist's MC and AC curves is paid by the consumer to the extent of the increase in the product price.

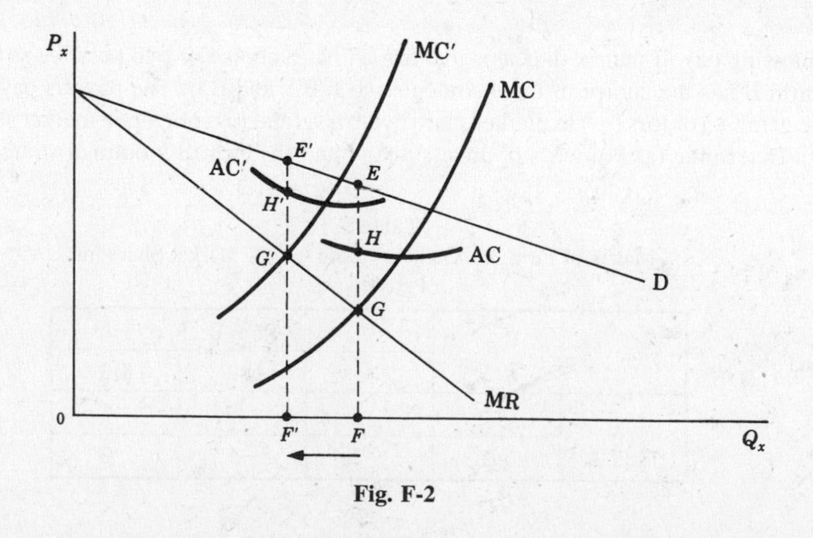

Fig. F-2

3. (*a*) Since cost curves probably differ under various forms of market organization, only a few generalizations can be made. First, the perfectly competitive firm and the monopolistically competitive firm break even when the industry is in long-run equilibrium. Thus, consumers get the commodity at cost of production. On the other hand, the monopolist and the oligopolist can and usually do make profits in the long run. These profits, however, *may* lead to more research and development and therefore to faster technological progress and rising standard of living in the long run.

(*b*) While the perfectly competitive firm produces at the lowest point on its LAC curve when the industry is in long-run equilibrium, the monopolist and the oligopolist are very unlikely to do so, and the monopolistic competitor never does so when the industry is in long-run equilibrium. However, the size of efficient operation is often so large in relation to the market as to leave only a few firms in the industry. Perfect competition under such circumstances would either be impossible or lead to prohibitive costs.

(*c*) While the perfectly competitive firm, when in long-run equilibrium, produces where $P = \text{LMC}$, for the imperfectly competitive firm $P > \text{LMC}$ and so there is an underallocation of resources to the firms in imperfectly competitive industries and a misallocation of resources in the economy. That is, under all forms of imperfect competition, the firm is likely to produce less and charge a higher price than under perfect competition. This difference is greater under pure monopoly and oligopoly than under monopolistic competition because of the greater elasticity of demand in monopolistic competition.

(*d*) Finally, waste resulting from excessive sales promotion is likely to be zero in perfect competition and greatest in oligopoly and monopolistic competition.

***4.** (*a*) The optimal and dominant strategy for firm A is A1. The reason for that is that the payoff for strategy A1 is greater than the payoff of strategy A2 (i.e., the values in row 1 are all larger than the corresponding values in row 2 of the payoff matrix).

(*b*) Given that firm A chooses strategy A1, firm B will chose strategy B2 because this minimizes firm A's gain, which is firm B's loss. Thus, each firm remains with the same market share that it had before. To be noted is that games, such as the above, where the gain of one firm represents the loss of the other firm (i.e., it comes at the expense of the other firm), are called *zero-sum games*.

5. (*a*) A profit-maximizing firm will employ an input as long as it adds more to total revenue than it adds to total cost. If L is the only variable input for the firm, the marginal revenue product of the additional unit of L hired (i.e., the MRP_L) is equal to the extra output of the additional unit of L hired (i.e., MP_L) times the marginal revenue of the firm (i.e., MR_x). That is, $\text{MRP}_L = \text{MP}_L \cdot \text{MR}_x$. As more units of L are hired, the MP_L, and thus the MRP_L, eventually declines. The declining portion of the MRP_L schedule is the firm's demand schedule for L when L is the only variable input of the firm.

(*b*) When L is only one of several variable inputs, the MRP_L curve no longer represents the firms demand curve for L. The reason for this is that, given the price of the other variable inputs, a change in the price of L will bring about changes in the quantity used of these other variable factors. These changes (called *internal effects*) in turn cause the entire MRP_L curve of the firm to shift to the right. The quantities of L demanded by the firm at different prices of L will then be given by points on different MRP_L curves. Thus, at $P_L = OA$ in Fig. F-3, the firm demands OC of L. At $P_w = OF$, the firm demands OJ. Joining point B on MRP_L with points such as H on MRP_L, we get d_L, the firm's demand curve for L

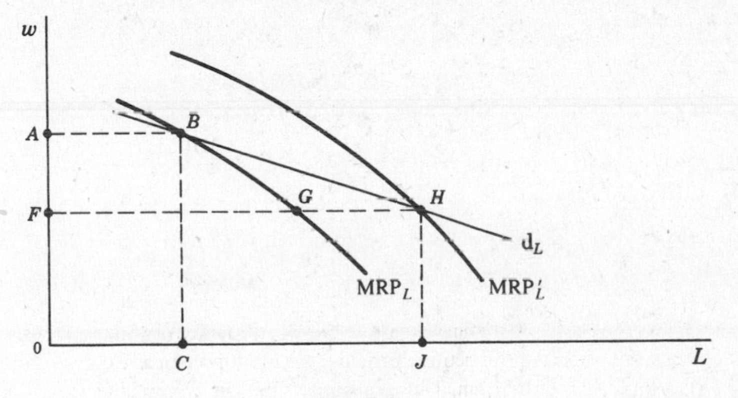

Fig. F-3

***6.** (*a*) The condition for Pareto optimum in production is that $(MRTS_{LK})_x = (MRTS_{LK})_y$. If this condition did not hold, the economy could increase its output of either X or Y without reducing the output of the other.

The condition for Pareto optimum in consumption is that $(MRS_{xy})_A = (MRS_{xy})_B$. If this condition did not hold, the satisfaction of either individual *A* or *B* could be increased without reducing the satisfaction or welfare of the other. This represents an unequivocal increase in social welfare. The condition for Pareto optimum in both production and exchange simultaneously is that $MRT_{xy} = (MRS_{xy})_A = (MRS_{xy})_B$. If this condition did not hold, a reorganization of the production-distribution process until this Pareto optimality condition holds would represent an unequivocal increase in social welfare. Pareto optimum is a necessary, but not sufficient, condition for maximum social welfare. For that, a social welfare function is also required. This is based on ethical or value judgments about the relative "deservedness" of individuals *A* and *B*.

(*b*) If industry X is imperfectly competitive, it will produce the output for which $MC_x = MR_x < P_x$. Thus P_x is higher, Q_x is lower, and fewer resources are used than if industry X were perfectly competitive. If another industry, say industry Y, is perfectly competitive, it will produce where $MC_y = MR_y = P_y$. Thus, $MRT_{xy} = MC_x/MC_y < P_x/P_y$, and so this economy does not reach Pareto optimum. Similarly, if the labor market is perfectly competitive while the capital market is imperfectly competitive, the least-cost factor combination in production is given by:

$$MP_L/MRC_L = MP_K/P_K \quad \text{or} \quad MP_L/MP_K = MRC_L/P_K > P_L/P_K$$

where MFC = marginal factor cost. Thus, $MRTS_{LK} = MP_L/MP_K > P_L/P_K$, and so this economy does not reach Pareto optimum.

(*c*) In order to achieve Pareto optimum the marginal social benefit must equal the marginal social cost, the marginal social cost must equal the marginal private cost. The existence of externalities and public goods will cause some of these conditions not to hold, and so the economy cannot reach Pareto optimum, even if perfect competition exists in every market. Furthermore, the economy will not reach a point of Pareto optimum when there are public goods. The reason for this is that if X is a public good, the economy is in equilibrium when $MRT_{xy} = (MRS_{xy})_A = (MRS_{xy})_B$. However, since individuals *A* and *B* can both use each unit of public good X at the same time, the equilibrium condition for maximum welfare is $MRT_{xy} = (MRS_{xy})_A + (MRS_{xy})_B$. Thus, perfect competition leads to the underproduction and the underconsumption of public goods and does not lead to a Pareto optimum point.

Theory and Problems of

MICROECONOMICS

Fourth Edition

INDEX

The letter *p* following a page number refers to a solved problem.